SUSPECT NO. 1

WARNING
This book includes content readers may find disturbing.

LISE PEARLMAN IS ALSO THE ACCLAIMED AUTHOR OF

THE SKY'S THE LIMIT:
People v. Newton, the REAL Trial of the 20th Century?
(2012)

AMERICAN JUSTICE ON TRIAL
People v. Newton
(2016)

WITH JUSTICE FOR SOME:
Politically Charged Criminal Trials in the Early
20th Century That Helped Shape Today's America
(2017)

CALL ME PHAEDRA
The Life and Times of Movement
Lawyer Fay Stender
(2018)

www.lisepearlman.com

The Lindbergh Kidnapping

SUSPECT NO. 1

The Man Who Got Away

by Lise Pearlman

REGENT PRESS
Berkeley, California

Copyright © 2020 by Lise Pearlman

[Paperback]
ISBN 13: 978-1-58790-495-0
ISBN 10: 1-58790-495-0

[Hardback]
ISBN 13: 978-1-58790-532-2
ISBN 10: 1-58790-532-9

[E-Book]
ISBN 13: 978-1-58790-496-7
ISBN 10: 1-58790-496-9

Library of Congress Cataloging-in-Publication Data

Names: Pearlman, Lise A., 1949- author.
Title: The Lindbergh kidnapping suspect no. 1 : the man who got away / by Lise Pearlman.
Other titles: Lindbergh kidnapping suspect number one
Description: Berkeley, California : Regent Press, [2020] | Includes bibliographical references and index. | Summary: "In the depths of the Depression, millions worldwide followed every twist and turn of the Lindbergh baby kidnap/murder. Yet what was reported was largely fake news. Nearly a century after undocumented immigrant Bruno Richard Hauptmann was executed for the dastardly crime, questions still linger. If the wrong man was convicted, who did it? When? Why? Where? How? The shocking answers this book suggests have eluded all prior authors. Extensive research into dusty archives yielded crucial forensic evidence never before analyzed. Readers are invited to reexamine "the crime of the century" with fresh eyes focused on a key suspect – a slim man wearing a fedora that obscured his face. He was spotted with a ladder in his car near the Lindberghs' driveway early that fateful night. The police let an insider who fit that description oversee the entire investigation – the boy's father, international hero Charles Lindbergh. Abuse of power, amorality and xenophobia all feature in this saga set in an era dominated by white supremacists and social Darwinists. If Lindbergh was Suspect No. 1, the man who got away, what was his motive? Who else was involved? Who helped cover up the crime? Read this book and judge for yourself"— Provided by publisher.
Identifiers: LCCN 2020019381 (print) | LCCN 2020019382 (ebook) | ISBN 9781587905322 (hardback) | ISBN 9781587904950 (paperback) | ISBN 9781587904967 (kindle edition)
Subjects: LCSH: Lindbergh, Charles Augustus, 1930-1932—Kidnapping. | Lindbergh, Charles A. (Charles Augustus), 1902-1974. | Hauptmann, Bruno Richard, 1899-1936. | Kidnapping—New Jersey—Hopewell—Case studies.
Classification: LCC HV6603.L5 P39 2020 (print) | LCC HV6603.L5 (ebook) | DDC 364.152/3092—dc23
LC record available at https://lccn.loc.gov/2020019381
LC ebook record available at https://lccn.loc.gov/2020019382

All rights reserved under International and Pan-American Copyright Conventions. No part of this book may be used or reproduced in any manner whatsoever without the written permission of the Publisher, except in the case of brief quotations embodied in critical articles and reviews.

Every effort has been made to credit sources and obtain permission where appropriate. If we have inadvertently used or credited material or images inaccurately or without applicable consent and they do not qualify as Fair Use under the U.S. Copyright Act, or are not in the public domain, please contact the publisher so appropriate steps may be taken.

Printed in the U.S.A.
REGENT PRESS
Berkeley, California
www.regentpress.net
regentpress@mindspring.com

Contents

Dedication ix
Map of Crime Scene x
Cast of Characters xi
Floor Plan of the Lindberghs' Farmhouse xvi
Introduction 1

ACT ONE 5
1. KIDNAPPED! 7
2. A Secretive Loner in the Spotlight 13
3. The Orteig Prize 24
4. The Search for the Perfect Mate 30
5. Hooked 40
6. America's Royal Couple 52
7. An Ominous Beginning 56
8. Back in the Air — Grounded by Tragedy 67
9. Getting Reacquainted with "Hi" and "Mum-Mum" 73
10. Little Charlie's Last Days 80

ACT TWO 93
1. The Police Arrive 95
2. The First 48 Hours 108
3. Hunting Worldwide for the Curly-Haired Baby ... 116
4. Confusion Reigns 128
5. Mystery Trips 135
6. Conflicting Sworn Statements 140
7. Hunches Backfire and Leads Go Nowhere 148
8. Wild Goose Chases 154
9. A Nation in Mourning 167
10. At the Morgue 177
11. Ashes and Smoke 185
12. Bizarre Developments 197

ACT THREE 207
1. Stymied 209
2. An Elusive Suspect 212
3. The Most Hated Man in America 216
4. Framing an Ironclad Case 225
5. Slew Footing Dr. Mitchell 231
6. "Death House" Reilly 238
7. Show Time 246
8. Picking the Jury 251
9. Aiming for the Chair 255
10. More Damning Testimony 260
11. The Defense 270
12. Condemned Without Mercy 277
13. Raising Doubts 283
14. Old Smokey 291

ACT FOUR 299
1. Kindred Spirits 301
2. "The High Priest of Biology" 309
3. A New Mission 316
4. A Breakthrough at the Lab 325
5. The Landmark Experiment 329
6. Hitler Embraces Carrel's "Ideal" Solution 335
7. The Culture of Organs 340
8. The Highfields Center for the Science of Man 347
9. From Hero to Villain 353
10. Carrel's Fall from Grace 358
11. Lindbergh Secretly Achieves his Goal 364

ACT FIVE 369
1. Assembling the Puzzle Pieces 371
2. The Squibb Lab Report 379
3. Breckinridge, Fisch and Cemetery John 387
4. Reconstructing the Crime 390
5. Maggots and Chemicals Tell a Tale 404

6. What Lindbergh Valued Most in Life 410
7. Accidental Admissions? 414
8. Conclusion 423

Epilogue 427

Appendix A: Affidavit of Dr. William M. Bass 432
Appendix B: The Squibb Report 439
Appendix C: Declaration of Dr. Peter Speth 458
Endnotes 473
Sources 536
Index 543
Acknowledgments 551

Dedication

This book is dedicated to Anna Schoeffler Hauptmann (1898–1994) who, in utter disbelief at the American justice system, lived through the prolonged nightmare of her husband's sensationalized arrest in September 1934 as the most hated man in America, his murder trial four months later, and execution in April 1936. She spent the rest of her long life fighting to prove the truth of his alibi: that Bruno Richard Hauptmann could not have committed the kidnap/murder of the only son of America's hero on the evening of March 1, 1932, in central New Jersey because her Richard was picking her up from work at a Bronx bakery when the crime occurred, as he always did then on Tuesday nights.

Despite all obstacles, nevertheless she persisted — and convinced a growing number of people, including both crime reporter Anthony Scaduto and investigative journalist Ludovic Kennedy, of the righteousness of her cause. Without Anna Hauptmann's dogged determination, the government documents her lawyers uncovered through the Freedom of Information Act, the expert assistance they obtained, and the interviews of aged participants and sleuthing by Scaduto and Kennedy, much of the information relied on in this book would have been lost to history. Hats off as well to New Jersey Governor Harold Hoffman, whose thwarted efforts to reinvestigate "the crime of the century" likely cost him his reelection but provided historians with a gold mine of clues.

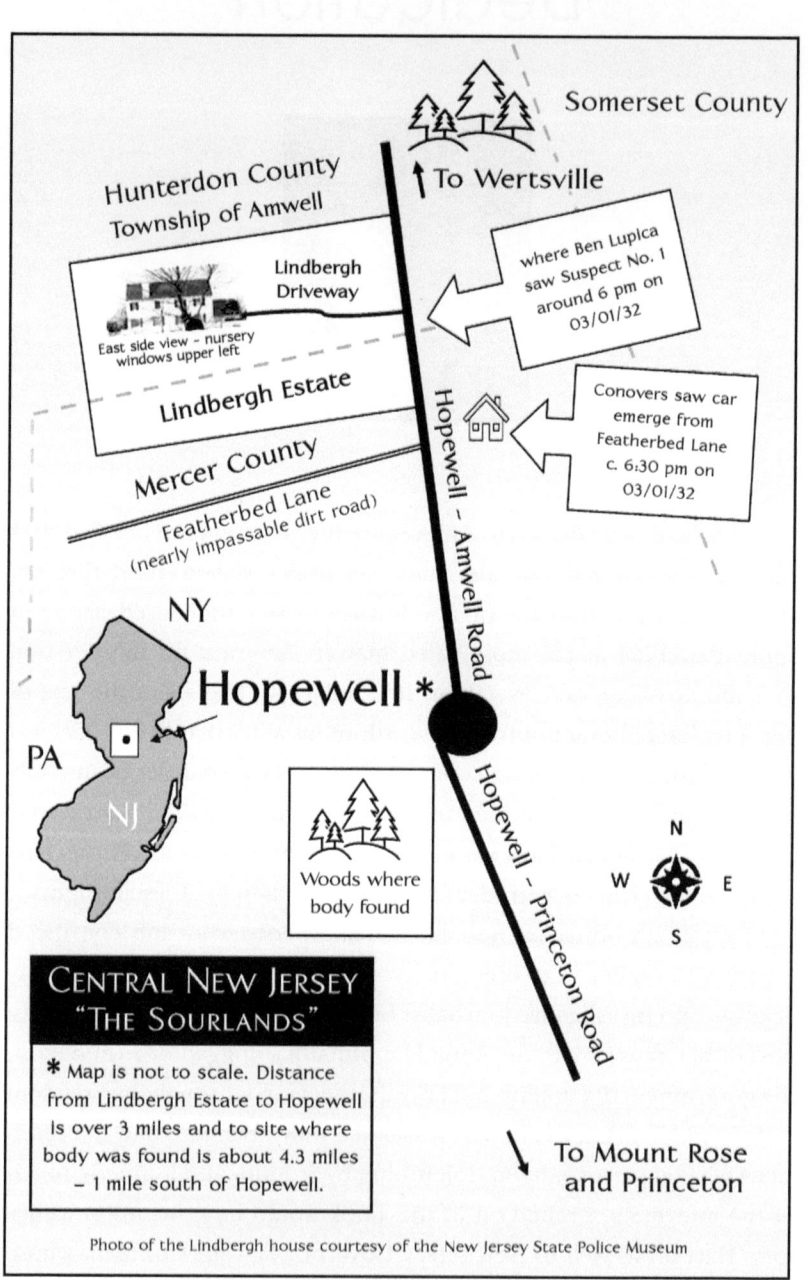

Cast of Characters

LINDBERGH FAMILY

Paternal grandparents August and Louisa Lindbergh (names taken by Ola Mansson and his mistress Lovisa Jansdotter Carlen after leaving Sweden for America in 1859. They later married.)

Charles August ("C.A.") Lindbergh, father of the aviator, born in Sweden. His birth name in Sweden was Karl August Mansson, the first of seven children of Ola Mansson and Lovisa Jansdotter

Evangeline Lodge Land Lindbergh, second wife of C.A., mother of the aviator and daughter of Detroit, Michigan, dentist/inventor Dr. Charles Land and Evangeline Land

Eva Lindbergh Spaeth, daughter of C.A. Lindbergh and his first wife. Her older sister, Lillian, died in 1916

Charles Augustus Lindbergh, pioneering aviator and victim's father

Anne Morrow Lindbergh, author, wife, navigator and co-pilot of the aviator, and victim's mother

Charles Augustus Lindbergh, Jr., firstborn of Anne and Charles. Delivered at Englewood estate of Morrow family on June 22, 1930. The couple had five more children from 1932 to 1945: Jon, Land, Anne, Scott, and Reeve.

Lindbergh household staff in New Jersey:

Betty Gow, nanny, who lived mostly at the estate of Anne's parents in Englewood, where the Lindberghs spent weekdays

Olly Whateley, chauffeur, butler and caretaker of the new Lindbergh farmhouse outside Hopewell, New Jersey

Elsie Whateley, Olly's wife and the Lindbergh's cook and housekeeper at the farmhouse

Family dogs: **Wahgoosh**, a white and black wire-haired terrier that lived with the Whateleys at the New Jersey farmhouse; **Skean**, a Scottish terrier that lived at the Morrow estate in Englewood and generally accompanied the family on weekends at their farmhouse

ANNE MORROW LINDBERGH FAMILY

Ambassador and Senator Dwight Morrow, Anne's father

Elizabeth Cutter Morrow, Anne's mother

Elisabeth Reeve (Morrow) Morgan, Anne's older sister

Dwight Morrow, Jr., Anne's brother

Constance (Morrow) Morgan, Anne's younger sister

Morrow household staff of 29 included:

Septimus Banks, butler

Violet Sharp, parlor maid

BRECKINRIDGE FAMILY

Henry Breckinridge, close friend and legal/business advisor to Charles Lindbergh

Aida De Acosta Breckinridge, Henry's second wife

Oren Root, Aida's son by her first marriage

Alva Root, Aida's daughter by her first marriage

NEW JERSEY STATE OFFICIALS

Gov. Harry Moore (1926–1929, 1932–1935 and 1938–1941)

Gov. Harold Hoffman (1935–1938)

Leon Hoage, investigator employed by Gov. Hoffman

NEW JERSEY STATE POLICE

Colonel H. Norman Schwarzkopf, Superintendent of the Agency

Lieutenant Lewis J. Bornmann

Captain John Lamb

Lieutenant Arthur Keaten

Trooper Frank Kelly, fingerprint expert

Trooper Joe Wolf

Sergeant Andrew Zapolsky

Jersey City detectives Harry Walsh and James Fitzgerald, assigned to assist the New Jersey State Police

KEY LOCAL LAW ENFORCEMENT FIGURES

Hopewell Police Chief Harry Wolfe and **Constable Charles Williamson**

Detective Ellis Parker

Oscar Bush, tracker

FEDERAL OFFICIALS

J. Edgar Hoover, Director of the Bureau of Investigation (now the FBI)

Elmer Irey, Internal Revenue Service executive who assisted in the Lindbergh ransom payment

Assistant Secretary of Labor Murray Garsson, who conducted his own investigation into the Lindbergh baby kidnapping

POLITICAL BOSSES AND MOB FIGURES

Jersey City Mayor Frank Hague

Owney Madden, a leading figure in New York's underworld

GO-BETWEENS TO THE KIDNAP GANG

Mickey Rosner, Salvatore Spitale and racketeer Irving Bitz

John Hughes Curtis, Virginia shipping company owner

William "Wild Bill" Donovan, World War I hero and lawyer friend of Henry Breckinridge

John F. "Jafsie" Condon, retired Bronx school principal

OTHER POTENTIAL SUSPECTS

Isidor Fisch, fraudster and business partner of Hauptmann

Jacob Nosovitsky, spy and former federal agent

Arthur Hitner, con man with multiple aliases

Gaston Means, former federal agent

HAUPTMANN FAMILY

Bruno Richard Hauptmann, prosecuted as the lone kidnap/murderer

Anna Hauptmann and their son **Manfred "Bubi" Hauptmann**

KEY MURDER TRIAL PARTICIPANTS

Justice Thomas Trenchard on assignment from the New Jersey Supreme Court

Attorney General David Wilentz in his first criminal trial

County Prosecutor Tony Hauck, who prosecuted John Curtis in June 1932 and Hauptmann in 1935 for crimes related to the kidnapping

Federal Wood Expert Arthur Koehler

Hauptmann Lead Counsel Edward "Death House" Reilly

Co-Defense Counsel for Hauptmann C. Lloyd Fisher, who also defended John Curtis in 1932

Fingerprint Expert Dr. Erastus Mead Hudson

ROCKEFELLER INSTITUTE FOR MEDICAL RESEARCH

Dr. Simon Flexner, First Director (1901–1935)

Dr. Alexis Carrel, Head of Experimental Surgical Research

Dr. Lillian Baker, serum production specialist

Dr. Albert Ebeling, tissue culture specialist

Dr. Raymond Parker, tissue culture specialist

Dr. Ralph Wyckoff, biophysics specialist and centrifuge expert

Floor plan of the Lindberghs' farmhouse. First floor.

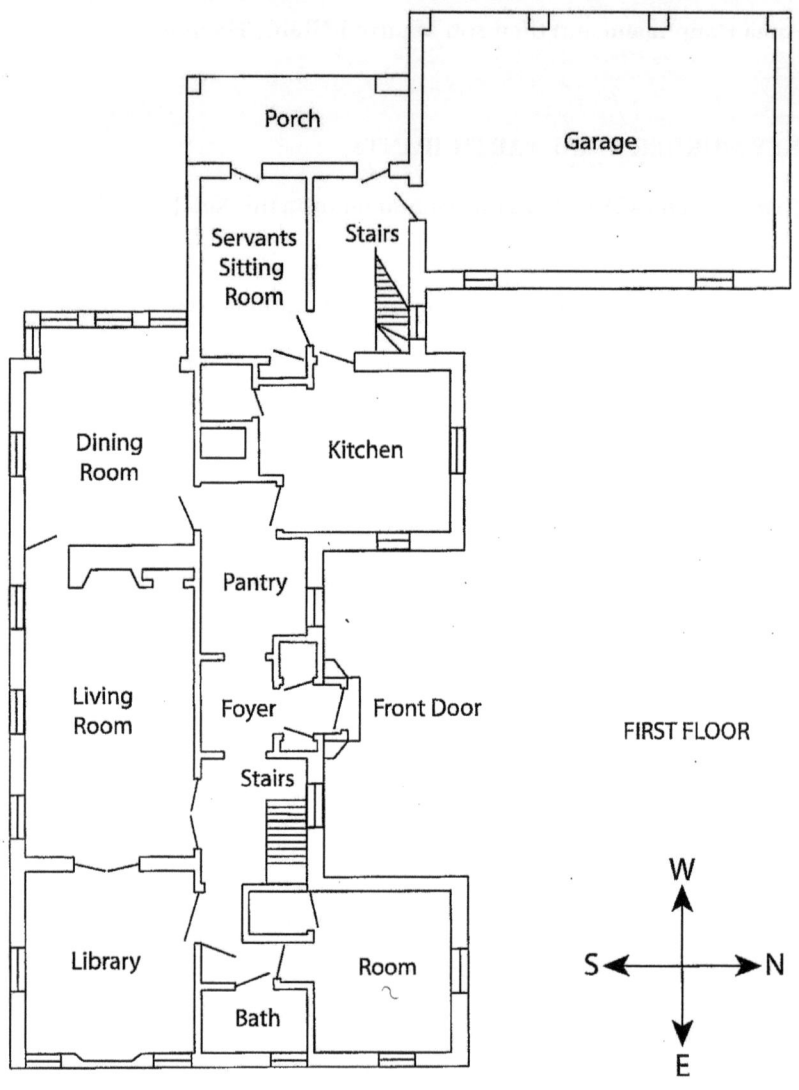

The site of the kidnapping.

Floor plan of the Lindberghs' farmhouse. Second floor.

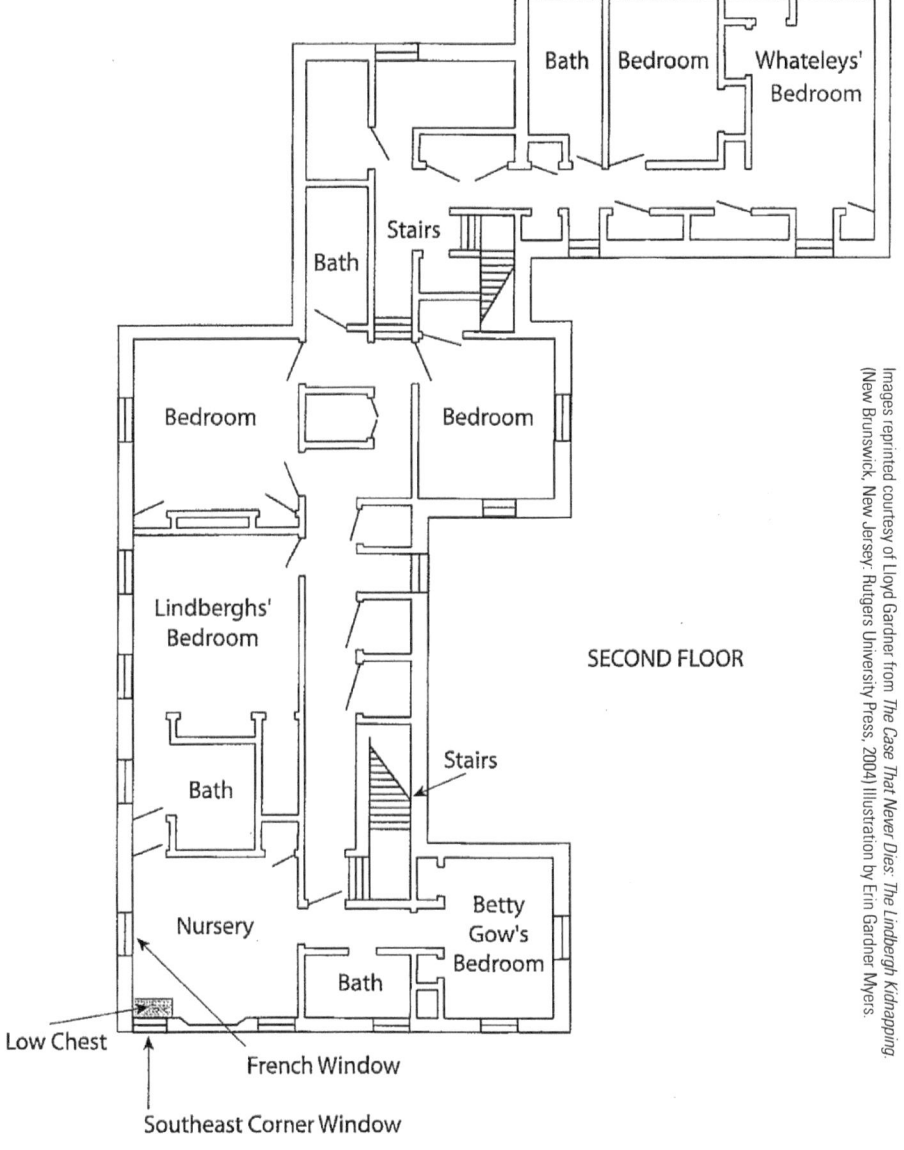

The site of the kidnapping.

42-year-old truck driver William Allen almost kicked away a small object as he stood under a tree to answer the call of nature in the woods off the Hopewell-Princeton Road on May 12, 1932. Looking more closely, he made a shocking discovery that the entire world would soon know. (Police photo taken an hour and a half later.)

INTRODUCTION

One drizzly Thursday afternoon in mid-May 1932, a truck driver on his way along a back road in central New Jersey pulled over at a remote location so he could relieve himself in the woods. Moments later, as the middle-aged African American stood under a tree branch, he stepped on something and started to kick it away. When he looked down, it startled him to see the foot of a small child sticking out of some leaves. He noticed the head face down in a hollow under the tree. The back of its skull had only a small bit of decayed skin on it and tufts of dirty blond hair partly washed by the ongoing light rain.

The driver called to his white co-worker to get out of the truck and come see. The body was missing both hands, one forearm and a leg below the knee. Though its chest was covered in a T-shirt, its lower torso and limbs were largely skeletal. Its sex could not be determined. The driver speculated that the rest of the body had "either decomposed or had been eaten by animals." This could well be the missing Lindbergh baby, the subject of an intense nationwide manhunt for nearly two-and-a-half months, found dead less than five miles from home. The two men then sped off to track down the local constable.

* * *

I began researching the Lindbergh baby kidnap/murder case when I started writing my first legal history book after I retired as a judge. The case became one of the chapters in my 2012 book, *The Sky's the Limit: People v. Newton, the REAL Trial of the 20th Century?* which compared the political and social significance of headline trials from 1900 to 1999 to that of a landmark 1968 death penalty trial. I also included the Lindbergh trial as a chapter in a follow-up book in 2017, *With Justice for Some: Politically Charged Criminal Trials of the Early Twentieth Century That Helped Shape Today's America,* which put famous criminal trials from 1900 through the Depression years in a different perspective — as a cultural backdrop to the divisive xenophobic, racial and ethnic issues we face as a nation today.

The Lindbergh "crime of the century" was an easy choice to include in both books. Among more than a dozen famous cases from 1900 to the Depression that were on every expert's list as a candidate for "the" trial of the century, the Lindbergh case mesmerized the widest audience. Record numbers of people followed its every twist and turn on radio, in newspapers and magazines and gatherings outside the hundred-year-old courthouse in the small town of Flemington, New Jersey. Its extraordinary saturation of news outlets rivaled the ubiquitous coverage of the O. J. Simpson trial in the 1990s.

Law Professor Gerald Uelmen was a member of Simpson's Dream Team. In his book *Lessons from the Trial: The People v. O. J. Simpson,* Uelmen observed a key feature of all the spellbinding trials in our nation's history: "The most remarkable aspect of every 'trial of the century' . . . has been the insight it provides into the tenor of the times in which it occurred. It is as though each of these trials was responding to some public appetite or civic need of the era in which it took place." The Lindbergh kidnap/murder took place during the height of the Depression. The context included a sharp rise in xenophobia in a national political environment dominated by white supremacists and social Darwinists, who feared the degradation of their race by an influx of immigrants. All of these factors figured in how that case played out. But most importantly, the case involved the world's first flying hero — a real-life Nordic demi-god — eleven years before Superman first appeared in the comics.

When police investigate various suspects, they generally consider motive, opportunity and means as well as later conduct demonstrating consciousness of guilt. Yet in the Lindbergh kidnapping case, the police only applied those criteria selectively and left many people questioning why they switched from blaming a professional gang with inside help to pinning the kidnap/murder on an accused lone actor. After German immigrant Bruno Richard Hauptmann was tried and executed, questions still lingered about Hauptmann's guilt or innocence, and what other persons might have been involved. Investigators also noted Lindbergh's odd behavior in the wake of the crime — conduct which either intentionally or negligently obstructed the police investigation.

Near the end of World War II, British military historian B. H. Liddell Hart invited his readers to open their minds to face facts that might be disquieting: "Nothing has aided the persistence of falsehood, and the evils that result from it, more than the unwillingness of good people to admit the truth when it was disturbing to their comfortable assurance." One key suspect the police focused on the day after the abduction was originally labeled by the FBI *"UNKNOWN PERSON NO. 1 (Man with Ladder Near Lindbergh Home)."* For shorthand, let us call him "Suspect No. 1" – a slim, unidentified man with what appeared to be "a thin face and long features." The man seemed American, not foreign, and wore a city dweller's stylish winter coat and fedora. He was seen at dusk with a sectional ladder in his car at the entrance to the Lindberghs' driveway. The police completely ignored one insider fitting that description who likely had both motive and opportunity. Instead, they bowed to prestige and political power and let control of the investigation be taken from them.

In this book, I take advantage of the distance in time to treat the boy's father as a potential suspect in his kidnap and murder; like all the others on the list, a fallible human being, not a demi-god. What impact did it have on the investigation to have the Governor of New Jersey assure Charles Lindbergh that he had full authority to direct the state police investigating a crime committed in his home?

Today, we have both the benefit of insights provided by previous scholars and sleuths, as well as a treasure trove of evidentiary puzzle pieces whose significance has been unrecognized until now. I invite you to join me in focusing on a key question police never pursued back in the spring of 1932 — was international hero Charles Lindbergh himself Suspect No. 1, the man who got away? Judge for yourself.

Charles Lindbergh testified as the star witness for the prosecution at the death penalty trial of Bruno Richard Hauptmann before a packed courthouse in Flemington, New Jersey in January of 1935. The jury is seated to the right behind the railing.

ACT ONE

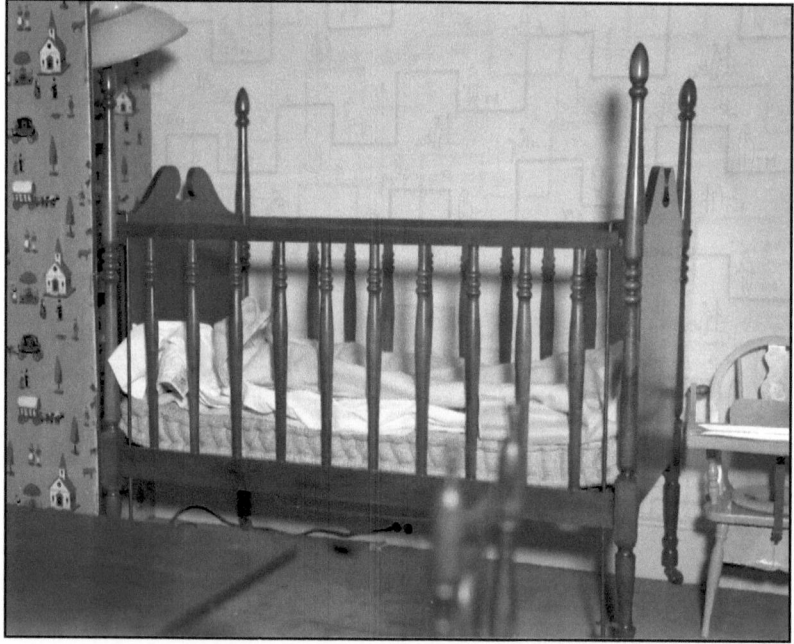

Nanny Betty Gow and the empty crib

1.
KIDNAPPED!

SCOTTISH nanny Betty Gow headed upstairs to the nursery on March 1, 1932, just before 10 p.m. to wake her twenty-month-old charge from his two-hour nap. Her routine at that hour started with taking him to the potty. Then Betty Gow would get him a snack and put him back in his crib for the night with his favorite stuffed animal. Sometimes his mother joined the nanny in this last trip of the day to the nursery. That Tuesday, when both of them had prepared the boy at 7 p.m. for his evening nap, nothing appeared out of the ordinary. But at 10 p.m. life in the Lindbergh household would erupt in chaos and never again be the same.

The twenty-eight-year-old nanny had been working for a year caring for the first-born son of American superstar Charles Lindbergh and his wife Anne Morrow Lindbergh. The little boy was the namesake of his famous father. Everyone in America, and most places around the world, knew Lindbergh's story by then — Minnesota farm boy turned fearless pilot. Heavily discounted as an amateur underdog in the death-defying race to complete the first nonstop intercontinental flight over the Atlantic, he outperformed the seasoned experts and accomplished the dangerous crossing before anyone else. His feat in late May 1927 heralded the dawn of a new era. After his solo transatlantic flight, Lindbergh was the object of idol worship of unprecedented dimensions, including frequent newsreel coverage of his flying exploits and his handsome likeness seen everywhere in America on envelopes. The image of his plane, "The Spirit of St. Louis," adorned air mail stamps.

Anything about Lindbergh was guaranteed to attract millions of readers, moviegoers and radio fans. When contemplating marriage in the fall of 1927, Lindbergh focused on the main lesson he had learned as a farmer. Being in his estimation one of the healthiest, most robust of studs, he wanted to pair himself with a woman capable of producing a dozen superior children. Yet, from the day in late December of 1927 that Lindbergh met Ambassador Dwight Morrow's two oldest daughters, the one he found by far the most alluring was Elisabeth. Her health would not have been up to his plan even had she welcomed his courtship. With Elisabeth in Europe in September 1928, and Anne totally enamored with him, Lindbergh wooed Anne instead.

When the couple married in 1929, press gathered outside Anne's father's mansion. The couple were clearly America's royalty, and Anne's first pregnancy became a national fixation. She spent most of the last two months in seclusion at her parents' estate. Her father was then ending his third year as Ambassador to Mexico. One of the prime movers and shakers in the Republican Party, in 1930 Dwight Morrow would be chosen to serve in a vacant Senate seat. As they awaited the baby's birth, publishers eager for a scoop were willing to pay $2000 (over $29,000 today) to any reliable source of information about the childbirth.

The baby was born on Anne's 24th birthday, June 22, 1930. The Lindberghs had already decided on a male heir's name: Charles Augustus, Jr. Counting on his superior genes, the father had the highest expectations for Little Charlie. Lindbergh jealously guarded their son's privacy but keeping the press at arm's length proved difficult. As soon as word got out the telegraph wires went crazy. Congratulatory messages deluged the Morrows' Englewood home, including some from heads of state. The note from Surgeon General Hugh Cumming expressed a sentiment many millions of people around the globe undoubtedly shared — a wish that the Lindberghs' son "may have as useful a life as his father."

Visitors thronged their front gate. More presents piled up in the mansion than they could possibly use. When the press received no pictures of the newborn, rumors circulated that the boy was horribly deformed from prenatal exposure to noxious fumes. To reassure the public, Lindbergh took a few photos of his curly-haired son and distributed them to the press. That only made them impatient for more. Very few would be shared after Charlie's first birthday.

The Lindberghs soon began searching for a remote location for the home they planned to build for themselves. After spending the first year of their marriage largely living out of suitcases, Anne told her family that she would be happy to be far from humanity where her husband could get back to his farming roots to relax. After conducting an aerial tour of central New Jersey, Lindbergh chose hilly acreage outside the small town of Hopewell in the densely wooded area of Mercer and Hunterdon counties that locals called "The Sourlands."

Though not far from Princeton University and trains to Manhattan, there were only three other houses within a mile of the nearly 400-acre tract. The area was "sparsely inhabited, difficult of access, thickly wooded and clogged with underbrush and . . . practically without organized police protection." The terrain was "almost inaccessible without a native guide." The town of Hopewell, more than three miles away, had just nine hundred permanent residents.

That fateful Tuesday night of March 1, 1932, Lindbergh was scheduled to be one of two widely advertised guests of honor at a gala in the Waldorf Astoria celebrating the hundredth anniversary of New York University. The planners panicked when he turned out to be a no show. Instead, he arrived at his New Jersey farmhouse late for dinner after having been gone since Monday morning. Anne was waiting for him at her desk in the living room, apparently unaware of the conflict in his schedule which Lindbergh would attribute to a calendaring error.

At about 8:30 p.m. the couple were served a hearty meal in the adjacent dining room by Phoebe "Elsie" Whateley and her husband Aloysius "Olly" Whateley, the only two other members of the Lindberghs' household staff besides nanny Betty Gow. At around 9 p.m. the Lindberghs headed briefly to the living room and then upstairs to the master bedroom. Neither then checked on their son in the nursery connected to their bedroom by the master bath.

Just before 10 p.m. Betty ended her visit with Elsie in the Whateleys' apartment over the garage and returned to the nursery. The lights in the nursery were off as Betty had left them just before 8 p.m. When she neared the crib, she was surprised not to hear the toddler breathing. She felt around the crib in the dark and found no child under the blanket, which was still pinned to the sheets as she had left it two hours earlier.

Betty immediately checked with Anne to see if she had Little Charlie with her, but Anne said, "No, maybe the Colonel has him." Colonel was the honorary title awarded to Charles Lindbergh by the government after his historic flight. Anne ran into the nursery and saw the crib was empty. By then Lindbergh was downstairs again in his study. Anne called down to her husband and chided him for taking the toddler when he knew Charlie had a cold.

Betty descended to the study to implore Lindbergh to confess if he was pulling another one of his famous practical jokes. When she reached Lindbergh, he was reading at his desk next to one of two study windows that faced east. The absence of drapes put the lighted room in sharp contrast to the deep black night. In response to Betty's anxious question, Lindbergh exclaimed: "The baby? Isn't he in his crib?" He bounded so precipitously up the stairs, he now had her quite scared. Lindbergh took a quick look in the nursery and rushed through the master bath to his bedroom. There Anne confronted him again, "Do you have the baby, Charles?" Anne vividly recalled him turning away. Biographer Susan Hertog would later report, "The silence confirmed her worst fears."

Lindbergh immediately grabbed his rifle from his bedroom closet. On his way out, he turned to his wife and said, "Anne, they have stolen our baby." Kidnapping of wealthy people's children for ransom was an all-too-common occurrence during the Depression. He then asked his wife to fetch Olly Whateley while Betty ran to tell Elsie that Charlie was gone. Elsie bounded up the other set of stairs by the kitchen to see what happened and found Anne in the nursery, still in her dressing gown, looking dazed. Elsie accompanied Anne back to her bedroom to change. Anne then opened a bedroom window and stuck her head out. She thought she heard a baby's cry, but decided it was probably the howling wind.

Elsie and Anne then joined Betty in the nursery with its light on to check under furniture and in every cabinet, closet and drawer where the toddler could possibly hide — to no avail. Nothing seemed amiss. As Anne knew, on Sunday afternoon the little boy had been left for a time to play by himself in the nursery. When he seemed too quiet, family friend Aida Breckinridge had gone upstairs to check on him and found Charlie had gotten out of the nursery into the bathroom at the end of the hall. She caught him in the act of pulling toilet paper from its roll and tossing it into the bowl. He squealed and raced back to his room.

Betty Gow said it was about quarter after ten when the two men rejoined the women and reported back no sign of the child: "We all searched all around the house, the closets and drawers in the cellar and attic and everywhere. . . . When we couldn't find the baby in the house the Colonel told Whateley to call the police." The alarm went out on the wire immediately:

> COLONEL LINDBERGH'S BABY WAS KIDNAPPED FROM LINDBERGH'S HOME IN HOPEWELL, NJ SOMETIME BETWEEN 7:30 PM AND 10:00 PM THIS DATE. BABY IS 19 MONTHS OLD AND A BOY. IS DRESSED IN SLEEPING SUIT REQUEST THAT ALL CARS BE INVESTIGATED BY POLICE PATROL. AUTHORITY STATE POLICE TRENTON NJ.

Colonel H. Norman Schwarzkopf responded immediately to news of the kidnapping with an all-points bulletin. He had been the head of the New Jersey State Police from its inception in 1921.

```
TRENTON NJ        GB 2507                                    3-1-32
                      POLICE INFORMATION
COLONEL LINDBERGS BABY WAS KIDNAPPED FROM LINDBERGH HOME IN
HOPEWELL NJ SOMETIME BETWEEN 7-30 PM AND 10-00 PM THIS DATE.
BABY IS    19 MONTHS OLD   AND A BOY.   IS DRESSED IN SLEEPING SUIT
REQUEST THAT ALL CARS BE INVESTIGATED BY POLICE PATROLS.
AUTHORITY STATE POLICE   TRENTON NJ.
10-46 PM    JWS-F                    NS              GB 2507
```

2.
A Secretive Loner in the Spotlight

ON MAY 20, 1927, when Charles Lindbergh took off on his unprecedented 33-and-a-half-hour solo flight to Paris from New York, he had little idea that this one journey would make him the object of the greatest media obsession in American history. The timing of his flight, and his ethnic background, made his super-stardom inevitable. "In an age of hedonistic materialism. he had shown courage and self-denial of a high order; in an age of corporations and committees he had acted alone." To insatiable reporters, Lindbergh's biography appeared perfect. The pioneering pilot was born on February 4, 1902, just over two years into the twentieth century. He was raised in part on a Minnesota farm at a time when most Americans remained farmers. He represented both the past and the future.

Fans thrived on any news about their hero that they could get their hands on. They learned that the blond, blue-eyed pilot was named for his Scandinavian father, Charles August ("C.A.") Lindbergh, except C.A.'s wife, Evangeline, spelled her son's middle name like that of the Roman emperor. Science had transformed the world since C.A.'s boyhood. Lindbergh's father had labored on a farm without any machinery before becoming a lawyer and Congressman championing farmers and laborers. His only son provided a comforting link between the past agrarian society and an unknown future shaped by new technology. What his worldwide admirers did not know was that Lindbergh "was shy and aloof, and wary, in his dealings with other human beings; he might be more spontaneous and wholehearted in his response to physical objects for the very reason that these did not demand that he respond and were, indeed, utterly indifferent to him."

Time magazine instituted the category of "Man of the Year" in 1927 and awarded it to the pioneering aviator, dwarfing Yankee Babe Ruth's mammoth sixty-home-run season. Scores of poems and songs honored "Lucky Lindy." Jubilant partygoers of all racial and ethnic backgrounds started doing the "Lindy Hop." Lindbergh was deeply offended. As biographers would later note, throughout his life Lindbergh would regard "most reporters and photographers with intense suspicion and resentment. He . . . insisted that they twisted his words or quoted them out of context, they took pictures of him and his family at unflattering angles, and their jostling and intrusive flashlights upset him."

Fans had no idea that the real Charles Lindbergh was far from the heroic figure reporters portrayed. They had no clue about the paralyzing fears Lindbergh had overcome, nor his nasty, antisocial habits or family scandals. Just three years earlier, he had shown up at Brooks Field in San Antonio, Texas, an unknown quantity in a beat-up commercial biplane. The Army Air Service staff greeting new recruits on March 15, 1924, had to be shocked when out popped a cocky college dropout just in time for flight school. Charles "Slim" Lindbergh's first assignment was to remove that junk heap from the premises.

Pilot training in the 1920s demanded great concentration and skill. Less than a third of the 104 recruits who showed up to boot camp that spring would complete the course. Lindbergh's brash attitude changed abruptly when he almost flunked out. For the first time in his life he hit his textbooks with a vengeance. By the following spring, Lindbergh became one of just 19 young men who earned their wings. He would be remembered as much for his pranks on the ground as for his superior flying ability.

When given time off, most recruits headed for speakeasies and the local whorehouse. Lindbergh never went along. If he was not holed up with reading assignments, the aloof Midwesterner preferred to spend his free hours on mischief. Historian Kenneth Davis characterized the stunts Lindbergh pulled as "more malicious than humorous." Learning that a cadet was deathly afraid of snakes, he hid a small, poisonous one in the fellow's bunk, taking care only that its venom would not be fatal. Another trainee who feared scorpions "might anxiously check his sheets almost every night for a nasty surprise." One well-endowed recruit who slept naked woke up with a start to find his penis painted green and a string tied to it, which Lindbergh had just convinced another recruit to yank. Those sleeping open-mouthed risked Lindbergh squirting their tongues with "shaving cream or hair grease."

When the troops gathered outside, Lindbergh created a trick with a sawed-off shotgun shell he placed under a chair and lit with a slow-burning, string fuse. When someone sat down, "the powder whoofed and the smoke shot upward." Decades later, the world-famous pilot recalled the victims' shocked reactions at boot camp as "delightful" to watch. At least one fellow pilot somehow found it amusing to recall that Lindbergh also attached a parachute to a dog and threw the poor animal off a hangar roof.

After interviewing men who trained with Lindbergh, Davis concluded: "[Lindbergh's] taste and talent for this kind of 'fun' [would] grow apace . . . passing beyond the bounds of sport into what, in the eyes of most observers, will appear a realm of crude, cruel aggression." As biographer Leonard Mosley similarly noted: "Life in the Army stirred Lindbergh's appetite for practical jokes, and they got rougher as he grew older."

When reporters quizzed Lindbergh about his personal life, he abruptly cut them off. Historian Kenneth Davis noted that Lindbergh strongly recoiled from "the absurd myth named 'Lindy' . . . his whole existence a melodrama shaped [by other people's] fantasies. His fame became, in this respect, his mortal enemy . . . No man had a greater passion for privacy than he."

One pair of family secrets the aviator was hell-bent on keeping was that his father was illegitimate, and that Lindbergh was not even his family's original surname. C.A.'s parents had not married until 1885, after they had seven children, C.A. being the first. C.A.'s father, Ola Mansson, had taken the name August Lindbergh when he fled Sweden in 1859 with his 20-year-old mistress Lovisa Jansdotter Carlen, and their baby son.

Mansson had served for more than a decade as secretary for Crown

Prince Charles of Sweden before getting caught in a major embezzlement scandal. He fled Stockholm to avoid prosecution. When he assumed a new identity in America, Mansson left behind a wife and seven children, the youngest of whom was just four at the time. Lindbergh never met his grandfather August Lindbergh, but likely learned about the scandals from two of C.A.'s older half-brothers who emigrated to Minnesota from Sweden in the 1860s and spent the rest of their lives in America.

Lindbergh's family proudly counted themselves of superior stock. As a child, Lindbergh relished the gruesome details of the Sioux Uprising of 1862 that included a massacre of white settlers at New Ulm, Minnesota. Pioneers of his grandfather August Lindbergh's generation vilified the Sioux to justify their own aggressive takeover of Native American lands. When C.A. Lindbergh was growing up, the frontier had moved West. The Chippewa were peaceful weavers and the Sioux no longer posed a threat. Still, C.A. told his young son, that when no adults were around, he and his friends "would hide in bushes and whoop like savages to frighten [their] sisters and their friends."

The future pilot's own earliest memories were from the year he turned three. The summer of 1905, two searing incidents occurred that stuck with the boy for life, and likely fueled his penchant as an adult for destroying the peace of mind of friends and family. His father often swam across the swift currents of the Mississippi River with young Charles on his back, both always stripped naked. One day, the small boy fell off into the rushing river. C.A. continued to shore and watched to see if his son would sink or swim. Luckily, after going under and starting to drown, the little boy managed to thrash himself to safety, shocked to see his father standing on the bank, never having made any effort to come to his son's aid.

Late on Sunday afternoon, August 6, 1905, came the second emotionally scarring event of Lindbergh's early childhood. After dinner, the little boy was playing in the parlor. Suddenly, his mother and their servants began screaming. A maid swooped him into her arms and brought him to the barn. The boy was by now greatly upset. He saw plumes of black smoke and tufts of flame coming from a third-floor window. Fire hoses could not reach that level of the house, but neighbors had time to bring out his mother's cherished piano and most furniture before the house burned to the ground.

To the little boy, the conflagration marked the end of an era. He lost all his toys in the attic. By year's end, his father suffered severe cash flow problems compounded by taxes assessed on his real estate holdings. The fire helped precipitate the final rift in a deteriorating marriage. His parents' separation when he was a small child was another well-guarded family secret.

Widower C.A. Lindbergh and Evangeline Lodge Land were mismatched to begin with: a middle-aged, small-town lawyer raised among immigrant farmers in rural Minnesota; and a refined schoolteacher 17 years his junior, whose father was a prominent dentist and inventor in Detroit. C.A. had been quick to propose to 24-year-old Evangeline in the fall of 1900 when they both lived in a rooming house in Little Falls. Evangeline had just arrived to teach high school chemistry. C.A. had a thriving law practice in town with his brother. When he met her, C.A. had just quit living in his townhouse with his judgmental widowed mother and put his two young daughters in boarding school.

C.A. knew the girls were desperate to come back to live with him. Marrying Evangeline would make that possible. C.A. also viewed her as an elegant asset to further his political ambitions. He had rarely met a woman college graduate, let alone one with a prestigious Bachelor of Science and Master's degree. The attractive brunette came from British, French and Irish stock. She had a beautiful figure, played the piano proficiently and had excellent social skills.

Evangeline's parents tried to dissuade her, but her father's recent bankruptcy made her especially concerned about financial security. The sophisticated Land family only met their stubborn Swedish son-in-law at the wedding at their home in March 1901. They found him "hard to approach and eccentric." Evangeline was at least as difficult in her own way — with a strong temper she likely inherited from her volatile grandmother. The strain on the newlyweds' relationship began shortly after their only child was conceived on their ten-week honeymoon out West.

Evangeline returned to Detroit for the birth of her son. She was still suffering from postpartum depression when she returned with her baby to Little Falls a month later. Her unhappiness was compounded by her prickly relationship with C.A.'s two daughters, who were closer in age to Evangeline than she was to her husband. Evangeline lashed out at C.A. in front of his family and acquaintances, alienating her Swedish mother-in-law and extended family with her superior airs and uncontrollable mood swings. Her stepdaughters called her "crazy" and claimed that she mistreated the baby. In later years, her daughter-in-law Anne Morrow Lindbergh watched Evangeline behave erratically as well, prompting Anne to conclude that her husband's mother suffered from a chemical imbalance.

Lindbergh grew up witnessing his mother's long memory for insults. She never forgave C.A. for guffawing at her when she fell off a galloping horse while riding side saddle because she found that more ladylike, or, on another occasion, when she slipped on winter ice in the town center and every passerby could see her underwear. Her son would exhibit both his father's juvenile sense of humor and his mother's thin skin and desire to inflict punishment for insults — real or imagined.

Well before the Lindberghs' house burned down, C.A. had begun cheating on his wife with a woman who worked in his office. The couple separated for good in 1906. C.A. relocated his principal office to Minneapolis and continued to see his mistress. Evangeline and her young son moved to a hotel in Little Falls and then shared a sparsely furnished room in a boarding house. The four-year-old boy spent a lot of unhappy time "looking out of windows." Once, he took the landlady's cat and dropped it out a third-story window "to see if it was true that it would land on its feet." The experiment worked.

Going forward, Charles alternated spending time alone with each parent as they battled for their son's loyalty with conflicting demands. Evangeline raised her son to value science. C.A. battled to raise his son to relish his tough, Swedish roots and prepare himself to endure any physical hardship. The couple's only child would always view himself as one half grounded in nature, the other in science.

The small boy clung to his father when visiting others. One close friend of C.A.'s later commented that his son was so exceedingly shy that it "made contact with other youngsters of his age next to impossible." His resentful mother reinforced the boy's isolation. He seldom had other children to play with. She disdained all their neighbors and did her best to avoid interacting with her husband's extended family.

In 1906, C.A. won a seat in Congress, where he would serve for five terms. Most winters Evangeline and Charles traveled to the nation's capital where they lived separately from C. A., who had brought his mistress with him to Washington. Yet he and Evangeline kept up appearances by attending official functions together. Their annual charade had to be confusing to their son.

Because of his parents' frequent moves, the boy wound up attending a dozen different public and private grade schools — none for very long. His mother would have preferred to avoid having her son keep being the awkward new kid in class, but C.A. would not commit to paying for private school over the long term. He felt it built character to attend public schools, getting his son ready for the challenges of life.

With all the disruption in his schooling, Lindbergh fell so far below his grade level he found school painfully humiliating. It made a strong impression on him that his Congressman father had originally found studying as tedious as he did. As a youngster, C.A. had often gone AWOL from school, much preferring "the freedom of the surrounding woods and water."

Charles spent most of his time in Washington with his mother. She found bitter satisfaction in bad-mouthing her husband for how little money he provided for their support. In front of their son, her husband called her a "blood sucker" and, at least one time, was so enraged he hit her. Evangeline, in turn, ended one shouting match about her husband's mistress by putting a gun to C.A.'s head. By the summer of 1909, Evangeline sought a divorce. C.A. told his sister he resisted for his son's sake. He also knew voters would never support a divorced man. Evangeline became persuaded that remaining the wife of a Congressman had some advantages.

Summers in Little Falls were far more to the boy's liking. C.A.

shared with his son a love of solitude. They both enjoyed walking in the primeval forests. Charles and his mother stayed in an uninsulated cabin built on the same site as their former home. The little boy created an "Indian lookout" by nailing cleats into a linden tree and later into a giant red oak tree the height of a six-story building overlooking the Mississippi River. He feared heights but found them irresistible.

Lindbergh's mother deeply disapproved of C.A.'s reckless attitude toward her only child. Evangeline had long attributed her husband's "sink or swim" approach to parenthood to his Swedish father, August Lindbergh, who had lost an arm in an accident and kept farming, priding himself for his own "independence and self-reliance." C.A. taught his son basic survival skills in the wilderness. Growing up among lumbermen, Lindbergh also picked up carpentry skills, which came in handy when left to his own devices. Before he was ten, the resourceful youth had built himself stilts, his own raft, and later, a wagon and a suspension bridge over a nearby creek.

Living mostly apart from his half-sisters, Charles became protective of his mother, despite her detached approach to motherhood. The bedtime ritual was a handshake, not a kiss. Few people other than her immediate family would ever get to know her well. For her son, she would remain practically the only female with whom he had any close relationship at all until he met his wife. Yet he also found making his mother panic highly entertaining. He would later derive similar pleasure taking advantage of opportunities to badly frighten his wife.

As a youth, Charles shivered in fear at night, often waking with a loud cry that prompted his mother to invite him to sleep on her bedroom floor. He was plagued by nightmares filled with unseen dangers: a robber with a dagger, a giant snake. Sometimes he seemed to be plummeting "from a tall cliff or building, plunging helplessly downward, nauseated by fear toward ugly death." His mother understood. Thunderstorms frightened her. Having her son sleep nearby let them both get through harrowing nights.

By the age of thirteen, Lindbergh had collected a small arsenal at the summer camp. It included his first rifle from Grandfather Land when he was six, another from his father the following year, a shotgun, a pistol, a revolver and a small saluting cannon with blank shells that his mother's uncle had given him. The weapons gave him a sense of security. Evangeline had by then become so disliked in Little Falls for her superior airs that some local hooligans took to intimidating her on occasion with warning shots. The bullets were fired way over her head as she neared her cottage. Her son then spent considerable time digging a trench by the riverbank, which he concealed with a lengthy mound of dirt in front of it. By the time he made use of his bunker, the mound would be overgrown with grass.

One day, likely in the late summer of 1915, Lindbergh and a friend hauled his weapons down to the bunker to take revenge on a man and several boys across the river who had just fired rifle shots within several feet of Lindbergh's raft. The group was celebrating its malicious mischief by singing a song about lynching. Lindbergh was quite familiar with "coon songs," which were hugely popular when he was growing up. He himself had learned from his mother's younger brother how to use burnt cork to darken his face like white singers then did while performing their racist sets. But the notion that he was the butt of such nasty humor provoked Lindbergh to paddle as fast as he could to shore to run to get his friend Bill Thompson to join him to seek revenge. Thompson was one of the two boys in the neighborhood whom Lindbergh palled around with. The two of them then hauled Lindbergh's weapons down to the bunker where they unleashed a barrage of fire that barely missed the heads of his harassers.

That fall, probably in retaliation, some unknown sniper killed Lindbergh's pet dog Dingo. In high school, the shy, gangly youth was not well-known or liked by other students. He was mortified when a teacher asked for his homework and he either had not done it or was ridiculed for a poor effort. He often fought with boys in the class who taunted him but could only "burn with slow anger over the sniggers of the girls." He did so poorly he was in danger of failing and could not bear to consider how demeaning that would be. Lindbergh lucked out. When the United States joined the Great War in Europe, President Wilson created a program for states to offer school credit for teenagers who took care of the family farm. Life-and-death decisions may have been more unnerving for Lindbergh because of his mother's penchant for naming many of their farm animals. But with help from his father's elderly tenant, the teenager designed and built sties with raised floors to keep his sows from accidentally killing their offspring. Veterinarians provided advice on how to euthanize disease-ridden, new-born calves by a heavy blow to the soft spot on their heads. Lindbergh corralled lambs that had gone astray, but then learned the harsh reality that bottle-feeding motherless lambs with cow's milk took time "you haven't got to give them." He could see verified before his eyes what his grandfather Land taught him about Darwin's law — survival of the fittest.

After grueling workdays, Lindbergh liked to read at night in the kitchen by the light of a kerosene lamp. He scanned headline stories in the *Minneapolis Tribune* and the Little Falls newspaper and pored over materials on farming. Starting in the winter of 1917, Lindbergh focused on a new serial in *Everybody's Magazine*, "Tam o' the Scoots," which featured a courageous Royal Flying Corps pilot on the western front.

Lindbergh had first become fascinated with airplanes when he was twelve and his mother took him to an airfield outside Washington, D.C. Born just a year before the Wright Brothers took their first brief flight, Lindbergh would feel drawn throughout his life to the latest machines that pushed the boundaries of human potential. "Science held the key to the mystery of Life; Science was truth; Science was power."

For several years, Lindbergh's maternal grandmother had come to stay with Evangeline and her grandson for a month each summer at the camp. But when she took sick with cancer, Mrs. Land started living with them year-round so Evangeline could care for her. Lindbergh remembered her later as a "kindly, quiet woman, wonderful with children."

With Evangeline and her ailing mother in the two bedrooms, Lindbergh made his bed on the uninsulated porch, burying himself under a pile of blankets. Staring at the starlit sky, Lindbergh remembered to keep his nose exposed, as his father had advised. Otherwise, his habit of pulling the covers over his head might risk tuberculosis — the disease that had cut short the life of his half-sister Lillian. Those winter nights on the below-zero porch helped him develop extraordinary endurance that would later come in handy as a pilot.

For added warmth, he wore his father's old winter coat to bed and kept his new dog curled up beside him. The terrier was named Wahgoosh — Chippewa for "fox" — and had quickly become the teenager's constant companion. One day, Wahgoosh went missing. The teenager located his beloved pet bashed to death with a crowbar and dumped in their well — his second dog lost to violence. By 1918, Lindbergh and his mother had made a number of enemies in their rural community who were likely capable of such cruelty.

In October of 1918, the sixteen-year-old saw billowing smoke covering the sky "as though a strange and titanic storm were brewing." More than fifty years later, he recalled it as "a rather terrifying sight." That gargantuan fire northeast of the farm turned out to be one of the most devastating in Minnesota's history. For Lindbergh, the experience likely brought back searing memories of watching his family's home at the same location burn to the ground when he was three and a half.

After his grandmother Land died of cancer in January 1919, Lindbergh and his mother left Minnesota with its bitter winters for good. Evangeline convinced her son to enroll in an engineering program at Madison, Wisconsin. She obtained a teaching job there, and a cheap apartment for them to share. Lindbergh joined ROTC and became an accomplished marksman. His mother cooked, kept house and ghost-wrote papers for him. Even so, Lindbergh flunked out. He then rode his motorcycle to Nebraska, where he had heard of a chance to apprentice himself at an airline company.

Soon Lindbergh talked his father into paying for an Army surplus "Jenny" biplane so he could eke out a living giving thrill rides at $5 a pop and performing as a barnstormer. C.A. only agreed to buy the plane on the condition that Lindbergh would fly him around Minnesota for a Senate race. After the political campaign failed, C.A. helped get his son into an Army pilot training program but did not live to see him graduate. That May of 1924, C.A. succumbed to a brain tumor during one last quixotic political campaign for governor. At the time, he and his son were estranged, and C.A. had no idea whether his offspring would make anything of his life.

3.
The Orteig Prize

AFTER Lindbergh graduated flight school in March 1925, he had no luck obtaining an army commission. One reason may have been that Lindbergh was involved just over a week before graduation in a spectacular mid-air collision with a plane piloted by one of his instructors. Amazingly, both men parachuted safely to the ground. Lindbergh soon turned to barnstorming in Missouri where he earned the nicknames "Daredevil" and "Lucky" and billed himself as "The Flying Fool." The tall, slender pilot preferred to answer to the nickname "Slim."

Lindbergh's base was Lambert Field in St. Louis, Missouri, a 170-acre tract that had just been transformed from a hot air balloon launching park. (It would later become the Lambert–St. Louis International Airport.) As a barnstormer, Lindbergh wowed spectators by "wing-walking" — deliberately facing his inner demons and trying to conquer them. But routine performance of that circus act only exacerbated his nightmares of falling to his death. More than thirty of the first forty American pilots had already died in crashes. Lindbergh soon tried a double parachute jumping trick to overcome his fears. He later described the risky stunt as "where life meets death on equal plane." He claimed that by forcing himself to leap into the open air and trust two chutes to open properly in succession, he finally began to sleep soundly through the night. He swore he never experienced nightmares again.

That fall of 1925 Lindbergh obtained a coveted job helping to establish private delivery of mail on a new air run between St. Louis and Chicago. The new company whose team he headed promised that they would make quick deliveries regardless of the weather.

To participating businessmen, the potential for advantage seemed staggering. They could make an offer on Monday afternoon and get a reply by mid-morning Wednesday — far sooner than most competition.

Pilots carried little more than the minimum amount of heavy fuel so they could maximize the mail load. The aviators were also encouraged to take their chances with stormy skies to fulfill the fleet owner's promises of speedy delivery. Until late 1926, Lindbergh was known mostly in the Midwest as a reckless airmail pilot. He often flew in bad weather. He lost two company planes in three months, parachuting out just before the engines died for lack of gas. Newspapers noted that Lindbergh might have set an all-time record of surviving four crashed planes. Fortunately, none of the planes killed or maimed anyone when they hit the ground.

While employed at Lambert Field, Lindbergh roomed with other pilots in boarding houses. His penchant for nasty tricks continued. He rigged colleagues' beds so they collapsed when they lay on them, poured freezing water over one roommate as he was getting out of the shower, and put frogs and toads in the other pilots' beds. When he had a rare passenger, he also repeated a stunt that nauseated his companion: whizzing straight up as they approached their destination — for no reason other than his whim — then plummeting straight down before leveling the plane and bringing it safely to ground. The experience must have been like taking a ride on Disney World's "Tower of Terror," only with unsuspecting participants given no choice to refuse the thrill ride.

To keep his head always clear, Lindbergh no longer drank alcohol or Coca Cola. He found their use had dulled his instincts for sharp thinking and interfered with physical fitness. He disdained smoking for similar reasons. He did not know — or care to learn — how to dance or make small talk and strongly disapproved of other frivolous behavior encouraged in the Roaring Twenties. He did occasionally go by himself to the movies to see war films. In September 1926, he happened to see a newsreel about a $25,000 prize he had somehow not heard of before. New York hotel owner Raymond Orteig had made the offer back in 1919 to the first pilot to fly nonstop between New York and Paris. No one had yet accomplished the feat.

Lindbergh soon talked several business clients into sponsoring his entry into that race. After a new monoplane he had his eye on proved too pricey, Lindbergh and his backers turned to Ryan Aircraft in San Diego, California, to have the company modify a mail plane to carry more fuel. The plane Lindbergh would immortalize as "The Spirit of St. Louis" also included a new twenty-horsepower engine and a gas tank in front of the cockpit to minimize the risk that Lindbergh would die in an explosion. The downside was that Lindbergh could only see ahead with a periscope or by leaning out the window.

Despite the time pressures they were under, Lindbergh could not resist playing practical jokes on the team constructing his new plane. He wired magnets to machine tools so anyone picking the tool up would get a shock. He also affixed explosives under the toilet seat in the shop so a loud bang would go off whenever someone sat on it. All of the aircraft crew must have realized Lindbergh bore a high risk of dying on this upcoming flight. Competitors considered a two-man crew essential and strongly favored planes with more than one engine.

Other entrants in the race possessed superior navigation skills and had much more flying time under their belts. Lindbergh had always relied on geographical clues like railroad lines and rivers to find his way. He had never flown over water before and simply planned to rely on dead reckoning. The main things in his favor over competitors were his phenomenal physical endurance, the fact that his plane would carry a substantially lower weight load than others, and sheer bad luck that disabled or delayed famous entrants like Navy Commander Richard Byrd, who had already flown expeditions to the North and South Poles.

* * *

It took nearly a day and a half of nonstop flight before the bleary-eyed pilot reached the European continent from New York. By the time he arrived the sky was pitch dark. Lindbergh initially passed over the lights of Paris, the Eiffel Tower and Le Bourget Field and had to circle back where automobile headlights lit the runway. He wound up with fuel to spare. From the moment of landing on the late evening of May 21, 1927, Lindbergh, the symbol, eclipsed Lindbergh, the man.

Timing was everything. The Coolidge administration used Lindbergh's achievement as a golden opportunity to redeem itself for a horrendous policy mistake two years before. Embracing Lindbergh as a national hero allowed top brass in the military to save face after prosecuting war hero Colonel Billy Mitchell in 1925 for speaking truth to power about America's unreadiness for future wars. Turf-defenders in the military had stubbornly ignored Mitchell's plea to develop an independent air force. After they ignored his dire warning, Mitchell bluntly accused the Navy and War departments of "almost treasonable" disregard for national defense. In a military "trial of the century" in October of 1925, Mitchell was drummed out of the service and ridiculed for his predictions about future national defense needs: a unified department of defense (such as the future Pentagon), protection of Pearl Harbor's fleet from a Japanese air attack (which caught Americans by surprise in 1941), and preparation for future wars in which unmanned missiles and planes would unleash bombs and chemical weapons on civilians.

Taking advantage of Lindbergh's sudden popularity, the Coolidge administration reversed course. The government decided to provide subsidies for much-needed airports at a critical time in the fledgling industry's development. On the Lone Eagle's voyage back to America, those accompanying him found themselves the subject of more practical jokes. Apart from the spectacular feat he had just achieved, those transporting him home knew little about the Midwestern pilot suddenly being thrust forward as a paragon of virtue.

A lavish display of destroyers, blimps, fighter planes and military bands greeted Lindbergh's arrival in Washington. The military provided him with a tailored uniform to wear for the occasion. Lindbergh had received the title of second lieutenant when he graduated from his army training. His title was upgraded to "Colonel" as part of the ceremonies in Washington that June of 1927. Yet by then Lindbergh had volunteer advisors who warned him that appearing in uniform would undercut his powerful image as a loner acting on his own. He rejected the uniform as ill-fitting and showed up in a suit — the first of many public relations ploys to cement his all-American image. Lindbergh would soon complain to a fellow pilot, "I was so filled up with this hero stuff, I could have shouted murder."

Americans across the country listened on their radios as Lindbergh received the honorary title of Army Reserve Colonel and a Distinguished Flying Cross from President Coolidge at a lavish military tribute in Washington, D.C., in June of 1927 following his historic flight.

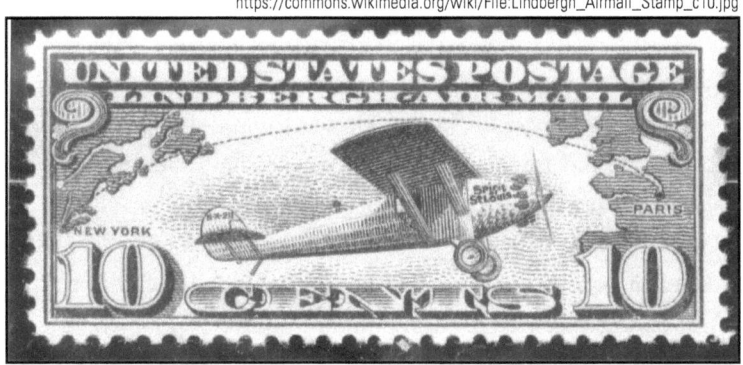

Over 20 million airmail stamps were issued with the image of the Spirit of St. Louis.

4.
The Search for the Perfect Mate

AFTER his historic flight, Lindbergh was viewed as the most eligible bachelor in the country, if not the world. Deluged by fan mail and hounded by autograph seekers, the Midwestern pilot was fawned over by women and teen-aged girls everywhere he went. The unwelcome attention started with a young Parisian woman who rushed up to plant a red-lipstick kiss on his cheek shortly after he landed at Le Bourget.

Star-struck girls who idolized "Lindy" had no idea that at age 25 he had never dated. Indeed, not long before, when he lived in obscurity with fellow pilot Philip "Red" Love in St. Louis, every time Love got on the telephone with a young woman he was interested in, Lindbergh "sang, shouted, whistled, stamped his feet — he banged things, dropped things, rattled things, screeched things" to force his frustrated roommate to end the call.

Facing hordes of reporters and fans on his return from Paris in May 1927, the reclusive pilot was woefully unprepared for the spotlight. He still had the uncouth habits of spitting on the ground in public and wiping his nose on his sleeve. He was tongue-tied when it came to small talk. He did not have his late Congressman father's affinity for glad-handing, nor had he ever absorbed his mother's social skills.

Philanthropist Harry Guggenheim immediately took the awkward new celebrity under his wing. The Swiss Jew headed the Foundation for Aeronautical Research. Guggenheim sequestered Lindbergh at his Long Island estate and helped Lindbergh acquire a suitable wardrobe and improve his social skills. Of greatest consequence, Guggenheim paired Lindbergh with his own attorney, Henry Breckinridge, for legal and business advice. The two became an inseparable team driven by unbridled ambition.

Breckinridge had his own far-reaching connections to powerful men. He was then 41 and in the prime of his career. The six-foot-one Ivy Leaguer, from a long line of bluebloods on both sides, was just a generation removed from the schism in his Kentucky family over the Civil War. Two of his father's brothers fought for the Confederacy, while his father became a Union officer, and later rose to the rank of Major General before retiring.

With his family connections, a Princeton college degree and a law degree from Harvard Law School, Breckinridge's career took off quickly. In 1912, he supported New Jersey Governor Woodrow Wilson (former President of Princeton) as the Democratic candidate for President. After Wilson won, he tapped Breckinridge to serve as Assistant Secretary of War — at the age of 27. Lindbergh was likely far more impressed that Breckinridge won a bronze medal in fencing in the 1920 Summer Olympics and was now training for the 1928 Olympics as the head of the U.S. fencing team. Breckinridge was also an amateur pilot. Lindbergh soon trusted Breckinridge implicitly with all his affairs.

So many accolades and opportunities had begun cascading upon the Minnesota barnstormer his head was spinning. After Congress voted Lindbergh the first medal of honor awarded a civilian, requests for endorsements poured in, totaling $5 million in what seemed like a blink of an eye. Lindbergh was immediately offered a starring role in a Hearst-produced movie opposite the newspaper mogul's mistress, Marion Davies. He accepted the offer but managed to wiggle out of it after Breckinridge convinced him he would regret it.

Chief among the proposals Breckinridge suggested Lindbergh should accept was Guggenheim's plan to bankroll a four-month promotional tour for commercial aviation. Lindbergh earned $50,000 visiting every one of the then forty-eight states, landing in over eighty cities that each honored him with a parade. By one later estimate, nearly a fourth of all Americans turned out to see him. Throughout this tour

Lindbergh was accompanied by a bodyguard, John Fogarty, a former detective, who had worked with one of Breckinridge's brothers when he was in the New York District Attorney's office.

Though Lindbergh turned down millions of dollars in offers, and donated gifts to museums, he accepted shares in new airline companies, which asked him to sit on their boards. Lindbergh soon also profited handsomely from his autobiography. Less than a year since he had scraped by, counting every penny, Lindbergh would become a millionaire, never in danger of going broke again. He made sure his mother was financially secure, too.

That summer and fall, Guggenheim introduced him to wealthy patrons who immediately embraced the national hero as one of their own. Lindbergh was of white Protestant stock at a time when control of America remained firmly in the hands of those with a similar religious and racial makeup. Of pure Nordic descent on his father's side, the tall blond pilot, was the very image the elite wanted to project of traditional wholesomeness, bravery, and self-reliance.

From his arrival in New York after his flight to Paris, in or out of his flight clothes, on or off the field, journalists and cameramen hounded the aviation pioneer. This was only the beginning of an insatiable media appetite for family photos and details of his background for newspaper editors to manipulate to fit the image of the hero the public craved to admire.

During his tour across America that summer, Lindbergh focused single-mindedly on expanding interest in commercial aviation. He was repulsed time and again by obsessed female fans who made off with souvenir pillow slips he had slept on or underwear they filched from his hotel laundry service. More than once someone absconded with his fedora left with a restaurant hat checker. He took to scowling at the camera and behaving rudely toward mobs of adoring fans. He soon began burning all the myriad letters he received without having anyone open them to sort out those he might wish to read and consider a reply.

Lindbergh remained surrounded by pretty young women almost everywhere he went. Yet he found it difficult to get beyond the awkward exchange of pleasantries. It got under his skin that the press wrote up any hint of interest he showed in the few females he found worthy of his attention. Some reporters even fabricated dates with women he had never met. For relief, Lindbergh turned to his usual source of amusement. He annoyed his new assistant Harry Bruno with practical jokes: "He'd put a fish in your camera, a blunt blade in your razor or switched the keys in your typewriter." The public never realized the extent of that nasty habit.

By late July 1927, *New York Times* reporter Carlisle MacDonald was nearing completion of the ghostwritten manuscript for Lindbergh's autobiography that Lindbergh had agreed to do in May. Lindbergh read the draft while secluded at Guggenheim's Long Island estate. He became incensed at MacDonald's presumptuous retelling of his life. Lindbergh remained at the estate while he set about rewriting the story in his own words. What disappointed Lindbergh most was that the ghostwritten draft left out all of his pranks. Rewriting the book that fall, the newly acclaimed paragon of "American idealism, character and conduct" took special delight in inserting some of his more memorable pranks, as well as racist anecdotes from his barnstorming days. In retelling some of his favorite stories, Lindbergh was careful to suppress incidents of his most sadistic behavior.

The "most notorious and cruel" of Lindbergh's practical jokes involved a younger pilot he recruited to his airmail team — Harlan "Bud" Gurney. One night when the two shared a room at a boarding house, Lindbergh filled the water pitcher with kerosene. Gurney quickly drank two dippersful from the pitcher before he realized he was not downing water. He wound up in the hospital with a severely burnt throat, lucky to be alive. Uncharacteristically, Lindbergh later regretted that he had not devised a more "moderate" practical joke to teach Gurney a lesson for Gurney's thoughtlessness in not doing his fair share of refilling the pitcher for the two of them. The near disaster did not dissuade Lindbergh from devising cruel tricks against other hapless victims.

As Lindbergh worked on his autobiography, *"WE,"* he mostly avoided all women except his mother. Yet the tall blond hero began seriously considering his marriage prospects. Lindbergh approached the issue of marriage and family scientifically. In the summer of 1927 Lindbergh had received a plaque from the Minnesota Eugenics Society "in recognition of his superior hereditary endowment." He felt he had a special obligation to pass on his acclaimed genes to help perpetuate the most advanced race of people. By then, eugenics had become firmly entrenched as "the religion of aristocrats" who believed "Western civilization was in danger of committing racial suicide as a result of the rapid reproduction of the unfit coupled with a decline in the birth rate of the supposedly 'better' classes."

Yet Lindbergh was also painfully aware of his lack of social skills: dancing, small talk and etiquette. Getting up the nerve to invite a woman to the theater or a restaurant totally baffled him. He did know what he wanted to avoid. He had been disgusted by the paid sex pursued by his fellow Army recruits. Lindbergh felt strongly the whorehouse was "not an environment conducive to evolutionary progress." He was just as nauseated by the one-night stands of his libidinous pilot buddies. Their dating habits did not reflect "selectivity, hardly any desire for permanence and children."

A year before Lindbergh's flight, prominent doctors, lawyers, politicians and professors launched an organization expressly devoted to improving the gene pool, the American Eugenics Society (AES). Both the AES and the more established American Genetics Association (AGA) counted among their members the nation's leading geneticists, strongly supported by powerful politicians and wealthy philanthropists, including the nation's two richest men, steel magnate Andrew Carnegie and oil baron John D. Rockefeller.

Lindbergh likely first became aware of the AES in 1926 when it started an annual national contest promoted in county and state fairs — places where barnstormers then often performed. Dubbed "Fitter Families for Future Firesides," these "Fitter Family Contests" awarded annual trophies through competition. The contestants vied for designation by AES doctors as the couple who produced "the most viable offspring based on physical appearance, behavior, intelligence, and health." Invariably, the winners were those of white Northern and Western European ancestry.

By the summer of 1927, Lindbergh's own elevated view of self-worth matched eugenicists' concept of ideal characteristics — narcissism that groupies reinforced everywhere he went. Looking for a wife in 1927, Lindbergh embraced the AES standard. He wanted a woman of "good health, good form, good sight and hearing." Biographer A. Scott Berg describes Lindbergh's formula as "more about animal husbandry than human relations. . . . emoting less about choosing a wife than a farmer might in selecting a cow." But Lindbergh saw human procreation through that same lens. He felt he had a special obligation to pass on his acclaimed superior genes to help perpetuate the most advanced race of people.

By his twenties, Lindbergh had clearly absorbed the knowledge that Nordic supremacy was a widely shared view. He, too, believed other races were inferior. Indeed, no one who came of age in the 1920s could escape the white supremacist message underlying the national agenda. In 1924, Congress passed a draconian immigration policy aimed at homogenizing the gene pool by excluding Asian immigrants and severely limiting the number of "Hebrews, Slavs, Catholics and Negroes" permitted to immigrate to the United States. Birth control advocate Margaret Sanger reduced the policy to a slogan: "More children for the fit; less for the unfit."

By the late 1920s, the widely publicized goal of eugenicists was both to purge the gene pool of as many people with "inferior" traits as possible and to encourage procreation by the best white families. Support for the eugenics movement hit its high point less than three weeks before Lindbergh's solo crossing of the Atlantic. That was when the United States Supreme Court issued a landmark ruling endorsing forced sterilization of those deemed unfit. The Supreme Court's ruling in *Buck v. Bell* prompted a major push to pass legislation to rid the country in future generations of "the socially inadequate" — defectives, dependents and delinquents. All of this coincided with the national campaign to encourage preferred white couples to compete in creating Fitter Families for Future Firesides.

It is easy to see how Lindbergh felt compelled to be part of the solution. Like Teddy Roosevelt, who had been C.A. Lindbergh's hero,

Lindbergh believed people exhibiting excellent family traits had a duty to intermarry and produce numerous offspring. Lindbergh considered it important to have a definite objective in mind before committing himself to a plan of action. He decided he could best help improve the gene pool by producing twelve children like himself. He focused on finding a marriage partner with "good heredity," a lesson learned from his "experience in breeding animals on our farm."

In the fall of 1927 when Lindbergh worked weekdays on rewriting his autobiography, Guggenheim continued his own mission. One wonders if he was inspired by the character Professor Henry Higgins in George Bernard Shaw's enormously popular play "Pygmalion" (later remade as the musical "My Fair Lady"). Guggenheim similarly planned to transform his houseguest from an uncouth barnstormer to the toast of high society. The debonair New Yorker had already fitted Lindbergh with a tuxedo and several hand-tailored suits. That fall, the wealthy philanthropist featured Lindbergh at numerous weekend parties held at the Guggenheims' Long Island mansion.

Lindbergh was still a virgin. He shunned women who wore too much makeup. He did not play tennis and found it awkward to learn parlor games or chat about movie stars or the latest styles. He was not comfortable holding doors open, discussing literature or escorting women to the theater. He studied girls' bodies to see if the clothes they wore might be obscuring defects in their builds. He invited some of them swimming to see for sure. But Lindbergh was wary of showing too much interest in a particular young woman. Otherwise, the newspapers were prone to instantly have them engaged.

While being feted at millionaires' private estates, it crossed Lindbergh's mind that one of their daughters would be a smart pick. He wanted a mate with a high-achieving father, a woman who would enjoy air travel and was game to assist him on future flights. He wanted a free-thinking girl, not a regular churchgoer with strong religious convictions. He also assumed she would be Caucasian. Guggenheim introduced the shy celebrity to a who's who of powerful men: Herbert Hoover, Orville Wright, John Rockefeller, and J. P. Morgan among them.

Dwight Morrow, whom Lindbergh had already met, attended

gatherings there as well. Morrow was a self-made man, who quickly mastered any subject he was assigned. J. P. Morgan had quickly nurtured Morrow's consummate negotiating skills. When Lindbergh was still in high school, Morrow, through Morgan's influence, had served as the top American civilian aide to General Pershing in France in World War I. (Morrow's path to riches exemplified the war profiteering C.A. Lindbergh had railed against at the time.)

When Lindbergh met his future father-in-law, Morrow occupied the powerful position of general counsel of Morgan's bank. Morrow was also one of the trustees of the Guggenheim Foundation for the Promotion of Aeronautics and had been one of the first dignitaries to greet Lindbergh on his arrival in Washington from Paris. Morrow then headed a board created by President Coolidge to elevate the air service to an Army Air Corps. At the time, an American war with Mexico loomed as a distinct possibility. The Coolidge administration hoped to avoid hostilities between the two countries.

On meeting Lindbergh, Ambassador Morrow instantly realized the pilot's potential value in smoothing relations with the nation's southern neighbor. That fall, Morrow invited Lindbergh to his apartment in New York and persuaded the pilot to take the Spirit of St. Louis on another international trip before donating it to the Smithsonian — an historic nonstop flight to Mexico City from Washington, D.C.

Anne Morrow first met Charles in December 1927, after her father engineered that public relations coup. At the invitation of Mexico's President, Lindbergh took off from the nation's capital on December 13, 1927, shortly after noon and flew through the night to Mexico City. Lindbergh emerged from the cockpit to yet another elaborate hero's welcome. Dwight Morrow brought the pioneering aviator back to the embassy and convinced his wife to invite Lindbergh and his mother to join their family for the holidays. At first, only the Morrows' two youngest children were present with their father and mother at the embassy: Dwight, Jr., aged nineteen and Connie, aged fourteen.

On December 19, 1927, the Morrows' two eldest daughters took the train to Mexico City to join their family for Christmas. Like their mother, both attended Smith College. Elisabeth, age 23, had already graduated and Anne, then 21, was in her senior year. Though Anne enjoyed her older sister's company, she could not help feeling inferior. Elisabeth was the taller of the two, and a striking blonde adept at witty conversation. (She was named for her mother, but the Morrows spelled her first name with an "s" instead of a "z.") Elisabeth seemed to draw beaux at will.

Anne was a petite brunette, pretty, but with her mother's less arresting features. Though athletic, she was bookish by nature, a tendency that filled her with self-doubt in mixed company. Anne did possess dazzling, violet-blue eyes, and two other things her older sister did not — excellent health and total infatuation with Lindbergh.

Ambassador Dwight Morrow

Elizabeth Cutter Morrow

Elisabeth Reeve Morrow

At the request of Ambassador Dwight Morrow, newly minted American hero Charles Lindbergh made an historic nonstop flight to Mexico City in December of 1927 From Washington, D.C. Invited to spend Christmas with the Morrows and their four children, he was instantly attracted to their oldest daughter Elisabeth.

5.
Hooked

AT FIRST, Anne had been irritated to learn that the close-knit family's Christmas holiday would include entertaining a famous stranger. She feared he would be boorish and put a damper on their activities. To her surprise, she found Lindbergh to be introverted. He seemed extremely young, though he was four years her senior. She noticed that he often withdrew into uncomfortable silence.

Lindbergh seemed instantly drawn to Elisabeth's beauty and vivacious personality. Anne wondered why it was that good-looking men inspired her older sister to perform "at her best and always . . . put me at my worst?" Whenever the Morrows and their guest went out in public, Anne observed that Lindbergh left everyone he met spellbound. She assumed he either symbolized "the most stupendous achievement of our age" or simply exuded "personal magnetism."

Soon Evangeline Lindbergh arrived from Detroit via San Antonio with great fanfare — transported to Mexico City in a Ford passenger plane flanked by five smaller planes for escort. The Morrow family greeted her at Valbuena Airport with a huge crowd that had gathered to watch the planes descend. Anne recorded in her diary how thrilled she was at the sight — "the tremendous excitement as of a strong electric current going through you." Photographers and reporters also mobbed the embassy on their return, shouting "Viva Lindbergh." Anne confided to her diary, "I can see how they all worship him."

Anne felt tongue-tied. She envied her older sister's conversational skill. During his stay, Lindbergh offered Elisabeth a ride in the three-engine Ford plane that had brought his mother to Mexico City. He extended the invitation to Connie and Anne, his mother, their Aunt Alice Morrow and a Ford engineer. The plane could seat them all strapped into wicker chairs in the cabin.

Arriving at the airport, Anne found the very sound of airplane motors "intoxicating." All three Morrow daughters found their modern magic carpet ride thrilling beyond belief. Lindbergh was so sure of himself and relaxed in the air. The lift-off left Anne breathless. She told her diary: "I will not be happy till it happens again." Elisabeth asked him at lunch if they could all learn to fly, and he encouraged them to get lessons. When Lindbergh departed on December 28 for a goodwill tour of South America, he left the family in awe. Anne later acknowledged that meeting Lindbergh completely altered "my world, my feelings about life and myself." She now felt that the sky was something open to her to possess as well, like a soaring bird or a winged unicorn.

When contemplating graduation from high school, Anne had fantasized about marrying a hero. Long after Lindbergh departed, she still felt his glow. Despite knowing she was his intellectual superior and far more sophisticated, Anne found herself magnetically attracted to him. Anne felt she had touched greatness. She thought he exuded "clean-cut freshness . . . complete absence of falseness . . . tolerant good humor." She was beguiled by "his smile, his attitude hands in pocket looking straight at you." At the same time, Anne realized Lindbergh barely noticed her. Being realistic, she expected him to remain utterly inaccessible to someone like herself.

Anne soon learned that her father had invited Colonel Lindbergh to join the family again that summer at their new vacation home on the island of North Haven, Maine. There, the family and guests could relax and enjoy swimming sailing, golf and tennis. Anne excelled at swimming and tennis. Their estate in New Jersey also boasted a tennis court and pool, but North Haven provided a much-needed respite for Dwight Morrow away from the intensity of Wall Street. Anne envied Elisabeth. She pictured yet another handsome young man falling under her sister's spell, while Anne stood by like a wall flower. Lindbergh was attracted to Elisabeth's "sparkling vivacity," while he barely noticed her younger sister Anne.

In the spring of 1928, Lindbergh made more headlines that Anne followed with fascination. While finishing up at Smith, she dated college boys who seemed all too commonplace. She resumed her focus in her last semester on classical literature and poetry, a concentration she disparaged as "utterly worthless compared to the world of Elisabeth and Colonel Lindbergh." Yet an essay and a highly imaginative story she polished that spring won Anne two coveted literary prizes.

Late in March Anne found herself at the movies in Northampton enthralled by the documentary, "Forty Thousand Miles with Colonel Lindbergh." It amazed her that she had met the hero of that film. On the way to the American Embassy in Mexico City, Anne and her mother got off the train in St. Louis in hopes of seeing the new Lindbergh exhibit at the Jefferson Memorial Museum, but they arrived too late for entry.

Anne kept thinking about Lindbergh. He was clearly someone from a different planet. "It is so *idiotic* to sentimentalize him, to see into his personality things we want to see there — things which could never, *never* be there. Everyone has made that mistake: he has been made a kind of slop bowl for everyone's personal dreams and ideals." Yet she did not heed her own warning. Soon, Anne was exclaiming to her diary that Lindbergh was "the last of the gods."

On her way back from Mexico to Smith, Anne studied the handbook, *Airmen and Aircraft*. Though she had played basketball in high school, she did not believe she had the physical endurance and coordination the book considered indispensable for pilots. She credited herself with excellent vision, but it dismayed her to read that an ideal pilot should have other attributes she considered herself to lack: fearlessness," "level-headedness at all times," and "adaptability."

In her spare time Anne got her license to drive and fantasized about flying again. She pored over issues of "Popular Aviation" and even wrote a few poems on the subject. In April, Anne and a friend stopped by an airfield near Smith College where Anne peppered an affable pilot with questions and wangled an invitation to sit at a parked plane's controls so she could try them herself. In early May, Anne talked her friend into going back. Despite heavy winds, a pilot took them up on a bumpy and noisy ride, but as they flew over the college, local hills, fields and neighborhoods, Anne "felt like God." It was "a shock of revelation, as if one suddenly saw the world upside down." Anne went up with a pilot twice more that spring, once joined by her sister Elisabeth.

Meanwhile, Lindbergh continued making front page news with his exploits, dodging reporters ever eager to track his moves. Anne read voraciously any news she could get of him, but still dreaded his visit that summer. She could tell that both her sisters had appealed to him more. She even imagined him marrying Connie in a few years' time, if he did not propose to Elisabeth.

In late April 1928, Lindbergh made banner headlines flying to Quebec through a snowstorm with a potentially life-saving antibiotic serum for rival pilot, Floyd Bennett. Bennett had been on his own rescue mission when he came down with a severe case of pneumonia in mid-flight, causing his hospitalization. Racing to Bennett's aid was just the type of high-risk, high-reward challenge Lindbergh thrived on. Only he could potentially make it in time — and there was some irony involved. Bennett had been favored, along with Commador Richard Byrd, to win the Orteig Prize in 1927 but got sidelined with a serious injury during a practice flight, leaving the field open to Lindbergh.

Lindbergh's courageous rescue mission deeply impressed Anne, though the medicine arrived too late to make a difference. In May, her idol flew from St. Louis to New York, but created the heart-stopping headline "Lindbergh Missing" after he failed to check in on arrival. The aviator was presumed dead, like so many hapless pilots before him, until he turned up and mocked the fake news he had engendered. Anticipating Lindbergh's next visit at the Morrows' new summer home, Anne fantasized about him once more, telling her diary it might be "sentimental hero-worship" but he was "the finest man I ever met." Yet she considered him "someone utterly opposite to me" and clearly outside of her world.

Lindbergh's schedule proved too busy to join the Morrow family in Maine. Then Anne learned from her aunt that he still planned to see Elisabeth that fall in New York. She concluded his marriage to Elisabeth was "inevitable." Anne confided to her diary: "That dream is peacefully dead — speedy burial advised." She and her sister Connie started speculating about who would come to Elisabeth's elaborate wedding.

If Lindbergh had tried to woo Elisabeth Morrow that fall, he likely would have faced a surprising rebuff. Earlier that year Elisabeth had made a pact with her close friend from Smith, Connie Chilton, to love each other and no one else. The two made plans to start a preschool together in Englewood, New Jersey. Her parents feared the young women had begun a lesbian relationship. The Morrows did their best to keep the pair apart. In September 1928, Elisabeth left on a trip to Europe.

Meanwhile, on Henry Breckinridge's advice, Lindbergh accepted a job at Pan American Airways and a position as technical advisor and board member at Transcontinental Air Transport, which later became Trans World Airlines. In exasperation at how much the media dogged his every move, Lindbergh told a colleague: "I'm going to quit! I'll go out of my mind if they don't stop pushing me." He completed his farewell tour in the Spirit of St. Louis with a flight from St. Louis to the nation's capital and returned to Manhattan where he often stayed with Breckinridge between travels.

Breckinridge was then newly married to his second wife, Aida, who was also an aviation pioneer of sorts. As a teenager in 1903 she took a few flying lessons from inventor and aviation pioneer Alberto Santos-Dumont and made a short hop on her own in his dirigible — the first woman in the world to fly solo in a powered aircraft. (It was a brief adventure. Aida accidentally landed it in the middle of a French polo match.)

The Breckinridges provided a welcome refuge from paparazzi and fans. Lindbergh now intended to move forward with marriage plans. Meanwhile, at Dwight Morrow's urging, Lindbergh ventured into politics. On October 3, 1928, the pilot endorsed Herbert Hoover for President. That same day, Lindbergh called the Morrows' home in Englewood and asked for Mr. or Mrs. Morrow or Elisabeth. Lindbergh learned that Elisabeth had gone to Europe, but that Anne was expected home later that night. He called back the next day and offered to make good on a flying lesson. Anne put him off because she was scheduled for minor surgery. The following week when they met up, her excitement diminished when the first thing he asked her was when Elisabeth would return from her trip overseas. Anne was his clear second choice.

Lindbergh wanted to avoid the press, so they agreed to a late morning rendezvous at the apartment house in Manhattan of a close colleague of Anne's father. Anne assumed they would grab sandwiches before heading out to Long Island in his new car to board his plane. She had dressed for the open cockpit flight in her mother's raincoat, an old wool top of her mother's, her sister Connie's riding pants, and her father's golf socks incongruously stuffed into high-heeled shoes. She carried a leather jacket in case she needed it in the open-air cockpit and apologized to Lindbergh for not wearing boots. Anne was both surprised and painfully embarrassed when Lindbergh brought her first to the Guggenheim mansion for an elaborate luncheon. All the other women showed up in high fashion. Before entering, Anne put on her smarter-looking red leather jacket instead of her raincoat. She proceeded to swelter through the unexpected ordeal.

The Guggenheim estate had its own landing field where Lindbergh said he would pick her up. Lindbergh then departed for Roosevelt Airfield to fetch his biplane. During his absence, the Guggenheims shocked Anne with stories of the stunts he had pulled on them while staying as their guest. One of his favorites was when they went canoeing. He would tip the canoe over to watch them get drenched and scramble for shore. Between the army and barnstorming, Lindbergh had developed a large repertoire of practical jokes he could not resist playing on anyone he spent significant time with.

Whatever misgivings Anne had about Lindbergh's immaturity went by the wayside when he came back with a helmet and pair of goggles for her to don for their aerial tour of the city and parts of New Jersey. He also showed her how to use a parachute in the unlikelihood they had to ditch the plane. Lindbergh then tested her ability to subordinate herself unquestioningly to his will. Once safely airborne, he instructed the petrified neophyte to take the wheel temporarily, assuring her it was safe. Despite her fright, she obliged. Anne pushed herself well beyond her comfort zone to do whatever he commanded.

Anne was soon writing to her sister Connie about the flying lessons but did not tell Elisabeth or their parents. Elisabeth was still in London, having taken to bed with recurrent pneumonia. Her mother had already heard about Anne being with Lindbergh at the Guggenheims and warned Anne that her father would not appreciate seeing her name turn up in newspaper gossip columns. Despite her excitement, Anne herself had developed major reservations about Lindbergh as a suitor. She considered him "terribly young and crude in many small ways."

While her parents remained in Mexico City, Anne and Charles visited the new family mansion, "Next Day Hill," in Englewood, New Jersey, under the watchful eye of the housekeeper. Lindbergh suggested that he and Anne take a drive through the local countryside. Anne later wrote a fictionalized account of a couple very much like herself and Charles on a similar driving date. The young man was also considered a "great catch," but terrible at small talk. Once he parked the car, he gave his date a lecture on carbon monoxide poisoning and then suddenly made "an awkward lunge across the front seat and blurt[ed] out a proposal of marriage. Astonished at winning such a prized beau, she accepts."

To escape for time alone together during their stay in Mexico with her family in the fall of 1928, Anne and Charles would disguise themselves and slip out a servants' entrance to avoid reporters. Despite how exhilarating it felt to be engaged to "the Prince of the air," Anne vacillated over her decision during the next couple of months. She sometimes felt there was a "hideous chasm" between her world and his.

By the end of the year Anne informed her parents she had agreed to marry Lindbergh. The Morrows were, by then, less than thrilled with the prospect. The Morrows were sophisticated and worldly-wise. Dwight Morrow was highly educated and read voraciously. He enjoyed stimulating conversations about politics and was partial to alcohol. Lindbergh was a college drop-out, poorly informed, but opinionated. He was also a teetotaler with a puerile sense of humor and few manners. When the family went canoeing, he would pull the same trick he had pulled on both the Guggenheims and Breckinridges. Anne found it tiresome.

Lindbergh's later claim that his choice of Anne Morrow to marry and bear his children was a product of careful study of her heredity did not match even cursory knowledge of her family's health history. Certainly, by the fall of 1928 he figured out that Anne was a sturdier choice for having children than Elisabeth. Elisabeth's slow convalescence from a second serious bout with pneumonia had the family quite worried. Lindbergh likely learned from Anne that Elisabeth had rheumatic fever as a child that left her with a heart murmur. Nor was her father a strong physical specimen. He stood under five-feet-five inches tall, suffered from chronic migraines, bouts of depression and digestive problems, and had one deformed arm.

As a teetotaler, Lindbergh also must have noticed Dwight Morrow's chronic drinking problem. Anne's mother, Elizabeth Cutter Morrow, was smart and industrious, but also prone to ailments. She was a twin, whose sister died as a child of tuberculosis. Elizabeth Morrow had another sister with severe developmental disabilities. Dwight Jr., the only son, had also been frail and sickly as a child. Some thought him manic-depressive. He had already been hospitalized several times. When Lindbergh met the young man, he stuttered, was subject to major mood swings and claimed to hear voices. He would collapse in a nervous breakdown in early 1928.

It seems obvious that Lindbergh decided to marry Anne despite her family's many health problems. He was a man of action with no real interest in courtship. Having been handed a golden opportunity to marry into a highly influential family, his primary concern was a spouse healthy enough to bear him the twelve offspring he envisioned, and so besotted and enthralled with him and with flying, that she would dutifully follow his every command.

Dwight Morrow asked Anne what she really knew about his background. He and his wife had courted for ten years before they married. At the time Anne was deaf to their concerns and overwhelmed by "merciless exposure" to the media. She later realized the unreality of it all made it extremely difficult for her to acquaint herself with "this stranger well enough to be sure I wanted to marry him." Yet when explaining to her younger sister Connie why she resolved all doubts in favor of marrying Charles, she confided, "Can't look in his eyes and do anything else." Anne's diaries from Christmas 1927 until their wedding in May 1929 revealed she was "besotted with physical desire" — a "powerful sexual attraction" for America's hero she could not resist had she wanted to. From the first time Anne shared the cockpit alone with the fearless pilot, the danger and excitement of flight acted like "an aphrodisiac."

That spring of 1929 Lindbergh took Anne on one of several flights to picnic in private in the Mexican countryside and lost a wheel in the rough terrain. He flew around for several hours to ensure that too little fuel remained to cause the plane to explode on impact when it landed back in Mexico City. The plane did roll over but did not catch fire. Lindbergh told their rescuers it was only a slight "mishap." Anne did not answer how she felt about it, but let her fiancé speak for her. He had already warned her against speaking honestly to interviewers, or even sharing her misgivings with those in their inner circle. He insisted that she also refrain from writing anything down that she would not want to go public.

Though Anne felt smothered, she ceased writing a diary for the next three years and self-censored her letters to friends and family. One biographer noted, "From now on Charles would be her voice." Lindbergh got Anne to fly with him again three days after their crash landing in Mexico City. He wanted to prove how safe they felt in the air. She honored his ban on expressing any contrary view, but she later wrote about similar harrowing experiences that each time left her vowing never to do it again.

In late April, as newspapers covered closely Anne's return by train from Mexico, the Morrows were preoccupied with her sister Connie's welfare — an incident that would become of interest again when Little Charlie disappeared. Connie went down to Mexico on her spring break and then returned to her boarding school in Milton, Massachusetts. On her return, she received a letter from an extortionist that warned she could wind up dead unless her father paid $50,000. The anonymous letter included reference to a Smith student who had recently gone missing (someone Anne knew). It also mentioned Anne and her mother's return from Mexico, which led police to suspect someone quite familiar with the family. The letter included a demand the police not be notified. Connie told her father, who summoned Connie home while he turned the letter over to the Milton police for investigation.

A follow-up letter in mid-May gave specific instructions where to leave the money in a crevice of a wall bordering an estate near the Milton boarding school. By then, all three of Connie's siblings had been apprised of the threat, as well as Anne's fiancé. Lindbergh gallantly offered to whisk his future sister-in-law in his plane to the family vacation home in Maine as a safe hideaway. Meanwhile, a young actress attended the school in Connie's stead. A box filled with paper instead of money was delivered to the designated drop-off spot. The Milton police kept the site under surveillance, but no one ever claimed the fake extortion payment. The police requested writing samples from the Morrows' circle of friends for purposes of comparison, but never found out who threatened Constance.

* * *

Despite repeated inquiries, the family kept the wedding date secret. At the groom's insistence, there would only be twenty guests. Given the Morrows' social standing they had likely wanted to invite hundreds. (When Connie had a coming out party in 1932, there were a thousand guests.) During the couple's short engagement, Lindbergh battled his prospective mother-in-law over the size and other details of the wedding, including his opposition to having a minister officiate. Anne surprised her parents by agreeing with her fiancé. Mrs. Morrow wrote in her diary: "He has her. And we have lost her."

Lindbergh's lawyer and close advisor Henry Breckinridge

Henry's second wife, Aida de Acosta Breckinridge

*Charles and Anne Lindbergh America's Royal Couple.
Photo taken in the summer of 1929 shortly after their marriage.*

6.
America's Royal Couple

ON MAY 27, 1929, the family gathered with friends at the Morrow estate in New Jersey, ostensibly for Mrs. Morrow's fifty-fourth birthday and to celebrate the return of Evangeline Lindbergh from an overseas teaching job. Except for the immediate family, the attendees at the Morrows' New Jersey home on May 27, 1929, had no idea they would be present at Charles and Anne's wedding. Even so, the press had gathered outside the gate of the Morrows' new estate just in case. The engaged couple distracted them with several trips back and forth in street clothes. Likely at Dwight Morrow's instigation, that morning Charles handwrote a will witnessed by his prospective father-in-law's secretary and Anne's sister, Elisabeth Morrow.

The first clue for guests of what they were about to witness occurred when Anne entered the room on her father's arm wearing a white chiffon wedding dress, lace cap and short veil. She carried a small bouquet from the garden. Lindbergh wore a blue suit. The minister then stepped forward. After a brief ceremony with no music, guests toasted the newlyweds. Lindbergh was asked to slice the wedding fruitcake. Unfamiliar with royal icing, he started hacking at the cake. At first, he made no headway through the sugary casing that created an almost impenetrable seal around the fruitcake. He must have felt someone had pulled a practical joke on him and was far from amused.

Neither Mrs. Morrow nor Anne had thought to look at the directions the specially ordered cake came with. The person cutting the cake needed to use a knife dipped repeatedly in piping hot water. Mrs. Morrow assumed the knife was too dull and offered to get her son-in-law a better knife. She then got the shock of her life. "He grabbed her by the wrist and growled 'No! No!' in a tone she had never heard before and would never forget." Lindbergh stubbornly kept sawing at the icing and managed to finish the task.

The entire ceremony and reception were over in less than half an hour. Anne slipped away from the guests to change into a suit to head off with her groom. She hid on the car's floor as Lindbergh drove by the throng of reporters at the estate's entrance. For the time being, they managed to keep the press entirely unaware of what had just taken place or where the two were headed for their honeymoon. Lindbergh had his plane readied for take-off, which fooled the press into heading to the airfield. The subterfuge continued with an exchange of vehicles arranged by Henry Breckinridge. The newlyweds then headed to the Long Island shore where Breckinridge had made sure there was a rowboat available for the couple to reach a thirty-eight-foot motorboat moored nearby.

Anne and Charles managed a few days of quiet motoring as they headed up toward Maine. He let his beard grow and donned grubby pants, a cap and sunglasses to disguise his appearance when he stopped to buy water. But the hunt for the pair was on. Word got out to reporters after they were spotted refueling the boat in Woods Hole, Massachusetts. From that point on, reporters dogged the couple to snag their photographs. Anne felt like "an escaped convict." Their daily life after the honeymoon remained extraordinarily public. Lindbergh's focus was on doing aerial surveys and helping organize travel plans for domestic and overseas commercial flights. The airlines he worked for encouraged as much hype of the new industry as possible. That meant extensive travel. On sidewalks or other public places, Anne felt like the two of them were "monkeys in a cage." She told her younger sister Connie that when speaking to the press she needed to be constantly alert not to reveal "anything at all personal or real."

When the Lindberghs ventured out they often disguised themselves to go unnoticed. Anne would stick all her hair up beneath her hat, wear goggles and heavy lipstick. Lindbergh had varying looks. He might appear as a poorly dressed country boy or wear his hair greased and parted down the middle, his eyebrows darkened and add a pair of glasses. Once on the way to the theater, Anne got her hair cut to a fashionable bob and wore glasses and lipstick but fooled no one. Her husband left at intermission. Life as celebrities was getting old fast. Newspapers and newsreels featured both men and women aviators, but none as much as the Lindberghs.

Anne missed her diary but kept her promise to her husband not to record any of her thoughts, not even during a week spent on vacation with President Hoover and his wife. Lindbergh's advisor Henry Breckinridge had already planted the seed in the celebrity pilot's mind that he, too, could aspire to be President someday. Then, Breckinridge could wield immense national power himself, perhaps as Chief of Staff or in a Cabinet position. Breckinridge likely suggested to Lindbergh that they might target a run in 1940, the first presidential election past Lindbergh's thirty-fifth birthday — the minimum age the Constitution set for a President. The thought stayed in the back of Lindbergh's mind, but, unlike his father, politics was not then his passion.

As reporters followed the Lindberghs around from airport to airport, they observed that he did not treat his bride with any noticeable consideration. Though slightly built, she lugged her own gear and boarded and deplaned without any offer of assistance from her spouse. Lindbergh generally acted as if she were just one of the guys. Anne did not want to be scorned for seeking special accommodations or for voicing persistent safety concerns. She remained stoic, stifling any complaints. Her husband at some point built her a ladder for getting in and out of the cockpit.

It was major news in August 1929 when twenty women pilots, including "Lady Lindy" Amelia Earhart, competed in the first, all-female air derby. Several suffered from carbon monoxide poisoning in their open cockpits. One lost consciousness and crashed and died in the Arizona desert. Unlike Earhart, Anne did not yet have an airplane pilot's license and considered herself simply a novice companion to her extraordinary husband.

Dwight Morrow worried a great deal about his son-in-law taking Anne out on so many risky flights and spending so much money on airplanes and travel. Anne had gained control of a considerable trust fund when she married in May 1929. That September, Dwight Morrow had his attorney prepare a will for Anne stipulating that on her death her estate would go in trust to any children of her marriage. If she had no children before she died, the proceeds of her estate would still not go solely to her husband, but be split equally among Charles, her two sisters and her brother. Morrow's aim was to ensure his son-in-law could not squander all of Anne's inheritance on new aircraft. Morrow may have also had concerns that Lindbergh's lucrative airline deals would not last. He might be a one-trick pony.

Charles was deeply offended. He told his father-in-law he would rather not accept any of the trust fund under those restrictions and asked Anne not to agree to her father's proposal. Anne did her husband's bidding. The Morrows then did an end-run around Lindbergh's objection by removing Anne as trustee and creating a new estate plan for her with the exact same distribution scheme — only without the need for Anne's signature.

In October, Lindbergh took Anne on a plane trip exploring the Yucatan. Inwardly, Anne yearned for "a home, family life, privacy, a baby." When the couple returned, they started thinking about a permanent home of their own. Originally, they considered coastal locations. Lindbergh was himself a millionaire by then, but far less wealthy than Dwight Morrow. Morrow's concerns about his son-in-law's financial security had to have magnified immensely following the devastating stock market crash in late October. By the following year, reports would surface that Lindbergh was hugely overpaid by Pan American and Transcontinental Airlines for technical advice lacking any substantial value and that he was simply "cash[ing] in on the name of Charles Lindbergh and the almost imbecile adoration of the American public."

7.
An Ominous Beginning

ANNE already knew she was pregnant when the couple looked at cliffside property on the edge of the Palisades not far from her parents' estate. Anne was concerned that, if they built a home overlooking the Hudson, in an unguarded moment their new baby might tumble into the river below. Her husband told her that "being a Lindbergh it will have more sense than that!"

Though Anne's first pregnancy soon became a national fixation, it had little effect on the couple's exploits in the air. She only grounded herself long enough to get over morning sickness. Charles could barely wait for her to accompany him to pick up a new plane on the West Coast in January 1930 and take it out for test spins. He expected her to help him set a new record flying across the country and then take another flight to Panama and Mexico.

While the Lindberghs were promoting air travel in California that January, a transport plane crashed on its way to Los Angeles, making national news. It killed all 16 on board. In a letter to her mother-in-law Anne confided that she sometimes feared they would be next. The aviator son of Lindbergh's sponsor Albert Lambert had died in a crash in 1929 while teaching others to fly. Such stories happened with disturbing frequency. But Anne trusted that Charles had excellent judgment regarding weather conditions suitable for flight.

For Anne one of the highlights of that trip was getting to know aviatrix Amelia Earhart better. To Anne's delight and her husband's consternation, the two women bonded when socializing at the home of a California airline executive. Anne noticed that her husband often displayed jealousy of anyone other than him commanding her undivided attention at a dinner or other gathering.

The Lindberghs' next stop was San Diego to visit his friend Hawley Bowlus, the manager of Ryan Aircraft, which had built "The Spirit of St. Louis." Bowlus had just designed his own large glider. Lindbergh pressured Anne into trying a solo flight to help counter the public's fear of flying. Anne feared being a sacrificial lamb, but acquiesced despite the fact she was then in her second trimester. Before the cameras, Anne forced herself to smile as a half dozen men worked the ropes to launch her off the side of the tallest hill in the area — a feat no one had tried before. Once aloft, Anne simply sat immobilized while the wind carried the glider down to an awkward stop. Yet, by staying aloft six minutes, Anne became the first woman to obtain a gliding license. Her husband was quite pleased. It would be decades before Anne would admit how petrified she had been.

On their return home in April 1930, Lindbergh raised eyebrows again by taking Anne — now more than seven-months pregnant — on a flight from Los Angeles to New York in an attempt to set a new record. Anne tried to set her mother's mind at ease. She was "crazy to get home . . . and have nothing ahead except June" when the baby was due. Anne was either being as reckless about her first pregnancy as her husband was or she could not figure out how to say no. In retrospect, she realized she was "tempting providence." Adverse weather conditions compounded what was already an extremely difficult undertaking. Yet Lindbergh stopped just once to refuel and resume his quest.

Lindbergh soared to 10,000 feet to show that getting above the weather was the best alternative for other pilots. But he had not packed along any oxygen. For the last third of the flight Anne was in agony, with a severe headache and nausea from the fumes, compounded by the lack of enough oxygen. She bore her misery in silence, so as not to spoil his chances at a record or prove she was just "a weak woman."

When they landed, Anne was fighting back tears and too ill to deplane without help. Yet the airfield was full of reporters. She insisted her husband get rid of the press as quickly as possible and rush her to a doctor. Curious as to the reason for Lindbergh's brush off, some reporters still lingered as his white-faced wife was lifted out and driven away in a limousine. Her doctor had Anne taken directly to the hospital, worried about the condition of her fetus. The doctor then ordered bed rest for the remainder of Anne's pregnancy. The next day's newspaper accounts mentioned Anne's poor condition upon exiting the plane. Lindbergh was livid. He thought the press should have just reported that the pair made the flight in fourteen and three-quarter hours, setting a new transcontinental record by three full hours.

That late spring of 1930, the Morrow household had its own small hospital ward. Dwight, Jr. was convalescing from his most recent breakdown; Elisabeth was resting from a mild heart attack; and Anne awaited her first born. With time on his hands, Lindbergh offered to take his father-in-law flying over Memorial Day weekend to help him with his new political campaign. Dwight Morrow had been appointed to a vacant Senate seat. He now had to compete in a primary race to win his party's endorsement for the next general election. For the first time in quite a while, the two men had reason to forget their differences. It thrilled Morrow to have his famous son-in-law take him airborne, publicizing his candidacy with a guaranteed crowd-pleaser.

As the impending birth of Anne's baby was the center of everyone's attention, Elisabeth left Englewood to convalesce at the family's estate at North Haven, Maine. She was depressed by the misfortune of her own failing health and fading prospects. She had just established the preschool in Englewood with her friend Connie Chilton a few months before but wondered if she should uproot herself and consider marriage after all.

Meanwhile, Anne tried to religiously follow her doctor's orders to stay home for the next two months. But her husband had other ideas. He talked Anne into sneaking out on June 9, 1930 — presumably against doctor's orders — to test a monoplane. It appalled Mrs. Morrow to see her son-in-law needlessly endanger Anne in her delicate condition, but Mrs. Morrow was powerless to intervene. Tempting fate again when Anne was even nearer her due date, the pair escaped the media on Thursday, June 19, 1930, and drove from Englewood to nearby Teterboro Airport. There, they took a short hop in his plane to Hartford, Connecticut, and back. One assumes Lindbergh brought along the ladder he had built Anne to make it easier to climb in and out.

Lindbergh had made arrangements for Anne to give birth in a private suite at a hospital in New York, but he cancelled those plans just before the baby arrived. Lindbergh refused to share any details. Newspapermen speculated that the baby must have been born early and, perhaps, did not survive due to injuries suffered before birth. So many reporters hovered at the gates of the Morrow estate that the Morrows hired twenty-four-hour guards. But the family remained mum.

To avoid revealing the highly coveted news to a telegraph operator, Lindbergh planned to use an assumed name when he notified his mother of her first grandchild's birth. He protected the message further by developing a code for the baby's sex. If it were a boy, the message would read "advise purchasing property"; a girl would be signified by "advise accepting terms of contract." Anne likely noted the difference in symbolism between the active way her husband characterized a prospective son and the passive language for a daughter. She feared that her husband would be extremely let down if they had a girl.

Photographers crowded by the gates of the Morrow estate for days as Anne's pregnancy neared its end. On June 22, 1930 — Anne's own twenty-fourth birthday — Dr. Everett Hawks delivered her new baby son at the Morrows' Englewood home. Charles Augustus Lindbergh, Jr., weighed 7 and ¾ pounds. The family obstetrician noted his head was quite large but told his grandmother that was like his grandfather's head.

Unlike her husband, Anne was totally absorbed in her new infant. It delighted her that the boy had features of both parents — a variation of their blue eyes, Anne's nose, his father's eyelashes, mouth and cleft chin. A household member told the press that the baby's hair was blond at birth, but that was not so. What the press would focus on more was whether the child had been born with serious health problems, which the family categorically denied. *New York Journal* reporter Laura Vitray later observed that "a great deal has been whispered from time to time about the Lindberghs' son not being normal, about its being deaf and dumb." She didn't believe it, and he showed no signs of either of those impairments. But the scarcity of pictures kept the rumors going.

Though the family never shared their son's medical records, it is quite possible that Charles, Jr. did have worrisome congenital issues.

The baby's pediatrician, Dr. Van Ingen, later described having diagnosed the Lindberghs' first-born at some point during his check-ups with "moderate" rickets. Van Ingen prescribed strong doses of Vitamin D — equal to 50 teaspoons of cod liver oil, almost 17 times what a child might ordinarily be given. In addition, Van Ingen suggested a sun lamp, and Anne made sure to take the boy out in the sun during the day. The baby's small toes curled in on both feet, he would be very late in developing teeth, he had unusually dry skin, and two other symptoms which could possibly indicate a far worse condition than "moderate" rickets.

Anne made many visits to the pediatrician during her son's short life. Yet the only medical record his pediatrician shared with the medical examiner after the boy's death was his 20-month check-up on February 18, 1932 — less than two weeks before he was kidnapped. Dr. Van Ingen reported that he made a note in that visit of the child's enlarged, "square" head and unclosed fontanel long after the soft spot in the baby's head would normally have closed. Back then, doctors depended on primitive x-rays which did not show much. There were no brain scans, ultrasounds or MRIs.

Although not diagnosed by Dr. Van Ingen, both the enlarged, "square head" and unclosed fontanel could potentially have been caused by hydrocephalus — an abnormal build-up of cerebrospinal fluid that, depending on its severity, can possibly lead to brain damage and premature death. Hydrocephalus may be inherited, sometimes caused by traumatic events in utero, including oxygen deprivation suffered at high altitudes, carbon monoxide poisoning, and sometimes by trauma to the head after birth. Modern brain shunts capable of draining the excess fluid and enabling hydrocephalic children to live long, productive lives were not introduced until 1949.

Except for insisting at the last moment that Anne should have their child at home in Englewood, Lindbergh had seemed indifferent to the birth of their new baby. Anne, meanwhile, doted on both her newborn and her husband. She was glad to see the baby's dark hair at birth soon give way to light hair like his father's. She wanted her husband to identify with their child. A few more photos were then circulated of a smiling blond cherub, with the baby looking the picture of health.

Infant Charlie was dubbed "The Little Eaglet." He quickly drew attention that rivaled that paid to his father — newsreels and stories featured in scores of magazines and newspapers, even a new song. France adopted the baby as an honorary citizen. Yet photographs remained few and far between. All through July of 1930 Anne remained at the Morrow estate with her newborn. Lindbergh flew other mail routes as a consultant but was impatient for Anne to feel ready to return to the air. She had not joined him for any long flights since late April. Even though the Lindberghs occupied a separate wing of the Morrows' Georgian mansion, he could not wait to be out from under his in-laws' roof and back in the sky.

Anne, in contrast, enjoyed tending to her newborn, despite finding it awkward at first to hug him. Anne had just read up on the latest child psychology advising against coddling babies too much. She knew her husband felt the same way. Anne still wanted to stay at home and "do nothing else but care for my baby." She soon began indulging her instinct to cradle her son in her arms and sing to him. Anne had a beautiful voice honed with frequent practice. It delighted her to serenade her son.

Reporters continued to dig for insights from the Morrow household staff. Whether staff spread information they were not supposed to share, or it was just the sparseness of photographs of "Little Lindy," the press continued to speculate about the Eaglet's condition. The preoccupation with their son's health greatly bothered both Anne and her husband. Indeed, some members of the media were now reporting with more regularity on Lindbergh's flashes of temper and rude behavior.

Lindbergh felt cornered at Englewood. By early August, Anne yielded to her husband's constant pestering that she join him again in his flights. The couple left their six-week-old infant in the care of a nanny as they flew for a several-day visit to the Guggenheims in Long Island. That was followed by other trips which took them away from Englewood for the better part of a month. Anne told her mother-in-law it felt like she boarded a plane straight from bed. In early September they flew to visit Evangeline in Detroit. Bad weather on their return trip compounded Anne's dread. She worried they were tempting fate.

By the time they returned, Anne and Charles had begun serious efforts to find a place of their own. Lindbergh's focus was on land in central New Jersey near Princeton. Lindbergh found a particularly appealing rural site with an adjacent field large enough to serve as an airstrip. Despite the property's relative isolation, there was also an express train from Princeton Junction to New York City twice daily for commuters. It took just over an hour each way. By car, the Lindberghs' new home was about two hours from the Morrows' estate in Englewood and up to half-an-hour's drive longer from Manhattan, depending on the traffic.

Lindbergh had deliberately focused his search for a suitable site on property near Princeton University. It seemed an ideal locale for the next phase of his career. Lindbergh first visited Princeton in 1928 by invitation from the brother of his transatlantic sponsor Albert Lambert. Back then, when given a campus tour, Lindbergh asked the university's president for permission to use its labs in the future for experiments. By 1929, Lindbergh had bought a number of biology books and purchased a high-powered microscope. He likely got strong encouragement to move near Princeton from his advisor and closest friend Henry Breckinridge.

Henry's middle name, Skillman, honored his mother's uncle by marriage, a Union surgeon who ultimately headed the Kentucky Medical Association. The Skillman family tree actually could be traced back to colonial days in New Jersey. Henry came from a long line of men who attended Princeton. Most of the Skillman men stayed to become prominent local citizens. The nearby town of Skillman, New Jersey, where the State Village for Epileptics was located, was named for another member of his mother's family tree.

In September 1930, the Lindberghs leased a two-bedroom farmhouse closer to Princeton in an unincorporated area called Lawrenceville near Mount Rose, New Jersey. Lindbergh observed to his delight that the rental property contained a field large enough to land a plane. There was also a road directly from Mount Rose to Hopewell so Lindbergh could easily check on progress in the building of his new home. Meanwhile, Dwight Morrow worried about protecting his grandson from intruders once Charles and Anne moved into their new home. Having already wrangled over trust funds for Little Charlie's education, the family patriarch's latest focus was household security at his son-in-law's and daughter's isolated farmhouse.

Every week, *The New York Times* covered the latest reports in a wave of lucrative kidnappings, averaging more than two a day nationwide since 1929. Morrow had become far more attuned to that risk after the incident in April 1929, described earlier, when an extortionist threatened to kidnap his youngest daughter. Police had never solved that crime. As the Depression deepened and kidnapping the children of the well-to-do skyrocketed, the multi-millionaire knew he and his wife remained prime potential victims. As newsreel darlings, Anne and her baby likely provided far more inviting targets.

The two-story rented farmhouse in Mount Rose came with servants' quarters. The Lindberghs soon hired a middle-aged, British couple, Aloysius "Olly" Whateley and Phoebe Mary "Elsie" Whateley, to take care of the farmhouse for them. Meanwhile, it did not take long before word leaked out to the Lindberghs' fan base about their rented farmhouse near Mount Rose and the larger farmhouse they were building in the Sourlands. Newspapers started covering the story of the layout and location of their new home in detail. Most intrusive of all was a spread in the *New York Sunday Mirror* revealing the floor plan and luring readers with the banner headline "THE LONE EAGLE BUILDS A NEST." When the Lindberghs stayed at the Lawrenceville property on weekends, they were tracked there by reporters.

At the rental farmhouse, Lindbergh established his own household rules akin to those observed at his family camp in Minnesota. He had the Whateleys bring dinner to the table all at once in bowls and serving platters. He and Anne and their guests could then help themselves, not be waited on like at her mother's mansion by servants bearing separate courses of food plated in the kitchen. With his huge appetite he must have found formal dining an irritating custom. At his insistence, the baby slept in the barn to build his endurance. Anne grew worried about the baby's safety from prying eyes. She saw to it that Little Charlie was constantly watched over in the barn by Elsie Whateley or herself, or

Betty Gow when she came down with the family for the weekend.

As a new mother, Anne fretted over parenting decisions for Little Charlie. Both Anne and Charles attended the third decennial Conference on Child Health and Protection in Washington, D.C., in November 1930, sponsored by the White House. Henry Breckinridge was both on the planning committee and chair of the legislation and physical education committees. Henry's wife, socialite Aida de Acosta Breckinridge, was Assistant Director of Public Information.

The Breckinridges counted themselves among the elite who enthusiastically promoted eugenics. This conference on child health was in part a think tank for developing public policy. The same eugenics groups which convinced the Supreme Court in 1927 to validate forced sterilization were even more focused than ever before on saving humanity from letting "citizens of the wrong type" procreate. By 1930, the American Eugenics Society had embarked on a national campaign to disseminate statistics that showcased the benefits of eugenics laws.

Anne and Charles were likely quite familiar by then with state fair Fitter Family Contest booths that used flashing red lights to compare birth rates of "able-bodied people" compared to what organizers called "degenerates." The exhibits aimed to horrify fairgoers with claims that capable children were only born "every seven and a half minutes, whereas a feebleminded child every 48 seconds, and a future criminal every 50 seconds."

The Washington, D.C., conference the Lindberghs attended featured a number of prominent eugenicists they already knew from New York and New Jersey, the hub of that movement for the past thirty years. They might have met the superintendent of Skillman State Village for Epileptics which was located near the new property they intended to build on. The village had a street in it named Morrow Drive in honor of Anne's father, who had served on two statewide oversight boards for New Jersey institutions more than a decade earlier. The Lindberghs already knew President Hoover, who himself was a strong proponent of eugenics. Their pediatrician, Dr. Philip Van Ingen, was on the panel that focused on medical care for children.

Of particular interest to the new parents, the conference also featured psychologists who taught the latest ideas about diet, sleep schedule and preschool education. Anne sat up front taking many notes, sometimes accompanied by Aida Breckinridge. The Lindberghs had already begun to follow the advice of popular psychologist John Watson on the care of infants and children. Dr. Watson recommended that babies should be fed on a strict schedule and woken up to change their diapers at 10 p.m. each night, to increase the likelihood they would then sleep through till morning. This practice would reinforce the notion of some of the policemen who later responded to the kidnapping that the crime had to involve insider knowledge.

SUSPECT NO. 1

Elsie and Olly Whateley were first hired to take care of the Lindberghs' rental home in Mount Rose, New Jersey, and cook and chauffeur for the Lindberghs when they spent weekends there. The Whateleys moved into an apartment above the garage of the Lindberghs' new farmhouse outside Hopewell in October of 1931.

Elsie Whateley

Olly Whateley

8.
Back in the Air — Grounded by Tragedy

THROUGHOUT 1931, the airlines continued to call upon Lindbergh to make promotional tours overseas and to comment on air safety. His reassurances to the public were especially desired in the aftermath of a major accident. One particularly spectacular crash occurred at the end of March 1931. Eight people perished after a propeller broke on a commercial plane in Kansas. Among the dead was legendary football coach Knute Rockne. Anne experienced visceral reactions to news like that, though Charles assured her the Kansas crash resulted from a freak accident.

By 1931, airline stock had dropped precipitously in value following the 1929 stock market crash. Yet Lindbergh remained reliably upbeat. He could be counted on as more of a cheerleader for increased air travel than a sober analyst. That spring, Lindbergh gave an optimistic guest lecture at Princeton on the extraordinary potential for aviation. Yet he was beginning to find some of his aviation assignments repetitive and boring. He was looking forward to a major trip which he had talked Anne into taking later that year.

Sometimes Lindbergh demonstrated strong support for his father-in-law. He showed up in early March of 1931 at a banquet at Princeton where Dwight Morrow gave the keynote speech. Despite Lindbergh's show of support, Morrow had reason for consternation. His son-in-law had just ordered a new, custom-designed sea plane to take Anne that summer across Canada to the Far East. The plane would be fitted with pontoons instead of wheels for its landing gear and hop from one water landing to another. Aside from the inherent risks, the plane would cost close to $18,000 (over $275,000 today). The frugal banker considered such expenditure hugely extravagant in the middle of the Depression.

While Lindbergh's new seaplane was being assembled for their next adventure, Anne was happier on the ground. Truth be told, she found flying with her husband often petrifying. Anne felt torn between maternal longings and her husband's demands. Yet incessant rubber-neckers invading their daily life were as frustrating to her as to her husband. Early that spring of 1931, Anne became furious when she learned from her family that fanatic "Lindy" devotees zoomed by her parents' estate and hit her beloved dog Daffin, leaving the white terrier near death as they sped off. The dog could not be saved. She wrote her sister Connie that Charles "wanted to shoot them."

Anne soon had two new dogs whose antics helped take her mind off the loss of Daffin. One was a short, Scotch terrier puppy they bought for themselves and named "Skean." Skean liked to follow Anne around during the day and sleep by the baby's crib. The other dog was a high-spirited fox terrier which arrived from Detroit as a gift from Lindbergh's mother. The dog was named Wahgoosh, like Lindbergh's childhood companion that had been brutally killed in Minnesota when he was a teen. Wahgoosh stayed with the Whateleys at the farmhouse. Skean lived with the Lindberghs in Englewood during the week and came down with them to the farmhouse when they spent weekends there. The baby soon knew both dogs by name. When excited, Skean yipped in "fierce little barks." Both dogs would later become of interest in the kidnap case.

Despite Anne's severe misgivings, Charles talked her into working with him that spring to get her own pilot's license. Breckinridge was on the board of an aircraft company based at Roosevelt Field in Long Island that made slow, three-seater biplanes marketed to barnstormers to take guests sightseeing. It had won an award for safety. The Bird Aviation Company had since relocated to Brooklyn and had just started marketing its third version. Lindbergh bought one to teach Anne to fly — again upsetting his in-laws at both the cost and the potential danger. Though he was spending his own money, the Morrows disapproved of his lack of a full-time job and spending habits. Mostly, they feared for Anne's welfare.

The lessons involved extensive hours away from their baby son each day as Charles trained Anne to pilot the small biplane. Anne hated it whenever they arrived home so late that she missed seeing her son before his bedtime. The lessons themselves became a nightmarish ordeal. She kept to herself the extreme frustration she felt when her husband forced her to repeat landings until she got them right. He also prodded her to complete radio operator training, which required mastery of Morse Code.

Decades later Anne acknowledged "how challenged, frightened and infuriated I was trying to satisfy my exacting instructor." Yet the results of her lessons were self-empowering and ultimately exhilarating. Very few women yet had the opportunity to do what she was being groomed for — and her instructor was the most famous pilot in the world. At last, Anne also had earphones to protect her from the engine noise.

In June 1931, Lindbergh received an honorary degree from Princeton for his pioneering role in aviation. As their departure date for the Orient approached, Anne was feeling conflicted about leaving her son behind. It had been such a joy to celebrate his first birthday with her family at their Englewood estate. By July, Little Charlie was beginning to take steps if someone held his hand. Yet he would not be led. He knew where he wanted to go. She marveled at observing each new stage of his infancy. Yet Anne could not bring herself to refuse another pioneering adventure with her husband.

Complete subordination of her will chafed sometimes, but Anne realized that it was also the lifeblood of their marriage. On the ground, Lindbergh could often be intolerable. He abhorred the arts, still played immature pranks and otherwise demonstrated his lack of savoir-faire. Apart from getting him to use a handkerchief to blow his nose, she mostly bit her lip. In the air, he could take her anywhere on the planet — like the fantastic voyages to exotic destinations she dreamed of as a child.

In late July 1931, the Lindberghs began their extended survey trip from Canada and Alaska to Siberia, Japan and China in their new float plane. Their mission included exploring possibilities for the fastest route from New York to Tokyo, but the trip was more for publicity than actual use by aeronautics teams. They left their thirteen-month old son at Anne's parents' mansion in Englewood.

The Morrows brought their grandson with them on their annual trip to their estate on the island community of North Haven off the coast of Maine. The toddler was accompanied by his new nanny Bessie Gow, who went by the nickname "Betty." Like the Whateleys, who had scant experience as household help, the twenty-seven-year-old Scottish immigrant had very little practice as a nanny before she was hired by the Lindberghs in late February 1931. The interview with the petite brunette at the Morrows' Englewood estate lasted only half an hour. After a week of overlap with the outgoing nanny, Marie Cummings, Betty had quickly gotten the hang of the precise regimen the Lindberghs required.

Before the trip to the Far East, Anne had often left her son alone with Betty at the farmhouse near Mount Rose, New Jersey with the Whateleys. Anne trusted Betty to take good care of the toddler and see to it that he got medical attention when needed. In the Morrows' privileged world, many well-to-do mothers similarly relied on nannies, but few, if any, took off on trips away from their baby as long as the several-month trip the Lindberghs were embarking on. Anne took Betty aside before they left and directed Betty to refrain from coddling the boy. Fearing the loss of her son's affections, Anne specifically warned Betty not to let Little Charlie become too fond of her.

Unlike his wife, Lindbergh never had qualms about leaving his son behind. He fully endorsed child psychologist Watson's view that pampering should be discouraged. It matched Lindbergh's own austere upbringing. If children were held and kissed too much, they turned into mama's boys. On their trip, Anne still greatly missed Little Charlie, cherishing the pictures of him she brought along and dreaming about him almost every night. Sometimes she got the pleasure of sharing the photos with women she met on their journey. Talking with others about her son's outgoing personality and the delight he gave her made Anne feel as if she were back in his presence. Her mother's letters helped a lot. Mrs. Morrow delighted in her grandson and gladly shared that he was now walking on his own. He also liked to take rides on the vacuum cleaner.

The Lindberghs reached the Republic of China in the aftermath of one of the worst floods in recorded history. The death toll from the

1931 months-long disaster along the Yangtze River would ultimately be estimated upwards of three-and-a-half million people with more than ten times as many severely impacted. Snow melt combined with heavy spring rains had precipitated constant flooding over the spring and summer of 1931, covering an area almost as big as New England. The disaster destroyed farmland and villages, leaving behind hordes of homeless and starving refugees devastated by outbreaks of cholera, malaria, measles and dysentery.

Chiang-Kai-Shek had only been the leader of the Republic of China for three years when the flood struck. He faced extraordinary pressure to provide disaster relief. He asked Lindbergh to extend his stay to help distribute food and medical supplies with his seaplane. Much to Anne's disappointment, Lindbergh agreed. When corresponding with her family back in the states, Anne mostly minimized the hardships of their prolonged trip. They sometimes slept in the cramped quarters of the plane and went days without bathing. An accident forced the couple to bail out in life preservers into the unsanitary Yangtze River. Anne's nightmare would be "to die screaming," but the emergency evacuation felt instead like an out-of-body experience. Lindbergh always encouraged Anne to make detailed notes of their flying adventures. She would chronicle this journey in her book *North to the Orient*, which became a best-seller when published in 1935.

When she left Little Charlie with Betty Gow, Anne had originally thought the Morrows would be spending the entire time they were gone with her son. She asked her mother to send pictures each month of the boy as he grew, despite her husband's reluctance to have their son photographed. The Morrows returned to Englewood in mid-September and left their grandson with Betty in Maine out of concern about exposing him to a polio epidemic in the New York area. Back in New Jersey, the Morrows were also immersed in politics.

Not surprisingly, Morrow's Senate campaign centered on ending prohibition. That proved overwhelmingly popular with the voters. Morrow himself still drank to excess and was now under a lot of stress. He died suddenly of a stroke on October 5, 1931, just after delivering a major radio speech. New Jersey's new Senator was only fifty-eight, a devastating loss to the family keenly felt by the Republican Party as well. Dwight Morrow's body was placed in an open casket in the library of his mansion so that colleagues, friends and family could pay their respects. An enormous funeral followed with his friend ex-President Coolidge among the distinguished attendees. Afterward, New Jersey's Democratic Governor Harry Moore offered Elizabeth Morrow her husband's seat for the remainder of his term, but she declined.

Anne was beside herself that she received the shocking news while on an American aircraft carrier in China. She immediately got her husband to cut short their overseas trip. Since their plane was then being repaired in Shanghai, they disembarked in Japan and returned via ship to Seattle. The slowness of their return must have been agonizing for Anne. They borrowed an airplane in Seattle to fly back to New York, arriving home on October 19 — two weeks after her father died.

9.
Getting Reacquainted with "Hi" and "Mum Mum"

A CHAUFFEUR drove Mrs. Morrow and her daughter Elisabeth up to Maine to bring Betty and Little Charlie back to Englewood. Left alone with Betty for a month, the toddler clung to his nanny, and she doted on him. While in Maine, she had his hair trimmed slightly and purchased a new outfit for him out of her wages. (No one had left her money for out-of-pocket expenses.) She was thrilled when his first word was "Betty." Anne would not be.

Following her husband's sudden death, Mrs. Morrow found great solace in being reunited with her grandson. When Anne and Charles arrived back at Englewood, a noticeable gloom pervaded the formerly happy household. Anne was still in shock and just beginning to grieve for her father, deepening her emotional reaction to seeing her son again. After being left behind by his parents for almost three months, Charlie did not recognize them. He cried when they approached, as he did with any stranger.

Upon returning from the Far East, Lindbergh was not happy that photographs of his son had been taken during the couple's absence. He immediately forbade any new pictures of his son, whose blond curls still partially obscured the size of his head. Starting at the end of October 1931, Lindbergh took steps to ensure no new photos of the Little Eaglet would be released to the press by the family.

As the Lindberghs settled back into their spacious quarters at the Morrow mansion that November, Anne was pleasantly surprised that her husband now took more interest in the boy. He fed him some toast with jam from his own plate, swung him "ceiling flying" and nicknamed him "Buster." Charlie called his father "Hi." The little boy enjoyed being swung in the air and asked his father to do it "den!" ("Again!"). Yet others noted that Lindbergh bestowed another, far less endearing nickname on his son — "It." Someone on the Morrow staff leaked to reporters that the little boy began repeating "It" among his very first new words after his father's return.

The Lindberghs could not wait to resettle in their secluded new home. Most of the work getting it ready for occupation had been done while they were on their trip to Asia. While it was under construction, a local man named Lee Hurley had been hired to watch over the property to prevent theft of building materials and supplies. Anne was especially concerned about how they would keep the public out of their property after the house was finished. Her father must have known that Lindbergh was paying a local man to protect the building site. Had he still been alive when the farmhouse was completed, Dwight Morrow would have been outraged to learn that his son-in-law refused Hurley's request to be kept on as a permanent guard.

The Lindberghs took a day trip to their new home on October 25, 1931, accompanied by Mrs. Morrow and Elisabeth. Access to the new property was difficult. Many roads were not marked; some were unpaved. For Mrs. Morrow's chauffeur from Englewood, finding the estate north of the small town of Hopewell was hard to do even during the day. Once you got there, you had to negotiate a long snake of a driveway before reaching the farmhouse.

The $50,000 French Provincial home was not visible from the public road. Its two-and-a-half stories consisted of two, two-story wings jutting out east and west from the main part of the building. Its large basement was fitted with special wiring so Lindbergh could build a laboratory there. The house was constructed of local fieldstones finished in white cement and, as yet, had no window coverings. The half story at the top remained an unfinished attic.

The Lindberghs' new home still had no beds, but that was soon remedied. On Halloween night, Anne, her mother and sister spent one night there with Little Charlie. Instead of having help from a nanny, Anne wanted time to bond with her son herself. But rising at 6:30 a.m. to change him and give him breakfast was not what she had in mind. She asked Elsie Whateley to get Charlie from the nursery and take care of him until Anne completed her own morning routine.

On the Sunday of their overnight stay, the family enjoyed leisure time with Little Charlie on the terrace. Anne may have already been following Dr. Van Ingen's advice to get the boy as much sun as possible. Anne planned to fill the downstairs study with her extensive book collection. Her husband's smaller collection, consisting mostly of scientific books, would be shelved in their bedroom. Originally, Anne had hoped to move into their new home before Thanksgiving, but it still needed painting inside. Anne thought the yard would look better with a bed of tulips by the house and put white ones in before winter hit.

Lindbergh had been home from their China trip only for a few weeks before he was off again on a two-week trip to the Caribbean for Pan-Am in mid-November. Anne declined to accompany him. She wanted to stay with her widowed mother in Englewood and reestablish a bond with her toddler without a nanny. Lindbergh agreed to give Betty Gow three-months' leave.

There was still no way to avoid constant public scrutiny of the Lindberghs' every move. One of the most widely read gossips of the time was syndicated columnist and radio host Walter Winchell. Two thousand newspapers around the world carried his column each day and twenty million people heard his Sunday night radio program. So, Anne must have felt acutely self-conscious when Winchell publicly announced that she must be pregnant again if she was not flying to Panama with her husband. Actually, Anne would not learn until December that she was pregnant with her second child.

Anne realized that her husband might feel otherwise, but she did not consider herself to be missing out by staying home while he flew solo to Panama. The last trip had been extraordinarily grueling, with three forced landings. She had always been close to her mother and wanted to be with the family as they grieved the loss of her father. She also delighted in seeing Charlie develop his father's grin. It pleased her immensely to hear Charlie call for "Mum Mum," or sometimes "Mummy," instead of "Betty." Anne enjoyed seeing her mother so delighted by Little Charlie as well. The little boy called his grandmother "Tee" after she had started letting him play with her golf tees.

Feeling extremely unwell by mid-November, Anne let her mother talk her into sending Little Charlie with Elisabeth to her preschool. Anne soon discovered that her concerns were amply justified. Charlie was only seventeen months old at the time — a full six months younger than any of the other preschoolers. The shy child with his baby curls was instantly viewed as an object of curiosity to the other tots. Bullied by some of the children and intimidated by others, Charlie could not defend himself from having his thick curls pulled, or from getting hit. He cried for the first few days. The school's psychologist suggested leaving Charlie by himself in a sandbox until he developed social skills. (One would think that an unlikely way to get the toddler acclimated to playmates.) Left alone, he did much better, content to play by himself.

People across the country again began speculating about Charlie's health. Rumors recirculated about him being traumatized in utero from "prenatal drumming of airplane motors." Maybe some parent at Elisabeth's day care started the rumor he was deaf. Or, perhaps, some staff member at the Morrows' Englewood mansion. There was also speculation the reason Little Charlie did not interact with other children was because he was mute. No such diagnosis could have been made by the doctor at the Little School who checked all the children's health once a week. Anyone who regularly interacted with the boy could tell that Charlie had an expanding vocabulary. To his mother and grandmother's delight, he had also begun to learn to count.

Meanwhile, at the end of November, Lindbergh stopped in Florida for an airline promotional event on his way back from Panama. Coming home, he got severely delayed navigating through heavy snowstorms and an icy gale, prompting reporters to call the Morrow house with false reports that calamity must have struck. Instead, he had detoured with unannounced stops on his trip north. Lindbergh returned home in the middle of the night three days later than expected. With him he carried the mangled body of a seagull that had gotten stuck in his plane's propeller. For some bizarre reason, he left the dead bird on the ground outside his and Anne's bedroom window for several days before it was disposed of.

Catching up with home life in his absence, Lindbergh reacted angrily to news that his son failed to defend himself at the preschool. Like his own father, he did not want to raise a weakling. In December, Lindbergh built a large wire pen in the yard of the Morrows' mansion. He then told Betty to dress his son warmly for the winter weather and put him in the pen with one of his toys "to fend for himself." Charlie sat bewildered by his isolation in the cold outdoors, crying off and on for hours. Betty could not take it any longer. She went to Anne and begged her to bring the boy in. Anne turned to her, with tears in her eyes and replied with resignation, "Betty, there's nothing we can do."

In late December 1931, Anne's morning sickness became compounded by food poisoning. The family spent that Christmas at the Morrows' Englewood estate, joined by Lindbergh's mother from Detroit. Charlie particularly enjoyed his gift from "Tee" — a wooden Noah's Ark with dozens of animals. The toddler and his father played with it for hours that day. Again, the next day Lindbergh made a game of testing his son's ability to name all the animals. Charlie was quite good at that, possibly surprising his father with his intellectual development.

There may have been a medical reason for Lindbergh to engage in that game with his son. If Lindbergh had learned by then that an enlarged head and unclosed fontanel could be signs of hydrocephalus, increased pressure of fluids on Charlie's brain could begin to cause mental impairment. So, checking on his memory would be a way to test that theory.

Likely highest on Lindbergh's list of concerns would have been whether all his children would turn out like Little Charlie. Lindbergh did not consider his firstborn an example of the fittest. Playing on the floor with his young son may also have brought back memories of the joyous days Lindbergh spent playing in the attic when he was three, before the twin horrors of nearly drowning and losing all his toys in the fire that destroyed his home.

The day after Christmas, Mrs. Morrow heard her grandson howling from the bathroom where he had been playing with his new rubber toys in the tub. Mrs. Morrow started screaming at her son-in-law, "sure that he had been ducking him 'to test his courage.'" Betty got to the bathroom first. She told Mrs. Morrow that she found "Colonel Lindbergh laughing his head off. He saw that the baby wasn't hurt, just frightened." Mrs. Morrow never really trusted Lindbergh afterward.

Anne heard a different version of the bathroom incident from her husband that she reported to her mother-in-law. Evangeline had given her grandson the bath toys as a Christmas present. Anne told Evangeline that Little Charlie had accidentally slipped in the tub while playing with the new toys. But that did not account for why Lindbergh was found chortling at the child's misery. Indeed, when interviewed many years later, Betty recalled "there was something about the Colonel — that little bit of sadism." Neither Betty Gow, nor Mrs. Morrow had reason to know of Lindbergh's terrifying "sink or swim" lesson at three-and-a-half from his own father.

The Lindberghs spent New Year's weekend at their new home with his mother and the Whateleys. Betty Gow joined them on the First. By then Little Charlie was accustomed to "Elthie" as one of his caregivers. It was Betty's first work assignment at the farmhouse, and she dreaded it. Once the family moved for good, gone would be her daily interaction with a score of other staff. Her new boyfriend would be upset, too. She would be stuck two hours away from him in the middle of nowhere.

As much as Evangeline Lindbergh enjoyed seeing her only grandson, she refrained from hugging or kissing him, something she remembered months later after it turned out to be the last time Evangeline ever saw him. To Anne, the last months of 1931 would in retrospect feel as if she were on a "swift-flowing stream . . . rushing headlong to the sheer drop of tragedy."

Animals from Little Charlie's Noah's Ark

Antique three-wheeled Kiddie Kar similar to the Kiddie Kar owned by Little Charlie

10.
Little Charlie's Last Days

AS THE new year began, neighbors thought the celebrated couple had not yet moved into their country estate. Mostly, Elsie and Olly Whateley stayed there alone with back up from another couple, Ambrose Titus and his wife, whenever the Whateleys left town. The Tituses may have given unauthorized tours to curious fans of the celebrity newcomer. The Lindberghs still spent weekdays at the Morrows' mansion in Englewood, but in January 1932, the Lindberghs started staying most weekends at their new home outside Hopewell. They brought Skean with them. Lindbergh called their new home "the farm," though he had no known plans for cultivating the property. The family came down on Saturday morning and stayed just two nights. The first weekend of February Mrs. Morrow came down to the farmhouse with them. The middle two weekends of February the family stayed in Englewood because of family colds. After weekends at the farmhouse, Lindbergh's destination on Monday mornings was Manhattan. His wife would separately pack up so Olly Whateley could drive her, Charlie and Skean back to her mother's estate in Englewood.

That same month, Lindbergh badgered Anne to accompany him to Los Angeles to an air race show. Though three-months pregnant with her second child, she grudgingly agreed. Her husband told Anne she was self-indulgent for wanting to stay home with her toddler, and the new baby when it came. It bothered him how thrilled Anne was to see her son now mimic everything said to him.

The little boy was very sure of his likes and dislikes, which he indicated with "uh huh" and "naw." He loved running around with the family dogs and playing with his new Christmas toys. He had his own three-wheel wooden scooter among the toys in his nursery. He enjoyed turning the crank on his music box all by himself. He also made Anne laugh when he bent over and viewed her through his legs. Charlie attended the Little School on and off through late February 1932, missing more than half of the sessions. The bullying apparently ended, and he began to enjoy the experience. Connie Chilton had noted in Little Charlie's January 1932 evaluation that he still preferred not to interact with other children. Instead he would carefully observe what they were doing and wait until they were out of the room to repeat their activities. His report card showed "good muscular coordination," but his "periods of concentration" were "very short," as one would expect at a year and a half.

Writing to her mother-in-law, Anne could not help going on at length about the delight she took in everything her son said and did. He enjoyed having "Tee" and Mum Mum read and sing to him, but Tee had just left on a trip to Mexico. "Tee — all gone." Charmed by her baby's determination and sense of humor, and eager to share her joy in his games and laughter, she rambled on for pages until her husband intervened. This was not the first time. Lindbergh did his best to discourage his wife from writing long letters to anyone, but especially resented her recent preference for Charlie's company to his own.

Anne had other recent occasions to sense her husband becoming quite tense. When he drove the family south for a weekend at their farmhouse outside Hopewell with the Breckinridges at the end of January 1932, their car got rear-ended by another vehicle. Lindbergh got out and banged his door shut. As he and the other driver exchanged irate accusations, Anne followed her own instincts and grabbed their toddler. Charlie noticed his father had left the car and said, "Hi — all gone."

Movie star and newspaper columnist Will Rogers reported on his own observations. An avid flyer himself, Rogers had befriended the Lindberghs in California. He and his wife visited the family at Englewood on Sunday, February 14, 1932 — just over two weeks before the boy disappeared. In a newspaper column in early March, Rogers noted the "affection of the mother and the father and the whole Morrow family for the cute little fellow . . . [with] almost golden [hair] . . all in little curls."

Rogers and his wife had watched Anne play with blocks on the floor with her son for an hour. Then Lindbergh repeatedly tossed a sofa pillow at his toddler while the little boy walked unsteadily in front of the adults. Each time Little Charlie got up and took a couple of steps, Lindbergh knocked his son to the floor — as if he were a carnival target. Rogers could not help but comment: "I asked Lindy if he was rehearsing him for forced landings. After about the fourth time of being knocked over he did the cutest thing. He dropped of his own accord when he saw it coming."

Rogers might not have found the game so amusing if he knew that Charlie suffered from rickets — a Vitamin D deficiency indicative of weak muscles, easily fractured bones and skeletal deformity. The Lindberghs' pediatrician would confirm that diagnosis later that same week. Maybe Lindbergh had kept knocking his son down so their visitors would not notice anything odd about the boy's gait. At the visit on February 18, Dr. Van Ingen had difficulty standing Charlie up straight for measurement at 33 inches. He also noticed that ". . . both little toes were slightly turned in and overlapped the next toe." More significantly, Dr. Van Ingen noted that Charlie had an enlarged "square head." The soft spot in the boy's forehead would normally have closed months earlier, but Charlie's fontanel still measured about ¾ inch in diameter. Though Charlie was tall and big-chested for his age, most other developments were far slower than Dr. Van Ingen routinely observed of twenty-month-olds. Dr. Van Ingen also noted that the boy's skin was "unusually dry all over his body."

Lindbergh had already begun issuing harsh commands for altering his son's behavior. When Charlie sucked his thumb, Lindbergh ordered special thumb guards put on him at night. The thimble-shaped wire caps were attached to a string tied around each wrist. This would be part of the nightly ritual from then on. (It might have been prompted by fear that thumb-sucking was the reason a couple of canine teeth were coming in at an angle.) Because of the rickets diagnosis, Dr. Van Ingen likely warned Anne and Charles that their child was quite fragile. He likely had already prescribed strong doses of Vitamin D, a sun lamp and plenty of exposure to sunlight. Those recommendations would remain.

To prevent Little Charlie from being teased as a "sissy" or have his hair pulled again, Anne arranged to get him his first real haircut a few days after his checkup. A local hairdresser was invited to the Morrow mansion to shear off his mop of curls. The rite of passage took place in his grandmother Tee's bedroom. Mrs. Morrow took clippings and saved them in an envelope. Very likely she also took before and after pictures despite her son-in-law's aversion to photos of Little Charlie. The next day, Anne and her mother came to the Little School to observe Little Charlie in his rhythm class. He was obviously having a great time attempting the various moves. Mrs. Morrow left on a trip out of state on Friday, February 26, not having any idea she would never see her treasured grandson again.

That Saturday, Aida Breckinridge's eighteen-year-old daughter Alva Root took the ferry from New York and joined Anne for lunch at the Morrows' Englewood estate. Alva had babysat for Little Charlie before and was invited to do so this weekend as well. Her parents and brother would join them at the Lindberghs' farmhouse. After lunch, a chauffeur from the Morrow estate drove Anne, Charlie and Alva to the new estate. Skean had somehow gone missing so they left without him. They arrived around 5:30 p.m. Anne was glad to give Betty Gow weekends off. (Betty was, too.) Alva had watched Charlie on other occasions. She and Anne set about getting him fed and put to bed at his usual 7 p.m. bedtime. The area was drenched with heavy rain driven by a chill wind.

Lindbergh spent the morning at the lab in Manhattan. Directly after lunch, he drove to Henry Breckinridge's apartment. The timing of their friend's arrival surprised Aida. She had understood that their plans were to leave in the late afternoon. But Lindbergh wanted to spend a couple of hours with Henry beforehand. They left New York around 4 p.m. Aida's son Oren would make his own way to the farmhouse from Princeton where he was a student.

When Lindbergh drove the Breckinridges to the new farmhouse, Olly Whateley and Wahgoosh came out to greet them in the garage. They found Anne in the living room by a roaring fire. Aida later recalled how much Lindbergh said he enjoyed having a home in the rural countryside as opposed to the city. The couple shared some tea while Alva went upstairs to the nursery, keeping Charlie company on the floor playing with his Noah's ark and alphabet blocks.

Anne and Aida soon came up to join Alva playing with Little Charlie in the nursery. He knew Aida as "Mimi." It pleased her that he seemed to remember her from her visit two weeks before. Soon, Elsie Whateley arrived with his dinner, and Charlie greeted her by name as well. He delighted in his "toast" and "applesauce" and sat down to eat and drink his milk without help. Aida was impressed at how rapidly the toddler's vocabulary was expanding. Anne then took him to wash up in his bathroom and dressed him for his evening nap in the crib with a stuffed rabbit to cuddle with. She opened a window slightly for ventilation and the two women and Alva came down to join the men for dinner.

The conversation focused on national politics. Their host seemed to be in particularly good spirits. Anne was distracted somewhat, thinking about her son's cold. Her husband had already established a household rule that Anne was not to check on her son after he was put to bed. After dinner she looked in on him once anyway and found him sneezing a lot. She, Alva and Aida went back up at 10 p.m. Charlie remained asleep when Anne lifted him from the crib to undress him and put him on his potty seat. Aida recalled that "he woke up crying quite hard in a rather high pitch."

After Elsie Whateley gave him some prune juice, Anne rocked him gently and sang him a favorite song as he bobbed his head to the tune. Anne then put her hefty toddler back in his crib for the night. The men came up to bed at 10:30 p.m. Alva would sleep in the nanny's room next to the nursery, and her mother and stepfather occupied a guest room at the end of the hall. Around 11 p.m. Lindbergh joined Anne in the nursery to give Charlie some nose drops. After all the lights were out, Aida and Henry were startled out of bed by what they thought were flashes of lightning. They ran from their room as the whole house experienced intermittent bursts of light. It turned out to be a practical joke. Lindbergh had a master switch set up that would operate all the lights in the entire house at once. He was toggling the switch for his own amusement to observe their frightened reaction.

When everyone else had gone back to bed, Aida went to check on her daughter and then stopped by the nursery. She adjusted the blanket and tucked the rabbit back in the crook of Charlie's arm. He looked quite peaceful. The next morning Anne realized that Charlie had slept better that night. Perhaps the medicine had helped. Elsie took him from his crib around 7 a.m., changed and dressed him. The whole group had breakfast in the dining room together, including Charlie. He fed himself his cereal and toast and got down from his chair to go ask Elsie for more. When he returned, he chased Wahgoosh around the table while the adults finished their own breakfast.

After breakfast, Lindbergh and Henry Breckinridge disappeared for a private talk in the library. Anne got her son's coat and hat. She and Aida then took the hefty toddler outside to play on the patio and get some sun. With his baby curls shorn, Aida noticed that Charlie now looked more like he was approaching three than two. At some point Aida's son Oren arrived from Princeton, where he was an undergraduate. Oren had spent many weekends with the Lindberghs at their rental home in Mount Rose and had been to the farmhouse outside Hopewell before. For a good hour Charlie entertained himself poking a stick in the dirt and running up and down. He still had a runny nose and started to fuss. They went in to let him have his lunch in the nursery.

Like his father, a cold did not affect his appetite. When he was ready for his nap, Lindbergh came up and adroitly administered the nose drops. Again, the little boy seemed to have no trouble sleeping. Later in the afternoon, the women took Charlie outside again with Wahgoosh, but his cold started to make him miserable. Back inside, Alva sat with him on the floor to play marbles. Lindbergh came by and chided the women for "fussing too much" about Charlie. He told Anne to take him back upstairs and leave him by himself in the nursery. Soon, the boy seemed too quiet. When Aida went to check on him, she found that Charlie had gotten out of the nursery into the bathroom all by himself. Apparently, none of the adults realized how dangerous it was to leave a toddler unattended — six adults and a teenager in the house, and Charlie could have accidentally drowned by falling headfirst into the toilet.

Anne, Alva and Aida then joined Charlie in the nursery and held up different miniature wooden animals from Noah's ark. He correctly named all of them — lion, tiger, giraffe, bear. Later, he got fussy again and Anne cuddled her son and sang to him. Her new favorite was the jazz song "All of Me." Aida noticed how exhausting it had been for the three women to keep up all day with the energetic boy. For Anne, that last weekend with Charlie would be a cherished memory she replayed over and over in her mind in an attempt to replace the horrific images that chilled her to the core after his death.

That Sunday afternoon, Aida noted that their host seemed restless. From time to time, he busied himself with various odd jobs around the house. Then he and Henry went out walking the grounds late in the day huddled in further private conversation. When they returned, the two men again holed up in the library with the door shut. Henry told her that he and Lindbergh were reading. That was not likely true. Later that spring, Aida shared with Lindbergh's mother something Henry had told her about his private discussions with Lindbergh the weekend before Charlie disappeared. Henry told Aida that Lindbergh had confided that he hated to leave Anne alone at the isolated farmhouse: "He worried that the baby might be kidnapped." (That sudden concern for Anne's and the baby's security at their isolated new home apparently was not relayed to Anne; nor, as far as is known, did Lindbergh ever tell the police he harbored that fear just two days before the kidnapping. The police might have wondered why he encouraged his wife to stay at the unguarded farmhouse Monday and Tuesday nights instead of returning to her mother's fortress in Englewood.)

At six, Anne and Aida went up to the nursery to get Charlie ready for his bath. The little boy was quite out of sorts but managed to eat the cereal and applesauce and drink the milk Elsie brought him. Anne had just put him in the crib when Charlie recognized his father's footsteps on the stairs. He greeted his father with: "Hi! Hi! Hi!" It made the women laugh. Then Charlie hid under his covers to encourage the adults to yell "Boo" so he would pop his head out again.

Anne loved how bold and playful her son was. Aida held his head still while Anne gave Charlie nose drops for his lingering cold. Unlike when his father administered the medicine, the little boy wriggled so much the effort was mostly unsuccessful. He then snuggled under the covers with his stuffed rabbit and went right to sleep. Shortly after the adults ate dinner, the Lindberghs drove Aida, Henry and Alva to catch an evening train at Princeton Junction back to Manhattan. Oren went back to Princeton. Meanwhile, Anne sent Olly Whateley to the store for some Milk of Magnesia for Charlie, which Anne thought might make him feel better.

If Lindbergh did harbor any fears of kidnapping, it did not stop him from leaving as usual on Monday morning without even looking in on his son. Lindbergh called Anne at the farmhouse later that day to ask that Anne stay there one more night even though he would not be returning. He did not tell Anne or Olly Whateley to take any extra precautions. Without a guarded entrance to the estate, except for an excitable terrier, security was negligible. The opposite was true of the fortress-like mansion at Englewood. With any reason for concern, Anne would surely have asked Whateley to drive them back to Englewood rather than stay at the ungated farmhouse without her husband or Skean. If worried about potential kidnappers, Lindbergh should have requested her to return that night to Englewood.

On that Monday, February 29, 1932, Little Charlie stayed inside from the wet weather as his cold got worse. He remained mostly with his mother. During the day, Anne went out for a couple of walks and left her son with Elsie Whateley. With her husband gone that night, Anne kept the doors open from the master bedroom to the master bath and nursery. She checked on her son several times.

The following morning Anne saw that Charlie remained congested. Lindbergh called to suggest that, for their son's sake, Anne should again stay at the farmhouse. He apparently made no mention of any fear of kidnappers. Lindbergh told his wife he would drive home from work to arrive in time for dinner. He gave Anne additional specific instructions regarding the baby's care, including another dose of medicine. Sleep-deprived and under the weather herself, Anne called the Morrow mansion in mid-morning and asked to have Betty come to the farmhouse to help with Charlie. The Morrows' butler answered the telephone and gave the message for Betty to parlor maid Violet Sharp. Sharp would later fall under police suspicion as a possible accomplice in the toddler's kidnapping. Betty arrived around 2 p.m. in a gusty wind and heavy rain.

Anne spent most of the afternoon with her son in the living room, reading and singing to him. She went out for a short walk after Betty arrived and stood under the nursery window at one point and tossed pebbles up against the glass to attract the nanny's attention. Betty brought Little Charlie to the window to wave at his mother. About 5:30 p.m. the toddler went looking for Betty in the kitchen. She took the little boy upstairs to his nursery, read to him and gave him some cereal at about 6 p.m., his normal dinner time.

Anne joined them in the nursery at 6:15 p.m. after her toddler had eaten. Little Charlie was still recovering from his cold. She and Betty made sure all three nursery windows were closed. They shuttered two of them, but the bolt on the pair of shutters on the east-facing window to the right of the fireplace would not lock even when both women yanked on the shutters together. It was a problem that her mother had observed on their last visit to the farmhouse the first weekend of February. Anne mentioned to Betty that the shutters would need to be fixed. They then gave the toddler nose drops and his medicine precisely as his father had instructed. Charlie disliked the medicine and spit some of it up. Somehow, they had not mastered Lindbergh's technique of getting his son to take his medicine without fuss or spillage. Betty got him another set of night clothes to change into.

Because he had a "croupy cough" Anne suggested that the toddler's chest be rubbed with Vick's VapoRub ointment as Mrs. Whateley had done for him on Monday. They wrapped a flannel bandage around Charlie's chest to keep the ointment from rubbing off on his new T-shirt and sleeper, but then decided he might not be warm enough. Betty remembered she had a flannel remnant of an old petticoat in her sewing pile. Anne left to fetch a needle and thread from Mrs. Whateley. When she returned, she played with her son while Betty cut the flannel and sewed Charlie another undershirt. The nanny sewed the shoulder seam on only one side so it could be easily removed over the baby's head. The two women then put the flannel T-shirt on Charlie. Betty then got him back into his new, store-bought undershirt. He was already diapered and had on rubber pants. Over the underwear, they dressed him again in Dr. Denton pajamas and put him in the crib.

The two women covered Charlie snugly with a sheet, two blankets and a quilt. It was already 7:30 p.m., half an hour later than the toddler usually went to bed. They knew Lindbergh wanted them to follow his instructions to a T. He usually arrived from work at about 7:45 p.m. He would expect his son to be asleep when he arrived. Betty thought the room might get too stuffy without ventilation, so she and Anne discussed opening one of the windows slightly. Anne said she normally opened the French window on the wall nearest the crib, but only after taking into account the direction of the wind. She headed downstairs as Betty unlatched the French window and opened it slightly for ventilation while the little boy slept. Betty secured its shutters again so they would not flap in the wind and turned out the light as she left.

Anne went down to her desk in the living room. Betty washed Charlie's clothes in the bathroom next to the nursery. The nanny checked in on Charlie again around ten minutes to eight, attached the thumb guards, and used two large safety pins to secure the blanket to the mattress. She turned out the light as she left and then turned out the light in her own bedroom across the hall. Betty went downstairs with the toddler's wet clothes to hang them to dry in the basement. On her way, she passed Anne in the living room. The nanny reported that Charlie was breathing more normally and had "gone to sleep unusually quickly." That was the last anyone would report seeing him alive.

Source: UCLA Leon Hoage Collection

The archivist of the Leon Hoage – Lindbergh Kidnapping Collection at UCLA identified the boy on the tricycle as being Charles Lindbergh Jr. shortly before the kidnapping. (https://www.library.ucla.edu/blog/special/2011/11/04/ evidence-in-the-crime-of-the-century.) If so, this photo was likely taken in January or February 1932 at the Little School (presumably by his grandmother or Aunt Elisabeth) and may be the only full-length photo of Charlie at 19–20 months. The tricycle appears to be a Colson Fairy Model No. 1, which was a popular high-end model in the 1920s and early 1930s. The boy on the trike looks about twice the height of this model's 16 inch front wheel: Charlie's height was 33 inches when last measured on February 18, 1932. Although this model was advertised for 3- to 4-year-olds, Charlie was very large for his age, exhibited good coordination according to his teacher, and had his own smaller, three-wheeler in his nursery. Lindbergh himself was fascinated with bikes as a child and would likely have wanted to foster similar mechanical aptitude in his son.

See: "1920s Colson Fairy Catalogue"
https://oldbike.eu/1911-colson-fairy-ball-bearing-velocipede-model-no-1/Fairy
See also: Children's Vehicles Holiday Advertisement 1930, p. 4
https://ohiomemory.org/digital/collection/p267401coll36/id/7002

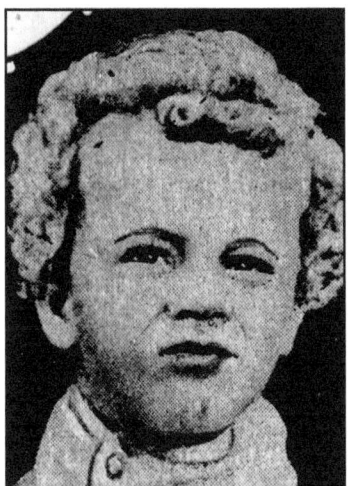

BEFORE

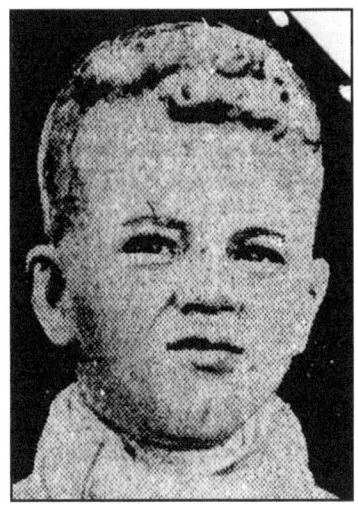

AFTER

Pictures published in early March 1932, depicting Little Charlie at 20 months

Pictures labeled here as "Before" and "After" are presumed to have been taken of Little Charlie on Thursday, February 23, 1932, less than a week before he disappeared. These were printed in several newspapers the week after he was kidnapped. The source of these photos was not reported but was likely his grandmother, Elizabeth Morrow, who kept locks of his hair in an envelope as a souvenir of his first haircut. (The envelope with her handwritten notations and the clippings themselves are now at Yale University archives. Yale also maintains in its Anne Morrow Lindbergh collection a typed list of photos of Charles, Jr. on Charles Lindbergh's stationery with a handwritten notation mentioning pictures taken at Englewood in February 1932).

ACT TWO

New Jersey State Police search the tall grass on the east side of the house in the daylight on March 2, 1932. The field was as overgrown as the one on the south side that led to Featherbed Lane. Lindbergh told them he found the three ladder pieces the night before 60 to 75 feet away from the house before the Hopewell police arrived with flashlights. According to Betty Gow, Lindbergh and Olly Whateley had run outside for maybe ten minutes after 10:10 p.m. while the women were searching inside the house before Whateley called the police. On March 2, the police recovered a chisel in the mud at a distance from the other finds.

1.
The Police Arrive

THE HOPEWELL police recorded that it was 10:22 p.m. when Olly Whateley first called to alert them that the Lindberghs' son was missing. The state police received a similar call at 10:25 p.m. State troopers, county detectives and local police had overlapping jurisdiction. The Lindbergh's large estate straddled both Mercer and Hunterdon Counties. Technically, the house itself was over the line in the township of Amwell in Hunterdon County; the town of Hopewell was situated in Mercer County.

Rushing from Hopewell, Police Chief Harry Wolfe and Constable Charles Williamson intercepted Olly Whateley headed to town to buy a flashlight. Since the policemen had flashlights, Whateley turned around and came back with the officers around 10:35 p.m. Lindbergh called the state police at 10:40 p.m. to alert them that he had found an envelope in the nursery. This was new information since the first call; no one had apparently yet spotted it when the police were first notified of the child's disappearance over fifteen minutes earlier.

Once the two local policemen entered the house, the nursery was the first place Lindbergh took them. Betty Gow said the room had been dark when she found the child missing at 10 p.m. just as it was when she left the room just over two hours earlier. Now the light was on. Lindbergh warned the two Hopewell officers against touching any surface. He wanted to leave the room as it was for the New Jersey State Police, including an unopened envelope on a windowsill to the right of the fireplace on the east wall. Lindbergh told Chief Wolfe that was where the kidnapper must have entered and exited. It was the one window for which the women could not make the shutters close when they put his son to bed earlier that evening. Lindbergh said he was in the study directly below the nursery from 9:30 until 10 p.m. and heard nothing unusual.

Looking around the room, it amazed the police chief that the nursery was full of undisturbed furnishings — quite a feat for a kidnapper to negotiate in the dark without knocking anything over. Chief Wolfe tried to figure out how that second-story window could have been the point of entry. The fellow would have had to stand on a ladder propped up against the house. Inside the room under the windowsill where the envelope lay sat a large chest, with a small suitcase on top and the roof of a wooden Noah's ark on its surface. The police chief observed a smudge mark on the suitcase and on the floor nearby. But Wolfe was more "surprised at what he did not see."

Having investigated many other crime scenes, Harry Wolfe expected much more evidence to be apparent this soon afterward. He saw no blood on the crib or the sheets or any place else. No handprints either. The standing screen that stood between the French window and the crib showed no signs of even having been moved. The window where the sealed envelope sat on the sill did not look like it had been forced open. The police chief concluded that to get through the window, a would-be kidnapper would have to be quite an acrobat to launch himself over the stack of obstacles without disturbing any part of it. There was no indication that the chest below that window had moved at all. The kidnapper would also have had to land on his feet in the dark without making any loud noise or disturbing any other furnishings.

Harry Wolfe considered the next step. He wondered how a kidnapper could possibly have carried a toddler out the same window without disturbing the chest that blocked his exit path. He later explained: "The culprit would have pushed it around in order to gain a secure foothold, he certainly would not have taken time to push the chest back into place, especially if he had a baby in his arms and was in the act of a desperate crime. But bear in mind — the chest had not been moved."

Lindbergh then took the policemen to the yard to view with the aid of their flashlights ladder prints under the nursery window. Because of the mud, workmen at the farmhouse had placed planks on the ground around the house to walk on. Without a flashlight someone out in that yard on that stormy night might have easily tripped. Lindbergh guided their way out 75 feet or so to a spot where the Hopewell officers' flashlights revealed a three-part sectional ladder — two parts lying together and one about 9 feet away. Constable Williamson was surprised that Lindbergh led them directly to the ladder. Lindbergh then pointed out to the two local policemen a dowel on the ground not far away. Back in the house at 10:53 p.m. Lindbergh called the state police again to say he had just located two ladders in the yard.

The head of the New Jersey State Police was 36-year-old Colonel H. Norman Schwarzkopf. (His son, American General H. Norman Schwarzkopf, would lead the Gulf War coalition in 1991 that ousted Saddam Hussein from Kuwait.) When Lindbergh's first call came into headquarters in Trenton, Schwarzkopf had sounded the alarm right away via a teletyped broadcast. With Lindbergh's blessing, the first all-points bulletin was issued well before any state police arrived at the scene. By 11 p.m., New Jersey State Police were stopping and searching all cars headed toward Manhattan via tunnel, bridge and ferries and at checkpoints on the highways to Pennsylvania. Every license plate number they saw was recorded.

The Coast Guard and all airports were also placed on alert. New Jersey Governor Harry Moore immediately sent telegrams to his counterparts in every state in the region seeking their help. The news was already on every radio station nationwide and set in type for shocking front-page headlines on March 2 around the world from Paris and London to Moscow, from Shanghai to Cape Town, South Africa and all the way to Sydney, Australia.

New Jersey State Trooper Joseph A. Wolf arrived twenty minutes after the local police. It was then about five minutes to eleven. He sent for other troopers to join him and interviewed all the members of the household. He noted in a detailed report that night that the ground was saturated at the time of the crime; it was "very dark"; the temperature was about 34 to 40 degrees Fahrenheit and "a strong wind was blowing." He also learned from Lindbergh that when Lindbergh first visited the nursery after Betty Gow reported his son missing from his crib, Lindbergh immediately noticed a window on "the east wall of the nursery was unlocked with the right half of the outside shutter open" and saw that a plain envelope sat on the sill. He told Trooper Wolf the "envelope had been left there by the person or persons who carried away his son."

Lindbergh assured Wolf that he did not disturb anything in the room but went outside accompanied by Olly Whateley and explored the grounds. Wolf reported that they found footprints near the nursery and the ladder "some distance from the house" on the east side of the house *before* Lindbergh instructed Whateley to call the Hopewell police, *before* the State police were alerted, and *before* Lindbergh sent Whateley to town to get a flashlight. The state police would never note the significance of this chronology or apparently wonder how the two men found anything in the yard that night in the pitch dark.

The State Police fingerprint expert, Trooper Frank Kelly, arrived from Trenton around midnight — the same time as Lieutenant Arthur Keaten and Major Charles Schoeffel arrived to take over command of the investigation as ordered by Colonel Schwarzkopf. Lindbergh summoned Betty Gow to bring a knife to the nursery for the fingerprint expert. She later testified that was the first time she saw an envelope on the windowsill. She left the nursery as others gathered around the fingerprint expert.

Kelly slit open the dime-store envelope to find a ransom letter in poor English. Lindbergh swore all those present to secrecy and had an officer read the note aloud. The note demanded $50,000 in small bills (about $730,000 today) for the boy's return and stated delivery instructions would be transmitted in two to four days. "We warn you for making anyding public or for notify the polise. The child is in gute care."

Colonel Schwarzkopf greatly admired Lindbergh and would eagerly do whatever he could for the national hero in the biggest case by far in the agency's history. Adhering to the warning in the ransom note was no longer possible. Police across the nation had already been notified. The State Police looked to Lindbergh for guidance on what to do next. Anne was reassured by the claim in the ransom note that her son was being cared for. It indicated the toddler was alive. The police had already observed there were no blood stains in the room — though one reporter would falsely claim otherwise. But Betty Gow had noticed something else that deepened her own anxiety. Although the toddler's crib blanket was still pinned in place, the sheets now bore small rips where they were pinned. It looked like Charlie had been roughly pulled out by his neck or head. She feared for his safety.

Both of the Lindberghs told Joe Wolf they heard nothing unusual from the time Lindbergh got home until they discovered their son missing. The state trooper wrote down that the child was 29 inches tall. He asked Lindbergh "whether he had any suspicion as to who committed the crime or whether he could recall any incident such as strange noises or actions of his dog which was in the house that night." His report that night summarized Lindbergh's response: "He had no suspect nor was he able to recall anything at the time by which he might be able to fix the time of the crime." The same was true of the Whateleys and Betty Gow — no odd noise heard by anyone in the house. Nor had their highstrung terrier ever barked until the police and reporters started arriving.

Kelly methodically went over every likely surface in the room for fingerprints. He was amazed to find none anywhere in the nursery, including the crib and the windowsill or on the ransom note. Even if the kidnappers wore gloves, some prints — primarily of Betty Gow and Anne Lindbergh — should have been left behind in the nursery. But no usable prints were found that night. One of the officers commented, "I'm damned if I don't think somebody washed everything in that nursery before the print men got here."

Lieutenant Louis Bornmann was sent to retrieve the ladder. It was so heavy it took him two trips to bring it into the house. Kelly found no fingerprints on it either. Amazingly, he could not even see any mud on the railings or rungs. In addition to alerting the police, Lindbergh had immediately summoned his lawyer Henry Breckinridge from New York. Henry and his wife Aida arrived around 2 a.m. after first detouring to Princeton University to ask Breckinridge's 21-year-old stepson, Oren, to join them. Although the Breckinridges had themselves been there twice, Henry did not think he could locate the farmhouse in the pitch dark without Oren's help navigating the countryside. Oren had heard the news of the kidnapping from the nursery over the radio but thought at first it must be a false rumor. As far as Oren knew when he left on Sunday, Anne and her son were planning to head back to her mother's estate in Englewood on Monday morning as they had always done before.

It turned out that Henry Breckinridge would not have had much of a problem that night finding the farmhouse on his own. The Lindberghs' property was lit up like a Christmas tree with all the lights on indoors, people milling around out in the yard with flashlights, and headlights of reporters' cars and police vehicles parked in the long driveway. That in itself was extraordinary for the locals. Only one out of ten families in the vicinity even had electricity.

Hearst reporter Laura Vitray and several other journalists had made a beeline to Central New Jersey from Manhattan as soon as they heard the startling news bulletin. The reporters found they had open access to the Lindbergh estate. They parked in its driveway and stood in the yard peering in on the family and staff in the uncurtained living room.

Soon Detective John Fogarty, Lindbergh's former bodyguard, arrived to assist Breckinridge. Both planned to stay at the farmhouse for as long as needed. Lindbergh turned down an offer from Princeton's President to head a search of the nearby area with college students. He rejected, as well, the suggestion that they immediately assemble a team of bloodhounds to scour the area. Instead, in the wee hours of the morning, Lindbergh formed his own small search party composed of three officers and several volunteers.

Vitray and her colleagues were leaving the estate at about 3 a.m. when they encountered Lindbergh standing by his car. He told Vitray's two male companions: "Boys, I rely on you to stay off the estate and not annoy me. For my part, I promise to give you a good break." He got in his car and called out "So long" with a smile and a wave. The reporters looked at each other in surprise: "Hell, that is what you would call nonchalant." Another added, "The Lindberghs are like that, they say. They never show any emotion, either of them."

Lindbergh's search party spent hours slogging through the dense, wet foliage on foot without anything to show for their efforts. Meanwhile, one of the first responders summoned a local trapper named Oscar Bush who had worked before as a deputy sheriff. Oscar was half descended from a Native American tribe and knew the backwoods better than anyone else. He arrived at the farmhouse around 4 a.m. on March 2 and made an important find: footprints under the nursery window and leading to the spot where the ladder was found.

Beneath the nursery window, Oscar spied a footprint from a woman's shoe. Anne Lindbergh then told the police she had stopped there on her afternoon walk on March 1 to toss pebbles at the nursery window to attract Betty Gow's attention so Betty would lift her toddler and Anne could wave to him. Outside, below the nursery, Oscar Bush found several large footprints and suggested they had been made by ribbed golf socks worn over men's shoes. Police took a photograph of one footprint that was estimated to be about twelve inches long and four and a quarter inches wide.

Corporal Wolf issued an immediate order for troops to protect foot prints from any damage. Oscar traced additional footprints that he was inclined to believe were from two different persons. They went from the ladder through the field on the east side of the house and turned south to an abandoned dirt road called Featherbed Lane. There, the tracks ended. Featherbed Lane ran parallel to the cinder driveway to the Lindbergh estate about a hundred yards south of the house. Both the lane and the driveway could be accessed only from the road from Hopewell that led north to Wertsville, New Jersey. Oscar told investigators that whoever crossed the Lindberghs' grounds in the dark had to know the property very well. "That ain't easy." Close by the footprints ending in Featherbed Lane were what appeared to be automobile tire tracks. Oscar told officers he thought two automobiles had been used in the kidnapping. Oscar assumed that the kidnappers would have known, as he did, that the only way to avoid the police was via the "isolated, muddy, almost impassable roads north to Neshanic."

The Lindberghs' nearest neighbors on the south side were the Conovers. The family reported seeing a suspicious car heading out of Featherbed Lane onto the Hopewell-Amwell Road around 6:30 or 6:45 p.m. on March 1. The driver turned off his lights as soon as the well-lit Conover house came into view, as if to avoid being seen. The incident struck the family as especially odd because the lane's entrance was posted with a sign: "Road impassable — drive at your own risk."

Oscar shared with police and reporters his conclusion of where the car on Featherbed Lane had headed on the night of the kidnapping:

"From the spot where those footprints headed at the Featherbed Lane, if you turn South you're headed toward Hopewell and pretty soon, if you've got anything to be afraid about or to hide, you'll be running straight into the arms of the police coming straight up from Princeton and Trenton.

If you turn north on the lane, you'll be coming into the Wertsville Road . . . a dead end for getting anywhere. But you can turn off it into the Neshanic Road at Zion. And there's no police up that way. For Neshanic is away back up in the hills, far from the police, but with good roads leading out . . . to Pennsylvania, to Summerville, New Jersey, or to Jersey City.

Or for that matter, you can drive on down again, through Skillman, with no one suspecting you, because you'd be headed the wrong way. . . ."

Oscar's sister Rebecca was also interviewed. She told a reporter: "Why don't they ask us people up here to help them find the baby? We know every inch of the ground. We know the places the police will never find. But none of us is going to butt into other folks' business until we're asked. Even if we found the baby, we'd be a-scared to say so for fear we'd be suspected of stealing him and maybe thrown into jail for the rest of our lives."

When Lindbergh returned to his estate in the early morning of March 2 after trekking through the woods to no avail, he saw reporters beginning to trample his yard. Unlike the rude attitude he often exhibited on prior occasions, he acted quite welcoming. He thanked reporters for their interest and had Elsie Whateley make sure there were ample sandwiches and coffee provided for them and the scores of state and local officers. The police had staked or boxed in the footprints and tire tracks, but efforts to maintain the integrity of the footprint evidence in the yard would quickly prove useless.

By then, Wahgoosh was barking almost nonstop. Lindbergh sent Olly Whateley to Hopewell several times to get more food. Lindbergh himself exhibited his usual huge appetite. He also readily joined in all discussions of what might have happened to the child, while his wife retreated from the invasion of her home. Three months pregnant with her second child, Anne felt disconnected from the trauma they were experiencing. It likely reminded her of a tragedy she endured at Smith when a good friend disappeared and was presumed dead: "A nightmare of reporters, papers, reports, clues, detectives, questioning." Now, her own house was invaded night and day. Anne was "only occasionally seen wandering like a distracted ghost between the rooms."

Yet while the details remained fresh in her mind, Anne wrote to her mother-in-law a chronology of what happened. She noted that Charles was downstairs in his study at 10 p.m. when Betty Gow announced Little Charlie was missing from his crib. Betty accused Lindbergh of perpetrating another of his pranks. "I did, until I saw his face." Anne concluded that her son could not have been kidnapped between 9:30 p.m. and 10 p.m. because her husband was already in his study and would have seen or heard something. Any footsteps in the uncarpeted nursery directly above would have been clearly audible. Anne accepted her husband's view that the crime had the look of professionals. Yet she knew that her own presence there on a Tuesday was by chance. She would not have stayed Monday and Tuesday night if her son did not have a cold. She assumed that the kidnappers must have closely followed their activities. It relieved Anne somewhat to consider the kidnapping well-planned. That gave her hope they were only after the money and would leave her son unharmed. Her first thought had been more dire — that it might be some "lunatic."

When the Lindberghs were staying at their rental home a few miles south the prior spring a peeping Tom had peeked in their window. He might have been an escapee from the nearby Skillman State Village for Epileptics. A substantial percentage of the state's diagnosed epileptics were segregated there on the mistaken belief they had incurable mental disorders. By the early 1930s, the village housed over 1200 inmates. Several of them had escaped over the past year, and not all had been caught.

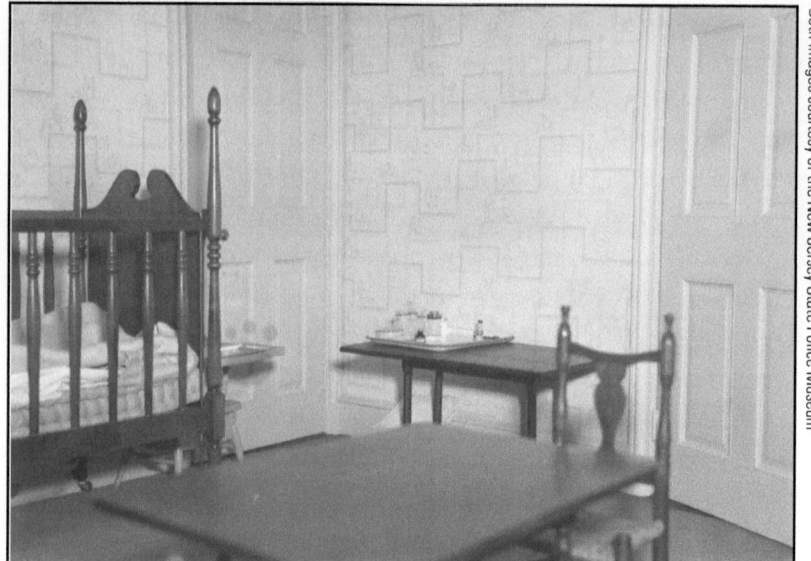

Above: The table with the medicine tray is between the two doors.

Below: The same table and chair in the center of the room looking toward the east wall and the window to the left of the fireplace.

*The three-wheel "Kiddie Kar"
parked in Little Charlie's nursery*

To the right of the fireplace behind the chair is the three-wheel Kiddie Kar State Trooper Joe Wolf described seeing on the night of March 1, 1932. To its right is the dresser, suitcase and roof of Noah's ark against the east wall beneath the sill where the ransom envelope was left.

https://www.ebay.co.uk/itm/Antique-KIDDIE-KAR-Trike-Scooter-Toy-By-H-C-White-Company-U-S-A-Patent-1918-/22347500324

Close up of the window to the right of the fireplace with a small dresser and suitcase under it and the roof of Noah's ark on the suitcase. Sitting on the sill is a stein. All appeared as they were when the nanny left the room at 7:50 p.m. The envelope with the ransom note was left on this windowsill.

Both images courtesy of the New Jersey State Police Museum

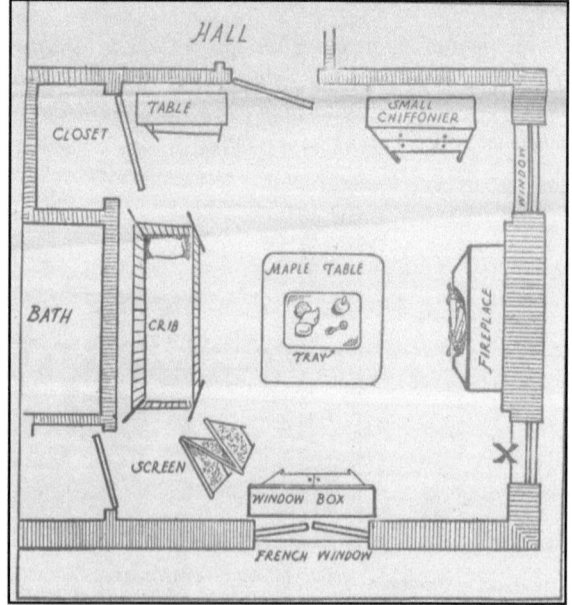

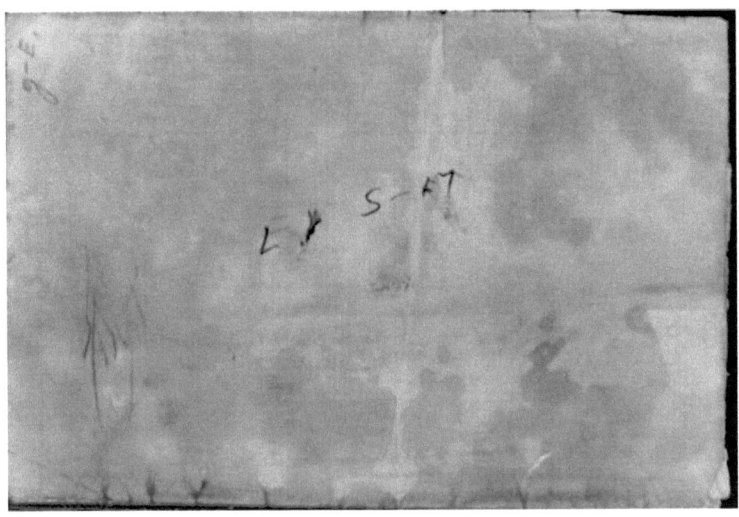

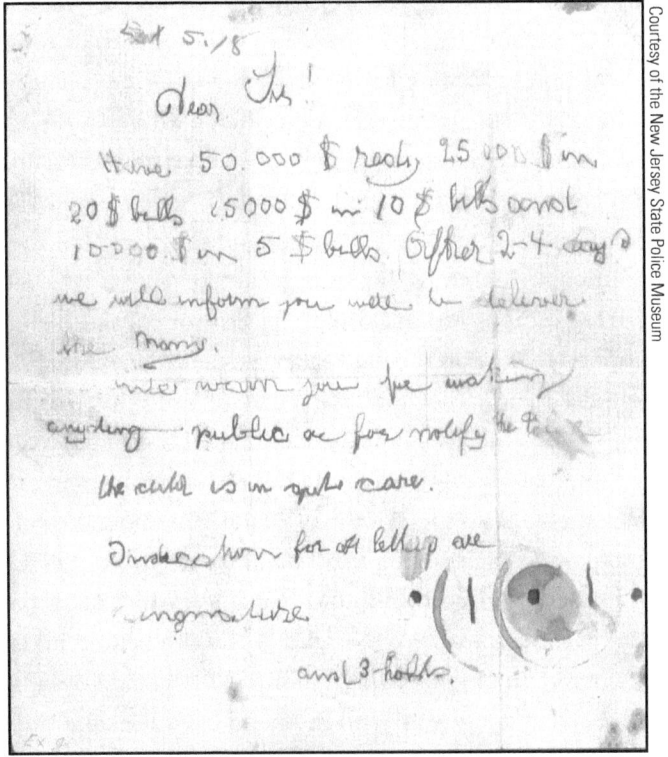

The dime-store plain envelope and ransom note left on the windowsill March 1, 1932, first opened by the state police at midnight.

2.
The First 48 Hours

BY NOON on March 2, the yard was swarming with over 400 newsmen and photographers as well as policemen. Scores of mattresses borrowed from Princeton University provided extra accommodations throughout the house. The most promising lead learned by the state police on March 2 was one the Bureau of Investigation later called "Unknown Person No. 1." A next-door-neighbor's son, Sebastian "Ben" Lupica, was brought to the estate to share a stunning breakthrough. He had just heard that morning about the kidnapping the night before. Lupica came at the suggestion of another neighbor and a reporter he met at the neighbor's house to tell the police what he had observed.

Lupica commuted to Princeton Academy from his parents' home. In addition to classes, he played baseball and ran track. On the afternoon of Tuesday, March 1, he stayed late for sports practice and returned from campus around 6 p.m. As he approached his turnoff, Lupica stopped to pick up the mail from the family mailbox. No other cars were then going either way. He started driving home again very slowly, partly due to the poor condition of that section of the road from the bad weather and partly because he was distracted by trying to read a letter. He estimated his speed was 8 to 10 miles per hour. Visibility was limited and darkness was setting in.

The Lindberghs' driveway was just half a mile south of his parents' farmhouse on the same side of the road. As Lupica neared his famous neighbor's home, the high school senior suddenly saw a dark blue or black Dodge sedan coming around the bend from the opposite direction, heading south. It had local Mercer County license plates like the plates on his own car. From its distinctive emblem and decorative radiator grill, Lupica recognized the car as a 1929 model.

The other driver was alone in the car and behaved strangely. When Lupica stopped and pulled to the right to give the driver ample room to pass, the driver instead braked to a stop on the left. Lupica saw that in the back of the Dodge sedan were at least two stacked ladders that extended partly over the front passenger seat. Though his view of the driver was obstructed, Lupica guessed that the man was about thirty-five to forty. The man wore a dark fedora and overcoat, which distinguished him as a city-dweller, not one of the locals. The man looked American, not foreign, and was clean shaven, with "a thin face and long features." The man did not wear glasses, but the evening shadows made it difficult to see him clearly.

Lupica told police that he did not get a good enough glimpse to believe he could ever identify this person. From the ladders, Lupica assumed the driver might be a window washer, though if so, he was clearly overdressed. In his rear-view mirror, Lupica saw the man wait for Lupica's car to get by before moving on. Lupica's remarkably detailed description included the type of spokes on the sedan's wheels. A farm woman in the neighborhood, Mrs. Henry Wendling, had a short while earlier seen a car of similar general description.

When Lupica volunteered his information, he did not know that a ladder of similar type had already been found abandoned in the Lindbergh's yard. The three-piece ladder had already been moved, but Lupica was brought back around 7 p.m. to see the ladder the police had found. He said it resembled what he had seen collapsed inside the Dodge sedan the evening before.

Despite sleep deprivation, Lindbergh had acted remarkably calm and collected almost the entire time since his son's disappearance — with a few noticeable exceptions. To Anne, her husband looked like a "desperate man" the first 48 hours after their son disappeared. Anne wrote to her mother-in-law that she was afraid to speak to Charles. Betty Gow, likewise, "had never seen him so changed." Yet to others the only time Lindbergh appeared anxious during the first couple of days was on the afternoon of March 2 when he was introduced to Ben Lupica.

Police told Lindbergh that Lupica was the neighbor's boy, who had seen a driver with ladders in his car near the estate the evening before. Though the Lupica farm was the next house past Lindbergh Lane headed north from Hopewell, the two had never met previously. In the 1990s, as an old man, Ben Lupica vividly recalled that meeting. He had been awestruck as a teenager with possibly vital information to share with the world-famous aviator in locating his missing child. But rather than praising the youth, "Lindbergh became agitated and distraught, and mumbled something about concern for his wife." He left the teenager standing there dumbfounded.

The night of March 2, the state police focused on finding Unknown Person No. 1, the driver of the car Lupica saw. They obtained from the Department of Motor Vehicles the official list of all owners of 1929 Dodge sedans in the county. Since Lupica felt he might recognize the sedan if he saw it again, officers took Lupica out all night until 4 a.m. the next day checking out likely vehicles. He then went home for a couple of hours' sleep and to Princeton for morning classes. At 10:30 a.m., police showed up at the Princeton Academy to take Lupica to look at Dodge sedans in the Princeton area. By the time those were eliminated, they had gotten only part-way through the list. Yet the police suddenly discontinued the search. Lupica could never fathom why they stopped looking.

Several other people who lived in the vicinity of the farmhouse reported to New Jersey police that they saw "strange automobiles near the estate at different periods of time just prior to the kidnapping." One of the most mysterious vehicles locals had seen was a blue-green sedan with New York license plates that hovered around the Lindbergh estate over the course of eight days ending on March 1. A nineteen-year-old music student who lived near Featherbed Lane said three men were in the out-of-state car and asked directions to the Lindberghs' home. A waitress in Pennington less than six miles south, also reported that three unfamiliar male patrons had shown up on both Friday, February 26, and Tuesday, March 1, 1932, asking directions to the Lindbergh estate.

Alfred Hammond, the Reading Railroad watchman at the Skillman Village crossing, spotted a similar trio in a car of a similar description — a light blue 1926 sedan with New York plates — on five mornings between February 25 and March 1 (excluding February 28, which was

Hammond's day off). A telephone lineman saw a car like that, too, not far from the Lindberghs' driveway. A woman from Zion said she saw a car of that description near the post office. It seemed to be on its way north. After March 1 no one saw it again.

Police also had other good leads. Archie Adam, Office Manager of the nearby State Village for Epileptics at Skillman, had been driving south toward Hopewell after work on March 1. Adam was not far from the Lindberghs' driveway at around 7:40 p.m. when he was forced to veer suddenly to keep from crashing into the second of two cars coming in the opposite direction. Adam did not see who was in the first car, but the second one had two men in it.

On March 2, Lindbergh subcontractor David Watson called police with some useful information. Watson had read about the shutters that could not be bolted on one of the nursery windows. He wanted to let the investigators know he had personally hung all of them and they all worked properly when he was finished. The house had only been completed in December 1931 — just shy of three months earlier. Watson had made a number of trips to check on his work. As a skilled carpenter he did not consider it possible that any windows he hung would already be warped — he would have noticed and fixed them. No police followed up with Watson.

Anne said she and her mother had noticed the problem with the bolt for that pair of shutters the first weekend of February. On the morning of February 29, 1932 — the day before his son disappeared — Lindbergh called a different subcontractor to fix the front door weather stripping. Yet he had never asked to have the nursery window fixed even though that window was routinely opened and shut twice a day.

While parents were often suspected of playing a role in crimes of this type, state officials didn't consider Lindbergh anything but a victim. Governor Moore visited the farmhouse to assure Lindbergh he would have full authority to direct the course of the investigation. Even before securing Governor Moore's blessing, Lindbergh and Breckinridge had not only excluded Hopewell Police Chief Harry Wolfe from any further role in the case but rejected assistance from veteran detective Ellis Parker as well. A nationally acclaimed master sleuth, Parker had earned his nickname "the Sherlock Holmes of New Jersey" by solving more than 95 percent of the 300 major cases he tackled in his decades-long career. Governor Moore had originally asked Parker to offer his help, possibly at the behest of Mrs. Morrow, since Parker was an old friend of her late husband.

As head of the investigation, what Colonel Schwarzkopf offered that the others did not was hero worship. Though he had never met Lindbergh before, Schwarzkopf later told a reporter: "There is nothing I wouldn't do for Colonel Lindbergh — there is no oath that I wouldn't break if it would materially help his well-being." When appointed to head the new state agency in 1921, Schwarzkopf had decided the men needed to have a motto to live by: "honor, duty and fidelity." He arranged for them to wear impressive, specially designed caps and light blue uniforms with orange trim. He also got the state to buy motorcycles and horses for their use and had them practice military drills. What he instilled most in his men was a military chain of command.

Newspapers at the time of Schwarzkopf's original appointment noted that the 25-year-old war veteran had no experience as a county or city policeman and no training on how to investigate major crimes. Skeptics assumed Schwarzkopf got hired because he was a friend of the governor's son and the governor was not keen on rigorously enforcing Prohibition laws. Even after more than a decade of operation, the New Jersey State Police had no veteran detectives or full-blown crime lab. Celebrated detective Ellis Parker told reporters that veterans like himself did not consider the state troopers with their spiffy uniforms to have any ability to handle a serious criminal investigation. Investigative reporter Noel Behn summed up Parker's view of the state police in 1932 as "glorified traffic cops."

One assumes that Governor Moore knew when he assigned Schwarzkopf to head the investigation into "the crime of the century" that Schwarzkopf was over his head and easily manipulated. Governor Moore himself likely took orders from the man who got him elected, the state's undisputed political boss, Jersey City Mayor Frank Hague. Hague was known as a consummate influence peddler, always open for business at the right price.

Hague demanded loyalty from all the many political candidates he backed for office throughout the state. Moore was an old friend of Hague's from Jersey City, who had been a city commissioner before he first got elected governor in 1926. By 1932, Hague's influence extended nationally.

The day after Lindbergh swore the New Jersey police to secrecy that a ransom note existed, he abruptly changed his mind. He told a reporter from *The New York Times* that he was prepared to pay the $50,000 demanded. The reporter asked Lindbergh for a recent photograph of the missing child so the newspaper could publicize it. The photo he gave the *Times* made the March 3 front page with the banner headline: "LINDBERGH HOPEFUL, IS READY TO RANSOM SON: NATION'S GREATEST HUNT FOR KIDNAPPERS PUSHED; ALL CLUES THUS FAR FUTILE: COUNTRY IS SHOCKED." The photo of Little Charlie seated in a chair was captioned, "Picture of His Missing Son, Given Out Yesterday by Colonel Lindbergh to Help in the Search. It Was Made About Two Weeks Ago." No correction was apparently ever offered by Lindbergh that the photo was not taken in February 1932 but in June of 1931.

Reporters soon learned that on the morning of March 3 an old barn burned down four miles from the Lindbergh estate. They asked the police if there might be some connection to the kidnapping but were told the police did not believe so. Despite being told that officers had combed the area, reporters began interviewing neighbors themselves and found that questioning by the police had been superficial and incomplete. Detective Parker determined he would continue his own unofficial investigation.

First 48 hours

Police ordering reporters to leave

Both photos courtesy of the New Jersey State Police Museum

The police move in

The Lindbergh three-car garage became temporary police headquarters

3.
Hunting Worldwide for the Curly-Haired Baby

POPULAR humorist Will Rogers wrote back-to-back newspaper columns published on March 3 and 4 focused on the calamitous news. He asked, "Why don't lynching parties widen their scope and take in kidnappings? They are ten times more premeditated and performed by more normal people." Rogers' wrath matched that of most people across the country — wanting to string someone up to put future would-be child snatchers on notice of the public's fury. Rogers noted that "the attention of the world" was all focused on the Lindbergh baby's safe return.

Anne's mother had arrived at the farmhouse with Anne's older sister Elisabeth on the morning of March 2. Before she arrived, Mrs. Morrow first made arrangements for guards for her youngest daughter Connie at Smith College. The widow's net worth was almost ten times that of her son-in-law. After hearing about the ransom demand for Little Charlie's return, she worried that Connie was at risk, too, because of the extortion threats Connie had experienced while at boarding school three years earlier. The state police made a file for this prior threat in connection with their current investigation. Federal investigators would also find it noteworthy since both demands were for $50,000 and had included similarly phrased complicated instructions for dropping off the money.

After making arrangements for Connie, Mrs. Morrow then contacted her son Dwight, Jr., at Amherst College. He would join the family at the Lindbergh estate. Mrs. Morrow reportedly took to bed almost immediately upon arriving at the farmhouse, shaken by the thought her only grandchild — the light of her life — was now gone. She assumed he was dead.

On Thursday, March 3, the Lindberghs distributed to the press an open letter to the kidnappers inviting communication through any intermediary the kidnappers chose, to facilitate the "immediate and safe return" of their child. The Lindberghs promised, in return, to hold the kidnappers harmless. At the same time, movies of his first birthday celebrated at the home of his adoring grandparents in Englewood were distributed to theaters nationwide to familiarize audiences with the Lindbergh baby's appearance in case they might provide clues to his current whereabouts. Lindbergh then gave two other snapshots from the summer of 1931 to Henry Breckinridge to have Colonel Schwarzkopf use them in a poster. The poster would not be distributed until March 11, The caption described the toddler as 29 inches in height and having curly blond hair. Like the picture given the *New York Times* and the newsreel clips from his first birthday, both descriptions were seriously outdated. When his parents brought him to his last checkup on February 18, Little Charlie measured 33 inches tall. His hair had been cut short a week before he disappeared.

Misled by the distributed photographs and first birthday film footage, police and amateur sleuths across the country began stopping practically every stranger with a blond, curly-haired baby. At work, in beauty parlors and barber shops, in diners and while sitting reading the paper on park benches, people speculated on who the dastardly criminals were, and when and if, the boy would be safely returned as promised.

Oddly, when later asked by reporters about the misdescription of the toddler's height and hair in the poster, Henry Breckinridge claimed responsibility. Breckinridge said he had consulted an outdated report from the boy's pediatrician. Having spent two recent weekends with the Lindbergh family, Breckinridge knew from his own observation that the twenty-month-old was large for his age. His wife Aida thought he looked over two-and-a-half. Nor did Breckinridge's claim explain why State Trooper Joe Wolf on the night of the kidnapping was told the missing child was 29 inches tall. Wolf had interviewed the Lindberghs for such details three hours *before* Breckinridge arrived on the scene.

Shortly after her arrival at the farmhouse, Mrs. Morrow gave an interview to a *World Telegram* reporter. Unlike her son-in-law, she agreed with the first responders that the crime looked like an inside job "perpetrated by someone familiar with the habits" of the household. She added, "perhaps the condition of the baby's health bore upon this kidnapping." Mrs. Morrow's comments should have interested investigators. Neither the Lindberghs nor the Morrow family had ever before publicly admitted that the boy might have health problems.

Hopewell Police Chief Harry Wolfe was likely open to infanticide as a potential motive, which Scotland Yard soon suggested be considered. This was too often the outcome of Scotland Yard's own investigations of reported child-snatchings from home. That possibility fit with Harry Wolfe's view that the boy did not get kidnapped out the nursery window. But the Hopewell Police Chief had quickly been taken off the case since the farmhouse was technically just outside his jurisdiction. After Colonel Schwarzkopf was put in charge, it was easy to get the star-struck state official to hand over control to Lindbergh and Breckinridge. Lindbergh invited the state police to move their headquarters to the farmhouse so they could coordinate closely with him.

While key local investigators were excluded, those from other jurisdictions were welcomed. Governor Moore immediately sent telegrams to police chiefs and top detectives both in New Jersey and across the country to convene an emergency meeting to solicit the best ideas of experts on kidnapping investigations on how to proceed. Fifty-four men gathered at the Governor's office on March 5, including several who flew in for the gathering. They then caravanned from Trenton to the Lindbergh estate to visit the scene of the crime and consult with the state police.

Among the group was only one mayor — political boss Frank Hague from Jersey City. The mayor of crime-plagued Atlantic City also sent a representative to the assemblage of high-powered lawmen. To the press, it presented a great show of political clout and coordinated sleuthing that masked the absence of real progress on the case. Before convening all that investigative brain power, Lindbergh and Breckinridge had first ensured that key evidence was not preserved, fresh clues were not followed, and local experts and Federal agents were practically frozen out.

Schwarzkopf immediately made Inspector Harry Walsh from Jersey City a lead investigator and appointed other Jersey City officers to assist him as well. It was well known that their mayor required all city employees to pay him 3 percent of their annual income — kickbacks euphemistically called "rice pudding." Boss Hague also demanded 30 percent of city employees' pay raises. He reportedly installed spies in his own police force to keep tabs on the department's activities and to call in favors.

After a decade in his position, Colonel Schwarzkopf had reason to know that Jersey City police officers who paid their mayor kickbacks did not likely live up to Schwarzkopf's high standards of "honor, duty and fidelity" — unless fidelity meant to Boss Hague. Somehow, the special unit consisting of State Trooper Cain and two Jersey City detectives assigned to investigate mysterious cars in the vicinity of Lindbergh's estate never found anything to report about.

Meanwhile, Schwarzkopf accepted Lindbergh's invitation to move police headquarters to the Lindberghs' garage for the duration of the search and to take over the servants' room and basement as well. Initially, ten uniformed troopers boarded on mattresses in the attic of the Lindberghs' home and another fifteen stayed nearby. Mrs. Morrow saw to it that meals for all these unexpected guests were delivered to the Lindbergh farmhouse from her own mansion in Englewood three times a day. Schwarzkopf ordered fifty or so more staffers to put aside their regular duties to join the team as dispatchers, telephone operators, guards, and clerks housed in the barracks a few miles away on the premises of Skillman Village. Reportedly, Lindbergh threatened to shoot any officer who pursued any leads without his prior approval.

From day one, the police had spent a lot of time thoroughly examining the ladder made from cheap pinewood and fir. With rungs spaced twenty-one inches apart — more than one-and-a-half times further apart than standard ladders — it seemed specially built for a very tall man. When put together, two sections reached just below the nursery window without any use of the third. When found in the yard, side rails of the ladder were partly split, as if the ladder had started to break from excess weight placed on it. After repeated testing, the police found that the ladder's rungs could not be relied upon to withstand more than 125 pounds of pressure. Yet it would have had to support both the weight of an adult and the 27 to 30 pound toddler. (It would have been far stronger if built with rungs 12 inches apart.) The rails and narrow rungs appeared clean — like new crating board — and the nails were shiny. It looked like this was the ladder's first use.

The impressions in the ground outside also showed that the ladder was set down to the side of the only unlatched nursery window in the lone spot where one could avoid being seen from the ground floor study. The officers wondered how the kidnappers knew exactly where to place the ladder. Veteran tracker Oscar Bush pointed out that the holes in the mud caused by the ladder's feet were much shallower than one would expect if they had to bear the weight of both an adult man and a hefty toddler coming down the ladder. He believed the ladder was a "bluff" meant to steer investigators away from suspecting an inside job. National radio host Walter Winchell was soon voicing that opinion, too. The police had found the use of three sections of ladder too tall to be of use in accessing the nursery but the use of just two sections seemed too short.

Right from the outset, Colonel Schwarzkopf discounted the misgivings expressed by his own officers, and the views of Oscar Bush and Hopewell's Chief of Police. Instead, Schwarzkopf accepted Lindbergh's suggestion that only a gang of hardened criminal immigrants would be daring and unfeeling enough to pull off the kidnapping. Schwarzkopf agreed with Lindbergh and Breckinridge that two or more sophisticated criminals had somehow found out that the Lindberghs were extending their stay at the farmhouse through Tuesday night.

Schwarzkopf decided the kidnappers must have used gloves and parked in a spot well-hidden from the house to assemble the thirty-pound ladder for use. Dozens of police already gathered at the estate had noticed one oddity in this theory. If the kidnappers were professional gangsters, why had they not bothered to cut the telephone line? A famous mystery writer published a different theory: the kidnapper was an exhibitionist "delighted by the enormous magnification of his ego such a crime would bring." Others found the entire kidnapping story hard to believe, but they remained in the minority.

Since the late afternoon of March 2, reporters had been excluded from the Lindbergh estate itself: first, by request that they leave, and then by a police guard station set up at the entrance to the driveway.

Reporters who had camped out near the Lindbergh estate were at first frustrated by having to share Hopewell's only public telephone at a soda and tobacco shop in town. The proprietor of Gebhart's diner greatly profited from his sudden popularity. Reporters would start using the shorthand "Gebhart's" to designate where they would meet, and all knew exactly where to head. Within a day, sleepy Hopewell would resemble Grand Central Station — overflowing with more than two thousand newcomers. New telephone lines were installed. The entire impoverished community enjoyed a huge economic boost from reporters, photographers, detectives, go-fers, telephone and teletype operators, volunteers, and thrill seekers. Locals did not appreciate a radio talk show host calling them hillbillies or potential suspects. A middle-aged resident named Peter Whitehead scoffed at the accusation: "They all think some of us took the baby; none of us would be smart enough to do that."

Despite the impressive call center set up after the kidnapping, the New Jersey State Police did not seem to be making much progress. Colonel Schwarzkopf even authorized a trip to Europe by his second in command, Major Schoeffel, to check on the background of household staff members at the Morrow mansion in Englewood as well as the Lindberghs' farmhouse and pursue other potential leads — all at taxpayers' expense. By the time it ended, the investigation would dwarf the cost of any previously undertaken. The media quickly grew frustrated with the confusing array of rumors and entertained each other with their own speculation.

Starting on March 3, Lindbergh and Breckinridge began bypassing the state police they had just put in charge. Instead, the two men established their own informal channels to contact the presumed gang of professional kidnappers who held Lindbergh's son for ransom. That morning, Anne Lindbergh noticed how strained and ashen Henry Breckinridge looked. She learned that Breckinridge was in the process of seeking help from mobster "Owney" Madden, as powerful a gangster in New York as the notorious Al Capone had been in Chicago before Capone went to prison for tax evasion. In reaching out to Madden, Breckinridge received assistance from a nationally prominent lawyer friend — William "Wild Bill" Donovan, a man to whom Schwarzkopf also happily deferred.

Donovan was one of the most highly decorated heroes of World War I. He would later head the Office of Strategic Services (OSS) during World War II — the predecessor of the CIA. In the 1920s, Donovan had served as United States Attorney in New York in the Harding administration and then as Assistant Attorney General in the Coolidge administration. In the spring of 1932, he headed his own law firm in New York City and was about to declare himself a Republican candidate for Governor.

Donovan sent an associate of his firm named Robert Thayer to contact crime boss Owney Madden. The young lawyer tracked down his speakeasy drinking buddy, Morris "Mickey" Rosner, who frequented underworld hangouts. Rosner had boasted in the past that his gangland connections would enable him to assist any friend victimized by kidnapping. As soon as Rosner arrived, Lindbergh and Breckinridge holed up with him. Breckinridge had Thayer create a hand-drawn copy of the ransom note for Rosner. It appeared to be an extraordinarily careless move since the ransom note had specified that it would be followed up with more instructions identifiable by the same unique "singnature."

The note had at its bottom a pair of interlocking circles with a red dot in the middle where they overlapped, several curved lines and three small holes in the paper. Such a complicated "singnature" would distinguish the real kidnappers from copycats sending any future communications. As later pointed out by historian Lloyd Gardner, "once the news was out, there would be scores (if not hundreds) of opportunists eager to cash in on the deal." Rosner shared the copied ransom note with two gangland associates who came at his invitation to the farmhouse on March 5 — Sicilian mobster Salvatore Spitale and racketeer Irving "The Little Guy" Bitz. Lindbergh authorized all three to act as go-betweens to share the ransom note with other underworld acquaintances, including Owney Madden.

The very next day Madden called to vent his anger at Rosner for bringing in Spitale and Bitz. That same Sunday Breckinridge's legal assistant Jim Phelan, called Lindbergh at the farmhouse and read

Lindbergh the contents of the next ransom note. Donovan's associate, Bob Thayer, was present when Lindbergh answered the call. It surprised him how cheerfully his host reacted. Lindbergh perpetrated practical jokes all evening.

Reporters could barely keep up with all the bizarre developments, including mystery trips Lindbergh made on March 2 and 3. Meanwhile, with so many troopers around the house, news leaked out of Lindbergh's behavior behind the scenes. It belied the image of a grieving father that the press was conveying to the public. Just two days after the Breckinridges arrived at the farmhouse Lindbergh had put dry ice down Aida Breckinridge's back. One morning, he sneaked into the Breckinridges' room to tie their clothes in knots before breakfast. While Lindbergh played pranks on his houseguests, police stopped hundreds of people with curly-haired babies looking somewhat like the photo in the newspapers. Officers detained some on sidewalks; others in their cars or other public places — not only in America but as far away as a train station platform in Prague. Hundreds of city dwellers on the Atlantic coast had their apartments raided after police heard they had a baby inside matching the photos released to the newspapers.

Heads of state sent their condolences. People across the country began mentioning the toddler every night in their prayers. Mothers started hugging their own children closer, afraid of having them snatched away. A nation bitterly divided between haves and have nots in the third year of the world's worst economic decline suddenly had one unifying mission — finding the loathsome gang who snatched their idol's only child.

It took a week before the police shared with reporters that the footprints outside the nursery had in fact led to car tracks on Featherbed Lane. Journalists then interviewed tracker Oscar Bush and reported his findings. Soon afterward, other stories appeared in the press discrediting Bush as an untrustworthy source of information and casting aspersions on his family as "a bad lot." That should have seemed odd. Aside from Oscar's reputation as the best tracker in the Sourlands, the car tracks he found in Featherbed Lane had later been confirmed by the Conover family who lived across the road.

Hopewell's Chief of Police also agreed with Oscar Bush that the kidnappers likely came from the north — and had help from locals. Harry Wolfe was quite dismissive of the state troopers who took over the investigation. He assumed they would get thoroughly lost if they penetrated more than half a mile from the road into the Sourlands. The state police did make some rough measurements of a few footprints on the grounds of the estate. They got at least one photograph, and apparently only one plaster cast, which somehow later got ruined.

This photo shows both the ladder police put up the next day and the planks workmen had left out on the ground near the house to avoid walking in the mud. In the dark, a stranger could have easily tripped on them.

This photo was taken of a footprint headed southeast from the Lindbergh farmhouse (toward Featherbed Lane) and estimated to be 12 $^{1}/_{8}$" by 4 $^{1}/_{4}$". The prints were found in the mud directly below the nursery window. These and other footprints observed nearby on March 2, 1932, led investigators to posit multiple kidnappers.

Gov. Harry Moore (center) offered a $25,000 reward from the state and assured Lindbergh that the aviator would have full authority to direct the investigation.

Gov. Moore called a meeting on March 5, 1932, of 50+ police chiefs, detectives and other invitees. The only mayor among them was Boss Hague of Jersey City, who had backed his friend Moore for governor.

Major Charles Schoeffel, the second-in-command at the New Jersey State Police, goes to London to investigate the background of household staff of both the Morrow family and the Lindberghs, but his agency ignores the suggestion of Scotland Yard to investigate infanticide.

Col. Schwarzkopf appeals to the public for information to help solve the kidnapping case.

4.
Confusion Reigns

ALTHOUGH the Bureau of Investigation had no jurisdiction at the time, Breckinridge contacted its director J. Edgar Hoover. (What we now call the FBI would not have "Federal" added to its title until 1935). When the agents arrived, Breckinridge and Lindbergh kept them mostly in the dark, refusing even to share with them the ransom note they had provided mobster Mickey Rosner.

On Lindbergh's behalf, the state police requested a photostatic copy of whatever the Bureau compiled on the case. The Bureau was left to glean information about the early stages of the state investigation from newspaper accounts, which were not always accurate. Reporters with contacts among the police and federal agents scratched their heads at the bizarre direction this case was taking.

Meanwhile, the family kept receiving stacks and stacks of mail — all screened by the police. By month's end Colonel Schwarzkopf would receive some 50,000 letters and telegrams "read, sorted, classified and evaluated" by a specially assigned detail. Many expressed sympathy, others clearly came from cranks and hucksters. The police switchboard in the garage remained inundated with telephone calls from across the country describing a curly-haired baby like the pictures from June 1931 that Lindbergh had just released to the press. Anne Lindbergh must have found answering such calls excruciating. Her son no longer looked like those pictures.

On March 9 and 10, 1932, some newspapers published variations of how Charlie might look currently. *The Philadelphia Inquirer* identified a recent picture of Charles Lindbergh, Jr., with curly hair as "how he normally appears." A second picture in both the March 9 and March 10 coverage looked like it could easily have been a photo taken the same day in what appears to be the identical sweater, but with his hair now cut. The likeliest source of these pictures was Mrs. Morrow.

The caption on the newspaper photo on March 10 informed

readers that this photo was how the boy *might* appear if the kidnappers disguised their captive. The reporter suggested that the gang would be motivated to camouflage the child because his image was now so "well-known in every corner of the United States." But, as any member of either the Lindbergh or Morrow household — or the Breckinridge family — could attest, the image of Little Charlie that had been given to the press on March 3 was way out of date and seriously misleading.

At the next press conference after these new pictures were published in several papers, Colonel Schwarzkopf told reporters for the first time that the child did in fact have his hair cut in late February. Yet Schwarzkopf assured the press that the child still looked much the same as in the photos Lindbergh originally distributed. Schwarzkopf had, of course, never seen the boy in person. A *New York Times* reporter wrote up the belated news about the haircut but thought the revelation so inconsequential it was buried near the end of a long piece dealing with more important updates. It was not inconsequential to Anne. She wished she had updated photos to mourn the engaging child her son had become instead of the old images of him as a baby. It compounded her sense of loss — the unreality of it all.

Hearst reporter Laura Vitray could not understand why these new pictures of an older looking toddler were not widely disseminated. She considered the boy's current appearance of vital importance to his safety. The misleading description would be compounded on March 11 when the police distributed thousands of posters across the country and internationally. Despite his reputation for meticulous attention to detail, Lindbergh never asked the police to replace the poster with a corrected description of his son. So, police and vigilantes in every jurisdiction kept looking for a curly-haired one-year-old four inches shorter than Charlie's height when he disappeared.

Meanwhile, reporters gathered a number of promising leads that looked to have been dropped by the police. Based on Ben Lupica's detailed account of the suspicious car and driver he had seen with the ladders near the Lindbergh estate, a few Hearst reporters put together an unofficial file and started to interview known owners of similar cars. But lacking sufficient information and authority, they soon gave up.

The Hearst reporters became convinced that the area in the

general direction of Skillman Village had yet to be fully investigated. Trapper Oscar Bush said that terrain was "ideal [for hiding] a kidnaped child because its maze of mystery was apt to discourage the hunt." The reporters bought boots for walking through the high underbrush and drove their car down Skillman Lane — the same lane where the reporter from *The Sun* had spotted a speeding sedan. Their excursion had "very interesting results." The reporters headed in an easterly direction toward Skillman Village and saw a number of old, abandoned homes that looked suspicious.

What excited the amateur sleuths the most was a conversation with a man who only stayed at his vacation cabin on weekends. He did not own a car. He always walked to his property from the train station in town. Yet he noticed when he arrived for the first weekend in March that someone had moved the wooden bridge he had built for use over a nearby stream. He had left the portable bridge on the stream bank, but found it put in place over the waterbed and reinforced so the stream could be safely driven over. The car's tracks were still visible in the soft earth and led back to Skillman Lane. The three reporters from Hearst's *New York Evening Journal* could not wait to return to the Lindbergh estate and relay their discovery to the New Jersey State Police. They never heard back whether anything came of their find.

In addition, Trooper William Kulikowski interviewed a Mrs. Bush of Skillman, who had seen suspicious activity at a vacant house owned by a man named Philip Catano. She told Kulikowski that she was previously interviewed on March 3 by another trooper and two plain clothes detectives. Although no one was supposed to be living at Catano's house any longer, she had observed cars with New York and New Jersey plates there until the night before the kidnapping. Then suddenly they were gone. On his return to headquarters, Kulikowski followed instructions to turn his report over to State Trooper Cain, who was working that angle on the case with two detectives from Jersey City. That was the last anyone heard about that lead.

State Police also had a report of two suspicious men coming out of the Lindbergh driveway onto the road to Wertsville two nights before the kidnapping. The two witnesses had remembered the license plate number, but what became of that investigation, if any, also remains unknown.

On March 7, *The Brooklyn Eagle*, one of the oldest and most widely read afternoon papers in the country, published a scathing critique of the Lindbergh investigation to date. Correspondent H. V. Wilkins revealed how perplexed the police were by the Lindberghs' dog Wahgoosh remaining silent on the evening of March 1. He wrote: "Lindbergh Pet's Failure to Give Alarm Points to Inside Job . . ." One wonders if he spoke to one of the police sergeants who was quite familiar with wire-haired terriers. They had extraordinarily accurate hearing and, in his view, the terrier would have immediately barked at any stranger unless his master called him off. That officer sent a memo to his superior suggesting the failure of the terrier to bark implicated the nanny in an inside job.

The police assumed that Wahgoosh (misidentified in the article as Trixie) would have barked at any sign of a stranger. That the dog did not bark — like the famous dog in a Sherlock Holmes mystery — appeared to be a valuable clue. (Lindbergh had by then convinced his wife otherwise. Anne now believed that Wahgoosh was simply too far away from the nursery to have heard the kidnappers entering the window and descending with their toddler.)

Wilkins summed up most of the evidence so far: "The failure of the dog to bark, the vagueness of the evidence of tracks of the kidnapers in the nursery floor and the fragility of the ladder, prompt the belief that the kidnaping of the Lindbergh baby was an 'inside' job." In that same article Wilkins reported another suspicious occurrence: someone dropped off a different watchdog owned by the Lindberghs at a kennel in Princeton on Saturday afternoon, February 27.

The Lindberghs' second dog Skean had not accompanied them when they headed to the farmhouse on Saturday. If Skean was left at a Princeton kennel, the reporter had the dog's breed wrong. Yet Skean was the only other dog that belonged to the Lindberghs. When Anne was chauffeured from the Englewood estate to the farmhouse, she thought Skean was off being walked in the park near her parents' mansion. It upset Anne greatly that chance had prevented Skean from being in his usual spot under the crib on Tuesday night. The excitable Scottish terrier would have yipped incessantly at any intruder. Skean would later be located and brought to the farmhouse the second day after the kidnapping. After *The Brooklyn Eagle* article came out on March

7, no state trooper ever had the opportunity to check whether Skean had just spent several days at a Princeton kennel.

On March 8, Lindbergh suddenly wrested complete control over the investigation from the police. That morning Lindbergh was overheard berating state police chief investigator Captain John Lamb, for answering the private line in the study, which Lamb had been standing near when it rang. Lindbergh told Lamb: "[Y]ou nor any other policeman is ever to touch any telephone in this house." Cutting off Lamb's startled response, Lindbergh added: "I am tired of all this slew footing. I want you police to realize you are here through my courtesy, so please refrain from interfering with my business." Lindbergh also "made it plain to the police he did not want his telephone tapped or his mail read."

Captain Lamb immediately headed to his men in the garage and ordered fifteen of the twenty-five to go back to their regular duties. Only ten would remain on the premises. Reporters understood the police were now "to all intents and purposes . . . out of the active picture, contenting themselves with minimal roles." Lindbergh also requested that the press stay "out of his path" while he and Breckinridge pursued the return of his son.

Sightseers had become so plentiful by then that the troopers and Hopewell police spent most of their time directing traffic away from the Lindbergh estate. Some folks were paying $2.50 apiece to barnstormers for an aerial view of the site of the infamous crime. Reporters remained nearby for whatever news they could glean from officials either in press briefings or by off-the-record conversations with talkative cops, some of whom were likely paid for information — then a common practice.

One of the United Press staffers assigned to Hopewell sent out a front-page wire story highlighting various rumors that the child was safe and about to be redelivered to his parents. The assumption was that delicate discussions were underway that very day of March 8 through back channels to the kidnap gang developed by Detective Fogarty and Breckinridge. Lindbergh explained he had "pledged to offer all possible protection to the kidnappers provided they return his baby." The United Press reporter noted: "in the parlance of gangland . . . the 'heat' has been turned off."

THE DOG THAT DIDN'T BARK

The Lindberghs' two dogs — Skean, a black Scottish terrier, and Wahgoosh, a black and white terrier — would have both been at the farmhouse on March 1, 1932, if Skean had not gone missing on Saturday. Skean normally slept under the crib. Wahgoosh slept in the kitchen. The fact that Wahgoosh never barked before the police arrived puzzled the first responders. The following week, reporters sought to find out from the State Police the exact whereabouts on the night of March 1 of "the little Scotch terrier, which was playmate and guard to the Lindbergh baby." That described Skean, not Wahgoosh. But the written question mentioned "the Lindbergh dog" and Col. Schwarzkopf chose to respond as if there were only one dog owned by the Lindberghs – Wahgoosh. The answer ("Ground floor, kitchen and pantry") did not mention Skean at all.

Eaglet May Be Disguised

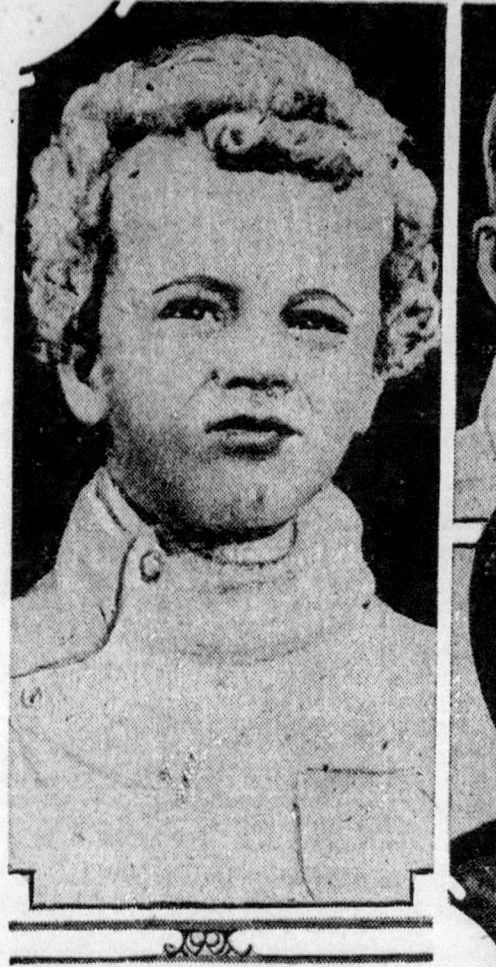

The appearance of baby Charles A. Lindbergh is now so well known in every corner of the United States that the kidnapers may have thought it necessary to disguise the child in one of the ways shown above. At the left is the child as it was when stolen from is home at Hopewell, N. J., and right, as he might appear if his abductors attempted to change his appearance.

This same photo and caption appeared in multiple newspapers the second week of March, 1932 without attribution.

5.
Mystery Trips

ON THURSDAY, March 10, United Press reporter Delos Smith reassured his readers that rumors of Lindbergh pursuing his personal mission to bring his son home were true: seven different reliable sources "connected with the Lindbergh kidnapping case" told him Lindbergh had secretly left his estate three times in the first three days of the week starting late Monday night. Each time Lindbergh disguised himself as a state trooper. (Smith's sources were likely themselves troopers). Smith noted that Lindbergh and his family had done their best "to confuse followers and conceal even the fact that he was away."

That same day, *The New York Times* reported on its front page a promising development: "Lindbergh Search Pressed Near Home: [Governor] Moore is Confident; Hunt in Rural Area 3 Miles from the Estate Seen as Move to Trace Kidnappers' Ladder." The article noted, "troopers hinted that [it] may in some way be connected to the ladder left behind by the kidnappers, and the alleged tracing of the wood used in its construction to the Skillman Village for Epileptics." That investigation oddly went no further.

The day before, a correspondent for *The Atlanta Constitution* had reported two strange developments at the Lindbergh estate at the beginning of the week. The first was that "two cars, one heavily curtained, set out of the back entrance to the estate, with two state troopers in each and dashed at high speed to Skillman." The other observation intrigued the reporter more. At 2 p.m. on Tuesday, Breckinridge left the estate on a secret mission and was gone for over eight hours. Breckinridge told the state troopers and police not to follow him and asked that they prevent others from doing so as well. When he returned after 10 p.m., he left again within half an hour and headed toward Princeton with a woman passenger presumed to be Mrs. Morrow. The front-page story considered these secretive trips hopeful indication of progress in Lindbergh's private efforts. The headline definitely piqued readers' interest: "Col. Breckinridge on Mystery Trip: Legal Advisor Demands Absolute Secrecy for his Movements; Returns, Dashes Away Again."

Avid readers would soon learn that Breckinridge attended a séance on March 6. This outreach to a clairvoyant was bound to spark even more public interest. While in a trance, the seer mentioned the second ransom note Lindbergh had received by mail. At the end of the session, receipt of a third note was predicted shortly — this time addressed to Breckinridge at his office. This peculiar turn of events might have been one of the reasons reporter Laura Vitray started feeling the press was being had. Confusion would soon arise as to whether the third ransom note was delivered on Sunday evening, or Monday or Tuesday mid-day in the mail. (Inspector Walsh later confirmed that the third ransom note was postmarked on March 7 and received in Breckinridge's office on March 8.) The envelope included a note asking Breckinridge to deliver the new ransom letter to Lindbergh. The United Press headline on March 8 mistakenly described Lindbergh as having accompanied Breckinridge on his secret mission that day. The author of the note had specified that a response be placed in the *New York American*. Rosner complied with a coded message for the personal section of the newspaper.

In his investigative report on March 10, reporter Delos Smith noted that Lindbergh's subterfuge in sneaking off the premises in disguise on his own mission was aided by "one member of the police" headquartered at the Lindbergh estate. Even so, Smith's informants recognized Lindbergh wearing glasses and an official leather jacket and hat. The trooper to whom they belonged had earlier reported the uniform missing from a peg in the hall nearest the garage where he had hung it. When that trooper complained to his superiors, word came back down from Captain Lamb to "forget it" — he would make sure the trooper was supplied a new uniform. The troopers were all ordered from then on "not to see too much" and be tight-lipped, only exchanging pleasantries with reporters.

The first time Lindbergh left on Monday night March 7, he reportedly sped down the private driveway in his own car at 11 p.m., almost running over two troopers assigned to guard the entrance. Not seeing the driver's uniform in the dark, one of the troopers had stood in the center of the driveway using his flashlight to get the car to stop. Instead, Lindbergh gunned his engine and the two guards "leaped and sprawled" to avoid getting hit as Lindbergh raced off north toward

Skillman Village – the opposite direction from the only other checkpoint at the first crossroads south toward Hopewell. On Monday night, Aida Breckinridge had stayed with Anne, who believed her husband was spending the night in the Breckinridges' room with Henry.

The press assumed these secret trips described by Smith meant Lindbergh and Breckinridge would soon negotiate the return of Lindbergh's son. Federal agents did, too. They had learned that Owney Madden had predicted in a call to Rosner two days earlier that the kidnappers would make contact again on March 8. Observers told Smith that around 9 a.m. on Tuesday they saw two men dressed as troopers in one car and two others dressed as troopers in another heavily curtained car who "set out of the back entrance to the estate . . . and dashed at high speed toward Skillman." Rosner later claimed that neither could have been Lindbergh or Breckinridge because both were conferring somewhere on the premises all morning. Yet Rosner was tied up answering the phone at the time so he was not in a good position to know. He then went out all afternoon so he could not vouch for either Breckinridge's or Lindbergh's whereabouts later in the day. Lindbergh did join police in his garage at mid-day when he gulped a quick lunch and was seen by reporters. But he may have left again because Lindbergh was reportedly seen returning to his estate at 4 p.m.

Smith heard that on Wednesday night, Lindbergh left at midnight and did not return until morning. Here, again Lindbergh had someone vouch for him remaining home — at least around 2:30 a.m. It was not Anne but an eccentric in his early seventies named John Condon, who had just offered himself as a new go-between for the national idol. Condon had called around midnight with news he believed the kidnappers had responded to an ad he had just placed in a local Bronx newspaper Likely, it was Breckinridge who told Thayer to invite Condon to drive straight to the estate to share that communication. Condon said he arrived between 2 and 3 a.m. from New York, which was when he said he first met Lindbergh, who provided him with army blankets to sleep on the floor of Little Charlie's nursery. (Rosner later stated that Breckinridge told him on Thursday a different version of their meeting, claiming that he and Lindbergh stayed up all night chatting with this stranger.) Condon would offer at least three varying accounts of that night in the nursery. He soon became known for never telling the same story twice the same way.

Thayer was still staying in the house and soon told troopers yet a different story: that Rosner and Breckinridge left together every day from Tuesday on and were gone long hours. Given all the conflicting accounts, all that we can say now about Lindbergh on Thursday morning is that no one ever disputed that he joined Anne and his house guests for breakfast. Wherever Lindbergh may have gone that week he did not tell Anne. She did not really know where her husband was much of the time. Anne wrote to her mother-in-law on March 8, "I hardly see C. at all." Anne believed he was holed up with detectives during the day and spent late nights on their telephone. She was proud of her husband for getting better rest during the day; "not wasting strength on petty things"; and putting himself in charge of the investigation like a shrewd military general "managing his forces."

Anne tried to keep her letters upbeat, but she was still shellshocked. Everywhere she went in the house were mattresses and pillows and troopers. Her desk was piled high with letters. She was constantly assaulted with the unreality of it all and could only focus on the hope of getting her cocky toddler back. If it was just a matter of money, that seemed quite possible. She counted on her husband to succeed.

Anne was more concerned about Breckinridge, who had barely gotten any sleep since March 1. She knew Lindbergh leaned heavily on his lawyer for advice. On Wednesday, Anne wrote to her mother-in-law again, cheered by reports the toddler remained unharmed. Both men seemed optimistic, but unhappy about all the headline stories claiming their boy had been found. By Thursday, she wrote: "There *really* is definite progress." She praised her husband for "handling things wonderfully." That day, likely on Lindbergh's orders, Schwarzkopf changed out all the remaining troopers in the house with replacements who had no prior contact with the press – quashing any further leaks.

Much to everyone's surprise, the secret activities did not result in the child's return. (Breckinridge would wait two-and-a-half years to explain to police his own mystery trip to Manhattan that Tuesday — with an implausible story.) Lindbergh never disclosed where his excursions took him, but a number of strong clues did surface over time.

WANTED

INFORMATION AS TO THE WHEREABOUTS OF

CHAS. A. LINDBERGH, JR.
OF HOPEWELL, N. J.

SON OF COL. CHAS. A. LINDBERGH
World-Famous Aviator

This child was kidnaped from his home in Hopewell, N. J., between 8 and 10 p. m. on Tuesday, March 1, 1932.

DESCRIPTION:

Age, 20 months　　　　Hair, blond, curly
Weight, 27 to 30 lbs.　　Eyes, dark blue
Height, 29 inches　　　Complexion, light
　　　Deep dimple in center of chin
　　Dressed in one-piece coverall night suit

ADDRESS ALL COMMUNICATIONS TO
COL. H. N. SCHWARZKOPF, TRENTON, N. J., or
COL. CHAS. A. LINDBERGH, HOPEWELL, N. J.
ALL COMMUNICATIONS WILL BE TREATED IN CONFIDENCE

March 11, 1932　　　　COL. H. NORMAN SCHWARZKOPF
　　　　　　　　　Supt. New Jersey State Police, Trenton, N. J.

Courtesy of the New Jersey State Police Museum

The New Jersey State Police distributed this poster internationally on March 11, 1932. Some countries received translated versions. The two pictures provided by Lindbergh date from the summer of 1931 when Charlie turned one. His height is misstated as 29 inches. He was 33 inches tall when he disappeared. His hair is described as curly, but Col. Schwarzkopf acknowledged to the press on March 10, 1932, that Charlie had his hair cut short a week before he was kidnapped. No corrected poster was ever distributed. Lindbergh had already caused clips of his son's first birthday home movie to be played in newsreels across the country, cementing the image of 12-month-old Charlie in the public mind.

6.
Conflicting Sworn Statements

THE POLICE interviewed Betty Gow at length in the farmhouse nursery on March 3 and had a stenographer record her answers. She told them that when she walked into the nursery at 10 p.m. she first closed the French window she had left open earlier in the evening. She then put on the heater before going over to pick up Little Charlie, whom she assumed was still asleep in his crib. At the time, Betty did not turn on the light, but simply left the hall door open so the room could be dimly illuminated by the light in the bathroom down the hall. When Betty found the crib empty, she asked Mrs. Lindbergh if she had her son and, when Anne said "no," Betty went downstairs to ask the Colonel if he knew where his son was and he said, "No, of course not."

Lindbergh immediately added: "Isn't he in his crib?" and ran past her upstairs to the nursery, felt around the crib, looked around and then went into his bedroom. Mrs. Lindbergh then came into the nursery. Betty said they searched everywhere in the house, including the attic *before* Lindbergh called the state police. She also told the police that Colonel Lindbergh was the person who found the ladder and that he was the one who saw the envelope on the sill.

That day the same three officers also took a statement from Olly Whateley. He said he had learned about 3 p.m. on Monday, February 29, that Mrs. Lindbergh was planning to stay that night at the farmhouse because of Little Charlie's cold. It was three hours later that Whateley first heard from his wife that Lindbergh would not be coming home Monday night. On Tuesday evening at ten, Whateley said he was in the servants' lounge outside the kitchen reading a newspaper. At ten past the hour Betty rushed in to tell him, "Quick, Whateley, the Colonel wants you. The baby is gone." Whateley raced upstairs to the nursery where he found the Colonel. Whateley told the officer: "He told me to hurry and call the police in Hopewell, which I did." Whateley made it sound as if summoning the police was the first thing he did, which did not match the information given Trooper Joe Wolf on the night of March 1. Apparently, no one quizzed Whateley about that discrepancy.

Whateley concluded his statement by saying: "I went back upstairs to the nursery and the Colonel told me to help him search the house which we did. [After they found nothing to report inside the house] the Colonel and I went out and searched the grounds and came back in about 10 or 15 minutes after failing to find any traces of the child." His wife was then upstairs with Mrs. Lindbergh.

The police already knew that Lindbergh sent Whateley to town for a flashlight around 10:30 p.m. and that Whateley met the Hopewell officers on the road and returned with them to the house at 10:35 p.m. That meant the prior search of the grounds by Whateley and Lindbergh had to have been done in the dark without a flashlight. In her own statement on March 3, Betty Gow said that Lindbergh found the ladder — which matched Constable Williamson's impression that Lindbergh knew where to find it before the Hopewell police arrived.

From March 10 through March 13, the New Jersey Police obtained an additional signed statement from Betty Gow, as well as statements from Elsie Whateley and the Lindberghs. They started with Elsie and a second interview of Betty. Elsie gave a detailed account of the evening. She corroborated that Betty was with her in the Whateleys' apartment until just a couple of minutes before 10 p.m. when Betty headed to the nursery.

Elsie confirmed that shortly after 10 she and her husband were urgently summoned by Betty to the nursery. Elsie thought it was around 10:30 p.m. when she helped Mrs. Lindbergh get dressed. Then, the two of them and Betty "looked into every nook and corner and every closet. . . . Mr. Lindbergh and Whateley went outside and searched around the grounds." Mrs. Whateley had the time wrong. Betty Gow repeated what she had stated on March 3 that the search of the house occurred *before* Lindbergh had Whateley call the police. Betty placed that search at about a quarter past ten. The call to the police was recorded several minutes later. Trooper Joe Wolf on Tuesday night reported that Lindbergh and Whateley went outside to search the grounds *before* Whateley called the police and then left to buy a flashlight.

Whateley had to have driven off the premises by 10:30 p.m. to meet the two Hopewell policemen on their way to the farmhouse. The three men arrived at the farmhouse at 10:35 p.m. and were greeted at the front door by Lindbergh. That made Elsie's estimate of 10:30 p.m. for the search of the house by all five people impossible.

Again, on March 10, Betty Gow went through the details of getting Little Charlie ready for bed on Tuesday night with help from his mother. She repeated her discovery of the little boy's absence from his crib at 10 p.m. and the thorough search they all conducted *before* Lindbergh called the police. But Betty added in this second statement a key piece of information she had left out of her first statement on March 3. She told the police that her first question to Lindbergh when she saw him sitting at his desk in his study was: "Colonel Lindbergh, have you got the baby? Please don't fool me."

On March 11, a week and a half after the kidnapping, the police separately interviewed Charles and Anne Lindbergh for a second time. By then, the police had also taken fingerprints from them both for purposes of elimination while pursuing prints of the kidnappers. This time they provided signed statements. Anne gave a fairly detailed description of the entire weekend that preceded her son's disappearance. She had been driven to the farmhouse by her mother's chauffeur with her toddler son and Alva Root, their teen-aged babysitter, on Saturday afternoon. Her husband drove down separately from Manhattan later that day with family friends Aida and Henry Breckinridge, Alva's mother and stepfather. Alva and her parents left by train Sunday night after dinner. Lindbergh left early Monday morning and called to say he was spending the night at the Morrow mansion in Englewood. He suggested Anne stay another night with their son at the farmhouse since Little Charlie had a lingering cold. On Tuesday, Lindbergh suggested she stay one more night and he would be home for dinner. He called at around 7:00 p.m. on Tuesday night to say he was running late.

It was about 8:20 p.m. when her husband honked his horn to announce his arrival. After dinner, the couple sat down in the living room for what Anne described as "a very short time, not more than a minute or two" before they both headed for their bedroom. She said they spent ten or fifteen minutes talking. Then Lindbergh drew a bath and dressed again at about half past nine and she drew one for herself. Then Betty discovered that Charlie was missing. When she asked where Anne's husband might be, Anne said: "I didn't know where Colonel Lindbergh was."

Lindbergh then gave his one and only signed statement to the New Jersey State Police. Unlike the detailed multi-page accounts of all three women, his was just a page long. Here, Lindbergh changed a key answer he had originally given the state police ten nights earlier. Instead of having heard nothing of significance, Lindbergh now had a different recollection. He said that after he and his wife finished dinner at about nine p.m.: "We went from the dining room to the living room where I heard a noise which I attributed to dropping something in the kitchen, such as a wooden box." Yet he did not investigate it. Differing with Anne, he said they remained in the living room for fifteen minutes, heading upstairs to the bedroom at 9:15 p.m. He did not say they went upstairs to talk.

Lindbergh finished his account: "I took a bath and after dressing went downstairs to the library where I read for a few minutes at a desk next to the window, just directly below the nursery window from which our son was taken." He acknowledged that Betty Gow ran down to ask him "Colonel Lindbergh have you got the baby? Please don't fool me." He said, "No." She said, "You must have the baby. He is gone." Lindbergh then said. "I went into the nursery and from the appearance of the bed clothes I felt sure that something was wrong. I immediately went into our bedroom and loaded a rifle."

Lindbergh said he then told Betty Gow to summon Olly Whateley: "I told him to call the Sheriff immediately and I waited upstairs while he made the call. After finding that the lines were not cut, I called Colonel Breckinridge in New York, then the State Police at Trenton. I left orders for no one to enter the nursery or walk around the house until the police arrived."

The police apparently never inquired further why Lindbergh said he instructed Whateley to make the call to the police immediately upon being summoned shortly after 10 p.m. The records of the local police showed they were first notified at 10:22 p.m. which matched Betty Gow's timeline, not Lindbergh's. Nor did police ask Lindbergh why, after grabbing his rifle, he waited *upstairs* while Whateley made the urgent call to the police from downstairs in the opposite wing. Lindbergh did go upstairs a second time into the nursery, which was when he shut the door and told the household not to enter it until the police arrived.

Two days later, Anne Lindbergh gave another statement which largely repeated the one she gave on March 11 — with a few noteworthy differences. This time she stretched the couple's brief time in the living room to possibly five minutes — still ten minutes less than her husband said they spent there. Anne added that when first asked by Betty Gow, she told the nanny it was "quite likely" that Colonel Lindbergh had taken their son. When he came into their bedroom, she asked him if he had the baby and "He did not answer me." Then she said, "Someone had already told him." When she passed him in the hall armed with his rifle, she "ran into the baby's room again looking through the bed clothes and closets." After Elsie Whateley helped her get dressed, they searched the house.

For unknown reasons, Olly Whateley was never re-interviewed. However, police did check his background. Before being hired by the Lindberghs, Whateley had only a few months of prior employment in America. His current job as a caretaker and chauffeur was new to him. His prior work history in England was as a machinist, jeweler, and munitions worker. The New Jersey State Police did not share with the Bureau any of these statements or other leads obtained so far, including Ben Lupica's key account of the man with the ladder. (The Bureau later found out about Ben and interviewed him on their own.)

On March 11, the New Jersey State Police had allowed questions to be submitted by reporters which the police then answered. After that date, no more Q and A took place — just bulletins from the New Jersey

State Police. It was obvious to reporters that the federal agents and the New Jersey State Police were not coordinating well in this investigation, but the press remained in the dark as to why. By the second week of March, the Department of Labor had also joined the turf battle. Rumors remained rampant that the kidnapping was an inside job — with fingers pointed at Betty Gow and her boyfriend Red Johnsen.

In mid-March J. Edgar Hoover privately met with an executive from Transcontinental Airways, Colonel Thomas Lanphier. Lanphier was a fellow pilot and friend of Lindbergh's. He was also a director, along with Henry Breckinridge, of the Bird Aviation Company, which made the plane Lindbergh bought for Anne in the spring of 1931. (Lanphier also knew mobster Owney Madden, to whom he had given flying lessons in 1932. In the summer of 1933, Lanphier would buy Madden's brewery, but may have only been acting as a front man for Madden's continued ownership interest).

Having been largely kept in the dark about progress in the official investigation, the Bureau eagerly chased after any information the agency could get. At the time Lanphier met with the Bureau Director, Hoover strongly suspected "some assistance from inside." He assumed that a stranger would have left the note in the crib if he planned to exit by the window. Hoover was determined to have his men solve it and help his agency gain jurisdiction over the wave of kidnappings across the country. A bill to accomplish that aim was then stalled in Congress.

On March 10, Lindbergh (apparently following Madden's wishes) abruptly decided to replace gangsters Rosner, Spitale and Bitz with his new acquaintance John Condon as the official go-between. Lindbergh then set aside $50,000 in a bank account for the ransom payment. Condon was a retired Bronx principal who had just launched his own quixotic effort to rescue Lindbergh's child. It was around midnight on March 9 that Condon had telephoned the Lindbergh residence to introduce himself and report a promising response he had just gotten to his own ad seeking to negotiate the toddler's safe return. Bob Thayer answered the phone and conveyed an offer for Condon to drive down from New York and spend the night. The next morning Condon became Lindbergh's new negotiator for that exceedingly delicate task

– without anyone vetting Condon first. A few days later, Lanphier called the Bureau's office in New York to suggest someone check on Condon's background. Lanphier requested that the Bureau provide him with whatever federal agents discovered about Condon. (The Bureau may not have known that on March 16 Lindbergh signed another authorization empowering lawyer Bill Donovan to pay the $50,000 ransom upon Charlie's safe return, presumably as an alternative to Condon, who had just been assigned that role).

When asked to investigate Condon, the Bureau had to assume Lanphier was acting for Lindbergh's benefit and the two were in close collaboration. So it was odd when Lanphier revealed to Director Hoover in their private meeting that Lindbergh had previously hidden his infant son in a closet as a joke. Lanphier also confided in Hoover that it was a closely guarded secret known only to Anne's doctors, the family, close friends and the Morrow household staff that Anne was now "quite deaf." Hoover may have wondered why a close friend of Lindbergh's would betray these family secrets.

Meanwhile, police began investigating the malfunctioning shutters. Mickey Rosner was still staying at the farmhouse on March 18 when he observed Colonel Schwarzkopf remove the shutters from the nursery window and instruct a trooper to send them out for fingerprint analysis. Detective Parker had his own sources within the state police. Still pursuing his own leads, Parker reportedly learned that the shutters were not warped; the police determined a screwdriver was used to disable the bolt, but never made that finding public. The shutters were not seen again.

Betty Gow and Red Johnsen

When police assumed the kidnapping was an inside job, they first focused on Betty Gow (pictured with Skean) and her boyfriend Red Johnsen.

7.
Hunches Backfire and Leads Go Nowhere

ANNE'S MOTHER was still staying at the farmhouse on March 22 when they received an early morning knock on the door. Anne had awakened her mother after Lindbergh called from New York about 1 a.m. to tell his wife to get dressed for a visitor she should let in. Anne mistakenly thought it would be good news about their kidnapped son. Instead, Special Assistant Secretary of Labor Murray Garsson wanted to interrogate Anne and all three of the employees. He arrived with an assistant at 3 a.m. and announced his intention "to break the Lindbergh case within 48 hours." Garsson had already grilled Betty's boyfriend, Red Johnsen, at length. Johnsen revealed that Betty had confided to him something Marie Cummings, the prior nanny, told her — that Lindbergh "used to hide the baby for a scare" before Betty had started working for him. When questioned by Garsson, Betty confirmed that Marie told her that story. Lindbergh had frightened both his wife and the nanny by concealing the baby in a clothes closet at the Morrows' home and pretending his son was missing. It had taken at least twenty minutes, perhaps closer to an hour, before he fessed up to that heart-stopping prank.

When Garsson demanded more information from Betty, she blurted out: "I was promised I wouldn't be touched!" Garsson pressed further and she said: "Colonel Lindbergh promised I wouldn't be touched." The questioning lasted past daybreak. Betty Gow admitted that Lindbergh had hidden his son more than once. Olly Whateley said that he had heard the same thing. Most distressing for Anne was that Garsson directed her to lead him to their incinerator where Garsson "began poking around in the ashes . . . leaving the plain inference that the Lindberghs themselves, had killed the youngster and burned the body." Shortly afterward, a call to the Secretary of Labor — reputedly at the direction of President Herbert Hoover — put an abrupt halt to Garsson's investigation. Garsson was then told that Lindbergh vouched for Betty Gow and she should "under no circumstances" be arrested.

IRS executive Elmer Irey, who later worked with Lindbergh on assembling and recording ransom funds, would ultimately take credit for shutting Garsson's efforts down. An official interviewed by the press attributed Lindbergh's promise to Betty Gow to "extreme eccentricity" due to concern that further interrogation of the nanny would somehow be breaching faith with the true kidnappers. More likely, Gow had observations she might have shared that Lindbergh didn't want divulged to the police. (On the night of the kidnapping Trooper Frank Kelly reportedly overheard Lindbergh tell Betty "to keep your mouth shut, or I will give you the kind of publicity you would not like.") Schwarzkopf then announced to the press that Red Johnsen was in the custody of immigration officials for his prior illegal entry into the country, but was cleared of any role in the kidnapping.

Meanwhile, it was newcomer John Condon, not Breckinridge's savvy colleague Bill Donovan, who remained the designated go-between to the kidnappers. Condon was well-known in his community as an outspoken oddball, who volunteered to work with prisoners. The retired educator may well have been steered toward Lindbergh by Owney Madden as someone who was gullible and easy to manipulate. Unlike Madden's anger at the choice of Spitale and Bitz, Madden raised no objections at all to this elderly schoolteacher from the Bronx acting as the new go-between.

Lindbergh gave Condon written authorization on March 12 to pay the kidnappers $50,000 ransom "on the condition that he sees my child and that it is returned to me alive." `Condon had already placed an ad in a local newspaper offering his own reward of $1000 to the kidnap gang and his services as an intermediary. The ad got twenty responses the next day, one of which he decided was from the genuine kidnappers. After Lindbergh accepted Condon's offer, Condon replaced his own name and address in future ads with the pseudonym "Jafsie" inspired by his three initials, J.F.C.

Condon kept up communications through ads and then fielded at least one telephone call purportedly from a gang representative. Condon could hear apparent cohorts in the background, one of whom spoke Italian. He was convinced he was dealing with the real kidnap gang. Condon planned on demanding proof the child remained in good health before paying any ransom, but, by the last week of March, Lindbergh was telling his wife they should consider dropping that condition before paying the ransom.

As ransom demand followed ransom demand into April, skeptical Hearst reporter Laura Vitray came to believe the motive must be political. She thought President Hoover's administration conspired with Breckinridge and the Lindberghs to divert national attention leading up to the 1932 election from "the grave economic disaster" that led to 18 million unemployed workers, while 1% of the population held 59% of the nation's wealth.

Six weeks into the investigation, Vitray made the bold accusation that the New Jersey State Police were working with "the powers that be" in high finance and the current administration to perpetrate an enormous kidnapping hoax. Vitray concluded that the child was "well and safe" and had been under no real threat from the start — the elites had just decided to hide behind "Anne Morrow Lindbergh's skirts" for a while. When William Randolph Hearst got wind of Vitray's intent to publish her exposé, he promptly fired her. Her conspiracy theory sounded to him like that of a crackpot. She turned around and cheekily dedicated "this true account of a national tragedy" to her ex-boss.

Shortly after Vitray's book came out, authors John Brant and Edith Renaud published their own effort to untangle fact from fiction: *True Story of the Lindbergh Kidnapping*. Ironically, the cover of the book displayed one of the deceptive photos of Charlie at age one without either author apparently realizing it was seriously out of date. Brant and Renaud noted "numerous complex, contradictory" reports and rumors that led to widespread confusion and "pandemonium" as Americans watched President Hoover and state governors offer their law enforcement resources to find the Lindbergh baby. The two authors felt America's hero and his stoic wife were disserved by the circus that the investigation had become. They pointed to territorial disputes among various law enforcement agencies, who often disagreed on strategy or contradicted each other on the facts.

Brant and Renaud were skeptical that the ladder was genuinely used in the crime: "Would the kidnappers have taken the chance of leaving a clew behind them — a clew with so much 'personality' as a home-made ladder for no other reason than to make it *appear* that they had used the ladder? That was a poser." If the ladder had been used, then police seemed to assume that: "One man inside, must have handed the child to another, waiting on the ladder. . . ." The astonished reporters commented: "An ordinary ladder, and a poorly made one! A bundle of wood and a few nails! *And yet the most important clew of all time!*"

Brant and Renaud believed that the police had followed up on these leads "but the clews simply added to the endless trail." The two investigative reporters noticed other ideas were shot down even though they had seemed to make a lot of sense. One came from the state game commissioner who volunteered several game wardens. Their participation was rejected in favor of troopers with no backwoods experience. The two journalists believed that a "quick, painstaking and expert" search should have indisputably taken place. Yet that did not happen.

Most troubling to them was the fact that three weeks after the kidnapping a suspicious car was found in an abandoned shack off Skillman Lane northeast of the Lindbergh estate. The shack reportedly had lumber in it of the same type as the ladder. The contractor who built the Lindberghs' new home named some other local potential sources of the wood used for the ladder. This was also reported in the *New York Times*. Brant and Renaud wondered why none of these suggestions had been pursued.

As their book was readying for publication, Brant and Renaud noted that a New Jersey State Senator was calling for a thorough investigation of the incompetent state police after the case came to its conclusion. Other reporters interviewed one of Lindbergh's close friends, who said Lindbergh was still confident his son would return alive "unless he died of exposure." That was an odd comment to make as ransom note after ransom note claimed the child was still alive and in good care — messages Lindbergh said he believed were sincere.

Lindbergh kept following other suggested leads for aerial and sea searches to locate his kidnapped son. Somehow new twists and turns to the story kept it on the front pages. The elaborate ransom scheme also had another impact. Mrs. Morrow became convinced — at least for the time being — that there was in fact a professional gang at work and her son-in-law was as innocent of any wrongdoing as her daughter.

When Elmer Hahn, the chief detective for Hunterdon County, suggested a thorough search of the Sourlands to smoke out all the local gangsters involved in black market applejack whiskey, he got nowhere. Hahn also suggested convening a grand jury to investigate why state troopers had impeded his entry onto the property with the local sheriff the night of the kidnapping. The idea of such an investigation got no traction.

In early April, special agent J.M. Keith reported to Bureau Director Hoover in frustration that Lindbergh was holding information back. Agent Keith believed Henry Breckinridge was acting "cagy" and was "the directing force" behind the investigation. "Lindbergh, it appears, takes no action unless advised by Breckinridge." The Bureau continued to lack any "coherent information as to what actually occurred at the Lindbergh home on the night of the kidnapping. . .. Our New York office has been running out blind." Agent Keith got the same runaround from Colonel Schwarzkopf, who never gave the Agency "any intimate basic details upon which this Bureau could conduct an intelligent inquiry."

Go-between John F. Condon aka Jafsie

8.
Wild Goose Chases

ON OR ABOUT MARCH 29, 1932 one of the thumb guards Charlie had been wearing when he disappeared turned up at the entrance to the Lindberghs' driveway — surprisingly untarnished. Bettty Gow spotted it when she and Elsie Whateley were on a walk. Inspector Walsh reported in a joint meeting of the State Police leadership with federal officials in May 1932 the significance of this belated find "in the middle of the road just about halfway between the two ruts" – where it could hardly be missed. (Surprisingly, confusion has arisen since as to the date of this important discovery. Whateley later testified it was March 29; Gow agreed with the prosecutor that it was "somewhere in the neighborhood of April 1" and answered "yes" to a follow-up question about her practice of taking walks in which the prosecutor incorporated April 1 as the date the thumb guard was found. Inspector Walsh reported that the thumb guard was spotted 29 days after the kidnapping. That would have been on March 30. The FBI timeline places the date as March 29, 1932.)

By April 1, ten ransom notes had been received, soon followed by two more. The demand was increased to $70,000. Lindbergh authorized Condon to deliver that increased sum "to whomever in his judgment he believes to be the kidnapper of my son." This replaced the prior instruction that Condon was to ensure the child's safe return to his parents before handing over the ransom money.

The eleventh note threatened to increase the gang's demand to $100,000 if they did not receive the ransom by April 8, 1932. The twelfth ransom note postmarked April 1, 1932 directed Condon to have the money ready by the next day. Condon confirmed the money was ready and received a thirteenth note hand-delivered to his home by a cab driver on April 2. Like a scavenger hunt, the note contained instructions to find another note under a table at a florist shop. There, Jafsie found a note directing him to St. Raymond's Cemetery in the Bronx, as the place to deliver the ransom. It ended: "Come alone and walk. I will meet you."

By then, Lindbergh had apparently depleted most of his liquid assets. Lindbergh told Condon he had to sell some of his airline stock at a steep discount to raise the cash and he had to borrow the rest. One of the first designated intermediaries (probably Mickey Rosner) later told a reporter that in March Lindbergh complained he had already spent a whopping $200,000 on the investigation. In today's dollars that would equate to two and a half million dollars *more* than the ransom demand. Lindbergh's legitimate expenses were far, far less. In the midst of the Great Depression, state and federal taxpayers were picking up the tab for the hugely expensive kidnap investigation that would amount to almost $1.2 million by the time it ended ($22.5 million today).

Elmer Irey, the head of the I.R.S. investigative unit, soon took charge of the ransom payment. (Irey had famously led the team that put mobster Al Capone behind bars for tax evasion in 1931.) Irey was aghast to discover that under Lindbergh's direction none of the bundles of ransom bills had their serial numbers recorded before they were packaged. Without doing so, the bills could not later be traced. Over Lindbergh's strong objections, Irey both insisted that all serial numbers be recorded, and that part of the ransom be made up of gold certificates.

Gold certificates were otherwise ordinary currency embossed with a special gold seal ensuring the recipient that the government had gold stored in its vaults that backed up its value. The gold seal readily distinguished those bills from others in circulation. IRS agents worked with staff at Morgan Bank to record and repackage all the ransom money. Lindbergh did win two concessions: "No police interference, and Dr. Condon was not to demand to see the baby before paying the money." Since he was the father, they acceded to this peculiar request. It was his money, but it made little sense to them.

Lindbergh then drove the money to Condon's home with Breckinridge tailing them. At Condon's home, they stuffed into a specially-built wooden box $50,000 in small denominations ($5, $10 and $20) — as the ransom notes demanded. In another smaller package, they placed 400 fifty-dollar gold certificates. Irey insisted on this because the larger denominations would be far more likely to raise suspicions when spent. There were 5,150 bills in all. Lindbergh accompanied Condon as he followed the directions to the cemetery rendezvous.

The press would only learn of this cemetery meeting after the fact. The same was true for the New York Police. By Lindbergh's specific request, the NYPD had also not been told ahead of time about an earlier rendezvous between Condon and the gang's purported representative on March 12 at Woodlawn Cemetery, which was also in the Bronx. The Bureau of Investigation's New York office also remained in the dark, never having viewed the ransom notes or received copies of any of them, despite asking to be apprised of all developments. Nor, at Lindbergh's specific direction, did the New Jersey police get involved. Lindbergh insisted that any police presence in either cemetery, no matter how well-concealed, might jeopardize the toddler's return.

On the evening of April 2, Lindbergh accompanied Condon to St. Raymond's but remained in the car parked on the street more than 200 feet away. Once Condon exited the car, he delivered only the larger box of less traceable $50,000 of the ransom money to the mystery man he had met before, whom Condon called "John." The box was wrapped in special paper and twine. Condon later claimed that he held back on the $20,000 in $50 gold certificates on his own accord, infuriating Irey for making it much harder to track how the money was spent. Condon said he was trying to save Lindbergh money, but it is unlikely the go-between would have made that decision on his own initiative, knowing the child's life might be in jeopardy. By refusing to have Condon ask for proof the child was safe before handing the money over, Lindbergh had insisted he was intent on "keeping faith" with the supposed kidnappers. If so, he would not let Condon make his own call to hold back close to 30% of the demand.

The ransom Condon delivered was still a hefty sum worth about $860,000 today. Cemetery John accepted the boxful of cash and smaller denomination gold certificates. In exchange, he handed Condon a fifteenth note that said the boy would be found on the "Boad Nelly" located "between Horseneck Beach and Gay Head near Elizabeth Island." So it was that Cemetery John was allowed to disappear with an enormous amount of ransom money with absolutely no guarantee that the child was still alive or would be recovered in exchange.

The location mentioned in the note was off the Massachusetts coast, coincidentally where the Lindberghs had honeymooned three years earlier. Lindbergh appeared thrilled with the news of his child's purported whereabouts. He quickly pursued the lead. Coast Guard ships were sent to that area and Lindbergh flew to the same location with Breckinridge, Condon and Agent Irey. The four men took off at dawn with Lindbergh piloting the plane. To Irey, Lindbergh looked "very cool and collected, but, like all of us, not . . . very optimistic."

Once they were in the air, Breckinridge asked to take over the controls, which Lindbergh must have anticipated. As soon as Breckinridge switched seats with Lindbergh and tried to manipulate the plane, he lost his composure. When Breckinridge sought to gain altitude, the plane descended. When he tried to descend, it went up instead. If Breckinridge tried to turn left, the plane headed to the right. Breckinridge could not fathom what was going wrong. Panic overcame Condon when he saw that Breckinridge lacked any control over their course. Condon started "yowling excerpts from the Song of Solomon" in the Old Testament. Hearing Condon's reaction, Irey had to be equally upset.

Lindbergh reacted with glee. He had switched the wiring as a practical joke. Then, when they arrived near the location where the Boad Nelly was supposed to be, Lindbergh took over the controls. They descended to approach each vessel they saw, but none matched the description in the directions given by Cemetery John for the recovery of Lindbergh's son. Apparently, none of the three men who accompanied Lindbergh found it disturbing that a supposedly desperate father would stage an elaborate, heart-stopping prank in mid-air on his way to a hoped-for reunion with his missing toddler. Breckinridge had gotten used to a number of Lindbergh's unnerving antics, but none had been this terrifying. The search off the Massachusetts coast in early April proved fruitless. Lindbergh called his wife to let her know. He told her "not to be discouraged," he still believed their son was alive. Others attempted to reassure Anne that it was more difficult to get rid of "a dead body than a live one."

Once the press learned Condon's identity, he became the object of ridicule for handing over such an extraordinary ransom payment with no results. Schwarzkopf grew suspicious of Breckinridge and contacted the state's Attorney General to investigate whether Lindbergh's lawyer might have played a role in the ransom scheme. Schwarzkopf had no apparent thought at the time that whatever Breckinridge was up to was sanctioned by Lindbergh. The police commander was blindly devoted to his hero.

In mid-April, soon after Lindbergh's fruitless search for the "Boad Nelly", *Science* magazine published a short, illustrated piece by Charles Lindbergh entitled "A Method for Washing Corpuscles in Suspension." Lindbergh's affiliation with the Rockefeller Institute's Division of Experimental Surgery headed by Nobel Prize winner Dr. Alexis Carrel was startling news. The world had no idea prior to then that the mechanical genius who designed "The Spirit of St. Louis" was now involved in medical research. Within short order scientists reading about the device would praise Lindbergh's contribution as of "immediate practical use" to lab technicians across the country.

Questions must have arisen immediately about how Lindbergh found the time to do such time-intensive lab work in the midst of an all-consuming search for his missing son. In early May, they got an explanation from *Science News-letter,* based on an update from the news service affiliated with *Science* magazine. Lindbergh had submitted the two-page description of an innovative centrifuge to the journal back in February before "the kidnapping of the Lindbergh baby rudely interrupted Col. Lindbergh's collaboration with the Nobel prizeman, Carrel."

In the meantime, Lindbergh had continued making headlines in the ongoing search for his son. By the third week of April, he had quit working with Condon and from then on only reached out to the kidnap gang through a wealthy volunteer from Norfolk, Virginia named John Hughes Curtis. Actually, Lindbergh had already been working with Curtis for a month on an alternative plan to ransom his son.

Curtis owned one of the largest shipyards in the south. In the third week of March, he had been approached by a New Jersey bootlegger Curtis knew only as "Sam." Sam shared with Curtis purported inside information about the kidnapping, including the floor plan of the Lindberghs' home. Sam told Curtis the gang would accept him as an intermediary to deliver ransom money in exchange for the Lindbergh's son. Curtis had never met Lindbergh and later said he only reluctantly became convinced by Reverend H. Dobson-Peacock, a local church deacon who knew the Morrow family, that Curtis had a civic duty to come forward. Dobson-Peacock had served as a pastor in Mexico City while Dwight Morrow was the Ambassador.

To Curtis, the situation seemed too bizarre, but the two of them drove up together from Virginia to the Lindberghs' home in New Jersey to offer their services. Curtis found Lindbergh's behavior off-putting, but felt sorry for his pregnant wife. Curtis agreed to meet with the kidnappers. Cautious by nature, he took detailed notes of the men and women he was introduced to and where he met them. He received repeated assurances from the people he met that the child was still alive. Lindbergh encouraged Curtis to negotiate for his son's safe return. The fact that Curtis and Reverend Peacock were undertaking this role went public on March 22, but where and with whom they met remained secret.

It was not until the second week of April that Curtis saw newspaper accounts about Condon and his own failed efforts to rescue Lindbergh's son. Curtis could not figure out why Lindbergh was simultaneously acting through two different intermediaries. Nor did he understand why Lindbergh never asked Jafsie to obtain proof his son was alive before paying out $50,000 to a mysterious man in a New York cemetery.

The State Police later learned that Curtis had already told Lindbergh that Sam and his gang had provided him with convincing evidence that they were the real kidnappers *before* the money transfer in the Bronx to "Cemetery John." Lindbergh had assured Curtis he found Sam's offer of proof credible. If so, police should have wondered why Lindbergh went ahead and authorized Jafsie to deliver $50,000 to Cemetery John — no strings attached. When Lindbergh embarked on his next odyssey, Curtis was convinced he was dealing with the "real" kidnappers in part by the fact they showed him several hundred dollars of gold certificates that matched newspaper accounts of serial numbers on the ransom bills. Somehow Cemetery John in the Bronx must have transferred this money to the gang Curtis met.

Sam told Curtis the child would be with a nurse on a boat called the *Mary B. Moss*. When Curtis suggested finding it by seaplane, the ace pilot balked for unexplained reasons and insisted on going out to sea by boat, guaranteeing a much slower search. Though the gang appeared to have implicated Olly Whateley as an inside accomplice, Lindbergh did not request that the butler be questioned again. He had earlier refused to allow lie detector tests on any of his household members and never reconsidered that decision.

Curtis later commented on Lindbergh's weird behavior on what turned out to be several forays out to sea over a three-week period. Lindbergh eagerly abandoned his anxious, pregnant wife at the farmhouse with the remaining police, his mother-in-law and other houseguests. He carried with him a repeating rifle which he said the State Police had loaned him to guard against being kidnapped himself. Yet, according to Curtis, Lindbergh did not act the least bit distraught, and slept a lot. Lindbergh told Curtis he wished the kidnappers would "hurry up" and he would, in turn, try to protect them. Curtis wondered why Lindbergh would want to safeguard a gang of professional criminals after all he had been through. Curtis was even more surprised when Lindbergh had their ship's captain set up a card table and told the captain he was "tired of hearing about the kidnapping — to hell with same, let's play cards."

The crew spent a couple of days on land at the end of the first week of May. On the weekend of May 7 and 8, Lindbergh met up with Henry Breckinridge and "Blackburn" (Schwarzkopf's code name) in New York. Then Lindbergh was joined by his wife Anne and the pair had dinner with the Breckinridges and other family friends in Manhattan and spent the night there as well.

On May 9, 1932 Lindbergh and Curtis transferred to another boat to continue to scour the seas for the mysterious *Mary B. Moss*. Meanwhile, Lindbergh kept pulling tiresome practical jokes on Curtis and the crew. Throughout their trip, Lindbergh was in contact with Colonel Schwarzkopf on an almost daily basis. Curtis left the boat on May 12 to go to Atlantic City to meet with another go-between Sam had put him in touch with. Toward the end of that day, Curtis received an urgent, coded message for Lindbergh to call Colonel Schwarzkopf.

Soon, the world would know the horrible news. Reporter Laura Vitray was dead wrong in assuming that the toddler was secretly unharmed and would wind up happily reunited with his parents.

Woodlawn Cemetery

Woodlawn Cemetery was the site for the first meeting of Condon with Cemetery John on the evening of March 12, 1932. Lindbergh insisted there be no police surveillance. Condon later provided many details about that bizarre, hour-long encounter. Cemetery John exhibited a "hacking cough" while answering Condon's probing questions regarding details of the kidnapping. Cemetery John then promised to provide the little boy's sleeping suit as proof he represented the real kidnap gang. Yet he kept inquiring whether "he would 'burn' if the baby were dead."

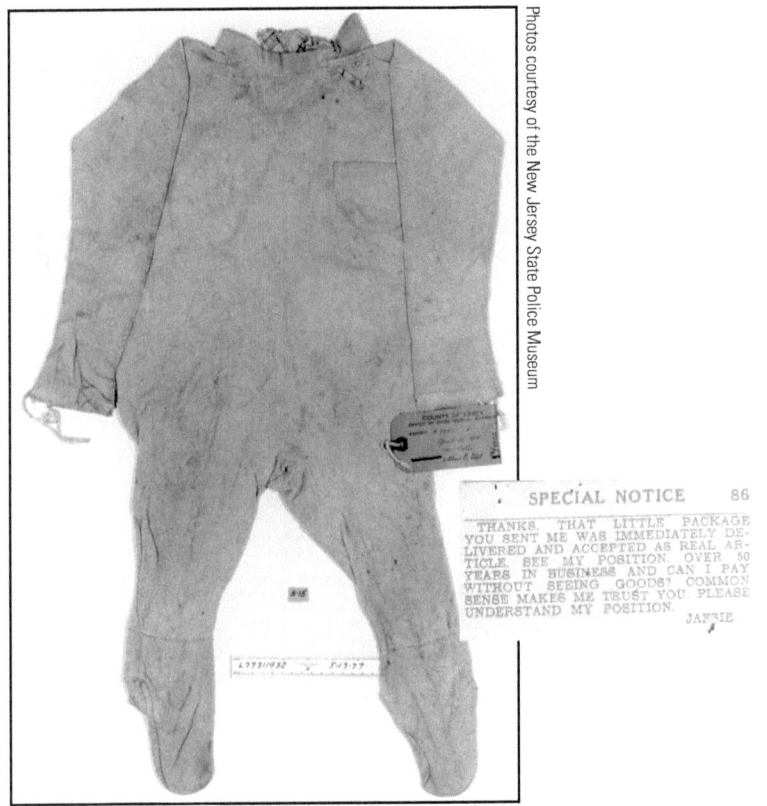

The Dr. Denton sleeping suit arrived inside an envelope mailed to John Condon on or about March 16, 1932 as proof Cemetery John was part of the real kidnap gang. Lindbergh identified the garment as his son's. Condon then published an ad signed "Jafsie" in the New York American on March 22, 1932: "Thanks. That little package you sent me was immediately delivered and accepted as real article."

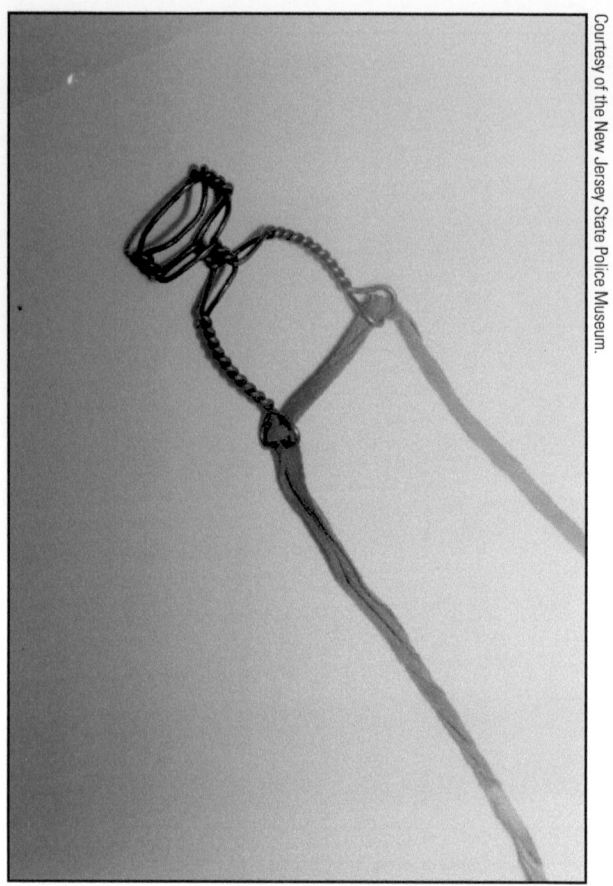

On or about March 29, 1932 — four weeks after the toddler was taken from his nursery — Betty Gow found in the Lindberghs' driveway one of the thumb guards Charlie was wearing when he disappeared. It was untarnished, surprisingly undamaged by cold and rainy weather.

ST. RAYMOND'S CEMETERY

Condon met Cemetery John inside St. Raymond's Cemetery while Lindbergh waited outside in a parked car. Lindbergh again insisted on no police surveillance. In exchange for the $50,000 ransom Condon received a note telling Lindbergh to look for the "Boad Nelly" off Cape Cod (near where the Lindberghs honeymooned in 1929).

John Hughes Curtis and the yacht Macron that Curtis and Lindbergh took out to sea.

9.
A Nation in Mourning

THE FALSE leads for Little Charlie's safe return ended abruptly in the mid-afternoon of May 12, 1932. After nearly two-and-a-half months of a nationwide search, a black truck driver accidentally found a small child's partly clothed, but badly decomposed body a few miles from the Lindbergh's estate. Not all of the descriptions of what happened, and when, in the next few hours completely match up. Most of the witnesses' statements fit the following chronology.

Just before 2:45 p.m., William Allen was driving a truck loaded with timber following his boss, Livingston Titus, and another employee as they traveled along the Hopewell-Princeton Road a mile from Hopewell. In the truck's passenger seat was Allen's white co-worker Orville Wilson. Allen stopped to go relieve himself in the woods and Titus kept going.

While Wilson stayed behind in the truck, Allen walked sixty or seventy feet into the dense woods and stood under a tree branch. There, he stepped on something that he started to kick away. When he looked down, he suddenly realized it was the skeletal foot of a small child sticking out of some leaves. He quickly noticed the head of the corpse in the same pile of leaves in about a three-foot long hollow under the tree. The corpse was face down. The back of the head was mostly skeletal, with a bit of darkened, decayed skin on it and tufts of dirty blond hair partly washed by the ongoing light rain. The skull had a halo of more tufts of similar hair around it. Allen could not see the face.

Allen called out to Wilson to get out of the truck and to come look, too. Allen wondered whether this skeleton could be that of the missing Lindbergh baby. He knew of no other missing children in the area, but he also knew there was a neighboring orphanage. Allen left Wilson by the corpse, warning him not to touch it and walked further into the woods to answer the call of nature that had caused him to stop in the first place. When he rejoined Wilson, the two got back in the truck and headed straight to Hopewell.

Allen's original statement would indicate they found their local constable, Charles Williamson, at the barber shop. (Allen later testified Williamson was actually located in a pool hall.) Upon hearing the news, Williamson raced to tell Chief Harry Wolfe, who was at a local garage having work done on his car. Allen had meanwhile gone with Wilson to deliver their load to a sawmill. The two officers drove to the sawmill and took Allen back to his discovery.

Arriving at the spot where the truck had stopped earlier, the pair of policemen immediately noticed a weather-beaten burlap bag on the roadside. They left it where it was and followed Allen to where the corpse lay. They gave the remains a good look before dropping Allen back in Hopewell. The Hopewell officers proceeded straight to the Lindbergh farmhouse to report their find to Colonel Schwarzkopf. The guard who stopped them at the gate telephoned Captain Lamb with the news. Lamb then ordered Detective James Fitzgerald from Jersey City to accompany Sergeant Andrew Zapolsky of the State Police to join the two Hopewell officers at the entrance to the Lindberghs' driveway. The four men then drove back together on the Hopewell-Princeton Road to the spot where Allen had stopped before.

When they emerged from their car, Fitzgerald saw the burlap bag just about ten feet away and Zapolsky noticed it, too. They then followed Williamson and Wolfe into the woods about 75 feet to the corpse partly buried in leaves under the tree. The decomposition was so advanced, the officers were not sure how the body could be identified. Fitzgerald then asked Zapolsky to get some sticks, which Fitzgerald put under the corpse to flip it over. Most of the face remained intact, the flesh color of a Caucasian, but it started to darken quickly.

All four officers — Zapolsky and Fitzgerald and Hopewell Police Chief Harry Wolfe and Constable Williamson — knelt down to get a good look at its features. Zapolsky had with him a photo of the missing child. According to New Jersey State Police historian Jim Fisher: "The size and apparent age of the corpse, its golden curly hair, the general shape of the head and the type of clothing on the body told them they were looking at the Lindbergh baby." That seems unlikely. Anne herself considered the outdated photographs of her son to bear little resemblance to her 33-inch toddler, who, by the time of his disappearance had an oversized head and new haircut and looked at least two-and-a-half. The swollen and distorted features of the corpse would have compounded the problem of identifying him.

Yet, Zapolsky and Fitzgerald did notice that, considering the advanced state of decomposition of the rest of the body, the face was amazingly well-preserved, which he and Fitzgerald attributed to it lying in the dirt. One eye was open; the other already putrefied. That suggested the head had previously lain on its side with one eye exposed, and that it might have been moved after death to the position it now occupied. Four hours later, the stench of decaying flesh would almost overpower the coroner and the county physician. Because of the rain that afternoon, any odor was apparently far less noticeable in the woods. The left leg was missing below the knee; both hands and one forearm were missing.

Fitzgerald and Zapolsky headed back to Hopewell with Chief Wolfe and Constable Williamson and called Captain Lamb from a public telephone. It was now 3:35 p.m. Captain Lamb dispatched four men to the site: two Jersey City investigators, Inspector Harry Walsh and Detective Robert Coar; Lieutenant Keaten of the New Jersey State Police and Sergeant Moffatt of the Newark police. Lieutenant Keaten was in charge, but Inspector Walsh had been given a principal role in the investigation since early March. Colonel Schwarzkopf had as much reason to be wary of Moffatt as he should have been of officers loaned to him from Jersey City. If anything, Newark police had a worse reputation than Jersey City police.

Newark was then widely known as the bootleg capital of America. Most of the city was under monopoly control by a Jewish kingpin named Abner "Longy" Zwillman, the Al Capone of New Jersey to Owney Madden's similar reputation in Manhattan. Zwillman's mob of hitmen and enforcers rivaled that of New York's Mafia. A local historian would later report that during Prohibition, Zwillman and other Newark gangsters could count on "almost open co-operation of police, prosecutors, and the courts, who were in [their] pay."

The two Hopewell policemen left the site of the corpse to go find Allen and Wilson to get their official statements. In his signed statement, Allen described seeing that "the skin was almost all off the head." He also reported seeing "one hole right in the top of it about the size of a quarter." From what he saw of the body he guessed: "The rest of it was either decomposed or had been eaten by animals."

Fitzgerald and Zapolsky had picked up the burlap bag by the side of the road and brought it with them when they went to look at the corpse. Lieutenant Keaten dispatched them to follow up on a different assignment, leaving four officers at the site. In their report later that day Walsh and Keaten said that upon their arrival, they made a "close examination of the body and clothing" and suspected it was the Lindberghs' child. But the truth was that at that time it was hard to tell if this decayed corpse really was Charles Lindbergh, Jr. or even if it were male. Though the face was preserved, what was left of the child's lower body was mostly skeletal and no longer wore any clothes. Its gender could not be determined.

The officers presumed that the missing limbs may have been gnawed off by "dogs or other animals" because they found nothing "to indicate what otherwise happened to these [parts of the body]." However, the corpse wore a double layer of undershirts. Walsh suggested they interview Betty Gow again to confirm what Charlie had been wearing when he disappeared. Inspector Walsh and Sergeant Moffatt headed to the Lindberghs' estate. Keaten and Coar stayed behind to guard the corpse.

The first stop at the Lindbergh estate was to see Colonel Schwarzkopf to get his permission to interview Betty Gow. Ever since Gow was grilled in late March by Murray Garsson, no household staff could be interviewed without Schwarzkopf's okay. Walsh did not tell Betty Gow about the corpse in the woods but got her to describe once more the two T-shirts she and Anne put on the toddler when he went to bed on March 1. Gow gave him the remnant of flannel she had used for the homemade T-shirt. She also cut a length of blue thread for them to take. It was Gow's identification of the T-shirts that clinched the identification of the body for the state police.

In the meantime, Colonel Schwarzkopf sent New Jersey State Police Sergeant Louis Kubler to photograph the body. Kubler arrived at 4:15 p.m. and flipped the body back to approximate its original position in order to take one of the photos. Colonel Schwarzkopf arrived with Walsh, Zapolsky and Moffatt and observed the corpse having been put face up again. By then, Zapolsky noticed that the face, which had been white when he first turned it over, had turned blue. Walsh compared the scalloped edge of the inner T-shirt to that of the remnant he brought. They appeared to be a match.

It was still drizzling. With Moffat's help, Walsh used a stick to move the body enough to cut off both T-shirts, which he placed in the burlap bag to bring to Gow for identification — the same bag that Troopers Fitzgerald and Zapolsky had picked up from the roadside and left by the corpse when they went off on another assignment. Walsh would later testify he was the officer who "found" the burlap bag near the corpse. Moffatt then accompanied Colonel Schwarzkopf back to the Lindbergh estate, leaving the other two men to guard the child's remains once more.

The police had serious doubts that the body had been there long. Once Coroner Swayze removed the corpse, state troopers were directed to remove 14 inches of earth, leaves and other debris just below where the remains had been and send it to a lab for analysis to determine if blood had seeped into the soil. Lab analysis could also determine the presence of any clothing fibers or other foreign material.

In his announcement to the press that night, Schwarzkopf said, "The body was in a bad state of decomposition. We could not tell how long the body had been lying there." He also said it was about 75 yards from the road (as Wilson did). Allen and others said it was about 60 to 75 feet. Prior to May 12, no one had reported ever seeing the burlap bag on the shoulder of the road about 4 miles from the Lindbergh estate. Colonel Schwarzkopf had himself noted in a report in early April that "a re-check of all the surrounding area was made by experienced detectives in a minute search of the territory for a radius of at least five miles." Volunteers had covered the territory, too, as had a troop of Boy Scouts. If the burlap bag —which was so easily spotted on May 12— had been there long, it was remarkable that every single person who scoured that area before missed it.

A neighbor who walked through that area regularly said he would have noticed the corpse had it been there since the beginning of March. A local farmer told reporters: "The troopers were all over the place. I believe they were right around the little grave." In the past, the farmer had seen buzzards in the area, "but none recently. . . . I believe the body was placed there lately. I haven't seen any buzzards flying around." Just a few hundred feet from the half-buried corpse was a cottage recently rented to a young man named Charles Maran, who happened to have done some work for Henry Breckinridge as a process server. Maran lived with his mother and stepfather; none of them reported seeing anything there, either.

From that site, the Lindberghs' house on the bluff was plainly visible day and night. If this crime was the product of careful planning, the police had to wonder when and how the corpse got to this readily discoverable location. It was about fifty feet from one of the newly installed telephone poles that had been set up specifically for tips and coverage related to the crime. It was also within a mile of the Mount Rose farmstead the Lindberghs had previously rented.

Schwarzkopf and Moffatt brought the undershirts to show Betty Gow. She immediately identified the sleeveless B. Altman shirt she had put on Charlie on March 1, as well as her own handiwork on the flannel T-shirt she had made from an old baby's petticoat. Aside from its scalloped edge and the same blue thread, Betty could also see that one side of the T-shirt remained unsewn, just as she had left it to make it easier to put on. She noticed that the garment was still stained by Vapo-Rub. She inquired where the items were found. They told her about the dead toddler in the woods. Betty fought disbelief. She thought Lindbergh had a promising lead when he joined John Curtis out at sea and would succeed in getting the kidnappers to release his son.

Once Betty Gow identified the two T-shirts, Colonel Schwarzkopf officially declared the kidnap investigation a murder case. It was now 4:58 p.m. on May 12 — more than ten weeks after the boy disappeared.

Colonel Schwarzkopf then tried to reach Lindbergh to let him know and had Newark Officer P.D. Moffat contact Mercer County Coroner Walter Swayze and have him come to the Lindbergh estate. Swayze was a mortician who had just become coroner in 1930. Though the farmhouse was located in Hunterdon County, the corpse had been found over the line in Mercer County.

Schwarzkopf next had the unenviable task of informing the child's mother and grandmother, both of whom were at the farmhouse. Colonel Schwarzkopf saw Mrs. Morrow first. She realized at once that her grandson had been dead all along, likely since the very night of his disappearance. Colonel Schwarzkopf accompanied the recent widow upstairs to find Anne in the master bedroom. Mrs. Morrow bleakly told her daughter: "The baby is with Daddy."

Anne asked how her son died. From the skull fractures, Schwarzkopf assumed the toddler was bludgeoned to death. Anne was stoic; she had already somehow sensed her son was dead. Yet she had held out hope until her mother's distraught announcement. In a daze, Anne started a letter to her mother-in-law shortly after Schwarzkopf left, letting Evangeline Lindbergh know the devastating news. Betty Gow's identification of the T-shirts worn by the badly decomposed corpse left her certain of her child's identity. She understood that her son was murdered by a blow to the head from which he died instantly. Anne was relieved "to know definitely that he did not live beyond that night." The autopsy had yet to take place.

Officers had already been dispatched to locate Lindbergh and get him to return. When Curtis had gotten off the boat to go to Atlantic City, Lindbergh had remained on their borrowed, double-masted sailboat and couldn't be reached. Schwarzkopf told Curtis to have Lindbergh call him for an important update and for Curtis to wait for a trooper to bring Curtis to the farmhouse for questioning. When the coroner arrived at the Lindbergh estate, a trooper took him to the child's body and Swayze transported the remains to the Mercer County Morgue in Trenton, which also served as his family mortuary.

Word had already begun to leak out by quarter past five of the dead baby found in the woods. Schwarzkopf notified his staff to alert the press that he would be conducting a conference in about an hour. Shortly after 6 p.m. Swayze arrived back at the morgue with the corpse. At 6:55 p.m., Schwarzkopf delivered the stunning news to a crowd of reporters. His men locked the doors to prevent anyone from racing for telephones and telegraphs before he finished.

By 7:30 p.m. the gruesome story went out on the wire, leaving millions of people tuned to their radios with no appetite for dinner. The Associated Press reported, "Child Killed By Two Blows On Head, Fiend Evidently Held Little Tot In His Arms While Striking Its Head." The reporters understood from Schwarzkopf's briefing that "some adult person held the baby tightly in his arms and deliberately hammered the head with the purpose of causing instant death." *The New York Daily News* ran a banner story the next morning, "BABY LINDY FOUND BEATEN TO DEATH." Locally, reporters and gawkers would soon swarm the wooded area where the corpse had been. An enterprising vendor even set up a hotdog stand on the nearby shoulder of the Hopewell-Princeton Road before police forced him away.

William Allen had meanwhile been summoned to the Lindbergh estate to give his statement. While he waited for the police to let the family know of his presence, Allen assumed that, despite their grief, they would express their gratitude to him for uncovering the murder. At least they now knew what had happened to the toddler and no longer held false hopes of reuniting with him. But Lindbergh was not home and neither Anne, nor her mother showed any interest in speaking to the black truck driver who found the body that Schwarzkopf had just announced was Little Charlie's.

When Lindbergh returned, he likewise never sought Allen out to thank him for immediately reporting the grim discovery to the police. When his son asked Allen excitedly, "What did he say to you, Pop?" Allen answered, "Not a damn thing. Not 'thank you' not 'kiss my ass,' nothing."

The homemade flannel T-shirt identified by Betty Gow as the one she made for Little Charlie from an old petticoat on the evening of March 1, 1932.

The sleeveless shirt Little Charlie wore the night of the kidnapping.

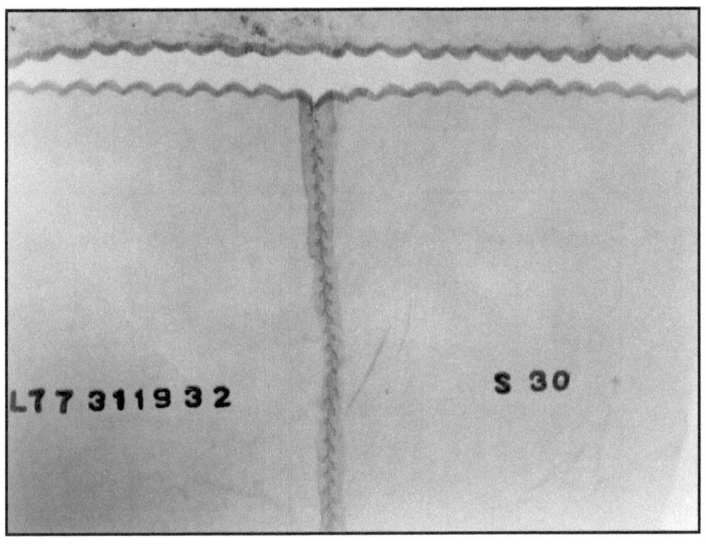

The scalloped edge of the remaining material in Betty Gow's sewing pile matched the scalloped edge of the homemade T-shirt found on the corpse.

Trial exhibits courtesy of the New Jersey State Police Museum

Photo taken of the corpse found in the woods after it was turned face up.

10.
At the Morgue

CORONER Swayze called the county's medical examiner, Dr. Charles Mitchell at his home in Trenton and summoned him to the morgue. The last time Dr. Mitchell had practiced in a hospital was over a decade earlier. It was a secret between Dr. Mitchell and Swayze that Dr. Mitchell had for some time been unable to perform autopsies himself. By age sixty, his hands had become too arthritic. For the past two years Mitchell had worked in tandem with Swayze. At Dr. Mitchell's direction, Swayze would do the actual hands-on examination of the corpse. Swayze then would type up the autopsy report and have Mitchell sign it. If testimony was later required, Mitchell would pretend he performed the autopsy himself. Swayze would not confess publicly to their arrangement for decades.

Even Swayze did not consider what he did in his morgue on the evening of May 12, 1932 with the remains of the "unknown baby" counted as an autopsy. That was how he labeled his first report since the identity of the body had not been confirmed by any family member. He did not open up the chest with shears as he normally would have done for a full autopsy. He thought of their effort that night as more of a preliminary "look-see." More tests were anticipated.

Outside the front of the mortuary a huge crowd was growing of both reporters and curiosity-seekers, all expecting Lindbergh to show up any moment. Inside, Swayze placed the remains of the corpse labeled "unknown baby" on the table and began the preliminary examination. At Mitchell's direction the preliminary examination took about an hour (Swayze's estimate) to an hour and a quarter or maybe an hour and a half (Mitchell's estimate). They started at 7:30 p.m., 45 minutes to an hour after Mitchell arrived. Mitchell later testified that the overpowering "odor made it impossible for a man to work over the child." No one else was present.

First, they measured the body's length and assessed its overall appearance. Mitchell observed that the forehead and skull circumference were unusually large. The remains appeared to have deteriorated from prolonged exposure to the elements. Mitchell could not tell the sex because the genitalia were among the many missing organs. But the pelvic bone looked to him more feminine than masculine.

The possibility that the child was held tightly and beaten to death with two successive blows to the head may have been Dr. Mitchell's first reaction. At least one newspaper so reported. But Dr. Mitchell soon noticed that the fractures on the left and right sides of the head were directly opposite each other. The one on the right side behind the ear was smooth, like a bullet hole. In the preliminary autopsy report it would be described as a "perforated fracture about a half inch in diameter on the right side of the skull posterior to the right ear." The much larger fracture on the opposite side of the skull went from the fontanel all the way behind the toddler's left ear and then split into two fractures. Dr. Mitchell quickly concluded that the fractures might have all been caused by one traumatic event.

Swayze measured the fontanel at about an inch in diameter. The report would note a hemorrhage on the inner surface of the skull underlying the fracture on the left side of the head. The "scalp was so badly decomposed that it was impossible to find any contusions or hemorrhagic conditions external to the skull." This matched Allen's description of very little skin on the top of the head.

Swayze sawed into the skull, which Mitchell noticed started to "come part of its own" and oozed brain matter. At Mitchell's request, Swayze spread the brain on the table to look for a bullet, but none was evident. Mitchell still assumed that the child was likely shot, but the bullet had been lost on the way to the morgue. Swayze had seen brain matter already oozing out of the fontanel when he brought the corpse in. They both noticed what looked like "a foreign substance, possibly a chemical or acid on the body." Swayze scraped it with a knife to look at it more closely. Whatever it was either never got analyzed or never got reported.

A hemorrhage under the fracture indicated the skull was fractured before the heart stopped pumping. Mitchell ruled out asphyxiation. There were no signs of strangulation. When they could not bear the smell any longer the two men went back to Swayze's house which was attached to the morgue. They both had stiff drinks while Swayze typed up their findings so far.

Pinpointing the date the child died did not seem possible. Instead, Mitchell gave a range of two to three months before it was found. Diagnosis of the cause of death — fractured skull due to external violence. When the pair had started the examination, the morgue was not guarded. At some point reporters gained access to the morgue and one took a photo of the corpse.

Walter Swayze's stepfather Frank Swayze arrived home wondering why there were reporters everywhere. When he found out the morgue was not guarded, Frank alerted his stepson and Dr. Mitchell to notify the police, who sent a sergeant and a patrolman. Frank also called the funeral home's teen-aged assistant, John Conlon, to help guard the morgue. At 10:06 p.m. one of the Swayzes called Schwarzkopf to have someone come to identify the "unknown baby."

Normally, Dr. Mitchell would invite the parents of a minor to perform that grim task. But Lindbergh was not yet back from his sea voyage and his wife Anne was considered in too delicate a condition. Schwarzkopf also did not want to subject Anne's mother to the gruesome sight. He asked Betty Gow to come instead and sent Captain Lamb, Detective Coar and Corporal Sam Leon to accompany her.

Sometime around 11 p.m., Betty Gow arrived at the morgue from the farmhouse and was escorted through a back alley to avoid the press. Mercer County Chief of Detectives James Kirkham had already arrived. Frank Swayze thought Gow showed up looking like a tart — wearing excessive makeup and chewing gum. He wanted to throttle her. For some reason, Dr. Mitchell stayed in the house when the Swayzes accompanied Gow into the morgue. When the sheet was lifted, she must have been horrified at the sight. The preliminary autopsy had already been performed. It is not known if brain matter remained spilled on the table.

Gow was only there five to ten minutes. She said that despite the bloated face, she could discern his dimpled chin, and, inside the mouth, the configuration of his sixteen teeth, two of which had just come in. She also recognized the blond hair. Gow had, in fact, been keeping a diary for his mother and grandmother of the baby's milestones, including when he cut new teeth. (The teeth were unusual. Two canines tilted somewhat "towards the incisors and were below the line of adjacent teeth.") Gow also knew her charge from the distinctive, overlapping small toes on the one remaining foot. (The autopsy report said the big toes overlapped, but that was likely in error).

The report did not include any analysis of when and how most of the child's organs went missing but stated that the only thoracic and abdominal organs that remained were the heart and liver. (Mitchell would later testify there was no stomach, no lungs. There were no kidneys. He did not list all the missing organs one by one, but said the only organs still found inside the corpse were the heart and liver, both in such condition they could no longer be examined.) Mitchell turned down assistance from a New York pathologist who was prepared to come to Trenton that night. No further analysis was apparently conducted, and no official photographs of the corpse were taken.

It was "the crime of the century" with the state police and federal agents in hot pursuit of the perpetrators. If a murder trial was later prosecuted, it could be compromised irreparably if they did not take all steps necessary to diagnose the cause, date and manner of death. Such pressure would presumably be magnified in this extraordinarily high-profile case. Yet the opposite seemed to be happening before the "look-see" even commenced.

Dr. Mitchell was not satisfied with an ID for the unknown baby provided only by the Lindberghs' nanny. Mitchell would not sign off on the identity of the corpse until Lindbergh came to see the corpse. Meanwhile, Dr. Mitchell went outside to talk to the press. Thoroughly inebriated, Mitchell was quite garrulous. He told the reporters he considered the brutal homicide likely resulted from a deliberate shooting sometime after the kidnapping.

Dr. Mitchell said he believed that the child had been originally hidden in a local hideout and murdered several days later when the police investigation got too close. He figured the body was disposed of in a hurry. The "peculiar condition" of the multiple skull fractures led him to believe one bullet likely caused all of the damage. Yet he also considered other possibilities. He told the press that the homicide could have resulted from being struck by an automobile, "banged against a tree or hit by a club or other heavy instrument." Having given the reporters lots to write about, Mitchell then went home to bed.

Reporters were anxious to witness the arrival of the grieving father, but Lindbergh was still en route. Henry Breckinridge, Breckinridge's wife, and John Fogarty had arrived at the farmhouse at about quarter past nine. Fogarty had been at the Breckinridge's apartment when he learned about the current buzz of activity in Hopewell and Trenton.

When the request was made that someone come to identify the "unknown baby" in the morgue it was likely Breckinridge who suggested Betty Gow. When Dr. Mitchell later insisted on Lindbergh himself coming in the morning, Breckinridge instead used a police telephone in the garage around 11:30 p.m. to contact Charlie's pediatrician to meet him at the morgue. Breckinridge also notified Jafsie and picked him up on the way. Meanwhile, Mitchell had gone home. When Coroner Walter Swayze learned that Dr. Van Ingen was coming, he called Mitchell to come back to the morgue.

Dr. Van Ingen arrived in Trenton around 1 a.m., bringing Charlie's medical records with him. He met up with Breckinridge and Mercer County's chief detective, James Kirkham. They entered the morgue together to join Mitchell and the Swayzes, while Jafsie waited outside with the throng of reporters. Dr. Van Ingen was shocked by the lack of professionalism in such an important case.

Dr. Van Ingen pulled out his file on the Lindberghs' son. The corpse, relaxed in death, had been measured at just half an inch longer than Dr. Van Ingen's own recorded measurement of 33 inches on February 18, which placed Charles, Jr. in the top half of the size chart for twenty-month-olds. (At that time, Charlie had balked at being touched and had difficulty standing straight.) Dr. Van Ingen noted the corpse had sixteen teeth like he mentioned in his own records, four of which were just coming in when Van Ingen saw the toddler two weeks before his disappearance. He had previously noted that the baby teeth were much slower in emerging than one would normally expect. (Generally, all of an infant's incisors appear by the age of one year.)

Viewing the skull, Dr. Van Ingen did notice "little locks of hair [which] was similar to the hair of the boy." The child's hair had been washed and it turned out to be "very light, flaxen hair." Despite some correspondence to features of his patient, Dr. Van Ingen found the remains too deteriorated to tell if this were truly the Lindbergh toddler. Breckinridge agreed with him. At the request of Detective Kirkham, Dr. Van Ingen wrote a note on the coroner's stationery: "The condition of the body is such that positive identification by me is impossible." Afterward he said that he also told Walter Swayze at the time that he could not identify the remains "if someone were to come in here and offer me ten million dollars."

Meanwhile, John Curtis, with whom Lindbergh had been at sea off and on for the last three weeks, was escorted to state police headquarters by a trooper who sped all the way from South Jersey. When Curtis arrived at the farmhouse around 2 a.m. he was immediately taken to the basement for grilling about his supposed contacts with the kidnap gang. The state police were then getting ready to interrogate John Condon and Mickey Rosner, too. The investigators particularly wanted to find out why Condon paid Cemetery John the ransom when the boy was already dead. All three former go-betweens were separated for questioning. Each accused the others of being a fraud, while their interrogators went from room to room comparing the men's stories.

Lindbergh had been reached by 7:30 p.m. May 12 to learn that his son's body had been found. Anne was told her husband would be home in three hours, at most. Contrary to her expectation, Lindbergh did not start out from Cape May, New Jersey until 9 p.m. and somehow did not arrive by his wife's side at the farmhouse until the wee hours of the following morning — sometime after troopers escorted Curtis there from Atlantic City. Why the trip took Lindbergh so long is not known. Instead of going straight upstairs, Lindbergh stopped to have a brief conversation with Curtis, who was being vigorously questioned by the police. Lindbergh then joined his wife in the master bedroom, finding her dissolved in tears.

Anne noticed that her husband seemed at a loss for words, but quite collected. She felt comforted by his reassurance that, if the baby died that night of March 1, it was already too late for them to make any difference. At least, Lindbergh told her, "I don't think he knew anything about it." At the time, Dr. Mitchell had already told reporters his belief that the child did not die on March 1, but had likely been shot or bludgeoned to death days later. So, if anyone had told Lindbergh upon his arrival what Dr. Mitchell had just told reporters at the morgue, Lindbergh had no known basis for reassuring his wife that their child had not experienced any terror before he died.

Anne tossed and turned for the remainder of the night as her husband sat observing her. Both Colonel Schwarzkopf and her husband could have been just trying to make her feel better with their assurances. Yet maybe something about her husband's reaction gnawed at her subconscious. She wrote the next day in her diary: "His terrible patience and sweetness and silence — terrifying."

Mercer County Medical Examiner Dr. Charles Mitchell kept it secret that arthritis prevented him from performing the autopsy of the "unknown baby" on May 12, 1932. Instead he supervised Coroner Walter Swayze doing the "look-see" that night. Dr. Mitchell's final autopsy report identified the corpse as Charles Lindbergh, Jr. and attributed death to external violence — either a gunshot or sharp blow to the head 7 to 10 weeks before the body was found.

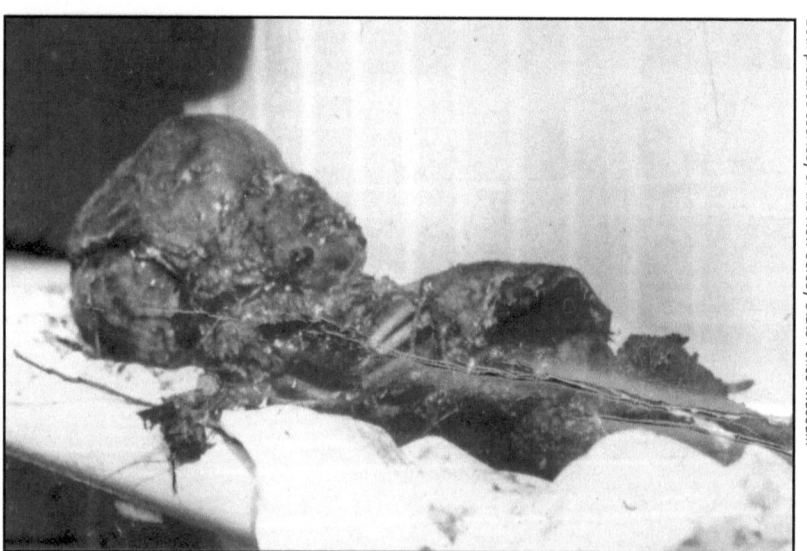

Only photo taken at the morgue by an unauthorized photographer who sold it on the black market. The face had been white when found and turned dark before it reached the morgue.

11.
Ashes and Smoke

THE DAY after the corpse was found, Schwarzkopf continued having his men investigate the site. Trooper Thomas Carmody found a crumpled piece of a page from a March 1, 1932 *New York World Telegram* stuck between two small limbs at the foot of a tree "about 50 yards further into the woods" from where the corpse had been found. That dated newspaper page wedged where it would not blow away could have been a sign the perpetrators were being too clever. Newspapers generally decompose in less than six weeks in a wet environment. The discovery of the still legible paper was made more than 10 weeks after March 1— a period which included a very wet spring. There is no indication that the police considered the condition of the newspaper a sign it could be a false clue placed there quite recently.

In addition to testing the soil, the burlap bag and the clothing, the police initially planned to have toxicology tests run to answer more unknowns about the homicide. Why such tests were not ordered immediately following the "look-see" was never explained. Instead, Frank Swayze announced on the morning of May 13 that the remains would be placed in a closed coffin. That same day, President Hoover reacted to the dreadful news of the child's death by ordering all federal agencies, including the Bureau of Investigation, to lend their support to find the perpetrators. By that afternoon Lindbergh told Schwarzkopf he wanted the boy immediately cremated, overriding the plans of the police to have tests done first. Outside pathologists strongly objected, but they were ignored. Dr. Mitchell insisted that Lindbergh view the corpse first, now much further decomposed.

In the meantime, the county physician let Detective Ellis Parker see the remains in the morgue. Coroner Swayze was present when Parker arrived but not Dr. Mitchell. Parker's reaction was that the child looked "subnormal." He was also puzzled by the advanced state of decomposition apart from the face. Parker soon checked weather reports dating back to March 1. The average temperatures were 37 degrees in March, 49 degrees in April and 55 degrees in early May. The temperature would have been cooler in that location because trees blocked the sun. Parker later consulted several pathologists who reportedly said it would take 70-degree weather for many days straight to produce such decomposition. Dr. Mitchell had more doubts of his own as to the corpse's identity after Dr. Van Ingen refused to identify the body as that of his patient.

A trooper told Mitchell that neither of the Lindberghs would be coming to the morgue, but Lindbergh later changed his mind. He arrived at the back entrance to the morgue around 4 p.m. on Friday, the 13th. In the presence of a score of men crowded into the embalming room, Lindbergh lifted the sheet from the corpse, and spent at most a minute and a half examining the child's remains.

First, to the astonishment of the hushed witnesses, Lindbergh asked for a sharp instrument so he could pry apart the swollen lips of the corpse. He seemed totally devoid of emotion as he counted the teeth and glanced quickly at the overlapping toes. When asked if he could identify the corpse, he announced: "I am perfectly satisfied that is my child." Dr. Mitchell believed Lindbergh simply wanted to get the process over with. Per Lindbergh's prior instructions to Colonel Schwarzkopf, the baby's remains were then delivered to a crematorium without any toxicology tests having been run. There would be no ceremony. Anne's grief was compounded by the lack of closure, but her husband's wishes ruled.

Expert observers were shocked when the police let a preliminary "look-see" stand in for a full autopsy and then allowed immediate cremation of the child's remains. Under New Jersey law an autopsy was then required for all homicides. The quick look-see did not come close to answering the questions about how and when the child died. Some still had doubts about the corpse's gender. Schwarzkopf's acquiescence in such irregularities again demonstrated Lindbergh's extraordinary clout.

Schwarzkopf followed the hearse to make sure it arrived at the crematorium safely. Lindbergh and Breckinridge waited behind to avoid the crowd outside. They then made a special trip of their own to visit the owner of the crematorium to ensure that no one would disturb the remains before they were picked up by Coroner Swayze to be delivered to Lindbergh. Lindbergh later scattered the ashes to the wind as he had done with his father's.

On the day after the cremation, Coroner Walter Swayze typed up an updated autopsy report identifying the corpse as that of Charles Lindbergh, Jr. He listed certain "marks peculiar to the Lindbergh baby" that conformed with the record made on February 14, 1932 [actually on the 18th] by his pediatrician, Dr. Van Ingen, including the 16 teeth and overlapping toes on the right foot, unclosed fontanelle, 33 1/2 inch body and "head larger than normal in child of twenty months, forehead prominent." Dr. Mitchell considered this update his official report.

Despite Dr. Mitchell's own lingering misgivings, he was willing to endorse the opinion that the remains were those of Charles Lindbergh, Jr. Detective Parker reached a different conclusion — that the pediatrician's doubts and the body's inexplicably advanced state of decomposition meant it was a substitute for the Lindbergh's child and was quickly cremated to prevent discovery of that fact. Parker may have known that medical training facilities hired grave robbers to supply "unclaimed bodies" for teaching purposes. It fit Parker's theory that a look-alike corpse would not have been too hard to find — even one with toes that overlapped.

The May 14 report incorporated more details of the bullet theory that Mitchell favored to explain the "suspicious opening" behind the right ear that was "somewhat rounded and resembled a bullet wound." Swayze reported that no bullet was found in the cranium, but "the fracture of the skull was directly opposite this opening." A bullet could have struck the skull on its right side and lodged inside after "striking the inner table of the skull." If so, it might have been lost in transit to the morgue since "the brains were exuding from the fontanelle." Advanced decomposition indicated "the child could have been killed and left at the point where it was found for a period of from seven to ten weeks." Since Charlie had been missing 72 days, Dr. Mitchell was placing his death at least two days after the night of his disappearance, possibly more than two weeks afterward.

Around 1 p.m. on May 14, a man who identified himself as Sergeant Doyle called headquarters from the nearby Skillman Village for Epileptics requesting a box of bullets. One would assume he might have been seeking to test out the bullet theory. But the purpose of that call would remain a mystery.

For some reason, the police kept the May 12, 1932 "look-see" preliminary autopsy report of an unknown baby, but not the official May 14, 1932 autopsy. The only photo would be unauthorized — one taken by a professional photographer whom Dr. Mitchell and Swayze may have let slip in while they were drinking. The state police were livid when they found out about the photo and quizzed both men. They swore the photographer and an accompanying reporter sneaked in and out on the evening of May 12 before they could prevent the intrusion. Mitchell and Swayze must have already been under strict orders not to have any photos taken. Lindbergh soon wrote a letter to the Trenton Police Chief directing him to find the commercial photo and destroy it, but it had already gone out on the black market.

Anne shared with her husband that their son's death shattered her belief in "the goodness and security of life." He told her it was "like war" and how disappointed he was at the failure of the kidnap search: "I hoped so I would bring that baby back." He focused Anne on looking forward instead of mourning their loss. She wrote in her diary: "We speak of the new baby and C's scientific work — two things of hope."

Less than a week after discovery of the child's body, the Assistant Director of the Bureau's New York office sat in a confidential conference with Colonel Schwarzkopf attended by ten other representatives of both agencies and a stenographer. The Agency executive asked about the autopsy findings regarding the child's skull fracture and was told: "The skull was not compressed, it seemed to be more or less of a clean break and some instrument of great weight must have hit it as there was no splintering." No one present questioned that conclusion, which matched Dr. Mitchell's alternate theory that death was caused by bludgeoning, which was similar to what Colonel Schwarzkopf had posited on day one.

At that meeting, Colonel Schwarzkopf also provided the federal agents with a chronology of the evening of March 1. He included in that briefing that both of the Lindberghs "were in communication with the Breckinridges" around 8 p.m. — supposedly at the farmhouse. Reaching Lindbergh was then of some urgency because Breckinridge had just received a frantic call about Lindbergh's failure to show up as one of two widely advertised guests of honor at the Waldorf Astoria gala. One of the first questions reporters had asked Schwarzkopf in early March was whether Breckinridge and Lindbergh communicated earlier that evening about Lindbergh being a no show at the Manhattan event. To forget he was to be a featured attendee at a gala was unlike him.

Breckinridge's 8 p.m. call on March 1 had great potential significance in unraveling the mystery of the kidnapping because it indicated further contact between Breckinridge and Lindbergh before Lindbergh's son went missing. Yet Schwarzkopf's description of the call was seriously misleading. There was zero evidence in the statements obtained by the state police that either of the Breckinridges talked by telephone with anyone at the farmhouse before Lindbergh arrived home at 8:20 p.m. that night. Anne and the Lindberghs' three employees reported only one call coming in during that time period — from Lindbergh himself at 7:00 p.m. to say he would be late for dinner.

The statements indicated that Lindbergh arrived home 20 minutes after Schwarzkopf told the Bureau that a call took place with Breckinridge. Lindbergh then went straight up to wash and then to dinner. If Breckinridge did call Lindbergh at 8 p.m. Lindbergh was at most twenty minutes from home, at some undisclosed location where Breckinridge knew his client could be reached.

At the same time as the state police met with members of the Bureau of Investigation, police had John Hughes Curtis in custody as a suspected hoaxer. Since the wee hours of May 13 Curtis had been kept locked up for nearly a week in the damp basement of the farmhouse. He spent a lot of his time staring at key evidence the police stored there — the makeshift ladder taken from the Lindberghs' yard on the night of the boy's disappearance and the clothes worn by the dead child.

It had been almost a month since Curtis left home on a mission to help Lindbergh retrieve his son. In an effort to speed his release, Curtis tried to get the police to follow up on his leads to the gang of seven that he insisted had led both him and Lindbergh on a wild goose chase. He gave them "minute descriptions of the haunts, hide-outs, boats, automobiles, furniture, wireless set, clothes, habits, voices and peculiarities of speech of six of the seven involved."

Curtis's companion, Reverend Dobson-Peacock, had seen two of the supposed gang members on April 21, 1932. The gang's designated contact brought the reverend to a hotel to meet an associate to discuss details of the upcoming exchange of the toddler for ransom. The police showed Reverend Dobson-Peacock a number of photos of known criminals. He picked out a serial con man named Arthur Hitner as the gang's liaison, and former federal agent Gaston Means as the other fellow he met at the hotel.

Though police did not believe Curtis, Curtis claimed he was just acting as a good citizen, spending his own money with no request for reimbursement. Curtis said that the reason he had kept such detailed notes was that he was wary of his new contacts. Curtis could tell most of the officers mistrusted him. After being grilled again all night on May 17, Curtis desperately wanted to get home. His wife was sick, his business was suffering, and he missed his children. Curtis was told that he would be released only if he signed a confession that the whole misadventure had been a hoax. Curtis was promised that this confession would not go public. Sleep-deprived and befuddled by Lindbergh's sudden aloofness, Curtis signed the confession. The next thing Curtis knew it was all over the front pages and he faced criminal proceedings for obstruction of justice.

Whether one thought Curtis was a genuine Good Samaritan or not, his arrest for obstruction of justice was just a side show. The real question was how to find and prosecute whoever committed the kidnap/murder. In the days after the discovery of Charlie's body, Lindbergh and Breckinridge worked with the police to stage the kidnapping the way Lindbergh had told them it must have occurred. A replica ladder was constructed, perhaps by Lindbergh himself. On May 19, the replica was placed on the outside wall of the house next to the nursery and a policeman repeatedly descended with a heavy sack that he could not help dropping. Anne watched in horror — for her it was living Hell.

That same day two federal agents met at the Lindbergh home with Schwarzkopf to see what he had in mind for the future direction of the investigation. The agents pointedly asked Schwarzkopf what his main objectives were in finding the killers now that the child's body had been discovered; what had already been done to pursue those objectives; what was left to be done; "and just how the various governmental agencies might best assist in this further work." To the agents' astonishment, Schwarzkopf "indicated no concrete objectives . . . no proposed plan of action, and . . . he apparently had none."

The Bureau continued its own investigation. Its files already included a category of potential suspects labeled "Lindbergh Household and Employees." The Agency summarized the background of the Whateleys, Betty Gow, Charles Jr., the family dog (misidentified as "Trixie") and Charles Jr.'s original nanny, Marie Cummings, who had left the Lindberghs' employ in the spring of 1931 before they began spending weekends at their new estate. The list excluded both Charles and Anne Lindbergh.

Unlike her husband, Anne Lindbergh's whereabouts on Monday February 29 and Tuesday March 1 were completely verifiable. She was at the farmhouse with her son and the household staff. Lindbergh later gave a general description of his activities in New York on Monday and Tuesday. He was never asked where he called from at 7:00 p.m. to say he would be late for dinner on Tuesday or where he took a call from Breckinridge at 8 p.m. before he arrived home.

Anne wrote in her diary that she wanted "the truth when they find it and I will face it and Justice should be pursued." She found some comfort in being told her son died so quickly that he did not bawl for his mother, but the subject was so painful, she choked with tears articulating her thoughts. Anne had become quite distracted recently by her pregnancy and numbed even more by her loss. She noticed how her husband's grief differed so markedly from her own. He focused on the case "incessantly," obsessed with police efforts to reconstruct the murder and search for the killers. She preferred to focus on her son's impish image and his laugh. It bothered her greatly that the only pictures of her son that she had to look at did not resemble the spirited child he had grown into. To Anne, Charlie was no longer an infant, but "a person . . . gay, full of power, sure of himself. . . ." It was hard to hold onto images of her vivacious toddler with so many "meaningless newspaper distortions" of his appearance impeding her memory.

Her husband's preoccupation with the details of their son's death was the opposite of what he was urging her to do. Charles told Anne how naive they were to trust in their security precautions; no one could guard against chance; and how much he had wished that his efforts to bring their baby home would have been successful. Yet, despite his father-in-law's warning, the only security precautions Lindbergh ever agreed to were two small dogs that yapped whenever they sensed something amiss. Anne found it a "cruel" twist of fate that chance had deprived them of Skean's company at the farmhouse that weekend. Within a week of her son's disappearance, she told her diary that she felt her son's death was "a poison working in my system . . . How deep will it eat into our lives?"

Anne consoled herself most by trying to relive her happiest moments with her son on the last weekend they were together. She saw her husband's reaction as far different from her own. "There is something very deep in a man's feeling for his son, it reaches further into the future." Charles kept telling her they "must find some way of making Time go backwards," so they could reclaim their prior life before tragedy struck. They agreed her current pregnancy was like "starting all over again."

The Lindberghs had received from Dr. Carrel a letter of condolence for their tragic loss. He urged Lindbergh to distract himself from his grief and demonstrate his courage by returning to assist Carrel as a volunteer at the Rockefeller Institute. Lindbergh told his wife he planned to return to resume lab work full time at the end of May. He suggested that Anne should dedicate herself at the same time to finishing her book on their 1931 journey to the Far East.

Somehow, in the two months following her son's kidnapping Anne felt that their first born still bound them together, that she and Charles "had never been so close as they were at his birth — except now, at his death." Yet Anne remained troubled by two observations. Her tulip bed at the new house had been trampled by the police, but the white tulips emerged anyway, all twisted and grotesque. The other was even more foreboding: not once did she observe her husband shed any tears for the loss of their son.

Once word got out, reporters and gawkers rushed to arrive at the spot where the body was found off the Hopewell-Princeton Road.

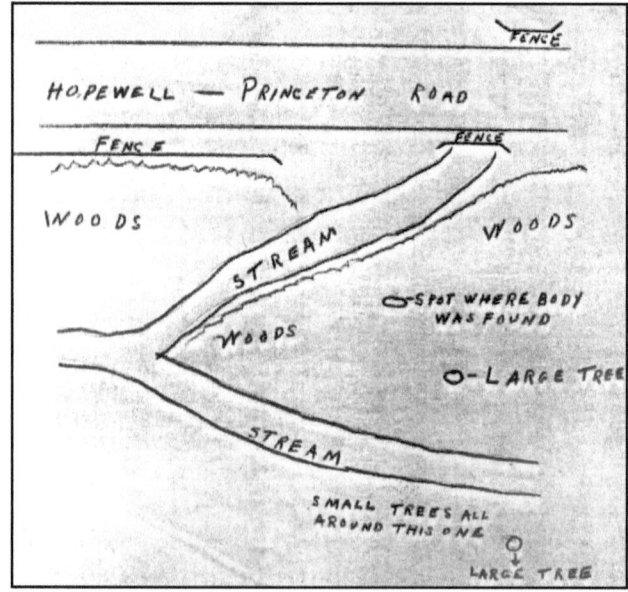

Police drew for their own use a rough map of the location.

Death certificate for Charles A. Lindbergh, Jr. signed by Coroner Walter Swayze: "fractured skull due to external violence." "Accident" and "suicide" were crossed out, leaving "homicide" as the cause of death at an "unknown location" "probably near Hopewell" "about March 1, 1932."

Left : Jersey City Detective James Fitzgerald
Center: Detective Robert Coar, Newark City Police
Right: Detective Harry Walsh, Jersey City Police.

All three were assigned to assist the State Police in the Lindbergh kidnapping investigation. When Walsh went back to Newark in August 1932, the federal Bureau Director in New York wrote a note to J. Edgar Hoover: "This is the most constructive action taken since the start of the case." Hoover added: "All too true!"

12.
Bizarre Developments

BY LATE May 1932, as distraught as they were at Charlie's death, the Morrow family was more focused on Elisabeth's failing health. Lindbergh talked her into being examined at the Rockefeller Institute. The doctors privately reported to Mrs. Morrow that Elisabeth's heart valve had suffered irreparable damage from rheumatic fever when she was a child. The doctors expected her to live another five years at most. Elisabeth was not told of this dire prognosis. She had her mind set on a trip to England that June with her mother, her brother and youngest sister Connie.

Meanwhile, the murder investigation continued to lurch from promising clues to useless dead ends. The Feds only had the word of the New Jersey State Police that local leads on the source of the ladder wood had been pursued. Agents in New York became increasingly concerned that the state police were playing hide the ball. (Several New Jersey detectives would later admit they never completed their investigations). A handwritten notation to an internal Bureau memo for the Director in late May 1932 ridiculed the way the New Jersey police had proceeded with the ladder: "It is a crime how the State Police handled this piece of evidence. It was originally the most valuable clue & and by bungling was made almost valueless."

On May 29, 1932, reporter Horace Wilkins of the *Brooklyn Daily Eagle* wrote a scathing headline story in the Sunday paper calling the investigation a "Series of Bad Blunders." Colonel Schwarzkopf was livid and immediately blamed the slam on leaks out of the Bureau's office, which the Bureau denied. Wilkins opened with the observation: "the known errors of omission and commission on the part of the investigating authorities brings into glaring relief the fact that from the start, the

Lindbergh case has been horribly bungled."

The reporter proceeded to summarize the most egregious errors. He started with: "Failure to get into immediate touch with a trained, recognized, scientific investigator the minute the baby was discovered missing." He explained, "Any policeman knows that the first few hours, minutes, of any criminal case are the most valuable. The Lindbergh investigators ran around in circles for at least 24 hours after the child was stolen. There was no head, no director, no plain common sense used."

Next, the reporter listed the failure to preserve clues to the kidnappers' identity. "A combination rustic constable, traffic cop, plumber and general handyman of Hopewell was in charge for the first few hours . . . He did nothing to safeguard evidence left behind by the kidnapers from being obliterated." The investigative journalist added: "One of the most glaring failures . . . was the lack of a thorough combing of the district about the Lindbergh home." He noted that bloodhounds could have been brought in, the National Guard and other volunteers could have led to the discovery of the corpse.

Wilkins bemoaned the lack of care surrounding the evidence of the crime: "The ladder, the footprints, the entire terrain about the Lindbergh home were [handled] . . . by the morbidly curious, newspapermen and photographers. Twelve hours after the child was discovered to be missing there wasn't an inch about the house which hadn't been trampled over, with every possible bit of evidence obliterated . . ." Wilkins seemed convinced that forensic tests could have supplied valuable clues or even solved the case if the evidence had not been mishandled.

The New Jersey State Police had never indicated whether they believed the heavy, ribbed socks worn by the kidnapper outside the nursery window were for the purpose of muffling the sound of footsteps or "to disguise footprints." The reporter wondered how an outsider could have known the Lindberghs would be staying there that weeknight. He speculated that ransom might not be the only possible motive. The article was forwarded to Director J. Edgar Hoover from the New York office. Hoover added his own note: "This is the most sensible analysis which I have seen of this case."

Hoover knew from his agents in New York that the New Jersey Police were still failing to share everything they had discovered. Among the investigations the State Police never completed was follow-up on the findings of a state expert named Squire Johnson, the assistant director of construction and architecture. He examined the ladder and concluded it was designed for a tall, agile person. It would have been "extremely difficult if not impossible for a short person or a tall person unversed in climbing to have negotiated," and was even harder going down "if both hands are not free."

Johnson also noticed a 3-foot maple dowel in Lindbergh's study that he called to Colonel Schwarzkopf's attention. It had the same ¾ inch diameter as the shorter dowels used in the ladder. Most telling in Johnson's report to Colonel Schwarzkopf was that Johnson had found similar paint-stained wood piled at the Skillman Village dump site. At a shack in the outskirts of Skillman Village he found more of the same type of wood and a set of chisels like the one found in the yard, but with one chisel missing of the exact same size. Johnson also found a Paige sedan under a lean-to that looked like a dark green automobile spotted near the Lindbergh estate on the evening of March 1, 1932 (a different car than the 1929 Dodge Ben Lupica saw at the foot of the Lindbergh driveway). Peeking inside, Johnson saw burlap bags like the one found on May 12 on the shoulder of the Hopewell-Princeton Road some 75 feet from the toddler's body.

The owner of the shack was a violent and mentally unbalanced man named Charles Schippell, whom Johnson thought was German. Police investigated and linked him to a number of unsavory associates, but somehow dropped him as a suspect. On June 8, 1932, both Colonel Schwarzkopf and the Assistant Director of the Bureau's New York office vented their frustration with each other. The Bureau executive scolded Schwarzkopf for hobbling the federal agency, noting that it "would be impracticable for this Division to conduct a comprehensive and intelligent investigation of the Lindbergh kidnaping case because . . . the Division has not received the significant facts ascertained and names of persons possibly suspected or concerned with the offense from the New Jersey State Police."

Schwarzkopf responded with news they hoped to break the case open on June 10 when they arrived at the Morrows' Englewood estate for additional investigation. They had already spoken at least once to all twenty-nine household employees. They wanted to question British parlor maid Violet Sharp once more because of major discrepancies in her prior interviews. Sharp was the staff member who had given Betty Gow the message to join the family at the estate near Hopewell on March 1. Sharp was known to be dating the Morrows' butler, Septimus Banks. His background was looked into as well.

Police had come to suspect Sharp of tipping off the kidnappers. When they returned to the Morrow mansion to interview her on June 10, Mrs. Morrow's secretary answered the door. As the police cooled their heels, they learned Sharp had just fainted and a doctor had been called. Soon Walsh arrived, too. Lindbergh and the doctor met the officers in the study with shocking news: Sharp was dead; Lindbergh found a can of cyanide and a used drinking glass and spoon in her room. Schwarzkopf then announced that Sharp's apparent suicide "strongly tends to confirm the suspicions of the investigating authorities concerning her guilty knowledge of the crime." He stated that Violet Sharp had already identified a companion named Ernest Brinkert as "her associate on the night of the kidnapping."

Lindbergh and Breckinridge supported Schwarzkopf's suspicions of Sharp but did not defend the tactics of the New Jersey State Police. Back in March, Lindbergh and Breckinridge had cast suspicion on Betty Gow by claiming the kidnapping occurred as early as 7:30 p.m. That could only be true if Gow was lying about checking on Little Charlie for the last time at ten minutes to eight. In April, Lindbergh had credited John Curtis's suspicions of Olly Whateley as the insider, but never had Whateley interrogated again. Lindbergh seesawed between pointing fingers at staff at the Morrow mansion in Englewood and his farmhouse outside Hopewell and, at other times, vouching for them all. No wonder the police were frustrated.

Mrs. Morrow told friends that she had no doubt of Violet Sharp's complete innocence of the police suspicions against her. Violet was popular among the staff and had been "absolutely devoted to the baby."

Mrs. Morrow publicly criticized Inspector Walsh and other investigators for their heavy-handedness. Walsh asked Lindbergh to come to his defense, but Lindbergh declined. That lack of support rankled deeply.

Within a week after Sharp's death, Congress would pass the previously stalled federal law against kidnapping, calling it "The Lindbergh Law." J. Edgar Hoover's men could now legally pursue kidnapping suspects over state lines, with *or without* local cooperation. Wasting no time, the Director of the New York Bureau office demanded copies of the New Jersey state investigative record to date. He got nowhere. Instead, the Agency wound up backing off after United States Attorney General William Mitchell ordered it to do so, a slap down likely orchestrated by Breckinridge and Lindbergh. Director J. Edgar Hoover got the message from Mitchell that since the Lindbergh kidnapping predated the federal law, that particular unsolved crime remained a state matter not within the Bureau's jurisdiction.

From then on, the Agency was only invited to help out the state police from time to time, mostly to track the dissemination of bills from the $50,000 ransom. Given the jurisdictional wrangle and inter-agency mistrust, it was not too surprising that, despite an unprecedented dragnet, enormous publicity, a renewed offer of a $25,000 reward from the New Jersey Legislature and many false leads, no real progress in the kidnap/murder case was made that spring.

By June, a rumor had come to the attention of both state and federal investigators that Anne's father had cut his namesake out of his will at Lindbergh's urging. The New Jersey police then considered the possibility Dwight Morrow, Jr. had a motive to kill his nephew as revenge against his brother-in-law. The malicious gossip was completely false. All four children were treated equally in Dwight Morrow's will. The only person Morrow fought with over distribution of family wealth was Lindbergh over control of Anne's trust money.

On the Morrow family's return from their overseas vacation the police called Dwight Jr. in for questioning without objection from Lindbergh. Quite possibly, the malicious rumor had been started by Lindbergh himself. Lindbergh may also have been the source of gossip investigated by the New Jersey Police that Dwight Morrow Sr. had an illegitimate son who might be a suspect. Nothing came of either accusation, but the episode must have exacerbated the often prickly relationship between Lindbergh and his mother-in-law.

By late June 1932, all that law enforcement had to show for their efforts to investigate the famous case was successful prosecution of John Curtis for obstruction of justice. The way that transpired was quite revealing about the extent of Lindbergh's enormous clout in his recently adopted county. Even Curtis's own local lawyer, C. Lloyd Fisher, had started out believing damning newspaper accounts before trial that Curtis had perpetrated a horrible hoax. Fisher was well-positioned to know how the community felt: he was President of the Hunterdon County Bar; had been a star athlete since his high school days; and was admired in social circles for his dancing talent and skill with a pool cue. Fisher also counted himself among Lindberghs' myriad admirers, having piloted a Jenny himself during World War I. When the Lindberghs bought their new property, Fisher had helped document title.

When asked to defend Curtis, Fisher already knew: "There wasn't a man or woman in the town whose sympathies were not one hundred percent with Colonel and Mrs. Lindbergh." All anyone in the county seat of Flemington had talked about since the second of March was the kidnapping. Fisher had already seen "little groups of anxious neighbors gathered daily on the steps of the . . . courthouse, on the veranda of the Union Hotel, in the stores and barbershops, and on the platform of the railroad station, to speculate on the day's developments."

Yet Fisher tried to keep an open mind when he was begged by Reverend Dobson-Peacock to go see Curtis in jail. Curtis's integrity was also vouched for by a number of other leading citizens of Norfolk, Virginia. When Fisher met Curtis, his own instinct was that Curtis was a community leader like himself who somehow got dragged into a dreadful situation not of his own making. Fisher quickly realized that the Virginia shipyard owner did not dream up the floor plan of the Lindbergh farmhouse and other inside information that "Sam" told Curtis, and which Curtis then believed implicated Olly Whateley as an accomplice in the kidnapping.

Curtis apparently impressed a few of the New Jersey officers who interrogated him as well. He told Fisher that Inspector Walsh and Lieutenant Keaten did not really believe Curtis had interfered with the investigation. Curtis said the two officers told him that Lindbergh himself was the one who had prevented them from capturing the man Condon paid $50,000 ransom in early April. According to Curtis, Walsh admitted the state police got much more accomplished whenever Lindbergh was not there to control the investigation.

On the advice of another veteran lawyer in the county named Harry Stout, Curtis had already gathered all the proof he could that the gang members he dealt with were real, not the product of his imagination. Fisher prepared to have Curtis take the stand to swear he signed the confession only under duress and to then describe in detail what the kidnappers looked like and where they met him. But Fisher realized something odd was happening when county prosecutor Tony Hauck abruptly switched theories on the eve of trial. Hauck now accepted that Curtis met the actual kidnappers but planned to convict Curtis anyway for obstruction of justice by interfering with their capture.

The new theory tacitly admitted that Curtis's confession to a hoax had no legs — too late to reverse the horrid impression already created in the jury pool. On the first day of trial, Fisher's jaw dropped when he saw Harry Stout sitting at the prosecution table as an advisor to Hauck, obviously having given away Curtis's planned defense. Worse yet, Lindbergh was Hauck's star witness and, with the court's permission, would sit throughout the trial at the prosecution table where no witness belonged. Fisher knew immediately that the case was lost. In his rural county: "Anyone who was on Lindy's side was a hero. Anyone who opposed him was a skunk." Here was Lindy himself bent on putting Curtis behind bars — and the defense Fisher had prepared no longer mattered.

Fisher fumed at the outrageous prosecution tactics and lack of notice but shifted gears and just put on a few character witnesses. Curtis was convicted, sentenced to a year in jail and assessed a $1000 fine. Fisher soon negotiated a compromise. The prosecutor would waive jail time if Curtis agreed to pay the fine. Curtis went home to his wife and children in Virginia wondering what awful things the police told Lindbergh to make Lindbergh turn against him. Folks following the news should have been wondering, if the kidnap gang Curtis described was not a hoax, why there was no follow up in pursuit of these murderers; and why no similar obstruction charge was ever filed against Condon. In fact, Lindbergh still praised Condon for his efforts even though Lindbergh lost $50,000 through Condon and nothing through Curtis. Lindbergh had held the reins in both bizarre adventures. He was now calling all the shots in the homicide investigation.

Anne grew concerned that summer how much her husband continued to fixate on details of the kidnapping and murder, while she remained overcome by grief. She was glad that he spent most of his time on lab work with Dr. Carrel. As the couple awaited the birth of their second child, Lindbergh kept reminding his wife "about the bigger picture." In August, Lindbergh confided to his wife that he had faith in a hereafter: "The more I go into science the more I feel that one cannot say that everything ends with the death of the body." By then, the Lindberghs had returned to the farmhouse outside Hopewell again with the added security of a police dog named Pal gifted to them by Dr. Carrel. (Carrel had for a long time been raising German Shepherds as a scientific experiment). Lindbergh soon re-christened the dog Thor like the Norse god.

Anne found living at the farmhouse again too painful. In anticipation of her delivery, she moved to her late father's apartment in Manhattan, which the tenant let her use for privacy instead of a hospital stay. It was a difficult childbirth in which Anne began hemorrhaging. She felt she might die, but somehow did not fear it. Her doctor then gave her drugs to put her into twilight sleep before delivering the baby.

Anne was overjoyed when she awoke to see her new son. She kept repeating her relief that he was "all right" until her husband said: "He has a wart on his left toe." Her mother mentioned the sadness of Little Charlie not getting to meet his younger brother. Anne wept copiously. The day after his second son's birth, Lindbergh suggested to Mrs. Morrow that he and Anne might give the farm property to the state for a children's home to create something positive out of their tragedy. Anne agreed. She did not want to forget her first-born but never wanted to live at the farmhouse again.

Anne's first outing after her second son was born was simply out in the yard at Englewood, carried there by her husband. Skean could not contain his excitement. Anne must have experienced another twinge of anguish that Skean had not been with Little Charlie that fateful night. Soon afterward, when cleaning out their possessions from their rural estate, Anne exclaimed to her diary that the reminders of their weekends there made her sick to death, "but I clutch at them madly . . . anything to keep from thinking."

Anne found her faith in humanity rekindled with a new child to care for. Yet neither she, nor her mother, wanted to let Charlie be forgotten. Her mother created a long list of cheerful memories of the little boy that she and Anne could cherish and keep distinct in their minds from time spent with the new baby. Like her mother, Anne wept for Little Charlie every night. She sometimes called the baby by his older brother's name. It took Anne and Charles more than a month to settle on the name "Jon."

That July, Anne's sister Elisabeth had written she had a new love interest. He was a Welshman named Aubrey Morgan, the wealthy son of a hugely successful department store owner, whom Elisabeth had first met in London in the winter of 1930. On December 28, 1932 Mrs. Morrow hosted an elaborate wedding for her eldest daughter at the family's mansion in Englewood. Dwight Morrow Sr.'s absence was keenly felt.

By the end of February 1933 Anne dreaded the press hoopla that would surround the first anniversary of her son's kidnapping. Anne still grieved Charlie's loss deeply and had nightmares about how he died. She took comfort from her husband's repeated assurances that "he did not suffer, he did not know, a blow on the head." She never questioned how her husband could be so sure. After a trip to the farmhouse in early February 1933 Anne wrote: "There is the difference between men and women. . . . I never accepted it . . . and I will never be through with it. . . . It stays frozen inside of me." Anne confided to her diary: "The punctuation of anniversaries is terrible, like the closing of doors, one after another between you and what you want to hold on to."

To distract her on the night of the anniversary, Charles lured her out in disguise to a Broadway show. The following month, Anne and Charles took a ten-day car trip to visit his mother in Detroit, leaving their eight-month-old son Jon behind. The couple again donned disguises. Anne thought her husband seemed "entirely free for the first time in six years."

ACT THREE

Pictured here in 1914 as newlyweds are Nobel-prize-winning vascular surgeon Dr. Alexis Carrel and his wife Anne de la Meyrie Motte Carrel, a widowed Parisian nurse. The photo was likely taken in New York where Dr. Carrel had headed a medical research laboratory for the Rockefeller Institute since 1906 and his wife assisted him for several years. By the time Charles Lindbergh started volunteering his mechanical expertise in Dr. Carrel's lab, Mme. Carrel had long since moved back to France where Dr. Carrel spent summers. Lindbergh met her when she came to New York in February 1932. He and Anne visited Mme. Carrel in Paris in 1933.

1.
Stymied

DESPITE leads from Curtis that could have been pursued by state police, the homicide investigation seemed to J. Edgar Hoover to be going nowhere. The Bureau itself remained mostly in the dark as ransom money turned up spent from time to time and no prime suspects emerged.

In early 1933, Lindbergh talked Anne into a plane trip to California, her first long flight since their second son's birth. They left baby Jon behind at her mother's mansion with a nurse and state supplied police bodyguard. The Governor was taking no more chances. The Lindberghs' journey would involve stopping in cities across the country, ending in California. Later that summer they planned a more extensive trip for five months overseas. Jon was then close to the same age as Little Charlie was when his parents left him for an extended trip to the Far East in the summer of 1931. Anne was torn but went anyway.

The couple were again feted by royalty as they explored four continents — traveling across Greenland and Iceland to Scandinavia before returning through the British Isles where they visited Elisabeth and her husband Aubrey Morgan at their home in Wales. When Anne and Charles saw Elisabeth again, she was clearly in declining health and contemplating a move to a warmer climate.

The Lindberghs then headed to the European continent before planning to fly to West Africa and Brazil. He was now researching the availability of primates for potential use as experimental subjects in ongoing lab research he was helping Dr. Carrel perform. In Paris, they visited Mme Carrel, whom Lindbergh had met in New York in February 1932. A decade earlier Mme. Carrel had moved back to France and generally only saw her husband when he joined her there each summer. She told Anne how valuable Charles was to her husband's research team. Anne told her sister Connie she was glad that Lindbergh's work for Carrel "made him happy, especially at the moment when life seemed unreal."

From Paris, the Lindberghs flew to Holland where they ran into such dense fog after leaving Amsterdam that Anne "was in sheer physical terror the whole time." Not for the first time, she swore if they survived this trip she would "never fly again." Though she often pined for home and resuming a normal life with her new baby, Anne could not bring herself to stop embarking on death-defying adventure after adventure at her husband's command. By then, Lindbergh had her largely distracted from their first son's death, assuming the mystery would never be solved. (When the couple later lived in exile, Anne would write a book about this adventure as well. *Listen! The Wind*, published in 1938, stayed on the best seller list for two years and won the National Book Award for nonfiction.)

The Lindberghs finally arrived back in New York in late December 1933 in time for Christmas with their son Jon and extended family. During their absence, no further progress had been made on the case. By March of 1934 communications between the Bureau and the New Jersey State Police had deteriorated to such an extent that only one lowly corporal on Colonel Schwarzkopf's staff was designated to interface with the Bureau. J. Edgar Hoover wrote to Colonel Schwarzkopf requesting access to the complete files the state had compiled on the unsolved case. Schwarzkopf sent back a terse reply: "When the Lindbergh case is finished I will be very glad to give you copies of everything you wish and will do my utmost to help you complete your file."

Hoover replied by return mail: "When the case is completed, the information which I have requested will be of practically no value to this Division." The Bureau Chief closed by expressing his intention to have his Agency carry on its independent investigation without help from the state police. Reinforcing Hoover's sense of frustration, Lindbergh himself intervened in May 1934 to further handicap independent efforts by the federal agency to make progress on investigating the kidnap/murder. When Lindbergh learned that the Bureau had decided on its own to interview a representative of the Morrow Estate, he immediately got on the telephone to the Director of the New York office. He made it clear that if the Agency wanted further interviews of "any member of the Lindbergh or Morrow household," the agents could not do so without supervision. They had to "first get in touch with the [New Jersey] State Police, so that an officer from that organization could be present at the interview." As the Bureau knew, Lindbergh had the New Jersey Police under his complete control.

Hoover's frustration hit its peak when his agents provided copies of all of their own reports to the New Jersey Police that summer and got none in return. He fumed in a memo to the Attorney General that cooperation between the two law enforcement agencies was not working both ways. The Bureau Chief told his own agents to be cautious from then on in what they shared with the New Jersey Police "in view of the obvious reticence on their part to furnish us with information which we request."

2.
An Elusive Suspect

THE MOST promising clue that had been developed since the spring of 1932 surfaced when a person turned in nearly $3,000 of marked bills on May 1, 1933 — the last day gold certificates were legal to circulate. It was unclear if the customer using the name J. J. Faulkner was male or female. When checked by police, no such person lived at the address on the deposit slip. For whatever reason, the fingerprints were not pursued by state police for a possible match. Federal agents were livid.

Almost two years of frustration and mockery made the New Jersey police desperate to solve the infamous case. New York police shared their concern. After the fiasco of losing the scent of J. J. Faulkner, the New York police made solving the crime once more their highest priority. They immediately followed up on the afternoon of September 6, 1934 when a bank teller on the Upper East Side reported receiving a $10 gold certificate from the ransom money in a deposit by a local fruit and vegetable vendor. Too many similar incidents of ransom bills spent in the New York area had never been timely pursued.

That same afternoon the police tracked down the vendor and learned the $10 gold certificate was received by an employee named Salvatore Levatino just the day before. It turned out that Levatino took special notice of the man who presented that large bill to pay for just a few cents worth of produce. Levatino told the police that the fellow was well-dressed in a royal blue suit and spoke English well with no discernible accent. Yet he speculated the man might have been Irish.

As detailed in the original police report, Levatino described the suspicious customer he had just interacted with as:

Trim and Athletic Build
Tall and Thin
About 5'11
Broad, but not heavy shoulders
About 155 or 160 lbs.
Long Thin Face
Pointed Chin
High Cheek Bones
Sunken Cheeks
Straight Nose, slightly flared at the nostrils
Very light Brown hair, not quite blonde.
Light Complexion
Clean shaven, no mustache
Straight thin lips

Levatino did not notice his customer's eye color, but described the man as having "fine white hands" that "did not appear to be those of a laborer." The officer who wrote up the report noted that the clerk's verbal sketch of the man who spent one of the ransom bills "coincided generally" with Condon's description of Cemetery John except for the accent. But Condon had thought Cemetery John might have been faking a foreign accent when they spoke in the spring of 1932.

Both Condon's and Levatino's descriptions could easily have fit a shady character by the name of Jacob J. Nosovitsky, who presented himself as a naturalized Russian. Nosovitsky was a repeat felon and former double-agent likely used as a jailhouse snitch. Author Noel Behn makes the case in his book, *Lindbergh: The Crime,* that Nosovitsky was both Cemetery John and J. J. Faulkner. Nosovitsky was well-known to Breckinridge's colleague Wild Bill Donovan and had also worked closely with J. Edgar Hoover on a failed attempt to bring the infamous 1920 Wall Street bomber to justice. Nosovitsky had also done some espionage in Mexico for Dwight Morrow's former employer J.P. Morgan Associates when Morrow was Ambassador there in the late 1920s. Nosovitsky claimed to be still owed $50,000 for his services and bore a grudge against Ambassador Morrow as a result of that episode.

Actually, although the police may not have realized it at the time, "Nosovitsky" was likely one of the many aliases of the American-born fraudster Arthur Hitner, whom Curtis and Reverend Dobson-Peacock had identified as a key member of the kidnap gang. Both Hitner and Nosovitsky listed themselves as born in 1889. Both were five-foot-ten with greyish eyes. Both had a history of criminal convictions for fraud for which neither served their full sentences. Each reportedly had an unusual background as a cosmetic scientist and government spy. They were also both known to be associates of former federal agent Gaston Means, who was also fingered as a gang member by Reverend Dobson-Peacock. Lindbergh admitted at Curtis's trial that he knew Hitner. Both Nosovitsky and Hitner were known by law enforcement to have inside information on the Lindbergh kidnapping. Neither was seriously pursued as a suspect even though Hitner grew up in America and was a white-collar criminal, who passed himself off as a doctor. Hitner's hands would have likely revealed that he was not used to day labor.

Hitner was also known to be back on the streets in September 1934. He had been in prison in the summer of 1933 for mail fraud when he made several startling claims about the case that got reported in the newspapers. Back then, Hitner had asserted that the kidnappers of the Lindbergh baby stole his car to use in the crime and later gave the car back; that he flew with Lindbergh in one of Lindbergh's aerial searches for his son; and that he knew the identity of the man who received the $50,000 ransom from Condon. It is not known whether federal or state police ever followed up on these assertions to either verify or discredit them. What is known is that, despite the importance of all the details they had just learned from Levatino, in memorializing key observations the fruit vendor made, the police omitted mention that Levatino said the man who spent the illegal gold certificate had "fine white hands" and no foreign accent. Even so, as disseminated, Levatino's description closely matched the one Condon gave of Cemetery John. This new lead looked highly promising. It immediately circulated as likely identifying the prime suspect in the ransom scheme. Yet the New York police soon arrested a man who did not fit the profile of Levatino's suspicious customer — and stopped looking for anyone else.

Nosovitsky's Mug Shot

3.
The Most Hated Man in America

On September 19, 1934, the New York police and New York federal agents arrested a stocky German carpenter of medium build who had workman's hands and a heavy accent. He had just bought gas with a different $10 ransom bill. Having misidentified scores of others who had ironclad alibis the officers nevertheless cockily confronted Bruno Richard Hauptmann: "So you're the Lindbergh kidnapper?" Hauptmann reacted in shock. Then another officer announced, "You're going to burn, baby." The team included James Finn, who just the week before had interviewed another produce vendor who described a customer spending a $10 ransom bill the same way Levatino had — well dressed with no discernible accent. (Finn had been added to the team at Lindbergh's request since he was a friend and former bodyguard.) Colonel Schwarzkopf immediately called the Lindberghs, who were visiting Anne's ailing sister Elisabeth in California: "Great news! No doubt of it, he's the guy we've been looking for." Lindbergh then told his wife: "They've got him at last."

The police tore apart Hauptmann's garage and made an explosive discovery. Nearly fourteen thousand dollars from the Lindbergh ransom money was hidden there. He claimed that the money came into his possession wrapped in a shoebox given to him for safekeeping by a friend and business colleague named Isidor Fisch. Hauptmann hosted a farewell party for Fisch in early December 1933 just before Fisch headed back to Germany. Hauptmann told police that Fisch described the box as containing important personal papers and asked him to hold the box until he returned.

The media immediately feasted on the news of Hauptmann's arrest

— an undocumented immigrant who lived with his wife and baby son in a second-floor apartment of a two-story house in the Bronx. No matter that Hauptmann lacked any criminal record since his arrival from Germany as a stowaway in 1925. If the police thought they at last had the man who killed the Lindberghs' child he was Public Enemy No. One. When police took Hauptmann across the street from the station that evening to get him some dinner at a restaurant, crowds had already gathered, shouting, "Kill him, crucify him!"

The potential for a lynching if police had let the mobs have access to Hauptmann was quite evident — in New York of all places. The city was the center of the national anti-lynching movement and protests against Alabama's efforts to execute the Scottsboro Boys. FDR's Attorney General, Homer Cummings, happened to be passing through New York that day and was asked if he believed Hauptmann was the culprit. Cummings responded, "I didn't know that anyone doubted it." Law enforcement would soon learn that their key sources doubted it very much. Condon, for one, told FBI agent J. Turrou that Hauptmann appeared "much heavier [with] different eyes, hair, etc." than Cemetery John.

The next night New York City Police Commissioner John O'Ryan signaled the monumental importance of the arrest by having Col. Schwarzkopf, as the head of the New Jersey State Police, and Bureau Chief J. Edgar Hoover join him at the podium for his press conference. Commissioner O'Ryan then announced that the combined efforts of his force, the New Jersey State Police and the Bureau of Investigation had succeeded in solving the Lindbergh baby mystery. Prosecution in New York for extortion was just the first step toward closure; New Jersey would soon be seeking Hauptmann's extradition for the kidnapping/murder.

Yet the Bureau privately acknowledged that the case had become "a three-ring circus and no ring master." Hoover was pleased that the Agency would shortly be bowing out "with dignity and not a part of any side-show." Two days after the murder indictment issued against Hauptmann on October 8, 1934, the Attorney General of the United States would formally end the active participation of the Justice Department.

Hauptmann's wife Anna immediately approached her friends and relatives for the name of a good lawyer and hired James Fawcett. On the day the grand jury convened, Fawcett went to the jail and spent four hours with Hauptmann and became convinced of his innocence. During that first visit, Fawcett asked Hauptmann to reconstruct as best he could his whereabouts two-and-a-half years earlier on March 1, 1932. Hauptmann realized the crime had occurred on a Tuesday. He insisted that he was working in New York that day and used his car that night to pick his wife up at 8 p.m. when she got off work as a waitress at a local bakery, as he always did back then on Tuesdays. The Hauptmanns named several witnesses who could prove that he picked Anna up on the evening of March 1, 1932.

The state of New Jersey proceeded to build its case against Hauptmann as the lone perpetrator of the crime of the century. Both the police and reporters were deaf to his claimed lack of knowledge of the crime and protests that he did not even know where the Lindberghs lived. As a result, an overwhelming number of the American people disbelieved Hauptmann's explanation of how he received the outdated gold certificates. The "Fisch story" was ridiculed even after it was corroborated by Hauptmann's friend Hans Kloppenburg who told the grand jury he saw Fisch hand a wrapped package shaped like a shoebox to Hauptmann at that December 1933 farewell party. Severe beatings from the police could not get Hauptmann to change his story.

District Attorney Samuel Foley immediately invited Salvatore Levatino and two other vendors who had described similar encounters to visit Hauptmann in jail to identify him as the mystery man who recently paid for produce with a gold certificate. Some newspapers reported that Levatino and the others said they could not identify Hauptmann as that customer. One paper claimed otherwise. However, if any of the vendors could have identified Hauptmann, both District Attorney Foley and, later, Attorney General Wilentz would have wanted that testimony. None of them were ever called.

Foley also asked Lindbergh to appear before the confidential grand jury proceeding on September 24, 1934 since Lindbergh had accompanied Condon to bring the ransom money to the cemetery on April 2, 1932. Lindbergh testified that he sat in the car the whole time

Condon was meeting with Cemetery John, but saw another man walk by whom he felt "sure was one of the actual group of kidnappers or connected with them." Lindbergh also said he heard a "voice of one man at a distance." A juror asked if Lindbergh might identify the man's voice as Cemetery John. Lindbergh responded: "It would be very difficult to sit here and say that I could pick a man by that voice." He had "a very distinct foreign accent," but Lindbergh only heard him briefly as he "simply called to Dr. Condon, 'Hey doc.'"

Two days after Lindbergh testified, District Attorney Foley asked Lindbergh to come back to his office "to see the man who kidnapped his son." Lindbergh arrived in disguise the next morning and Foley made Hauptmann repeat the words spoken by Cemetery John. Lindbergh left without saying anything. Two weeks later Lindbergh testified before a New Jersey grand jury and claimed that hearing Hauptmann in Foley's office made him recall Hauptmann's voice as that of Cemetery John. Condon, who had met twice with Cemetery John, disagreed with Lindbergh. Condon still could not identify Hauptmann as the man he gave the ransom money.

Other aspects of the case against Hauptmann also had reporters scratching their heads. *The New York Daily News* ran an article entitled "Lindbergh Sleuths Make Up Theories to Suit All Tastes." District Attorney Foley endorsed the idea that Hauptmann "could have climbed the kidnap ladder" while J. Edgar Hoover disagreed completely: "It was built for someone else" and could not support Hauptmann's weight. Foley believed there was more than one kidnapper, while an inspector from the Bronx insisted Hauptmann had no accomplice.

Two years earlier, when no suspect had yet been identified, the New Jersey State Police had hired Dr. Erastus Mead Hudson to look for latent fingerprints on the ladder. He had carefully taken the ladder apart and used a new technique employing silver nitrate to reveal hundreds of usable prints not visible through standard procedures. Most of the prints came from police officers and reporters who handled the ladder after it originally was tested and found to have no visible prints. But with the new technique, Dr. Hudson had found one person's prints on the ends of the rungs that he had just disassembled for the first time. That person had to be whoever constructed the ladder. (The state police never shared this with the Bureau. The Feds were led to believe that only unusable smudges were found that would be impossible to compare to legible prints in the Bureau's system.)

Dr. Hudson had concluded that the prints he found were those of the kidnapper. He had been quite surprised not to be contacted when Hauptmann was arrested in September of 1934. It prompted him to call a local New Jersey police officer, who said "We got our man." When Dr. Hudson asked if Hauptmann's prints were found anywhere on the ladder, the officer said, "No." Hudson responded, "Then you'll have to look further." The officer said, "Good God, don't tell us that, doctor!" This must have caused immediate alarm all the way up the chain of command. Shortly afterward, all the fingerprints were washed off by order of someone at State Police Headquarters.

At the end of September 1934, Sir Harold Nicolson, Dwight Morrow's biographer, visited Lindbergh and his in-laws at the Morrow mansion in Englewood and noticed with surprise Lindbergh's seeming lack of interest in the efforts to extradite Hauptmann from New York for the murder of his son: "The Lindbergh case is still front-page news. It *must* mean something to him. Yet he never glances at them and chatters quite amiably on Roosevelt [charging the airlines with profiteering off air-mail contracts]."

Actually, in Nicolson's presence, Lindbergh was masking an intense interest in the headline case. Anne had noticed that his current fixation paralleled in its intensity his obsession with controlling the course of the initial investigation in the spring of 1932. "He plunged again into long conferences with police, lawyers and advisers . . ."

The police knew that Hauptmann had lied to them when first arrested. Originally, he claimed he only possessed a handful of gold certificates. Only after confronting him with their find of a hidden stash of nearly $14,000 in ransom notes in his garage did he admit to placing them there. They also found an illegal pistol he owned. Hauptmann had originally denied having any criminal record in Germany. The police soon learned the truth. Hauptmann had fled Germany for America in 1925 to avoid returning to jail for parole violation. He had committed several burglaries and a robbery with a friend when he was a nineteen-year-old jobless veteran of World War I. Yet in painting him as a hardened criminal in America, the police only had proof Hauptmann knowingly possessed an illegal gun and outdated gold certificates, not that he kidnapped and killed the Lindberghs' son or committed any other crime in his adopted country.

Hauptmann's first lawyer, James Fawcett, was not a specialist in criminal law, but he was a hard worker undaunted by death threats for representing such a vilified defendant. He hired an investigator to help him locate and interview witnesses and obtain employment records that could corroborate Hauptmann's alibi. With Condon and Lindbergh unable to identify Hauptmann as Cemetery John before the Bronx grand jury, there was only weak evidence Hauptmann was involved in the ransom scheme and none linking him to the kidnap/murder. Even the date and county of death was left uncertain by the autopsy and death certificate. Hauptmann could not be tied to any prints. His blue 1930 Dodge sedan was not among the thousands the police had recorded headed to New York late on March 1, 1932.

Most problematic was that Hauptmann's car did not match Lupica's description of the car he saw with a ladder early on the night of the kidnapping. Lupica told authorities it was a 1929 Dodge with wooden spokes on the wheels. Hauptmann's 1930 sedan had wire spokes. Lupica also reported seeing a spare tire on the sedan's rear and no trunk. Back in 1931, Hauptmann had permanently attached a large wooden box to the rear of his car before taking a cross-country camping trip that summer with his wife and friend Hans Kloppenburg. The trunk was still in place when he was arrested. Yet, as later noted by author Noel Behn, in the short time leading up to Hauptmann's trial, a suspicious "pattern" developed: "the emergence of physical evidence helpful to the prosecution and the disappearance of evidence helpful to Hauptmann."

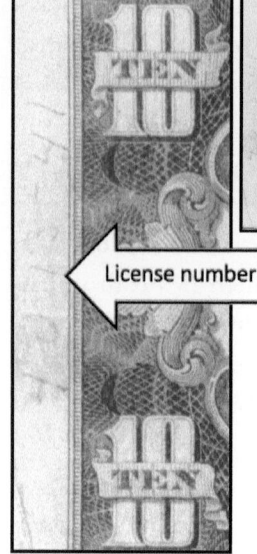

A gas station attendant wrote Hauptmann's license plate number on the left margin of this outdated gold certificate used to buy less than $1 worth of gas in the Bronx on Saturday, September 15, 1934. On Tuesday, the 18th, a bank teller identified it as part of the ransom money and alerted the police. Investigators obtained Hauptmann's name and address from the DMV, followed his car and arrested him the next day.

After police arrested Hauptmann, they found nearly $14,000 more of the ransom money hidden in his garage. Headlines immediately proclaimed him the Lindbergh kidnapper — caught at last. Crowds outside the police department shouted, "Kill him! Crucify him!!"

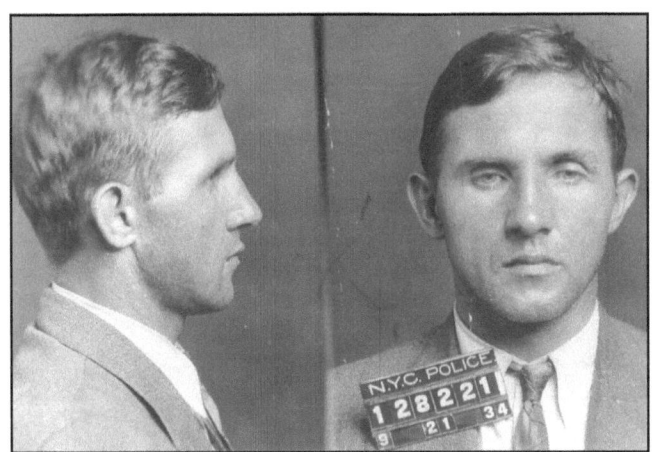

Bruno Richard Hauptmann arrest photos

Hauptmann's garage that the professional carpenter constructed himself with his landlords' permission was torn apart after police found nearly $14,000 in gold certificates from the ransom money hidden in it. (The workmanship appears far superior to that of the "kidnap" ladder.)

4.
Framing an Ironclad Case

AS THE felony/murder case sped to trial in New Jersey less than four months after Hauptmann's arrest in New York, national radio hosts and newspaper reporters, including Walter Winchell, prepared to head to Flemington. Winchell no longer cared that he had derided the ladder as unusable back in March 1932 when the prevailing theory was an inside job. He could not wait to have a seat at what might be the greatest show of the century. It would provide a guaranteed feeding frenzy for the media.

Despite the public presumption of Hauptmann's guilt, Wilentz still had major problems to overcome to ensure the carpenter's conviction and execution. Neither kidnapping nor accidental death during a kidnapping was a capital offense. To ensure that Hauptmann faced the electric chair, Wilentz and D.A. Hauck worked closely with Breckinridge and Lindbergh. Instead of a kidnap charge, the grand jury was asked to indict Hauptmann for felony burglary. Accidental death during a burglary constituted murder. Exercising questionable gamesmanship, Wilentz asked the grand jury in Flemington to charge Hauptmann with unlawful entry into the nursery and making off with the Dr. Denton pajamas the toddler was wearing. The alleged theft of that inexpensive sleeping suit would be the springboard for condemning Hauptmann to death.

The dubious theory was that even though stealing the child's pajamas was a petty offense, Hauptmann's intent was "felonious." That argument was based on the fact that the common law historically had not distinguished grand theft from petty theft. Since a kidnapping death could not send Hauptmann to the electric chair, a creative "felonious intent" charge for pinching the Dr. Denton's the toddler was wearing just might do the job. (It did not seem to bother the prosecutors that the pajamas had been returned.)

When reporters later asked about the unusual collaboration of Lindbergh and his lawyer in prosecuting the case, Wilentz denied that Lindbergh played a far greater role than other crime victims. To the contrary, as Anne knew, her husband "follow[ed] every detail of evidence and testimony to be given" in lengthy meetings with his advisors, the police and the prosecutors.

The New Jersey State Police hoped railroad watchman Alfred Hammond could identify Hauptmann as one of the three suspicious men Hammond had seen in a light blue New York car at the Skillman Village crossing on five mornings preceding the kidnapping. Hammond could not do so. Yet, he identified Isidor Fisch as a member of the trio. Wilentz found that of no use. Hammond would not be called to testify.

One of the witnesses Wilentz planned to use to identify Hauptmann as "Cemetery John" would be taxi driver Joseph Perrone. In the spring of 1932, Perrone had told the police that he could not recall any physical characteristics of the man who paid him to deliver a letter to a residential address in the Bronx and would not know him if he saw him. But Perrone did say the man seemed to be faking an accent. Later, he picked out over twenty different men who did not resemble each other as the man who paid his cab fare.

To prevent that from happening again, when Perrone was brought in to see Hauptmann in custody, an officer told Perrone: "There isn't a man in this room who isn't convinced he is the man who kidnapped the Lindbergh baby." Federal agent Sisk reported to superiors that the New York inspector "practically coerced Perrone into identifying Hauptmann." Even so Perrone testified before the grand jury that his passenger had brown eyes. Hauptmann's were blue.

Dr. Condon was even more problematic. After viewing over 100 photos, he identified two men who proved to have been nowhere near New Jersey the night of the kidnapping, and tentatively identified several other men including Isidor Fisch. Condon also had said that

Cemetery John convinced him that the kidnappers were a gang of six, including at least one who spoke Italian. Unlike Lindbergh, Condon continued to resist pointing the finger at Hauptmann before the New Jersey grand jury, despite heavy police pressure.

Condon had already confirmed to a federal agent he was sure Hauptmann was *not* Cemetery John. Wilentz threatened Condon himself with prosecution. When Condon left without making a public statement, Wilentz was quoted as telling a reporter from the *New York Daily News*, "You can surmise what you please." The following day the Associated Press ran with the headline: "Condon Names Hauptmann as Ransom Taker," The *Brooklyn Daily Eagle* believed it had a similar scoop: "HAUPTMANN IDENTIFIED BY CONDON AS 'JOHN': Educator Sure Prisoner Was Ransom Agent."

Fortunately, for Wilentz, back in those days, prosecutors could play their case close to the vest. Although the New Jersey State Police compiled 90,000 pages of documentation during their investigation, Hauptmann's lawyers never had access to *any* of it. With all of the conflicting statements regarding the Lindbergh baby kidnap-murder and the write-ups in police files on various suspects, ample ammunition existed to raise far more than a reasonable doubt of Hauptmann's guilt that did not get turned over to his lawyers. All this time, Lindbergh and Breckinridge were overseeing the build-up of the prosecutor's case against Hauptmann.

When the police tried to beat a confession out of Hauptmann, he insisted his friend Isidor Fisch gave him a wrapped shoebox for safekeeping in December 1933. Hauptmann said he put the box on the top shelf of his kitchen closet and did not open it until August 1934. Only then did he discover the box contained bundles of gold certificates. Hauptmann swore he had no idea of the source and was ridiculed for his "Fisch story."

The Kitchen Closet

Isidor Fisch died in Germany in March 1934. Before he left in December 1933, he had been engaged in several fraudulent schemes in the New York area. A number of witnesses later identified Fisch as having a connection to the Lindbergh kidnapping.

Isidor Fisch

Extradition Conference

Seated left to right D.A. Foley, New Jersey Gov. Harry Moore and Atty. Gen. Wilentz. Col. Schwarzkopf is standing behind Gov. Moore.

Extradition to New Jersey was only possible if, in addition to the ransom money found in Hauptmann's garage, evidence tied him to the kidnapping itself. Suddenly, with the offer of reward money, alleged eyewitnesses began to surface.

Wilentz had just been appointed Attorney General in early 1934 and had never tried a criminal case. He and his team of lawyers worked closely with Charles Lindbergh, his lawyer Henry Breckinridge and Col. Schwarzkopf to ensure they convicted Hauptmann for the kidnap/murder of Lindbergh's son.

Attorney General David Wilentz

Peacock had the primary responsibility for the labor-intensive job of reviewing hundreds of witness statements and proposed trial exhibits. The team also included Hunterdon County prosecutor Anthony M. Hauck, Special Asst. Atty. General George K. Large (who had started out on the defense team); and Asst. Attys. General Joseph Lanigan and Richard Stockton III.

Asst. Attorney General Robert Peacock

5.
Slew Footing Dr. Mitchell

ONE OF Wilentz's biggest remaining problems was Dr. Mitchell. Contrary to newspaper reports, Wilentz wanted to call the medical examiner to establish the cause of death as due to an accidental fall from the kidnap ladder — as Lindbergh had insisted from mid-May 1932 — despite the conclusion to the contrary in the autopsy. Dr. Mitchell still embraced the theory that the toddler was killed by a bullet sometime in the days following the kidnapping. Mitchell repeated the bullet theory under oath at both the New York and New Jersey grand jury proceedings against Hauptmann. He had also so testified at a different criminal proceeding in 1933 attended by Lindbergh.

That 1933 trial was a fraud prosecution in Washington, D.C. against ex-federal agent Gaston Means — the same man identified by Reverend Dobson-Peacock in the spring of 1932 as part of the Lindbergh baby kidnap gang. (Means had also worked for the Burns Agency with spy Jacob Nosovitsky in the 1920s). Means was convicted of bilking millionairess Evelyn Walsh McLean out of more than $100,000 in the spring of 1932 for his purported services as yet another go-between to the Lindbergh baby kidnappers. (Means was never prosecuted for being identified as one of the members of the kidnap hoax identified by Curtis and Reverend Dobson-Peacock). When cross-examined in the Means trial, Dr. Mitchell testified that the only way he could consider attributing the skull fractures of the corpse to an accidental fall would have been if the child landed on an extremely hard surface like a concrete sidewalk.

Wilentz had to hope the jury would be too riled up to consider that a free fall into mud from a second story window was not the same as smashing one's full weight on a hard, flat surface. Tellingly, there had been no large imprint in the mud below the nursery on the night of March 1 to indicate a man carrying a burlap bag with a hefty toddler had just fallen there, nor any sign at all that a bag weighing at least 27 pounds could have been dropped there just hours before the police arrived. Colonel Schwarzkopf had his men reconstruct the kidnapping with a bundle weighing the same as the child. An officer went up the ladder, took the bundle and descended again. Three times in a row, he was unable to stop himself from slipping on the ladder and dropping the bag.

Adopting Lindbergh's theory of the crime also did not account for the small hole behind the corpse's right ear. To support that theory, Wilentz relied on a claim first raised in September 1934 by Major Schoeffel of the New Jersey State Police. He testified before the Bronx grand jury that Lieutenant Keaten accidentally punctured the skull with a stick while helping the coroner remove the corpse from its shallow grave on May 12, 1932. Major Schoeffel claimed that Coroner Walter Swayze was told about the accident right after it happened. Swayze denied this account.

In talking with the press, Colonel Schwarzkopf backed Schoeffel's version, insisting that both Swayze and Dr. Mitchell were told about the stick incident on May 12, 1932. Schwarzkopf also claimed that he had always believed the crime was perpetrated by a lone actor — aiming to match Lindbergh's sudden shift from blaming a professional gang for the crime. Schwarzkopf was willing to do whatever Lindbergh asked him to do, apparently including to bear false witness.

Undermining Schwarzkopf's and Schoeffel's assertion, the officers who viewed the corpse on May 12, 1932, including Keaten, had all turned in statements that same day. None reported noticing a small hole behind its right ear, let alone causing it. Dr. Mitchell immediately rejected Schoeffel's grand jury testimony as absurd. The skull was too thick and hard at that spot behind the ear for anyone to puncture it with a misdirected stick. Tellingly, Lieutenant Keaten never came forward to swear he had made that hole. Meanwhile, police were sent to the site of the corpse to look further for a lost bullet. At the New Jersey

Grand Jury proceeding on October 8, 1934, Dr. Mitchell again testified to the bullet theory. Colonel Schwarzkopf told reporters that the police disagreed with the medical examiner. He added pointedly, Dr. Mitchell "may be asked to supplement his report at the trial." Supplement was not the right word; Mitchell was then being pressured to recant his findings and medical opinion on the cause of death.

As trial preparations progressed, Mitchell still clung to the idea a single bullet had likely caused the skull fractures. A Bureau of Investigations expert in ballistics agreed with him. Lieutenant Robert Hicks opined in a published article that if punctured by a stick the hole would have a pronounced jagged edge, not be nearly perfectly round as a bullet would make. Hicks assumed that Hauptmann was the perpetrator and placed a handkerchief between his small gun and the child's head to prevent gunshot residue on the skull. The New Jersey police ridiculed Hicks's analysis.

If Dr. Mitchell testified to his original conclusions at trial, he could torpedo the entire theory of the indictment against Hauptmann. The May 12 autopsy report that attributed death to external violence also stated that Dr. Mitchell could not pinpoint the date of death better than two to three months before the body was found. The final autopsy report on May 14, 1932 modified the timing of the death to seven to ten weeks prior to the body's discovery, placing death at the earliest two days after the kidnapping, quite possibly up to mid-March. Yet Wilentz sought to prove that the toddler died immediately on the evening of March 1, 1932 from an accidental fall off the kidnap ladder — not due to homicide up to a fortnight later at a different location. Dr. Mitchell was decidedly not helping that cause.

If the toddler had actually died where the body was found, jurisdiction over the murder trial would belong in Mercer County. The charges in Hunterdon County would have to be dismissed and refiled for trial in Trenton. Lindbergh and prosecutor Hauck both knew from their experience in the Curtis trial in 1932 that Hauptmann's death penalty conviction was practically assured with a rural jury in Hunterdon County. Unlike other county prosecutors, District Attorney Tony Hauck had a reputation for never dismissing a case of his own accord, even with scant evidence to support a conviction. Hauptmann's execution was less assured from a more urban jury convened in the state's capitol.

Somehow, Inspector Harry Walsh of the Jersey City Police (who had left the team back in August of 1932), suddenly offered to testify at Hauptmann's trial that he was the one who accidentally caused the hole behind the corpse's right ear. Walsh swore it happened when he was cutting off the T-shirts from the corpse. He claimed he told Colonel Schwarzkopf at the time but did not tell the coroner or Dr. Mitchell. There were many reasons to disbelieve Walsh. He had signed the same original joint report as Lieutenant Keaten regarding their activities on May 12, 1932, which made no mention at all of a hole behind the right ear. When Swayze arrived, he could see no damage done by the police in their movement of the corpse. Walsh also never explained why neither he nor Colonel Schwarzkopf came forward to contradict Dr. Mitchell when he first announced his bullet theory on May 12, 1932 or when he later testified to it in the Gaston Means trial.

The Bureau of Investigation was aware of a more compelling reason to discredit Walsh's new claim. As a key member of the state police murder investigation team, Walsh had attended the confidential joint meeting with Colonel Schwarzkopf and members of the New York office of the Bureau a week after the body was found in mid-May 1932. Neither Walsh nor Schwarzkopf made any claim at that joint meeting just days after the corpse was found that the rounded hole in the skull of the homicide victim had been made by Walsh, Keaten or anyone else poking the corpse with a stick.

Wilentz also needed to convince Dr. Mitchell to disavow another finding in his May 12 autopsy report. It indicated there was so little scalp left on the skull he could not tell if there had been external bleeding as well as internal hemorrhaging. External bleeding supported death by homicidal violence that could hardly have occurred at the Lindbergh estate or at the site by the Hopewell-Princeton Road where the body was found. The burlap bag that the prosecutor claimed the kidnapper used to transport the toddler from his crib showed no signs of blood, nor was any found in the nursery, the toddler's clothing, on the ground outside, or in the soil and leaves in the woods beneath the body. Wilentz wanted Mitchell to shut the door on the possibility of external hemorrhaging. Mitchell obliged.

Insight into Dr. Mitchell's complete rejection of key findings in his autopsy report would be provided after he testified again in 1937 about the May 1932 autopsy. The occasion was a criminal trial charging veteran detective Ellis Parker and his son with coercing a false confession to the Lindbergh baby kidnapping from a disbarred New Jersey attorney named Paul Wendel. Mitchell was called to identify the corpse once more because Parker asserted that the body found in the woods was deliberately disfigured by Wendel to prevent its identification.

As part of his testimony for that 1937 trial, Dr. Mitchell claimed that when viewing the badly decomposed corpse in the morgue he immediately recognized the pelvis as that of a small boy. The opposite was true — when Dr. Mitchell had not been able to ascertain the sex of the unknown baby, he thought the pelvis looked more feminine than masculine. After testifying in the Parker trial, Mitchell admitted to an interviewer how much pressure he was under to reverse his medical opinion: "I'd 've been crazy to tangle with Lindbergh. Why, with his power, he could have ruined me — and don't think he wasn't just the boy to do it!"

The New Jersey Grand Jury

In Lindbergh's testimony before the Hunterdon County Grand Jury he claimed he recognized Hauptmann's voice as the one he heard yell two words to Condon at St. Raymond's Cemetery two and a half years before. At the time, Lindbergh sat in a parked car more than 200 feet away. At that same grand jury proceeding, Condon still could not identify Hauptmann as Cemetery John even though Condon had two lengthy conversations in person with that man.

Chief Defense Counsel Edward Reilly (center) and his new stationery.

6.
"Death House" Reilly

FROM the day of Hauptmann's arrest, newspaper extras printed banner headlines: "'LINDY CASE' SOLVED, $13,000 RECOVERED", "Bail denied as web tightens around alien." Anna Hauptmann and her husband were worried Fawcett was not up to the challenge of defending him. When Hauptmann was extradited to New Jersey to face murder charges, Anna took up the offer of newspaper mogul William Randolph Hearst to pay for a veteran criminal defense lawyer to replace Fawcett. The Hauptmanns were impressed with misleading news of Edward Reilly's successes in prior high-profile criminal cases.

Hauptmann bore no ill will toward Lindbergh. He expressed sympathy for both parents of the deceased child. The carpenter loved his own fourteen-month-old son "Bubi" so much he could not imagine their grief. He assumed the police talked Lindbergh into identifying him as Cemetery John and thought he owed his predicament to bungling and unethical officers. Hauptmann was looking forward to his day in court, trusting his alibi witnesses and the justice system.

What the beleaguered couple did not realize was Hearst's motive. Hearst knew how much his readers adored Lindbergh and clamored for Hauptmann's conviction of the heinous crime. Hearst made sure his media empire portrayed Hauptmann as a villain who deserved to die. For nearly thirty years, Hearst's yellow journalism had thrived on salacious crime stories. Back in 1913, Hearst had famously incited working-class whites in Atlanta to an uncontrollable thirst for mob "justice" by lynching Jewish factory manager Leo Franck for a murder that history would show Franck did not commit. In the early 1920s, just as the Prohibition Era was launched, Hearst provoked a nationwide crusade against Hollywood megastar Fatty Arbuckle for the death of an actress. Arbuckle became the face of Hollywood debauchery despised by good, churchgoing Americans. The actor wound up prosecuted three times and ultimately exonerated — thanks to good lawyering. In the process, Arbuckle's career was ruined, but Hearst remained unrepentant. He claimed that the coverage of Arbuckle's prosecutions sold more papers than the sinking of the Lusitania, which helped precipitate America's entry into the Great War.

Again, with the Lindbergh kidnap/murder prosecution, Hearst knew exactly how best to deliver what the public craved — Hauptmann's execution for the death of their hero's infant son. Central casting could not have done better than a defendant who had fought for the enemy in the Great War, an undocumented German immigrant with a criminal record. Edward Reilly was flamboyant and over-the-hill, a cynical choice to spike newspaper sales once more. Hearst expected Reilly to enflame the public against his own client as a dire warning against other would-be kidnappers. Hearst had no doubt of Hauptmann's guilt. The newspaper mogul knew Reilly's pomposity and flashy suits would likely alienate a rural New Jersey jury where Reilly was not even licensed to practice law. The Hauptmanns had no idea Reilly was an alcoholic with a string of recent failures in New York courtrooms. His newest nickname was "Death House" for the clients he lost to the electric chair.

Reilly accepted a flat fee from Hearst in exchange for providing the Hearst newspapers exclusive defense stories through the upcoming New Jersey trial. The paper provided no money for hiring experts. Nor did it cover the cost of transcripts, which Hauptmann could not otherwise afford. Reilly himself was a great fan of Charles Lindbergh and had kept a photo of the aviator proudly displayed on his office desk ever since Lindbergh's historic flight. During the trial, Reilly would tell a federal agent that he "knew Hauptmann was guilty, didn't like him, and was anxious to see him get the chair."

The Hauptmanns quickly became demoralized with their new counsel when Reilly barely made a pretense of consulting with his client to prepare for trial. Indeed, from the end of October when he was hired until the beginning of the trial in early January, Reilly only made four token trips to see Hauptmann. Each visit to his client in jail was extraordinarily brief. All four visits together added up to less than forty minutes. Each time, Reilly reeked of alcohol and left Hauptmann feeling so devastated he lay down and sobbed.

Reilly spent more time replacing his letterhead and ordering new business cards and notepads for trial. His new stationery featured an embossed, three-section, red ladder trumpeting himself as chief defense counsel for "The Lindbergh-Hauptmann Trial." The business card was the same; his legal pads were simply imprinted with a red ladder. He bought extra stationery with the red ladder on it for Hauptmann, telling the press Hauptmann could use it to respond to fan mail. That had to have compounded his client's misery. Aside from the lack of faith Reilly displayed in Hauptmann's innocence, Hauptmann found it deeply offensive that anyone could think a craftsman like himself would ever build such a shoddily constructed ladder.

The only hope Hauptmann had was the accomplished local Flemington lawyer who was brought in to assist in the defense, C. Lloyd Fisher. Having represented John Hughes Curtis in 1932, Fisher had far more knowledge of the puzzling background of the case than Reilly did. Fisher visited Hauptmann often and believed strongly in his innocence. But even Fisher's visits were severely handicapped. He was not permitted to have a single private conference with his client — there was always a policeman within earshot. The police also decided to let Anna Hauptmann visit her husband in jail — not out of sympathy, but so they could eavesdrop on the couple's conversations in case he made any admissions. The assigned officer was fluent in German. No admissions occurred. Instead, the Hauptmanns engaged in gallows humor, joking about how Isidor Fisch had gotten them into this fix. They still expected to prove the police had the wrong man.

Lloyd Fisher recruited two other lawyers to assist in the defense, splitting $500 three ways for their share of fees — all that Anna Hauptmann had left. But the two men were both strong additions to the team. Egbert Rosecrans was president of a neighboring county's bar association and Fred Pope had handled numerous murder cases both as a defense lawyer and former prosecutor. Yet Fisher, Pope and Rosecrans knew, as Lindbergh and the prosecution team did, that the entire Flemington community anticipated a guilty verdict. In fact, of the three, only Fisher believed in their client's innocence. Pope later said he joined the team for the publicity. (A fourth lawyer, retired Judge George Large, started out on the defense team, but reportedly received $8,000 to switch sides after learning the defense strategy.)

Fisher could tell the case against Hauptmann appeared manufactured. Just before Hauptmann's arrest the police had been on the lookout for Cemetery John as a tall, slender white-collar criminal who spoke perfect English and had just cashed a recorded gold certificate to pay for a few cents' worth of produce. But journalists turned on a dime to enflame the public against a stockier immigrant carpenter with a heavy German accent and the hands of a day laborer. The press displayed no concern that at the time of Hauptmann's arrest for possessing ransom money there was zero evidence he had been in or near the Lindbergh farmhouse around the time of the kidnapping.

Fisher did not know that the first two handwriting experts consulted by the police initially rejected Hauptmann as the author of the ransom notes. But Fisher had to be aware that neither John Condon, nor Lindbergh could originally identify Hauptmann as Cemetery John. Apparently, neither could Levatino, the sidewalk vendor who had most recently seen the prime suspect. Unbeknownst to any of Hauptmann's lawyers, on September 28, 1934 Breckinridge had implicated Isidor Fisch to the police as a member of the kidnap gang — not Hauptmann.

Fisher did learn from fingerprint expert Erastus Hudson that after comparing Hauptmann's fingerprints to those on the ladder, the police concluded they did not match. Their response was to erase all prints from the ladder. Also, it was public knowledge as of September 1934 that medical examiner Charles Mitchell was still insisting that his original opinion of the cause of death was correct. The FBI knew as well as the New Jersey State Police that the "kidnap" ladder could not hold the weight of a grown man carrying a hefty toddler. (J. Edgar Hoover also assumed that the flimsy ladder had been taken apart and put together so many times while in police custody, it was likely rendered useless as evidence.)

Within a short time, the prospects for convicting Hauptmann dramatically improved — starting with Lindbergh's testimony before the New Jersey grand jury on October 8 when he suddenly recognized Hauptmann's voice as Cemetery John. Yet Condon remained unsure.

Wilentz needed more evidence to tie Hauptmann to the kidnapping. The New Jersey State Police were hell bent on finding it. New York police had searched Hauptmann's apartment on the day of his arrest and found wood in the garage but none of it matched the ladder. At least 36 state and federal investigators also checked the landlord's basement and attic over the next week. None "found anything remotely connected with the case." Federal wood expert Arthur Koehler was summoned to New Jersey in late September 1934 to help out.

Koehler's lab was affiliated with the University of Wisconsin where he had obtained his master's degree the same day Lindbergh received an honorary degree as one of its most celebrated former students. Koehler volunteered in 1932 to review wood samples from the infamous kidnap ladder and to try to trace their sources. Yet it was not until 1933 that he was invited to partner with Lieutenant Louis Bornmann to embark on that Herculean task. Koehler's November 1933 report suggested that two rails might have been obtained from a Bronx lumberyard. After Hauptmann's arrest, Koehler became far more confident he was right. He assumed another rail came from flooring in "an attic, shop, warehouse or barn." (Back in March of 1932 that same rail looked to Erastus Hudson like it came from a crate.) Interviewed on his arrival in September, Koehler told the press he hoped to determine whether Hauptmann's tools were used to make the ladder.

After teams of investigators saw nothing of note in the attic, Bornmann claimed in a backdated report he made a remarkable find on September 26: an 8-foot gap in the floor next to a board matching the very ladder rail Koehler assumed might have come from an attic floor. Yet Bornmann waited nearly two weeks until *after* Koehler's grand jury testimony on Oct 8th before bringing Koehler to the attic. Koehler became convinced Bornmann was right. The Feds and Hauptmann's lawyers were denied access to see for themselves. When this explosive new evidence surfaced just before trial Hauptmann accused the police of manufacturing it. To the public and the press, the carpenter's fate looked sealed as chief defense counsel "Death House" Reilly handed out "kidnap ladder" business cards and chatted up reporters.

While the murder prosecution headed toward trial, Anne

immersed herself in writing *North to the Orient*. Lindbergh took time from his work at the Rockefeller Institute to read and comment on her drafts. Harold Nicolson returned for a visit in November and Mrs. Morrow threw a reception for him and invited eighty neighbors. After they left, Nicolson remained with just his secretary, Mrs. Morrow and Anne in the Morrows' large living room when he was surprised by Lindbergh suddenly making his presence known from the garden. "A sepulchral voice broke in on us from outside the window: 'Have they all gone?' And in vaulted Lindbergh who had been watching from outside." Nicolson may have been envious because he had also found the reception hard to endure. Yet it gave him a glimpse of Lindbergh's extreme distaste for social interaction.

Though Nicolson found Lindbergh cool and hard to penetrate, he could tell that Dwight Morrow's death and the little boy's murder still deeply affected both Anne and her mother. During Nicolson's visit that fall, he praised Mrs. Morrow's strength and courage as she focused on Elisabeth's worsening health. Betty Morrow shook her head: "Courage? Do you know I cry about that baby of ours every night even now? That is not courage!"

Despite the joy of being with her son Jon, Anne's grief remained near the surface. When she read of a young girl kidnapped and found in a shallow grave with her head bashed in, Anne cried uncontrollably, grateful her husband worked late and did not see how upset she had once again become. Then came news Elisabeth had to have her appendix removed. After the operation Elisabeth suffered another bout of pneumonia that Anne feared would be fatal. Mrs. Morrow flew out to California to be with Elisabeth, who succumbed on December 3.

The funeral was held at their parents' Englewood mansion in the same room where Elisabeth had been married just two years earlier. Anne decided she had to keep moving forward day to day with her emotions in check. In January, Hauptmann would face trial. Anne vowed not "to disappoint C. at the Trial." Her husband had made it clear how much Hauptmann's conviction meant to him.

Courthouse on Main St. Flemington, New Jersey

Inside the Courthouse

Tours were given of the empty courthouse on weekends. Passes were hard to come by when the court was in session.

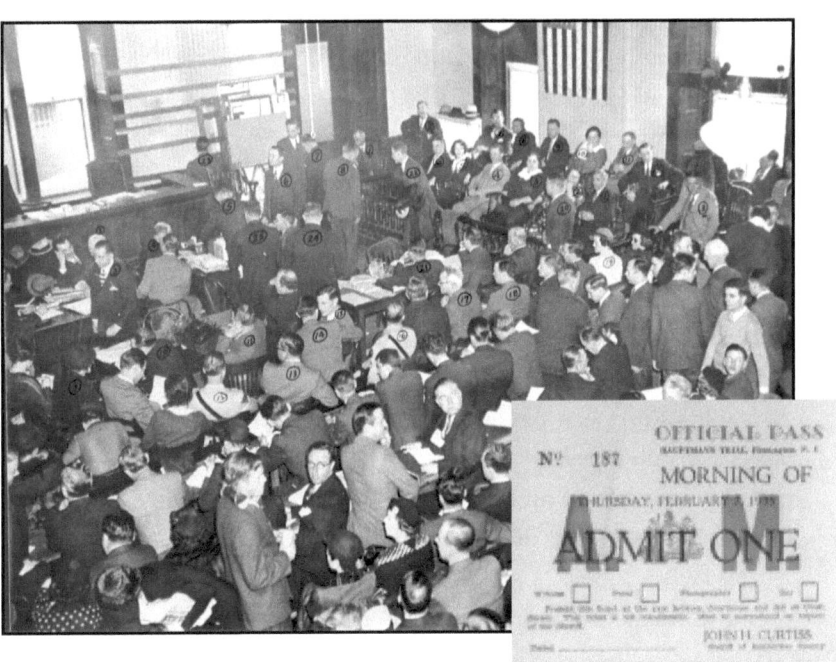

7.
Show Time

FROM the time Bruno Richard Hauptmann arrived at the Flemington jail to face trial for his life state police made sure the public viewed him as the worst criminal in the world. Despite no evidence that Hauptmann was violent or posed an extraordinary risk of flight, the state surrounded Hauptmann's cell day and night with a seventeen-man guard. Fisher estimated it cost the state $30,000 (over $560,000 today) just for that excessive security. The newspapers were no better. Nine out of ten already referred to Hauptmann as "the criminal" and presumed he would be executed for the murder of Lindbergh's son. Headlines like "Definitely Link Kidnap Ladder to Hauptmann's Home" did not help. Fisher noticed that public outrage even impacted the annual tradition of having the Flemington children's choir sing carols to prisoners in the courthouse. This year, the children were forbidden to sing either near the jail or by the local boarding house where Anna Hauptmann and her son had moved.

The "trial of the century" was anticipated to resemble a media circus far more than a judicial proceeding. It exceeded all expectations. From the outset, the personnel of the Hunterdon County Courthouse were overwhelmed, as was the town itself. Before trial began on January 2, 1935, Flemington had a population of 2700. Over 400 reporters and photographers showed up, including correspondents from over 20 leading European papers. Reporters booked solid every hotel and motel for miles around. Prostitutes flocked there, too. Some 60,000 sightseers converged on Flemington. Locals eagerly rented out rooms in their homes for five dollars per night.

Newsreel cameras were sneaked into the courtroom with a microphone hidden in a corner of the jury box facing the spectators.

Household names Damon Runyan, Edna Ferber, and Heywood Broun were among the major writers hired to cover the trial. Americans across the country became glued to their radios. Famed New York lawyer Sam Leibowitz — the Clarence Darrow of his generation — summarized its highlights each night for a major radio station, sometimes prefacing his comments with reference to Hauptmann being "one day closer to the electric chair."

The courtroom had six benches for spectators designed to hold up to about 250 people. Often, more than 500 shoehorned themselves in. Both the prosecutor and the defense handed out more than 100 witness "subpoenas" simply as a way to secure seats for celebrities like Ginger Rogers, comedian Jack Benny and Elsa Maxwell, who arrived from Manhattan in chauffeur-driven Rolls-Royces. In a converted attic, cable and overseas telegraph operators described the daily proceedings to millions of others around the world. Wires allowed direct filing of stories not only in Paris, London and Berlin, but Buenos Aires and Sydney, Australia. Small planes and express trains transported photographs and film footage daily to New York.

Souvenir hawkers sold all types of memorabilia, from Lindbergh photos purportedly autographed by their hero to tiny wooden "kidnap" ladders. The hotel across the street offered dishes named for the prosecutor and key witnesses. At least one suburban New York paper resisted and simply published photos from the trial instead of the running negative commentary. It was a minor protest in light of the insatiable public appetite being fed by "droves of sporting writers, society scribblers, magazine authors, short-story specialists, scenario specialists, sob-sisters, sobbing brothers, actors, chorus girls, lawyers, doctors and psychiatrists, Broadway columnists and managing editors."

Though Lindbergh declined to be interviewed, his remark to a high government official made it into the newspapers: "There can't be any doubt about it. They have the right man." Both Prosecutor David Wilentz and Chief Defense Counsel Edward Reilly gave interviews to the press during the trial. The judge or their own sense of propriety should have precluded both from commenting at all.

Hauptmann's lawyers understandably sought a change of venue

due to the overwhelming prejudice from pretrial publicity, but it was denied. Negative coverage throughout the country surpassed in volume the total reporting in any Olympic games up to that time or even coverage of the truce ending the Great War. One judicial critic looking back in 2004 suggested: "Hauptmann would have needed a change of venue to Baghdad to get a fair trial."

Hauptmann's lead lawyer Edward Reilly suffered from syphilis. He would often party at night with a prostitute and show up at trial with a hangover. Reporters were well aware of Reilly's nighttime activities since a number of them were similarly engaged. Scalpers hawked trial tickets. Bettors gambled mostly on the trial's length, not its outcome. Oddsmakers pegged the chances of conviction at 20 to one. The only suspense was "whether Hauptmann would get the chair or life imprisonment."

The judge who presided over the trial was 71-year-old Justice Thomas Trenchard of the New Jersey Supreme Court, who sat by assignment in Hunterdon County. He had also overseen the grand jury indictment in October. In his long career, Judge Trenchard had issued eleven death sentences while conducting more than ninety murder trials. Almost every day of the Hauptmann trial Judge Trenchard would warn the overcrowded courtroom that he would have the bailiffs remove spectators if they could not keep quiet, but he never made good on his threats. In the meantime, the courtroom suffered four broken windows and frequent eruptions of laughter, noisy chewing of candy bars and side conversations. In fact, reporters sometimes talked so loudly that witnesses could not be heard.

Although Lindbergh would be a key witness for the prosecution, from the outset, the judge surprisingly allowed the aviator to sit at the prosecutor's table, only a few feet from the defendant. Besides Lindbergh, Wilentz allowed other high-profile guests to be seated at the prosecution table, including Henry Breckinridge.

Hauptmann, quite pale and thirty pounds thinner than when arrested, got to wear a suit and tie at the trial, which was far better than jail clothes. Yet he looked "hollow-cheeked, corpse complexioned" as he sat sandwiched between two hefty troopers. A reporter for *The Brooklyn Eagle* contrasted Hauptmann's appearance to Lindbergh's.

Hauptmann "seemed dull, spiritless, disinterested" while "Lindbergh was red-cheeked, health flushed, bright-eyed, alert, almost merry at times. He seemed to have put on weight." Fisher had only once before seen a witness be allowed to sit with the prosecutor — Lindbergh at the 1932 Curtis trial. Here, the special privilege was of far greater consequence. Fisher objected but could not get Justice Trenchard to prohibit this strong signal to the jury which side should have their sympathy.

The Trial Jury

The first juror chosen said he had not made up his mind about the case "any more than anybody else." He became the foreman.

8.
Picking the Jury

ONE hundred fifty prospective jurors were called to the courthouse. The state used former Judge George Large, who had switched sides, as a paid jury consultant. The state also paid a number of investigators $100 apiece to check the background of everyone on the entire jury panel and supply confidential notes like "Very good type. Has remarked Hauptmann should get the chair;" "good type . . . father-in-law state police," "good type . . . easily led." These contrasted with undesirable jurors like the one who "stated state has weak case against Hauptmann. . . OUT."

Hunterdon County Prosecutor Tony Hauck made sure to ask each potential juror if he or she was capable of imposing the death penalty. Observers took note that Lindbergh wore a .38 in a shoulder holster inside his suit jacket — seated just four chairs away from Hauptmann. The gossip in the courthouse that day was that Lindbergh intended to take justice into his own hands if the panel lacked the courage to send Hauptmann to his death.

Fisher asked potential jurors if they had read accounts of the case or heard anything on the radio or in talking with others that caused them to have a negative opinion of the defendant. He also focused on the jurors' understanding of the rule of law that put the state to the burden of proof beyond a reasonable doubt. Though reporters considered this portion of the trial tedious, Lindbergh "seemed keenly interested in everything that went on, frequently leaning over to whisper to those in front of him." Yet when a reporter asked about Lindbergh's outsized role in the prosecution, Wilentz denied it was unusual. "Lindbergh has nothing to do with conducting the case. He is the complaining witness; it is his privilege to make suggestions if he wants to. We will give them the consideration that goes to any complaining witness."

The first juror chosen was a married father of four, who said he had not made up his mind about the case "any more than anybody else." Charles Walton, a 44-year-old semi-professional baseball player and machinist, became the foreman. Four women made it onto the jury, which was quite unusual at the time for a death penalty case. They ranged in age from 39 to 50. All were mothers and none were employed outside the home. Three of the six alternates were also women. For this jury, Wilentz planned an emotional appeal and his team assumed housewives would especially identify with Anne Lindbergh as a grieving mother.

The eight white men ranged in age from 25-year-old steel mill foreman Robert Cravatt to 60-year-old farmer Philip Hockenbury. Three of the men had no children. Hockenbury would be seen dozing more than once during the trial. The jury members were officially supposed to be sequestered during the trial in the Union Hotel across from the courthouse, but that was also the hub of reporters and radio commentators. The jury was not allowed to read newspapers or turn on the radio but ate its meals in the same dining room as all other hotel patrons, only separated from the boisterous crowd by a thin cloth screen that reached neither to the ceiling nor the floor.

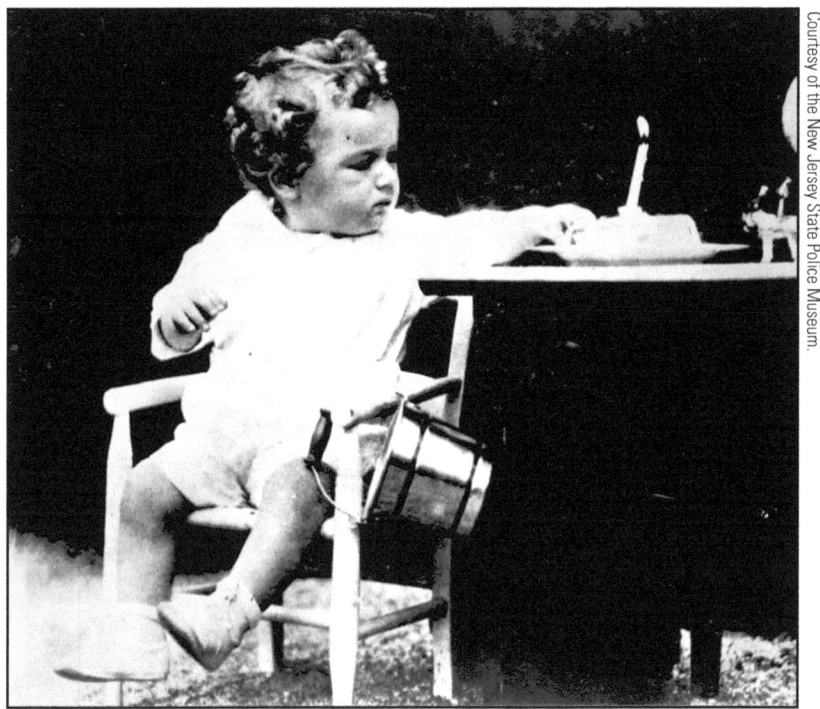

*Hauptmann Trial Prosecution Exhibit 6
(photo from first birthday June 22, 1931)*

Anne Lindbergh took the stand on the first day of trial and identified this photo of her son Charles A. Lindbergh, Jr. as the kidnap victim in answer to Wilentz's questions about his age, appearance, and health on the night of March 1, 1932. Anne swore he was then in good health with no mention of his medication. Privately, she found photos like this made it hard for her to remember what her son looked like when he disappeared — more than eight months after this photo was taken.

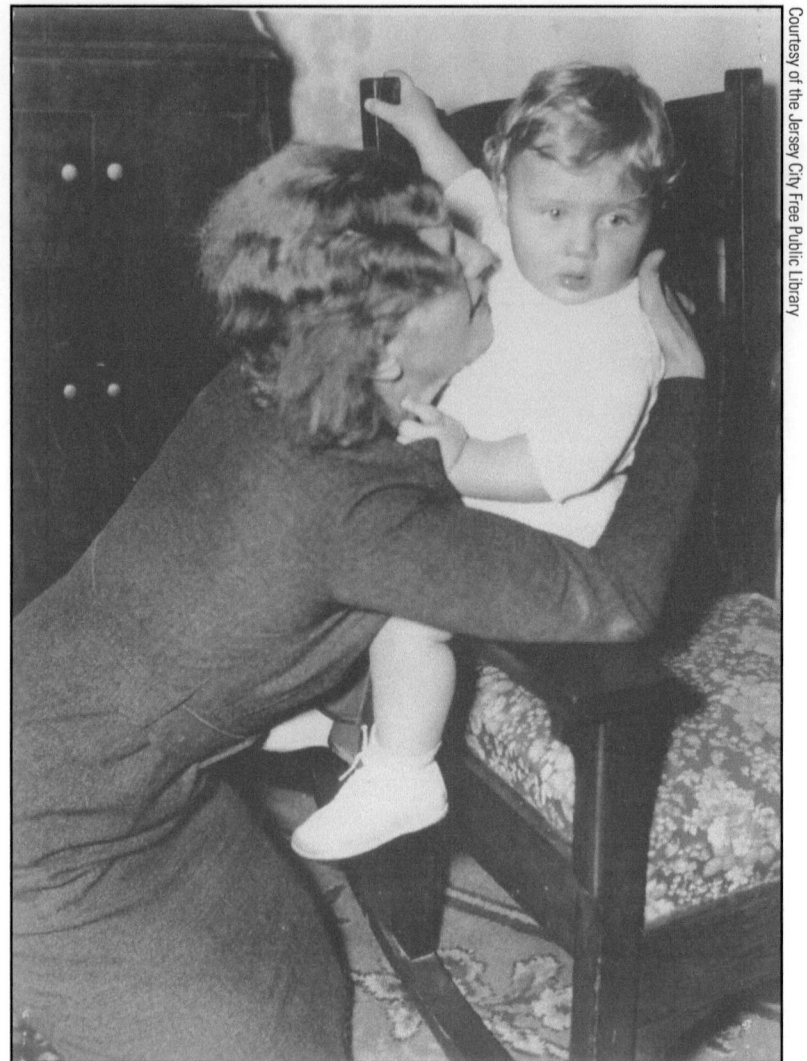

Anna Hauptmann with her son 'Bubi".

Hauptmann kept a photo of his son Manfred in his cell, whom he and his wife called "Bubi". Hauptmann told his wife not to bring Bubi with her so Bubi would not have nightmarish memories of his father behind bars. Hauptmann empathized with the Lindberghs for the loss of their son, knowing how much he loved his own toddler.

9.
Aiming for the Chair

NINETY witnesses would be called for the state. Though Hauptmann spoke English haltingly, he declined a translator. Daily transcripts for a death penalty case of that length were essential. The state ordered expensive Stenotypes that were available to read within a quarter of an hour after each witness testified. The defense could not afford to buy any transcripts. The court reporter decided to offer Hauptmann's lawyers a free copy but Wilentz refused to allow that courtesy, leaving the already handicapped defense team at an even more severe disadvantage.

Wilentz began his opening statement promising to prove Bruno Richard Hauptmann guilty of felony murder — accidental death of the Lindbergh toddler during a bungled burglary and kidnapping. He assured the courtroom he would prove that Hauptmann climbed into the nursery after casing the house for weeks, grabbed the child, and left the ransom note. The ladder broke as he descended with the baby in a sack, causing him and the child to fall — Lindbergh's theory of the homicide. To get the jury and courtroom full of Lindy fans to recoil in horror, Wilentz imagined the toddler "instantaneously killed" when the ladder broke and "down he went with this child" somehow inflicting a fatal blow upon contact" — with no outcry or physical evidence outside the house to back that claim up.

Wilentz also told the jury Hauptmann carried both the ladder and the child for many yards (a combined awkward load of more than sixty pounds) before dropping the ladder on the grounds of the estate. Since the child he intended to hold for ransom was accidentally dead, Wilentz suggested that Hauptmann left the body "at the very first convenient spot . . . in a hastily improvised and shallow grave and he went on his way to complete the rest of his plans. . . ." ("Convenient" did not match the wooded area where the body was found 75 feet off a back road a mile south of Hopewell if Hauptmann was supposedly in a hurry to head back north to his home in the Bronx.)

Anne Lindbergh attended that first day and was on and off the stand quickly. At Wilentz's request, she recited her activities on the night of March 1 and described how she and Betty Gow dressed her son for bed. She identified for the record a picture of her son from his first birthday party in June of 1931 — over eight months before he disappeared. The date of the photo was left unstated. She was not asked if that was what he looked like when last seen on March 1, 1932. Prompted by Wilentz, Anne swore that her son was in good health when he disappeared, despite having widely advertised back in early March of 1932 that her son was taking Viosterol, a prescription-strength medicine for Vitamin D deficiency.

When Anne described Betty Gow finding the crib empty many women in the courtroom burst into tears. Anne admitted that she never saw any envelope on the nursery windowsill, although she and Betty Gow were the first to enter the room after her son went missing. Reilly declined to ask Anne Lindbergh any questions at all out of deference to her grief.

The prosecutor now planned to prove that Hauptmann was himself "Cemetery John" through three witnesses: Lindbergh, John Condon, and cab driver Joseph Perrone. Lindbergh followed Anne to the stand, only testifying for about an hour. Observers noticed that he had taken off his gun. Lindbergh said he spent the day of March 1, 1932 in New York on various activities. No precise details were elicited. He largely agreed with Anne's testimony but swore that after dinner he heard a crashing sound while seated in the living room with his wife just after 9 p.m. He testified that just over an hour later on his first or second visit to the nursery, he found the ransom envelope.

Lloyd Fisher recalled that in Curtis's prosecution in June 1932 Lindbergh testified that he believed a gang had committed the crime. At that time, his lawyer Henry Breckinridge also credited Condon's description of the gang as "three men and two women, one night nurse and one day nurse." Now, Lindbergh confounded Fisher by insisting Hauptmann was the lone perpetrator. The jury paid rapt attention when Lindbergh confidently identified Hauptmann as Cemetery John based on having heard Hauptmann repeat the words "Hey Doctor" in September at the New York prosecutor's office, the phrase Lindbergh said he heard Cemetery John call out to Condon more than two-and-a-half years before. Actually, before the grand jury, Lindbergh had recalled the phrase he heard as "Hey Doc."

Death House Reilly was too enamored of the aviator to cross-examine his hero about such extraordinary hearing ability that most pilots lacked. Yet two days later a *New York Law Journal* editorial challenged the credibility of anyone making such a claim. J. Edgar Hoover also read Lindbergh's testimony and considered it completely unworthy of belief. (After the trial Hearst reporter Adela Rogers St. Johns polled the jurors. They said they made up their minds about Hauptmann's guilt right then.)

Watching her husband on the stand, Anne saw for herself how he impressed everyone with his apparent integrity. (No one in the courtroom but Lindbergh had any idea he was accused of brazenly committing perjury ten years earlier in a court battle over the principal asset in his father's estate. Nor did it occur to the packed courtroom that Lindbergh might have reason to lie. Even Hauptmann blamed the police, not Lindbergh, for convincing their star witness to point the finger at Hauptmann as the voice of Cemetery John).

The next two witnesses after Lindbergh were John Condon and the taxi driver. Police did not admit it, but they considered Condon mentally unstable. He and the cab driver had already proven themselves totally unreliable witnesses. The police also knew that Hauptmann's driver's license showed he weighed 175 pounds in 1932, not 160 pounds as Condon had described Cemetery John to them. The carpenter now on trial for his life also had no disfigurement at the base of his thumb that Condon had described seeing on the man he met.

Condon had resisted for months pressure from the police to say that Hauptmann was the go-between for the ransom gang Condon met in two cemeteries in the spring of 1932. Yet with Lindbergh sitting at the prosecution table having just named Hauptmann as "Cemetery John,"

Condon did the same. Like Lindbergh, Condon never mentioned having seen another man acting as look-out at St. Raymond's as they had both done previously in confidential grand jury proceedings and statements to the New Jersey State Police. Nor did Lindbergh or Condon mention that Cemetery John left three footprints in soft dirt when he climbed over a low fence at St. Raymond's and that they immediately had a plaster cast made of one of them. That preserved footprint did not match Hauptmann's foot size. (The Bureau was meanwhile sitting on scores of conflicting interviews of Condon, many of which the defense could likely have used to destroy him on cross-examination.)

Betty Gow had returned to Scotland back in August of 1934 and came back for the trial at state expense. Elsie Whateley was still employed by the Lindberghs. Both women then took their turns on the witness stand. Olly Whateley had passed away in May 1933. Reilly focused on casting suspicion on the butler/chauffeur as Violet Sharp's lover, both accused of acting as inside accomplices to the true kidnappers. His widow would have none of it — she and Olly spent all of their spare time together. Lindbergh told his wife that Betty and Elsie both did a good job on the stand.

Yet Betty described searching the room with the other two women. She also mentioned that she did not see the envelope until after the police arrived and Lindbergh summoned her to bring a knife to the nursery for them to open it. (Gow did not mention that the women had not noticed any smudge marks anywhere when they first searched the room). Betty said that she did not know what Lindbergh's movements were for several minutes before the police arrived. The defense was ill-prepared to cross-examine either woman because they had been denied access to the farmhouse to view the crime scene and never saw the two women's statements to the police.

The First Week of Trial

Betty Gow (left) and Elsie Whateley (right)

A "Who's Who" of Reporters

Walter Winchell alone had 50 million followers in print and on radio

10.
More Damning Testimony

THE SECOND week of trial brought heavy snows, but tickets inside remained in high demand. Everyone the prosecution had lined up was expected to deliver damning testimony developed by the prosecution team over the past few months. Yet the defense did score a few points. A Manhattan movie-theater ticket taker falsely testified that Hauptmann was the suspicious patron who paid for his ticket with a recorded $5 bill on the evening of Sunday, November 26, 1933. At the time, Loew's cashier Cecile Barr told investigators she believed the patron was American. November 26, 1933 also happened to be Hauptmann's birthday that he celebrated at home in the Bronx with friends.

Wilentz had many more witnesses in his arsenal. He had told the jury in his opening statement that Dr. Mitchell's testimony would be key. Wilentz first used Inspector Walsh and Trooper Zapolsky to mislead the jury to believe the burlap bag was found near the corpse, not by the side of the road some 75 feet away. Wilentz knew Reilly and Fisher did not have access to internal records showing the truth. Then, Wilentz had Inspector Walsh testify he made an accidental hole in the corpse behind its right ear while removing the toddler's T-shirts. The defense, of course, had no access to the report Walsh signed on May 12, 1932 which made no reference whatsoever to any such accident. Nor did the defense know about the meeting Walsh attended with Colonel Schwarzkopf a week after the body's discovery to share their findings with federal agents where Walsh again made no such claim. The stage was set for Swayze and Mitchell to testify.

Coroner Swayze swore that he only assisted Dr. Mitchell, prompting Reilly to dismiss him without asking any probing questions whatsoever. Dr. Mitchell's unorthodox conduct of a "look-see" autopsy performed by the lay coroner was thus not uncovered. Reilly should at least have asked Swayze some more questions about the official death certificate he himself completed. Swayze had signed the death certificate on May 13, 1932, the day after the "look-see" autopsy. In that official document, he described the fatal injury having occurred at an "unknown" location." He listed the date as "about March 1, 1932," and the death as due to homicide that occurred somewhere "probably near Hopewell, N.J."

During the lunch break, one of the lawyers on Wilentz's team was overheard by a relative of defense team member Fred Pope "coaching Dr. Mitchell to make sure above all else to testify that death was instantaneous." Both Wilentz and Lindbergh knew what Dr. Mitchell had stated in his testimony at the Gaston Means trial in May 1933 — that "the child died within probably 48 hours, at least, following the disappearance from its home." This time, Dr. Mitchell testified the boy died instantly. On cross-examination Mitchell denied he had ever attributed death to a bullet wound. He claimed that he had just previously described the small hole as bullet-shaped. Even so, Reilly found an opening to question the peculiar state of the corpse when found. Dr. Mitchell mentioned that when they sawed open the skull it started separating on its own. (Skulls normally stay hard in the ground for many centuries). Reilly compared this child's skull to an orange peel. He said he would return to that subject with further questions, but never did.

Making sure Hauptmann got the blame for felony-murder took scores more witnesses. These included three investigators who knew another suspect with fine hands and no accent had passed ransom money just two weeks before Hauptmann's arrest — NYPD Detective James Finn (who had been promoted right after the arrest), federal agent William A. Seery, and New Jersey State Trooper William Horn. One accountant gave elaborate testimony demonstrating how Hauptmann must have spent the entire $50,000 ransom. J. Edgar Hoover received daily reports from two agents who came every day to observe the trial. Hoover considered the accountant's reconstruction totally unconvincing. Wilentz had to know he was working with a house of cards. (Ransom money was still turning up sporadically during the trial and would do so after it ended.)

Wilentz also put on evidence that Hauptmann wrote Dr. Condon's telephone number and address on a closet wall. (Reporter Tom Cassidy later claimed that the scribbled phone number was his own prank written when the press had free access to the apartment that was denied to the defense. Other newsmen confirmed Cassidy's boast.)

With great flair, Wilentz presented three witnesses who were all promised reward money for placing Hauptmann in the area of Hopewell on or shortly before the day of the kidnapping. Millard Whited had twice given the police statements in March of 1932 that he had no information to offer about the crime. When he pointed out Hauptmann as a stranger he saw lurking around Hopewell before the kidnapping Schwarzkopf had reason to know that was a bald-faced lie, as did Lindbergh and Breckinridge. Wilentz likely did, too.

Wilentz also called Charles Rossiter, who had given a prior statement about a stranger he met on Saturday night, February 27, 1932 standing in the dark outside a parked car on the Hopewell-Princeton road. (Rossiter had previously told police the man did not look like Hauptmann, but described a shorter man who might have been Isidor Fisch.) On cross-examination, Rossiter could not describe the make of the car but said it had a rear tire holder. He did not realize Hauptmann's sedan had a protruding wooden trunk but Reilly asked no questions about that important detail. The last, lately discovered "eyewitness," 87-year-old Amandus Hochmuth, had cataracts in both eyes. Two days earlier, Hochmuth had given a statement to Asst. Atty Gen. Peacock that he could not be sure Hauptmann was a man he saw driving a green two-door near the Lindbergh estate around 10 a.m. on March 1. (Hauptmann's blue sedan had four doors.) Hochmuth mistakenly thought a neighbor (Lupica) saw that same green car. Within 48 hours, Hochmuth was convinced to swear the man was Hauptmann. *(Wilentz knew that D. A. Foley had admitted Hauptmann showed up for work that morning in Manhattan).*

Anne Lindbergh got most of her news of the trial's progress from her husband who was there every day. Anne came back to the trial only once — when her mother vouched for Violet Sharp's character. Anne noticed how "tired, bewildered" and "pathetically bedraggled" Mrs. Hauptmann looked. Anne also saw the defendant's "pale profile" when she peered through the crowded courtroom.

Two types of expert testimony provided further damning evidence against Hauptmann. The state put on eight top-rated handwriting experts to say they were sure Hauptmann wrote all of the ransom notes. (The cost of these experts was roughly the entire budget of the defense.) But all of them relied in large part on misspellings in Hauptmann's samples similar to those in the ransom notes. Hidden in the police files was a statement from Colonel Schwarzkopf revealing that the police did offer Hauptmann spelling "help" on the samples just as Hauptmann would testify in court. The defense had no access to either Schwarzkopf's admission or the original opinion rendered by two of the experts that Hauptmann was not the author.

The defense had made preparations to put on medical experts at trial to challenge whether the toddler found in the woods was, in fact, the Lindbergh's kidnapped child. The cremation of the corpse before a full autopsy greatly helped fuel that suspicion, along with other oddities observed about the body on May 12 and 13. Then Reilly shocked his co-counsel by stipulating that the corpse was that of the Lindberghs' son without requiring proof. Lloyd Fisher was livid. During a break outside the presence of the jury, Fisher yelled at Reilly: "You are conceding Hauptmann to the electric chair" and stomped out of the courtroom.

Lt. Bornmann took the stand and falsely testified that September 26, 1934 — the day he made his alleged discovery — was the first time any officer had gone up to the attic. Bornmann claimed a floorboard caught his eye because its color looked the same as rail 16, but even after all the fingerprints had been chemically removed from the rail the two boards were different hues.

Koehler was the state's last witness. He explained how he traced wood from two rails of the ladder to a Bronx lumberyard where Hauptmann sometimes worked. (At the time, police considered Condon a possible suspect). The defense still lacked access both to the attic and to

Koehler's less certain conclusions in his November 1933 report. J. Edgar Hoover considered Koehler's analysis to have major holes in it but was most bothered to learn *when* Koehler completed his report. The New Jersey State Police had withheld that report from the Bureau, despite repeated requests in 1934 for all information in their possession.

To clinch the case, Koehler impressed the jury with charts and analysis identifying a missing section of floorboard from the attic above Hauptmann's apartment as the source of ladder rail 16. Koehler pointed to similarities he saw in the growth rings of rail 16 and a section of attic floorboard removed by Lieutenant Bornmann – but downplayed the differences. Rail 16 not only lacked a tongue and groove and differed in color, it was 1/16th of an inch *thicker*, more than an inch-and-a-quarter *narrower* and showed no signs it had previously rested on floor joists. If Koehler played devil's advocate, he might have considered a simpler explanation of rail 16's origin than assuming Hauptmann climbed up into the attic to obtain a one-by-six floorboard he then downsized to approximate the size of a cheap, one-by-four available at any lumberyard. All six rails were almost exactly two meters long; the thickness of rail 16 matched a metric standard. If the lumber used to make rail 16 originated in a foreign country, that could dovetail with the belief in March of 1932 that the ladder was made from a repurposed shipping crate.

One wonders if it crossed Koehler's mind that key parts of his analysis depended on Bornmann's honesty. Bornmann certainly had the opportunity after Hauptmann's arrest to give rail 16 a distinctive, nicked surface with Hauptmann's old plane as Koehler had already announced he would be looking for. Did Koehler wonder why Bornmann waited almost two weeks after Koehler's arrival to take him to see the attic — the day *after* he testified before the grand jury? In helping to place the nail in the coffin of the most hated man in America it is doubtful Koehler gave serious thought to the possibility he was being used.

Hauptmann could not help being outraged by Koehler's testimony. He insisted he was being framed by the police. What offended him most was that anyone could believe an accomplished carpenter like himself would go to such absurd lengths to construct such a poor excuse for a ladder. Governor Hoffman would later also become convinced that the ladder was tampered with by the police after they took over the Hauptmann's apartment.

Prosecution Witness Amandus Hochmuth

Amandus Hochmuth first came forward when a reward was offered in late 1934. He was legally blind. His daughter had told police and reporters he had no firsthand knowledge about the kidnapping. Yet, after visiting the jail, Hochmuth told Asst. Atty. Gen. Peacock that Hauptman resembled a man with a ladder he saw driving a dirty green, two-door car near the Lindberghs' about 10 a.m. on March 1, 1932. At trial, Hochmuth swore he recognized Hauptmann as the man driving that green car in "the forenoon." (Wilentz knew D. A. Foley had admitted in earlier court proceedings that Hauptmann was in Manhattan all morning.) Gov. Hoffman later tested Hochmuth's eyesight and found he could not tell a vase from a woman's hat at ten feet.

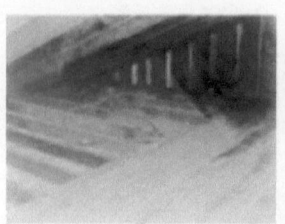 

Landlord's attic above Hauptmann's apartment with rail 16 placed to show where it could have once been part of that floor.

Before and After Koehler

rail 16   S-226

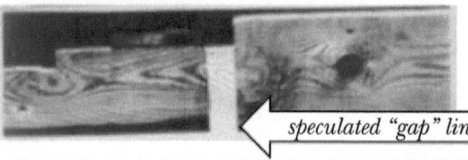

speculated "gap" lines

The top trial photo (left) is a close-up taken before Koehler began comparing rail 16 to S-226. The lower photo was taken later to show the jury how the (now darker) surface grains might link through an "artist's rendering" of the assumed missing piece. Koehler knew that these "grain" lines on the "gap" piece were speculative.

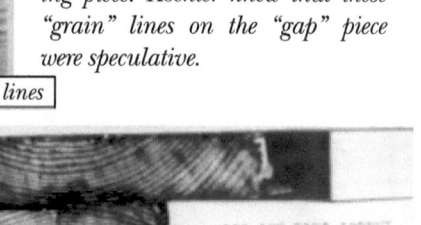

Above: Trial photo comparing ends of rail 16 (dark board) and S-226 (lighter board) after Koehler shaved the ends of both and superimposed one image on the other. In the picture it is hard to tell rail 16 was thicker than S-226.

Koehler testified that the ring patterns on rail 16 and S-226 showed they must have come from the same 20-foot length of pine lumber – a conclusion other experts challenged.

Below: A cropped photo Koehler later published with an article defending his opinion while the case pended on appeal. The wood hues and tree rings look matched but the boards themselves seem not to be fully aligned. Besides the light color, rail 16 also appears narrower than S-226 when the opposite was true.

Board from attic floor. | Ladder rail No. 16

All photos courtesy of the New Jersey State Police Museum

The Ladder

The "kidnap" ladder is now on exhibit at the New Jersey State Police Museum with a then uncommon ¾ inch birch or maple dowel attached. A second birch or maple dowel had been found in the grass nine feet away near the ladder's third section. The ladder itself was made of cheap pinewood and fir. The police soon realized it could not hold more than 125 pounds of weight without cracking. The first responders thought it was a ruse and pursued the theory it was an inside job before Lindbergh persuaded Col. Schwarzkopf otherwise.

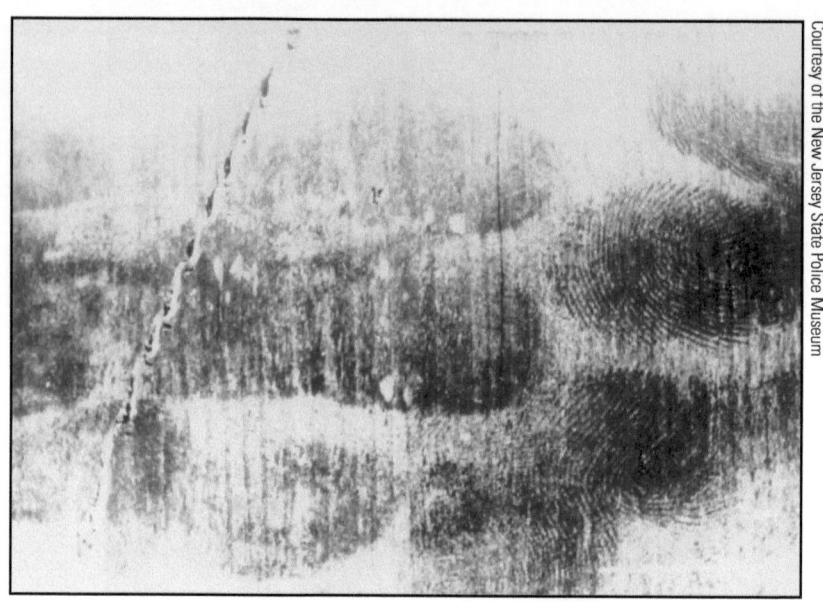

Exculpatory Ladder Fingerprint Testimony

Defense expert witness Dr. Erastus Hudson had originally been hired by the New Jersey State Police in 1932. When Hauptmann was arrested in 1934, Hauptmann's prints were nowhere to be found on the ladder, including the prints Dr. Hudson had earlier observed on an inside joint that could only have been made by the person who constructed it. For some reason, the state produced at trial just one photo of a set of unidentified prints on the ladder's surface. By the time of trial, they had erased all prints on the ladder itself, including the prints on the inside joint that would have implicated someone other than Hauptmann. Hudson was handicapped in testifying for the defense at trial because the ladder's inside joint had been cleansed of prints. (In cross-examining Hudson, Attorney General Wilentz indicated that Lindbergh's prints had previously appeared somewhere on the ladder).

The State's Handwriting Experts

The state put on eight top-rated handwriting experts at a cost roughly equal to the defense team's entire budget. In testifying that they were sure Hauptmann wrote all of the ransom notes, the state's experts relied in part on similar misspellings in his writing samples. The police did not tell these experts that the police had offered Hauptmann spelling "help."

11.
The Defense

IN HAUPTMANN'S defense, Erastus Mead Hudson testified that Hauptmann's prints were not found anywhere on the ladder. By then the police had erased all prints, but kept a box of photos of latent prints in their files. At trial, Wilentz only produced one photo of prints to quiz Hudson about: "Don't you know that Colonel Lindbergh, whose hands touched it — that his fingerprints were never revealed by your process?" Hudson replied, "I don't know that, sir." Wilentz was trying to cast doubt on Hudson's expertise — but Hudson's job had only been to make latent prints visible. The State Police were responsible for analyzing the prints. The police had never disclosed to the defense that they had identified any of them. Wilentz's question implied Lindbergh handled the ladder while it was in police custody. If so, this was poor police practice and at odds with Lindbergh's remarkable restraint from touching the ransom envelope to avoid contaminating evidence. Wilentz was also acknowledging that the police knew the prints they erased included Lindbergh's. He obviously assumed everyone on both sides considered Lindbergh beyond reproach.

Neighbor Ben Lupica testified for the defense that the dark car he saw with the ladders in the back had New Jersey plates with an "L" on it. Yet Wilentz confronted Lupica with a newspaper story claiming Lupica had identified Hauptmann. The article was false. Flustered, Lupica testified that Hauptmann "resembled the driver" although Hauptmann was stockier than the man Lupica had repeatedly described to the police and the Bureau as slim. (Decades later, Lupica recalled the trial as a sham. He knew other locals received money for fingering Hauptmann. He had been offered some as well if he retracted his statement about the 1929 Dodge, but he refused.)

Anna Hauptmann testified for the defense that her husband came to pick her up around eight p.m. on March 1, 1932 as he always did to take her home on Tuesdays and Fridays, the nights she worked late. Other alibi witnesses included two strangers: one, August van Henke, recalled stopping a man walking a German Shepherd in the Bronx on the night of March 1, 1932 because the dog resembled his own German Shepherd that had gone missing two weeks earlier. The pair both spoke German. The man with the dog said his last name was Hauptmann and offered to bring van Henke to a nearby bakery to prove the dog's ownership. By then, van Henke realized the dog was not his and left for home. At trial, van Henke identified the man he met as defendant, Bruno Richard Hauptmann. A patron of the bakery named Louis Kiss recalled the date because it was a week after his seven-year-old son's emergency admission to the hospital with a severe kidney problem. Mr. Kiss was sitting with his back to the door when a large dog ran in followed by a man who called out to the waitress (Anna Hauptmann) in German "Jemand wollte das dog – das Hund – nehmen." Mr. Kiss translated what he had heard: "Somebody wanted to take the dog!"

Some of the witnesses Reilly brought to the stand had not been well vetted but Wilentz's team had found little to impugn these two men's testimony. Even Hearst reporter Adela Rogers St. Johns was impressed. In her write-up that day for the *New York Journal* she observed: "If I had happened to be on the jury, I would have listened very carefully to Mr. Kiss because I had the conviction he was telling the truth." But other papers reported the news differently. *The Los Angeles Times* described the cross-examination of Mr. Kiss as a "hard blow" to the defense.

Hans Kloppenburg was also a key defense witness. He provided corroboration that Hauptmann was home playing music with friends the night of April 2, 1932 when Cemetery John received the ransom money at St. Raymond's. Kloppenburg also testified that he saw Fisch handing Hauptmann a package at Fisch's going away party in December 1933. But this time, Kloppenburg had been warned by Wilentz not to describe the package as looking like a wrapped shoebox. Instead, Kloppenburg just gave the jury a physical description of the package: "about five to six inches, high, and seven, eight wide [by] about fourteen inches." Wilentz ridiculed Kloppenburg's memory.

The last two defense witnesses were a general contractor and a veteran carpenter. Their years of experience made them sure rail 16 could not have come from the attic floor, which the landlord had testified was completed in 1926. The two experts listed a number of reasons, including the contractor's observation that rail 16 had no marks on its underside showing it had ever lain on any joists.

In rebuttal, the state put on more witnesses — including a Fisch family member flown in from Germany at state expense — to undermine the claim Isidor Fisch was involved in the ransom scheme. Wilentz also wanted to address a problem that had arisen when Dr. Hudson was on the stand. The prosecutor had not been able to get photos into evidence that rail 16 had four square-cut nail holes back in March of 1932. Hudson was adamant only one such hole existed then (which was why he thought it had previously been a piece of a large crate).

In response, Wilentz put police photographer George Wilton on the stand. This testimony should still have given the judge pause because Wilton did not take any of the photos and provided no back up for his testimony that he made the enlargements on March 8, 1932. Wilton told the jury he assumed either Trooper Kelly or Kubler took the originals. Both had already testified and neither claimed to have done so. Kubler was not even assigned to the case until March 10th. Wilton also admitted he saw changes to rail 16 and other ladder parts while in police custody.

The defense objected that the state was only offering Wilton's word when these damning enlargements were made, despite having better evidence to date them that it was not producing. Indeed, anyone familiar with early coverage of the case should have questioned why enlargements would have been made on March 8, 1932 of any ladder part. That very morning Lindbergh had wrested control of the investigation from the state police and publicly promised "all possible protection to the kidnappers provided they return his baby" — prompting a reporter to write "the heat" was now "off." Justice Trenchard let the enlargements in anyway.

Wilentz then put on Harold Betts, a federal wood expert from Washington, D.C. who testified that he examined the ladder in late May 1932 and noted four square-cut nail holes in rail 16. The noose had been tightening on Hauptmann day by day ever since the grand jury indicted him for murder on October 8. The packed courtroom eagerly anticipated closing arguments.

The Defense Team at Trial

Back row left to right: Reilly, Hauptmann, Dep. Sheriff Hovey Low, Lloyd Fisher and Egbert Rosecrans. In front is Corporal Julius O'Donnell.

Anna Hauptmann assists Fisher with trial prep as her cousin looks on.

Hauptmann confers with Fred Pope, who admitted that he joined the defense for the publicity.

Hauptmann confers with Lloyd Fisher — the only lawyer on the defense team who believed in Hauptmann's innocence.

Ben Lupica testified that he saw a dark blue or black 1929 Dodge sedan with an L on the New Jersey plate like his own Mercer County car had (plus 4 other digits). It appeared to have dark wooden spokes (see inset). Lupica noted a sectional ladder across the passenger seat and a spare tire on the car's rear, but no trunk. He also described the car's blue winged emblem and high, decorative radiator grill.

Hauptmann's 1930 Dodge Sedan

Hauptmann's blue 1930 Dodge sedan had New York plates. Lupica said the car he saw did not have a trunk on the back. It also did not have wheels with wire spokes. The spare tire for Hauptmann's car was not on the rear of the car but attached to the mudguard on the driver's side. The police photo (upper left) shown to the jury displayed only the passenger side of Hauptmann's sedan – after police removed the trunk Hauptmann built in 1931. (In 1932 the trunk was painted black and had no canvas cover. Hauptmann also described the two back tires as having white bands in 1932.)

AP photo taken Sept. 20, 1934 – the day after Hauptmann's arrest

Alibi Witness Hans Kloppenburg

Hauptmann's good friend Hans Kloppenburg testified that he was with the Hauptmanns on the evening of April 2, 1932 playing music with a group of friends at the Hauptmanns' apartment. If believed, it provided Hauptmann with an alibi when Condon met in St. Raymond's Cemetery with Cemetery John. Kloppenburg also testified that he saw Isidor Fisch hand a package to Hauptmann at a party at Hauptmann's apartment in December of 1933.

12.
Condemned Without Mercy

CLOSING arguments took place in early February 1935. Hauck went first. He pointed to Hopewell resident Millard Whited's identification of Hauptmann. Hauck insisted that Whited "did not just come and tell a story in 1934 and 1935, but he described that very man the very next morning after the baby was taken from its crib." In fact, the opposite was true. Back in the spring of 1932 Whited had repeatedly denied he had seen anyone suspicious on March 1 or the days leading up to it.

Wilentz began his own argument by assuring the jury he was bound by ethics: "For all these months since October, 1934, not during one moment has there been anything that has come to the surface or light that indicated anything but the guilt of this defendant, Bruno Richard Hauptmann, and no one else. Every avenue of evidence, every little thoroughfare that we traveled along, every one led to the same door: Bruno Richard Hauptmann." Yet the state's own former expert Erastus Hudson had pointed to fingerprints on an inside joint of the ladder not matching Hauptmann's as proof they had the wrong suspect. Hudson had also found only one old nail hole on rail 16 which made him believe it came from a crate. The State never produced a cameraman to testify he filmed four such holes. In his summation, Wilentz simply told the jury the key photographs must have been taken within 48 hours of when George Wilton swore he made the enlargements.

After defense lawyers focused on the infant's failure to cry out, Wilentz abandoned his efforts to prove Hauptmann accidentally killed the toddler while descending the ladder. Instead, Hauck and Wilentz offered a new theory — that the child had his life brutally snuffed out inside the nursery before Hauptmann ever descended. "He smothered and choked that child right into insensibility." Wilentz suggested the child's head hit the headboard as he was yanked from the crib and that the chisel might have been used "to crush the skull." (As the police knew, no blood had been found anywhere in the nursery or on the chisel, which had been etched with someone else's initials.)

The prosecution's new theory of how the homicide occurred presented a quite different scenario, with no corpse, physical evidence or autopsy to back it up. Wilentz did his best to whip the jury to a frenzy by painting Hauptmann as "an animal lower than the lowest form in the animal kingdom . . . with ice water in his veins . . . the vilest snake that ever crept through the grass."And he sealed Hauptmann's fate with Lindbergh's voice identification: "If Colonel Lindbergh says that is the man, men and women that is good enough."

The defense team challenged Wilentz's closing argument as unsupported by the evidence but got nowhere with Justice Trenchard. Reilly in his own closing statement raised many obvious questions and attributed the crime to a gang acting with insider help. By that time his arguments fell on deaf ears. By its end, the trial had cost the state $150,000 (about $2,800,000 today) — three times as much as the most expensive criminal trial previously prosecuted by the state. The investigation itself had cost the state and federal governments $1,181,000 ($22.5 million today). All through the many objections by both sides during the trial, Justice Trenchard had mostly upheld the prosecutor's position. He even overruled objections to admitting the ladder into evidence without requiring the police to put anyone on the stand to prove that the ladder remained as it was originally found and had not been tampered with after the police took custody of it. (The erasure of fingerprints itself constituted tampering).

As the trial drew to its close on February 13, 1935, observers watched Justice Trenchard steer the jury toward conviction with his comments and tone of voice in summing up the evidence and the defense arguments:

> It is argued that the kidnaping and murder was done by a Gang . . . with the help of one or more servants. ***Now do you believe that? Is there any evidence in this case whatsoever to support this conclusion?***
>
> "Does not the evidence satisfy you that at least a part of the wood from which the ladder was built came out of the

flooring of the attic of the defendant?"

It is argued that Dr. Condon's testimony is inherently improbable and should be in part rejected by you. But you will observe that this testimony is corroborated in large part by several witnesses whose credibility has not been impeached in any manner whatsoever. *Upon the whole, is there any doubt in your minds as to the reliability of Doctor Condon's testimony?*

The Defendant says that these ransom bills, moneys, were left with him by one Fisch, a man now dead. *Now do you believe that?*

Justice Trenchard suggested that the jury should give particular weight to Amandus Hochmuth's testimony: "Mr. Hochmuth lives at or about the entrance of the lane that goes up to the Lindbergh house. He testified that on the forenoon of that day, March 1st, 1932, he saw the defendant at that point driving rapidly from the direction of Hopewell . . . that he had a ladder in the car, which was a dirty green. This testimony, if true is highly significant. Do you think that there is any reason, on the whole, to doubt the truth of the old man's testimony?" (Both sides knew of several good reasons to disbelieve Hochmuth.) The defense team included the judge's instructions in their long list of prejudicial trial errors to make their record for appeal. They likened the atmosphere in the courthouse to the ancient Roman Circus Maximus. With no real hope of acquittal, they still had faith that an appellate court would take a fair look at the case. After the jury went into deliberations, a restless crowd of ten thousand outside the courthouse began yelling "Kill Hauptmann."

At home that night, Lindbergh himself marveled at Justice Trenchard's bias in favor of the prosecution. The dinner guests at the Morrow mansion included Sir Harold Nicolson, who had just returned to conduct more interviews for his biography of Dwight Morrow. Lindbergh confided to Nicolson that the judge clearly signaled his disbelief in Hauptmann's defense with sarcastic points of emphasis that "sounds all right when read in print. But what he actually said was "Do you believe THAT?" (Justice Trenchard would receive many letters after the trial critical of his conduct.)

As the group sat down to be served in the Morrows' elegant dining room, the jury had been deliberating Hauptmann's fate for about five hours. A radio was left on in the pantry and another in the drawing room to get the announcement as soon as the verdict was reached. When no word came during dinner, they all headed to the drawing-room to look over family photos for Nicolson's biography. He noticed "they were all rather jumpy." (Nicolson did not know Anne was especially on edge. She had been reduced to tears just two days earlier by her husband for failure to live up to his expectations of how she should behave.) Nicolson moved to another room to privately interview Dwight Morrow's nephew for the biography he was writing. An AP reporter at the courthouse thought he had the scoop. He reported that the verdict was guilty and the sentence life imprisonment. This became the next headline in a thousand affiliated newspapers. Soon the jury returned to court and rendered their verdict. Betty Morrow popped her head in the door of the room where Nicolson was conducting his interview. He wrote in his diary: "She looked very white. 'Hauptmann,' she said, 'has been condemned without mercy.'"

Everyone reentered the drawing room where they could hear on the radio the "diabolic yelling of the crowd. . . . Anne looking very white and still. 'You have now heard' broke in the voice of the announcer, 'the verdict in the most famous trial in all history. Bruno Hauptmann now stands guilty of the foulest . . . .'" Anne interrupted the announcer's description of the crime: "'Turn that off, Charles, turn that off.'"

The group then headed to the pantry where Lindbergh sought to explain the case to Nicolson, not sure if he had followed it closely as a Brit. But to Nicolson, Lindbergh seemed bent on reassuring everyone present with his take on the case: "'There is no doubt at all that Hauptmann did the thing. My one dread all these years has been that they would get hold of someone as a victim about whom I wasn't sure. I am sure about this — quite sure.'" Nicolson, who prided himself as a careful observer and note-taker, apparently never reflected on the fact that he wrote in his diary that night that Lindbergh used the word "victim" to describe the man the police fingered for the crime.

Lindbergh proceeded to review the murder trial "point by point." His calm recapping of damning evidence impressed Nicolson. Lindbergh left no doubt in Nicolson's mind that the right man was convicted:

It seemed to relieve all of them. He did it very quietly, very simply. He pretended to address his remarks to me only. But I could see that he was really trying to ease the agonized tension through which Betty and Anne had passed. It was very well done. It made one feel that here was no personal desire for vengeance or justification; here was the solemn process of law inexorably and impersonally punishing a culprit."

Nicolson could see that Anne had been horrified by the sound of the blood-thirsty gathering outside the Flemington courthouse. Lindbergh commented, "That was a lynching crowd" which Nicolson knew was still a regular feature of the American South. Nicolson thought an acquittal of Hauptmann after all the effort that went into his prosecution would have had a "bad effect on the crime situation in the country . . . [giving] all gangsters . . . . a sense of immunity. The prestige of the police has been enormously enhanced by this case." The next day, Nicolson noted for his diary one last comment Lindbergh made to him the night before. After having sat in close proximity to Hauptmann throughout the trial, the aviator observed that the German carpenter was a "magnificent-looking man. Splendidly built. But that his little eyes were like the eyes of a wild boar. Mean, shifty, small and cruel."

That satanic characterization of Hauptmann was not the jury's overall impression. It turned out that the jurors had immediately voted to convict but had taken time to consider whether to recommend leniency. After hearing sixteen hours of testimony, Hearst reporter Dorothy Kilgallen thought one of the women on the jury had a crush on the good-looking carpenter. On the first sentencing ballot, two men and one of the women reportedly voted for life imprisonment. The jury then kept deliberating until they all agreed on the death sentence.

For the *New York Times* the conclusion of the trial still raised too many questions, as it did for First Lady Eleanor Roosevelt. But Anne Lindbergh's reaction to her husband's reassurances was exactly what he hoped. With the trial ended, that chapter of their lives was over. It was time for their family to start anew — Charles, Anne and their two-and-a-half-year-old son Jon.

Justice Thomas Trenchard

Justice Thomas Trenchard of the New Jersey Supreme Court was assigned to conduct the trial. He had also overseen Hauptmann's grand jury indictment in October 1934. In his long career, Justice Trenchard had issued 11 death sentences in 90+ murder trials. He made key rulings favoring the prosecution, particularly in admitting the ladder without proof of chain of custody. Even Lindbergh noted Trenchard's thumb on the scales when the judge sarcastically commented on Hauptmann's defense in his instructions to the jury: "Do you believe THAT?"

13.
Raising Doubts

ANNE was extremely happy that they were spending the entire summer of 1935 with her family at their island home in Maine. Sir Harold Nicolson joined them at North Haven for a few weeks as he continued to work on his biography of Dwight Morrow. Nicolson noticed that Lindbergh's behavior with his almost three-year-old son Jon was quite aggressive. He saw how Anne Lindbergh "could not bear to watch when her husband flung their child into the pool and watched him struggling in the water." (Several years later, Lindbergh challenged eight-year-old Jon to a long-distance swim together in the Long Island Sound beyond Jon's endurance. Jon nearly drowned. It was not his father who came to his rescue, but a lighthouse keeper who tossed out a rope to haul the boy to safety.)

In August, the Lindberghs got shocking news that their friend Will Rogers died in a sea plane accident on take-off in Alaska with world-renowned pilot Wiley Post. Back in 1931, Post had won fame circling the globe with a co-pilot. He then repeated the achievement solo in 1933, garnering acclaim that echoed Lindbergh's own. Then, five days after Rogers and Post lost their lives, Anne feared she would die in a terrifying trip through thunderstorms. Yet she understood why her husband liked to say, "nothing can be accomplished without taking any chance at all." Shortly afterward, she waved good-bye to her husband as he took off on another solo flight. Anne then realized that "without C., I would lose life and the whole purpose of life." She desperately needed to believe in her husband, or she lost all sense of self-worth.

Self-doubt soon began to recede. In September, Anne published *North to the Orient*, which would climb quickly to the best-seller list. Anne had been given great encouragement in her writing by Sir Harold

Nicolson. He considered her to have extraordinarily keen powers of observation and talent at expressing herself. Anne wanted to pursue more writing projects. She realized that when she had accompanied her husband to exotic destinations overseas, she felt patronized. She got tired of being treated as simply a sidekick whose own rudimentary flying skills were simply better than one might expect for a female. She assumed that was all behind her now — the agony and torment of long journeys in the air separated from her son. She wanted to find a new home and settle down.

On October 5, *Liberty* magazine published a cover article by Hauptmann's former lawyer Edward Reilly asking whether Lindbergh would save Hauptmann from the chair. On October 9, 1935, the appellate court rejected Hauptmann's challenge to his conviction. Hauptmann's last chance was with the New Jersey Board of Pardons presided over by new Governor Harold Hoffman, who already had familiarity with the case from Hoffman's days as head of the New Jersey Department of Motor Vehicles. Under his guidance, the department had fruitlessly checked thousands of cars just after the kidnapping occurred. Lindbergh may have known that Governor Hoffman and Detective Ellis Parker were old friends, and that Parker had reached out to Hoffman during the investigation for his help in pursuing clues to the kidnapping. Hoffman had, in fact, started out his career as a police reporter for his hometown newspaper.

Hoffman had been sworn in as governor during the Hauptmann trial. From what he had already learned, he was greatly troubled by the prosecutor's evidence, and the manner in which the case had been handled. He received a letter from the Morrow family pediatrician, Dr. Van Ingen voicing concerns about the identity of the corpse, presumably with Mrs. Morrow's permission to share his views. Governor Hoffman obtained confidential reports and letters of support from Ellis Parker, Squire Johnson and other volunteers, including fingerprint expert Erastus Hudson. Johnson told Governor Hoffman he knew "personally, of some perjured testimony that the State Police gave which you also know of. . . . It can also be assumed that the testimony given by some of the other witnesses was also perjured, and. . . the prosecution would have winked at it."

The second week of October, the Lindberghs were enjoying themselves at North Haven again with three-year-old Jon when Charles suddenly sprung travel plans on Anne that totally devastated her. He was just asked to undertake another Pan Am trip to the Pacific that would probably take two months. Anne knew her husband's estimate would likely stretch out much further and they would have to leave Jon behind again at Englewood. She burst into tears. For a fleeting moment, she wished she were newly pregnant so that she would have an excuse not to go.

Anne dreaded the terror of a sixteen-hour flight through darkness over the Pacific Ocean to Hawaii, reliving nightmarish experiences she had endured on prior trips. Anne also anticipated it would take a long time to readjust to a daily routine on their return as she had unhappily experienced before. Her husband pressed her to support him once more, arguing that it would be the highpoint of his international flying career. In desperation, Anne asked her husband how he could interrupt for months his important medical research work with Dr. Carrel at the Rockefeller Institute. Carrel had just made the cover of *TIME* magazine the month before for an ambitious book, *Man, The Unknown*, and his efforts to prolong life through the potential of organ transplants. But Lindbergh convinced his wife he would get little done on his research project with Dr. Carrel that fall. There was too much horrible news coverage, stress and gloom while Hauptmann's last appeal played out. As far as the Hauptmann case was concerned, he told Anne there was nothing they needed to be present for — their job was over. Remaining in New Jersey would only increase the intensity of media focus on Hauptmann's impending execution.

Anne recognized the logic of her husband's proposal for a final lengthy tour of the Far East as a climax to his pioneering role in aviation history. Drying her tears, she reluctantly endorsed it. She knew her feelings mattered little. Anne criticized herself for wanting to stay home, and for thinking her budding writing career merited any consideration as a counterargument to such an important journey. She rationalized that this one last trip would be at most a six-month delay to settling into a new home and a more sedentary existence.

Then just as suddenly the next day Lindbergh decided not to go on the Pan Am trip, telling Anne his change of heart had nothing to do with her feelings. Anne was glad that her emotional reaction was not what dissuaded him. No, her husband simply decided the trip was designed by Pan Am more for organizational purposes, not pioneering work, and it did not suit him. Someone else could do a fine job of it.

Following Hauptmann's arrest in September 1934, Ellis Parker had told Harold Hoffman that the police "have got the wrong man." A week after Hauptmann's appeal was turned down, Governor Hoffman paid a secret visit to the death row inmate to see if he could elicit a confession and answer lingering questions about who else must have been involved in the kidnapping gang. Governor Hoffman brought along Ellis Parker's bilingual secretary to take notes and translate from the German since Hauptmann did not speak fluent English. Hauptmann offered to take a lie detector test or truth serum; he urged further investigation of the case. Hauptmann asked about footprints that did not match his and about the absence of any fingerprints in the nursery and the erasure of prints found inside a joint of the ladder. Governor Hoffman came away largely convinced of Hauptmann's innocence and increasingly concerned about Lindbergh's own behavior, though he dared not say that publicly. When the New Jersey Court of Pardons met on October 29, the Governor told them of his puzzlement about aspects of the case and suggested they visit Hauptmann, too, since a request for pardon "will soon be in our laps."

State police wood expert Squire Johnson encouraged Governor Hoffman to keep digging into the case. Johnson did not believe that all potential suspects at Skillman Village had been followed up on as the Bureau had been told. Lindbergh likely got wind of Governor Hoffman's concerns shortly after Hoffman voiced them to other members of the Board of Pardons. Anne confided to her diary that in early November 1935 her husband seemed "unhappy, restless — must get away from Englewood" for undisclosed reasons.

Then on December 5, 1935, Governor Hoffman made headlines confirming to a reporter that he had reopened the kidnap case. Two days later, the Governor issued a formal statement. He began by acknowledging: "The case of Bruno Richard Hauptmann is one with which the dimensions of American justice will be measured by all Americans and the world." Governor Hoffman cited "thousands of rumors" about evidence not revealed at the trial that "must be set to rest . . . to make sure that justice is done. . . . No person participating in this crime can be allowed to escape the full penalty."

That same evening Lindbergh shocked Anne by telling her they might be going "abroad to England or Sweden for the winter, or longer. . . . Be ready to go by the end of the week—at twenty-four hours' notice." While Anne packed up her life, Lindbergh made arrangements through Dr. Carrel for introductions to medical researchers in England so he might carry on additional experiments abroad.

Meanwhile, Lloyd Fisher told the press he intended to subpoena the records of the Department of Justice, expecting to show that expert testimony was fabricated. The head of the New York Bureau office wrote J. Edgar Hoover that the Attorney General considered such a request for confidential Bureau files "preposterous." A newspaper article pointed out that Koehler had only linked one rail of the ladder to Hauptmann. There was no proof rails 12 and 13 came from the lumberyard where Hauptmann had worked, and more questions had been raised about whether rail 16 originated as an attic floorboard.

Before Governor Hoffman could have Lindbergh and his family questioned further, they were gone. Three days before Christmas, they secretly boarded a freighter to England. Anne previously had told her mother that she, Charles and Jon would be spending Christmas in Detroit with Evangeline Lindbergh. Mrs. Morrow accepted the explanation they needed to get on with life and that the change of plans for an extended trip overseas was to avoid unwanted press attention as Hauptmann's execution approached.

Anne, for her part, was grateful not to battle with her husband over whether to bring their three-year-old overseas with them. She did not want to repeat their prior arguments over her not wanting to leave Jon behind, and earlier, over her wanting to stay at home with Little Charlie. Her husband liked to joke that he ran the household like a benevolent dictatorship.

Lindbergh gave a *New York Times* reporter an exclusive interview on the reporter's promise not to publish the fact they had departed until after their ship sailed. Lindbergh said there had been recent threats to his son Jon, and he feared for Jon's continued safety (a concern he did not voice two months earlier when he proposed leaving his son behind while he and Anne took an extended trip for Pan Am).

When the *New York Times* broke the news of the Lindberghs' departure, outraged Americans accused Governor Hoffman of driving their beloved hero into exile to protect his family from having to relive the horrendous crime. Soon after the Lindberghs left, Governor Hoffmann took over Hauptmann's lease from Bornmann and conducted his own investigation. After multiple tests, including a new Ultra-Violet technique, Hoffman's expert concluded that the evidence linking the ladder to the attic had been manufactured after Hauptmann's arrest. Though Koehler was familiar with UV as a valid technique, he was not convinced. To resolve the dispute, the parties agreed to one last test at Columbia University. These results were inconclusive.

Yet further questions raised by witnesses implicated other men in the crime. Alfred Hammond, the night watchman for the railroad, identified Isidor Fisch as one of three suspicious men he had seen at the Skillman Village railroad crossing on four dates in late February and again on March 1, 1932. Hammond said Hauptmann was not one of them and told the governor he had shared that information previously with the state police. A night watchman at St. Raymond's Cemetery on April 2, 1932 had also identified a photo of Fisch. This account could have correlated with the lookout Lindbergh described.

Ellis Parker informed Governor Hoffman that he had verified that Fisch spent some of the ransom money in November 1933 for an expensive boat ticket back to Germany the following month. The governor also received intriguing information from a prominent Cuban lawyer named Arturo Gonzales providing another possible lead linking Fisch to the ransom scheme. Gonzales worked for the German consulate in Havana in the early 1930s. He said that sometime between the kidnapping and Hauptmann's arrest a man came to the consulate who wanted to exchange recorded American dollars for pesos. The man showed

Gonzales a letter purportedly signed by Isidor Fisch, a name which did not then mean anything to Gonzales. The man who had the letter with him claimed to be Fisch's friend. Gonzales thought he could recognize this man if he saw him again.

Governor Hoffman received another affidavit that implicated someone other than Hauptmann as Cemetery John — a rather tall and thin man with blue eyes, who called himself Edilberto Borelli. (The description of Borelli generally matched Condon's description of Cemetery John.) According to the purser of a cruise ship bound for Chile on April 8, 1932, Borelli had hurriedly arrived by plane from New York to board the ship in Panama. Purser Humberto Pastori was surprised that the man possessed three passports but no visa. But what struck Pastori most was the extraordinary amount of cash Borelli carried. He deposited $30,000 in fives, tens and twenties for safekeeping on board (just six days after $50,000 in small bills was paid to Cemetery John in a Bronx cemetery). Borelli also talked obsessively about the Lindbergh baby kidnapping and claimed the perpetrator was on board. Pastori said he alerted the captain. The captain directed Pastori to give a report about this suspicious passenger to a company executive when the ship returned to New York later that month. Pastori swore he did so and was told in no uncertain terms to keep his mouth shut.

Another intriguing letter received by Governor Hoffman was signed "J.J. Faulkner," now claiming Hauptmann was innocent. (None of the handwriting experts employed by the state against Hauptmann had ever clained Hauptmann was the person who signed "J.J. Faulkner" on the deposit slip for nearly $3,000 in ransom money on May 1, 1933.) March of 1936 was the first time someone calling himself J.J. Faulkner had resurfaced since the spring of 1933. Hoffman's investigators believed that Faulkner was really the ex-spy and felon known as Jacob Nosovitsky, a connection Governor Hoffman wanted to pursue. In addition, the Governor received from J. Edgar Hoover an anonymous letter that had been sent to the FBI claiming Lindbergh engineered the kidnapping and death of his own son. It included some demonstrably false accusations but Hoffman believed it was worth looking into. Hoffman shared it with Attorney General Wilentz. All of these new potential leads were to no avail.

Gov. Harold Hoffman

The New Jersey Board of Pardons is shown on its way to the hearing in which Hauptmann was denied relief. Gov. Hoffman was the only member who believed there were too many unanswered questions about the case.

14.
"Old Smokey"

OVERWHELMING opposition to Governor Hoffman's and Lloyd Fisher's efforts to reinvestigate the case proved too powerful. Despite last minute appeals, Hauptmann was scheduled for execution in the electric chair on March 31, 1936. Outside the prison a large crowd gathered as the invited guests arrived, including thirty members of the press. Police officers who had participated in the investigation included Captain Lamb, Lieutenant Keaten and Inspector Walsh, accompanied by FBI agent Hicks. Yet Lloyd Fisher came running into the prison with surprising news. A grand jury investigating disbarred lawyer Paul Wendel's possible role in the case got the warden to postpone Hauptmann's date of execution three more days.

Hauptmann then wrote an article for *Liberty* Magazine to be published afer his death: "Why Did You Kill Me?" In it, Hauptmann summarized his life story and the evidence at trial that he had so much trouble believing resulted in his conviction. "I suppose that there will be in that chambers some of those who have had part in the preparation of my case for the prosecution. It is my belief that their suffering, their agony, will be greater than mine. Mine will be over in a moment. Theirs will last as long as life itself."

That Friday night, April 3, all the invited guests returned and took their places in the chamber. Lloyd Fisher came back one last time to bid Hauptmann good-bye. The minister gave Fisher a note Hauptmann had just written in German. His client now felt his soul full of "the love of Christ" and at peace "with no malice or hatred in my heart." Though he was "dying an innocent man" he felt his death would be purposeful if it helped abolish capital punishment.

Clad again in execution pants, with the crown of his head newly shaved, Hauptmann asked for a moment to view his two-year-old son Bubi's picture one more time before four guards marched him into the death chamber. Just prior to being strapped into the chair, Hauptmann made one final statement: "Ich bin absolut unschuldig an dem Verbrechen das man mir zur Last legt." The German-speaking Lutheran minister who accompanied Hauptmann into the execution room translated for the condemned man: "He says that he is absolutely innocent of the crime that has been laid at his door."

The straps made a cracking sound at 8:44 p.m. as the executioner repeatedly turned the wheel that sent three fatal jolts of electricity into Hauptmann's body. A plume of smoke emitted from Hauptmann's head as he slumped in death at 8:45 p.m. Within minutes, a half a mile away in a hotel room, Fisher's secretary told Anna Hauptmann the dreaded news. Anna locked herself in the bathroom and sobbed uncontrollably.

The execution made front page news in London as well as elsewhere around the world. The *New York Daily News* used its whole front page to display an artist's rendering of the execution under the banner headline "BRUNO DIES IN CHAIR." Just a week and a half after Hauptmann's execution, Lindbergh started openly debating with his British hosts whether he should go back and reform American politics. Like his lawyer Henry Breckinridge, Lindbergh had strong views about the state of the union. After Dwight Morrow died in October 1931, Lindbergh had felt free to assume the mantle of the family politician.

Lindbergh began testing his wings taking positions on public affairs with Populist speeches like his father had made about redistribution of wealth. Dwight Morrow would likely have been apoplectic, but the speeches resonated. Lindbergh's renewed interest in politics in the spring of 1936 was likely piqued by knowledge that Breckinridge was then launching a challenge to Franklin Delano Roosevelt for the Democratic presidential primary. Yet for now, Lindbergh decided to pursue "the bent of my mother's family rather than the bent of my father and follow mechanics and not politics." He was set on moving forward with Alexis Carrel's quest to lay the groundwork for organ transplants. Like Carrel, Lindbergh observed an overlap between the scientific experiments they were working on and the political reality of the ongoing Depression.

It may not have escaped Anne's notice at the time that Hauptmann's execution could have figured into her husband toying with the idea of returning so soon to America. But she likely was as much in the dark as the public that her husband had been sent a coded message from Henry Breckinridge that spring about getting police files on the kidnap/murder case transferred to Lindbergh's custody. Colonel Schwarzkopf and Attorney General Wilentz readily agreed to do so.

Anne's own thoughts about the conclusion of the case would remain private. Biographer Dorothy Herrmann noted: "her published diaries and letters for 1936 make no mention of either Hauptmann's execution or the crime that led up to it." It never occurred to Herrmann that Anne's husband hovered over her when she decided what to publish from those diaries and letters. One thing Anne should have realized is that by early April of 1936, their son Jon's safety was no longer the paramount concern Lindbergh had claimed just four months earlier when they abandoned the United States for England.

Still troubled by all the unanswered questions about the kidnapping, in July of 1936, Governor Hoffman put his own investigator, Leon Hoage, to work on the state's payroll to thoroughly reinvestigate the case. (Hoage had been working for Hoffman unofficially for at least several months before then). It would take Hoage another eight months to review the accumulated evidence and try to make sense of it.

Besides getting access to police records, Hoage received a photo of a small boy on a tricycle to follow up on. He believed it was taken of Charles Jr. shortly before he disappeared. Its date and subject are disputed to this day, but the photo fueled suspicion that the Lindberghs' son was still alive and the corpse belonged to a different child. That was what Detective Ellis Parker still believed. In a series of articles published in 1938, Governor Hoffman relied on Hoage's research to expose the many holes in the case that resulted in Hauptmann's execution. In his criticism of the trial, Hoffman quoted a New York trial lawyer who condemned the case as judicial lynching:

"[I]n the record compiled at the trial there is no more evidence that the man is guilty of murder than there is that you or I am. . . . No reasonable man can believe that an adult and a baby can fall off a ladder into soft mud without making an impression in the mud. No reasonable man can believe that the baby, in falling, can have its skull crushed in three places by the wall of a house or the rungs of the ladder without its brains and blood staining either the wall or the ladder, or the sleeping suit in which it is clad. In the alternative no reasonable man can believe that baby can be done to death in its cradle with a chisel without either the bedclothes or the chisel retaining any evidence of the deed."

Hoffman came to believe that Olly Whateley had been withholding information about the kidnapping and that Whateley's sudden death in May of 1933 was suspicious. Violet Sharp's apparent suicide also raised questions. Hoffman pointed out that despite millions of dollars spent and years of man hours "the crime of the century" remained shrouded in mystery:

"It was never proved that the child was killed on the Lindbergh premises. No one knows to this day, with the exception of those who participated in the crime whether the baby was smothered in his crib, whether its skull was crushed with the chisel or against the house or by a fall . . . or whether it was killed in some other way. No one knows whether the child was killed in Hunterdon County, where the trial was held, or in Mercer County, where the body was found. Neither is there proof that the baby did not meet its death in some other place than either of these counties."

Governor Hoffman ended his analysis of the case with many still-unanswered questions. In 1937, the American Bar Association had issued a scathing report on the unfairness of the publicity in the Hauptmann trial, calling the behavior of the press and radio commentators: "Perhaps, the most spectacular and depressing example of improper publicity and professional misconduct ever presented to the people of the United states in a criminal trial." In 1938, Governor Hoffman would predict: "Someday someone may supply the irrefutable answer to the question molded from all the enigmas of the Lindbergh crime: Did the wrong man die in the electric chair?"

Thousands gathered outside

Photographers were not allowed inside the prison. Newspapers sent sketch artists instead. Hauptmann was escorted to the electric chair by a Lutheran minister to whom he handed a note in German: his soul was full of "the love of Christ" and he was at peace "with no malice or hatred in my heart" even though he was "dying an innocent man." Hauptmann felt his death would be purposeful if it helped abolish capital punishment. Anna Hauptmann was staying at a hotel nearby and broke down in uncontrollable grief when she got the news of his execution.

Death Watch Trenton April 3, 1936

Reporters housed in a temporary newsroom in the prison waited for word Hauptmann was dead.

A huge crowd gathered outside the prison gates on April 4, 1936 to gawk as a police escort accompanied the hearse that would carry Hauptmann's body from the prison to a funeral parlor in New York City. Taking the casket out of state honored his widow's request. New Jersey forbade a public funeral for executed felons. His casket was then transferred in the dead of night in a second hearse to the Fresh Pond Crematory in Long Island where Anna Hauptmann and close to thirty friends and family held a private ceremony. Despite all precautions, word had gotten out. Some 2,000 people assembled across the street from the crematorium in case there might be something to see.

"Old Smokey"

"Old Smokey" is now on display at the New Jersey State Police Museum. Its most famous use was to execute Hauptmann on April 3, 1936. This electric chair was first put in place in 1907 to replace hanging. From then until 1963, 159 men were electrocuted by the state. New Jersey switched to lethal injections in 1983 and, in 2007, abolished capital punishment — in part based on studies that some of those convicted and condemned to death were in fact innocent. To this day, one out of every 25 death row inmates are eventually exonerated. Too often, the real perpetrators have eluded any punishment.

ACT FOUR

Nobel Prize-winner Dr. Alexis Carrel

The Rockefeller Institute for Medical Research

1.
Kindred Spirits

LINDBERGH took special notice of the artificial respirator that Dr. Paluel Flagg brought with him to attend his son's birth on June 22, 1930. Sometimes newborns needed mechanical help breathing. Lindbergh asked Dr. Flagg if Anne's sister Elisabeth might benefit from a similar mechanical pump for her weak heart. Earlier that summer, she had become ill again and left Englewood for the Morrows' summer home in Maine to recuperate. Dr. Flagg told Lindbergh he did not have that expertise, but he had worked as an intern years before for Dr. Alexis Carrel, a Nobel Prize-winning experimental surgeon at the Rockefeller Institute for Medical Research in New York. Carrel would be the right person to ask if any such device were feasible.

The day after Thanksgiving Lindbergh put on dark glasses and his fedora before heading to New York's upper East Side with Dr. Flagg to meet Dr. Carrel. Since November 1906, the vascular surgeon had been a fixture at the Rockefeller Institute for Medical Research, the nation's first institute dedicated to biomedical advancement. The institute's first director, Simon Flexner, hired Carrel at age 33 to head the experimental surgery department within months after it was fully launched. By the time Carrel arrived in America from his native France, he had already perfected a technique for joining blood vessels with tinier, more effective stitches than ever before — opening the door to huge advances in vascular surgery. By late 1930, when Lindbergh met the Nobel-prize-winning surgeon, Carrel's scientific achievements had made his name almost as well known to the public as Albert Einstein's.

Lindbergh had already become acquainted with the Rockefeller family whose philanthropy funded all the research. The family patriarch invited the nation's hero to his home in 1928, and sponsored Lindbergh's failed effort that spring to deliver life-saving serum to a fellow pilot in

Quebec. But Lindbergh had never been inside the five-story building in Manhattan which housed the institute. To avoid being spotted, Lindbergh and Flagg took the precaution of using a side entrance. Alerted ahead of time, Carrel's staff lined up at the windows on the top floor to be the first to see the famous pilot approach the building.

Upon meeting Lindbergh that first day, the five-foot-three Frenchman used his pince-nez to gaze intently up at the far taller man's face. Carrel wanted to see if he could get a sense of Lindbergh's soul before deciding that this was a man he could work with. Carrel believed in phrenology, a pseudoscience founded on the belief that personality traits were reflected in the physical features of the head. Looking down, Lindbergh got a close-up view of Dr. Carrel's mismatched brown and blue eyes. To Carrel, Lindbergh appeared the very embodiment of the Nordic supermen Carrel thought should people the earth in the future.

Lindbergh had grown up at a time in America that may have marked the height of white supremacy since colonial days. American politicians and captains of industry supported both genocidal practices at home and colonialism as foreign policy. Just four years before Lindbergh's birth, the United States annexed the Philippines, Guam, and Puerto Rico, won control of Cuba and acquired the Hawaiian Islands as a territory — what British poet Rudyard Kipling called "The White Man's Burden." In 1900, President McKinley ran for reelection with Spanish-American War hero Teddy Roosevelt and won handily with the slogan: "The AMERICAN FLAG has not been planted in foreign soil to acquire more territory but for HUMANITY'S SAKE."

During the next two decades, efforts to improve the human race through selective reproduction became the secular religion of those in power. In 1911, the American Breeders Association created a special new eugenics committee "to study and report on the best practical means for cutting off the defective germ-plasm of the American population." Dr. Carrel was among the leading doctors, political scientists, sociologists, judges and lawyers who lent their endorsements. Lindbergh's own father, Congressman C.A. Lindbergh, proudly proclaimed his membership in "the American Academy of Immortals" — white men of distinction listed in a Who's Who of that era.

Support for eugenics mushroomed in 1916 after New York lawyer Madison Grant published *The Passing of the Great Race*. As a Swedish immigrant, C.A. Lindbergh likely kept a copy in his home library. In it, Grant declared, "The Nordics are, all over the world, a race of soldiers, sailors, adventurers, and explorers, but above all, of rulers, organizers, and aristocrats." Grant feared the mixing of races. He proposed sterilizing "undesirables who crowd our jails, hospitals, and insane asylums." His aim was to cleanse the gene pool of "an ever-widening circle of social discards . . . [and then] weaklings rather than defectives, and perhaps ultimately . . . worthless race types." Leading high school biology texts soon advocated the adoption of the same techniques for humans as those employed to improve livestock. Five races of men were identified with European and American Caucasians representing "the highest type of all."

In the 1920s, efforts took off to reshape the American gene pool to strengthen the white population that had lost so many promising young men in the Great War. In 1922, Princeton Professor Carl Brigham published *A Study of Human Intelligence*, arguing that Army IQ tests developed during the war somehow "proved that the Nordic race was intellectually superior to Negroes, Jews, Italians and other ethnic groups." That same year, Dr. Harry Laughlin, the head of the influential Carnegie Institute Eugenics Records Office in New York, spearheaded a campaign for a model national law for compulsory sterilization. Included among the targets of Dr. Laughlin's model law were first and foremost those he labeled "criminalistic" (including the "delinquent and wayward"). Dr. Laughlin's list of undesirables extended to: "inebriates, the blind and deaf (and those with severely impaired sight or hearing), persons with deformities (including crippled persons), the insane, dependents (including orphans), ne'er-do-wells, the homeless [and] tramps . . .."

Dr. Laughlin and his colleagues in the American Eugenics Society were thrilled at their success when Justice Oliver Wendel Holmes delivered the 8-to-1 majority opinion for the high court in *Buck v. Bell:* "It is better for all the world, if instead of waiting to execute degenerate offspring for crime, or to let them starve for their imbecility, society can prevent those who are manifestly unfit from continuing their kind." That 1927 ruling prompted a major push to pass legislation to rid the country in future generations of "the socially inadequate" whom lawmakers labeled defectives, dependents and delinquents.

Eugenicists had been battling state courts since 1911 over the constitutionality of involuntary sterilization laws. They estimated as many as ten percent of Americans were of inferior stock and constituted "an economic and moral burden to the country." (With such laws validated, some 64,000 Americans, mostly women, would be sterilized from coast to coast from the first decade of the twentieth century through the 1960s.)

Lindbergh likely had concerns about his own son. Although Anne's obstetrician had said that the boy's oversized head at birth was similar to his grandfather's, reporters kept speculating whether he suffered damage in utero. The suggestion that it was Lindbergh's fault for taking his pregnant wife on a flight across country that caused her to suffer from oxygen deprivation made his blood boil. Media fixation on his son's health was one of the many reasons he had wanted to build a new home secluded from reporters' prying eyes. It was also likely why the Lindberghs joined the Breckinridges at the decennial children's health conference in Washington just the week before Thanksgiving.

Dr. Carrel likely knew just about everybody that the Lindberghs had just met at the conference. He had been a featured speaker at eugenics gatherings for over two decades, warning about the "serious menace" of diseases of the mind, "chiefly because they profoundly weaken the dominant white races." Carrel was among the medical experts consulted on those to target with involuntary sterilization laws. By 1930, he had long since been recognized as one of the most prominent proponents of eugenics in the world. But engaging with Dr. Carrel on that topic could wait. Lindbergh was focused on one thing only as he met the famed surgeon that day in November 1930 — trying to save Elisabeth's life.

Carrel sat patiently over lunch in the cafeteria with his two guests as Lindbergh poured out his ideas for a heart pump. Lindbergh appreciated being taken seriously by such an eminent surgeon. Carrel immediately saw major problems with Lindbergh's proposal, but was impressed with the aviator's enthusiasm. Back in 1910, Carrel had written up his attempt to achieve coronary bypass on a dog only to see the animal die. He told Lindbergh that attaching a mechanical pump to a human heart would invite infection and likely damage the delicate tissue. The main problem was that doctors still had no way of keeping a patient alive for the time it would take for surgeons to repair that patient's defective heart.

Carrel explained that one could operate on an anesthetized dog's or cat's heart for five minutes and bring it back, but after ten minutes they often "lost their soul." He claimed that, in his experience, humans could be resuscitated up to twenty minutes after their hearts stopped without experiencing brain damage — a highly dubious observation. Carrel was prone to exaggeration.

Carrel took Lindbergh and Flagg to the lab after lunch. First, he had the pair wash their hands thoroughly and each don a black gown and hood. Carrel did the same. One of the reasons Carrel insisted on donning black outfits in the lab was they made specks of dust easier to see. A hygienic environment was essential to keep the experiments germ-free. Yet one wonders how fastidious Carrel was. He sometimes absent-mindedly wore the black lab coat to the building's cafeteria.

Once inside, Lindbergh saw rows of caged cats and dogs with their backs shaved. He instantly became enthralled by the macabre experiments being conducted in the institute. Carrel and his staff would sometimes expose animals to infectious diseases kept in test tubes to see which medicines worked on the animals. Some had open wounds on which Carrel was testing out various antiseptics. (Lindbergh would soon be inspired to shave his own dog Skean for a several-week experiment, rendering the poor animal jumpy and afraid of human contact until its fur grew back.)

Carrel opened a refrigerator to show Lindbergh and Flagg jars that contained preserved animal organs. At extremely low temperatures some organs removed before or shortly after death could be kept alive independent of the body from which they were harvested. Carrel knew that skin could stay viable far longer than other organs; bones could maintain their transplant viability for eighteen hours if kept at zero degrees. Carrel described how in 1910 he had discovered that blood vessels from one animal could be grafted successfully to another animal two months later if, in the meanwhile, the blood vessels were refrigerated properly in saline solution or petroleum jelly. Carrel could easily excise organs from vivisected animals, but he had not yet been able to keep whole organs viable long enough for transplant, except by grafting a freshly obtained extra organ to a living animal.

Touring Carrel's lab opened Lindbergh's eyes to the world of medical research with both animal and human subjects. Since 1911 Carrel had experimented with isolating human tissue in vitro. Carrel showed Lindbergh the rudimentary "perfusion" pump an assistant had designed to keep organs oxygenated with circulated blood serum. He explained that in experiments to date organs quickly became infected and necrotic — dying within days. Lindbergh examined the pump closely and believed he could do a much better job.

After describing his tissue experiments, Carrel showed his famous visitor and Dr. Flagg another room housing mice he had been breeding since 1928 for a generously funded study of environmental effects on cancer. Carrel's mousery used at least twelve thousand, short-lived mice to test Darwin's theory of evolution by letting the dominant males kill weaker ones. He then mated only the largest and most disease-resistant mice. One of his key assistants in the mousery, Dr. Albert Ebeling, had been working under Carrel's supervision for nearly two decades.

Back in 1913, Ebeling had been focused on helping Carrel cultivate human tissue in vitro. Watching Ebeling conduct his mouse experiments, Carrel confided to Lindbergh: "If I could do the same tests on humans, I might produce a man who could jump twenty feet in the air and live to be two hundred." (In June of 1932, the medical facility's Board of Directors announced the expensive mousery would be discontinued.)

Although a shared zeal for eugenics was not the reason Lindbergh sought out Dr. Carrel, the pair soon bonded over that passion as well. Carrel lived in a bachelor apartment in New York. He invited his new protégé to join a dinner group in the city called the Philosopher's Club. The elite group included the leading proponents of eugenics as well as a Columbia University dean and future Supreme Court Justice

Benjamin Cardozo, among other luminaries. When given an opportunity to share his views, Carrel spoke forcefully on the bold topic that preoccupied him more and more — how to save the world from further degradation of its gene pool and foster a superior race. His ideas would later be captured in his 1935 best-seller *L'Homme, cet Inconnu* (*Man, The Unknown*).

Carrel firmly believed that the Western world was failing because the "white race was drowning in a sea of inferiors." Carrel considered the "ideal solution . . . to suppress each of these individuals as soon as he has proven himself to be dangerous." Carrel felt strongly that medical science should not be focused on reducing the mortality rates of all humans, but only those deemed worthy of reproducing. He held the same view of political goals. The West was in decline because Socialist governmental programs like those being advocated to help millions of America's needy citizens during the Depression "interfered with natural selection" by "coddling the unfit."

Biographer Walter Ross would later note that "except perhaps Carrel" Lindbergh seemed to exhibit "no real warmth" for any of his many acquaintances throughout his career. Ross also noted that Carrel exercised "tremendous influence" over Lindbergh "not all for the good." Carrel was already planning to write at length about societal restrictions on who should be allowed to procreate and who should be "humanely and economically disposed of in small euthanistic institutions supplied with the proper gasses . . . Why preserve useless and harmful beings?" In the category of "those who should be dead" Carrel included "the weak, the diseased and the fools." He suggested that it would be most "effective to kill off the worst and keep the best, as we do in breeding dogs . . . the old order must die so that the new order lives." Among leading eugenicists of the time, Carrel was hailed as an impassioned visionary.

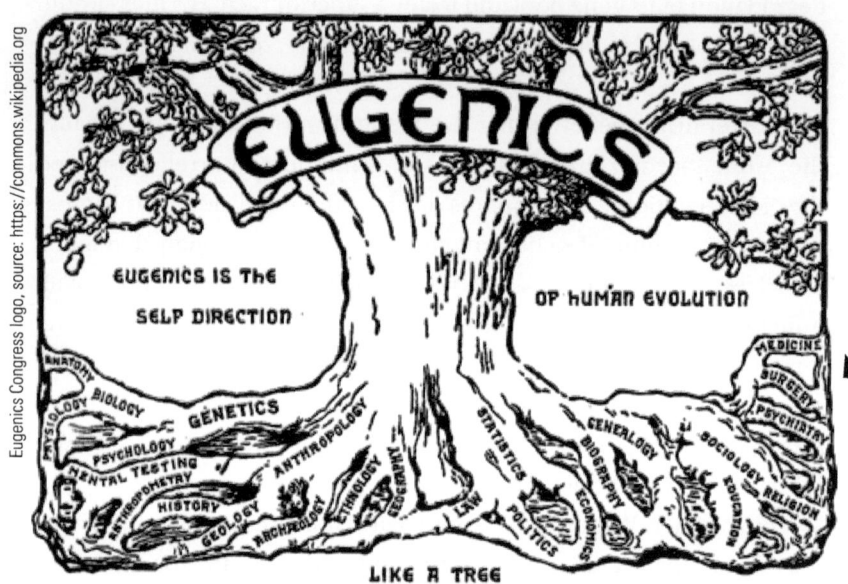

This is the logo from the Second International Eugenics Congress in New York in 1921. Research surgeon Dr. Alexis Carrel was among its most prominent members. He had helped organize the first such conference in London in 1912 with Darwin's son as its honorary head and Winston Churchill among the ardent attendees. The arrow points to surgery as one of the roots to the eugenics tree of evolving human life. Following World War I, efforts to improve the human race through selective reproduction became the secular religion of white Anglo-Saxons in power in England and the United States.

2.
"The High Priest of Biology"

WORKING with such a world-renowned scientist as Carrel and his talented research team gave Lindbergh a unique opportunity to leverage his own mechanical know-how to help launch the possibility of organ transplants. Dr. Carrel exuded self-confidence. Actually, his early medical career had taken a disastrous turn in France just four years before Flexner hired him. As a surgical resident in Lyons, Carrel drew the wrath of both medical colleagues and the Catholic Church following an embarrassing incident in 1902.

Carrel had volunteered to accompany pilgrims headed to Lourdes for a miracle cure for debilitating illnesses. He expected to discredit claims that the spring at the holy site had extraordinary healing powers. Instead, he bore witness to the immediate recovery of a deathly-ill young woman after she was sprinkled with holy water. A newspaper article quoted Carrel acknowledging the event as a miracle, which he immediately disavowed. He claimed that the cure was baffling, but not proof of divine intervention. From then on, he became a target of ridicule by both French scientists and Church leaders for taking a position neither side endorsed. Efforts to reconcile science and religious miracles would intrigue him throughout his life.

Speaking only French and discouraged about his future in his own country, Carrel emigrated to Montreal and then to Chicago. In his first practice in the United States, he had patients assigned to him, but much preferred working with colleagues conducting animal vivisections. He stopped seeing patients in 1905 and began focusing on experimental blood vessel surgery, mostly using dogs, as Carrel had some experience with before he left France. From his first days at the Rockefeller Institute, Carrel enjoyed great latitude in the conduct of his department. Secrecy shrouded experiments that might well appear callous and sadistic to outsiders or staff with weak stomachs. The supply of animals the institute kept for experimental use included stray cats and dogs that staff paid neighborhood volunteers twenty-five to fifty cents apiece to round up.

In his first few years at the Rockefeller Institute, Carrel weathered adverse publicity generated by anti-vivisectionists. The key in fending off animal cruelty charges was to rebut claims that he subjected cats and dogs to "unnecessary suffering." Among the accusations was that he severed limbs from dogs and left them to die while he transplanted the limbs to other dogs to see if they would take. Carrel defended himself in a sworn statement that his team sedated a dog into unconsciousness before amputating its leg and that death occurred either just before or right after the amputation while the dog remained unconscious. Carrel had earlier worked with American surgeon Charles Guthrie who infamously transplanted a severed dog's head to the neck of another living dog without success.

Members of the press changed their dim view of Carrel's handling of laboratory animals in 1908 when he saved the infant daughter of a well-known physician by a daring transfusion from her father. Other colleagues put their animal experiments to good use in addressing diseases that then plagued New York and other cities. Soon, both the press and the general public accepted the assurances of research scientists that the suffering they inflicted was necessary and kept to a minimum. Instead of "do no harm," experimental surgeons focused on the lesser harm. The medical community received high praise for developing break-throughs to reduce recurrent epidemics of smallpox, dysentery, cholera and other deadly diseases. In fact, looking back today, observers have noted that over the past century, approximately four out of five Nobel prizes in medicine were awarded for experiments with animals.

All along Carrel engaged in unabashed self-promotion. In 1910 he succeeded in maintaining a dog's carotid artery in cold storage for 72 days before successfully transplanting it. The dog lived another five months before it was vivisected. That same year Carrel and colleague Montrose Burrows published a series of articles on their newly coined study of "tissue culture." The pair harvested specimens of tissue from mammals and kept the samples viable for days bathed in blood plasma. By placing the specimens inside clear glass structures lab workers could observe how they functioned and grew.

In 1911, Carrel made an extraordinary presentation at a conference of surgeons in which he boasted of successful interspecies surgery. He had transplanted a human kidney to a dog that lived another two years. No one apparently asked how he obtained the human donor. (In 1909, Carrel had inquired of authorities if condemned prisoners could be experimented upon.) Ever since the experiments of army surgeon Dr. William Beaumont in the 1830s, American physicians had been taught Beaumont's Code — to only work with living humans after receiving their informed consent which could be withdrawn at any time. Yet Beaumont's Code was often ignored if the patients lacked the power to protect themselves. Dr. J. Marion Sims, the "father of modern gynecology," gained his pioneering insights into obstetrics by performing experiments without anesthesia on African American women slaves.

Under Dr. Flexner's leadership, the Institute fostered human research as well as animal research. Throughout the early twentieth century, doctors often engaged in experiments subjecting unknowing patients to disease, pain, mutilation, and even death. One of Carrel's colleagues would be sued in 1913 after he injected adults and children with supposedly inactive syphilis to develop a skin test. In 1931, Rockefeller pathologist Cornelius Rhoads wrote a letter boasting he killed eight Puerto Rican patients through cancer injections as a step toward exterminating their race. A public scandal resulted. Rhoads claimed he was being sarcastic. The Institute rose to his defense in what Puerto Ricans considered a whitewash. A government investigation found no wrongdoing.

Most infamous was the 40-year, federally funded study by both Rockefeller and Johns Hopkins researchers that started in 1932 and involved untreated syphilis in hundreds of unsuspecting black sharecroppers. The men treated at Tuskegee University were told only that the government was providing them with free medical care; 600 syphilis sufferers were given only placebos.

In the second decade of the twentieth century, Carrel and Burrows gained recognition for hugely expanding laboratory study of cultured embryos to "the cultivation of all kinds of tissues, embryonic and adult, amphibian, mammalian and human, normal and pathological." Carrel learned that human tissue quickly died after removal. The possibility of human organ transplants continued to tantalize him. Yet the method remained elusive. Other pioneering experiments included unsuccessful attempts to preserve human sperm. Carrel enjoyed testing the limits of his imagination of what might be possible.

In 1912, for his pioneering work in vascular surgery, Carrel became the youngest person ever to be awarded the Nobel prize for Medicine and Physiology. It was a moment of great personal triumph. It also marked the first time the prize went to a scientist based in the United States, establishing him beyond any doubt as the Rockefeller Institute's greatest star. (Dr. Guthrie was a leading contender as well, but colleagues assumed that the notoriety over his failed dog head transplant ruined his chances.) That same year the *New York Times* lauded Carrel's successful human skin grafts using infant tissue coated in Vaseline and kept in cold storage. Healing leg wounds was a talent Carrel would later put to great use when the French government called him to serve during World War I to patch up soldiers who suffered extensive burns.

In 1913, Carrel married an accomplished French widow, Anne de la Meyrie Motte, who had a nine-year-old son. The couple would have no children together. The two first met when she accompanied pilgrimages to Lourdes. At the time they married she was working as a nurse for a surgeon in Paris. The couple moved to New York where Mme. Carrel volunteered in his laboratory and helped write up the results of key experiments. Yet she grew increasingly homesick. During World War I, they both served in French hospitals and then returned to New York. In 1922, Mme. Carrel moved back to France where the Carrels soon bought an island home off the coast of Brittany with proceeds from his Nobel prize. Her husband joined her there each summer but kept working the rest of the time doing research for the Rockefeller Institute in New York and New Jersey.

Since 1912, Carrel had amazed the scientific world by keeping living tissue pulsating in a specially designed, clear glass flask. He announced that the tissue came from an embryonic chicken heart. He and his staff periodically cleansed the flask of waste and then added nutrients to this self-regenerating tissue, which he dubbed his "immortal" chicken heart. Beginning in 1913 Carrel's team took pictures of the cultured cells at equally spaced intervals so progress over time could be directly observed. He realized that by projecting the photos one after another every few seconds cell behavior could be observed on a movie screen. At conferences with other scientists his films awed both colleagues and reporters.

Carrel boasted to the press that his chicken-heart experiment would lay the groundwork for human organ transplants. He was confident that the same method of preservation would apply to most human body parts. Not until decades later would research scientists conclude that the original tissue Carrel put in the flask had not survived as he had boasted. It was additional tissue that he or his staff added over time that got him accolades for a break-through he had not achieved. Experiments in the 1960s would show that living cells of all types have only so much capacity for reproduction, replicating themselves generally fifty times before they died. But that discovery did not take away from Carrel's other medical achievements transforming vascular surgery.

Though medical research scientists like Carrel relied heavily on animal experiments, Carrel was among those who believed the best information could only be derived from studying the organs of humans themselves. In fact, Carrel's personal files from January 1932 contain a handwritten note suggesting his most famous experiment begun in 1912 may have gone far further than the public was led to believe. A newspaper clipping acknowledged the twentieth anniversary of harvested embryonic chicken-heart tissue still pulsating in vitro. The word "chicken's" from the headline is crossed out, and "human" is written in blue ink over it. (Back in the 1910s Carrel had acknowledged experimenting with human embryos as well as those of lower animals. In 2018, Rockefeller's medical researchers announced they were conducting similar experiments in which they observed the growth of hybrid cells created by transplanting cells from human embryos into chicken embryos).

The use of discarded human embryos remains controversial in the 21st century. Back in the early twentieth century far less information became public knowledge when human guinea pigs were subjected to experimentation. Doctors then were far less regulated in that era of medical "paternalism — physicians presumed they knew better than others and had no qualms experimenting on patients without permission or even despite objections, all for the sake of science." People who were most available for experimentation were prisoners or patients in hospitals, asylums or orphanages. All that doctors needed was the consent of the men or, more rarely, women in charge of such institutions. By 1911, Dr. Carrel had already begun cultivating relationships with institutional administrators in New Jersey. By 1912, key executives of the Skillman Village for Epileptics provided the exhibits for the first International Eugenics Conference that Carrel helped organize. During the next three decades, Skillman and Vineland Villages remained laboratories for gathering data to support Carrel and other leading eugenicists.

Like his prominent French colleague Serge Voronoff, Carrel urged researchers to conduct more human experiments because no other animal came close to providing data as valuable. Voronoff argued for the creation of special hospitals in each city to create organ banks with refrigerated, healthy body parts replenished on a regular basis by victims of accidental death. Carrel had a more daring ambition. In his 1925 journal Carrel wrote: "Si nous ne risquons jamais rien, nous ne gagnerons jamais rien. Le conservateur qui désire etre toujours à l'abri, en sûreté, est un etre desséché." In English: "If we don't risk anything, we never gain anything. The conservative who always wants to be in a shelter, in safety, is a dried up being." His next journal entry was in the same vein. Translated to English it reads: "Don't pay attention to criticism. It comes generally from men who never have done anything and who rejoice if defeat follows your action, in order to use that defeat to justify their own propensity to do nothing."

Carrel recognized that the biggest hurdle was that, unlike with animal experimentation, society did not condone deliberate killing of any humans in the interests of science:

> "One has not done it for man until now, due to the difficulty of the subject and the impossibility of applying to human beings the methods that have succeeded for the improvement of the animal kingdom. . . . [T]he problem is infinitely more complex when it is a question of ameliorating the human organism with its extremely powerful and delicate nervous system, held as one is to respecting individual liberty."

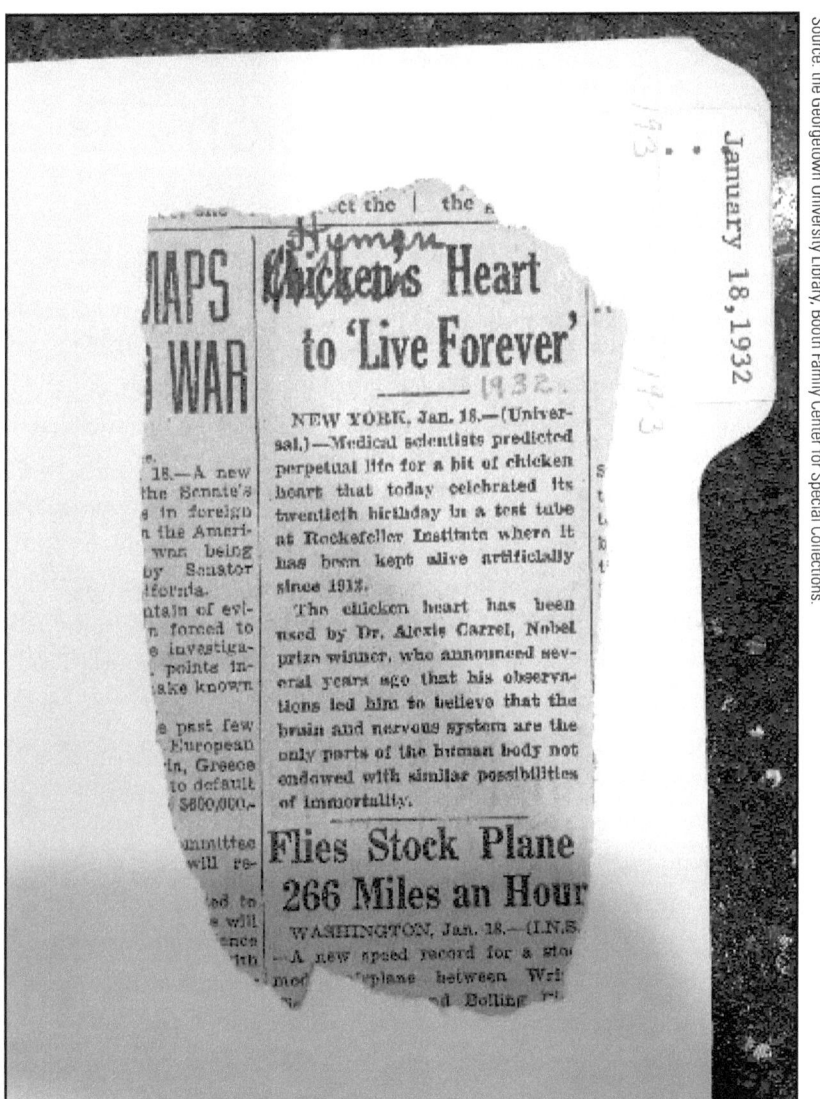

Annotated newspaper clipping in Dr. Carrel's files dated January 18, 1932 celebrating the 20th anniversary of Carrel's world-famous 1912 "chicken-heart" experiment. The article noted Carrel's boast that the same result would occur for most human body parts. The word "chicken's" is crossed out in pen in the heading and "Human" handwritten over it.

3.
A New Mission

WHEN he returned to New Jersey from his first visit to the Rockefeller lab in Manhattan, Lindbergh quickly sketched out his own design for a perfusion pump. He then delivered it to Carrel's glassblower, Otto Hopf, who operated a lab in the basement of the Rockefeller Institute headquarters. Lindbergh must have felt he was working against time to save Elisabeth's life. In January 1931 Lindbergh began secretly driving to the Manhattan lab as the surgeon's guest worker. Soon, Lindbergh realized that regular access to the lab was worth the long commute. Biographer A. Scott Berg notes: "Lindbergh put in long weeks in Carrel's laboratory . . . If he [Charles] could not put aside a day to get into the city, he would work in one of the laboratories at Princeton." Lindbergh was soon trusted with his own keys to the Manhattan lab so he could come and go at all hours. Such access to an inner sanctum of the secretive research facility was highly irregular, but after nearly a quarter of a century at the Rockefeller Institute Carrel had become "the pet" of its directors. Wealthy patrons of the institute provided Carrel with "almost anything that he wanted" because they were "so awed and gratified by his world fame."

Lindbergh felt similar wonderment in Carrel's operating room as he experienced as a child visiting the basement lab where his mother's father practiced taxidermy. Grandfather Land had given Charles a lifelong belief in science as God. Lindbergh's mother likely also told her son about her maternal grandfather Dr. Edwin A. Lodge, who conducted experiments in homeopathic medicine. (Evangeline likely did not share that in 1862 Dr. Lodge was prosecuted for manslaughter after a black servant suddenly convulsed and died in his home. Dr. Lodge had given the woman over forty drops of poisonous woodbine as an experiment because the vegetable had some perceived healthful properties. Part of Dr. Lodge's defense was that he had also tested the homeopathic remedy in much smaller doses on himself and his children. Dr. Lodge was acquitted.)

Though Lindbergh kept to himself at the lab, Carrel's teammates were thrilled to have the celebrity on board. Every time he signed his name on lunch slips the autograph was grabbed for a souvenir. The staff also learned to tolerate Lindbergh's practical jokes. His favorite was putting a full water bucket above a laboratory door so the next person who opened it would get drenched.

On January 21, 1931, Lindbergh also made a secret visit to the Carnegie laboratory and Eugenics Records Office in Cold Spring Harbor, where he met Dr. Laughlin and other leading eugenicists. They probably did not expect him to know much about their field, but it flattered them to host such a celebrity. It was common knowledge that Lindbergh had never finished college, so they were impressed with pointed questions and interest in their heredity exhibits. He had obviously boned up on the subject before his arrival.

Of greatest urgency to Lindbergh, however, was saving Elisabeth. When he first came to Carrel's lab, he wanted to observe how the prototype perfusion device operated. Carrel wasted no time scheduling a cat vivisection. His surgical suite at the Rockefeller Institute was quite elaborate. Animals were first taken to a room where they were etherized, and their fur shaved off the area where the incision would be made. In the next room, staff sterilized the animals' skin. The surgery team got themselves ready in another room. Last, and most important, was the operating room itself, which was painted gray with black floors. Since the department was located on the top floor of the Institute, the operating room took advantage of natural lighting from a large skylight.

A sterilization team headed by Carrel's chief nurse had the task of steaming instruments for two hours beforehand. They then protected the instruments with a black sheet while spraying the room with bacteria-killing disinfectant. Perfusion pumps and other equipment were kept scrupulously clean to avoid the risk of infection once an organ or blood vessel was mounted in the central chamber on two insertable glass tubes (cannulas) — one that admitted blood serum, the other that allowed waste to escape.

Carrel was proud of the fact that his assistant Dr. Ebeling had figured out how to manufacture cannulas just under three inches long and only half a millimeter in diameter (less than two-hundredths of an inch). These tiny tubes could be inserted into rabbit and cat arteries without puncturing their delicate walls. Each cannula had sterilized rubber tubing on one end. To keep air from getting in, they were soaked in a filtered isotonic salt solution known as Ringer's Solution. A special, tiny clamp known as mosquito forceps was needed to manipulate the cannulas during the operation. Sometimes, the team also required a special plate made of a thin sheet of mica to hold a particularly delicate specimen.

The subject of the experiment remained covered in a black sheet while awaiting the operation. A nurse kept handy more Ringer's solution and bacteria-killing disinfectant for use during the operation, as well as gauze pads and sterile cellophane. Carrel and his assistants washed up thoroughly and dressed in their black gowns and hoods. Rubber overshoes were also available to minimize the potential for contamination. Only their eyes could be seen through slits in the hoods, adding mystery to the life and death drama they regularly performed. To a later generation, their garb might call to mind a scene from the satanic movie *Rosemary's Baby*.

Lindbergh was awestruck at the opportunity to join the surgical team in the darkened surgery. Watching Carrel closely as the surgeon bent over the trunk of an etherized cat, Lindbergh could see that Carrel concentrated so heavily on his task that his eyelids rarely flickered. Carrel manipulated the tiny mosquito scissors with practiced agility as he cut the cat's arteries and sewed up the ends with silk thread — a skill he sometimes performed with just one hand. "Then came the quick, confident motions of Carrel's scalpel" as he excised an organ with connective tissue and blood vessels, demonstrating both "precision and economy of effort." Carrel had mastered his impressive knotting technique by training himself to use an index finger and middle finger to tie two strips of catgut together so tightly the knot could not be manually undone. He practiced by first placing the catgut in a small box where he presumably could not see what his fingers were doing.

Lindbergh noticed that Carrel checked to see if any blood remained in a removed artery segment. If so, the surgeon used finger pressure to remove it before inserting silk threads in each end, making a slit in the segment and washing off any further blood that came out of it. Then Carrel inserted each cannula, being careful to avoid letting air in before tying the silk thread. Only then was the specimen ready for transfer to the perfusion pump.

As a teenager, Lindbergh had experienced the omnipresence of death on his farm. He had already decided, "There was nothing good about death; it was terrible." It reinforced his trust in science rather than a religious God. Observing Carrel and his staff in action made Lindbergh feel he could "see across the border separating life from death. . . . The boldness of these biological inquiries shook the pilot to his core." Lindbergh was drawn like a magnet to watch blood be drained from an animal while its heart still pumped and lungs inflated and contracted in a vain effort to keep the creature alive. The transition from life to death happened right in front of his eyes.

Among Carrel's most daring experiments with cats were those in which he cut out the cerebrum — the part of the brain that controls higher functions like memory — but left the animals alive. As a result, each "decerebrated" cat lost its ability to learn from experience. Starting decades before Lindbergh met him, Carrel had attempted to see if cats could be revived after being put in cold storage. He found that the brain could not survive that process. He then hit upon the idea of eliminating a fully functioning brain while the rest of the animal was kept alive refrigerated in a special solution. Carrel described his technique as whole-body perfusion. Lindbergh saw the results of a brain-dead cat whose eyes still functioned and could still be fed and use its claws.

After the organs were harvested, Lindbergh observed the next step performed by Carrel's team. One lab technician was charged with placing specimens in the perfusion pump. That assistant also prepared sections of tissue for viewing and photographing under a microscope. Another key participant was Dr. Lillian Baker, a then rare female medical research doctor whom Carrel had relied upon to assist his department for more than a decade in both the satellite laboratory in Princeton and the Rockefeller Institute's headquarters in Manhattan. Dr. Baker oversaw the vital task of preparing the serum needed for the pump. A few technicians under her direction ensured smooth operation of the pump and helped Dr. Baker track the results of each experiment.

Lindbergh wanted to assist, too, but had trouble at first figuring out at what point the possibility of bacterial contamination was introduced. He watched several more organ experiments with the perfusion pump before diagnosing a design problem: a moving piston touched the serum in the pump. That was what gave rise to infection. Lindbergh soon improved the design enough that the new device could stay sterile. Yet once tested with newly harvested organs, the new pump was no more effective in keeping organs pulsating with "life" than the one it replaced. Undaunted, Carrel invited Lindbergh to keep trying.

When Lindbergh became Carrel's protégé, the two connected both as men of science and at the spiritual level. Carrel likely knew that in pagan witchcraft the color black is traditionally used for communication with the dead, yet also signifies a new beginning. Like Carrel, Lindbergh had personal experience to draw on for belief in the occult. In the last leg of his historic flight, Lindbergh had an out-of-body experience where his mind and spirit seemed independent of his physical being. As he later wrote in his Pulitzer-Prize winning book *The Spirit of St. Louis*, the cockpit seemed populated by talking ghosts he saw all around him through "one great eye" without shifting his gaze. Since then Lindbergh had regarded death in a new light, not as final but "the entrance to a new and free existence which includes all space, all time." Lindbergh worked by himself, often past midnight. Each time he designed an improved model perfusion pump, Carrel was eager to obtain organs to test it.

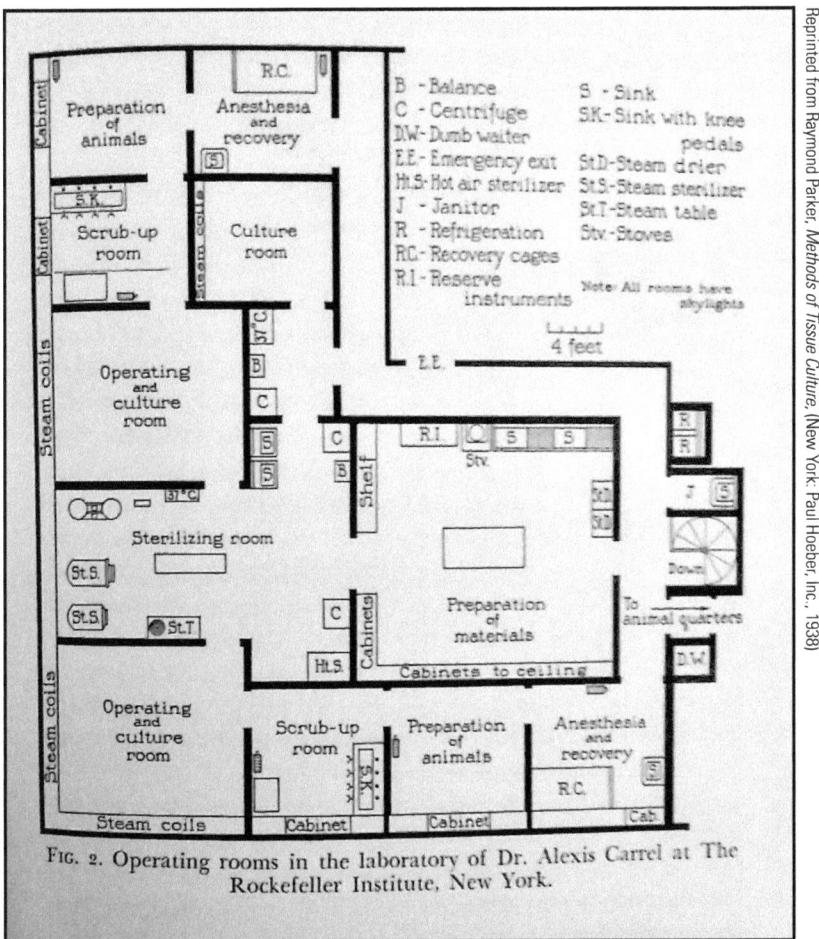

FIG. 2. Operating rooms in the laboratory of Dr. Alexis Carrel at The Rockefeller Institute, New York.

Realizing that the operating facilities Carrel's team had been provided at the Rockefeller Institute's headquarters were far more elaborate than most research doctors could expect, Carrel's assistant Dr. Raymond C. Parker wrote a manual providing diagrams of how similar experiments could be conducted in a three-room, five-room or six-room operating suite by doubling up on compatible activities.

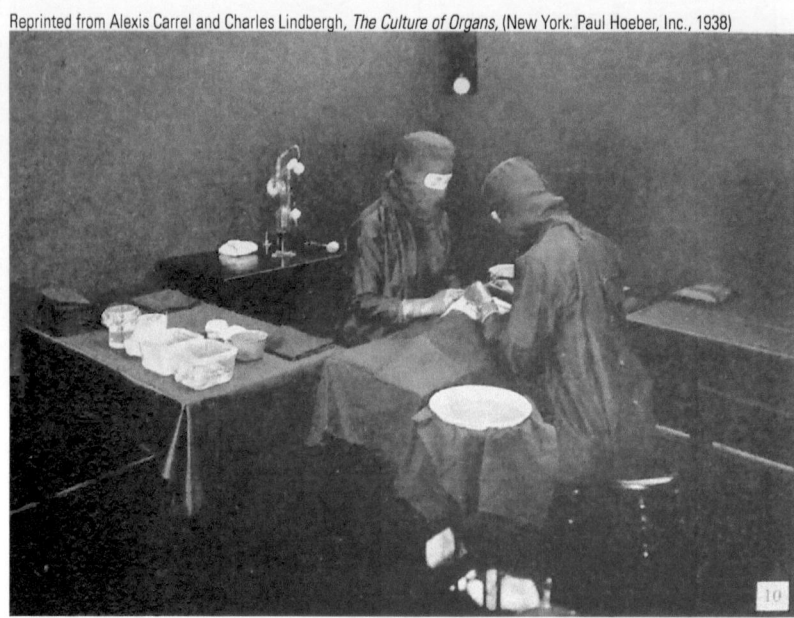

Reprinted from Alexis Carrel and Charles Lindbergh, *The Culture of Organs*, (New York: Paul Hoeber, Inc., 1938)

Inside Dr. Carrel's Operating Room

Carrel used extraordinary precautions to ensure a bacteria-free environment for his perfusion experiments — black gowns and hoods were worn by all team members in the operating room. The walls were painted gray and the floor black so any specks would be more visible.

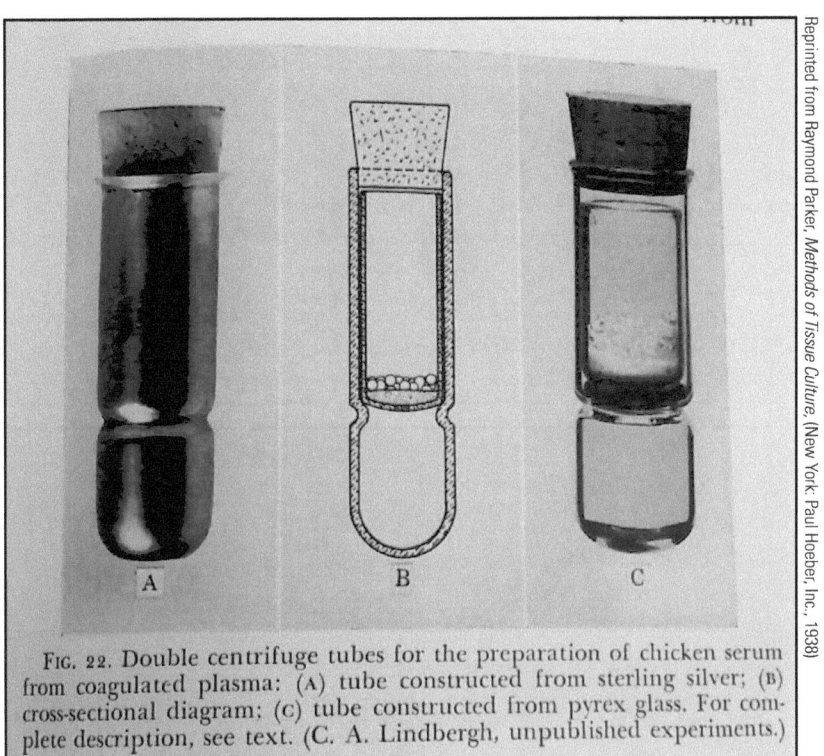

FIG. 22. Double centrifuge tubes for the preparation of chicken serum from coagulated plasma: (A) tube constructed from sterling silver; (B) cross-sectional diagram; (C) tube constructed from pyrex glass. For complete description, see text. (C. A. Lindbergh, unpublished experiments.)

Lindbergh's double centrifuge tubes. One of Lindbergh's innovations was to introduce white sand into the centrifuge to streamline the cleansing process.

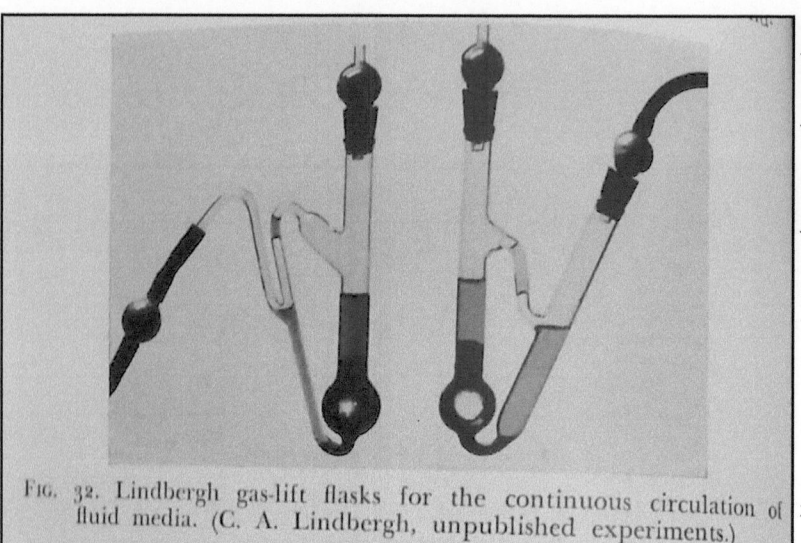

FIG. 32. Lindbergh gas-lift flasks for the continuous circulation of fluid media. (C. A. Lindbergh, unpublished experiments.)

FIG. 33. Lindbergh gas-lift flasks assembled as in use (Compare Fig. 32).

Lindbergh's "gas-lift" perfusion flask

In the preface to his book, Methods of Tissue Culture, *Dr. Parker thanked Lindbergh for allowing him to publish the first photos of Lindbergh's apparatus.*

4.
A Breakthrough at the Lab

LINDBERGH'S volunteer work at the Rockefeller Institute remained a well-kept secret throughout 1931, even after the Institute published an anonymous article describing an early model of Lindbergh's improved perfusion device. Carrel was excited about another development as well. At a scientific conference later that year, Carrel's long-time assistant Dr. Albert Ebeling presented a new technique for measuring chemical changes in cells. Ebeling reported the exciting news that Carrel's lab technicians believed they could create a "virtual" motion picture for measuring chemical changes in cell life.

Carrel saw great potential for filming organ perfusion in Lindbergh's device. But the slowness of creating the necessary serum was a major impediment that needed to be addressed first. Using the subject's own blood increased the chances of keeping a specimen alive in the pump because it was the most compatible source of oxygenation available. Yet blood was of no use once it coagulated. To prevent coagulation in the perfusion pump, Carrel's associate, Dr. Lillian Baker, created a serum from blood by washing off the corpuscles and isolating the plasma. She then combined the plasma with Phenol red dye and other additives. If the subject was too small to provide sufficient blood for the serum needed, Dr. Baker would make a special serum from ox blood instead.

Lindbergh had noticed when he first started working at the lab that technicians engaged in a two-step process to perform that task. First, at the end of every vivisection they drained the animal's blood. Then it would be cleansed and converted to serum. Working with Dr.

Ralph W.G. Wyckoff, who specialized in centrifuges at the Rockefeller Institute, Lindbergh designed an improved conical centrifuge that could perform both steps at the same time. By different sized openings on each end, Lindbergh regulated the flow to leave corpuscles suspended inside the chamber.

Lindbergh completed his last test on dog blood on February 24, 1932. The centrifuge process was now far faster than before. Carrel could not wait to announce to the medical world that Lindbergh had just revolutionized a task routinely performed in research labs several times per day. The fact "a college dropout with no formal training in biology could . . . immediately begin producing world-class work" for the Rockefeller laboratory was "less astounding than it sounds." While major developments had occurred in applied science and technology in the last few decades, researchers in medicine lagged woefully behind. As noted by Lindbergh biographer Joyce Milton: "Bio-engineering was in its infancy."

Ever the showman, Carrel wanted to reveal Lindbergh's affiliation in spectacular fashion. Keeping the collaboration with Carrel and his team secret until the article about Lindbergh's invention was published would guarantee that the news drew extraordinary attention. No members of the public were then aware that the aviator's mechanical genius had any application beyond aviation. The huge improvement in the speed of washing fresh blood Lindbergh had just achieved was critical to moving forward with the next stage of Dr. Carrel's perfusion experiments. At first, Lindbergh shared with his wife some of the details of the laboratory work that kept him so excited. He told her of seeing chicken heart tissue pulsating in a glass vial and watching cats be vivisected to learn more about blood flow. She preferred to be spared the gory details.

Mme. Carrel, who had lived in France for the past decade, made a special trip to New York to join her husband in February. Anne Lindbergh wrote to her mother-in-law to share how thrilled her husband was to work with Carrel at the institute. She had "never seen him as happy" as when he was at the lab. Lindbergh had just taken a break from his lab work to fly Mme. Carrel and the Ebelings on a short trip. It seemed to Anne that he had quickly made friends at the Institute, but he was "very secretive and shy" about what they were doing, though she realized it had something to do with blood work.

On Saturday morning, February 27, 1932, Lindbergh left the Morrow Estate to drive to work at the Rockefeller Institute before he picked up the Breckinridges that afternoon and headed to the farmhouse to join Anne and his son. When Lindbergh left the farmhouse Monday morning, the 29th, he went back to the institute. He may have dined with the Carrels. Where he stayed that night is uncertain. Lindbergh returned to spend some part of Tuesday at the lab before coming back to the farmhouse for dinner. His son disappeared later that night.

On March 3rd, the Lindberghs made public the missing toddler's diet and a description of strong medicine for rickets the child took daily. For his own use, Dr. Carrel created a separate file at his lab to include both a newspaper clipping of that diet and a retyped copy headed "Diet Given by Mrs. Lindbergh to her son, March, 1932."

Meanwhile, Lindbergh worked hand in glove with the state police during the media circus that developed around efforts to find the boy alive and return him to his parents. When the announcement of Lindbergh's centrifuge invention and his affiliation with the Rockefeller Institute became public in mid-April, both he and Carrel indicated that Lindbergh did all of that work before the end of February. Undisclosed internal documentation at the institute suggested otherwise.

DIET GIVEN BY MRS. LINDBERGH TO HER SON,
MARCH, 1932.

One quart of milk during the day.
Three tablespoonfuls of cooked cereal morning and night.
Two tablespoonfuls of cooked vegetables once a day.
One yolk of egg daily.
One baked potato or rice once a day.
Two tablespoonfuls of stewed fruit daily.
Half a cup of orange juice on waking.
Half a cup of prune juice after the afternoon nap.
Fourteen drops of medicine called Viosterola during the day.

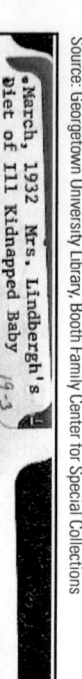

Charles, Jr.'s Diet

This is a typed copy in Dr. Carrel's files of the diet published by the Lindberghs on March 3, 1932 to try to get the kidnappers to follow to keep their son healthy until he was reunited with his parents.

5.
The Landmark Experiment

ON LEAP DAY, February 29, 1932 — the day before Little Charlie disappeared from his nursery — Carrel's department billed the institute for exceptionally expensive new lab equipment to implement Wyckoff's new method for filming living cells. Carrel's chief nurse ran interference with the institute's bureaucracy. The experiment was one Carrel had awaited with great anticipation. Mme. Carrel likely stayed to lend a hand with this important project.

For the upcoming experiment, two lab assistants would be specifically assigned to photograph sections of tissue placed on slides. In addition to Lindbergh, the key members of Carrel's team included Dr. Raymond Parker, who conducted his own fibroblast experiments on animals and humans, and Dr. Lillian Baker, who was the serum specialist for both Drs. Parker and Carrel. (Dr. Parker would later become famous for his contribution to the Salk polio vaccine.)

Dr. Parker later described in a manual how Carrel's team conducted carotid artery experiments. Two tables were set up — one for the instruments, the other for the subject to be operated on. The procedure was essentially the same for mammals as it was for chickens. The participants scrubbed up and put on their protective gear which, for maximum protection from bacterial contamination, included sterile gowns, rubber gloves, and rubber footwear. (Lindbergh may have had to order his shoes specially to fit his unusually large 11D feet.) The etherist meanwhile strapped the subject face up to the operating board and placed a towel over it before taking it to the operating room. Parker instructed other researchers who wished to replicate their experiments that a chicken should be etherized "just enough to keep it fairly quiet." No different instruction was suggested when operating on mammals.

Carrel needed the help of several assistants. During the carotid artery operation, the etherist held the subject's neck steady while another assistant managed the bleeding tubes. Each tube had been lined in advance with paraffin and chilled. Dr. Baker's role was to have each tube of drawn blood refrigerated as soon as it was obtained. Then the blood would be run as quickly as possible through a centrifuge to separate the plasma and create serum. One of Lindbergh's duties was to make sure there were no problems with the speedy operation of the centrifuge. He had made an improvement to its filter system using white sand.

To begin the operation, the neck area was swabbed with iodine and covered with a four-and-a-half-foot black cotton sheet. (Since medical linens were typically white, it was likely dyed in house.) The sheet had a narrow, five-inch-long oval opening that Carrel placed directly over the neck area where he intended to make his incision. Carrel used forceps to clamp the cloth on both ends of the opening to the subject's skin. Carrel then used a scalpel to cut through the skin of the neck and clamped the skin to the sheet. Next, Carrel made another incision into the tissue below the skin to free a segment of a carotid artery from muscle and connective tissue. Once the artery segment was freed, Carrel tied one end of it and clamped the other.

Carrel used a minute glass cannula to draw blood and worked with tiny curved needles to make very fine sutures. After removing any blood, he cleansed the segment before inserting the cannulas that would be used to keep serum circulating once the segment was placed in Lindbergh's perfusion device. Only after the artery segment was isolated did the assistants start collecting blood in paraffin-lined glass tubes to make the serum in the centrifuge. Then the experiment shifted to transferring the segment aseptically to the perfusion device, circulating serum through it, and recording what the team observed. Lindbergh again would be on standby in case there were any mechanical problems with the perfusion device. While the larger tissue segments were perfusing, Carrel's team also prepared small mica discs coated with drops of plasma and phenol red dye for study under a microscope. (Mica was used because it has some similar properties to glass but is much stronger. In addition to being easy to cut into small pieces, the mineral is highly resistant to extreme temperatures and chemicals, including strong acids.)

Earlier, in the operating room after Carrel finished excising a segment of carotid artery, Dr. Parker began his own experiments — harvesting living muscle tissue to study fibroblast outgrowth under a high-powered microscope. Fibroblasts produce the principal connective tissue (collagen fibers) throughout the bodies of animals and humans that are also key to wound repair. Dr. Parker's role was to grow colonies of fibroblasts out of the muscle tissue obtained from one or more limbs of the subject.

As Dr. Parker later described in a manual, the first step to create slides with living fibroblasts required him to surgically remove a section of a limb, peel back the skin and expose the muscle. Then Dr. Parker severed a section of muscle to dice into tiny fragments. Each fragment would then be placed on an oval depression slide and bathed in glucose solution. Then he would prepare mica coverslips, each with a drop of plasma, transfer the fragment to the coverslip and add a mixture of tissue extract and isotonic solution. A new depression slide would then be placed on top of the mica coverslip and the sandwiched fibroblast fragment would be flipped over — to be sealed with melted paraffin, labeled and examined as the injured muscle gave rise to a colony of fibroblasts. To prevent the fibroblasts from dying, it would be necessary to repeat the process to transfer the fragments every few days to a new slide.

In early April, Carrel reported exciting results to the institute's board. His team had just kept a segment of harvested carotid artery alive for a full month. Carrel did not identify the artery's donor, except to convey that during the past year Carrel's team had focused their vivisection experiments on both animal and human subjects. Carrel's month-long carotid artery experiment was later included in the official history of the Rockefeller Institute's medical accomplishments over its first half century. This experiment would likely not have been noteworthy unless it was human. Two decades earlier, Carrel had kept a dog's carotid artery viable in his lab refrigerator for 72 days before transplanting it it for use in a successful heart bypass operation on another dog. When accepting the Nobel Prize in 1912, Dr. Carrel had envisioned future opportunities for life-saving operations on people with defective heart valves. Preserving a compatible human donor's blood vessel might allow a surgeon to use it to create a temporary bypass – permitting the time needed for open-heart surgery to repair a patient's valve.

In the April 1932 report, Carrel thanked five key team members, including Drs. Parker and Baker, but gave the lion's share of credit to Charles Lindbergh. Lindbergh's technical assistance had been essential both on the pump and the centrifuge. That was apparently why Carrel started the landmark experiment only after Lindbergh completed his modifications to the centrifuge in late February 1932 that reduced the serum-processing time down to 12 minutes.

In early May 1932, the press was told that Lindbergh took a hiatus from his lab work in March and April to concentrate on finding and rescuing his son. But that cannot be determined from his detailed diary. He regularly logged daily entries in his personal diary, including flight information and notes on experiments. His diary omits the entire month of March and the first half of April — the time during which the historic carotid artery experiment took place. It jumps from the end of February to mid-April and early May where Lindbergh entered details about his futile searches at sea with Curtis.

Carrel's own diary was published by his widow in the mid-1950s when Lindbergh was assisting her with Carrel's papers. Some of the text chosen for the jacket cover of Carrel's diary is telling, as are a few unredacted entries written in March and April of 1932. The back of the book jacket describes the Nobel-prize-winner's major achievements. As translated, one blurb states: "In 1932, impassioned by Carrel's work, the aviator Charles Lindbergh put himself at Carrel's disposal. The two men pursued together research on the long-term culture of living tissue transported out of their milieu." Their actual collaboration began more than a year earlier. The book jacket was apparently referencing some important milestone in 1932 that evidenced Lindbergh's total devotion to his mentor which Mme. Carrel may have been present to witness. Everyone working on the project kept it hush-hush. Their results would not begin to be publicized until 1935.

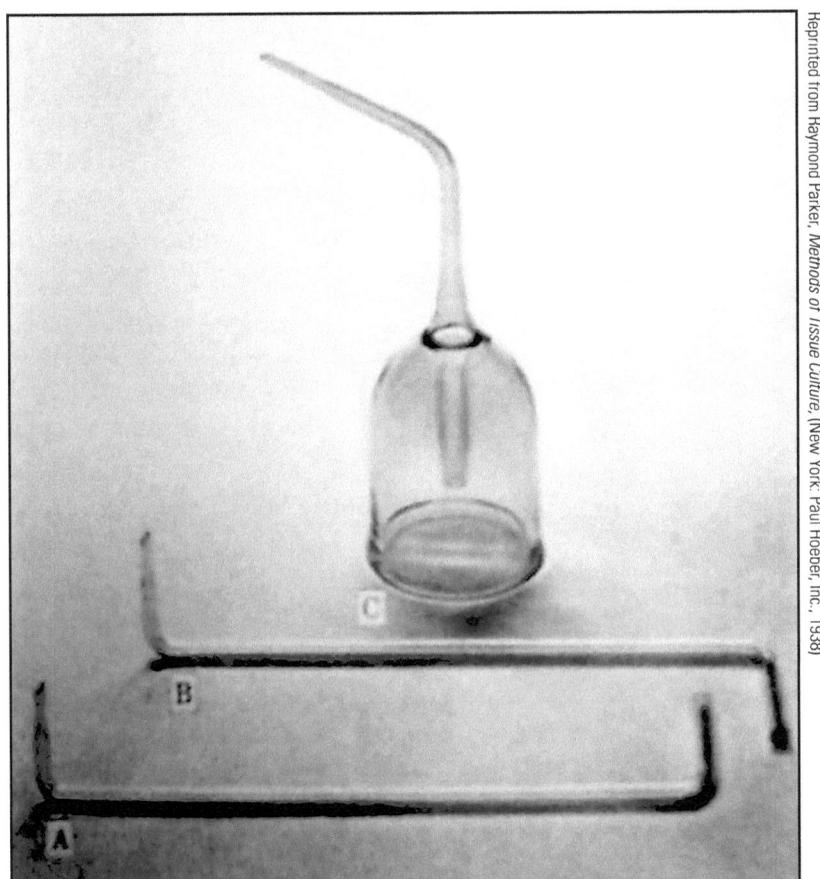

Glass bleeding cannula used in draining blood from carotid arteries in Carrel's lab (from Raymond Parker's 1938 book, Methods of Tissue Culture.*) Parker noted in the preface that most of the equipment had been in regular use in Carrel's lab at the Rockefeller Institute for the past ten years. A glass bleeding cannula of this type was likely used to drain blood in the March 1932 carotid artery experiment with an unidentified donor.*

Lindbergh's perfusion pump could only hold a tiny organ, often a thyroid gland, but according to the caption of this photo in The Culture of Organs, *this particular perfusion pump contains a cat's ovaries and fallopian tube.*

6.
Hitler Embraces Carrel's "Ideal" Solution

BEFORE the Lindberghs left the country for England in December 1935, Carrel's book, *Man, The Unknown*, was well on its way to becoming an international best seller. It would go into sixty printings including a condensed version in *Reader's Digest*. Along the way it drew some pointed criticism questioning whether "mercy killing" was ever justified even for those incurably ill. Columbia University Dr. A. A. Brill warned that "no matter how humanely applied . . . it would revive the dormant sadism [of primitive societies] and destroy the sacredness of life." Yet the enthusiasm for Carrel's bold vision of a utopian society drowned out Brill and other Cassandras.

Man, The Unknown's enormous popularity in America — second only to the Pulitzer-prize-winning novel *Gone with the Wind* — capped the major educational effort by leading American eugenicists to get the public on board with involuntary sterilization of the "unfit." Carrel's book was also received enthusiastically in Europe, particularly by Adolf Hitler, whose own recent involuntary sterilization laws were modeled after those in a number of American states. The Secretary of the American Eugenics Society greatly admired how the Germans made "compulsory" what "many far-sighted men and women in both England and America have long been working earnestly toward." Joseph De Jarnette, a nationally known proponent of involuntary sterilization, famously exclaimed: "The Germans are beating us at our own game."

What Hitler likely focused on most was Carrel's argument that societies wishing to create a superior race should "euthanize" misfits. Carrel was not suggesting mercy killing or assisted suicide as the term is now understood but putting to death undesirable people for the general good. Carrel recommended exterminating unwanted categories of people in "small, euthanistic institutions." Besides killers, armed robbers, kidnappers, and those diagnosed with incurable mental illness, Carrel endorsed the view that infant mortality was natural selection at work — caring for sickly neonates saddled society with an unnecessary burden. Nature intended such babies to die.

In 1936, when Carrel's best-seller was translated into German, he added special recognition of the Nazi regime's progress in implementing his vision of a more utopian society: "The German government has taken energetic measures against the propagation of the defective, the mentally diseased, and the criminal. The ideal solution would be the suppression of each of these individuals as soon as he has proven himself to be dangerous." Carrel was openly urging Hitler to "suppress" groups who were perceived to endanger the gene pool. He even called it an "ideal solution," foreshadowing Hitler's Final Solution that marked Jews and gypsies for extermination.

At the time, Lindbergh remained determined to move forward with Carrel's quest to uncover the secret to immortality through organ transplants. He and Anne were then renting a centuries-old estate owned by Harold Nicolson where Lindbergh was conducting his own experiments. Nicolson was well aware of Lindbergh's new preoccupation. Nicolson had been staying with the Lindberghs and the Morrows back in June 1935 when Alexis Carrel first published a summary of the pioneering work his research team at the Rockefeller Institute had been focused on for the past few years. Lindbergh had then become the center of press attention with Carrel's stunning announcement that the key to the Rockefeller team's success was improvements to a perfusion pump that Lindbergh designed. As Carrel expected, the revelation also led to many questions from the scientific community.

The article Carrel wrote in June of 1935 was quite short and devoid of details. He noted that 26 experiments had been conducted with the Lindbergh "life chamber" for as long as twenty days "without infection or blockages in the system." Carrel was confident that the tiny organs they tested could have been kept living "indefinitely." Yet that would await future developments. The only repeated success Carrel then reported was in temporarily sustaining thyroid glands. Scientists could not wait to find out more details and see how the experiments the pair had conducted might be improved upon to enable entire adult human organs to be kept viable outside the human body, advancing the possibility of organ transplants.

Anne was thrilled for her husband: "I am glad to have it known and glad, in a way, for the publicity on this thing . . . as though the right values were being set for his other achievements. Every act of his is not a fluke, not chance, not charm and youth and simplicity and boyishness, but the expression of a great mind that can turn its search light in more than one direction." She had hoped the new direction her husband's interests were taking would lead to a more settled homelife in the future but instead he had uprooted them to England. There, Lindbergh immersed himself in further experiments, including unsuccessful attempts to create a prototype for a mechanical kidney.

In the spring of 1936, Lindbergh's flying expertise was tapped once more. He was asked by the American military attaché in Berlin to accept an invitation from the Nazi government to tour German airplane factories. The Germans invited the Lindberghs to stay for the 1936 Summer Olympics in Berlin. Lindbergh made several trips that year during which the Nazi government gave him tours of their airplane factories, let him pilot a new model, and deliberately misled him as to their airplane production and aerial warfare capability.

At the opening ceremonies of the Summer Olympics in August 1936, the Lindberghs were seated in the same luxury box as Hitler. It was the first Olympiad to be televised. German Jews were prohibited from participating. Many Americans urged a boycott but did not prevail. Some athletes from countries around the world saluted Der Fuhrer as they entered the stadium, as if the event were solely in his honor. One American author in attendance noted the ominous fanaticism exhibited by the crowd, transforming the international celebration of athletes almost into a "scary . . . cult of personality." Yet despite Hitler's fanaticism, Anne Lindbergh found the German dictator quite personable and not self-aggrandizing. Her husband considered moving the family to Germany.

As the Nazi government assumed, Lindbergh went back to England greatly impressed. Lindbergh then helped convince British Prime Minister Neville Chamberlin to appease German aggression with the Munich Accord, which France also signed. At the time, Lindbergh fervently believed that Germany's aerial capability far exceeded that of all other European countries put together.

The second week of August 1936, Dr. Carrel and Lindbergh demonstrated the perfusion pump at an international gathering of experimental cytologists in Copenhagen, Denmark. At the demonstration, Carrel and Lindbergh amazed attendees by showing how they had kept a cat's thyroid viable for 28 days in Lindbergh's device and then successfully transplanted it into another cat. But trouble lay ahead. Since the end of 1935, it had been clear that Rockefeller's new director of medical research, physiologist Herbert Gasser, was interested in "put[ting] the squeeze" to Carrel's work by cutting funding to Carrel's lab. While Carrel was in Copenhagen, his head nurse wrote to him in alarm. Over her objection, Dr. Gasser insisted on sending a team of outside scientists to review the records of Carrel's experiments.

After Lindbergh fled the country, Carrel's team had successfully conducted over 200 additional experiments with a variety of organs — mostly spleens, thyroids and kidneys. Over 100,000 hours were devoted to Dr. Carrel's vivisection experiments before the team was through — using hundreds of hand-blown perfusion pumps. Gasser obviously suspected that Carrel had crossed the line into forbidden territory. At the same time, Carrel had concluded that he could never keep nerve tissue alive. Carrel had originally thought brains lasted forever; it was only other human body parts that might need replacement. But as 20th century doctors extended more and more lives, Carrel observed that mental decline was as predictable a phenomenon among geriatrics as the development of physical infirmities. Surgically replacing organs while brains deteriorated would only result in a huge number of senile centenarians.

For Gasser, it was a moral issue. He was half-Jewish and had been appalled ever since Carrel had given a standing-room only speech about "The Mystery of Death" at the New York Academy of Medicine in

December 1935. That speech included condemnation of medical practices that prolonged the lives of persons "who should be dead . . .the weak, the diseased and the fools" who encumbered civilized societies. Some of the Jewish doctors at the Institute had friends and relatives already fleeing the Nazi regime — the country where Carrel's chilling ideas for purifying the white race found the warmest reception.

Gasser began disbanding Carrel's vivisection support team in 1936, leaving Carrel free to research, write and lecture, but without sufficient resources to continue his surgical experiments. In June 1937, Gasser convinced the institute's board to force Carrel himself to leave by adopting a mandatory retirement policy at age 65 effective July 1, 1939. Carrel was the only staff member then approaching that proposed cut-off. He accused Jewish administrators at the Rockefeller Institute of aiming to replace him with "one of their own."

As the Lindberghs extended their stay in Europe, Lindbergh grew more openly pro-German, creating friction with their British acquaintances. In 1938, Lindbergh accepted an Iron Cross medal of honor from the Nazi regime. That same year, Nazi government representatives came to Michigan to bestow the only other award they gave to an American by honoring 75-year-old Henry Ford with the Grand Cross of the German Eagle — the highest medal Nazi Germany awarded to foreign nationals. Hitler was inspired by the efficiencies of Ford's assembly lines for mass production. Hitler also admired Ford's strident anti-Semitism.

While Lindbergh considered relocating to Berlin, Carrel remained in high demand in Europe both as a speaker and a researcher. His wife, Madame Anne Carrel, had been active for years in successive right-wing political parties in France. Carrel thought he might find a suitable post under either Mussolini's Fascist government in Padua, Italy or Hitler's government in Berlin. Carrel did not doubt that both Fascist governments would highly value his work even if it was no longer appreciated by the Rockefeller Institute.

7.
The Culture of Organs

IN THE summer of 1937 Carrel returned to his island home in France. He realized that if perfusion work were to continue — as Lindbergh was intent on the pair of them doing — they would need extensive help from researchers outside the Rockefeller Institute. Carrel began drafting a manual on how to replicate and expand upon the results of their perfusion experiments. He brought Lindbergh in to write the chapter on the mechanics of the perfusion pump. Documenting their successes to date might well develop funding sources and convince other research doctors to conduct similar tests.

The Culture of Organs would wind up being published in June 1938. In the spring of 1937, Lindbergh decided to travel to India to find out more about the extraordinary longevity experienced by revered elders of a Hindu sect, who believed the body was capable of rejuvenation through consuming a "nectar of immortality." Lindbergh talked Anne into flying with him, although she was then six-months pregnant. The pair flew over the Alps to Rome and Athens and on to India on an uncharted course in extremely hazardous conditions. Much to Anne's dismay, it evolved into being a ten-week trip in which she longed to return to her four-and-a-half-year-old son Jon, whom they had again left behind. The ordeal culminated in a long flight back when she was eight-months pregnant. They returned to England the second week of April. Her son Land was born there on May 12, 1937, a date that for Anne must have evoked mixed emotions. It marked the fifth anniversary of the discovery of her first-born's corpse.

That summer, the Lindberghs returned to the United States for the first time since their hasty departure eighteen months earlier. Anne could not wait to introduce her newborn son Land to her family. Lindbergh anxiously planned ahead for more work with Carrel. Madame Carrel, who accompanied her husband to New York that winter, told Lindbergh that a small island adjacent to the one the Carrels owned was now on the market. The two islands actually connected by a sand bar in low tide. Lindbergh pounced on the offer. Anne would just have to tag along.

The purchase had to be handled through French nationals posing as the new owners since the island could not legally be transferred to foreigners. The Lindberghs first occupied the unheated island home in late June 1938, bringing along their two sons and household staff. By then, the Lindberghs' third son Land was just over a year old, and Jon was turning six. Anne found that Carrel was even more controlling than her husband. Lindbergh happily deferred to his mentor after they moved to the island as Carrel dictated the boys' diet and daily schedules. He even gave instructions to Anne on breastfeeding her toddler.

Anne grew increasingly miserable, unable to meet Carrel's exacting requirements of a nurturing mother and overwhelmed at the effort to keep her household staff from mutinying over the demands Carrel placed on them for the children's care. Her offer to assist her husband in the book he was writing with Carrel was rebuffed. Excluded from working with the two men, Anne also found Madame Carrel exceedingly difficult to take. The surgeon's wife dabbled in hypnotism and interpretation of personal auras. She examined both Anne and Charles, finding that he exhibited signs of supernatural powers, while Anne was found wanting in all respects. Meanwhile Madame Carrel was invited to participate in documenting the perfusion projects, while Anne was blocked from offering any advice on editing the book.

In June 1938, Lindbergh and Carrel published *The Culture of Organs* mostly as a how-to handbook to encourage more researchers to advance the specialty from its infancy. Promoting their achievements with the Lindbergh perfusion device in lectures on the subject, Carrel boasted that "practically every important organ had been studied." He concealed his own current lack of enthusiasm for the perfusion project after seeing brain tissue quickly die inside the pump's central chamber.

Lindbergh remained fixated on the original mission he and Dr.

Carrel had embarked upon. In England, he had been pursuing the possibility of using hypothermia and perfusion of entire bodies to move forward with his goal of open-heart surgery. In promoting the idea, Lindbergh explained that he and Carrel planned to use monkeys or apes to test the new device. Lindbergh's proposal did not generate much enthusiasm among British medical researchers. Yet great excitement in the media accompanied the release of the handbook on the breakthrough experiments.

In June 1938, *TIME* magazine featured Carrel and Lindbergh posing with the pump in its cover story. A colleague of Carrel's at the Rockefeller Institute later commented that the two men's celebrity status blew up their achievement "out of all proportion." The *New York Times* reacted with excitement at the announcement that the experiments involved a thousand organs including "hearts, lungs, livers, spleens, [and] reproductive organs." In the book, Carrel noted that his collaboration with Lindbergh started in 1931 when Lindbergh designed his first Pyrex perfusion pump that provided a sterile environment. Every time Lindbergh developed an improved pump, Carrel arranged to test it on excised organs and blood vessels small enough to fit in the chamber. Carrel boasted that improvements Lindbergh made allowed the Rockefeller team to move forward with cultivating "entire organs . . . in vitro [which] have not only been found to remain alive, but to modify their structure and their function."

Carrel's focus on vivisecting humans as well as animals had been revealed to the institute's board in his April 1932 annual report. But the new management after Simon Flexner retired in 1935 disapproved. Later, when the official history of the institution was written, the author lauded Carrel's pioneering technique for organ transplants, but noted that the surgeon was not able to use that technique on humans. Carrel was not licensed as a physician in New York or New Jersey. At the Rockefeller Institute he was employed as an experimental research surgeon, never a practitioner.

Yet the lack of a license apparently had not stopped the surgeon from experimenting with human beings. *The Culture of Organs* acknowledged that Carrel's team tested numerous human specimens in

Lindbergh's perfusion device from both living and recently deceased subjects: "It happens today that organs removed from the human body, *in the course of an operation* or soon after death can be revived in the Lindbergh pump and made to function again when perfused with an artificial fluid." [Emphasis added].

While Carrel spoke in the alternative — "in the course of an operation [i.e. vivisection] or soon after death" — he made clear his own strong preference was for removing organs from living donors. Elsewhere in the book, Carrel describes human arteries as thicker than those of animals and provides a how-to section on preparing both animal and human organs for isolated perfusion. Carrel summed up his team's achievements to date:

> Although the cultivation of organs is still in the early period of its history, it is firmly established on a large number of experiments. . . . These techniques are opening to experimental investigation a forbidden field: the living human body. . . . And still vivisection is considered by certain people as not very far from being criminal.

Lindbergh well knew that Carrel had developed a source of living human subjects. In fact, in early March of 1935, E. P. Earle of the New Jersey State Board of Overseers of mental institutions asked Dr. Carrel in a letter: "When are you and Col. Lindbergh going to Vineland with Commissioner Ellis and me to look over some of our feeble-minded 'prospects'?"

David Friedman, author of *The Immortalists: Charles Lindbergh, Dr. Alexis Carrel, and Their Daring Quest to Live Forever,* realized with horror that the only project both Carrel and Lindbergh were working on together that Earle could have been referring to was harvesting organs for perfusion in Lindbergh's pump — "experiments on live humans, maybe even without their informed consent." Friedman may not have realized, as Carrel biographer Dr. David Hamilton later did, that by the mid-1930s, at least some of the tiny organs for perfusion in Lindbergh's device came from neonates, or that the only consent then deemed necessary for any "feeble-minded prospects" from New Jersey institutions was that of institutional overseers like Earle and Ellis.

Friedman understood that "donors" were routinely drained of blood to make the serum needed for successful perfusion. He tempered his revulsion by assuming that Carrel and Lindbergh were only planning in March 1935 for potential experiments in the future and had not already undertaken any human vivisections. This is belied by Carrel's own statements in the 1938 handbook that he had already undertaken some operations on live human subjects. The fact that 27 of the 36 different types of specimens were identified as coming from lower animals suggests that the remaining nine were likely human specimens. Indeed, the casual tone of Commissioner Earle's letter makes it appear that the topic of "feeble-minded prospects" was one he had discussed with Carrel before, and that he expected Carrel and Lindbergh to welcome the offer.

In the mid-1930s, the Superintendent of Skillman permitted experimentation on inmates by other visiting doctors studying Scarlet Fever and pneumonia. There were many suspicious deaths at Skillman in those Depression years. The county then kept track of investigated deaths in two categories: deaths at Skillman Village, and everywhere else in Somerset County. With less than two percent of the population, Skillman Village accounted for a whopping 35% of investigated deaths in Somerset County in the early 1930s.

As time passed, its reputation only got worse. By the end of the next decade the press would expose Skillman Village for patients "thrown into the dark closet of neglect" rendering it "New Jersey's most tragic institution" and "the snake pit of New Jersey." (The derogatory term alluded to a semi-autobiographical best-seller, *The Snake Pit,* and award-winning 1948 movie of the same name which explored a woman's harrowing life in a New York mental institution.)

The question does not appear to be whether the pair used persons labeled "feeble-minded" as vivisection subjects, but when they started doing so. The landmark carotid artery experiment in the spring of 1932 may well have been among their first. The pair were more than eager to do further organ and tissue culture experiments if they could get the backing.

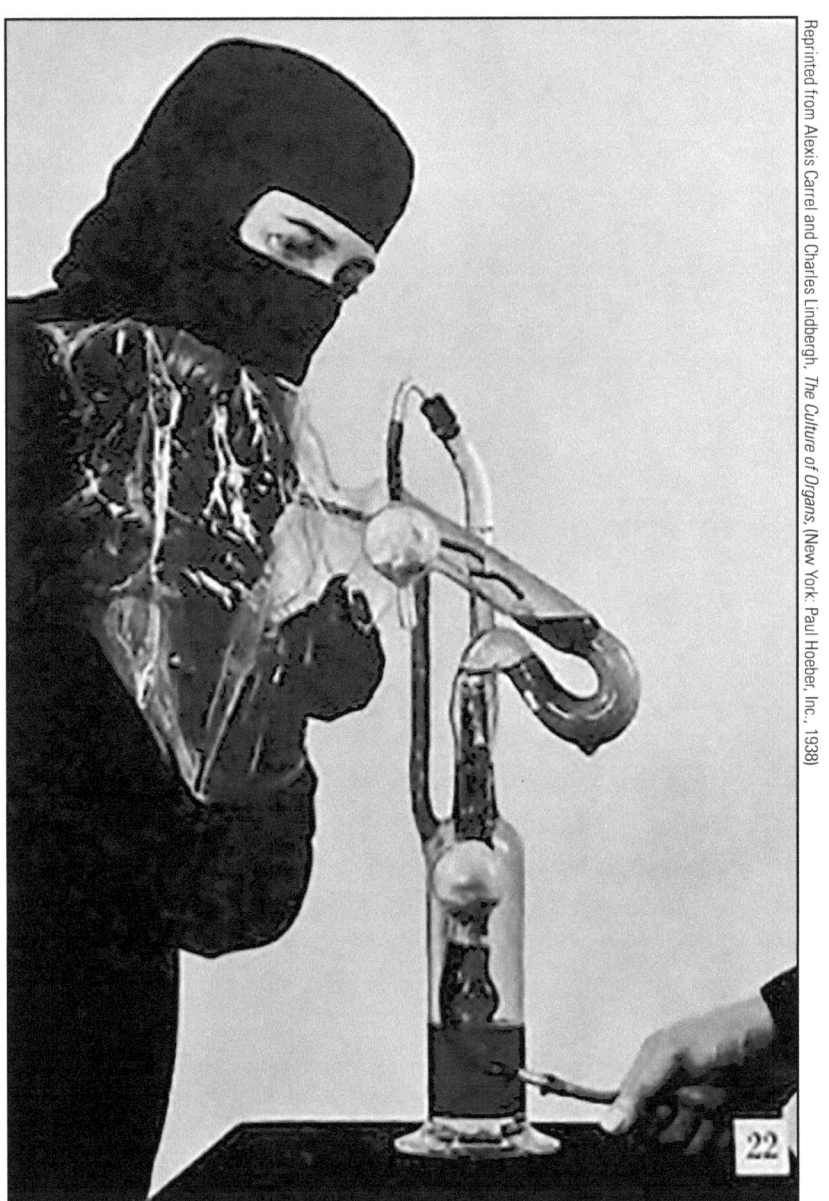

Putting an organ into the perfusion chamber.

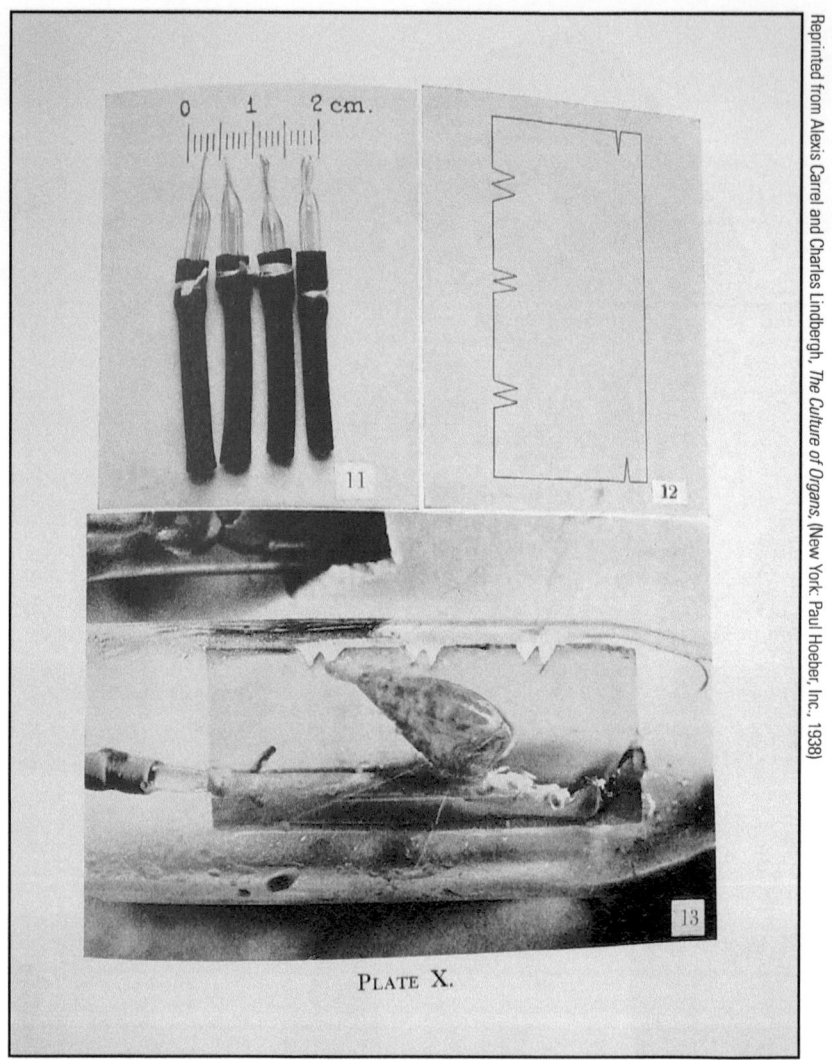

Carrel's Carotid Artery Experiment

Upper left (Figure 11) are cannulas with rubber handles. All specimens were tiny. The .5 mm size was inserted into excised artery segments of small animals and human subjects (likely infants). The diagram in the upper right (figure 12) shows a mica plate needed for delicate specimens. Though undated, Figure 13 displays a carotid artery that was likely the subject of the historic experiment Carrel's team conducted in the spring of 1932.

8.
The Highfields Center for the Science of Man

IN 1933, while Charlie's murder investigation was still active, Lindbergh made arrangements with the overseers of Skillman Village to transform his estate into a state charitable institution focused on children's welfare. Lindbergh originally intended to name it "Sourland Mountain Farm, Inc." but was persuaded to go with something less grim. It may have been Anne who suggested the name "Highfields." Lindbergh created a five-member board of trustees to oversee the charitable institute: himself and Anne; Henry Breckinridge; sociologist Owen Lovejoy, who was then the Executive Secretary of the Children's Aid Society; and Abraham Flexner (Simon Flexner's brother) who was the Director of the Princeton Institute for Advance Study.

Both Flexner brothers were strong admirers of Carrel's genius and believed in his mission to accomplish a break-through in achieving organ transplants. In turn, the Flexner brothers were among the select secular Jews that Carrel and Lindbergh considered worthy of inclusion among the elite of society. Abraham Flexner seemed the perfect choice for launching Carrel and Lindbergh's new institute. He had focused his career on vastly improving the quality of medical care in America by modernizing the country's medical schools. To achieve his aim Flexner had coaxed hundreds of millions of dollars from Rockefeller, Carnegie and other wealthy philanthropists to fund world-class, merit-based programs.

The papers of incorporation were approved by Commissioner William J. Ellis for the State Board of Control of Institutions and Agencies, in June of that year. The announcement was void on specifics as to the intended use of the property. Ellis told the press: "The actual working out of the details of the school need not be described in the incorporation papers."

Lindbergh had probably first met Ellis at the national children's health conference he and Anne attended with the Breckinridges in November 1930. Ellis chaired the committee on physically and mentally disabled children and was among several key New Jersey officials invited to that event as overseers of institutionalized mental patients and other persons labeled "defectives." Their charges were a primary concern of the ABA's long-standing eugenics subcommittee on population control. Ellis was a former colleague of Anne's father, Dwight Morrow, on two different state oversight committees.

At that 1930 conference, Lindbergh likely was also introduced to the director of South Jersey's Vineland Village (originally called the Training School for Feeble-minded Boys and Girls). As Lindbergh had undoubtedly already come to appreciate, all of these facilities played important roles in supporting medical research by Dr. Carrel and other members of the eugenics movement. By the 1930s, the two villages each had a long history of serving as a "major clinical laboratory, where eugenics theory was tested and validated" by doctors from various institutions, including the Carnegie and Rockefeller institutes.

Newspapers across the country quickly got word that the children's welfare center would be called "Highfields" and that it would serve as a "living memorial" to the Eaglet "to protect little ones from sickness and unhappiness." But no reporters linked the proposed institution to a pronouncement earlier that same week by Simon Flexner. Flexner had just gone public endorsing human as well as animal research: "The medical investigator today takes all of animated nature as his legitimate field of exploration. There are no closed compartments in nature into which man, animals and plants can be separately placed. All are related organically and, as we may say, physiologically and pathologically." (In fact, under Flexner's watch, medical researchers at the Rockefeller Institute had experimented with human guinea pigs as well as animals for over two decades.)

From day one Lindbergh likely had in mind experimental use of children for medical research. Trustee Lovejoy apparently so understood because he reached out to Simon Flexner for suggestions before Flexner retired as Rockefeller's Director of Medical Research in December 1935. Before secretly departing for England later that month, Lindbergh changed his will to provide that if he and Anne died, Princeton University would inherit his estate. He most likely conferred with Abe Flexner about Princeton collaborating with Alexis Carrel on future plans for Highfields. For the past two decades Princeton University had strongly supported the controversial animal vivisection program Carrel oversaw at Rockefeller's Princeton facility – including lobbying heavily in 1915 for the change in state law to permit such experiments.

For the next couple of years, the trustees took no further action to develop the institute. In retirement, Simon Flexner continued to endorse Carrel's and Lindbergh's perfusion work, offering high praise for *The Culture of Organs*. While the book was still in galleys in mid-January of 1938 Dr. Carrel invited Commissioner Ellis to meet with him and Lindbergh at the Rockefeller Institute in Manhattan. At the time, Lindbergh was temporarily back from Europe and working at the lab. They gave Ellis a tour featuring their current research projects and discussed their upcoming collaboration with Skillman Village. Ellis told them he greatly enjoyed conferring on "possible ways and means of correlating the researches which you and Dr. Carrel are conducting with some of the practical problems in our institutions." Lindbergh, in turn, thanked Ellis for the "excellent" report and other "useful information" Ellis had provided to Dr. Carrel and himself.

The following month, Dr. Carrel wrote to a doctor doing cancer research to suggest that experimental work could be done on malignant tumors with the Lindbergh perfusion device. Carrel emphasized that breakthroughs in studying cancerous tumors would require collaboration with a "hospital that could supply human tumors and human organs." He copied Lindbergh, perhaps assuming that cancer research could be added to their own institution's lab work with the perfusion pump. Carrel's response appears based on the model he had developed with Lindbergh, reaching out to Skillman Village to partner with their new research institute – presumably to supply experimental subjects.

That spring, Lindbergh had as his highest priority helping Carrel relocate as the July 1 closing date of his lab at the Rockefeller Institute approached. Carrel had been dreaming for some time of creating his own Institute of Man with a team of experts focused on perfecting the human race. He and Lindbergh would be among its founding fathers, not only helping develop ideal social policies, but continuing their organ culture experiments.

Timing must have seemed perfect to attract media attention to the new project. Lindbergh's perfusion device was featured at the 1939 World's Fair in New York. Promoted as the second biggest fair in American history after the 1893 Chicago World's Fair, one of its purposes was to reveal what science had in store for the future. On opening day that April 200,000 fair attendees witnessed the first live public television broadcast — a welcome to the fair from President Roosevelt. For the entire time the fair was open, the Hall of Science showcased Lindbergh's perfusion device as its star exhibit. Attendees could line up to stare in awe at a dog's thyroid, the shape of a narrow butterfly, held in suspension in one of the glass pumps Lindbergh had designed. Signage promoted the medical breakthrough as "the principal instrument for the investigation of the mystery of the age — the first laboratory approach to the problem of enabling man to live indefinitely."

The exhibit averaged 600 to 800 fascinated visitors per hour during the week and 1000 to 1200 per hour on weekends. By then, three key research assistants of Carrel's had relocated to the Lederle Laboratories in New York. One or more of them manned the booth at the World's Fair every day to answer questions about Lindbergh's device. At Lederle, these researchers kept the "chicken-heart" experiment going after new management had forced Carrel's retirement. Behind the scenes, Carrel was then badmouthing the Rockefeller Institute's new leadership for dismantling his surgical team and trying to kill the perfusion project.

In the summer of 1939, Abraham Flexner's fund-raising committee began soliciting donations for the proposed Science of Man Institute. To entice donors, Lindbergh and a few close associates prepared a brochure. One of the selling points was that contributors would sponsor tissue culture experiments by Carrel and Lindbergh at Skillman

Village — clearly signaling the pair's intent to continue conducting experiments like those that *TIME* magazine had extolled in 1938 for facilitating future organ transplants through Lindbergh's "life chamber." The organizers of Highfields estimated they needed to cover annual expenses of $50,000 to $100,000 per year ($900,000 to $1.8 million today) to sustain the foundation.

Though Lindbergh was still trying to minimize public knowledge of his own plans to participate in the foundation, the brochure promised donors that both Carrel and Lindbergh would invest significant time in the day-to-day lab work in virology and tissue culture. Donors were assured that the team would draw all of its scientific conclusions from "observable data" already arranged to be conducted at nearby Skillman Village for Epileptics.

Tabloids speculated that the famed pair contemplated whole organ transplants — a bionic man reporters sensationalized as a Carrel-Lindbergh robot. After major donors to the proposed institute failed to materialize that summer, Wyckoff wrote to Lindbergh that he and Ebeling needed to know as soon as possible if the Highfields project was still a go. Lederle Laboratories was pressuring them about their future, and they could not reach Dr. Carrel. Lindbergh assumed the funding problem was due to mounting anxiety over the potential for war in Europe. He suggested to Abraham Flexner in late August 1939 that plans for the Science of Man Institute be put on hold "until the crisis has turned one way or the other."

As it turned out, both the Science of Man Institute and the 1939 fair in Queens ended in financial failure. In the case of the World's Fair, most Americans were too poor to buy tickets. Then came the war in Europe. Had the Nazis won World War II, Highfields might have gotten the funding it needed.

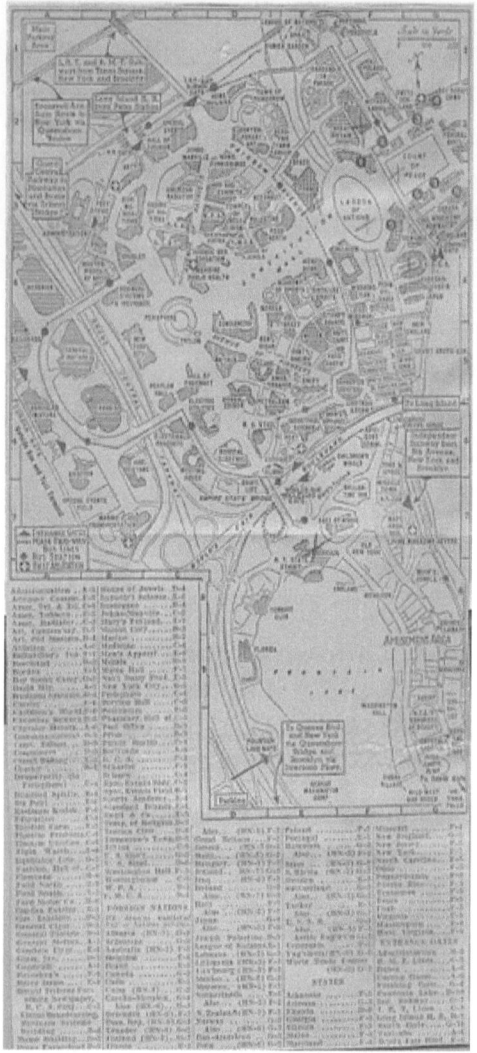 

Thousands thronged to see Lindbergh's perfusion pump at the 1939 New York World's Fair

Signage promoted the medical breakthrough by Dr. Carrel and Charles Lindbergh as "The principal instrument for the investigation of the mystery of the age — the first laboratory approach to the problem of enabling man to live indefinitely." The exhibit averaged 600 to 800 fascinated visitors per hour during the week and 1000 to 1200 per hour on weekends.

9.
From Hero to Villain

JUST a few days after Lindbergh and Carrel put the Highfields Science of Man project on hold, Germany shocked the world on September 1, 1939, by invading Poland, violating the Munich Accord and precipitating war with England and the French Republic. Lindbergh immediately began speaking against American involvement in the war. He was forced to resign from the military. President Roosevelt was already doing all he could to find ways to support the Allies with supplies and consultants while publicly proclaiming American neutrality.

The news from Europe was greatly unsettling to many Americans. In May 1940, the Germans attacked and quickly defeated the French army. Nazi troops took two million soldiers prisoner. The Germans used two-thirds of the French soldiers as forced labor. By mid-June, the Nazis occupied Paris after French officials fled. A new, conciliatory French government was established in the south of France, headquartered in Vichy where it nominally remained in charge of French citizens and colonies. The Vichy government collaborated with the Nazis occupying northern France as a growing French Resistance sought to undermine the Nazis and provide vital information to the Allies. German demands on the Vichy government included rounding up Jews, Communists and other targeted undesirables for exile to concentration camps.

Before the war, Lindbergh had been far more of a Nazi sympathizer than Carrel, though Carrel told friends that if the choice were between Fascism and Communism, he preferred Fascism. Carrel spent the summer of 1940 in New York. Lindbergh convinced him to take an offer from the new Vichy government to head his own institute in Nazi-occupied Paris — The French Foundation for the Study of Human Problems. It would be based in the same building that had formerly housed a branch office of the Rockefeller Institute. The Vichy government offered Carrel a huge budget of 40 million francs to pursue his goals for ideal citizens. Carrel expected a great deal of freedom in putting the theories of his eugenics book into practice in his native land. The Vichy regime made his 1935 best-seller, *L'Homme, cet Inconnu,* required reading.

By 1940, rumors of the horrors of Hitler's concentration camps began to spread in America. Meanwhile, Lindbergh embarked on more speaking engagements that year aimed at keeping America out of the European war. The majority of Americans sympathized with the British but remained opposed to joining the war. However, support for Great Britain was growing, due in large part to the efforts of the Lindberghs' brother-in-law Aubrey Morgan and his second wife, Anne's younger sister Connie. Aubrey Morgan had been tapped in 1939 to start mustering American enthusiasm for backing the British if war broke out in Europe.

Mostly with their own money, the Morgans soon employed a staff of reporters at the British Press Service in Rockefeller Center. The news group gathered stories from abroad on a weekly basis to bolster American awareness of the imminent peril facing Great Britain. Dubbed the "Clip Club," the news group was initially overseen by Connie Morgan. It ultimately evolved into the British Information Services with Aubrey Morgan at its head.

By the following spring, strain escalated between the Morgans and the Lindberghs over their opposing views on the United States entering the European War. In May 1940, when the Nazi army invaded Holland, Lindbergh took to the airwaves to castigate "powerful elements" who planned to profiteer from sales of arms to the British. Many fellow countrymen, including his lawyer Henry Breckinridge, were appalled by Lindbergh's insistence America simply stand by while the Nazis took over the rest of Europe. Breckinridge immediately quit representing the Lindberghs as their attorney. Even this sharp break with his closest confidante since 1927 did not deter Lindbergh from his latest mission.

In September of 1940, two Yale graduate students founded the isolationist organization, America First, as a platform for their idol Charles Lindbergh and other anti-war speakers. Lindbergh had already spoken on their campus in favor of maintaining American neutrality in the European conflict. One of the group's founders was Kingman Brewster, a graduate student at Yale who traced his ancestry back to the Mayflower. (Kingman Brewster would become President of Yale decades later.) America First soon boasted 800,000 members, attracting strong critics of President Roosevelt and his New Deal legislation, anti-Semites and pacifists from both the political left and right.

That fall, Anne Lindbergh completed a booklet sharing her own views on the divisive war issue — *The Wave of the Future*. Like Carrel, Anne embraced neither Fascism nor Communism, but considered totalitarian regimes inevitable. Anne's pamphlet wound up being published shortly after she gave birth in October 1940 to the couple's fourth child, their first girl, whom they named Anne Spencer Lindbergh. Anne naively did not anticipate the instant denunciation her booklet would receive. Roosevelt's Secretary of the Interior publicly condemned *The Wave of the Future* as "the bible of every American Nazi, Fascist . . . and Appeaser." The booklet further alienated Anne's sister Connie and her husband Aubrey. Some old friends began avoiding Anne. Mrs. Morrow counted herself among the Anglophiles. Her efforts to reason with her older daughter fell on deaf ears.

Wild Bill Donovan also spoke out to condemn Lindbergh's unwillingness to take a stand against German aggression. Still, Lindbergh remained popular among isolationists. He quickly became America First's most prominent speaker with strident attacks on FDR. Lindbergh did not hesitate to levy charges of malfeasance against the President and call for FDR's impeachment and removal from office. Despite the opposition of America Firsters, FDR convinced Congress in the spring of 1941 to pass the Lend-Lease Act authorizing extensive support for the Allies, including war ships and planes.

Speaking in Des Moines, Iowa, on September 11, 1941, Lindbergh gave his most incendiary speech yet. His wife had read it ahead of time and warned him against it. Lindbergh echoed Henry Ford's view that Jews were pushing the country to join a war that would be detrimental to the nation. Lindbergh severely criticized Anglo-Saxon opposition to the Nazis as self-destructive. He urged his countrymen to fight the "yellow peril" and threats from "black and brown, not ourselves." He addressed "the Jewish problem" and told Americans that they should not listen to those alarmed by rumored atrocities in Europe. He urged his audience to be clinical in their approach to the war: "We must be as impersonal as a surgeon with his knife."

The majority of Americans now recoiled from both Lindberghs in horror. Jewish philanthropist Harry Guggenheim had already become estranged from his former protégé even though Guggenheim had previously been among the minority of Jews opposed to entering the war. Lindbergh's pro-Nazi speeches succeeded in alienating Abraham Flexner as well. In distancing himself from Lindbergh, Flexner wrote: "I am sorry about Lindbergh for he has ruined his life. He is a nice boy whom I know well, but he is uneducated and was completely taken in [by the Nazis]."

Biographer A. Scott Berg described Lindbergh in 1941 as exhibiting "messianic fervor." He wrote that by December of that year, "many Americans considered the aviator nothing short of satanic — not just a defeatist but an anti-Semitic, pro-Nazi traitor."

Folk singer Woodie Guthrie captured the growing national aversion to Lindbergh with lyrics to a new song: "Hitler wrote to Lindy, said 'Do your very worst.' Lindy started an outfit that he called 'America First.'" In fact, the political movement was not new. "Protect America First" had been the slogan used in 1924 on the third-party, Farmer-Labor ticket on which C.A. Lindbergh had signed up to run for Governor of Minnesota. Both he and Henry Ford had opposed World War I for similar reasons to those Lindbergh currently articulated — to keep whites from decimating each other and losing their global advantage over other races.

Lindbergh's September 1941 speech made some members of America First so uncomfortable they resigned the organization when it refused to repudiate his comments. Many Americans were already incensed that Lindbergh had sat in Hitler's box at the 1936 Olympics and later accepted a medal of honor from Der Führer. After the bombing of Pearl Harbor in December 1941, the United States officially joined the war on the side of the Allies. America First promptly disbanded.

When Lindbergh tried to regain his commission, President Roosevelt refused. The Lindberghs remained stateside and had their fifth child, Scott, in 1942. As war continued on two fronts, Lindbergh found a way to volunteer his services to help fight Japan. Though Lindbergh had been blackballed by the FDR administration from most military defense contracts, the Ford company invited him to serve as a technical consultant for the company's airplanes in the Pacific. Lindbergh then finagled his way, without Roosevelt's knowledge, into flying with fifty combat missions over Japan in 1944, training American pilots on fuel efficiency to extend their range.

In 1944, against her husband's advice, Anne published a novella, *The Steep Ascent,* a fictionalized account of a pregnant American aviatrix and her British pilot husband who barely survived a harrowing flight across the Alps. It was clearly based on their own trip to India in the spring of 1937 in her last trimester before giving birth to Land, an experience Anne had found almost unendurable.

10.
Carrel's Fall from Grace

AFTER December 1941, Lindbergh lost contact with Carrel. As Nazi atrocities became better known, support for American eugenics laws began to plummet. A strong push in that direction came from more liberal jurists then sitting on the United States Supreme Court. The high court for the first time recognized a fundamental right of individuals to procreate and declared that laws seeking to take such right away demanded strict scrutiny. In contrast, Carrel's bold ideas for improving the gene pool of France continued to receive generous support from the Vichy government.

While in Paris, Carrel had little direct interaction with the Nazis. Yet to the extent he differed with them philosophically, he did not challenge the banning of Jewish medical staff in his institute. Nor did he participate in the Resistance or raise any concerns in July 1942 when nearly 13,000 Jews were rounded up near his Paris headquarters for deportation to concentration camps. In fact, for his grand plan to reshape his country's future, Carrel gathered demographic data on the current population, including race, ethnicity, and disabilities. In Germany, children with disabilities had already been taken from their families on the pretext that they would be cared for by the state. With heartbreaking regularity, parents then received condolence letters telling them that their children had died of pneumonia. In the government's hands in Paris, the detailed information Carrel collected on French citizens similarly raised the "potential for grim consequences."

From 1942 to 1944, Axis troops also occupied Southern France where the Vichy government was headquartered. Carrel continued his work under far more difficult conditions. He became despondent not hearing from formerly close friends in the West, including Lindbergh.

But Lindbergh was concerned that any correspondence with Carrel would be intercepted. In August 1944, after the Allies succeeded in retaking France, the new French minister announced Carrel's immediate removal as one of the first essential steps of "purification" of government programs following ouster of the Nazis. The minister promised to make unspecified major changes in Carrel's institute.

Carrel's dismissal was instant news on Paris radio. It revived previously ignored criticism in America of how dangerous Carrel's recommendations were in his 1935 book *Man, The Unknown*. One editorial at the end of August 1944 labeled Carrel more evil than Hitler for urging that society be purged of undesirable members based on recommendations from a sequestered elite council. Instead of one "fanatic Fascist," Carrel was advocating that great races of the future be dictated by "a group of Hitlers" shut off from human society.

A week later the new French government named Carrel to the press as a Nazi collaborator whom they intended to prosecute based on "important new evidence." Among the projects Carrel had undertaken during the war was a study of the effects of poison gases. It was also reported that he had under his charge institutionalized mental patients. Suspicion arose that he gassed some of them to death when war-time food shortages made that seem expedient — the very euthanistic solution he had suggested in *Man, The Unknown*. Carrel denied the charges, but he and his wife abandoned their apartment and took refuge with a friend.

Carrel's abrupt dismissal followed by serious criminal charges soon hit the front pages of the *New York Times* and *The Herald Tribune*. *Newsweek* featured an article entitled "Collaboration Camp." The news accounts reminded readers of the close links between Lindbergh and Carrel. Former co-workers at the Rockefeller Institute told reporters it was quite possible Carrel had actively assisted the Nazis.

The news alarmed Carrel's long-time devoted secretary in New York, who still handled correspondence for him. Kathleen Crutcher immediately reached out to retired Director Simon Flexner for help on Carrel's behalf. Flexner, then 81 and himself in declining health, sent an urgent telegram to Secretary of War Henry Stimson seeking his intervention. Flexner cited Carrel's prior decades-long record of medical achievements in America. Stimson promptly sent orders to General Dwight Eisenhower, as the head of the European Theater of Operations, to prevent the new French government from taking Carrel into custody. The 71-year-old doctor was then dying of cancer at his friend's home. No further action was taken against Carrel by the new French government. He died on November 5, 1944.

The next spring, following the Allied victory in Europe, Lindbergh headed to Germany as a representative of the United Aircraft Company on a mission headed by the American military. Officially, Lindbergh did so to help review and report back on German war plane and rocketry factories. He left Anne behind, pregnant with their sixth child. Upon arriving in May 1945, Lindbergh visited France first, ostensibly as a detour to determine for himself if the stories of Carrel's Nazi collaboration were true. The aviator did not speak French and all of his activities in Europe had to be authorized by the Secretaries of the Navy and the Army.

FDR had died in April 1945. The military mission President Truman dispatched to Europe that May included Wild Bill Donovan as the head of the OSS. Between World War I and World War II, Donovan had been part of a cadre of trusted lawyers and business executives who gathered foreign intelligence in Europe for the U.S. government. During the war the OSS had been tracking Nazi atrocities. It was Donovan's idea to have trials at the war's end charging crimes against humanity. Donovan returned to Europe in the spring of 1945 to interview death camp survivors and prepare for the Nuremberg trials.

Presumably, OSS agents in Paris were already pursuing any evidence supporting the explosive charges of Carrel's complicity. Lindbergh told the press that he saw a copy of the charges while in Paris and considered them without merit. The copy he saw had to be in translation. Somehow, the charges themselves and any underlying documentation went missing, apparently never to surface again. Proof of Carrel's collaboration would have proved highly embarrassing to the Allies as they started bringing charges against German doctors.

After the war's end, as Donovan had urged, Great Britain, France, the United States and the Soviet Union jointly created an international military tribunal at Nuremberg to make an example of Nazi atrocities. The "Doctors' Trial" went first. Hitler's personal physician Karl Brandt and 22 other Nazi doctors and administrators faced charges that included the secret "negative eugenics" program started in 1939 to gas to death mentally ill patients and disabled children.

When defending Brandt at trial, his lawyer argued that the gas extermination program simply followed a recommendation from Dr. Carrel's best-selling 1935 book. That did not keep Brandt from being convicted and executed. Yet he and the other medical defendants represented only a small percentage of the doctors and staff who committed atrocities during World War II. Many additional suspects, including "Angel of Death" Josef Mengele, either fled to escape prosecution or, like Alexis Carrel himself, died during the war.

The Doctors' Trial had implications for the boundaries of medical ethics beyond condemning mass extermination of civilian prisoners. The judges at Nuremberg grappled with the core belief research doctors in America like Alexis Carrel shared with Nazi doctors: that physicians who engaged in experimental research were entitled to risk the lives of human subjects and sometimes sacrifice them for the greater good of mankind.

Nazi physicians were accused of forcing thousands of war prisoners to undergo life-threatening experiments. Medical researchers tested their resistance to disease, various types of poison, extreme cold and heat and deliberatedly inflicted other almost unimaginable trauma, often without anesthetics. (Mengele had gone further and performed shocking experiments on nearly three thousand identical twins, more than 90 percent of whom died.) Like Carrel, these fanatic research doctors believed that previously forbidden human experiments would greatly benefit the scientific community and the master race. Most of their involuntary human guinea pigs either perished or were permanently disabled or disfigured.

Sixteen of the medical defendants were convicted and received sentences of lengthy imprisonment or execution. Carrel may have been acquainted with another physician later convicted of collaborating with the Nazis in committing war crimes – naturalized American Edwin Katzen-Ellenbogen, a Polish Jew by birth, who had run a controversial laboratory at Skillman Village in 1911.

The judgment at Nuremberg included an historic list of ethical principles to divide permissible medical experimentation from barbaric crimes against humanity. These principles were deemed to override any nation's conflicting laws and to disallow the defense of "just following orders." Chief among the ethical requirements for use of human guinea pigs was informed consent. Perhaps, not too surprisingly, the Nuremberg principles were not all immediately endorsed by the American Medical Association or U.S. government. (The Tuskegee syphilis experiment was ongoing at the time.) Nor have all of the Nuremberg principles ever been codified by any country.

The United States government did begin banning the use of federal funds for experiments that put children at high risk solely for the benefit of others. Yet prior work remained shrouded in secrecy. Lindbergh had to be particularly concerned about exposure because *The Culture of Organs* boasted that he and Carrel had occasionally perfused human organs from living donors. All of Carrel's experiments were well-documented, filling shelves of notebooks in his office at the Rockefeller Institute. The bulk of such records presumably remained under lock and key in New York. Madame Carrel returned to New York in 1945 to handle her husband's estate in America. Lindbergh offered his assistance.

Lindbergh stayed close to Madame Carrel for years afterward, particularly focused on Dr. Carrel's papers. "He helped her by clearing the New York apartment, and characteristically made a careful inventory of its contents, including a catalogue of Carrel's books." Likely, he also sifted through Carrel's professional correspondence. Lindbergh also took charge of reviewing Carrel's boxes of medical records and extensive personal papers at the Rockefeller Institute. Somehow most records of Carrel's human experiments disappeared. Critics of Carrel's ethics were left with mostly vague allegations against a dead man. In the two decades following the end of World War II, Lindbergh and others were successful in restoring Alexis Carrel's reputation as a brilliant pioneer in vascular surgery.

In 1969, to honor his lifetime achievements in medical research, the French named a medical institute in Lyons for Carrel. Four years later the centennial of Carrel's birth was celebrated in both France and the United States. Lindbergh spoke at a 1973 conference in Carrel's honor in Washington, D.C. In France, Carrel's achievements were celebrated by naming a street for him. Yet by the 1990s, just the fact that Carrel's 1935 book strongly encouraged the Nazis to undertake their ethnic cleansing programs caused Carrel's name to be removed from the Lyons medical institute and the street. Today, his legacy is mixed. In retrospect, medical historian Dr. Michael Nevins views Carrel as both a "medical marvel" and a "moral monster."

11.
Lindbergh Secretly Achieves his Goal

AFTER the war ended, Lindbergh moved his family to Darien, Connecticut, an exclusive suburb of New York where restrictive covenants then prevented both Jews and blacks from becoming his neighbors. Biographer Leonard Mosley alluded to Lindbergh's Dr. Jekyll and Mr. Hyde quality during the Cold War: "Sometimes in this period of his life, Charles Lindbergh seemed like an actor in a small-town repertory theater who has to play most of the male parts in the script, one moment twirling his mustaches as the villain of the piece, a few minutes later reappearing as the blue-eyed hero."

Anne started seeing a psychiatrist for depression. Her husband appeared quite threatened by the prospect of Anne revealing her inner thoughts without him acting as a filter. It was the first time in more than two decades she ignored his efforts to keep her from speaking unguardedly. She wrote an essay about how she felt about their marriage in middle-age: "high and dry in an outmoded shell, in a fortress [that] outlived its function." Lindbergh tried to get his wife to quit seeing the psychiatrist. He even moved out of their bedroom and refused to speak to her for a couple of months. Anne kept up her appointments with Dr. Rosen, the same psychiatrist who had helped her younger brother.

Yet Anne still collaborated on a joint project with her husband. In 1953, Lindbergh published *The Spirit of St. Louis* to critical acclaim. With Anne's deft editing, it won the Pulitzer Prize, which he dedicated to her with the acknowledgement "she will never realize how much of this book she has written." Even so, the couple would increasingly live separate lives. After the war Lindbergh had resumed a major role in developing America's air commerce. In 1954, President Eisenhower made him a Brigadier General in the Air Force. Then Lindbergh traveled the world for Pan American Airways, spending months each year away from Anne and his children.

In 1955, Anne published her own classic book of essays, *Gift from the Sea*. It topped the best seller list, but she was greatly disappointed when her husband failed to show up at the party to celebrate its release. Anne confessed to her sister Connie the belated realization that she and Charles were "badly mated." Anne had by then embarked on a long affair with a physician who became a close confidante. Anne ended their affair in 1958 after realizing she simply could not bring herself to divorce her husband.

Lindbergh continued to go on long trips abroad year after year. Anne suspected her husband was unfaithful but had no idea of the extent of his infidelity. Under an assumed name, from the late 1950s through the late 1960s, he secretly fathered seven illegitimate children by three mistresses in Germany. His total number of offspring almost rivaled his grandfather Ola Mansson's achievement. Two of the mistresses were sisters. All three had been put in touch with the world-famous aviator when they let it be known they would like to bear his children. So many German men of their generation had died in World War II, the women were eager for even a small percentage of Lindbergh's time and attention. The three women knew his true identity, but their children did not learn it until they grew up.

In a partial about-face in his later years, Lindbergh also found a new passion. On his 1945 visit to Germany, Lindbergh had been taken to see a Nazi death factory. Though the Nazis had tried to blow up crematoriums and gas chambers before the Allies arrived, some evidence of their huge extermination campaign remained, including mass graves that horrified him. Lindbergh also saw evidence of American atrocities in Japan. He started to question whether civilization was always progress. In the 1960s, he emerged as a global advocate for protecting wildlife threatened by human activity. In 2007, author David Friedman commented on Lindbergh's changed world view by the time he was in his sixties: "The person who once tried to save the world by saving white civilization would now try to save the world from white civilization."

Lindbergh visited Africa again and began to question his prior conclusions on racial superiority: "Who is to say the record of future evolutionary ages will prove the black to be less progressive than the white?" He thought history indicated otherwise. Yet Lindbergh still strongly supported the American Eugenics Society and believed in natural selection — survival of the fittest, which he assumed he himself exemplified. Through the 1960s Lindbergh secretly continued splitting his time between his American and German families.

During the years he lived his double life, Lindbergh failed to return to Anne's side when she had a difficult knee operation and had to hobble around afterward on crutches. He also missed Scott's high school graduation and Land's wedding in 1960. Yet in 1965 Lindbergh made sure he was available to make several trips to the Harper & Row publishing house to review galleys of a biography of Carrel.

Anne's psychiatrist, Dr. Rosen, told her that her husband's long trips showed that he was running away from old age and intimacy. She felt that Dr. Rosen was right to point out that her husband's "compulsive outward orderliness" compensated for "inward disorderliness" and attributed his "compulsive need to travel" to "the loss of their first born, whose death he never fully mourned." He had forbidden Anne to even mention their first son's name to any of their children. When each sibling heard at some point in school or from some other source about the infamous 1932 kidnapping, Lindbergh took that child aside and explained briefly that the man who killed their older brother had been tried and executed. Lindbergh made it clear that he did not want the subject discussed within the family. Anne felt differently and continued her own self-examination. She said, "I want first of all . . . to be at peace with myself." She referred to having absorbed "shocks . . . [that] tend to crack the hub of the wheel."

Sadly, her younger daughter Reeve later also lost a young boy around the same age as Charlie. Reeve's son Jonny died of a fatal seizure during the night in his crib at Anne's home in Connecticut shortly before the boy's second birthday. As they waited together for emergency medical assistants to take his body to a funeral home, Anne commented that at least Reeve got the opportunity to grieve her son's loss, unlike Anne: "I never saw my child's body, after he died," she told Reeve. "I never sat with my son this way."

Anne did not add that the family held no memorial service for her firstborn son. Anne's pain had been magnified by her husband forbidding her even to keep recent pictures of Charlie taken shortly before he died. Her husband's efforts to erase Little Charlie from both of their memories simply carved the little boy more deeply into her soul. Reeve understood that she and her mother were now taking the time to mourn the death of both toddlers.

In 1966, Lindbergh had been stung by revelations in the published diary of Harold Nicolson that characterized Lindbergh as a strong Nazi sympathizer leading up to World War II. The aviator responded in 1970 by publishing *The Wartime Journals of Charles A. Lindbergh* which only reinforced Nicolson's observations. Lindbergh still stubbornly insisted American involvement in World War II was a mistake. He displayed open admiration for the Nazis even years after all their atrocities had been laid bare. The book was spurned, but it served as a catalyst for him to get his wife to publish her own diaries.

Anne had kept a diary from her college days through most of World War II except for a three-year gap demanded by her husband from 1929 to 1932. In a preface to her first volume, Anne wrote that diaries "reveal the writer" with the truth of her contemporaneous feelings laid bare not "veiled or colored." Yet that was highly misleading. When her writings were prepared for publication, her husband was watching over her shoulder the whole time. That gave him the opportunity to shape her revelations and remove observations he considered problematic.

Lindbergh was not only a hard taskmaster with his wife, he was extremely competitive with his children. One biographer noticed that, even at 69, when tramping across a pasture with two of his sons, Lindbergh suddenly challenged them to a race "to prove he was still their physical master, and either he was indeed or they let him think so, for he beat them blind."

When Lindbergh's oldest surviving son Jon married and his wife became pregnant, Lindbergh urged them not to name the new baby after himself. Lindbergh did not count Charlie as his first child. He called Land, not Jon, his "second son." Lindbergh feared that "[t]he naming of your first boy 'Charles' would, without doubt, create undesirable and dangerous newspaper publicity connecting him with the tragedy of 1932 — which was probably itself caused by excessive publicity." Jon's baby turned out to be a girl so that possibility was avoided.

Why Lindbergh felt the tragedy of his first son's death resulted from the media frenzy over his birth is open to more than one interpretation. Some insight might be provided from one of his bitterest arguments with his wife. Lindbergh reacted with outrage when Scott married a Belgian film actress and gave up his American citizenship. Anne defended their youngest son's life choices, including racing around Europe in an MG sports car. In one hot exchange, Lindbergh insisted that Scott needed to be more careful about putting his life at risk: "Machinery doesn't forgive." Anne shot back, "Neither does the unconscious."

ACT FIVE

Dr. Charles H. Land with grandson Charles circa 1905. Dr. Land captioned it: **"Me and My Best Chum."**

Charles Lindbergh developed a lifelong belief in science as God watching his grandfather, dentist and inventor Dr. Charles Land, experiment in his basement where he also practiced taxidermy. Photo circa 1900.

1.
Assembling the Puzzle Pieces

ANNA HAUPTMANN spent the rest of her long life trying without success to prove her husband's innocence. In 1981, outgoing New Jersey Governor, Democrat Brendan Byrne, ordered the New Jersey State Police to make public the 90,000 documents and exhibits they had accumulated in the kidnap case. In 1982, to see if the now decades-old remains found in the woods had been misidentified, Anna Hauptmann's attorneys hired Dr. William Bass, the human bone specialist who founded the University of Tennessee Anthropological Research Facility colloquially known as "The Body Farm."

Dr. Bass came to the New Jersey State Police Museum to examine a dozen small bones the museum still maintained from the site where the corpse was found. Mrs. Hauptmann hoped he could determine that the bones could not have been those of the Lindbergh child. Dr. Bass found to the contrary, that ten of the bones appeared to be foot and hand bones of the typical size of an 18-to-24-month old male. These findings were not inconsistent with the corpse being Charles Lindbergh, Jr. Two of the bones belonged to a mid-sized bird that had been gnawed by predators. None of the human bones had tooth or claw marks. No one at the time realized that Dr. Bass's conclusion suggested that wild animals might not account for the missing organs of the corpse. If that assumption by the first responders was wrong, a more sinister answer suggested itself.

The first clue something was off about the kidnapping story was that nothing seemed amiss in the nursery. This indicated a possible inside job. Then, the Hopewell police were led by Lindbergh out in the pitch dark in a beeline to the discarded ladder 60 to 75 feet from the house across a muddy field thick with tall grass — when he had no flashlight before they arrived. Col. Schwarzkopf failed to follow up when alerted by his own wood expert that Johnson saw a dowel in Lindbergh's den similar to the unusual ones used for the ladder.

Most tellingly, for two months in the spring of 1932 the whole country was looking for a baby who looked much different from the toddler when he disappeared. In the summer of 2019 forensic expert artist Melissa Cooper examined several photos of the Lindbergh baby: the one taken at his first birthday that the Hauptmann jury saw; a photo (likely taken the same day) posted on the History Channel; and the two photos reproduced in the ubiquitous poster in the same outdoor setting at Englewood. She compared them to the unattributed March 1932 newspaper photos depicting the child "as he was when stolen from his home" and what he would look like "if disguised" by the kidnappers. Cooper opined that it was the same child more fully developed as a 20-month old. She observed that "the shape within the eye area, his mouth, his hairline and the direction of the hair growth appear especially similar."

We also know that just a week before the kidnapping Anne arranged to have her son's hair cut at his grandmother's house in Englewood so he would no longer look like "a sissy." Five days before that, his pediatrician measured Charlie as then 33 inches tall. Yet in March his father authorized police to describe his missing son as only 29 inches tall in posters distributed nationwide and had apparently already given the same misinformation to police on the night he disappeared. In contrast, Aida Breckinridge described Charlie at twenty months as looking over two-and-a-half when she saw him post-haircut at the Lindberghs' home that last weekend of February.

Another oddity was the private meeting between Lindbergh's close colleague Thomas Lanphier and J. Edgar Hoover in mid-March 1932, a time when Lindbergh himself was freezing the Bureau out of meaningful participation in the hunt for his missing son. If that meeting occurred behind Lindbergh's back that was one thing. If it occurred at Lindbergh's instigation, it was another. Lindbergh could have assumed the Bureau already knew about him hiding Charlie in a closet at the Morrows' home a year earlier. The incident was known not only by family and staff but also revealed to the State Police. Lindbergh could have prompted Lanphier to confirm that practical joke simply to convince Hoover that Lanphier was a reliable source. That would put in a different light Lanphier's revelation to Hoover that Anne's hearing was impaired.

Back then, few pilots flying in open cockpits wore headsets and many suffered serious hearing impairment from repeated exposure to noise. If true, partial deafness made Anne a less reliable earwitness to the events on the evening of March 1. Yet no one else ever confirmed that Anne suffered from hearing loss. Indeed, it might have occurred to J. Edgar Hoover that if anyone's hearing was impaired it would more likely be Lindbergh's, given how many years he had spent flying in a noisy open cockpit.

Convincing Hoover not to credit Anne's hearing would reinforce Colonel Schwarzkopf's belief that Lindbergh alone heard a cracking noise between 9 and 9:15 p.m. on March 1, 1932 that he thought came from the kitchen in the west wing of the house. If investigators concluded that the sound of crating boards breaking must have come from the opposite direction — outside the nursery — it conveniently gave Lindbergh an alibi. Yet Anne otherwise seemed to pick up sounds perfectly well that night: a car on the gravel at 8:15 p.m. despite the wind; her husband's car horn around 8:20 p.m.; the rustle of the high wind when she looked out her bedroom window shortly after 10 p.m. Her statements to the police were also consistent with what the Whateleys, Betty Gow, and Lindbergh told the state police the night of March 1 – no one reported hearing any sharp noise that evening that might pinpoint the time of the crime. Since her son's disappearance, Anne had fielded phone call after phone call without apparent difficulty, talking to people about her missing toddler.

J. Edgar Hoover would remain skeptical of Lanphier's story and suspicious of Lindbergh. Yet there is no evidence that the FBI ever seriously pursued evidence of infanticide like Murray Garsson of the Department of Labor had tried to do. With Lindbergh and Breckinridge guiding the official investigation by the New Jersey State Police, Schwarzkopf made no effort whatsoever to follow up on Scotland Yard's suggestion to investigate that theory. And so it was that Lindbergh's activities during the days leading up to his son's disappearance were never fully explored. Here is what could have been pieced together.

Since December 1930, Charles Lindbergh secretly worked at the Rockefeller Institute helping Alexis Carrel and his medical research team with technical support for perfusion experiments. Finally, on February 24, 1932, Lindbergh succeeded in isolating plasma many times faster than lab technicians had performed the task before. Lindbergh was still hard at work at the lab in Manhattan on Saturday morning February 27 and back on Leap Day, Monday February 29. That was the same day Carrel's department submitted an unusually large charge for parts to assemble an innovative camera to film living tissue samples under a microscope. Lindbergh and the Carrels may also have dined together Monday night.

Lindbergh had left his wife and son at the New Jersey estate on Monday morning when he went to the Rockefeller Institute's headquarters in New York. He called Anne later on Monday to tell her to stay that night at the farmhouse instead of returning to Englewood as she normally would have done. On Tuesday morning, Lindbergh called Anne again to tell her to spend Tuesday night at the farmhouse and gave her specific directions on the dosage of medicine to give their son at bedtime for his cold. That evening Betty Gow remarked to Anne Lindbergh how soundly Little Charlie had fallen asleep within twenty minutes of his 7:30 p.m. medicine dose. The police apparently never checked what was in that medicine or how big a dose was given him on Tuesday evening at Lindbergh's specific telephoned instruction.

Lindbergh returned to Carrel's lab on Tuesday for part of that day, too. He uncharacteristically failed to show up at a gala dinner that night in Manhattan for which he was a guest of honor. Instead, he headed back to New Jersey at an unknown time. The police quickly learned that at dusk that evening a neighbor's teen-aged son, Ben Lupica, saw in the dimming twilight a 1929 Dodge with local plates proceeding in an odd manner at the foot of the Lindberghs' driveway. The driver appeared to be a "slim" white man wearing a city dweller's winter coat and a fedora that masked his features. Lupica did not know his new neighbor went by the descriptive nickname "Slim." The next day Lupica recognized the kidnap ladder found by police in the Lindberghs' yard as similar to the one he had seen in the car at dusk the night before. The police should have kept looking for that 1929 Dodge. Though Colonel Schwarzkopf never followed up on "Unknown

Person No. 1," he kept Lupica's description of the man and the car in his own slim file of promising leads.

Henry Breckinridge's behavior should have raised further suspicions. If the police had interrogated the Lindberghs and the Breckinridges about their recent interactions, they could have discovered that the two couples had spent a lot of time together shortly before the Lindberghs' son disappeared. That included the last weekend of January and most of the last weekend of February. On the afternoon of February 27, Lindbergh went straight from the lab to Henry Breckinridge's apartment and holed up with him for hours. The Breckinridges then rode with him to Lindbergh's farmhouse where the two men spent much of the time in private discussions. Apparently, the police never learned from Aida Breckinridge what she later was told by Henry — that the weekend before Charlie disappeared, Lindbergh was concerned his son would be kidnapped. The police might have wondered why neither man mentioned this to Anne and why Lindbergh himself took no precautions whatsoever. Instead, he called his wife on Monday to tell her he would not be coming home that night, but that she should remain at the secluded farmhouse with their son.

The police also should have wondered where Lindbergh was on Tuesday evening, March 1 at 8 p.m. when he got a call from Breckinridge. Lindbergh had told Colonel Schwarzkopf that Breckinridge alerted him by telephone that the sponsors of the gala were frantic because he failed to show up as a guest of honor at the Waldorf Astoria for the widely advertised event. Breckinridge obviously knew where to call Lindbergh, even though the aviator was not home yet. Lindbergh had to be somewhere near his estate in order to arrive at the farmhouse around 8:30 p.m.

By the time Lindbergh arrived home, Anne and Betty had given the boy his medicine and put him to bed. Both women then followed Lindbergh's standing instructions not to enter the nursery between 8 p.m. and 10 p.m. Lindbergh exhibited no interest in checking in on his son. Immediately upon being notified the child was no longer in his crib at 10 p.m., Lindbergh blamed a gang of kidnappers, grabbed his rifle, and then called the police and his lawyer — all long before opening the mysterious, unmarked envelope he said he found on a nursery window ledge.

Lindbergh's lack of curiosity as to what was in that envelope should have raised suspicions. He announced his son had been taken by a gang of kidnappers *two hours before* anyone in the house supposedly knew the plain envelope found in the nursery contained a ransom note. Indeed, no one else reported seeing the ransom note the first time they entered the nursery. Lindbergh only called the police to alert them about it after the women had thoroughly searched the room and found nothing unusual. Betty Gow later swore that the first time she saw it was at midnight when Lindbergh was asking the police to open it.

Investigators should also have inquired why Breckinridge and his wife packed suitcases and rushed back to the rural estate hours *before* the mysterious envelope was ever opened. One reason could have been that Breckinridge and Lindbergh already knew what the envelope contained and anticipated that the Breckinridges needed to stay at the farmhouse for the prolonged, fruitless investigation that followed.

Indeed, to give credence to the kidnap gang theory locals quickly reported numerous sightings of three suspicious men during the week leading up to the kidnapping and the day it occurred. Two witnesses even mentioned that the men asked for directions to the Lindbergh estate. It seems quite possible in retrospect that their aim was to be spotted. Lindbergh and Breckinridge could have hired them for the very purpose of drawing attention to themselves and their New York license plates and then disappearing from sight after the kidnapping.

During the first week of March a second and third ransom note arrived while Breckinridge openly solicited go-betweens with underworld connections supposedly to locate and negotiate with the kidnappers. This created a flurry of news coverage to a presumably delicate situation. (What no one ever noticed was a mix-up in timing. The coded ad responding on Lindbergh's behalf to the third ransom note was prepared and published before Breckinridge received the ransom note in the mail. It was strong evidence the whole ransom scheme was a hoax.) The police and reporters then heeded warnings not to follow either Breckinridge or Lindbergh on secret missions that were expected to result in the boy's recovery. When no progress resulted, one piece of startling news should have been pursued. Lindbergh had been spotted several times leaving home disguised as a trooper.

On March 10, a reporter verified with multiple sources that Lindbergh wore that costume when he raced from his home toward Skillman Village that Monday evening, not to return until morning; that he was gone again much of Tuesday; and then once more from midnight on Wednesday to some time on Thursday morning. The informants were likely troopers on night watch. They were fairly sure it was once again Lindbergh.

The police had a source of clues where Lindbergh might have gone if they had looked into his ongoing project with Dr. Carrel's experimental surgery team. But the Rockefeller Institute was one place the authorities never evinced interest in investigating. Carrel took detailed notes and documented his ground-breaking experiment with film footage and still photos, which would have been still available.

In his report to the Rockefeller board in April 1932, Carrel gave special credit for that just-completed experiment to team member Charles Lindbergh, for mechanical expertise in modifying the perfusion pump and centrifuge no one else on his staff possessed. Yet during all of March and early April 1932 when this experiment took place Lindbergh led his wife Anne to believe he took a complete break from his work at the lab to hunt for their son. Lindbergh's missing diary entries for March and most of April might have been enlightening. Carrel kept his own diary of his lab work, of which only three entries from March of 1932 were later published. All three focused on the need for scientists to study living humans and to focus on improving the quality of the race instead of just expanding its quantity. These entries mirrored speeches Carrel was already giving at the Philosopher's Club. In early April 1932 Carrel wrote in his diary about studying living organisms "directly" and not by "anatomical and physiological study in . . . repose." Carrel was saying that he learned far more from vivisection than scientists ever did from autopsies when the organs were no longer functioning.

When Lindbergh embarked on repeated searches at sea for his son with volunteer John Hughes Curtis from late April through early May, the public assumed the pair were together that entire time. But on the weekend of May 7-8, Lindbergh took a break to head back to New York.

He met up with both Breckinridge and Colonel Schwarzkopf before dining Sunday evening with Anne and the Breckinridges. The Lindberghs spent that night in Manhattan. He did not return to head out on another boat with Curtis until May 9. When the toddler's body was found in the woods on May 12, Lindbergh was off at sea again. The police suspected the body had only recently been placed in the woods because the whole area had been previously searched more than once. The burlap bag found by the side of the road could hardly have been overlooked.

The police should have considered the corpse's location peculiar for another reason. It was exactly where tracker Oscar Bush had pointed out any kidnapper with brains would not go on the night of March 1, 1932. Turning south from the Lindbergh estate, "you're headed toward Hopewell and pretty soon, if you've got anything to be afraid about or to hide, you'll be running straight into the arms of the police coming straight up from Princeton and Trenton." Lindbergh said he heard the sound of cracking wood around 9:15 p.m. A kidnapper from New York making that much noise would be far more likely to dump the body in the Sourlands directly north than to head south through town to find some other woods where he could get rid of the body and then make a U-turn. Had the authorities been open to it, there was a far more logical explanation of when the corpse was dumped where it was found.

The police later learned from a local man named Herman Veidt that he saw three suspicious men enter the woods off the Hopewell-Princeton Road a few nights before the body was found on May 12. He said the sightings came around midnight on May 4, 6, 8, and 10. It is unclear if Veidt saw three men each time. Once, he spotted a man coming out of the bushes carrying a "white cloth." The police apparently never followed up on that extraordinary report. Yet the gap in time between the discovery of the body and Lindbergh's arrival to identify his son's remains had left the state police briefly handling the homicide in a professional manner. The fourteen inches of soil removed from the vicinity of the corpse contained more hidden clues of what happened than has previously come to light — critical evidence that should lay to rest the theory on which Hauptman was tried and convicted.

2.
The Squibb Lab Report

IN THE analysis E. R. Squibb & Sons Laboratories sent to Col. Schwarzkopf on May 27, 1932 technicians reported no blood found anywhere. Knowing that would be disappointing news, the director of the lab stated: "it is of great regret that the results were practically barren of any significant clues which in our opinion would be of value in the investigation of the case now under consideration." Director John Anderson, M.D., a veteran research physician, made it sound as if nothing of consequence had been found in his staff's careful examination. That was not true.

The police delivered a large envelope marked "Hopewell" to Squibb on May 20, 1932 without indicating exactly where it came from. The contents included a well-worn left "rubber" overshoe with an inside length of 11¾ inches and inside width of 4 ⅛ inches. This would correspond to a man's shoe size between 11 and 12 ½, which was then unusually large. (In that impoverished rural area men generally owned heavy-duty boots for outdoor work, not rubbers. However, rubber overshoes were then worn in high-end medical laboratories, probably including Squibb.) The heel of the rubber contained particles of leaf, dirt and coal. The possible sources of those particles could have been analyzed just as was later done with particles found on the chisel left in the Lindberghs' yard.

That was not the only clue among the items gathered in the envelope. It also contained a left-handed leather glove with a canvas cuff. The glove had several kinds of dirt inside it: "small white sand particles . . . a few larger black particles, a few yellowish particles and black material." Squibb technicians also found particles of slag and coal dust in much of the soil, on the clothing, burlap bag and other items that were "distinctly different" from the other soil the lab received.

It could have been "boiler slag" which is only produced when coal is combusted in a specialized wet-bottom boiler – a luxury few but the extremely wealthy invested in during the Great Depression.

The burlap bag found by the roadside bore the stamps "ANIMAL FOOD" and "0224 OJL." This was traceable – perhaps to a nearby farm that for some reason also used an expensive, wet-bottom boiler. One of eleven fleshless human foot and hand bones was found in the bag. The rest were found in dirt and leaves near the body. Squibb technicians identified the single bone found in the burlap bag as belonging to an infant – like the other human bones they analyzed. The evidence examined by the Squibb lab suggested the child was not brought directly to those woods from his nursery on the night of March 1. That may have been the reason Attorney General Wilentz did not offer the Squibb report in evidence at Hauptmann's trial, or make that report available to the defense.

Two bird bones found in the soil indicated that the bird was devoured there by predators. Yet the detailed Squibb report did not mention any teeth marks on the human bones, one of which was pulverized to confirm it was human. Nor did Squibb identify any animal scat. (In 1982, without having seen the Squibb report, Dr. William Bass specifically noted there were no signs of trauma on the human bones, which he concluded all likely came from the same 18- to 24-month old.) Thus, there was no evidence wild animals had attacked the corpse to account for its missing organs. Indeed, there was no blood at all found in the burlap bag, soil, leaves or other materials Squibb examined. This indicated the burlap bag had transported the corpse to the woods, but only long enough after death that the foot and hand bones had already lost their flesh and separated from the body. This should have ruled out the corpse arriving in the woods on the same night the child was kidnapped.

Squibb examined a "strip of lavender paper 2-3/4 inches x 3/8 inch" found near the corpse. There may have been a reason why this premier lab did not express these dimensions scientifically. This strip matched a standard size of litmus paper – 70 x 10 millimeters. For many years Squibb itself had been selling similar-sized pH indicator strips in a variety of colors, including light purple.

The lab also analyzed a tiny, slightly oblong white disc which it described as 15/64 of an inch by 17/64 of an inch. In metric, its diameter would be almost exactly 6 millimeters, the same size as a standard coverslip used in medical labs. The technicians noted that it "appeared to be made of synthetic material," but was "insoluble in acid." It had taken microscopic examination and chemical testing for Squibb to determine the hard disc was not made of bone, cartilage or shell. (No mention was made that the disc might be a piece of mica, a mineral resistant to acids then used in labs as an alternative to glass coverslips.)

A Squibb doctor observed that the disc was coated with a substance "which looks very much like dried blood" but was determined not to be blood. A similar blood-like stain was found on both T-shirts that also tested negative for blood. This coincidence indicated a possible link between the corpse and the items found nearby.

In addition, a handkerchief was found at the site with "three small red stains . . . which have the appearance of a dye. . . . None of [these] stains . . . have the appearance of blood[.]" The Squibb report did not mention that this dye could be Phenol Red, then commonly used in labs as a pH indicator. Dr. Anderson's own lab had used phenol in past experiments with filtered animal blood and plasma. At the time, Squibb also routinely used centrifuges to process blood for the serum needed to inoculate children against polio. Over the past several weeks Carrel's team had several times made national news heralding Lindbergh's innovation revolutionizing the speed of that centrifuge process — including a review in *TIME* magazine. Lindbergh's ground-breaking article on April 15 noted that his experiments had been conducted with a mixture of filtered blood components and Phenol Red. (This mixture likely resembled blood, although technically it was not blood.)

Here was Dr. Anderson in late May 1932 — just weeks after Dr. Carrel's and Lindbergh's stunning announcements in Anderson's own field — with death scene evidence that might be linked to Carrel's lab. Squibb technicians should have considered whether they were looking at a 6-millimeter mica coverslip coated with a mixture dyed with Phenol Red and compared it to the unidentified stain on the T-shirts worn by the corpse. Both the corpse and the disc had been found dumped less than 10 miles from the Rockefeller Institute's Princeton lab. It was now public knowledge that the homicide victim's father volunteered in Dr. Carrel's lab experimenting with blood products containing Phenol Red. Why did Dr. Anderson dismiss these findings as providing no meaningful clue to solving "the crime of the century?"

Another possible clue not highlighted in the report was an unidentified, tar-like substance on a deteriorated towel bagged by the police. Squibb itself sold tar oil as a medicinal supplement and for experimental use by other labs, including the Rockefeller Institute. The same distinctive, dark soil found on the burlap bag was found in one other place – inside one finger of a pair of discarded brown gloves. One of those gloves contained a wrist hair that was mostly white but brown at the tip, matching a hair found on one of the T-shirts removed from the corpse.

The gloves appeared worn through in two places. The right glove had a small hole in the tip of the middle finger, the left glove had a small hole at the tip of the forefinger. This suggested the gloves were worn while doing repetitive needlework using those two digits – which required unusual dexterity. By the gloves, a piece of board was found wrapped with a dirty towel. Squibb identified another item in vague language: a 52-inch by 8-inch strip of "loosely woven . . . originally white" cotton cloth, parts of which were "discolored black." This cloth contained faint pink stains that were again determined not to be blood; it also had 20 holes in it, the largest of which was five by two inches.

Oddest of all, the report listed six pieces of "waste material" weighing from 6 to 74 grams (more than two-and-a-half ounces) with no indication what these items were. In his cover note, Director Anderson assured Col. Schwarzkopf that nothing larger than 3/64 of an inch (about one millimeter) escaped examination. The report described how even minute particles were sieved repeatedly. The failure to identify these six large objects was a glaring departure from an otherwise detailed analysis.

In addition to the items recovered from the woods and surrounding areas, the Squibb lab also analyzed the Dr. Denton sleeping garment that had been mailed to Condon in mid-March as proof that the kidnappers had Lindbergh's child. The report noted that the outfit had been washed. It, too, showed no blood, but the technician found "deposits of very fine black particles assumed to be of rubber under surface of 5 buttons and in fabric under these buttons and where center back button was torn off." This could have resulted if whoever removed that sleeping suit from the toddler was wearing black rubber gloves – like those medical technicians then wore.

Taken together, the many items Squibb analyzed suggest that the kidnapped child may have been taken alive to a medical lab in March and then stripped by a technician of his pajamas. Whenever the boy died, it was apparently not in either the burlap bag or the woods where his severely decomposed body was dumped but no blood was found. Nor was there any physical evidence that the corpse had been attacked by wild animals. Yet rubbish found at the site hinted at what could have transpired before the corpse was placed face-down in the hollow under the tree. The discarded items seemed to implicate: an older person with mostly white wrist hairs, highly practiced in using a needle and thread with a middle finger and index finger while wearing protective gloves; and possibly one or more associates who worked with mica coverslips, litmus paper, red dye, a blood-like substance, tar-oil, and a cotton sheet dyed black with a 5-inch slit cut into it. The rubber overshoe fit someone with extremely large feet who may have participated in experiments highly sensitive to bacterial contamination.

Contrary to Anderson's assertion that his technicians found nothing of consequence to the murder investigation that then preoccupied the whole country, they found a great deal of evidence that could have helped solve the crime. It is impossible to believe that Dr. Anderson and his staff did not have any clue about the source of that trash. More likely, Dr. Anderson deliberately chose to obscure what they discovered. The analyzed materials not only pointed to death at a different date and location than March 1 at the Lindbergh estate, they might have linked both removal of the pajamas and the dumping of the decomposed corpse to the staff of a high-end medical laboratory.

Despite all its shortcomings, the Squibb report provided the police with vital information about the homicide. With the report in hand in late May 1932, Col. Schwarzkopf must have known it corroborated his original assumption that the body had only recently been placed in the woods, and now knew that it was no longer bleeding when placed there. The report also contradicted the assumption the child's head fractures occurred at the estate on the night of March 1. Schwarzkopf's own men had seen no blood in the Lindberghs' nursery or the ground outside; the report disclosed that the burlap bag had never transported a bleeding toddler. Schwarzkopf should also have noted that the dimensions of the unusually large "rubber" were remarkably similar to the measurements of the footprint outside the nursery the night of the kidnapping.

When the police arrested Bruno Richard Hauptmann in the fall of 1934, they should have considered the Squibb lab findings. Hauptmann was a carpenter who wore a size 9 shoe. He was accused of hurriedly dumping the corpse in the dark of night on March 1, 1932 right after leaving the Lindbergh estate. He then supposedly fled in the opposite direction to his home in the Bronx before the police set up region-wide checkpoints. Hauptmann could hardly have transported a toddler with a fractured skull in the burlap bag, dumped the body on March 1, and left a fleshless bone in the discarded bag without a trace of blood.

By January 1935 millions of people worldwide were anticipating the conviction and execution of "America's Most Hated Man." Director Anderson of E. R. Squibb & Sons Biological Laboratories must have known that the German immigrant's death penalty trial was based on a theory that the analysis by his prestigious lab did not support. Yet Anderson did not come forward. The Squibb lab had an ongoing business and professional relationship with the Rockefeller Institute. Anderson himself conducted lethal animal experiments and shared Carrel's strong belief in medical advancement even if it entailed loss of life. We cannot determine now if Anderson took those factors into account, but we do know that since late May of 1932 he had in his hands key evidence that could have later saved Hauptmann from the electric chair. Yet Anderson maintained his report was "barren of any significant clues."

Pictured here are black rubber gloves doctors wore in the 1930s.

The Squibb lab report analyzed the Dr. Denton sleeping suit that the kidnappers mailed to John Condon in mid-March 1932. Squibb found fine black rubber particles on the underside of five buttons as well as on the sleeper's back flap where one button was ripped off. Dr. Carrel's surgical team routinely wore surgical rubber gloves.

Left to right: Asst. Atty. General Robert Peacock; Trooper John Lamb; and County Prosecutor Anthony Hauck

In prosecuting Hauptmann, the state likely did not realize the sleeping suit mailed to Condon by the kidnappers may have implicated Carrel's surgical team instead.

3.
Breckinridge, Fisch and Cemetery John

THE BUREAU had additional information by mid-May 1932 that, if state and federal investigators had been working together to solve the crime, would have been another key lead. May 13, 1932, the day after the child's body was found in the woods, was when someone using "B.D." as an alias wrote a letter to the Secret Service providing clues to the kidnap/murder. Among other assertions in his letter, B.D. claimed that Henry Breckinridge had seen the man who received the ransom money from Condon on April 2, 1932, i.e., Breckinridge should be able to identify Cemetery John. One assumes that after Hauptmann's arrest on September 19, 1934, federal agents in New York shared their information about Breckinridge with the New York police. On September 28, 1934, the New York police called Breckinridge in for questioning. Most likely, they wanted to see if he could identify Hauptmann as the man who took the ransom money on April 2, 1932 after Lindbergh and Condon were unable to do so. Breckinridge instead gave the police a statement that a mystery man came to his office on March 8, 1932 that he now believed was likely Isidor Fisch.

Breckinridge described the man who came to his office as 5' 6" or 7" and "about 120-25 lbs." He had dark eyes with pupils that dilated and contracted as he seemed "under mental and emotional excitement as he discussed the case." The man spoke with "little or no foreign accent but was obviously a foreign type." He wore glasses, had a dark complexion and black hair and "strongly resembled photographs of Fisch" Breckinridge had just seen in the *New York Evening Journal* and an international newspaper. (Fisch was far too small and had the wrong color eyes to be the man Condon called Cemetery John).

Breckinridge told police what intrigued him about his strange visitor on March 8, 1932 was the man's apparent knowledge of the third ransom note just delivered that day to Breckinridge's office. As reported in the press on March 9, 1932, Breckinridge had just sped up to New York from the Lindbergh estate on a largely secret mission. Reporters believed he was meeting with the kidnappers at Lindbergh's direction. But Breckinridge waited another two-and-a-half years before he told police he spent hours on both March 8 and 9, 1932 with this suspicious fellow, including having a meal together to pump the man for information.

The man insisted that Breckinridge "must deal with 'us'" which Breckinridge assumed could refer to the kidnap gang. Most ominously, Breckinridge recalled: "With a peculiar glint in his eyes, he stated that I must realize that the needs of science must be served, and that human life was of no consequence in comparison with the needs of science." He concluded the man was a "maniac of the degenerate Leopold and Loeb type" — the infamous Chicago teenagers convicted in 1924 of kidnapping and murdering Loeb's cousin for the thrill of getting away with a perfect crime. Breckinridge claimed to have told his secretary at the time that if this man "had anything to do with the Lindbergh case the child would be killed or had been killed." Yet Breckinridge then willingly met with the man again a day or so later. The following Saturday Breckinridge dispatched Condon to meet the kidnap gang's representative which resulted in the rendezvous in Woodlawn Cemetery. Condon told Breckinridge that the sleeping suit would be sent as proof and had to have also shared with Breckinridge and Lindbergh what Condon later told investigators: that "Cemetery John" kept asking if he would "burn" if the child were already dead. Yet Breckinridge still kept his own ominous conversation on March 8 from the police while a nationwide manhunt continued in full gear.

In his September 1934 account, Breckinridge tried to justify his secretive behavior up to then based on his concern back in March of 1932 that if word got out his visitor was roughly handled by the police it might discourage others from coming forward with useful information. This account made little sense. If Breckinridge had reason to be concerned in March 1932 that the child was already dead, why did he help his client pay an enormous ransom on April 2 without any proof Lindbergh's son was still alive?

The police should have checked their own records. On May 17, 1932, after the child's dead body was discovered, Breckinridge was brought in to give grand jury testimony about the case. At the time, Dr. Mitchell had just concluded in his autopsy that the homicide occurred seven to ten weeks prior to May 12. Breckinridge had to know he had highly relevant testimony to give about a possible suspect. He mentioned in that testimony that he received a third ransom note at his office, but never referred to his maniacal visitor that same day.

Breckinridge further testified before the grand jury that his efforts that spring were aimed at doing "every possible thing that might lay the basis of future evidence" against the kidnap gang. When asked about the progress of the homicide investigation, Breckinridge said he did not know if the New Jersey police might have anything that "might be of some use or aid" to the New York police investigating the ransom scheme in the Bronx. All the while he concealed vital information he later claimed to know firsthand.

The police could easily have discovered that Fisch had applied for a passport the week before Breckinridge testified in front of the Bronx grand jury. The date might have riveted their attention — May 12, 1932 — the very day the body was discovered. Fisch then planned to leave the country two months later but wound up staying in the U.S. for another year and a half before his trip back to Germany in December 1933. When shown Fisch's photo, several other witnesses would identify Fisch in connection with the crime, including the watchman at the Skillman railroad crossing the week leading up to the kidnapping; a guard at St. Raymond's Cemetery on the night of April 2, 1932; a Cuban official who reported seeing a letter Fisch signed seeking to exchange ransom money for Cuban pesos; and a ticket seller who identified Fisch as a passenger who spent ransom bills in November, 1933, for his fare back to Germany.

It was telling that Breckinridge had such clout in his own right and as Lindbergh's lawyer that the police never pressed him to explain his conflicting accounts and bizarre behavior. But by late September 1934 all that the police apparently cared about was that Breckinridge's statement was not going to help convict Hauptmann as the lone perpetrator of the kidnap/murder. Publicly revealing that Lindbergh's own lawyer believed he met Isidor Fisch as a representative of the kidnap gang on March 8 and 9, 1932 would have reinforced Hauptmann's "Fisch story." Breckinridge's startling police statement on September 28, 1934 would remain undisclosed for decades.

4.
Reconstructing the Crime

BOTH the first responders and outside pathologists consulted by Detective Ellis Parker believed the body had not been left in the woods since March 1, 1932. An educated guess can still be made today as to when and where the boy died, why the corpse was planted in the woods, and why the burlap bag was dropped by the road to make it easy to find. This is where the decades I spent as a trial lawyer and judge came in handy. I have had extensive experience weighing evidence and evaluating witness credibility. I am also well-practiced in considering arguments for and against suppositions and spotting holes in logic. That all helped in assessing the many theories about this case that other authors have put forth over the years. After reviewing all the material I could find that appeared pertinent, here is my theory of what likely happened.

Lindbergh was unhappy with a weakling son as his firstborn. Intense press coverage of the Eaglet already included speculation that the baby had suffered prenatal damage when Anne inhaled toxic fumes on the couple's record-setting flight across country in April 1930. Lindbergh's refusal to let pictures be taken of Little Charlie after the fall of 1931 was because of the boy's oversized head. Lindbergh dreaded the press that would follow as his boy grew larger and more obviously abnormal in appearance. If Charlie was hydrocephalic, Lindbergh may have assumed his son would die young. As a teenager during World War I, Lindbergh had turned to farming magazines for breeding advice. He internalized the American Genetics Association's recommendation to rid himself of weak animals and breed only the sturdiest.

Lindbergh had another motive — jealousy of his wife's time and attention. Since he first courted Anne, he counted on her as a companion in the air, his navigator, radio operator and faithful chronicler of their exploits. Anne originally thought of herself in similar terms — as a page to a crusading knight. Once she had her first child and became pregnant again, Anne no longer wanted that life. She told her husband she planned to stay at home with Little Charlie and the new baby they were expecting. Lindbergh was not willing to accept that.

All during 1931 when Lindbergh was working closely with Dr. Carrel, what to do about his sickly son must have weighed heavily on Lindbergh's mind. Despite being childless himself, Carrel was never reticent to express his strong views on child-rearing that included the belief weak infants were meant to die. Carrel also made up his mind that year that it was time for the next bold step in his research: to advance his knowledge of the way human body parts interacted through vivisection experiments using Lindbergh's perfusion device. Carrel was already in touch with New Jersey institutional overseers ready to offer "feeble-minded" guinea pigs. Carrel suggested to Lindbergh that one of the first human sacrifices in the perfusion device be Lindbergh's son. Carrel's wife knew well what happened next: "impassioned by Carrel's work . . . Lindbergh put himself at Carrel's disposal."

Carrel had already convinced Lindbergh they were on the path to obtaining the secret to immortality — and saving Elisabeth. Time was of the essence. Lindbergh might well have felt like Abraham offering the Almighty his son Isaac — not to the Biblical God but to the God of Science with Carrel as the chosen instrument. Through twisted logic, that was how "the Eaglet" might live up to expectations of greatness like that achieved by his father.

The vivisection would take place at Rockefeller's secluded Princeton lab. Then they needed the child to go missing for a couple of months to allow the body to decompose and appear to have been attacked by wild animals. Lindbergh knew he had to disguise the death to fool the public, his wife and her family. He confided his plans to another devoted eugenicist, his advisor and close friend Henry Breckinridge. Anne's sensibilities had to be considered on top of the need to avoid the risk of public condemnation and criminal exposure. Lindbergh and Breckinridge hit upon the idea of a fake kidnapping since such crimes against wealthy families were already common occurrences in the Depression. Revenge on the press was one of the side benefits of the scheme. Reporters would run rampant with the fake news and generate enormous sympathy for the national hero.

After he was kidnapped, the toddler likely was taken to a nearby hideaway in the outskirts of Skillman Village to be transferred from there by car to Rockefeller's Princeton lab. Breckinridge, perhaps with the aid of Donovan, made arrangements in January 1932 through Owney Madden for several con men to help with the fake ransom scheme, none of whom were told Lindbergh's true aim. Lindbergh and Breckinridge knew that Skillman Lane provided a great place for a few accomplices to hide out in one of the abandoned homes there.

A secluded house on Skillman Lane was also where Lindbergh could have escaped observation while constructing the ladder from crating board used to deliver lab supplies to Rockefeller's Princeton facility from overseas. Maybe at the time Lindbergh was thinking that a homemade "kidnap" ladder might lead the police to attribute the crime to an escaped inmate. (Had police kept the fingerprints their own expert, Dr. Erastus Hudson, found on an inside joint of the ladder they would have likely matched Lindbergh's. But the police were ordered to erase them in the fall of 1934 — likely at the instigation of Lindbergh himself when Dr. Hudson alerted the police that the prints would prove Hauptmann's innocence).

Circulating a copy of the unique "singnature" throughout the underworld was a good way to create confusion. Owney Madden likely orchestrated that part of the scheme for them. Paid cohorts including Arthur Hitner, Gaston Means and Isidor Fisch, would be counted on to fool go-betweens like Curtis and Condon, as well as eyewitnesses, and guarantee continued front-page media coverage of the bizarre crime. (Curtis became collateral damage, framed by Lindbergh).

Lindbergh and Carrel likely planned the abduction for Leap Day 1932. The symbolism would have greatly pleased both men. That also fits with Lindbergh not asking Anne to stay over at the farmhouse again on Monday night until that evening and then telling her the next morning to stay one more night. Over the weekend of February 27-28, Lindbergh and Breckinridge had ample time together to work out final details of the deadly plan. By then, three or more cohorts (likely including Fisch) had moved into an abandoned house on Skillman Lane and were spotted driving in the area. Because of a few loose ends that needed attending to, the kidnapping was moved to March 1. Lindbergh did not forget about the gala that night at the Waldorf Astoria, he had to skip it to carry out his part of the crime.

Lindbergh called his wife on Tuesday morning to give her specific instructions on the dose of medicine to give Little Charlie that night when he was put to bed. Lindbergh had presumably doctored it over the weekend and wanted to ensure there was no danger Little Charlie would wake up when grabbed from his crib. That afternoon, Lindbergh drove back from Manhattan to switch cars at the Princeton lab. There he borrowed a 1929 Dodge with local plates. He then picked up the ladder likely stowed in a shed on Skillman Lane and drove the last few miles expecting not to see any traffic at all. It startled Lindbergh when Ben Lupica's car came by when Lindbergh was at the foot of his own driveway. Lupica got a good look at the car but not the driver. A thorough police investigation in the next few days might have traced that Dodge's ownership to a team member of Carrel's at the Princeton lab. Lindbergh put a stop to that investigation.

When Lupica continued to his own home, Lindbergh then parked in Featherbed Lane and sneaked onto his own property. By then it was dark. He put on his golf socks over his shoes to disguise his footprints. He likely set up only two sections of the ladder leaving the third section in the yard near Featherbed Lane. He put the feet of the ladder precisely under the nursery window he had tampered with earlier that month so its shutters would not close. He held the ladder in place only long enough to leave imprints on the ground before taking the ladder down and leaving it in the yard near the other section. The ladder had started to crack when he stepped on it, but on that windy night no one inside heard that happen. The staff were likely then in the kitchen on the far side of the house. Setting up the decoy ladder prints did not take much time. Avoiding getting caught by members of the household was well within his bag of tricks as a long-time prankster.

By then it was around 6:30 p.m. Lindbergh was spotted exiting Featherbed Lane by the Conovers, his nearest neighbors on the south side as he headed out of Featherbed Lane onto the Hopewell-Amwell

Road. They noticed that the driver turned off his headlights as if to avoid being seen, but did not realize who was behind the wheel. Lindbergh then drove the borrowed Dodge back to the Rockefeller Lab. He called his wife at 7:00 p.m. to tell her he would be late for dinner and remained at the lab for the next hour. That is where the 8 p.m. phone call from Breckinridge to Lindbergh could likely have been traced. Lindbergh then got back in his own car and arrived home without the household having any idea that he did not come directly from Manhattan.

When Lindbergh got home for dinner, the stage was set. He likely arrived a few minutes before he honked his car horn to allow him to take care of a final detail or two in the yard. Anne thought she heard his car on the gravel around 8:15 p.m., but then became unsure when she heard him press the horn at 8:20 p.m. All Lindbergh needed to do at that point was wait until the Whateleys and Betty Gow were back in the other wing after dinner — all according to their known routine before Betty was allowed to return to the nursery at 10 p.m. to check on Little Charlie.

After the couple finished dinner and had just sat down for a minute or two in the living room, Anne must have been surprised that her husband suggested they go immediately upstairs to their bedroom. But she was used to following his dictates. They spent fifteen minutes together in the bedroom and then both headed for baths, also something Lindbergh likely could count on Anne doing. He went first. After locking the door, he simply ran the bath water. Then he sneaked into the nursery, pulled his unconscious toddler out from under his blankets and left him still asleep down in the study. Lindbergh then returned upstairs to reenter the master bathroom through the nursery and emerge in his dressing gown to get dressed.

Planning in advance to go out in the stormy night after taking his evening bath also explains why Lindbergh got fully dressed again — an odd decision he was never questioned about. (Lindbergh purposefully made sure Skean was left elsewhere at either Englewood or a Princeton kennel. Skean would have ruined the plan if the dog was in his customary spot by the crib and started yipping when the little boy was taken). After moving his son down to the study, Lindbergh then only had to wait until Anne was in the bath in order to head back downstairs to complete the kidnapping.

Until Lindbergh went downstairs around 9:30 p.m. that whole side of the house had been dark from ten minutes before 8 p.m. Opening the shutters of his study's window and turning on the light made him visible for some distance eastward. Lindbergh walked outside with his sedated son to meet his accomplices who had parked in Featherbed Lane. Historian Lloyd Gardner noted evidence of "sightings that night of cars leaving the area of the Institute [Skillman] on the way to (possibly) Highfields."

No one else saw Lindbergh hand off his toddler. Betty Gow and the Whateleys were then on the west side of the house and Anne was taking a bath. Wahgoosh had no reason to bark. No stranger entered the house. The accomplices then returned to Featherbed Lane and drove off unnoticed. (On March 2, 1932, tracker Oscar Bush saw evidence of two cars that had just parked in Featherbed Lane, as well as multiple footprints across the yard from the farmhouse to the lane).

Lindbergh walked back inside to his study while Anne was still in her bath. He had enough time to get settled in his desk chair by the window with a book and affect surprise at 10 p.m. at Betty Gow's news of his son's disappearance. By then, his cohorts easily had returned the short distance back to the house they were staying in on Skillman Lane. Lindbergh gave the men some extra leeway by delaying the first call to the police until 10:22 p.m. (Police records belied his statement that he had Olly Whateley alert the police immediately after viewing the empty crib at 10 p.m.)

Lindbergh also had the opportunity to plant the ransom note in the nursery. In their alarm, both Anne and Betty did not focus on their own knowledge they had not seen any envelope when they thoroughly searched the nursery shortly after 10 p.m. A few minutes later, Lindbergh ostentatiously closed the hall door to the nursery, telling his wife and household staff he wanted to preserve evidence for the police. He was instead in the process of manufacturing evidence. He had just placed the envelope on the windowsill with gloved hands so he could point it out to the police on their arrival after he led the two officers to "find" the ladder in the yard that he had planted there along with the chisel and dowel.

All Lindbergh had to do a few minutes later to finish setting the scene was to enter the master bedroom and head to the master bath, locking the bathroom door behind him. While Anne likely assumed he was using the facilities, Lindbergh exited through the other door of the master bath that opened into the nursery. He then wiped prints off every surface with no one to observe him doing it because the door from the nursery to the hall remained shut. Then he returned to his bedroom through the master bath. At 10:35 p.m. he headed downstairs to greet the Hopewell police on their arrival.

Lindbergh later told state policemen that he had waited by himself upstairs while Whateley was downstairs telephoning for help. Lindbergh was upstairs shortly after 10:20 p.m. when Whateley made successive calls to the local and state police. That was when Lindbergh had to have been busy erasing fingerprints in the locked nursery. (This dovetails with Betty Gow's later testimony that she did not know where Col. Lindbergh was for several minutes before the Hopewell officers arrived.)

Police Chief Harry Wolfe immediately deduced it was an inside job. When Lindbergh and Breckinridge took charge of the investigation, they were able to exclude Wolfe and other skeptical veterans like Ellis Parker and federal agents. Lindbergh also ensured that reporters obliterated the car tracks on Featherbed Lane, trampled footprints in the yard and tainted fingerprint evidence on the ladder. Leaving a ¾ inch dowel in his study similar to the two used in the ladder was a mistake. Though Col. Schwarzkopf later dropped that inquiry, the dowel's length puzzled their wood expert. Both it and the two ¾ inch diameter dowels used with the ladder likely came from standard Army Air Corps supplies unavailable to the general public.

Some state troopers who stayed on the case found Lindbergh's behavior quite suspicious. As Inspector Harry Walsh reportedly later admitted: "He was just too big to bring down." Unique among all Americans in the early 1930s, Charles Lindbergh could probably have shot somebody on Fifth Avenue in broad daylight and gotten away with it.

On March 3, likely at Anne's insistence, the Lindberghs published Little Charlie's diet and the medicine he was taking. Dr. Carrel created a special file in his office for that information. That made sense if he planned to experiment with the child's organs. Otherwise, creating that file on Little Charlie's diet had no discernible purpose. The boldest part of all came the following week.

While the press focused on Breckinridge's seance on March 6 and mystery adventure in New York the following Tuesday, Lindbergh disguised himself as a trooper. He concealed from his wife where he was off to and raced from his home toward Skillman late Monday night March 7 until morning, part of Tuesday, and possibly again sometime in the wee hours of March 10, returning in time for breakfast. His actual destination was Rockefeller's medical research lab in Princeton. Carrel needed Lindbergh to attend the historic vivisection to make sure no problems arose with the centrifuge or perfusion pump that required his mechanical expertise to fix. And Lindbergh was thrilled to participate.

The risk of being followed necessitated elaborate subterfuge. After dressing as a trooper, Lindbergh took a circuitous route to thwart anyone who might be tracking his path. But he had warned off the press and no one else could be expected to be driving in the vicinity that close to midnight. It was only 12 miles from Skillman Village to the Rockefeller lab near Princeton. Dr. Carrel and other team members would have already arrived from Manhattan by train to Princeton Junction, during the day on Monday. As Carrel was the director of the institute's experimental surgery department, his team's comings and goings to the satellite laboratory did not attract special attention.

From Carrel's perspective, the vivisection of Lindbergh's son was the highlight of their perfusion experiments to date; for Lindbergh, it was proof of his passionate devotion to Carrel's mission to unveil the key to immortality. Being present in the lab as body parts were examined and filmed following the vivisection also gave Lindbergh the extraordinary opportunity to contrast his son's undeveloped sperm cells to his own sperm under a high-powered microscope. (The boy's testicles were among the missing body parts. Carrel mentioned in *The Culture of Organs* that he and Lindbergh harvested testicles, but not successfully. Lindbergh later marveled about viewing his own swimming sperm through a microscope, noting sperm on the microscope slide did not last long.)

Breckinridge's role was to provide a major distraction by speeding off from the Lindbergh estate to New York for a secret meeting on March 8, 1932. Breckinridge was then prepping Cemetery John (likely Hitner) with inside information to prepare for the first meeting with Condon in

Woodlawn Cemetery. Breckinridge later implicated Fisch as the stranger he met in his office on March 8, 1932 who spoke cryptically of the needs of science requiring human sacrifice. Back then, the toddler was still assumed to be alive. In retrospect it appears that Breckinridge was well aware that the child had been vivisected that very morning.

In his April 1932 annual report, Carrel identified Lindbergh as a key member of the team that had just completed an historic month-long carotid artery experiment. The vivisection of Lindbergh's son on March 8 would have provided a month of observation for Carrel to report back to the Rockefeller board before mid-April. Lindbergh was key in more ways than one if he supplied his own child as the subject of that experiment.

By March 11 Lindbergh decided to improve his alibi for the kidnapping. He pretended he and Anne had spent fifteen minutes in the living room after dinner and, while seated there, he heard a noise like a crate breaking. Lindbergh relied on the gullibility and hero worship of Col. Schwarzkopf to sell that account of when the kidnapping must have occurred. (His wife was too honest to stretch their time in the living room to fifteen minutes. She amended her statement to the police at her husband's instigation to say they may have sat there five minutes.)

When Erastus Hudson revealed scores of unidentified prints on the ladder in mid-March of 1932, Lindbergh may have started getting nervous. Otherwise, how does one explain why the investigation he controlled never sought to identify those prints when money was no object in solving "the crime of the century"? Hudson's independent efforts to locate large pinewood crates reinforced with a cleat secured by a square-cut nail could have concerned Lindbergh as well. Too much focus was now on the consensus in March of 1932 that the ladder looked like it came from new crating board. Perhaps Lindbergh feared that Hudson might trace the origin of rail 16 to a crate of foreign supplies delivered to the Princeton facility or a shipment to himself from China.

That entire spring the ladder sat in Lindbergh's basement where it would have been easy both to plane the edges of rail 16 to make it look like it had once been tongue and groove floorboard and to add three more square-cut nail holes on its face. (There is a dispute to this day whether the rail originally had one square-cut nail hole in it or four).

Doctoring the rail could redirect searches for its origin away from a crate to the pinewood floor of a barn, attic or warehouse as wood expert Arthur Koehler would later assume. Misdirection was a hallmark of Lindbergh's and Breckinridge's game plan.

Throwing away $50,000 in April was a hugely expensive way to make it look like Lindbergh was genuinely eager to get his son back, but it succeeded in convincing his skeptical mother-in-law, as well as the public, that the ransom scheme was real. As some of the money turned up in scattered locations, state and federal investigators focused considerable resources on trying to hunt down whoever spent it. Meanwhile, Lindbergh and Breckinridge could count on a gullible press eager for sensational headlines to compound the confusion. But they also relied on deliberate misinformation. From day one, Lindbergh described his son as 29 inches tall and disseminated pictures of a curly-haired infant at age one instead of what Little Charlie really looked like when he disappeared — a nearly three-foot-tall active toddler with a new haircut. The ubiquitous posters succeeded in implanting the idea of a helpless baby stolen out the window of his nursery that has lasted to this day.

In late March and April of 1932 — the very time that Little Charlie's remains were lying undiscovered with most of his internal organs missing — Dr. Carrel's diary sang the praises of harvesting tissue and organs from living organisms, including humans, to isolate them for study. He reveled in the insight scientists could obtain from vivisection versus anatomical studies of animals and humans with their organs in a "state of repose" — i.e., subjects which were dead before their organs were harvested. Most likely the corpse stayed somewhere on the premises of the Princeton facilities of the Rockefeller Institute. Only staff and rare invited guests visited that secluded farmland property. The strong smell of chemicals and carcasses of vivisected animals would likely have masked any odor from the decomposing corpse that could have attracted attention elsewhere.

It was Lindbergh's plan all along to have the corpse found at some point to put an end to the convoluted ransom scheme. Putting the toddler's two T-shirts back on the child's chest after death ensured the nanny would recognize the boy's clothing once the body was discovered.

Lindbergh knew that as March turned to April and April to May, Anne would remain obsessed with finding the boy alive. Once the child's body was found and identified, Lindbergh correctly assumed he could convince her to resume their prior lives, something he was quite anxious to do.

It was not hard to pick a suitable remote site off a seldom-used road between Hopewell and Princeton where the corpse could be dumped. Lindbergh was familiar with the woods off the same road south of the farmhouse he had rented the year before. It was also an easy drive from the Princeton campus of the Rockefeller Institute. Maybe Lindbergh and Breckinridge even thought ahead of time to make sure the body was found over the line in Mercer County so Coroner Swayze and Dr. Mitchell would conduct the "look-see" autopsy rather than a county pathologist elsewhere who might do a more thorough job.

Meanwhile, Lindbergh had constructed an alibi for himself in taking to sea on still another false lead. Since he secretly took a break from that excursion on the night of May 8, he actually might not have had an alibi for when the child's body was deposited in the woods. Dumping the body together with other lab discards could have been their undoing, but that oversight did not go public — one of the benefits of Carrel's and Lindbergh's enormous clout and the fact that Lindbergh was allowed to take full charge of the state investigation.

Leaving the corpse's head and a leg partly exposed was intentional — to ensure that the corpse was spotted. That was why the burlap bag was left as a giant clue by the roadside. That probably occurred on May 10 — the last night Herman Veidt saw suspicious activity at that location. By then Lindbergh was back at sea so he would have an alibi when someone discovered the corpse. There was some risk that the remains would not look like a carcass attacked by wild animals, but speedy cremation could, and did, prevent exploration of a different theory of what happened. No surgical incisions were noted but neither Swayze nor Dr. Mitchell was looking for any. They were not permitted to conduct a full autopsy. The Squibb lab report could have shed considerable light on the homicide but there is no indication the police ever shared that report with Dr. Mitchell.

Watching his son die on Carrel's operating table in March of 1932 explains why Lindbergh felt compelled to tell his wife that same summer: "Man has always feared the unknown, and yet when he has understood it, it has been good, not evil." Anne knew he was referring to his work in Carrel's lab and their joint quest for the secret to immortality, but likely never reflected deeply on why he was focused on good and evil. Lindbergh had no reason to believe his wife thought animal vivisection was evil. She knew her husband participated in experiments involving drained animal blood and admired his pioneering work with Carrel. But Lindbergh had to know his wife would have been aghast if she learned he helped Carrel vivisect any human infants, let alone her own beloved Charlie — even to save her sister Elisabeth. Lindbergh convinced Elisabeth to undergo a medical evaluation at the Rockefeller Institute in May of 1932. He likely hoped to find out if she was a viable candidate for open-heart surgery. One assumes the doctors considered her too weak to survive such an invasive procedure, and that Dr. Carrel's technique for creating a temporary bypass would have to await another potential patient.

When Anne visited the Rockefeller Institute in early 1933, Carrel made a point of assuring her: "It is really excellent, what he has done here. This [experiment with a perfusion pump] has not been done before." Carrel had used a perfusion pump for many years before Lindbergh ever came to the lab. What Carrel cryptically described to Anne as not having been done before her husband's arrival most likely referred to the successful maintenance of a human carotid artery in vitro — the landmark experiment in Lindbergh's "life chamber" conducted from early March to early April 1932. If so, Anne had no clue Carrel was referring to the sacrifice by her husband of the couple's firstborn son for "the needs of science."

By 1934 the bungled investigation appeared unlikely to ever be solved. But when Hauptmann by chance began spending ransom money late that summer and got caught, most people were ready to accept that the German immigrant carpenter must have been guilty. The police, even more than most other Americans, wanted the saga behind them. The State police put themselves at Lindbergh's disposal, wiping the ladder clean of prints and manufacturing evidence implicating Hauptmann in the creation of the ladder, offering Hauptmann spelling "help" that would persuade experts Hauptmann authored the ransom notes, and paying three men to belatedly identify Hauptmann in 1934 as a stranger they saw near the Lindbergh farmhouse in late February and on March 1, 1932. With the help of Attorney General Wilentz, the police also pressured Dr. Mitchell to recant his testimony about the time and manner of death and bullied Condon into joining Lindbergh in agreeing to identify Hauptmann as Cemetery John. All that effort paid off.

Yet eight years after Hauptmann's execution, Lindbergh must have had great fear of being exposed by records left behind following Carrel's death in the fall of 1944. He partnered with Madame Carrel as she went through Carrel's personal papers. Lindbergh knew that the groundbreaking experiment Carrel performed in March 1932 was well-documented, including with extensive film footage. Most daily records kept of experiments with human organs somehow disappeared in the next several years as did most of Carrel's and Lindbergh's diary entries for the spring of 1932. But Lindbergh could not erase everything. *The Culture of Organs* had already been published with human vivisection included in it and a photo of a carotid artery experiment that appeared to date from the spring of 1932. At the time, Carrel and Lindbergh were immensely proud of their initial achievements. After the Rockefeller Institute disbanded Carrel's team, they desperately wanted to encourage other medical researchers to follow in their footsteps with human vivisection experiments. In 1939, Dr. Anderson hired Parker to head Squibb's new virology lab and staffed it with several other former Rockefeller medical researchers.

Earlier in 1938, Carrel's colleague Dr. Raymond Parker had published with Carrel's blessing a more detailed manual. It described the operation of Carrel's lab over the past ten years, explained how to set up a similar vivisection lab and told researchers how they might replicate the tissue and organ experiments conducted by Carrel and his colleagues at the Rockefeller Institute. Parker's book included a photo of four unpublished experiments by Carrel of human leukocytes preserved in their own serum. By the third edition in the 1960s those photos and accompanying caption were eliminated from the book.

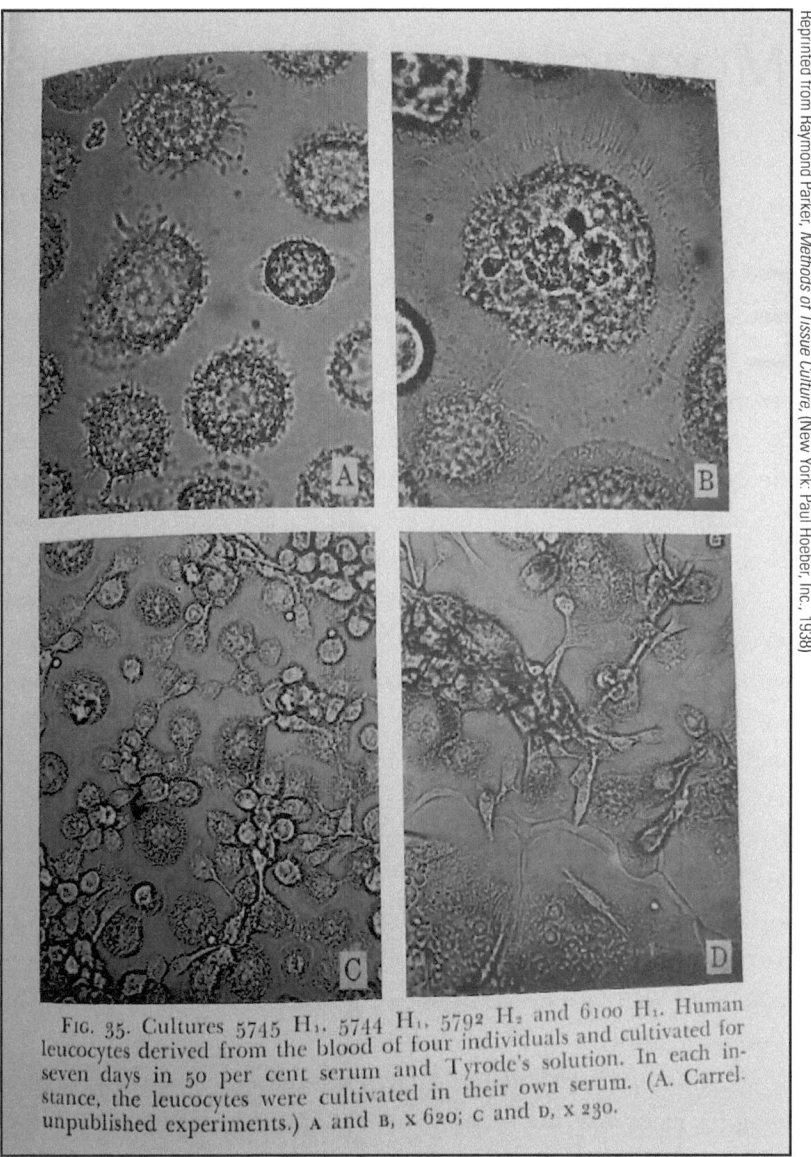

FIG. 35. Cultures 5745 H₁, 5744 H₁, 5792 H₂ and 6100 H₁. Human leucocytes derived from the blood of four individuals and cultivated for seven days in 50 per cent serum and Tyrode's solution. In each instance, the leucocytes were cultivated in their own serum. (A. Carrel, unpublished experiments.) A and B, x 620; C and D, x 230.

This photo in the first edition of Dr. Parker's book, Methods of Tissue Culture, *shows human leukocytes bathed in their own serum from an unpublished Carrel experiment. By the third edition, this photo and reference to Carrel's unpublished human experiments had disappeared from the book.*

5.
Maggots and Chemicals Tell a Tale

EVIDENCE that Little Charlie's heart kept beating while his organs were removed was provided by the hemorrhage Dr. Mitchell noted inside the skull beneath the fractures. When the surgery was over, a misleading cause of death could have been faked by hitting the right side of the head with a blunt instrument while he still lay on the operating table. Experts on a PBS special in 2013 opined that both the small hole behind the right ear and the fractures likely resulted from a blow to the head while the child lay on a flat, hard surface.

Another explanation for the small, rounded hole behind the ear was recently suggested by forensic pathologist Dr. Peter Speth, a nationally renowned forensic expert and veteran of more than 2,000 death scene investigations. If Carrel diagnosed the toddler as hydrocephalic, he might have wanted to drill a hole behind the right ear to see if he could set up a successful shunt with vein segments to drain off excess fluid on the brain. Carrel had performed similar experiments with hydrocephalic dogs about 25 years before. In 1908, Dr. Harvey Cushing attempted to replicate Dr. Carrel's shunt on a hydrocephalic baby, but the infant died. No one was known to have succeeded since. Dr. Carrel would have been quite eager to have a human guinea pig to conduct such an innovative procedure himself.

Carrel could have had time to fit in such an experiment before pursuing his main objective – and his wife might have even served as the boy's nurse. But Lindbergh prevented a full autopsy and later joined Mme. Carrel in purging most of her deceased husband's records of human experiments. So, we cannot know. Yet when pediatric surgeon Dr. Lauren Schwartz participated in a 2016 reexamination of the case, she assumed the boy was hydrocephalic and that the corpse's internal organs were surgically removed postmortem to disguise that fact. She did not believe wild animals would leave behind the heart and liver while devouring other organs. Dr. Speth and the experts he consulted consider the available data to point instead to vivisection.

Dr. Speth noticed that no teeth marks were mentioned in the the autopsy or Squibb lab report, nor were any large bones from the missing limbs found at the woodland site. Dr. Speth took special note that out of all the bags and baskets of dirt, twigs and leaves and other evidence recovered at the woodland site, Squibb technicians reported finding maggots within only a few "small masses" of soil. No other maggots and no insect eggs or puparia were found. He also noted that none of the people who viewed the body back then mentioned seeing any insect activity on or around the corpse. Only one person claimed otherwise — two-and-a-half-years later. That was when Inspector Walsh took the stand in Hauptmann's trial and testified that he accidentally poked a hole in the corpse's skull with a stick — which Dr. Mitchell had previously sworn was impossible to do.

Walsh testified that he used a stick to turn the corpse over because the corpse was covered in a "veil of vermin." Yet the joint report Walsh filed with State Police Lieutenant Keaten on May 12, 1932 made no mention of seeing any insect activity on the corpse or of puncturing the skull. To the contrary, Walsh and Keaten reported they made a "close examination" of the face and suspected it was the Lindbergh child. No one who observed the corpse that afternoon mentioned any necrophagic activity at all — not the two laymen who found the body; nor several other state officers who guarded the body before the coroner removed it; nor Hopewell's police chief who filed his own detailed report. Such a nauseating sight as a host of maggots feasting on the body would likely have been noted in one or more of the police reports.

Dr. Speth observed that truck driver William Allen and his co-worker said they spent five minutes staring at the corpse before they headed off to the local constable. In Dr. Speth's experience, people unused to seeing maggots feeding on a corpse tend to gag and turn away at such a sight. That did not happen. Half an hour later, Sergeant Zapolsky and Detective Fitzgerald were the first to turn the body face up and bend down to take a hard look at its features. Zapolsky found that, unlike the darkened corpse, the face was white and remarkably preserved. Zapolsky compared what he saw to a photo of the Lindbergh baby that he had brought with him from police headquarters. Hopewell Police Chief Wolfe and Constable Williamson joined in the effort to determine if this face looked like that of the missing baby. None of them indicated that this scrutiny of the face happened through a veil of vermin.

Dr. Speth concluded that Walsh's testimony that he saw a "veil of vermin" was simply not credible. When discovered, the head was face down with most of its features remaining intact. That indicated that the entire time it lay in the woods it had likely been lying face down. Just one eye had begun to decompose. Only after the police turned the corpse over did the face start to darken. Lying in that position until the police turned it over, the corpse would not have left easy access to the thoracic and abdominal organs for animal predators to attack. If maggots or other necrophagic insects had been present in droves on the afternoon of May 12 — as Walsh later claimed — they would have already invaded orifices of the head. Yet the autopsy listed no such evidence.

Dr. Speth also notes that had there been a host of maggots such as Inspector Walsh described, they would have still been present in great numbers when the body was taken to the morgue. That would have likely meant maggots dropping to the floor during the autopsy and crunching under foot. Instead, Dr. Speth observes that: "The complete absence of blow fly and other carrion insect activities on and about the body is contrary to the known scientific succession of necrophagic insects, considering the stated prevailing conditions on and about the body." The absence of maggots was confirmed by the photographer who took the only picture of the corpse at the morgue.

The most likely explanation under the circumstances for the lack of necrophagic insect activity was some type of unnatural intervention, most notably a chemical. Dr. Speth concluded that the presence of one particular chemical would have easily accomplished that result: "ethyl ether, a known anesthetic utilized in the 1930s during vivisections. No necrophagic insect would feed on a corpse containing ether."

Based on Dr. Speth's preliminary observations and review of other evidence cited in this book, Dr. Bass now believes that it is quite plausible Charles Lindbergh Jr.'s organs were surgically removed in a vivisection experiment — invalidating the entire premise of Hauptmann's conviction. Since anthropologist Dr. William Bass was only asked in 1982 to examine the remaining bones held by the New Jersey State Police for identification purposes, he had never rendered an opinion on the cause of death or even reviewed the autopsy and Squibb report.

Dr. Speth was not done analyzing the homicide. It puzzled him greatly how the face was mostly well-preserved when the body was found. On the evening of May 12, 1932, Dr. Mitchell had observed at the morgue: "The facial muscles had still not deteriorated, although the body generally was in a bad state of decomposition." Dr. Speth noted this was the reverse of the expected result after a freeze/thaw cycle which occurred in March and early April 1932 in that part of New Jersey. Freeze/thaw weather accelerates decomposition of the face compared to internal organs. Here the exact opposite happened.

Dr. Speth noted that Hauptmann's defense team had one or more experts prepared to testify at his murder trial in 1935 that the corpse appeared to have been embalmed, but none of them wound up being called to the stand. (There is no available record of what such opinion was based on.) Dr. Speth similarly concluded that only application of some chemical to the face explained how the facial features remained lifelike while the body greatly deteriorated.

At the morgue on the evening of May 12, Dr. Mitchell also noted that the face was quite discolored. Dr. Speth was more interested in how the face had looked when first discovered. Sergeant Zapolsky testified that the face had turned from white to blue between the time he and Detective Fitzgerald first turned it over that afternoon and when they came back an hour later. Detective Fitzgerald gave a slightly different description when interviewed by Assistant Attorney General Peacock in December of 1934. Fitzgerald recalled the part of the face that had been face-down in the dirt was "more or less of a pink" when turned over and "after the air hit it, it became dark."

"White" and "more or less of a pink" likely just reflected two different ways of describing the hue of a typical Caucasian toddler's face. But Zapolsky testified that the face very shortly turned blue. He said it twice for emphasis. Fitzgerald's description that it turned "dark" after the air hit it did not specify the shade of discoloration. Whether the face turned blue or simply darkened, Dr. Speth wanted to figure out why it would discolor so quickly the day the body was discovered. If Fitzgerald was right in assuming that the cause was exposure to air on May 12, how had the remains been transported to the woods without the face turning dark like the rest of the body had done? If Zapolsky was more accurate, what would cause the face to turn blue?

Dr. Speth's sleuthing paid off. He noted that the police reports filed the day of May 12, 1932 indicated it rained lightly all afternoon. Dr. Speth assumed that the rain could have triggered a chemical reaction with whatever preservative had been applied to the face. One possibility was tannic acid, a well-known skin preservative in the 1930s. Several people connected with the Lindbergh kidnapping/murder case likely had some prior knowledge of the use of tannic acid to preserve animal skin. Isidor Fisch was apprenticed to a tanner in Germany for three years as a teenager and later worked as a cutter for a furrier in New York; Arthur Hitner and Jacob Nosovitsky (who may have been the same person) both reportedly claimed expertise as cosmetic chemists; and Charles Lindbergh, whose mother taught chemistry, attributed his own lifelong passion for science from time spent with his grandfather, Dr. Charles Land, who practiced taxidermy in his basement as a hobby.

Dr. Speth discovered that tannic acid was also used in medical research. A former intern of Dr. Carrel's had begun using tannic acid for wound care in the early 1920s and Dr. Carrel's lab had been making its own use of it by then. Tannin is sometimes mixed with iron salts. A dry tannic compound could have been applied by a cloth or other means. What matters most is what happens to a tannic compound containing iron salts when it is diluted with water. That gave Dr. Speth an "aha" moment. When dissolved in water, tannic acid that contains iron salts turns dark blue or dark green. That could explain why Sergeant Zapolsky found to his amazement that the face had turned from white to blue an hour after exposure of the face to ongoing drizzle.

Another possibility Dr. Speth considered was copper sulfate, which turns blue when it absorbs water. The question of precisely what preservative was applied cannot now be determined. But Dr. Speth is quite confident that only some sort of chemical intervention explains the well-preserved facial features. Had a full autopsy been conducted far more light could have been shed on this issue — which Lindbergh precluded by having the body immediately cremated.

Dr. Speth also considered two other attributes of the body found in the woods. The preservation of the entire head was noteworthy — it was contrary to what he would expect to find if animals had attacked the body. Like the well-preserved face, the intact right leg and, particularly, the right foot with all of its toes and toenails in place, was in marked contrast to the mostly skeletonized lower body and scattered bones of the left foot. He also noted the absence of any left leg bones or arm bones anywhere in the area. That reinforced his assumption the body had been transported after those limbs were detached. The patch of non-discolored skin on the right foot that Dr. Charles Mitchell described in the "look-see" added further evidence of human intervention. Dr. Speth concluded that the right foot could only have remained as found if it had been wrapped since the child's death to preserve the foot with its unusual overlapping toes when they would otherwise have naturally separated from the foot as the toe bones on the left foot had done.

Given the other evidence that has been uncovered that points to the child's vivisection, it would not be surprising if the plan from day one was to apply a preservative to the face and to wrap the remaining foot to ensure positive identification of Little Charlie two months afterward when the greatly decayed body would conceal the fact most of his organs had been harvested before death.

It is easy to picture Sherlock Holmes himself doffing his deerstalker hunting cap in tribute to Dr. Speth. From the peculiar lack of evidence of maggot activity on the corpse, he deduced both that the child might have been etherized before death, and that Inspector Walsh had to be lying when he testified to a veil of vermin on the corpse in the woods. From the unexpected preservation of the right foot, Dr. Speth concluded that had to be purposeful. Most impressively, he deduced that a chemical preservative applied to the face best explained why the face turned from white to dark blue in the rain.

6.
What Lindbergh Valued Most in Life

IN HIS critically acclaimed alternate history, *The Plot Against America*, author Philip Roth has Lindbergh winning the Presidency in 1940 instead of Roosevelt getting reelected. Then Lindbergh keeps America out of the European War; Hitler wins; and America turns into a Nazi puppet state. Lindbergh did not live to read Roth's 2004 book or see the HBO miniseries in 2020, but he might have held similar fantasies. What Lindbergh really wanted toward the end of his life was to retell his life story his own way. In his 70s Lindbergh set about publishing his memoirs — his look back at his life's mission and accomplishments. Lindbergh considered "genetic inheritance" of "critical importance." To his way of thinking, "nothing attainable by man has as great value" as family planning. How did his first-born fit into this theme?

Lindbergh prefaced his very first mention of his namesake with a paragraph praising Alexis Carrel's unparalleled exposure to life and death through his surgical practice and tissue culture experiments. "In Carrel, spiritual and material values were met and blended as in no other man I knew." In Lindbergh's mind, his son and Carrel were intertwined. Over the course of many years, Lindbergh created several drafts of a rough, working manuscript more than two thousand pages long. It contained scores of autobiographical notes that he kept closely guarded. In 1957, to get himself started, he prepared a meticulous, 35-page chronology of friends, birthdates of children, names of pets, anecdotes, family homes and other details of almost his entire life. The list was, indeed, exhaustive, with one "remarkable" exception noted by curator Brian Horrigan of the Minnesota Historical Society. Lindbergh totally omitted from even passing reference in that 35-page list the kidnapping of his first son and the unprecedented lengthy investigation and "trial of the century" resulting in Bruno Richard Hauptmann's execution.

Much of the material was then placed under lock and key in the Yale University archives that Lindbergh had arranged for America First co-founder Kingman Brewster to establish once Brewster became Yale's President. The rest of the manuscript either travelled with Lindbergh, or was kept at his home in Darien, Connecticut. Anne had seen little of the manuscript for his memoirs because Lindbergh said he wanted to finish it first. That was far different from when he welcomed Anne's editing expertise for *The Spirit of St. Louis* that played a pivotal role in Lindbergh winning a Pulitzer prize.

Despite their difficulties over the past two decades, in 1974 Anne remained constantly at her husband's bedside when he underwent treatment for terminal lymphoma at Columbia Presbyterian Hospital in Manhattan. Approaching death, Lindbergh still declined to ask Anne for any help in finishing his manuscript even though he knew she could correct many of his mistaken memories and improve the book's polish with her superior editing skills. Instead, "the last American hero" called publisher, Bill Jovanovich of Harcourt, Brace & Jovanovich, with a special request.

For decades, Harcourt Brace had published almost all of the books Anne and Charles had authored. Not long before his hospitalization Lindbergh had been using an office in the Harcourt Brace Building to review the manuscript and write the preface for his Congressman father's authorized biography by Professor Bruce Larson. (Scholar Grace Nute had completed most of the research and writing of that biography decades earlier but was fired because she refused to whitewash family scandals.) While writing the preface to Larson's book, Lindbergh met privately with Bill Jovanovich in the publisher's office to raise the subject of his memoirs but did not share any of the manuscript with Jovanovich at the time.

When Lindbergh summoned Jovanovich to the hospital in August

1974, Anne was with her husband. She left the two alone in his private room since she could tell she was not wanted. Lindbergh then asked Jovanovich to look at 400 pages of draft chapters in a well-worn satchel by his bed that he had traveled the world with for thirty years. Jovanovich took the material home and stayed up all night reading. The next day, he told Lindbergh he was a "superb writer"; that the book was "written surely and with distinction"; and that what he had read so far "remarkably conjoined the events of [Lindbergh's] life with reflections and speculations." Even though Lindbergh had authored several other autobiographical works, this memoir clearly merited publication. After two days of negotiations, Jovanovich promised that he would personally edit the material and that Lindbergh's drafts would be used as source material "without being bound by the dates of their composition" to establish their sequence. Lindbergh knew his days left were few in number. He managed to arrange a special flight to his home in Hawaii where he died later that month.

Jovanovich put in 600 hours over the next two years on the "intricate" editing job, not counting work put in by his co-editor at the Yale Library and three other colleagues. *Autobiography of Values* did not see release until two years after Lindbergh's death. In the preface, the publishing magnate fulfilled another promise to his late author. Jovanovich assured readers that "the work was [Lindbergh's] own [with] parts of the text . . . subject to editing consistent with his purpose." Jovanovich took credit only for "the cutting of the manuscript and the insertion of words and phrases and punctuation to make bridges between certain sections." Widow Anne Lindbergh was thanked only for contributing some family photos.

Most striking after all that editing work was how many easily correctable factual errors the memoir contained. As a pilot, Lindbergh was known as a stickler for accuracy. He never forgot the lesson he learned in the army that attention to detail when preparing for flight could be a matter of life and death. When it came to reportage, Lindbergh read every word carefully and pounced on any error, "unforgiving of the most trivial mistake or exaggeration."

Jovanovich had once urged Lindbergh to read a laudatory biography by magazine editor and publisher Walter Ross only to receive back from Lindbergh 79 typed pages of asserted factual errors. Biographer A. Scott Berg later noted that when Lindbergh wrote about his own unhappy childhood, "the most painful memories of his first eighteen years were subjected to selective amnesia." Lindbergh's descriptions of early experiences in his life were "riddled with errors, with major events forgotten and entire years mixed up."

Telling the truth would have been both excruciatingly painful and would have exposed many secrets Lindbergh intended to take to his grave. He had just gone to great lengths to ensure that the authorized biography of his father published in 1973 hid both his father's illegitimacy and his grandfather's embezzlement scandal. His own mistresses and seven illegitimate children would not be revealed for decades. So, what principles did Lindbergh focus on in his *Autobiography of Values*? He considered its chief message for his children "the importance of genetics in mating." Yet Lindbergh's own family provided questionable evidence of that. As Berg later noted, "at least two generations of Lodges and Morrows had been afflicted with mental illness," and both Lindbergh's father and father-in-law died relatively young.

In the book, Lindbergh described family planning as the highest of goals. But other than picking Anne for his spouse over her sister Elisabeth, Lindbergh took no special effort to ensure his first child was born healthy. Instead he convinced Anne to take considerable risks to herself and the fetus during her pregnancy. The only way family planning could be linked to Little Charlie was his death, if Lindbergh credited himself with ensuring that his son's sperm never entered the gene pool.

Following her son's death, Anne observed that her husband took a similar long view — one unlike her own: "There is something very deep in a man's feeling for his son, it reaches further into the future." Reading Lindbergh's last book with that in mind provides troubling signs that Lindbergh believed the greater good was served by Little Charlie's early demise.

7.
Accidental Admissions?

WHAT Lindbergh had to say in his memoirs — after decades of opportunity for reflection — provides important evidence both of his conduct in the spring of 1932 and his mindset. While other circumstances suggest that Lindbergh should have been a prime suspect in his son's disappearance, if his own later statements are either provable lies or incriminating admissions, they signal consciousness of guilt. In New Jersey, as elsewhere in the United States, there is no statute of limitations for murder. So, Lindbergh appeared to have good reason to be quite careful about who got to see his private notes.

Of the 400 printed pages of Lindbergh's memoir, only 13 paragraphs describe the three-year saga that the entire nation endured along with the Lindbergh family. Just a handful of pages cover the period from the fateful night of March 1, 1932 when "a tragedy took place that was to affect our lives forever" to February of 1935 when Bruno Richard Hauptmann was sentenced to death for the "crime of the century." Lindbergh specifically instructed Bill Jovanovich not to rearrange the order of events in his memoirs. So, it was by design that his description of the shattering of "all material values" in the lives of himself and his wife when his first son disappeared followed directly in his memoirs after a tribute to Carrel's efforts to uncover the mechanics of life through organ perfusion experiments.

Even more telling are the paragraphs that follow. Despite a detailed memory for most other experiences as an adult, Lindbergh's recollection of the night his son disappeared is riddled with misstatements, serious omissions and outright lies. If this were before a jury, the panel would be instructed to consider whether Lindbergh had a reason not to tell the truth; whether he otherwise demonstrated a good memory; whether anyone else corroborated his account; and whether he previously did or said anything contradictory.

For starters, Lindbergh's memoir greatly distorted his role in the investigation generated by the infamous crime. The aviator said he forsook flying to collaborate with federal, state and local police to search for the kidnapper. But that was mostly untrue. Lindbergh took lengthy flights with his wife while the investigation continued in 1933 and 1934. Nor did he collaborate with the Bureau of Investigation or local police while he was still in New Jersey. At Lindbergh's instigation, Hopewell's police chief was immediately removed from the case after Chief Wolfe suggested the kidnapping was an inside job. Lindbergh not only shut out the Bureau almost entirely, he bypassed the New York police in setting up the rendezvous with Cemetery John, and reportedly threatened New Jersey State Police with loss of their jobs, even death, if they pursued methods of investigation he did not approve.

Lindbergh also complained in his memoirs that the extraordinary publicity during the search subjected his family to such high threats of extortion that he had to protect his second son Jon with an armed guard. Yet in the next breath, Lindbergh described how he and his wife Anne left Jon behind to undertake a five-month-trip overseas when Jon was still an infant — apparently without any second thoughts. That was about the same age as they had first left Little Charlie for several months in 1931, leaving the 16-month-old clinging to his nanny unable to recognize his parents on their return.

Lindbergh mentioned that he and his wife were visiting California in September 1934 when Colonel Schwarzkopf of the New Jersey State Police left him a message that they had just arrested a new suspect. Lindbergh did not repeat in his memoir what he told his wife after hearing that news. Despite all the wrong men previously arrested and let go, he was sure before he left California that this time the police had the actual culprit. Less than four months later, in January 1935, it was Lindbergh's confident testimony that Hauptmann was Cemetery John that convinced the jury to condemn Hauptmann to death — without the defense ever learning the aviator had apparently made up his mind back in California before he ever heard Hauptmann speak.

If the truth was that Lindbergh conspired to kidnap and murder his son himself, cover that crime up and ultimately frame Hauptmann for it, the trickiest part of his memoir for Lindbergh to write was the part about the night of his son's disappearance. Lindbergh started the passage about his son by invoking the reader's sympathy once more: "Our son, Charles, Jr. . . . was twenty months old, blond, blue-eyed, and just beginning to talk."

Little Charlie was not just beginning to talk; he had quite a large vocabulary. He was also quite agile. Most of the time, Lindbergh showed little interest in his toddler. In the spring of 1931, he pestered Anne to spend long days away from their infant son while she took several weeks of piloting lessons which often brought them home after his son was put to bed for the night. He then talked her into leaving their son behind for months while the pair resumed their ambitious plane travels together. Even on their return Lindbergh insisted his son be put to bed before he arrived home for dinner.

The memoir's effort to pull at readers' heartstrings over the loss of his toddler thus seems oddly out of character. Anne noticed that her husband never shed a tear over their son's death. While the boy lived, on several occasions persons in the household observed the new father behaving in a hostile manner toward his firstborn. Just months before his son's short life ended, the aviator was said to have repeatedly derided Little Charlie as "It." Nanny Betty Gow and Anne were appalled when Lindbergh left the 17-month-old penned in the yard one winter day as punishment for being a cry baby. That Christmas, Betty and Mrs. Morrow strongly suspected Lindbergh of dunking the boy in a tub, leaving the toddler screaming and his father laughing at his plight.

After invoking readers' sympathy, Lindbergh then proceeds to make many mistakes describing the investigation and trial. These are particularly noteworthy since he was obsessively committed to orchestrating both aspects of the homicide prosecution. By the time he completed his memoirs, Lindbergh had many sources to consult on any particulars he might have forgotten.

In his 1968 critique of biographer Walter Ross's chapter on the kidnapping, Lindbergh wrote: "He gives many details in these pages that I cannot either deny or verify, at least from memory. I assume he achieves about the same degree of accuracy he has in the previous portions of this book." Lindbergh was implying that Ross committed many factual errors in describing the 1932 crime. Actually, Ross largely adopted Lindbergh's own version of the night of the kidnapping and subsequent events leading to discovery of the child's body. Ross's account was indeed questionable, but Lindbergh presumably did not consider the source.

Most recently, in 1973 Lindbergh had the opportunity to review his wife's diaries and letters for the period 1929-1932 and could refer to passages in *Hour of Gold; Hour of Lead* to refresh his memory. Nonetheless, Lindbergh seriously misdescribed in *Autobiography of Values* what happened that fateful night of March 1, 1932. Lindbergh wrote that he and his wife were together in the parlor on that stormy night when:

> I went upstairs to the child's nursery, opened the door, and immediately noticed a lifted window. A strange-looking envelope lay on the sill. I looked at the crib. It was empty. I ran downstairs, grabbed my rifle, and went out into the night, first to the nursery end of the house. Under the lifted window I saw a ladder, and saw that it was broken, Obviously, it had collapsed as the kidnapper descended. It looked as though it had been made out of new crating boards.

First, Lindbergh had not been sitting with his wife in the parlor when he decided to check on his son. He had been in the study alone reading at a desk by the window when his son's nanny came rushing in at 10 p.m. and accused him of hiding Charlie as a practical joke. Anne was then upstairs. Betty Gow is not mentioned as being present at all in Lindbergh's account in his memoirs of the night of the kidnapping. Nor does Lindbergh mention his wife's immediate assumption that he was pulling yet another juvenile stunt. His editors also failed to note these blatant errors, though both facts appear in *Hour of Gold, Hour of Lead*, which Harcourt Brace itself had published in 1973 — just one year earlier. (Elsewhere in Lindbergh's memoirs, the editors had put an asterisk by Lindbergh's description of when the famous couple's engagement was made public, based on his wife's mention of the correct date in those very same diaries.)

Lindbergh's description of what happened when he went outside with his gun to look for presumed kidnappers is particularly revealing. Lindbergh said that when he arrived at the east side of the house in the dark: "under the lifted window I saw a ladder and saw that it was broken. Obviously, it had collapsed as the kidnapper descended." But at the time Lindbergh attributed the crime to a gang, not a lone actor — a gang he testified at the trial of John Curtis in June 1932 he still believed was responsible for the crime. It was not until the fall of 1934 that Lindbergh switched theories to convict a lone man for the kidnap/murder.

More tellingly, there was no cracked ladder under the nursery window when Lindbergh ran out into the yard. According to Corporal Wolf's March 1, 1932 report, Lindbergh claimed to have found the ladder in sections on the ground some 75 feet away from the house in the pitch dark before the local police arrived with flashlights. Was this key passage in Lindbergh's memoir the product of an old man's false memory or an actual vivid memory of seeing the ladder up against the house the evening of March 1 that he no longer realized he should still keep secret?

If Lindbergh correctly remembered that he saw the makeshift ladder against the house before the police arrived, there is only one explanation that makes sense. Lindbergh secretly put the ladder up under the nursery window shortly after 6 p.m. to make imprints. That could have been when the ladder cracked just by him stepping briefly on one of the rungs. He then could have carried the ladder 75 feet away and left the premises — only to pretend he did not arrive home from New York until 8:20 p.m.

There are three other points to note about Lindbergh's description of the ladder on the night his son was kidnapped. He said it looked like it had been made out of new crating boards. That was a remarkably keen observation by a father running frantically in the dark in pursuit of a gang he thought had just grabbed his toddler son out the nursery window. Lindbergh's description in his memoirs of a ladder made from new crating boards once again matched Erastus Hudson's assumption that rail 16 looked like it came from a large new crate. Lindbergh may have forgotten that the State convinced the jury that Hauptman made the ladder based on expert testimony that rail 16 was ripped from the attic floor above Hauptmann's apartment.

Mentioning that the ladder rails looked like crating board dovetailed conveniently with Lindbergh's formal statement to the police on March 11, 1932 asserting for the first time that between 9 and 9:15 p.m. on March 1, he heard a sound like a falling wooden crate. Yet Lindbergh mentioned no such distinctive noise to the police officers who interviewed him on March 1 within hours of his son's disappearance. The same was true of every other member of the household – no one reported hearing anything at all that might identify precisely when the crime occurred that night. Ten days later Lindbergh claimed for the first time that he alone had heard a clatter while seated in the living room that he thought came from the direction of the kitchen in the west wing of the house.

The police were never convinced that a noise attributed to something falling in the kitchen pinpointed the time a ladder must have broken outside the nursery in the opposite direction. But they never considered whether Lindbergh's statement was itself potentially incriminating. Lindbergh told the police he heard that odd cracking sound more than 45 minutes before anyone noticed his son missing on March 1 and more than an hour before a ladder was found lying in the yard that, not coincidentally, appeared to be made from crating boards. Investigators never questioned why Lindbergh's comment just happened to provide him an alibi. Less gullible police might have found the specificity of Lindbergh's belated claim itself suspicious for placing him in the living room at the time the toddler ostensibly was carried off by a stranger descending a makeshift ladder made with crating boards.

Lindbergh states in his memoir that when he entered the room shortly after 10 p.m. he noticed the window was open. That did not match Betty Gow's repeated statements to the police. She said the first thing she did at 10 p.m. was to close the French window she had left open for ventilation at 7:30 p.m. The east windows were both closed when she left before 8 p.m. and were still closed when she returned at 10 p.m. That was one of the reasons the police had originally doubted the kidnap story and thought it was an inside job. They immediately questioned how anyone climbing out that window with a heavy toddler onto a rickety ladder could have stopped to close a window after he exited. They also wondered why an escaping kidnapper would go to that bother.

The whole point of leaving a ransom note was to advertise a crime had just been committed. Kidnappers were in it for the money. But Lindbergh's effort to inject the possibility that Betty Gow was wrong, and the window was left open made less sense. Several early investigators were convinced that the heavy wind that night would have whisked away an envelope placed on the sill, and the wind would have left the shutters of an open window flapping loudly — something no one had reported hearing even though several adults had been upstairs in the hall by the nursery and in the adjacent master bedroom suite since shortly after 9 p.m.

Lindbergh testified at Hauptmann's 1935 trial that he might not have seen the envelope on the windowsill until his second visit to the nursery. He had reportedly told Trooper Joe Wolf on March 1 that he saw it there immediately on his first trip into the room. But that was implausible. If he had seen it on his first quick visit, but nevertheless left it undisturbed, at least one of the women should have seen it when they searched the room thoroughly after Lindbergh ran outside with his rifle. Betty Gow said she never saw the envelope until after the police arrived. Anne also testified that she did not see it. Crediting Lindbergh's trial testimony, the envelope was apparently first spotted on the sill sometime *after* Lindbergh had *already* blamed kidnappers by exclaiming: "Anne, they've stolen our baby."

Lindbergh's memoirs raise another question of what he did when he saw a "strange" plain envelope on the nursery windowsill following his son's disappearance. He demonstrated complete lack of curiosity about its contents. Lindbergh was the only one who was ever alone in the nursery after his wife, Betty Gow and Elsie Whateley searched it. That was when he could have placed the note there before shutting the door and warning the others not to enter the room until the police showed up.

Lindbergh also wrote in his memoirs that he was surprised that the telephone line had not been cut. It was the police, not Lindbergh, who had openly questioned why professionals would not have taken the obvious step of cutting the phone line to delay notification of authorities. Lindbergh also blamed reporters for obliterating evidence of footprints and tire marks without taking any blame for allowing hordes of reporters to trample the crime site. Tellingly, Lindbergh continues his reconstruction of the late night of March 1, 1932: "I realized there was no use going into the woods or trying to follow along roads. The night was too dark and stormy to see or hear anything. I returned to the house and put in an emergency call to the State Police."

We can take his word he knew there was no use looking for his son in the woods, but it was not too dark for him to claim he found the ladder and chisel in tall grass without a flashlight. The truth was that Lindbergh rejected offers of a thorough search that night by woodsmen with bloodhounds, by the National Guard and by volunteers from Princeton. He did form his own small search party to tramp around in the woods, long after the state police arrived.

Lindbergh also wrote that thousands of cars were stopped and searched by police. He failed to mention that the police only stopped cars going out of the area — not in the obvious direction of Skillman Village where mysterious cars were observed coming and going that night. Lindbergh makes no mention at all in his memoir of the 1929 Dodge Sedan with a local county license plate at the foot of his own driveway at 6 p.m. that police suddenly quit looking for. Neighbor Ben Lupica could never understand why police abandoned their search for the sedan driven by "Unknown Person No. 1" dressed in a city dweller's coat and fedora, whom Lupica saw at dusk transporting a sectional ladder.

Autobiography of Values would not have survived edits for accuracy by Anne Lindbergh. Nor would it have passed the Pinocchio test of serious biographers. Throughout his life, Lindbergh pursued mechanical advances to push the limits of human achievement. He never embraced traditional values like truth-telling and the Golden Rule. He had no compunctions about lying to save face, and, time and time again, took sadistic pleasure in causing pain and anguish to friends, family and associates — with special venom reserved for the media.

The memoir was a tribute to his strongest held belief — commitment to the creation of a master race to which he assumed he belonged. Lindbergh accepted the view of social Darwinists like Dr. Carrel who believed weak infants, like individuals with chronic disabilities and criminals, did not deserve to live and pass on their genes to future generations. Much later on a family African safari in the mid-1960s, he told his daughter Reeve that a baby elephant left behind by the herd was meant to die. It appeared to be an allusion to his own firstborn. Yet ascribing the death of perceived weaklings to fate came from the father who swore on the stand in January 1935 that his toddler son was in excellent health when he disappeared.

If Lindbergh did conspire to kidnap and murder his own son, *Autobiography of Values* demonstrates he never had any regrets for the child's murder, for the hell he put so many innocent suspects through, the torment to which he subjected his wife, for the extraordinary waste of public resources and turmoil he caused in a national Depression — or for orchestrating the legal lynching of Bruno Richard Hauptmann.

8.
Conclusion

SO, WHAT should the FBI have looked into? How about starting with a nursery where a violent crime had just been reported that showed no furniture out of place; the apparent erasure of fingerprints in the nursery by an insider after the kidnapping was discovered; and a ladder that could not possibly support a 160+ pound man carrying at least 27 pounds of extra weight. The FBI could also have considered that first responders saw no evidence that anything fell in the mud outside the nursery; and that before Hauptmann's trial Dr. Mitchell had repeatedly sworn the skull fractures could not have occurred from a two-story fall into mud. The corpse and burlap bag could hardly have been lying where they were found for over two months without being spotted. A state police officer himself noticed the oddity of the well-preserved face turning white to blue. If the FBI had access to the Squibb report far more questions would have been raised.

Motive would have been another fruitful area of inquiry. Charles Lindbergh obsessed over raising superior offspring. He had forbidden any recent photos of his son, quite possibly because the boy's oversized "square head" became more evident as he got older. Lindbergh had already faced press rumors of jeopardizing the baby's health by recklessly exposing Anne to toxic conditions in their record-setting flight across the country when she was pregnant. His mother-in-law strongly hinted as her first reaction that she believed the child's health could have been a motive for murder. She had witnessed her son-in-law behave cruelly to his child on more than one occasion. Scotland Yard had seen parents commit infanticide many times before.

Lindbergh's actions had the impact of thwarting the investigation from the start — allowing the destruction of footprints and tire tracks, preventing follow through on mysterious cars coming and going near the estate and from Skillman Village. Lindbergh oversaw the state police who failed to follow up on multiple leads implicating Isidor Fisch as one of three strangers seen driving near the rural estate just before the kidnapping.

John Curtis provided detailed descriptions of six people who purported to be members of the kidnap gang, who displayed as proof some of the recorded ransom money and a floor plan of Lindbergh's home. Lindbergh swore at the time that he believed Curtis. Yet only Curtis was prosecuted for leading Lindbergh on a wild goose chase for his dead son's safe return. (Means was convicted in 1933 for a different hoax related to the kidnapping.)

In the largest manhunt in American history, why were such credible leads to other suspects abandoned? Those odd choices make the most sense if Lindbergh and Breckinridge hired several criminals in early 1932, including Isidor Fisch and Arthur Hitner, to pose as a kidnap for ransom gang in a hoax to distract the public from Lindbergh's true intent. Even assuming the co-conspirators had no idea of Lindbergh's actual aim, Lindbergh could not risk having the police pursue evidence of either Cemetery John's true identity or Fisch's connections to the crime.

Concern about exposing the two men also would explain why Lindbergh rejected staking out the mail boxes in the area from which ransom notes had been mailed; was extremely resistant to having the numbers on the ransom bills recorded; and vetoed alerting the New York police about either cemetery rendezvous, or having the New Jersey police conduct surveillance. If it was a ruse, Lindbergh could not risk having cohorts caught in the act and confess.

After cremating his son, Lindbergh openly returned to his lab work, and got his wife to resume her role as his navigator and radio operator soon after the birth of their second son. The question remains whether this was all part of a plan Lindbergh hatched after realizing that "the Eaglet" was not his ideal progeny, but a weakling who might not live to adulthood; and the boy's vivisection might help save Elisabeth's life and the lives of other people Lindbergh and Carrel deemed far more worthy.

While the toddler was presumed to be alive, deference to his famous father was understandable, though poor practice. Once the child was dead, not considering a prime suspect with easy access to commit such an inside job was inexcusable. The FBI has since documented that a parent was to blame for more than half of all reported infanticides. Of those committed at home, nine out of ten are perpetrated by a family member. By the end of the twentieth century, even millionaire parents reporting a child's abduction and death at the hands of mysterious strangers remained prime suspects. That was what happened in the still unsolved kidnap-murder of JonBenet Ramsey in 1995, which generated a similar media circus as the Lindbergh baby kidnapping. Back in the 1930s, however, influential parents were treated with far greater solicitude. No officer wanted to be blamed for potentially endangering the child of the nation's royal couple by ignoring the father's requests to back off. But once a body was found, it was a homicide case for which the corpse would be the most important evidence. Ordering the body cremated was another act in obstruction of justice that Lindbergh and Breckinridge collaborated on.

People in the Depression desperately clung to their heroes as well as their anti-heroes. Movie theater owners in 1933 and 1934 had already noted newsreel audiences giving far greater applause to bank robber John Dillinger, as the gangster version of Robin Hood, than to President Roosevelt or Charles Lindbergh. But politicians and yellow journalists had at the same time found it extremely easy to rouse public ire against undocumented immigrants. They were, and remain today, a recurring target.

Just before Hauptmann's arrest the police had been on the lookout for Cemetery John as a tall, slender white-collar criminal who spoke perfect English and had just cashed a recorded gold certificate to pay for a few-cents-worth of produce. But journalists turned on a dime to help direct public fury at a stocky carpenter with a heavy German accent and the hands of a day laborer. None of them seemed concerned in the slightest that at the time of Hauptmann's arrest for possessing ransom money there was *zero* evidence that he had been in or near the Lindbergh farmhouse around the time of the kidnapping. That was also when medical examiner Charles Mitchell still insisted, as he had since May 12, 1932, that the child was likely either shot or hit with a blunt instrument, and ruled out death from an accidental fall out the nursery window on the evening of March 1, 1932.

The defense and later New Jersey's governor maintained that, except for Hauptmann's possession of a portion of the ransom money, the evidence mounted against Hauptmann at trial was all manufactured by the police or coerced by the prosecutor. If fingerprints found on the inside joints of the ladder had instead conclusively proved the public's all-American hero constructed it, such news could only be met with widespread shock and incomprehension. The possibility that Charles Lindbergh might have callously arranged for his son to be killed for "the needs of science" was beyond almost anyone's belief. Nor could hardly anyone be expected to accept the possibility that a surgical team led by Nobel-Prize-recipient Alexis Carrel of the world-renowned Rockefeller Institute collaborated with Lindbergh and his blue-blooded lawyer Henry Breckinridge to carry out that crime.

Imagine the public's reaction if they became persuaded that an enormous hoax had been played on them; that when key authorities were assuring them who the evildoer was they had an ulterior motive; that the prosecutor's proof implicating Hauptmann as the kidnapper contained perjured testimony and doctored evidence; and that instead of ridiculing Governor Hoffman for seeking to reopen the case, the public, too, should have been thinking critically and demanding that investigators reexamine the clues that could have revealed the truth.

In the throes of the Great Depression, unprecedented sums of public money appear to have been grossly misused to ensure a scapegoat died for the heinous crime — all in a display of the raw power of money and influence when so many Americans were destitute and powerless. How do we feel now about the institutional cover-ups? The gullibility of the fawning fourth estate of mainstream journalists, who allowed the truth to be buried in lies and fake news? The failure of law enforcement at all levels — state and federal — to pursue the horrendous probability that Charles Augustus Lindbergh was Suspect No. 1?

Epilogue

The New Jersey State Police and the FBI both kept many key documents from public view for decades. In 1977, the State Police reexamined the evidence analyzed in the Squibb lab report and concluded it "enhanced the positive identification" of the body as Lindbergh's son and provided no reason to question Hauptmann's guilt. The 1977 report doubled down on the theory that "the decomposition and dismemberment" of the body occurred "at the scene where the body was found" without explaining why no blood was found at the site or in the burlap bag. Nor was any mention made of the medical lab materials police found by the corpse or the black rubber residue on the buttons of the little boy's pajamas.

In *Top Secret: FBI Files on the Lindbergh Baby Kidnapping*, published in 2001, files on the case that the Agency had already made public under the Freedom of Information Act appeared in a single, edited volume. But the title was seriously misleading. The book did not contain the most revealing Agency records that had truly been "top secret." Confidential memos to and by J. Edgar Hoover would not be declassified for another two years. The memos revealed mistrust between the New Jersey Police and the FBI that kept the Agency mostly out of the loop during the entirety of the state's investigation; the astonishment of the FBI Chief at the state's extraordinarily botched handling of the case; and the unparalleled political clout wielded by Lindbergh to prevent the Bureau from pursuing its own independent investigation. Federal agents assumed he was hiding something. But even in 2001 the FBI did not want these suspicions known to the public, presumably because it could give the Agency a black eye for never acting on its knowledge.

Indeed, the Department of Justice currently has in distribution a simplistic Kindle version of the famous case that buries all of the FBI's suspicions of an inside job and makes it appear that the Agency had no doubt that the ransom scheme was genuine; that Condon was always certain that Hauptmann was Cemetery John; that Hauptmann was properly tried and executed for the crime; and the case was thereby solved. *The Lindbergh Kidnapping Case As Told by the FBI* fails to disclose the Agency's own confidential reports that contradict the glib story recited within the booklet's pages, including its knowledge that the New Jersey State Police improperly coached witnesses to do the state's bidding.

Chief among those who continue to this day to justify Hauptmann's execution is former FBI agent Jim Fisher, who felt compelled to refute recent published charges that the New Jersey State Police mishandled their most famous investigation. Yet in his 1987 book, *The Lindbergh Case*, Fisher stated five principal assumptions he made in concluding Hauptmann was guilty. All have obvious, major deficiencies which implicate not only Fisher's reasoning, but that of every other person over the past three decades who has treated Fisher's book as a trustworthy resource. These include his assertion that the New Jersey State Police conducted a thorough investigation of the crime and that Hauptmann had a fair trial.

Just as J. Edgar Hoover did not pursue Scotland Yard's suspicions of infanticide, the Department of Justice won't go anywhere near there now. The Bureau knew since day one that Lindbergh appeared to be hiding something. The FBI should have considered it odd that the child's pediatrician, Dr. Philip Van Ingen, was not called to testify at Hauptmann's trial and that the May 14 autopsy — which the Bureau had received a copy of from Dr. Mitchell — was not offered into evidence. It should have been even more suspicious that the New Jersey Police kept no copy of Dr. Van Ingen's pediatric records used to identify the corpse.

J. Edgar Hoover probably rationalized his silence about his suspicions of Lindbergh's complicity because he did think Hauptmann was in on the ransom conspiracy. Less charitably, keeping a file on Lindbergh could prove useful in the future just as Hoover found when tracking the secrets of so many other prominent Americans. Freedom of Information Act inquiries have since laid bare that from the day of Hauptmann's arrest, the Bureau withheld from public view critical information in the Agency's possession that might have enabled Hauptmann's acquittal, including what it knew about the white collar suspect who spent ransom money; the prosecution's manipulation of experts on handwriting and wood; and the state's suppression of fingerprint evidence on the ladder.

J. Edgar Hoover believed from the outset that more than one

person had committed the crime with "some assistance from inside." Historian Lloyd Gardner noted that Hoover ran into direct opposition from Lindbergh in pursuing that line of inquiry. "The two men never completely trusted each other after Lindbergh interrupted one of Hoover's special agents as he attempted to question Betty Gow." Lindbergh had promised her she would not be questioned — another instance of obstruction of justice.

In 2002, New Jersey Police Museum archivist Mark Falzini made a startling discovery about a small table the museum had received many years earlier from a man in Plainfield, New Jersey less than thirty miles north of Hopewell. On the desks's underside was a purported confession in German of someone claiming he was part of the Lindbergh baby kidnapping gang. The anonymous confession also asserted that Richard Hauptmann was not involved. Authorities at first considered the message a hoax, but Falzini discovered that screw holes in the table brace matched perfectly with the three puncture marks in the ransom notes. Other peculiar aspects of the ransom notes also pointed to use of that desk as the surface on which all of the notes were written. Calls followed for DNA tests on the desk, envelopes and other evidence from the kidnapping trial. The state refused to conduct any. In May 2003, the State Police Museum allowed the Estate of Anne Lindbergh to retrieve key evidence from the museum's exhibits related to the victim, including the child's thumb guard, sleeping suit, and T-shirts.

In 2016, a television series called *Chasing Conspiracies* focused viewers on the "shadowy boundaries . . . between fact and fiction." Its third episode, "The Vanished" featured the Lindbergh baby kidnapping as one of several famous criminal cases whose details remain shrouded in mystery. Both archivist Mark Falzini and historian Lloyd Gardner were interviewed — two leading experts on a crime that has confounded sleuths for more than eighty years. The program explored Lindbergh's possible collusion in the kidnapping of his own son. Gardner put forward his hypothesis that Lindbergh was involved in the crime. Gardner believed that the pioneering aviator suffered from an extreme form of narcissism, believing himself to be a Nietzschean superhero, and could not abide fathering a sickly child. His son's oversized head was just one of several signs that the boy had developed serious health issues likely associated with hydrocephalus.

Pediatric neurosurgeon Lauren Schwartz agreed that details from the autopsy were consistent with the supposition that the child suffered from macrocephalus, an enlarged brain, possibly compounded by hydrocephalus. Gardner assumed Lindbergh wanted to have his son institutionalized to keep any deformities from public knowledge. Psychiatrist Raj Persaud noted that if Lindbergh were an extreme narcissist, he could have reacted with profound hostility to his namesake son not living up to his image of perfection, possibly prompting Lindbergh to become "very dangerous" and capable of "very dark behavior."

Gardner considered Hauptmann either an innocent victim or just a bit player in the kidnapping. He guessed that the plan to institutionalize Charles, Jr. went amiss when the child was accidentally killed. Dr. Schwartz also commented on why the corpse wound up with so many missing organs. She suggested that the selective removal of organs did not reflect an attack by wild animals but suggested surgical removal of internal organs after death to prevent a proper diagnosis of his health problems.

By the 21st century, Lindbergh had enough detractors that he became the inspiration for Philip Roth's novel, *The Plot Against America*, that HBO turned into a 2020 TV miniseries. Lindbergh was also the principal inspiration for the hero turned evil ace pilot in the PIXAR movie "Up!" Perhaps the most comparable character is X-Men member Jean Grey in the 2019 science fiction movie *Dark Phoenix*. Like Grey, Lindbergh's traumatic childhood left him capable of exploitation, in her case by a villainess bent on having her own people take over the planet — not unlike Carrel's vision of a superior race.

All biographers of Charles Lindbergh and his wife Anne accept that Lindbergh was innocent of any involvement in the crime. But are they wrong? J. Edgar Hoover's own secret memoranda — not made public for another sixty years — summarized evidence the Bureau Chief accumulated. Hoover learned early on that Lindbergh had already concealed his baby son in a closet for almost half an hour in 1931 and that in March 1932 his mother-in-law immediately suspected the child's health was a motive for killing him. Hoover knew it was possible a man of Lindbergh's stature could pull off a kidnapping hoax involving his own son. He knew that big lies could create their own alternate "truth." Not wanting to take on such a popular hero, Hoover kept quiet about his knowledge that there was far more to the story than ever came to light.

Anne Lindbergh cooperated with investigative journalist Ludovic Kennedy in the early 1980s as he sought to prove Hauptmann was innocent and framed by the police for her son's kidnap/murder. In the introduction to his book, *The Airman and the Carpenter: The Lindbergh Kidnapping and the Framing of Richard Hauptmann*, Kennedy thanked Anne profusely for her cooperation. He noted her assurance "that if in fact a miscarriage of justice did take place, and notwithstanding any difficulties this might create for her and her husband, it should not be glossed over."

Long after her husband's death, in an interview with biographer Susan Hertog, Anne again made cryptic references to the explosive issue. The pilot's widow seemed preoccupied with linking Lindbergh with the myth of Icarus, flying too close to the sun and plummeting to the earth. Like Lady Macbeth, Anne obsessed about her own unclean hands in perpetuating the public perception of the two of them over the past sixty years: "I feel an aversion to . . . the falsity of public images. . . Every image is a 'sin.'" Then she added, "I want to set the record straight. That's all I have left of him." Hertog noted that when it came down to it, "Anne loved Charles passionately and, though willing to forgive his frailties, she could not bear to portray him as he was. If meeting Charles was Anne's moment of rebirth, exposing him would be akin to suicide."

Was Lindbergh the mastermind of the kidnap and murder of his own son? Consider whether in his then secret lab work with Dr. Carrel, he had motive, means and opportunity to carry out that crime. Most of all, focus on why several witnesses confirmed to a reporter that Lindbergh disguised himself late on March 7, 1932 and disappeared on a secret mission without ever revealing where he went. Yet persons under his sway swore he remained at home all week. Who was telling the truth? Why was there a gap in his daily diary for all of March and half of April? Was his subsequent conduct that of a man searching desperately for his only child, or a man engaged in a cover-up? Why did he order his murdered son's body cremated before a full autopsy could be performed? You be the judge.

APPENDIX A
Affidavit of
Dr. William M. Bass

Knox County, Tennessee Affidavit of William Marvin Bass III.

Under penalty of perjury, I, William Marvin Bass III, declare as follows:

1. I am a forensic anthropologist with a specialty in the research of human osteology and human decomposition, and the founder of the University of Tennessee Anthropological Research Facility colloquially known as "The Body Farm" – a forensic facility uniquely devoted to research on human decomposition. I currently live at ▮▮▮▮▮▮▮▮▮▮▮▮▮▮▮▮▮▮▮▮▮▮▮▮▮▮▮▮ Though retired from teaching, I am still associated with the Tennessee Anthropological Research Facility as a professor emeritus. Attached hereto as Exhibit A is a true and correct copy of my 20-page curriculum vitae.

2. For more than fifty years I have served as an expert assisting federal, local, and non-U.S. authorities in the identification of human remains. In June of 1982, at the request of attorneys for Anna Hauptmann, the widow of Bruno Richard Hauptmann, I undertook to examine a dozen small bones then retained by the New Jersey State Police in Trenton, New Jersey in an evidence box related to the Charles Lindbergh, Jr. homicide investigation. Since the original investigation of the crime in May of 1932, the bones had only been reexamined once before in 1977 by my former mentor, Dr. Wilton Krogman, at the request of New Jersey's Attorney General. By the time I was retained on behalf of Anna Hauptmann, I had already examined thousands of skeletons and assisted with over one hundred forensic cases. I was then head of the Anthropology Department at the University of Tennessee where I had already created what later became known as "the Body Farm." At the time, I was also President of the American Academy of Forensic Sciences physical anthropology section.

3. Attached hereto as Exhibit B are two pages of photo copies I arranged to be printed in July 2019 from slides I have retained of four of the photographs I took on my visit in June of 1982 to the New Jersey State Police Systems & Communications Building in Trenton, New Jersey on behalf of Anna Hauptmann. Upon my arrival, I was taken to the basement of the state police building where a clerk brought me an evidence box with five glass vials inside it, one of which had cracked and been repaired with clear tape. The vials were repurposed cigar preservers, each sealed with a cork stopper. On the first page of photos the top one was taken outside of the New Jersey State Police headquarters in Trenton, New Jersey. The bottom photo shows the desk in the basement of that building where I undertook the examination of the contents of the cigar tubes which contained the bones. The top photo on the second page of photos attached as Exhibit B shows four bones I identified as human bones. I also

Knox County, Tennessee Affidavit of William Marvin Bass III.

identified six of the other bones as human bones. The bottom photo on that page shows the two remaining bones that I identified as bird bones.

4. In 2004, I published a book called *Death's Acre: Inside the Legendary Forensic Lab the Body Farm Where the Dead Do Tell Tales.* (New York: Berkley Publishing Group, 2004). Chapter One of that book contains a summary of my findings in June 1982 on behalf of Anna Hauptmann. I hereby reaffirm the following finding I then made with respect to the bones pictured on page two of Exhibit B.

> "Two of the bones were clearly animal in origin: a two-inch piece of rib from a good-sized bird, perhaps a grouse or quail, and a small vertebral arch, probably from the same bird. Both of these bore tooth marks on them."

5. Chapter one of my book *Death's Acre* also describes my findings with respect to the human bones. I hereby also reaffirm the following findings regarding the human bones:

> "Of the ten human bones, the largest of them – the calcaneus, or heel of the left foot – was about an inch and a quarter in diameter; to the untrained eye, it could have passed for a piece of gravel. Four of the bones were from the left foot; two were from the left hand; and four were from the right hand. Despite the passage of half a century, decayed tissue, dirt, and even a few hairs clung to several.
>
> Intact and undamaged, the bones bore no signs of trauma, no indication of cause of death."

Had there been signs of tooth marks on the human bones as I had found on the two bird bones, I would have noted them.

6. My assignment in June 1982 was to attempt to ascertain the identity and age of the human whose bones I examined. I based my opinion solely on visual observation of the ten bones that had been preserved. In childhood, skeletons are androgynous: There is no way to determine the sex of a skeleton; all you can do is measure and compare the bones you are examining with the size and development of other known specimens. I brought two definitive reference books with me to the New Jersey State Police building for that purpose: *Radiographic Atlas of Skeletal Development of the Foot and Ankle* and a companion volume, *Radiographic Atlas of Skeletal Development of the Hand and Wrist*. These two books contained careful studies of children's hand and foot bones based on hundreds of X rays. I hereby reaffirm the

Knox County, Tennessee Affidavit of William Marvin Bass III.

conclusion I reached in June of 1982 as described in chapter one of my book, *Death's Acre*:

> "According to the measurements in those studies, the hand and foot bones I removed from the glass vials were slightly larger than those of an eighteen-month-old male and slightly smaller than those of a twenty-four-month-old male. It took less than an hour for me to reach the same conclusion that my mentor, Dr. Krogman, had reached five years before me: There was nothing in the bones themselves to refute the notion that these were all that remained of a Caucasoid male child, aged twenty months. A twenty-month-old Caucasoid male child named Charles Lindbergh Jr.: The Eaglet."

7. In *Death's Acre* I speculated that the tooth marks on the two bird bones were "possibly from the same dog or dogs who had gnawed off the hands of the dead child hidden in the forest." My basis for that speculation was knowledge that the decomposed body found in the woods on May 12, 1932 was missing some body parts -- including both hands -- and that the police assumed wild animals had attacked the corpse while it lay undiscovered in the woods. I never examined any bones of the corpse other than the ten foot and hand bones I examined in June of 1982. My understanding was that the body was cremated within hours after Charles Lindbergh identified the corpse at the morgue as that of his son. I have never formed an expert opinion on whether any of the child's bones that were cremated bore any signs of predation or how long it lay in the woods before it was discovered. As stated above, the ten hand and foot bones I did examine were intact and undamaged with no visible signs of trauma.

8. I have read materials provided me by author Lise Pearlman supporting the theory in her manuscript, *Suspect No. One: The Man Who Got Away*, that Bruno Richard Hauptmann was wrongly convicted and executed for the Lindbergh baby kidnapping and murder. She suggests that the child's missing organs were surgically removed, not eaten by predatory animals as previously had been assumed. I had never considered that shocking possibility before, but her analysis of the evidence is logical and well-documented. Based on these materials, I believe it quite plausible Charles Lindbergh secretly arranged for his own son's removal from the Lindberghs' New Jersey home on March 1, 1932 for vivisection experiments conducted

Knox County, Tennessee Affidavit of William Marvin Bass III.

by Dr. Alexis Carrel of the Rockefeller Institute for Medical Research.

Executed on November 25, 2019 at ████████████ Tennessee.

████████████████████████

William M. Bass III

ACKNOWLEDGMENT

State of Tennessee
County of Knox

On this 25 day of November, 2019, before me personally appeared William M. Bass known to me to be the person described in and who executed the foregoing affidavit and acknowledged that he executed the same as his free act and deed, for the purpose therein set forth.

Betty Krachey
Notary Public

[Appendix A, Exhibit A curriculum vitae omitted]

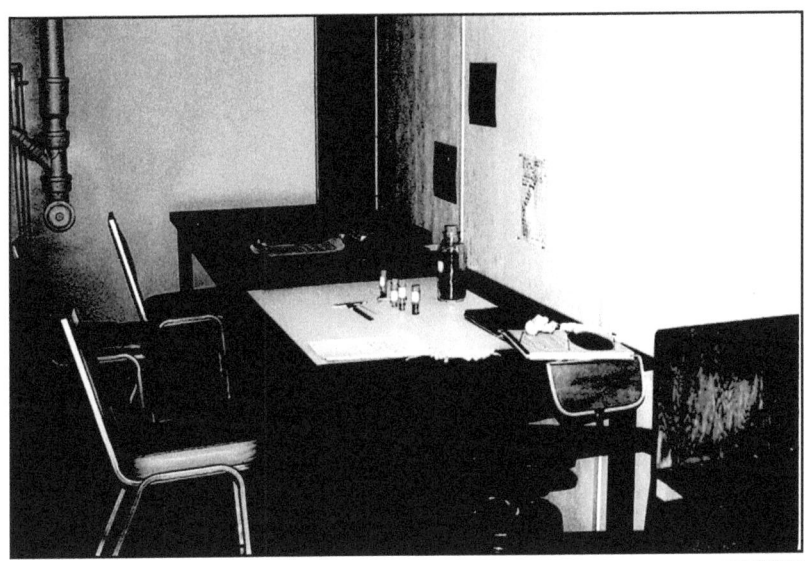

Appendix A, Exhibit B

SUSPECT NO. 1

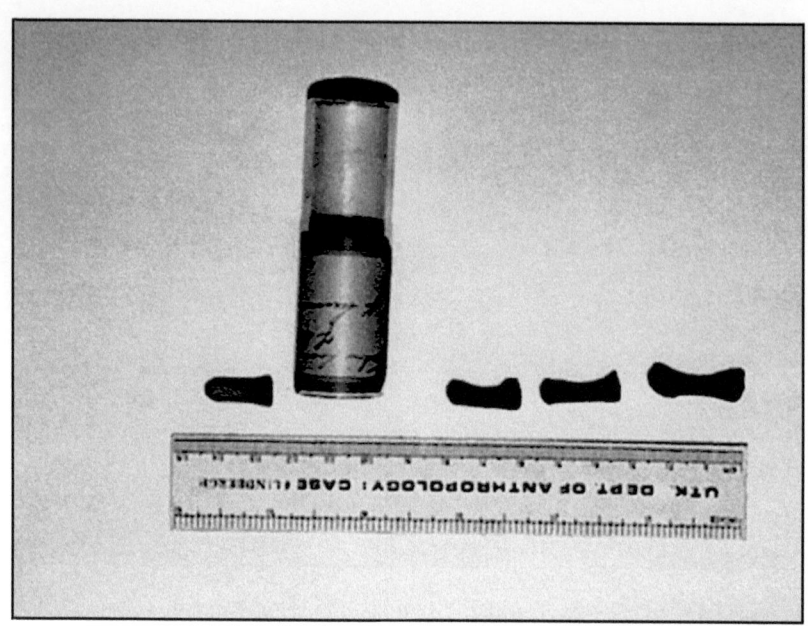

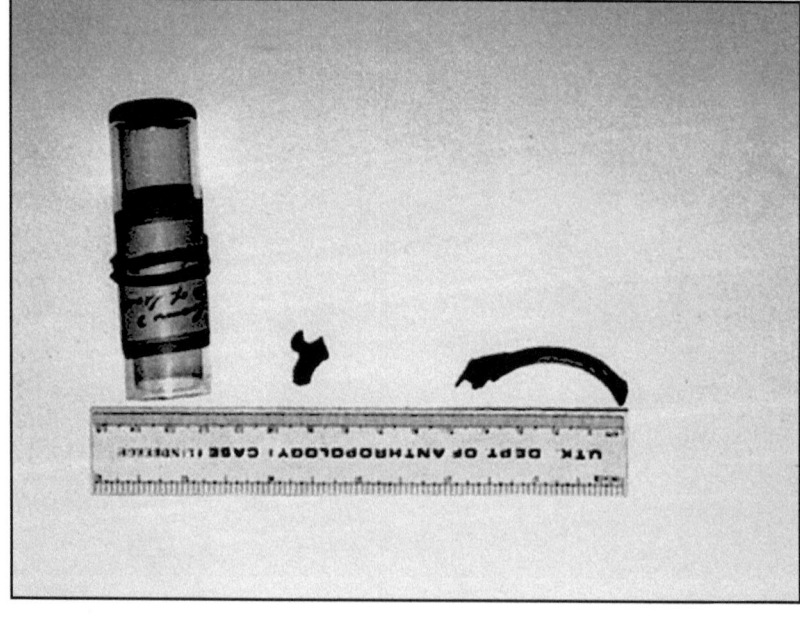

APPENDIX B
The Squibb Report

E·R·SQUIBB & SONS
BIOLOGICAL LABORATORIES
NEW BRUNSWICK, N.J.

JOHN F. ANDERSON, M.D.
DIRECTOR.

May 27, 1932

Colonel H. Norman Schwarzkopf,
Superintendent, State Police,
Trenton, N.J.

Dear Sir:

    In accordance with the request transmitted to us through Sergeant Kubaler of the New Jersey State Police, we made a detailed examination of various materials and objects delivered to our Laboratories on Monday May 16, 1932 by Sergeant Louis Kubaler.

    Examination has also been made of certain materials delivered by Sergeant Kubaler on May 23rd., and also certain materials and objects delivered by Mr. Kelly to our Mr. Holaday on May 20, 1932. These examinations included the following, the results of which are shown in the individual reports attached hereto, bearing corresponding numbers in Roman numerals:

    I. Examination of five bags of soil described as having been dug to a depth of 14 inches at the site where the body of Charles A. Lindbergh, Jr. was found on May 12, 1932.

    II. Examination of three baskets of leaves labeled as collected from the ground in the immediate scene where the body was found.

    III. Examination of clothing removed from body of child.

    IV. Examination of Dr. Denton sleeping garment received in 10 x 13 inch envelope labeled "#10 Morristown Hdqs."

    V. Examination of burlap bag containing leaves and hair found near body.

    VI. Examination of pair of cotton gloves and towel.

    VII. Examination of strips of burlap and piece of table cloth delivered in waste paper basket.

    VIII. Examination of handkerchief delivered in envelope marked "#11 Handkerchief".

-2-

As regards the finding of any significant clue the results of these examinations are essentially negative. The 5 bags of soil and 3 baskets of leaves were examined in such a manner that no significant object larger than about 3/64 of an inch in its greatest dimension could have escaped detection. No pin or other piece of metal was found. No blood stain was found on any of the garments or other fabrics examined. Tests for blood spots on the undershirt and band removed from the body and on the sleeping garment were made by Dr. Leonard with negative results.

One toe nail and nine foot bones corresponding to 8 toe bones and one calcaneus from a child's foot were found in the soil and leaves. One of the bones was positively identified by Dr. Leonard as human bone with the precipitin test. Four of the six bones found in the five bags of soil were embodied in masses of the soil. All bones were completely devoid of any adherent tissue. All soil scraped from the bones was identical in its characteristics as revealed by microscopic examination to that in the five bags or with that in the three baskets of leaves. All objects removed from the soil and leaves have been placed in labeled tubes or bottles.

Fibres of the same type as in the fabric of the burlap sack found near the body were matted to the shirt and band. Stencil marks were identified on this sack. The sack was spotted with soil common in its microscopic characteristics to that of the immediate location and with a black humus soil not found on any other object examined. A small amount of "dirt" was found inside a finger tip of one glove which was similar to the black soil on the sack with the exception that there was a lesser proportion of humus and the sand granules were of smaller average size. A white and brown hair characteristic of human wrist hair was found at the wrist seam inside of one glove.

In addition to the 8 reports numbered in Roman numerals, referred to above, there is also sent herewith a copy of the notes made by our Mr. B.G. Thomas as a record of his examination of the articles listed below which were delivered to me in my office at 3-20 p.m. May 20,1932 by Mr. Kelly with a verbal request for examination and identification of any blood spots if such could be found. Also a copy of Mr. Thomas' notes made as a record of the examination of soil delivered in a card board box labeled "One dozen pint Ball Fruit Jars" and the following written on a white paper pasted on top of the box "To Squibb's Laboratory New Brunswick Dr. Anderson or Mr. Holaday Monday May 23,1932".

One envelope 9¾ x 13 inches - Printed on upper left hand corner "State of New Jersey, Department of State Police, Trenton, N.J. Printed in pencil on front of envelope "Hopewell".

Contents as follows: one large rubber for left foot with mass of leaves and fibrous material in the heel, one torn leather glove with cotton cuff for left hand, one piece white bag material 18¼ x 33 inches, one piece soiled cloth 7 x 31 inches, one piece of soiled cloth 38½ inches long in two strips.

-3-

One filing envelope 11¾ x 9¼ x 2" tied with ¼" ribbon - labeled in pencil on flap "Dr. Anderson" and on front "Communications".

Contents as follows: one handkerchief 9 x 9¼" with blue border design, one piece soiled loosely woven cotton cloth 52 x 8", one piece light brown cloth 6" long x 1" at greatest width, 1 torn leather glove with cotton cuff for left hand, six masses of waste, one piece torn very dirty white paper approximately 16 x 4½".

N_0 indications of blood stains were found on any of the articles examined by Mr. Thomas. Much of the soil on these articles is characterized by particles of cinder, slag and coal dust. The types of soil found on these articles and that received in the fruit jar box on May 23rd are distinctly different in microscopic characteristics from any of the soil found on the articles described in sections I to VIII of this report.

The examination of these various materials and objects has been very painstakingly carried out and the examination has been most minute, most of them being done by our Mr. B. G. Thomas and our Mr. H. A. Holaday. In addition certain tests looking to the identification of material as of human origin were carried out in detail by our Dr. George F. Leonard.

It is of great regret that the results were practically barren of any significant clues which in our opinion would be of value in the investigation of the case now under consideration.

Very truly yours,
E. R. SQUIBB & SONS.

JOHN F. ANDERSON M.D.
DIRECTOR.

JFA.RE.

I

I. Treatment and Examination of soil received in five burlap bags.

The following mechanical operations were carried out by Mr. T. D. Gerlough

(1) All the soil from the five bags was spread out over an area of 12' x 12' x 2" to dry.

(2) The soil was broken up with a rake and when sufficiently dry was screened through a 4 mesh sieve.

(3) The fine portion was then further screened - part through a 16 mesh sieve and part through a 20 mesh sieve.

(4) The fine dirt, i.e. the material less than 16 or 20 mesh, was examined after each screening.

(5) The material which did not pass through the 4 mesh sieve was further dried and broken up and then screened through the 4 mesh sieve.

(6) The final lumps greater than 4 mesh, consisting mostly of gravel and rocks, were carefully examined by hand and then washed clean.

The following exhibits were obtained by means of the above described examination of the soil.

(1) A piece of plain brown paper about 6" x 9/" soiled with grease or oil - microscopic examination negative - no food particles found.

(2) A strip of lavender paper 2-3/4" x 3/8" - microscopic examination negative.

(3) a piece of wool fabric about $1\frac{1}{2}$" x $\frac{1}{2}$" irregular outline corresponding to piece of edge material from underarm of undershirt found on body.

(4) A piece of wool fabric about 2" x 1" irregular outline corresponding to piece from edge of shirt found on body.

Soil from 5 burlap bags.

(5) Four phalanges and two metatarsel bones corresponding to foot of infant. One of these bones found loose while sieving soil. Four of these bones found embedded in lumps of greyish black soil which were dried and broken up a second time for the second screening on the 4 mesh sieve. The sixth bone was found on washing the gravel and rock. One of the phalanges was cut into small pieces, extraced with ether, ground to a powder, the powder extracted with physiological salt solution and the salt solution submitted to Dr. George F. Leonard for a precipitin test for human protein which was found by Dr. Leonard to be strongly positive. This bone was thus identified as human bone. Microscopic examination of the soil adherent to the bones revealed no particles not common to the soil in which the bones were found.

(6) One piece red pepper about 3/4" x 1/2".

(7) Four small pieces less than 3/4" x 3/4" of white material which appears to be very thick paint scale. Has the odor of paint and contains lead carbonate.

(8) Moist lump of soil about 3/4" x 1/2" containing a few fine light brown hairs corresponding to locks of hair found in leaves and hairs on shirt.

(9) A small mat of fibers corresponding to the burlap bag number 02240.J.L.entwined with rootlets.

(10) A small white round disk slightly oblong 15/64 in. wide x17/64 in. long by 1/32 in.thick - edges smooth. Flat surface on both sides coated with a dark reddish black crackled homogeneous material which looks very much like dried blood and is dark red under the surface. This material however is not blood. It is insoluble in water and salt solution in which finely divided particles of the material were allowed to soak over night, - gave a negative precipitin test. (tested by Dr. Leonard).

Microscopic examination and staining test (crystal violet) indicate that the white object is not composed of bone or cartilage. It is insoluble in acid and therefore not composed of shell. It appears to be composed of some synthetic material - but probably not of the nature of celluloid or pyralin - since the material does not swell or dissolve when allowed to remain in acetone. It may be a casein derivative since it dissolved to some extent in caustic soda and the solution gives biuret test. The solid material also gives a strong xanthoproteic acid test.

(11) With the addition of a piece of acorn, and two small pieces of shell similar to snail shell the above listed items include all foreign objects found in the five bags of soil. No pins or pieces of metal were found.

II.

—3—

II. Examination of Leaves and Soil contained in the three baskets on each of which was pasted a strip of white paper bearing the following typed description "Leaves collected from ground in immediate scene where body of kidnaped Charles A. Lindbergh, Jr. was found on May 12, 1932 just off Princeton-Hopewell Road in Mount Rose, Mercer County, N.J."

The following operations were carried out by Mr. T. D. Gerlough.

(1) The material in each basket was carefully and thoroughly examined.

(2) The matted leaves were pulled apart, leaf by leaf and after inspection deposited in another container.

(3) The soil with the leaves was also hand picked into small bits and then placed on a 20 mesh sieve and dirt sluiced away with water.

The following exhibits were obtained from the three baskets of leaves by means of the above described examination.

(1) One toenail which corresponds to the large toe of a small child. Found in the greyish black top soil.

(2) Two phalanges corresponding to foot of infant were found on the sieve.

(3) One phalange and one calcaneus corresponding to foot of infant were found in small masses of the greyish black top soil with the leaves. In the portion of the top soil in which the bones were found putrifaction and decomposition were evident. Numerous maggots were present. Dirt scraped from the bones is seen by microscopic examination to be characteristic of the soil in the bags and with the leaves (i.e. consists of fine sand mostly white grains and humus).

(4) One small rib bone and a portion of vertebra with which the rib articulates were found in the greyish black top soil. These two bones have the appearance of chicken bones and are differentiated from any of the foot bones in that all of the latter are oily whereas the rib and vertebra are not. They are thoroughly bleached out. The wide flat portion of the rib bone is torn for a distance of 1/2" with a hole 1/32" diameter punched through as if by a round tooth.

(5) Piece of woolen fabric 1" x 1¼" same knit as undershirt found on body.

(6) Mass of leaves and soil (5 oz. air dried) with numerous curly light brown hairs loose and in locks identical to those found on undershirt. Hair found intermixed with disintergrated and partially decayed wet leaves and also embedded in small masses of wet greyish black top soil. No signs of blood in soil or on leaves. This soil of the same character as scraped from bones except that it contains a higher percentage of humus.

(7) A small additional amount of hair - fine light brown curly hair - was found scattered through the leaves.

(8) Piece of paper towel about 2 x 1". Yellowish stain on paper and small spot of adherent dark brown material on paper not identified.

The above list includes all foreign objects found in the 3 baskets of leaves.

Examination of exhibits by H. A. Holaday assisted

III

III. Examination of Contents of Collapsable brown filing envelope 15 x 10" tied shut with ribbon knotted between two eyes in the flap of the envelope. The following label typed on white strip of paper pasted on side of envelope, "Clothing removed from body of small child, later identified as the kidnaped Charles A. Lindbergh, Jr. Body found in woodland just of Princeton-Hopewell road, Mercer County, N.J. on May 12, 1932."

Contents of envelope - woolen infant's undershirt or vest bearing W. Altman & Co. tag and woolen garment hand sewed with blue thread and pinned at shoulder with safety pins.

Woolen undershirt plastered with mud. Quite a few fine light brown curly hairs were matted into the mud both inside and outside of the garment. A few small clots of material which had somewhat the appearance of blood stains was found on the inside of the garment about $\frac{3}{4}$ inch below the arm pit. This portion of the garment was cut out with scissors submitted to Dr. Leonard who extracted the material with physiological salt solution and conducted tests for blood which were reported as negative. The cut piece of the fabric was pinned back to the garment after the extraction was completed.

One white hair 5/8" long tapered at the end and one hair 7/16 in. long white at one end, shading into brown at the other end were found on the garment also two brown fibres of jute 5/8 in. long corresponding to the fabric of the burlap bag stencilled "0224 O.J.L.". No additional fibres of this type were found on the garment. One blue fibre was found which corresponded to the thread with which the other garment was sewed.

Woolen garment hand sewed with blue thread - pinned at shoulder on one side with two medium sized safety pins. Garment but full length on one side. Garment matted with dirt, leaves and quite a few hairs both inside and outside. Three areas on the garment (one on outside of garment 2 inches from center and 1 inch below the neck, one on inside of garment 2 inches in from the cut down the side and even with the neck, and one on inside of garment 3$\frac{1}{4}$ inches from the bottom and $\frac{3}{4}$ inches in from the edge of a U shaped area cut or torn out at the edge,) appear as though they might have been stained with blood. The first described area 2 inches in from the center of the neck was cut out with scissors and submitted to Dr. Leonard who extracted the material with physiological salt solution and conducted tests for blood which were reported as negative. The cut piece of fabric was pinned back to the garment after the extraction was completed.

One white and dark brown hair 1-1/8" in length gradually tapered at the brown end was found on the garment - has the appearance of an animal hair. Three jute fibres corresponding to the fabric of the burlap bag stencilled "0224 O.J.L." were found on the inside of the garment. The fibres were 2$\frac{1}{2}$", 1-3/8" and $\frac{1}{2}$" in length.

Examination of exhibits by H. A. Holaday assisted by B. G. Thomas

IV.

IV. Examination of Contents of Envelope 10 x 13 inches labeled "#10 Morristown Hdqs."

Contents consisted of a child's sleeping garment marked "No. 2 Dr. Denton sleeping garment 28 inch," on a printed tag sewed inside the front of the neck.

Garment in good condition - no holes and all buttons intact excepting left outside back button at hip pulled out with piece of fabric and piece from strip of cloth sewed under fabric as button reinforcement.

Feet of garment clean and pressed flat as though garment had not been worn since laundered. Seven out of the nine button holes show no evidence of having been used since the garment was washed. Two button holes slightly spread (i.e. center button hole back flap and third button hole from top in back). Deposit of very fine black particles assumed to be of rubber on under surface of 5 buttons and in fabric under these buttons and where center back button was torn out. Deposit assumed to be rubber because it is partly soluble in carbon bisulphide and insoluble in ether.

Spots and stains. Yellowish brown stain about 3/4 x 5/8" in front of left shoulder immediately below neck band, up to and including seam on neck band. Stain penetrates fibres.

Faint yellowish stain 1 inch below and 2 inches to left of front pocket.

Small yellowish stain between two middle buttons on back - also similar stain one inch below neck band and 3" from right shoulder seam and 1½" below neck band and 2" from right shoulder seam.

Neck band somewhat darker than remainder of garment - appears to have been soiled before it was washed the last time.

None of the above described stains have the appearance of blood stains. A piece of the fabric containing the first described stain was cut out with a scissors and submitted to Dr. Leonard who extracted the material with physiological salt solution and conducted tests for blood which were reported as negative. The cut piece of fabric was pinned back to the garment after the extraction was completed.

Some lavender colored spots were inadvertently made on the back of the garment while examining the buttons and fabric under the microscope. The spots came from traces of crystal violet dye which were present on the microscope stage.

Examination by H. A. Holaday assisted by B. G. Thomas

SUSPECT NO. 1

V. Examination of Burlap Bag 36 inches long by 27 inches wide containing mass of leaves and hair which weighed 4 oz. when air dried.
(Bag as received was turned inside out)
A card board tag bearing the following typed description was tied to the bag: "Burlap sack found near body of Charles A Lindbergh Jr. in woodland off Princeton Hopewell road in Mount Roase Mercer County N.J. on May 12th 1932".

(1) Markings

    a) Stencil "0224 O.J.L." on inside of bag as received 12" from top.

    b) Stencil "ANIMAL FOOD" on inside of bag as received 8" from bottom.

    c) Bag stiched together with white cord (1/32 in. thick) same stick as used on side and bottom of bag. White stiching extends 2½ inches in from unsewed edge 6 inches from top and parallel to top.

    d) Similar stiching 4 inches from top beginning 1 inch in from sewed edge of bag and extending for 1 inch parallel to top.

    e) Tuft of white cord (3/32" - 10 thread) in good condition sewed into fabric 4 inches from unsewed side and 7 inches from top of bag.

(2) Materials on bag.

    a) Careful examination of the entire surface of the bag on both sides of the fabric failed to reveal any evidence of blood stains.

    b) Clump 3/64 inches in diameter of black particles having the characteristics of coal found in side seam - 6 inches from bottom of bag.

    c) Plant hull - 3/64 x 11/64" - looks like oat hull found 6 inches from bottom and 1¼ from side seam on outside of bag as received. Broken pieces of hull of similar appearance found along bottom and side seams.

    d) Bag soiled with reddish brown soil and with black soil. In some places the black soil overlies the reddish brown soil. The reddish brown soil consists mostly of fine sand with a small proportion of fine humus and corresponds to the types of soil found in the baskets of leaves and in the 5 bags, whereas the black soil on the bag is characterized by a large proportion of humus and the sand particles are 3 to 6 times larger than most of the sand particles found on the bones and in brown dirt on the bag - also many of the larger grains are colored yellowish brown as contrasted to the preponderance of white granules in the brown soil.

Results of examination of leaves, twigs, and soil found inside bag.

(1) No evidence of blood stains on the leaves or twigs.

(2) Numerous fine curly light brown hairs and locks of hair corresponding to that found on undershirt from body matted with leaves and pressed between leaves.

(3) Found one phalange corresponding to foot of infant.

Examination of exhibits by H. A. Holaday and assisted by B. G. Thomas

VI. Examination of Contents of Filing Envelope 12 x 9½ x 1-1/3 inches labeled #12, Gloves, Hopewell.

Contents consisting of piece of board 5¼ x 3½ x 3/4 inches placed between a dirty cotton towel and a pair of brown cotton gloves, wrapped in newspaper.

Towel - 35½ x 20½ inches - ¼ inch hems on short sides - very much weathered and rotted. Irregularly soiled with grey, black and brownish materials with numerous scattered specks and droplets of black tar like material - no signs of blood stains could be detected. No hair was found on this towel. Numerous small holes in the fabric - which appear to have been eaten out by insects.

Cotton Gloves - dyed brown. Knit material, inner surface of fingers fleece like. Dye not faded or "washed off" inside of gloves. Dye irregularly faded and "washed off" on outside - particularly palm of left hand and most of back of right hand and parts of palm of right hand. Fabric in fairly good condition - is not rotted. Small holes (probably worn through) in tip of middle finger of right glove and forefinger of left glove.

No evidence of blood stains were detected on inside or outside surface of either glove.

A number of fine white flakes were found on the inside surface of each glove. These corresponded in appearance under the microscope to flakes of dandruff.

A curved white hair 7/16" long with part of hair root was found at the wrist seam on the inside of one glove. This hair is white at the root and is gradually tapered and brown colored at the tip end. For a short distance beginning 11/64 inches from the tip the hair shaft bulges to about twice the diameter on either side of bulge.

Very small tufts of fibre were found on the inside of the gloves which correspond to the fabric of the above described cotton towel.

A small amount of loose "dirt" was found and collected at the tip of the inside of the third (ring) finger in one of the gloves. This "dirt" corresponded in appearance (i.e. type and color of sand particles) to the black soil found on the burlap bag except that the size of the particles average somewhat smaller and the proportion of humus was much less than in the black soil on the burlap bag. A different type of soil was found throughout the fibres of the gloves inside and out. This soil corresponds to the soil received in the 5 bags.

Examination by H. A. Holaday assisted by B. G. Thomas

VII

VII. Examination of Contents of Brown Waste Paper Basket

Contents of Basket: One 22 foot strip of burlap, one 5½ foot strip of burlap one piece blue striped table cloth.

Burlap strip 22 feet in length and 4 to 5 inches in width. Jute threads run parallel to the strip.

Burlap strip 5½ feet in length and 3½ inches in width. A piece of burlap 1 foot in length sewed to one end of the strip.

Many irregularly outlined soiled areas on both strips of burlap. The soil found by microscopic examination to consist essentially of humus material with rootlets and vegetable matter and a small proportion of fine white sand. The proportion of humus in this soil is much greater than that found on the burlap sack or in the 5 bags of soil or the three baskets of leaves. No sign of any blood stain was found on either burlap strip.

Piece of cloth 20" x 25" two sides hemmed - irregular edge on two sides as if torn. Piece looks like the corner of a cheap loosely woven cotton table cloth. Blue border on each edge approximately 6½ inches wide consisting of 5 stripes of blue leaving 4 stripes of white. Laundry tag 1-7/8 " x 3/8" fastened at one corner with metal fasteners. Tag is stamped "XX 612" the last numeral is very faint and not identified with certainty. No indication of blood stains on this piece of cloth.

Examination by H. A. Holaday assisted by B. G. Thomas

VIII.

VIII. Examination of Contents of Envelope 7½ x 10½ inches labeled "#11 Handkerchief."

Contents consisted of one white cotton handkerchief 15 x 16 inches with ¼" hem. No laundry marks.

Fabric in good condition. No signs of decomposition of the cloth. No mildew. No fine grains of sand (i.e. soil) found between threads of fabric as with other exhibits. Light brown colored stains of irregular outline as follows: Small spot at each of two corners on same side, one spot about 4½ x 2" - edge of spot in about 3" from a third corner, one spot 9 x 4½" extending from middle of edge on one side toward center. One faintly stained spot about 4" toward center from the fourth corner. These stains penetrate into the fibres of the fabric and appear to be slightly oily. Three small red stains 3/32" diameter which have the appearance of a dye. Two spots of mucous discharge on faintly stained area, one spot of mucous discharge on two larger stained areas and one spot of mucous discharge with almost no stain. None of the stains on this handkerchief have the appearance of blood stains.

Examination by H. A. Holaday assisted by B. G. Thomas

SUSPECT NO. 1

Copy of record of examination by Mr. B. G. Thomas of the following articles by Mr. Kelly delivered to H. A. Holaday in his office in the Biological Laboratories of E.R. Squibb and Sons, New Brunswick, N. J. on May 20, 1932.

Examination of contents of Envelope $9\frac{1}{2}$ x 13".

Envelope marked "Hopewell" and in left upper corner, when opening to left hand side "State of New Jersey
Department of State Police
Trenton, New Jersey"

Loose dirt in envelope consisted of coal dust and larger, white, yellowish, and red mineral particles. On microscopic examination many of the particles were aggregates of small white particles and black material. The articles were loosely wrapped in a brown paper 33" x 19".

Article 1. Rubber for left foot. The soles were red and the red rubber extended $\frac{3}{4}$" up sides above the soles. There was a band of gray rubber at the top which was 7/32" wide. The length of the bottom of the rubber was $12\frac{1}{2}$" on the outside and $11\frac{3}{4}$" on the inside, the width of the sole was $4\frac{1}{2}$" on the outside and 4-1/8" on the inside. The outside width of the heel was 3-5/8", and the inside width was 3". The rubber was in poor condition. It was torn on the inside of the foot for $5\frac{5}{8}$". The tear began $6\frac{1}{2}$" from the back seam and extended down to 1/8" of the red rubber on the side and thence toward the toe of the rubber ending 3/8" from red rubber on side. 3 pieces of rubber were missing on the inside of foot which were 2 areas of red, 11/16" x 2/16", and the other 17/32" x 11/32" in the shape of a V and a piece of gray band approximately $1\frac{1}{2}$" long at the top of the rubber. The lining on the inside of the rubber was torn 4 places. A piece of rubber was missing on the side corresponding to the outside of foot, beginning $10\frac{1}{4}$" from back seam. The red portion of the rubber missing was approximately 7/8" x 3/8" and the black portion of the rubber was 1" x 3/8". The rubber was torn 1-9/16" back from the missing portion next to the red. The lining of the rubber was torn.

A mat of fibrous material was found in the heel approximately 3" x $2\frac{1}{2}$" x 1". Leaf, dirt, and coal particles were also found in the heel of the rubber. The dirt found on the leaf in the fibrous material on microscopic examination consisted mostly of fine small particles of sand and humus. The particles were mostly white a few of which were yellow to red in color. The fibrous material was not identified. There was a considerable amount of coal dust in the dirt. There were six pieces varying in size from 4/32" to 13/32". There was no evidence of blood on the rubber or on microscopic examination.

Article 2. A leather glove with canvas cuff for the left hand. The lumps of dirt found in the glove on microscopic examination consisted mostly of small white sand particles and a few larger black particles, a few small yellowish particles and black material.

The thumb seam of the glove was ripped on the palm and the back side. A seam was ripped on the back of the hand of the glove where the two middle fingers were sewed. A piece of canvas for the back of the hand of the glove was missing. The canvas tore very easily. No signs of blood stains were found on the glove on microscopic examination.

-2-

Article 3 A piece of rag 38½" long, in 2 strips. The shorter strip was 24½" long and torn, the hole measured 15¾" long. There was a machine stitch of white cotton sewing thread along the long edge. Most of the stitch was ripped out. White thread was sewn through the cloth in 4 places 1¾" from the machine stitch and 5 to 5½" apart. There were two button holes 5½" apart which were in line with the 4 above stitches. One of the button holes was 5" from the ripped end. Parts of fabric were discolored a light brown. The microscopic examination of the above discolored areas disclosed a large number of small white sand particles and a few small black particles embedded between and on the fibres of the cloth. The non discolored portion of the cloth on microscopic examination had only a few small black particles embedded between the fibres.

Article 4. A piece of white bag, 33 inches by 18¼ inches. White cord was sewed along the long edge. Six areas of the cloth were discolored which appeared like brown rust. The discolored areas were irregular in shape and from 2 to 6 inches in diameter. On microscopic examination the red color penetrated into the fibres of the cloth and small black particles were on the fibres of the cloth.

There were 4 black, gray greasy and oily appearing spots 1 to 5 inches in diameter on the cloth. On microscopic examination there were many fine white sand granules in the mesh of the cloth, few yellowish brown, reddish and black granules.

There was no evidence of blood stains on the cloth.

Article 5 Grayish black soiled cloth, cloth originally white. The cloth was 31 inches long and 7 inches wide. There were numerous small holes in the cloth. On microscopic examination there were many fine very small granules mostly white between the fibres of the cloth. There were also a few to moderate number of small black particles. There was no evidence of blood stains.

-3-

Examination of contents of yellow envelope folder type 11½" x 9¼" x 2" tied shut by ribbon ¼ inch wide. Labeled "Communications Dr. Anderson".

Article 1. Handkerchief white with blue and black edging. The colored edge of the handkerchief was 2 inches wide. The handkerchief measured 9" x 9¼" and was in good condition, that is no holes in cloth and it was strong. A large portion of the handkerchief, approximately ½, was discolored a light brown and there were many small light brown lumps of dirt on the light brown areas. On microscopic examination of the above areas and soil there were many fine white and light brown sand particles and a small number of small dark particles. On one side the handkerchief there was a brownish black material appearing to be soil. Microscopic examination of the smudge showed it consisted mostly of black particles with a moderate number of small light brown and white particles. There was no evidence of blood stains on the handkerchief.

Article 2. A piece of soiled waste weighed 36 grams and approximately 5½" x 2½". There were no signs of blood on the waste on microscopic examination. Dirt was shaken out of the waste. There were 6 pieces of klinker or slag like material ranging from 1/8 to 1/2 inch in diameter. The fine material consisted of moderate sized particles. On microscopic examination the particles were chiefly aggregates of small particles which were mostly black. There were a few clumps of white and light brown particles which were of moderate size. There were a few larger particles of black material as some of which resembled coal and others as if they were clinker or slag. The dirt was gritty.

Article 3. A dirty piece of waste which weighed 50 grams when in a ball measured 4½" x 4". The dirt was shaken out of the waste. There were 18 pieces of cinders or slag shaken out which measured 1/8 to 1/2" in diameter. On microscopic examination the appearance of the dirt was the same as the dirt from article 2 above. There were no signs of blood stains on the waste.

Article 4. A dirty piece of waste which weighed 6 grams. The dimensions were approximately 3½" x 5" larger. The dirt was shaken out of it which was small and gritty. There was one piece of clinker or slag, 7/16 in. diameter. On microscopic examination the appearance of the dirt was the same as for articles 2 and 3. There were no signs of blood stains on the waste.

Article 5. A dirty piece of waste which weighed 58 grams. The dirt shaken out was gritty and consisted mostly of a few fine particles (about 5 particles 1/8" to 1/4"). On microscopic examination the material was the same in appearance as the dirt from articles 2, 3, and 4. There were no signs of blood stains on the waste.

Article 6. A piece of waste which was relatively clean and weighed 62 grams and was approximately 12" x 4". The dirt shaken out was gritty and consisted mostly of fine particles but there was one piece of cinder or slag which was 3/8" long. On microscopic examination the particles were mostly small and black and white and a few brown and a very few red particles. There were also many larger particles of above materials or aggregates of the above materials. No signs of blood stains on the waste material.

—4—

Article 7. A clump of waste material which weighed 74 grams. The dimensions were approximately 8" x 5". The dirt was shaken out of the waste and was gritty and cinder like in character. It was composed of black, yellowish white to dark red particles. Microscopically many of the particles were larger than observed from the other pieces of waste. The larger pieces of white particles were more numerous than those from the other samples of waste. A few blades of dried grass, leaves and stems of vegetable matter were in the waste. Part of the waste material was slightly greasy in appearance. There were no signs of blood stains on the waste material.

Article 8. A soiled piece of cotton cloth 52" x 8". The cloth was lossely woven and originally white in color. There were 26 holes in the cloth, the largest of which was 5" x 2". The cloth tore easily. There was a faint pink stain 4" from one end next to two small holes which was not blood. There was a faint pink stain near the edge of the largest hole which was not blood. There were brown stains around edge of largest holes and also other smaller and holes and on cloth 5½" from one edge. On microscopic examination the stain penetrated into the fibres and did not appear like blood. 12" from one end there were approximately 10 small particles which appear to be old food.

There were clumps of dirt with fibres and hair matted in it on one end of the cloth. The hair was darker in color than that found in the burlap sack (O224 O.J.L . with leaves in it). The hair was curly. A few white hairs were also present, which were not identified whether they were human or some type of animal resembling human hair. A clump of dirt was removed 12" from the other end. It had fibres and hair matted in it. There was a small clump of the above type still left on the cloth about 1 inch from where the other clump was picked off. A clump of dirt with hair and fibres in it was picked off the cloth approximately 2 inches from the largest hole.

Parts of the cloth were discolored with brown soil which on microscopic examination showed numerous small particles mostly light brown color some white and few black. The parts of the cloth discolored black showed on microscopic examination numerous small particles which were mostly black and relatively few white, brown and red particles. There was no positive evidence of blood stains on the cloth.

Article 9. A strip of light brown cloth which was 6 in. long and the widest portion was 1 inch. On microscopic examination there were numerous small particles embedded between the fibre of the cloth. The particles were nearly all either white or black in color. There were no signs of blood stains on the cloth.

Article 10. A piece of irregular torn dirty white paper which was approximately 16 inches long and 4½ inches wide. On microscopic examination the paper was covered with numerous small particles which were mostly white and black with a few slighly larger brown and reddish brown rounded particles. There were no signs of blood stains on the paper.

- 5 -

Article 11. A leather glove with canvas cuff to fit the left hand. The fingers, thumb, and palm of the glove were made of leather. The back and cuff of glove were made of canvas. The leather parts of the glove were covered with a black grimy dirt which was slightly greasy in appearance. On microscopic examination the leather was covered with numerous small black particles and few white particles and occasional reddish-brown particles. There were also a few larger particles of white with brown and black particles in it and also brown and light brown color areas in the larger white particles. The dirt on the canvas portion of the glove on microscopic examination was of the same type as on the leather portions. The glove was approximately $11\frac{1}{2}$" long from finger tip to end of cuff and $4\frac{2}{4}$" wide across the palm of the hand. There was no evidence of blood stains on the glove.

-6-

Dirt or soil from pasteboard box (1 doz pint Ball Fruit Jars) labeled: "To Squibb Laboratory, New Brunswick Dr. Anderson or Mr. Holaday, Monday, May 23, 1932".

The soil was light brown in color and the clumps were easily broken between the fingers. On microscopic examination soil was composed almost entirely of small sand particles mostly white and light brown in color. There were a moderate number of reddish brown particles present. No humus visible under the low power of the microscope. This soil was distinctly different in appearance from any of the other soils examined except the light brown soil on the loosely woven cotton strip 52" x 8" wide in envelope marked "communications Dr. Anderson" and also on the handkerchief in same envelope.

Soil scraped from portion of burlap bag (0224 O.J.L.) stained black and compared microscopically with dirt from the waste material appeared different, that is, the former had many times more fine white and light brown sand particles in it. A few of the larger particles resembled those found in the waste material.

APPENDIX C
Declaration of Dr. Peter Speth

Certification declared by Peter Speth, MD
May 27, 2020
In the matter of the circumstances surrounding the death of
CHARLES A. LINDBERGH, JR.

Peter Speth, MD, being of full age, does hereby certify and declare as follows:

Your Declarant was contacted by retired California Judge, Lise Pearlman, in January 2019. Judge Pearlman has been investigating the available documentary evidence and circumstances surrounding the alleged abduction and death in the spring of 1932, of the 20-month old Charles A. Lindbergh, Jr. Bruno Richard Hauptmann was tried and convicted of abducting and murdering the child, and was executed in 1936 in the electric chair in a New Jersey State Prison. Your Declarant was asked to consider the evidence, as described and obtained at the woodland scene where the body was found and during the ensuing autopsy, and interpret that data from a forensic pathological and taphonomic standpoint. The ultimate question that would be asked here is whether the forensic analysis by this Declarant comports with the conclusions reached at the time in convicting and executing Hauptmann.

A. Credentials

Your Declarant is competent to all matters stated herein. I am a licensed physician, certified as a Diplomate in anatomic, clinical, and forensic pathology by the American Board of Pathology, with specialized training in forensic neuropathology; a Fellow in the American Society for Clinical Pathology, the College of American Pathologists, the National Association of Medical Examiners, and the American Academy of Forensic Sciences. I served as County and Assistant State Medical Examiner in the States of California and New Jersey, with hands-on, expert participation at more than two thousand death scene investigations, taking witness statements and evaluating evidence. Your Declarant has performed several thousand autopsies in determining and certifying the circumstances, cause, and manner of death in violent, suspicious and unusual deaths. I have been qualified as an expert in these matters in State and Federal Courts and have continued to practice as a forensic pathology expert consultant for Defense and Prosecution since my retirement.

Of particular relevance here is my first-hand, routine experience in determining time-since-death at death scenes, including those with decomposed bodies. I have lectured on this subject matter and published a review for the International Association of Identification. In all my cases involving forensic entomology and forensic anthropology/taphonomy, after my initial on-scene evaluations and analyses based on my training and experience, this Declarant has then always consulted with those having expertise in these specialized areas to refine and/or correct my determinations. Having reached out also in preparing this Declaration, in particular, I am extremely grateful for the assistance and encouragement I received from Marcella H. Sorg, PhD, William Rodriguez III, PhD, William M Bass, III, PhD, Alison Galloway. PhD, John R. Wallace, PhD, and Jason H. Byrd, PhD. I wish to also thank Gretchen R. Dabbs, PhD, Sherah Vanlaerhoven, PhD and Lauren M. Weidner, PhD.

B. Evidence considered by Declarant

The May 12, 1932, preliminary autopsy report of an "unknown baby;" the FBI transcription of the May 14, 1932, autopsy of Charles A. Lindbergh, Jr.; photos taken by the police at the site and by a photographer at the morgue; evidence summarized by Judge Pearlman of prior searches of the area and of the theory of the crime that became the basis for the murder conviction of Bruno Richard Hauptmann; police reports and witness statements obtained by the New Jersey State Police on May 12 and 13, 1932; the activities at the morgue over the next two days; the statement of Herman Veidt to the police about suspicious activities he had seen on May 4-10, 1932, at that location; the May 4, 1932, letter from family pediatrician, Dr. Philip Van Ingen, to Elizabeth Morrow; Dr. Van Ingen's hand-written note on the stationery of Coroner Walter Swayze on May 13, 1932, regarding the identifying features of the child; Dr. Van Ingen's statement taken on November 21, 1934, by Assistant Attorney General Robert Peacock regarding identifying the baby; the January 1935 testimony of the medical examiner Dr. Charles Mitchell, Inspector Harry Walsh of the Jersey City Police, and Sergeant Andrew Zapolsky of the New Jersey State Police; a description by Detective James Fitzgerald of the Jersey City Police Department of his first sighting of the corpse on May 12, 1932, as contained in a transcription of the statement given by Fitzgerald to Assistant Attorney General Robert Peacock on December 4, 1934; a page-one, February 21, 1935, article in The Record-Argus, Greenville, Pennsylvania "Challenge Identity of Body as Lindbergh Baby"; the daily minimum, average, and maximum temperatures and precipitation obtained from the National Oceanic and Atmospheric Administration (NOAA) for the period from March 1, 1932, to May 12, 1932, in Somerville, New Jersey (which lies about 17 miles north of where the corpse was found and, when examined with contemporary weather data, compares well with the weather in the area where the corpse was found; the May 27, 1932, Squibb lab report from Director John Anderson to Colonel H. Norman Schwarzkopf, Superintendent of the New Jersey State Police; and an affidavit of Dr. William Bass dated November 25, 2019. (Attached as Exhibit A hereto is a chart which I prepared of the relevant weather conditions. Attached as Exhibit B hereto is a photo of the corpse taken between 4:15 p.m. and 4:30 p.m. on May 12, 1932, after the corpse was turned face up).

C. Introduction

Forensic taphonomy is the study of the stages of decomposition as it applies in a forensic context. There is a generally accepted succession of these stages that varies in its time-line and its manifestations, dependent on temperature, environment (buried, ground surface, submersion, etc.), precipitation/humidity, clothing/covers, body size/habitus, etc. This succession involves autolysis of the body cells, microbial putrefaction with bloat/purge, active decay and skeletonization/ disarticulation, with variations such as adipocere and mummification. Under appropriate conditions, it also involves a succession of carrion insects and possibly animal predation, also depending on temperature, precipitation, environment, etc.

The evidence in this case was examined from a forensic taphonomic standpoint. Marked deviations were noted. What follows describes these deviations, with interpretations wherever possible.

D. Opinion re: absence of necrophagic (carrion) insect activity

a. The favorable conditions for necrophagic insect activity

(1)   The corpse was found by truck driver William Allen around 2:45 p.m. on May 12, 1932, lying prone (face down) in slightly hollowed out, dark soil, and minimally covered with leaves, in a central New Jersey forest with tree canopies over it. The location was about 75 feet in from the edge of a road, Princeton-Hopewell Road. A burlap bag was found by the side of that road and then picked up by two state policemen and brought to the site of the body.

(2)   It is apparent that the corpse had been only recently transported to the woods in that burlap bag (see below). Namely, Col. Schwarzkopf had overseen a thorough search of a 5-mile area in April which included that woodland site. Neither that search nor any other since March 1. had turned up the body or the burlap bag by the roadside. Police interviews of locals on May 12 also indicated none of those interviewed had seen the body or burlap bag previously. It is possible that the statement of Herman Veidt could pinpoint the deposit of the corpse to the time period from May 4 to May 10.

(3)   The general stage of decomposition of the body, as described at the scene and during the subsequent autopsy, can be characterized as post-bloat putrefaction/active decay. But – contrariwise to the general stage of decompositional discoloration, the face appeared on initial inspection at the scene to be well-preserved, and a "section" of skin on the relatively preserved right foot was described at autopsy as Caucasoid by not displaying that discoloration (both to be discussed below). Also, the medical examiner and a photographer who were in the morgue with the body that evening both described the body as having a stifling, pungent odor of decomposition.

(4)   Scalp hair was still present on the head, except over the back of the head. There was general decomposition of the musculature except in the face. The liver, the heart and the brain were described as still present and in place. The intact brain was found to be pudding-like in consistency when the fractured skull was opened at autopsy. The left lower leg, the left hand and the right forearm were missing at the scene, but there was no disarticulation of the mandible, skull or cervical spinal column.

(5)   The corpse was wearing two, waist-length shirts that bore no blood stains and no tooth or claw marks.

(6)   The temperatures in May 1932 (see Exhibit A), and the location where the corpse was found (less than 5 miles from the Lindbergh home), and the stage of odoriferous putrefaction, with relatively preserved facial features, were ideal for carrion (necrophagic) blow fly ovipositioning (egg-laying) during a few rain-free days after the corpse's arrival at that location, and for the subsequent early development (succession) of maggot instars, involving at least two prevalent carrion blow flies, P. regina and also C. vicina (family Calliphoridae).

(7)   There was light rain on May 12 (see exhibit A), when the body was found and recovered, and before that, there had been slight rain on May 7 and 8, 1932. The corpse was shaded by the canopy -- it was found face down, with the body and face in a slight hollowing out in the forest dirt and with some leaves strewn on the baby's back.

b. What was recovered from the scene

(1) After initial discovery on May 12, 1932, the body was rolled over onto its back from the prone position in which it had been found -- this occurred at about 3:15 p.m. Close to an hour later, it was returned face down in order to be photographed in the approximate position in which it had been first discovered. It was then turned face up again for additional photos (including the one attached hereto as Exhibit B). After the photographs were taken, its two shirts were removed by Inspector Walsh before the corpse was transported to the morgue.

(2) All of the surface debris (leaves, twigs, clumps of dirt and other debris) from around and under the corpse was collected and placed in three "baskets," and submitted to the Squibb Lab, where the contents of the baskets were examined. Three phalanges and a calcaneus, all said to have been from the "foot" of an "infant," were found by Squibb Lab in those "baskets". The bones were said by Squibb Lab to be devoid of "any adherent tissue." Two "thoroughly bleached" bird bones were also found, described by Squibb Lab as demonstrating what would be the typical gnaw marks of scavenging predators.

(3) The dirt to a depth of 14 inches under and around the body was recovered and transported in five "bags" to the Squibb Lab for examination. Four phalanges and two metatarsal bones, said by Squibb lab to be "foot" bones, all from an "infant," were found in those "bags." These bones were also said by Squibb Lab to be devoid of "any adherent tissue."

(4) The burlap bag in which the police assumed the body was transported (since it was found by the edge of the road abutting the woods where the body lay), contained leaves, twigs, dirt and one small phalanx. There is no mention in the Squibb report of any adherent tissue. The Squibb lab reported it as corresponding "to [the] foot of [an] infant."

(5) The Squibb lab pulverized one of the bones from the five bags of dirt to confirm by precipitin test that it was human.

(6) Dr. William Bass, in 1982, examined the ten remaining human bones and the two bird bones. He confirmed that all of the human bones were of a child aged 18-24 months, two from the hand and the other eight, foot bones of that child. Dr. Bass noted that the human bones were **"intact and undamaged"**...devoid of "tooth marks" like those which he had noted on the two bird bones, i.e. the ten human bones were devoid of any predatory gnawing. He also noted that "decayed tissue, dirt and even a few hairs clung to several."

c. What was actually found relevant to the anticipated necrophagic insect activity

(1) Contrary to the anticipated scientific expectations, considering the above-described conditions, there was no evidence whatsoever of any blow fly activity (eggs, maggots, puparia, pupa shells) or necrophagic beetles/beetle shells, anywhere on the body surface, notwithstanding an odor of putrefaction that would attract blow flies during rain-free times while the body lay in the woods. There was also no evidence of blow fly activity on the preserved left eye and front of the face or under the protective two shirts, or at the body-ground interface, or within the body (notwithstanding the still-present liver and heart, the liver a favorite source of nutrition for blow fly maggots) or in the debris and dirt around and under the body (with one exception to be described next) or in the burlap bag in which the body was apparently transported, albeit with one residual, disarticulated, decomposed human foot bone.

(2) The three "baskets" of surface debris received by the Squibb Lab on May 16, 1932, were examined at some point in time before May 27, 1932, when the report of Director John Anderson issued. Two of the phalanges found in those three baskets, and as stated in the Squibb Lab report, devoid of "any adherent tissue," were described as being "oily." They were embedded in small masses of grayish black topsoil, the latter showing "presence" of "putrefaction and decomposition," (very likely the result of decompositional liquefaction see page), and the "presence" of "numerous maggots." These were the only maggots Squibb technicians mentioned finding in any of the materials they analyzed.

(3) No witness statement or police report regarding May 12, 1932, mentioned the presence of any maggots or any other type of "vermin."

(4) At the morgue, there were at least five persons actively involved in the autopsy room. The body had a stifling, pungent odor of decomposition described by at least two of those present. There is no evidence that any persons at the morgue described seeing any maggots or any other type of "vermin."

(5) In January 1935, Jersey City Inspector Harry Walsh testified in the death penalty trial of Bruno Richard Hauptmann. Walsh testified that when he arrived at the site of the corpse on the afternoon of May 12, 1932, the body was covered in a "veil of vermin." Walsh's own May 12, 1932, report made no such observation.

(6) Contrariwise, Sergeant Zapolsky testified at the same trial that an hour before Walsh had arrived on the afternoon of May 12, Zapolsky had bent down close to the corpse after it was turned face up so that he could compare a photo that he had brought with him of Charles Lindbergh, Jr., with those features of the corpse that were still preserved. Zapolsky did not describe any impediment to viewing the features of the corpse or any vermin present.

d. Conclusions regarding the lack of necrophagic insect activity

(1) It is the opinion of this Declarant (and supported by the forensic entomologists contacted by this Declarant) that the maggots found only in those two small masses of grayish black top soil, had been opportunistically laid there, in isolation, by flesh flies (also known as dung flies in the family Sarcophagidae). Flesh flies characteristically are attracted by the odor of carrion, dung, decaying material, or open wounds of mammals. In contrast to blow flies, they directly deposit hatched or hatching maggots instead of eggs.

(2) Apart from the flesh flies just described in subparagraph (1), no maggots were found by the Squibb lab. No maggots at all were reported by at least a dozen persons who arrived at the scene on May 12 and who, to varying degrees actively participated in the identification, guarding and removal of the corpse to the mortuary that afternoon. The complete absence of blow fly and other carrion insect activities on and about the body is contrary to the known scientific succession of necrophagic insects, considering the stated prevailing conditions on and about the body (see exhibit A). The most likely explanation under the circumstances is some type of *unnatural intervention, most notably a chemical*.

(3) As stated above, the burlap bag was found by the Squibb Lab to contain a disarticulated phalanx of a child. Dr. Bass later determined the appearance and stage of decomposition of that bone were indistinguishable from the disarticulated bones found in the baskets of dirt and bags of surface debris – all belonging to a child between 18 months and 24 months old and consistent with that child being a male.

(4)   The burlap bag also contained similar leaves, twigs and dirt as those found near the body. The burlap bag, like all other materials analyzed by the Squibb lab, showed no traces of blood. It is therefore reasonable to assume that the body was placed in that bag for transport, but that the body had already decomposed before being placed in that bag; and that the corpse had spent some previous length of time decomposing in a similar habitat to that where it was found (based on the presence of leaves, twigs and dirt in the burlap bag that accompanied the body); and that therefore the temperatures were similar at that prior location. Accordingly, relying on the data in exhibit A, the conditions in that prior location during the latter two-thirds of April and during the first few days in May 1932, were somewhat less ideal than in the remaining week of May at the final location, but still adequate for blow fly ovipositioning (egg-laying) and subsequent succession of blow fly maggot instars, puparia and also carrion beetles. However, to be described below, some type of roof or covering protected the body at that location from rain and also at that location possibly from insects.

(5)   Walsh's uncorroborated testimony in 1935 that he observed a "veil of vermin" on the corpse in the woods on May 12, 1932 -- that no one else ever reported -- does not match the extensive experience of this Declarant as it relates to the public reaction to maggots. Those who are not familiar with maggots react in disgust and turn away as quickly as they can. One can hear maggots in their masses "munching." The whole area of involved tissues seems to be moving.

(6)   Yet the statements of the two truckers who found the body indicate the two men stared at the corpse for five minutes to see if they could identify it. Sergeant Zapolsky, who arrived half an hour later, testified that he turned the body face up and compared it to a photo he brought along of Charles Lindbergh, Jr.

(7)   Furthermore, had there been a veil of maggots on the corpse in the woods, those maggots would still have been present in large numbers on the corpse at the morgue. They tend to drop off the morgue table to the floor and crunch under one's feet. None were reported at the morgue. There was no revolt and disgust by the many observers and participants — there surely would have been had there been a "veil of vermin.".

(8)   Discrediting Walsh's trial testimony and crediting all the other evidence, this Declarant assumes that although some maggots were found in soil near the corpse, there was no necrophagic activity on the corpse itself.

(9)   Based on the evidence summarized by Judge Pearlman, there is at least one credible explanation for the absence of necrophagic activity on the corpse -- **ethyl ether**, a known anesthetic utilized in the 1930s during vivisections.

(a) No necrophagic insect would feed on a corpse containing ether. (The only known fly that genetically is protected against ether is a fruit fly, which has no bearing here).

(b) There are numerous published articles reporting levels of ethyl ether in postmortem blood and organ tissues. But there are no scientific articles that I could find describing postmortem ether in decomposed bodies.

(c) However, Dr. John Butts, the now-retired former chief medical examiner for the state of North Carolina for almost a quarter of a century, personally sent information to this Declarant regarding a case that he himself had certified in which ethyl ether was detected and quantitated in the brain of a body in advanced putrefaction (the skull was intact). Notably, there was no evidence of maggot activity at the time he examined the body, nor any residual evidence of such.

E. **Opinion re: Preservation of the face in contrast to the rest of the putrefied/decaying body.**

a. **Facts and observations considered by Declarant:**

(1) As described above, the disarticulated phalanx found in the burlap bag was determined by Dr. Bass to match those hand and foot bones found in the baskets and bags of soil, leaves and twigs recovered from the site of the corpse. Two of the bones were found by the Squibb lab to be "oily" with presence of "putrefaction and decomposition." These facts indicate that the stage of decompositional disarticulation had occurred already before the body was transported in the burlap bag, in keeping with post-bloat putrefaction/ active decay.

(2) And, in his official May 14, 1932, autopsy, Dr. Mitchell determined that the body, apart from the face and a "section" of the foot (see below), exhibited signs that it had been undergoing decomposition for seven to ten weeks. The condition of the disarticulated human bones, some described as "oily" by Squibb Lab and several displaying "decayed tissue" years later, would be consistent with seven to ten weeks of decomposition, again in keeping with post-bloat putrefaction/active decay.

(3) And, as stated above, it had been raining lightly when truck driver William Allen found the body around 2:45 p.m. on May 12, and it was still raining when Zapolsky returned around 4:15 p.m. with Col. Schwarzkopf. This rain, as will be explained below, may be a critical factor.

(4) **Observations by the first responders at the woodland site and later by Dr. Mitchell at the morgue**: The body was face-down in the slightly hollowed-out dirt, with some leaves on its back. The body was turned face-up by Sergeant Zapolsky and Detective Fitzgerald when they had arrived at the scene in the woods around 3:15 p.m., using a stick to flip the corpse. Their initial observations at the scene disclosed remarkable preservation of the face. But there was an extraordinary change of color after the face had been exposed to the rain for an hour or more. Dr Mitchell noted later in the autopsy that there was a lack of deterioration of the facial muscles in contrast to the general stage of decomposition of the muscles of rest of the body,

   (a) Detective Fitzgerald, in his statement to New Jersey Attorney General Peacock, stated: **"One eye was deteriorated and the other eye was open. ... The face was partly decomposed. ...The color of the face was more or less of a pink."** Sergeant Andrew Zapolsky testified at Hauptmann's death penalty trial: **"...the face that was in the ground was preserved; when we turned it over it was white..."**

   (b) Zapolsky then left and returned with Colonel Schwarzkopf, Inspector Walsh and another officer around 4:15 p.m. The corpse had just been placed face down again for a photograph to approximate how it looked when first spotted, and then it had been flipped face up again. What they then noticed is reflected in Zapolsky's testimony at trial: **"...and then when we returned from Hopewell [the face] turned blue. We found it was blue."** Fitzgerald in his statement to AG Peacock stated: **"...After the air hit [the face], it became dark..."**

   (c) Dr. Mitchell's preliminary autopsy report confirms the darkening of the face that had been noted at the scene after the face had been turned up into the rain. But Dr. Mitchell notes preservation of the facial musculature and features (including lips and tongue, albeit swollen): **"The facial muscles, the only ones of the body that had not deteriorated.... General decomposition of the muscles of the entire body and other soft tissues except the face, but marked discoloration and some disfigurement of this part of the body due to softening of the eyeballs and a swollen condition of the lips and tongue."**

(d) Dr. Mitchell later testified at Hauptmann's trial that when he saw the corpse at the morgue the night of May 12, 1932: "...**The facial expression was quite good on this child. The facial muscles had not deteriorated, although the body generally was in a bad state of decomposition.**"

b. **Seeking an explanation for the preservation of the face in light of all of the above facts and observations**

(1) There is no question that the face had to have been preserved in some manner, and that would have involved some type of chemical intervention. In determining the identity of such chemical – it would have to be a chemical whose preservative action would be rapidly reversible by quickly becoming dark (according to Fitzgerald) and, in fact, more specifically, becoming blue (according to Zapolsky). Also, it would have to be a chemical that could be applied directly to the face and be held or replaced there (e.g. with a cloth) for the duration of 2 months.

(2) In further support of the intervention of a preserving agent to the face is the freeze/thaw cycle that occurred in March and early April 1932 (see Exhibit A), in that area of New Jersey. Forensic taphonomy has established that such a freeze/thaw cycle usually acts to cause accelerated decomposition from "outside-in," meaning the exterior (especially the face) versus the interior organs. Here the exact opposite occurred.

(3) Simple exposure to air, when turned face-up (as Detective Fitzgerald suggested), was given consideration by the declarant. But declarant dismisses that idea, because the face had already been exposed to air during transport in the burlap bag, not to mention the presence or absence of exposure to air at whatever prior site the baby had been.

Furthermore, if it were just a matter of exposure to air, then the frontal parts of the body (chest and abdomen), that had also been in the same prone position as the face, should have undergone the same change when exposed to air. Instead the chest and abdomen were in a decomposed state of post-bloat putrefaction/active decay. Finally, simple exposure to air does not explain the face turning "blue" as Sergeant Zapolsky observed.

(4) This Declarant suspected embalming chemicals. In fact, a newspaper article at the time reported that one or more defense experts for Hauptmann had been prepared to testify at his trial that they believed the corpse had been subjected to embalming, but they were never called to testify.

(5) Many chemicals have been considered for embalming over centuries. Two are considered:

(a) <u>Tannic acid</u>

i. Tannic acid immediately came to mind, used for ages in tanning and preserving hides. Tannic acid acts by precipitating proteins and cross-linking the collagen peptides in the skin. It is available as a brown powder. Tannic acid in solution had been considered as a substitute embalming fluid for centuries. But, in that regard, among other serious disadvantages, it has a very slow reaction time, with only superficial penetration to achieve the preservation (the epidermis would not be preserved, maintaining the features of the underlying dermis). **The preserving reaction is temporary, and readily reversible, and tannic acid is highly soluble in water.**

ii. The tannic acid powder could readily have been placed on a cloth over the face, initially and even on repeated occasions. More than one piece of cloth was, indeed, found in the dirt and leaves transported for analysis to the Squibb lab. Discolorations on these pieces of cloth were observed by Squibb technicians but not diagnosed. Tannic acid's properties satisfy the requirements of enduring for 2 months, being rapidly reversible and darkening the dermis as the tannin was washed away by the rain after the face was turned face-up and exposed to the rain. The surrounding and subjacent microbial putrefaction would have rapidly extended to the face as the crosslinking of peptides were reversed.

iii. Problematic is the issue of turning blue. Ferric iron salts would have to have been added to the tannic acid powder in order for the face to have turned blue when exposed to the rain. This reaction was well-known at the time.

(b) **Copper sulfate:**

i. Copper sulfate has also been used in tanning and preserving hides. It is an astringent, **highly soluble in water**, and available as a white powder. It had been considered for embalming, but has the same deficiencies as tannic acid in that regard. These deficiencies, just as with tannic acid, would be suitable to fit the sequence being discussed here. Therefore, it could have been applied to a cloth over the face for 2 months, reversible immediately upon being exposed to the rain.

ii. However, copper sulfate is hydroscopic (not as efficient, however, as copper chloride), and is therefore used as a desiccant. **It turns deep blue as it absorbs water.** The problem that this Declarant cannot readily resolve here is that the humidity in the air and moisture in the dirt during such a two-month exposure, would probably have caused the copper sulfate to turn blue before the discovery of the body unless some type of moisture-proof cloth could have been used.

(6) Whatever chemical was used, it would not only require the placement and replacement of a cloth of some type to hold the chemical against the face, but also, as elucidated at D.d,(3), it would also require protection from rain by either a roof and/or a covering during the long postmortem interval until the child was found. The question that this declarant needed to answer is how this could be accomplished. There certainly could have been a roof and/or covering at the prior location. But an explanation is needed for the ultimate location where the body was found. The latter can readily be explained by the statement provided by Herman Veidt -- between May 4th and May 10th he had seen person or persons entering the woods from the road late in the nights at the location where the child was ultimately found -- he had never seen such activity prior to those nights. This statement is immensely important when one considers that it rained on May 7th and 8th (see exhibit A) -- the preserving chemical needed to be protected from rain.

F. Opinion re: The Caucasoid "section" of skin on the non-skeletonized preserved right foot

a. Facts and observations considered by Declarant:

(1) Dr. Mitchell, in his preliminary autopsy report, stated:

"...a section of skin on the right foot which had not become discolored indicated a child of the white race."

(2) This area on the right foot was the only area of "skin" thusly observed by Dr. Mitchell as consistent with the "white race." Namely, the face was dark by the time he examined it in the morgue, albeit, with preserved musculature and features.

(3) But also, the entire right foot, remarkably, was the only part of the four extremities that was preserved, with almost intact dermis covering the subjacent tissues. This is especially apparent in one of the photos taken at the scene (exhibit B) when the child had been turned over onto its back. To understand the photo, it should be explained that, as the child was turned over onto its back, the right leg flipped over the upper left leg (the lower left leg was disarticulated), displaying the quite intact right foot.

b. **Seeking an explanation for the "section" of skin on the foot with Caucasoid features and the preservation of the right foot**

(1) Based on declarant's personal experience and confirmed when consulting with taphonomic experts, this "section" of "skin" on the foot probably does not represent "skin," but more likely light-colored dermis, remaining after preceding characteristic decompositional skin slippage. As such, it is not specific for Caucasian (as, for example, noted when the skin is thermally damaged in Afro Americans).

(2) As stated above at D.d.(3) and at E.b.(6), there was a roof and/or covering at the prior location, and possibly a covering initially at the final location during the rain on May 7th and May 8th (see exhibit A) when, as is apparent from Herman Veidt's statement, there was revisiting of the scene at night during that time-span by person or persons, who could have transported the body there in the burlap bag.

(3) But that does not yet explain the preservation of the right foot. Again, based on declarant's personal experience and confirmed when consulting with taphonomic experts, the only reasonable explanation is that the foot was tightly wrapped. And, that would not happen by way of merely "covering" the body. That would require intent. And, of course, that had to have been removed during a short prior time-span before the body was found.

(4) Just as it can be presumed that the motive for preserving the face was to assure ultimate identification of the child, so also was the intent in preserving the foot. It is no coincidence that the nanny, Ms. Betty Gow, the family pediatrician, Dr. Van Ingen, and Charles Lindbergh himself, identified the body in large part by the unique situation of the little toe on the right foot overlapping with the adjacent toe. Therefore, it could not be risked that the foot decompose and disarticulate.

G. **Additional evidence of intervention in the normal process of decomposition**

a. **Selective organs missing:**

(1) Not only is there a disparity between the preservation of the face, on the one hand, and the post-bloat putrefaction/active decay of the torso and limbs, on the other hand (as described above), but there is also a discrepancy regarding the internal organs.

(2) The sequence in which the organs undergo decomposition is such that the gastrointestinal tract, pancreas and lungs are the first to undergo advanced decomposition (although they may still be noted in their collapsed states). When experimentally sampling biomarkers and their availability during decomposition, by determining the cumulative daily degree hours versus the postmortem interval, it has been determined that the kidneys survive the longest, followed by the liver and the heart.

(3) The liver and the heart were still described as present at autopsy which, based on the above, should be expected to be present (albeit discolored, flabby/mushy) in bodies found in the post bloat/active decay stages of decomposition. Dr. Mitchell testified that "the heart was in such a condition it couldn't be examined" and that "the liver also was present but not in a condition to prove anything as a form of pathology on it."

(4) On the other hand, the kidneys were absent, and during the normal process of decomposition, the kidneys are the longest to survive and should have been present. The most likely conclusion is that the kidneys were selectively removed during etherized vivisection. There is no other reasonable explanation except the question of animal predation (see next section).

b. Absence of animal predation

(1) The left leg below the knee, the left hand and the right forearm and hand were not found with the corpse or in its surroundings, despite extensive, repeated searches. And, they were not in the burlap bag. That strongly suggests that they did not reach the final site still attached to the body and they were not transported to the final site in the burlap bag.

(2) The bones on the right foot are still attached. Therefore, the four foot bones that ended up in the dirt and debris where the body was found, and the one in the burlap bag, must have come from the missing left foot. But it seeks an explanation how the five foot bones from the left foot were available and yet the two very much larger lower left leg bones were missing. That is not readily explained by either animal predation or undisturbed decomposition.

(3) Furthermore, there was no evidence of any predation on the found foot and hand bones, and no mention of predation in Dr. Mitchell's autopsy report. There was no animal scat in the dirt and debris carefully examined at the Squibb Labs.

(4) With regard to the missing kidneys --- the autopsy report provides no details regarding the lower torso and pelvic region. Careful analysis of the four photos taken at the scene and the one taken at autopsy reveals that the skeletal structures below the costal margins are openly exposed without overlying soft tissues, exposing the lumbosacral spinal column and pelvic bones -- most likely representing decompositional changes in accord with the skeletonization of the extremities. However, one can see in the photos that the exposed costal margins and pelvic bones show no predatory gnawing or other alterations from animal predation.

(5) This again raises the question as to why the liver was still present. It not only was readily accessible to insect necrophagia (as discussed above), but also to animal predation, yet the liver was present. But the kidneys are absent.

(6) There never is certainty that a body will be subjected to animal predation --- there are many variables. However, the following needs explaining:

　　(a)...the body was found in a rural location in this New Jersey forest with available animal predators, and presumably they were also available at the prior location;

　　(b)...there was the absence of evidence of predation on the body, clothing (T-shirts) and bones; absence of animal scat in the dirt/debris when examined at the Squibb Lab.

　　(c)...there was the unexplained absence of the intervening left lower leg bones;

　　(d)...there was the unexplained absence of the kidneys, yet the presence of the liver.

(7) Finally, there was also the fact that the head was preserved in its entirety, i.e. no characteristic animal predation of the head. Namely, another very important identifying feature was the child's known large, "square-shaped" head, prominent forehead (bossing) and open anterior fontanel. In fact, Dr. Van Ingen's handwritten note to Swayze referred to those features for identification, as well as the findings by Dr. Mitchell in his autopsy report.

(8) When all of the above are combined cumulatively with the other evidence presented in this Declaration, it reinforces the conclusion that there was no animal predation. Instead it speaks for interventional vivisection by skilled and knowledgeable person or persons and that the body in all likelihood had been etherized.

H. Final Comment

In the opinion of this Declarant, the cumulative impact of this Declaration is that there was no "veil of vermin" on the corpse. There is strong circumstantial evidence consistent with chemical interference, such as that from ether known to have been used in vivisections. There were interventions, such as the preservation of the face, which cannot be explained as part of the normal stages of decomposition -- that were enacted by person[s] with specialized skills and knowledge and with access to a preservative chemical such as tannic acid. The transport of the body in advanced decomposition in a burlap bag in May, the missing kidneys and the apparent absence of animal predation are also elements involved in the death of Charles A. Lindbergh, Jr., that are contrary to the "theories" on which the carpenter, Bruno Richard Hauptmann, was tried and convicted of murder. Those *"theories" are completely inconsistent with the evidence that I have presented in this Declaration.*

I declare under penalty of perjury that the foregoing is true and correct.

Executed at ▮
in the State of New Jersey on May 27, 2020.

Date: *May 27, 2020*

Peter Speth, MD

Forensic consultations

EXHIBIT A

Weather Conditions: March 1, 1932 to May 12, 1932
Somerville, New Jersey
Obtained from NOAA

March

Max	Av	Min	Precip (inches)
9	6	3	0
15	8	1	0
16	7	-3	0
7	3	-1	0
15	6	-3	0.1
7	3	-1	1.08
3	-1	-5	0.11
-1	-5	-8	0
-1	-6	-10	0
2	-5	-10	0
7	2	-3	0
6	0	-7	0
3	-2	-7	0
3	2	-7	0
0	-5	-10	0
7	-2	-11	0
2	0	-1	0.60
7	2	-3	0
13	3	-6	0
9	4	-1	0
2	-1	-4	0.05
15	6	-3	0.52
11	3	-4	0
14	6	-3	0
13	4	-4	0
17	8	0	0.14
13	**10**	7	0
10	6	1	2.38
11	5	-1	0
16	6	-4	0
15	**10**	5	0.34

April

Date	Max	Av	Min	Precip (inches)
1	**15**	8	1	0
2	**19**	9	-1	0
3	**23**	**14**	6	0
4	**13**	5	-2	0
5	**16**	6	-5	0
6	**18**	9	0	0
7	**19**	**10**	1	0
8	**14**	8	2	0
9	7	7	6	0
10	8	7	5	0.57
11	8	6	3	0.13
12	**12**	8	4	0.52
13	6	2	-1	0
14	**12**	7	1	0
15	**12**	4	-4	0
16	**15**	6	-4	0
17	9	4	-1	0
18	**15**	**10**	4	0
19	**20**	**10**	0	0
20	**23**	**11**	-1	0
21	**24**	**14**	3	0
22	**27**	**15**	3	0
23	**23**	**14**	6	0
24	**17**	8	-2	0
25	**13**	**10**	7	0
26	**24**	**17**	9	0
27	**15**	9	3	0
28	**19**	**10**	1	0
29	**24**	**12**	1	0
30	**25**	**16**	7	0

May

Date	Max	Av	Min	Precip (inches)
1	**19**	**17**	**13**	0.80
2	**18**	**14**	**10**	0.24
3	**21**	**12**	2	0
4	**24**	**14**	4	0
5	**19**	**16**	**13**	0
6	**21**	**16**	**11**	0
7	**18**	**14**	**10**	0.24
8	**13**	**11**	**10**	0.19
9	**17**	**13**	9	0
10	**15**	**11**	6	0
11	**16**	**11**	6	0
12	**16**	**12**	9	0.27

Legend
Bold Black: =/>10° in C.   *Red italic: </=Freezing in C.*

13.

EXHIBIT B
Photo of child on its back (supine) next to where it had been found face-down
(overall photo, and cropped closeup of foot)

**Right leg is crossed over left upper leg showing relatively intact right foot
(only four toes visible due to the known overlapping of the fifth toe)**

Endnotes

ABBREVIATIONS USED IN ENDNOTES

AC Alexis Carrel
AML Anne Morrow Lindbergh
AV Autobiography of Values (New York: 1978)
BMAU *Bring Me a Unicorn* (New York: HBJ,1972)
BDE The Brooklyn Daily Eagle
BOYHOOD *Boyhood on the Upper Mississippi* (St. Paul: MNHS, 1972)
BRHT Trial transcript of The State of New Jersey vs. Bruno Richard Hauptmann, Hunterdon County Court of Oyer and Terminer, 1935.
CA Charles August Lindbergh (CAL's father)
CAL Charles Augustus Lindbergh
CAL Jr. Charles Augustus Lindbergh, Jr.
CO The Culture of Organs (New York: Paul B. Hoeber/Harper & Brothers, 1938)
DWM Dwight W. Morrow (AML's father)
ECM Elizabeth Cutter Morrow (AML's mother)
ELLL Evangeline Lodge Land Lindbergh (CAL's mother)
ERM Elisabeth Reeve Morrow Morgan (AML's older sister)
FBI Federal Bureau of Investigation
GUBSC Georgetown University Libraries Booth Family Center Special Collections
GFS *Gift from the Sea* (New York: Pantheon, 1955)
HBJ Harcourt Brace Jovanovich publishing company
HSB Henry Skillman Breckinridge, CAL's lawyer
HGHL Hour of Gold, Hour of Lead (New York: HBJ, 1973)
JEH J. Edgar Hoover, Director of the FBI
LMAG Liberty Magazine
LOC Library of Congress, Washington, D.C.
LROD Locked Rooms and Open Doors (New York: HBJ, 1974)
MD Memorandum for JEH, Director of the FBI
MNHS Minnesota Historical Society
NJSP New Jersey State Police
NJSPM New Jersey State Police Museum Archives
NYDN The New York Daily News
NYT The New York Times
SCMFP Morrow Family Papers, Sophia Smith Collection, Smith College, Northampton, Mass.
SSL The Spirit of St. Louis (New York: Charles Scribner's Sons, 1953).
WE "WE" (New York: Harcourt Brace & Co. 1938)
YUAML Anne Morrow Lindbergh Papers (MS 829). Manuscripts and Archives, Yale University Library.
YUCAL Charles Augustus Lindbergh Papers (MS 325). Manuscripts and Archives, Yale University Library.

Dedication

Source of photo of Anna Schoeffler Hauptmann: https://images.findagrave.com/photos/2003/25/7088745 1042769330.jpg

Introduction

"either decomposed or had been eaten by animals": statement of William Allen to the NJSP, May 12, 1932, NJSPM.

"The most remarkable aspect . . ." From Gerald Uelmen, *Lessons from the Trial: The People v. O.J. Simpson*, Kansas City, Missouri: Andrews and McMeel, 1996), 208–09.

"Nothing has aided the persistence of falsehood . . ." from B. H. Liddell Hart, *Why Don't We Learn From History?* (New York: Hawthorn Books Inc, 1971), 26.

"UNKNOWN PERSON NO. 1 (Man with Ladder Near Lindbergh Home)," Thomas Fensch, ed., *Top Secret: FBI Files on the Lindbergh Baby Kidnapping* (The Woodlands, Texas: New Century Books, 2001) 342-345.

ACT ONE

1. KIDNAPPED!

"may have as useful a life . . ." From Hugh S. Cumming, letter to CAL, July 10, 1930, YUCAL.

"sparsely inhabited . . .": Fensch, ed., *Top Secret*, 97. The FBI's original source of most information was newspaper reports.

"almost inaccessible . . .": Laura Vitray, *The Great Lindbergh Hullabaloo*, (New York: William Faro, Inc., 1932), 28.

"No, maybe the Colonel has him" "Do you have the baby Charles" and "The baby? Isn't he in his crib?" From Betty Gow, March 1932 statement to NJSP, NJSPM.

"The silence confirmed her worst fears": Susan Hertog, *AML, Her Life* (New York: Nan A. Talese Doubleday, 1999), 164, n.34, citing AML statement to the NJSP, March 13, 1932.

"Anne, they have stolen our baby" "We all searched all around the house." From statement of Betty Gow, made to Lieutenant John Sweeney and Detective Hugh Strong of the Newark Police, March 10, 1932, 4, NJSPM.

She thought she heard a baby's cry. From statements of AML made to the NJ State Police March 11 and March 13, 1932.

When he seemed too quiet. source: Aida Breckinridge undated statement, account of Feb 27/Feb 28, 1932, Reminiscence of Aida Breckinridge and speech by Henry Breckinridge, 1932 February 27, undated, YUAML.

Text of police bulletin, Mark Falzini and James Davidson, *New Jersey's Lindbergh Kidnapping and Trial*, (Charleston, South Carolina: Arcadia Publishing, 2012), 226.

2. A Secretive Loner in the Spotlight

"In an age of hedonistic materialism . . .": Ludovic Kennedy, *The Airman and the Carpenter: The Lindbergh Kidnapping and the Framing of Richard Hauptmann* (New York: Viking Penguin, Inc., 1985), 26.

"was shy and aloof . . .": Davis, *The Hero*, 14.

"most reporters and photographers . . .": Leonard Mosley, *Lindbergh: A Biography* (Garden City, New York: Doubleday & Company, 1976), 3.

"Remove that junk heap . . .": Richard Bak, *Lindbergh: Triumph and Tragedy* (Dallas, Texas: Taylor Publishing Company, 2000), 32.

"more malicious than humorous," "might anxiously check his sheets . . . ," "shaving cream or hair grease," "Lindbergh's taste and talent. . .": Davis, *The Hero*, 117.

Venom not fatal. Mosley, *Lindbergh: A Biography*, 57.

The incident with the cadet whose penis Lindbergh painted green was one Lindbergh himself relished telling even 35 years later. CAL's remarks on his biography by Walter S. Ross, August 1, 1968. Charles Augustus Lindbergh Papers, 1913–1987, Charles A. Lindbergh and Family Papers. MNHS.

Dropping the dog off the roof was recalled by Glen "Steve" Thomas in a chain letter circulated among 20 or so pilots who remained in touch from their 1924 army training days in Texas. From "Gang letters" 1932–1937, October 11, 1932, Box 31, file 986, YUCAL.

"the powder whoofed" . . . "delightful" to watch from CAL's remarks on his biography by Walter S. Ross, August 1, 1968–August 23, 1969. Charles Augustus Lindbergh Papers, 1913–1987, Charles A. Lindbergh and Family Papers. MNHS.

"Life in the Army stirred Lindbergh's appetite . . .": Mosley, *Lindbergh: A Biography*, 57.

"the absurd myth . . .": Davis, *The Hero*, 245.

Pioneers vilified the Sioux. See Theodore Blegen, *Minnesota: A History of the State* (Minneapolis, Minnesota, 1963) 282; Bruce L. Larson, *Lindbergh of Minnesota: A Political Biography* (HBJ, 1973), 8 and 297, n. 11.

The primary sources for describing Lindbergh's earliest memories were CAL, *Boyhood*, and Davis, *The Hero*, 23–24.

"hard to approach and eccentric": Mosley, *Lindbergh: A Biography*, 20.

Her stepdaughters called her "crazy": Hertog, *AML, Her Life*, 16.

Source for Anne Morrow believing her mother-in-law suffered from a chemical imbalance: Berg, *Lindbergh*, 498.

"looking out of windows" "to see if it was true . . .": Mosley, *Lindbergh: A Biography*, 9.

" . . . made contact with other youngsters of his age next to impossible." From interviews with non-family, Mr. and Mrs. A. M. Opsahl on Charles A. Lindbergh, Sr., compilation by Grace Lee Nute, Charles A. Lindbergh and Family Papers. MNHS.

"the freedom of the surrounding wood and water": Larson, *Lindbergh of Minnesota,* 10 and note 18.

"blood sucker" and source of description of Evangeline holding a gun to her husband's head: Berg, *Lindbergh,* 39.

He told his sister he resisted for his son's sake. From interviews with family members, [interview with] Mrs. Robert Herron [Ellen LaFond Herron] by Grace Lee Nute, September 9, 1937. Charles A. Lindbergh and Family Papers. MNHS.

"sink or swim" approach . . . independence and self-reliance": Hertog, *AML: Her Life,* 14.

"from a tall cliff or building . . . ": Davis, *The Hero,* 27.

"burn with slow anger over the sniggers of the girls": Mosley, *Lindbergh, A Biography,* 25.

"you haven't got to give them": CAL, *SSL,* 382.

"Science held the key . . .": Hertog, AML, *Her Life,* 18 citing CAL, *SSL,* 319.

"a rather terrifying sight": CAL, *Boyhood,* 24

Lindbergh flunked out. While other sources only indicate he dropped out, the most accurate source appears to be Richard Bak, *Lindbergh, Triumph and Tragedy: An Illustrated Biography* (Dallas, TX: Taylor Trade, 2000), 16, citing Feb. 1922 letter to ELLL from CAL's academic advisor, P.H. Hyland.

3. The Orteig Prize

The spectacular mid-air crash is described in Bak, *Lindbergh: Triumph and Tragedy,* 33.

"where life meets death on equal plane": Mosley, *Lindbergh, A Biography,* 39, 399–400, quoting CAL description of his historic flight citing both *"WE"* and *SSL.*

"almost treasonable" disregard for national defense: Edward W. Knauppman et al., *Great American Trials: From the Salem Witch Trials to Rodney King* (Detroit, Michigan: Visible Ink Press, 1994), 320.

"I was so filled up with this hero stuff . . .": Kennedy, *The Airman and the Carpenter,* 27.

4. The Search for the Perfect Mate

"sang, shouted, whistled, stamped his feet . . .": Davis, *The Hero,* 137.

"He'd put a fish in your camera . . .": Mosley, *Lindbergh, A Biography,* 126.

"most notorious and cruel of his practical jokes": Davis, *The Hero*, 136.

"moderate" practical joke to teach Gurney a lesson. From CAL's remarks on his biography by Walter S. Ross, August 1, 1968–August 23, 1969, 34. Charles Augustus Lindbergh papers, Charles A. Lindbergh and Family Papers. MNHS.

"in recognition of his superior hereditary endowment.": Source: Finding Aid to Charles Fremont Dight Papers, 1883–1984, Eugenics Files, Correspondence and related papers, undated, 1920–1928. MNHS.

"not an environment conducive to evolutionary progress"; "selectivity, hardly any desire for permanence and children": CAL, *AV*, 121.

"the most viable offspring . . .": Gur-Arie, Rachel, "American Eugenics Society (1926-1972)." Embryo Project Encyclopedia (2014-11-22). ISSN: 1940-5030 http://embryo.asu.edu/handle/10776/8241.

"good health, good form . . .": CAL, *AV*, 119.

"more about animal husbandry . . .": Berg, *Lindbergh*, 193.

"the religion of aristocrats" who believed "Western civilization was in danger . . .": Nevins, *A Tale of Two Villages: The unknown story of New Jersey's major role in promoting eugenics theory which indirectly led to sterilization of more than 65,000 Americans and to mass murder in Nazi Germany* (New York: iUniverse, Inc., 2009), 13.

Nordic supremacy was a widely shared view. A major boost to the eugenics movement occurred after World War I when the United States emerged as the only global superpower. In 1922, Princeton Professor Carl Brigham published *A Study of Human Intelligence*, in which he argued that Army IQ tests developed during the Great War "proved that the Nordic race was intellectually superior to Negroes, Jews, Italians and other ethnic groups." Nevins, *A Tale of Two "Villages*, 44.

"Hebrew, Slavs, Catholics and Negroes"; "More children for the fit; less for the unfit": Nevins, *A Tale of Two Villages*, 13–14, quoting Margaret Sanger.

"inferior" traits: Dr. Laughlin believed that millions of people deserving sterilization superficially appeared normal. He and his colleagues estimated as many as ten percent of Americans were of inferior stock and constituted "an economic and moral burden to the country" (Nevins, *A Tale of Two Cities*, 16). With such laws validated, some 64,000 Americans, mostly women, would be sterilized from coast to coast from the first decade of the twentieth century through the 1960s.

The landmark Supreme Court ruling was in *Buck v. Bell* (1927) 274 U.S. 200. In his majority opinion, Justice Oliver Wendell Holmes famously declared: "Three generations of imbeciles are enough. It is better for all the world, if instead of waiting to execute degenerate offspring for crime, or to let them starve for their imbecility, society can prevent those who are manifestly unfit from continuing their kind." 274 U.S. 200, 207. In fact, in the case before it, the state of Virginia had given carte blanche to doctors it hired to decide who got labeled an "imbecile" and who did not. However loosely defined, it was clearly misapplied to teenager Cary Buck and her baby. *Buck v. Bell* upheld 8-to-1 the involuntary tubal ligation of teenager Carrie Buck based only on a state-employed doctor labeling both Carrie (who had given birth to a baby after being raped) and her mother "feeble-minded and promiscuous." This characterization of the family later proved unfounded. "the socially inadequate" — defectives, dependents and delinquents: Edwin Black, *War Against the Weak: Eugenics and America's Campaign to Create a Master Race* (Washington, D.C., Devon Press, 2003), 159.

"good heredity"; "experience in breeding animals on our farm": CAL, *AV,* 118.

5. Hooked

All but two quotes of AML in this chapter are from BMAU 83–85, 96–97, 103–04, 118, 127, 135, 146–47, 167, 219. The two exceptions are: "this stranger well enough" (AML, *HGHL,* 13); "Can't look in his eyes and do anything else" (AML, *HGHL,* 13 [letter to sister CCM, February 8, 1929]).

"sparkling vivacity": CAL, *AV,* 123.

Attempt to save the life of Floyd Bennett. In 1926, Bennett and Commander Byrd had received Congressional medals of honor for being the first to fly over the North Pole that May (although they reportedly later confessed they did not get that far).

"an awkward lunge across the front seat . . .": Joyce Milton, *Loss of Eden: A Biography of Charles and Anne Morrow Lindbergh* (New York: Harper Collins Publishers, 1993), 169, referring to AML's 1962 novel *Dearly Beloved* (Chicago, Illinois: Chicago Review Press, 1990 by arrangement with Harcourt, Inc.), 31.

"From now on Charles would be her voice": Hertog, *AML: Her Life,* 93.

"He has her and we have lost her." ECM, diary entry April 6, 1929, SCMFP, https://findingaids.smith.edu/repositories/2/archival_objects/143140

6. America's Royal Couple

The handwritten will was to be opened only in the event of Charles's death, and provided for his mother to receive $100,000 and Anne the remainder, including all his trophies loaned to the Jefferson Museum. Wills of Charles Augustus Lindbergh, 1929–1955, YUCAL.

"He grabbed her by the wrist . . .": Berg, *Lindbergh,* 202, quoting ECM diary entry May 28, 1939. Diaries, 1937–1946, SCMFP, https://findingaids.smith.edu/repositories/2/archival_objects/143141 Accessed April 16, 2020.

"an escaped convict": AML, *HGHL,* 7.

"monkeys in a cage": AML, *HGHL,* 106.

"anything at all personal or real": AML, *HGHL,* 53.

The thought stayed in his mind. In CAL *WJ,* 274-275, Lindbergh mentions that he was urged to run against FDR in 1940 but decided he valued his privacy too much to consider it. See also Mosley, *Lindbergh,* 319; Davis, *Lindbergh: The Hero,* 389.

The disagreement over the trust fund for AML is detailed in Joyce Milton, *Loss of Eden: A Biography of Charles and Anne Morrow Lindbergh* (New York: Harper Collins Publishers, 1993) 189-190.

"cash[ing] in on the name of Charles Lindbergh": Berg, *Lindbergh*, 218, citing a column by an unnamed Toronto reporter in a summer 1930 edition of *The New Yorker*.

7. An Ominous Beginning

"being a Lindbergh it will have more sense than that!" AML, *HGHL*, 137.

Amelia Earhart witnessed perhaps the only instance of AML standing up for herself to her husband in the early years of their marriage. The two women were chatting in the kitchen of an airline executive in Los Angeles, both drinking a glass of buttermilk. Lindbergh apparently got jealous of their comradery. He started dribbling water from his own glass onto her blue silk dress, leaving ugly spots drop by drop in a clearly deliberate manner. Anne soon repositioned herself and got her revenge by whirling to empty the rest of her glass of buttermilk all over her husband's suit. Shocked by his wife daring to retaliate, on this occasion at least, Lindbergh decided to laugh off the incident. Dorothy Herrmann, *Anne Morrow Lindbergh: A Gift for Life* (New York: Tickner & Fields, 1992, 1993), 61-62.

Anne feared being a sacrificial lamb. From AML, *HGHL*, 126.

"crazy to get home . . .": AML, *HGHL*, 131.

"tempting providence": AML, *HGHL*, 10.

just "a weak woman": Herrmann, *AML: A Gift for Life*, 64–65, quoting AML's recollection.

The ladder for Anne to make it easier to climb in and out. Bak, *Lindbergh: Triumph and Tragedy*, 111. Photo caption: "Anne Morrow is helped out of a plane on one of her early flights with Lindbergh. Once she and Charles became flying partners he built a little ladder to help his short-statured wife climb in and out."

He talked Anne into sneaking out . . . to test a monoplane. An alarmed doctor wrote an op ed criticizing a newspaper editorial for making light of that potentially hazardous flight and for applauding the decision to have a home birth instead of going to a hospital where mortality rates for women and newborns were far lower. The editors dismissed his safety concerns with their caption, "Naturally the Specialists Think They are Indispensable," *The Evening Sun*, June 26, 1930, 23. What the doctor was pointing out is that Anne Lindbergh did have specialists in attendance, which hardly anyone else could afford; hospitalization for most women was far preferable because it enabled emergency care.

. . . a short hop in his plane to Hartford, Connecticut and back. Source: "LINDBERGHS TO NAME SON AFTER FLIER; MESSAGES ARE POURING IN: "Cancels Hospital Plans," *The Record*, Hackensack, New Jersey, June 23, 1930, 1.

"advise purchasing property"; "advise accepting terms of contract": AML quoting CAL in letter to ELLL, AML, *HGHL*, 137.

Dr. Hawks noted that the baby's head was large. Memories of CAL Jr., notes by ECM, c. 1932 YUAML.

"a great deal has been whispered": Vitray, *Hullabaloo*, 180.

"moderate" rickets": Lloyd Gardner, *The Crime of the Century: The Enduring Mystery of the Lindbergh Kidnapping* (Now and Then Reader, LLC: Kindle 2015), Kindle loc. 1180.

The child's enlarged, "square" head. Source: Gardner, *The Enduring Mystery*, Kindle location 1175–1222. Gardner notes that Dr. Van Ingen's use of the term "square" in describing the child's head might refer to a condition sometimes today called "toaster head." "Toaster head" (medical term "plagiocephaly") describes a skull that appears flattened on both sides; it could result from a variety of causes and might date from birth.

. . . sometimes [caused] by trauma. See Gerald So, Barry Kosofsky and James Southern, "Acute Hydrocephalus Following Carbon Monoxide Poisoning," Case Report, Pediatric Neurology, Volume 17, Issue 3, October 1997, 270–273 https://www.sciencedirect.com/science/article/abs/pii/S0887899497000970. Sometimes, hydrocephalus is acquired after birth from a serious disease, but CAL Jr. was only diagnosed with rickets – no other serious affliction.

"do nothing else but care for my baby": AML, *HGHL*, 10.

HSB great uncle by marriage: "Social and Personal", *The Daily Leader* (Lexington, KY) Oct 20, 1898: 6, col 1; Johnson, E. Polk. *A History of Kentucky and Kentuckians*, Vol. 3, (Lewis Publishing: chicago/nyc, 1912) 1483.

N. Y. Sunday Mirror headline re "The Lone Eagle" : see Friedman, *The Immortalists, Charles Lindbergh, Dr. Alexis Carrel, and Their Daring Quest to Live Forever,* (New York: HarperCollins, 2007) 51. The paper is now out of print.

"citizens of the wrong type" procreate: Nevins, *A Tale of Two "Villages,"* 38.

. . . what organizers called "degenerates"; "[born] every seven and a half minutes, whereas a feebleminded child every 48 seconds, and a future criminal every 50 seconds." Source: Gur-Arie, Rachel, "American Eugenics Society (1926–1972.)." Embryo Project Encyclopedia (2014-11-22). ISSN: 1940-5030, http://embryo.asu.edu/handle/10776/8241.

8. Back in the Air -- Grounded by Tragedy

Charles "wanted to shoot them": AML, *HGHL*, 152.

When excited, Skean yipped in "fierce little barks": AML, *HGHL*, 296.

"how challenged, frightened and infuriated I was . . .": AML, *HGHL*, 9.

"become too fond of her": Berg, *Lindbergh*, 227.

. . . outbreaks of cholera, malaria, measles and dysentery. Source: Chris Courtney, *The Nature of Disaster in China: The 1931 Yangzi River Flood* (Cambridge University Press, 2018).

"to die screaming": AML, *HGHL*, 199–200 [letter to ERM, early October 1931].

9. Getting Reacquainted with "Hi" and "Mum-Mum"

"ceiling flying"; "Buster"; "Hi": AML, *HGHL*, 205 [letter to ELLL December 1931].

do it "den!" ("Again!"): AML, *HGHL*, 202 [letter to ELLL November 12, 1931].

repeating "It" among his very first new words. From John Brant and Edith Renaud, *True Story of the Lindbergh Kidnapping* (New York: Kroy Wen Publishers, Inc., 1932), 12.

to hear Charlie call for "Mum-Mum" or sometimes "'Mummy' instead of 'Betty.'" From "Lindbergh Baby Called His Mother 'Mum-Mum': Anne Had Golden Locks Shorn So He Wouldn't Be a 'Sissy:' 'Most Beautiful Child I Ever Saw,' Says Barber," *Lancaster New Era*, March 10, 1932, 22.

"Mummy" instead of "Betty": AML, *HGHL* (diary entry Feb. 7, 1932).

"prenatal drumming of airplane motors." Source: Clinton Gilbert, "Spiking an Absurd Rumor the Lindbergh Baby is Deaf," *The Daily Mirror of Washington*, *The Dayton Herald*, November 21, 1930, 4; "Writer Blasts Rumor That Lindbergh Baby Is Deaf," *Des Moines Register*, November 29, 1931, 6.

The dead seagull anecdote is from a memorandum by ECM's secretary, Marguerite Junge, memories of life at Next Day Hill, 7, NJSPM.

"Betty, there's nothing we can do": Berg, *Lindbergh*, 234.

"sure that he had been ducking him. [Betty] found Colonel Lindbergh laughing his head off. . . Betty recalled there was something about the Colonel — 'that little bit of sadism'": Berg, *Lindbergh*, 234, quoting Betty Gow and ECM.

"swift-flowing stream . . . rushing headlong to the sheer drop of tragedy": AML, *HGHL*, 11.

10. Little Charlie's Last Days

"unauthorized tours": see Melsky, *Vol I*, Kindle loc. 747 and note 202.

January 1932 evaluation of CAL, Jr.: Constance Chilton and Mary Ellen Riber, "Charles Lindbergh: age 17 months," January 6, 1932, "Lindbergh, Charles Augustus, Jr.," YUAML.

"Uh-huh"; "Naw"; "Tee — all gone"; "Hi — all gone": AML, *HGHL*, 226 [letter to ELLL, February 7, 1932].

"Affection of the mother and the father . . ."; "I asked Lindy if he was rehearsing him for forced landings": Will Rogers, "WILL ROGERS RECALLS A GOLDEN-HAIRED BABY TODDLING ABOUT THE LINDBERGH NURSERY," *Daily Telegrams, Vol. 3: The Hoover Years*, (Stillwater, Oklahoma: Oklahoma State University Press, 1973) 1749, March 2, 1932, 17.

The source of the quoted observations by pediatrician Dr. Philip Van Ingen were his sworn statement in 1934 and a May 1932 letter. Dr. Philip Van Ingen, statement taken November 21, 1934, by Assistant Attorney General Robert Peacock, 1; Van Ingen letter to Mrs. Morrow, May 4, 1932, 1, NJSPM.

"he woke up crying quite hard in a rather high pitch"; "fussing too much" about Charlie . . .": undated statement, account of Feb. 27/Feb. 28, 1932, Reminiscence of Aida Breckinridge and speech by Henry Breckinridge, 1932 February 27, undated, YUCAL.

"Lindbergh Baby Called His Mother 'Mum-Mum'": *Lancaster New Era*, March 10, 1932, 22.

Mrs. Morrow saved the shorn locks in an envelope. She later labeled the envelope to identify the clippings it contained as her grandson's hair cut by Mrs. Erna Scholtz in ECM's bedroom at Next Day Hill. Mrs. Scholtz was a local hairdresser. ECM apparently estimated the date of the haircut sometime later. She guessed it might have taken place on February 23, 1932. (That matched generally with the interview Mrs. Scholtz gave the press two weeks later that she cut the boy's hair a few days before the kidnapping.) "Hair clippings, envelope that held (1932)," YUAML, Box 67A. Very likely she also took before and after pictures despite her son-in-law's objections. Family records indicate that photos of the child were taken at Englewood in February 1932 that were never given by Lindbergh to the press. "Photo lists and orders, circa 1932, undated," YUAML 67A, folder 8. [A note states they were "all blank" but that seems belied by the photos newspapers printed in early March.]

Source of Aida's observations on Feb 27-28, 1932: Aida Breckinridge undated statement, account of Feb. 27/Feb. 28, 1932. Reminiscence of Aida Breckinridge and speech by Henry Breckinridge, 1932 February 27, undated, YUCAL.

"He worried that the baby might be kidnapped." The source is an undated and unsigned 14-page handwritten memorandum on the stationery of the Hotel Pennsylvania in New York, attributed by Yale archivists to Evangeline Lindbergh. She came to her son's farmhouse from Detroit for an overnight visit on May 14, 1932. The memo appears to have been written during that trip. Among other things, it memorializes information obtained from "Charles" and "Anne" and from Aida Breckinridge about the weekend before the kidnapping. The memo also notes her own personal observations of the police exhibits of clothing taken from the corpse that were stored in the basement of the farmhouse. "Memorandum re kidnapping and death of Charles Augustus Lindbergh, Jr. in 1932," 1, YUCAL.

"Hi! Hi! Hi!": Aida Breckinridge undated statement, account of Feb. 27/Feb. 28, 1932. Reminiscence of Aida Breckinridge and speech by Henry Breckinridge, 1932 February 27, undated, YUCAL.

"croupy cough"; "gone to sleep unusually quickly": AML March 10 and March 13, 1932, statements to Newark Police Lt. John Sweeney and Det. Hugh Strong, NJSPM.

The identification of the UCLA photo as CAL Jr. is disputed. See lindberghkidnapproboards.com, http://lindberghkidnap.proboards.com/thread/992/leon-hoage-files-ucla.

ACT TWO

1. The Police Arrive

Lindbergh called the State Police again . . . : Michael Melsky, *The Dark Corners of the Lindbergh Kidnapping, Vol I*. (West Conshohocken, Pennsylvania: Infinity Publishing, 2016) Kindle Loc. 1236, n. 395, citing report of Lt Dunn.

That was where the kidnapper must have entered and exited. . . . : Joseph A. Wolf, "Major Initial Report," March 1, 1932, NJSPM.

But Wolfe was more "surprised at what he did not see." . . . The culprit would have "pushed it around." From Lloyd Gardner, *The Case that Never Dies* (New Brunswick, New Jersey: Rutgers University Press, 2004), 25 and n. 40.

"Very dark" . . . "a strong wind was blowing": Source: J. Wolf Report, March 1, 1932, NJSPM.

Text of ransom note, Jim Fisher, *The Lindbergh Case* (New Brunswick New Jersey: Rutgers University Press, 1997), 18.

The same was true of the Whateleys and Betty Gow: J. Wolf Report, March 1, 1932, NJSPM.

"I'm damned . . . ": Gregory Ahlgren and Stephen Monier, *Crime of The Century: The Lindbergh Kidnapping Hoax* (Boston: Brandon Books, 1993, 20.

"Boys I rely on you . . . The Lindberghs are like that": Vitray, *Hullabaloo*, 22.

Footprints under the nursery window. Source: Vitray, *Hullabaloo*, 54; Brant and Renaud, *True Story of the Lindbergh Kidnapping*, 52-54.

Police took a photograph . . . The measurements were approximated, 12 to 12 $^1/_8$ inches long, 4 to 4 ¼ in wide. The trooper used markings on his flashlight to approximate the length, and the width of his palm to approximate the width. Nuncio Degaetano, testimony. BRHT reel 1, part 002, 28–32 (435–443), NJSPM.

"That ain't easy": Vitray, *Hullabaloo*, 103.

"isolated, muddy, almost impassable": Fensch, *Top Secret*, 83–84.

"Road impassable — drive at your own risk": Fensch, *Top Secret*, 164.

"From the spot where those footprints headed . . . ": Vitray, *Hullabaloo*, quoting Oscar Bush, 57.

"Why don't they ask us people . . .": Jane Dixon, Baby Strong Enough for Present Ordeal": *The Boston Globe*, March 10, 1932, 22.

"A nightmare of reporters": AML, *BMAU*, 107 [diary entry February 1928].

"only occasionally seen wandering": Mosley, *Lindbergh: A Biography*, 409.

"I did until I saw his face": AML, *HGHL*, 227 [March 2, 1932, letter to ELLL].

Her first thought had been more dire, some "lunatic": AML, *HGHL*, 226 [March 2, 1932, letter to ELLL].

Mistaken belief they had incurable disorders. New Jersey had been one of the first handful of states to place mental patients in institutions to isolate them from society. Epileptics were placed in the same category on the theory that epilepsy was a form of "feeblemindedness" that was incurable and caused aberrant behavior — ignoring such famous historical figures as Julius Caesar, Peter the Great, Fyodor Dostoevsky, and Lord Byron. Some historians have thought Joan of Arc was epileptic, too. It took another decade before medications for epilepsy changed that widespread perception and began to replace the stigma and isolation with more appropriate treatment.

Not all had been caught. See Minutes of the Board of the New Jersey State Village for Epileptics, Skillman NJ, Nov. 1930–1933, 386. New Jersey State Archives.

2. The First 48 Hours

A farm woman in the neighborhood . . . From Brant and Renaud, *The True Story of the Lindbergh Kidnapping*, 63.

"a desperate man": AML, *HGHL*, 229 [diary entry March 5, 1932].

"had never seen him so changed": Kennedy, *The Airman and the Carpenter*, 112 (based on an interview with Betty Gow).

Lindbergh became agitated . . . : Ahlgren and Monier, *Crime of the Century: The Lindbergh Kidnapping Hoax*, 274.

strange automobiles near the estate. From Brant and Renaud, *True Story of the Lindbergh Kidnapping*, 62–64.

A waitress in Pennington . . . : Vitray, *Hullabaloo*, 164.

Alfred Hammond sighting: Melsky, *Vol I*, Kindle loc 92, n. 1, citing NJSP report "Re: Alfred Hammond and Suspects in Auto."

"There is nothing I wouldn't do for Colonel Lindbergh": Mark Falzini, *Their Fifteen Minutes, Biographical Sketches of the Lindbergh Case* (New York: iUniverse, Inc., 2008), 83.

"glorified traffic cops": Behn, *Lindbergh: The Crime*, 83.

A consummate influence peddler: Hague's only legal source of income was his mayoral salary of $7500 to $8500. Yet he somehow acquired two mansions and lived extravagantly, acquiring the nickname "King Hanky-Panky" which referred to his expensive signature suits, not his notorious corruption. From Jack Alexander, "Boss Hague, King Hanky-Panky of New Jersey," *The Saturday Evening Post*, October 26, 1940 [edited by GET NJ 2002], http://www.cityofjerseycity.org/hague/kinghankypanky/index.shtml. When he died in 1956, his estate was valued in the millions. "Boss Frank Hague," November 2011, https://gardenstatehistory.blogspot.com/2011/11/boss-frank-hague.html.

NYT March 3, 1932 banner headline: "LINDBERGH HOPEFUL, IS READY TO RANSOM SON: NATION'S GREATEST HUNT FOR KIDNAPPERS PUSHED; ALL CLUES THUS FAR FUTILE: COUNTRY IS SHOCKED." Caption of photo: "Picture of His Missing Son, Given Out Yesterday by Colonel Lindbergh to Help in the Search. It Was Made About Two Weeks Ago." *NYT*, March 3, 1932, 1.

An old barn burned down: "Lindbergh Search and Ransom Moves Forward on Ninth Day," *NYT*, March 11, 1932, 1.

3. Hunting Worldwide for the Curly-Haired Baby

Will Rogers, "WILL ROGERS RECALLS A GOLDEN-HAIRED BABY TODDLING ABOUT THE LINDBERGH NURSERY," *Daily Telegrams*, Vol. 3, 1749, March 2, 1932, 17.

Connie Morrow extortion threat link, see "Letter of Warning Sent to Lindbergh," *NYT*, March 4, 1932, 8; "Link a Ransom Note to Morrow Threat," *NYT*, March 9, 1932.

"immediate and safe return": Walter S. Ross, *The Last Hero: Charles A. Lindbergh*, (New York: Harper & Row, 1968), 200, reproducing the open letter.

"perpetrated by someone familiar with the habits of the household": Inside Job Seen by Mrs. Morrow," *The World Telegram*, March 3, 1932, NJPM, "Kidnapping of Lindbergh Baby was an 'Inside Job', Mrs. Morrow Believes," *The Courier* (Waterloo, Iowa), March 3, 1932, 1.

Newsreel footage of first birthday source: "Lindbergh Baby Shown in Theatres," *Brooklyn Times Union*, March 4, 1932, 4.

"rice pudding": Andrew Jacobs, "Power Broker Jersey-Style," *NYT,* April 30, 2000, https://www.nytimes.com/2000/04/30/nyregion/power-broker-jersey-city-style.html

Lindbergh threatened to shoot: Anthony Scaduto, *Scapegoat: The Truth about the Lindbergh Kidnapping* (London: Secker & Warburg, 1977), 43, citing Hearst reporter Adela Rogers St. Johns as his source of the quote from another reporter.

After repeated tests of the ladder: The FBI's official summary report states: "Tests were conducted by the New Jersey State Police to determine what weight the ladder would hold, and the consensus of opinion among a number of officers present at the test, was the ladder would not hold a weight much over one hundred and twenty-five pounds." From Fensch, editor, *Top Secret,* "Summary Report in re Unknown Subjects Kidnaping and murder Charles A Lindbergh, Jr." (N.Y. File 62-3057) Physical Evidence," 141.

He believed the ladder was a "bluff": "Reveal Secrets of Lindbergh Kidnapping Investigation," *The Chicago Tribune* April 11, 1932, 2. "The shallowness of the impressions left by the ladder under the nursery window in the soft, wet loam that had been deposited as the base for a lawn indicated that no man had been on that ladder."

The kidnapper was an exhibitionist: Brant and Renaud, *True Story of the Lindbergh Kidnapping,* 69, quoting Joseph Gollomb.

" . . . none of us would be smart enough": "Resident of 'Badlands' Near Lindbergh Home Declares no one There Could Be in Kidnaping," *Marysville Journal Tribune,* March 9, 1932, 1.

Donovan sent Thayer to an associate of Owney Madden: In mid-May 1932 the Bureau received information it deemed credible that Madden had been secretly involved in the ransom scheme since January 1932. If so, it was likely either Donovan or Breckinridge who had already recruited Madden, and Thayer was just used for public cover. From FBI Summary Report (N.Y. File 62-3057), 306.

Thayer was at the farmhouse when the call was received: Robert Thayer personal notes, March 6, 1932, Robert Helyer Thayer Collection, Lindbergh, Charles A. Kidnapping Case, LOC, message quoted verbatim in Melsky, *Vol. I,* loc. 681, n. 179.

Lindbergh's March 2 and 3, 1932 mystery trips source: "Hunt for Baby Centers in New Jersey," *Brooklyn Times Union,* March 3, 1932, 1, 2.

"a bad lot": Melsky, *Vol. I,* Kindle location 2160 and n. 735.

4. Confusion Reigns

The state police requested a photocopy of whatever Bureau compiled: from Memorandum of telephone call from J. Edgar Hoover to Colonel Schwarzkopf, March 4, 1932, FBI Files Classification 7-1, Record Group 65, Box 1, Section 1, Serial No. 48, NJSPM.

50,000 letters and telegrams "read, sorted, classified and evaluated": from H. Norman Schwarzkopf, Personal File, April 7, 1932, NJSPM.

Charles Lindbergh, Jr. as "how he normally appears": "How Lindbergh Baby Would Appear in Varying Disguises," *The Philadelphia Inquirer,* Mar 9, 1932, 7.

his image was now so "well-known in every corner of the United States": "Eaglet May Be Disguised," *Republican & Herald,* March 10, 1932, 4.

news about the haircut buried: F. Raymond Daniell, "Lindbergh Search and Ransom Moves Fail on Ninth Day," *NYT*, March 11, 1932, 1.

Vitray considered the boy's appearance of vital importance: Vitray, *Hullabaloo*, 83–84.

"Lindbergh Pet's Failure to Give Alarm Points to Inside Job . . ." and summary of the evidence: H.V. Wilkins, "Dog's Silence At Kidnaping Puzzles Police," *BDE*, March 7, 1932, 3.

Someone dropped a Lindbergh dog at a Princeton kennel: Wilkins, "Dog's Silence At Kidnaping Puzzles Police," *BDE*, March 7, 1932, 3. Melsky has a chapter in *The Dark Corners Vol I* that is entirely focused on the two dogs.

Anne thought Skean had been off being walked in a park: When Henry Breckinridge was asked in his grand jury testimony in the Bronx in May 1932 if the dog took sick before the kidnapping, Breckinridge did not answer the question directly. Instead, he said, "The dog was in the other place" – not away. (HSB Grand Jury Test., May 17, 1930, 30, NJSPM.) In that same session, Breckinridge claimed a hazy memory of events he witnessed earlier that spring and said other information was hearsay. In this instance, he answered the questions about Skean categorically despite not having any firsthand information on that subject since the Breckinridges came directly from their apartment in New York to the Lindbergh farmhouse late on the afternoon of February 27, 1932. See Aida Breckinridge, account of Feb. 27/Feb 28, 1932, "Reminiscence of Aida Breckinridge and speech by Henry Breckinridge, 1932 February 27, undated," YUAM.

"I am tired of all this slew footing": *United Press*, "Lindbergh had a Tift [sic] with State Police," *Republican and Herald* (Pottsville, PA) March 8, 1932, 6.

Lindbergh "did not want his telephone tapped or his mail read": Bates R. Raney, UPS, "COL. LINDBERGH MADE THREE MYSTERIOUS TRIPS SINCE LAST MONDAY TO FIND HIS CHILD," *Republican and Herald*, Pottsville, Pennsylvania, March 10, 1932, 1, 4. Lindbergh's private line in his study was installed when the house was built. Behn, *Lindbergh: The Crime*, 128.

stay "out of his path": *United Press*, "LEAVES HOPEWELL FOR SIX HOURS WITH ADVISER COL. HENRY BRECKINRIDGE," *Marshall Evening Chronicle*, Marshall, Michigan, March 8, 1932, 1. [This reporter was one who was misled to believe Lindbergh accompanied Breckinridge that day, when others saw Lindbergh leave earlier disguised as a state trooper].

"the 'heat' has been turned off": *United Press*, "Gates Wide Open at Lindbergh Home," *Republican and Herald*, March 8, 1932, 1.

The Dog That Didn't Bark: "Progress Toward Early Return of Kidnaped Baby Reported by Both Police and Col. Lindbergh:," *Atlanta Constitution*, March 9, 1932, 1, 6 ("Dog's Silence Puzzles.")

5. Lindbergh's and Breckinridge's Mysterious Excursions

Quotes are from Delos Smith, "Lindbergh Made Mysterious Trips," *Republican and Herald*, Pottsville, Pennsylvania, March 10, 1932, 4. "Secret Trips by Lindbergh are Unofficially Reported; Say He Wore Officer's Coat," *Marysville Journal Tribune*, Marysville, Ohio, March 10, 1932, 1. His unnamed sources were likely troopers stationed at the estate.

Those who concealed Lindbergh's absence: one was Frank Kelly whose odd account of a 5 a.m. summons by Lindbergh was contradicted by his superiors (see note below). Two others were Mickey Rosner, the "small time Mafioso" who then served as Lindbergh's private secretary; and John, Condon, a man possibly suffering from dementia "who never told the same story twice". (Falzini, *Their Fifteen Minutes*, 31, 75).

Article re tracing the ladder to Skillman Village: F. Raymond Daniell, "Lindbergh Search Pressed Near Home: [Governor] Moore is Confident," *NYT*, March 10, 1932, 1.

"two cars, one heavily curtained . . .": "Col. Breckinridge on Mystery Trip: Legal Advisor Demands Absolute Secrecy for his Movements; Returns, Dashes Away Again," *The Atlanta Constitution*, March 9, 1932, 1. [*The Atlanta Constitution* did not place Lindbergh with Breckinridge on this outing and appears to have that right. Other papers reported that Lindbergh had left the estate earlier for Skillman disguised as a trooper].

"Col. Breckinridge on Mystery Trip: Legal Advisor Demands Absolute Secrecy for his Movements; Returns, Dashes Away Again," *The Atlanta Constitution*, March 9, 1932, 1.

Ransom notes 3 and 4 received on March 8 by Breckinridge: see Walsh statement, joint conference NJSP/FBI May 18, 1932, 10. Oddly, Trooper Frank Kelly wrote a report dated March 8 claiming Lindbergh summoned him at 5 a.m. to check these notes for prints – contradicting the formal report of his superiors that the notes had not yet arrived in the mail.

Mickey Rosner's observations in this chapter source: Morris Rosner, Untitled, unpublished mss., circa 1932, pp. 1, 49-51, NJSPM.

Delos Smith quotes are from Smith, "Lindbergh Made Mysterious Trips," *Republican and Herald*, March 10, 1932, 4.

Condon's arrival: see May 13, Statement of John Condon (Taken in Hopewell, NJ) [made to Inspector Harry Walsh (Jersey City Police) and Inspector Keaton (NJSP), NJSPM.

"set out . . . and dashed at high speed . . . ": "Col. Breckinridge on Mystery Trip: Legal Advisor Demands Absolute Secrecy for his Movements; Returns, Dashes Away Again," *The Atlanta Constitution*, March 9, 1932, 1.

He was seen returning . . . : "Secret Trips by Lindbergh are Unofficially Reported; Say He Wore Officer's Coat," *Marysville Journal Tribune*, Marysville, Ohio, March 10, 1932, 1.

Condon's arrival: see John Condon, *Jafsie Tells All! Revealing the Inside Story of the Lindbergh-Hauptmann Case* (New York: Jonathan Lee Publishing Co. 1936) 30-35. Investigators doubted his credibility as does NJSPM archivist Falzini. See Falzini, *Their Fifteen Minutes*, 31.

"not wasting his strength"; "managing his forces": from AML, *HGHL*, 231 [letter to ELLL March 8, 1932].

"There *really* is definite progress . . ." [emphasis in original]": AML, *HGHL*, 232–233 [letter to ELLL, March 10, 1932].

Replacement of troop force source: Bates Raney, UP, "Col. Lindbergh Goes on Three Mystery Trips—Fact That Baby is Still Missing Officially Confirmed." *News-Record* (Neenah, Wisconsin) March 10, 1932, 1.

6. Conflicting Sworn Statements

Elsie Whateley statement . . . : Statement of Elsie Whateley to Lieutenants John Sweeney and Hugh J. Strong of the Newark Police Department, March 10, 1932, NJSPM.

Betty Gow statements to NJSP March 3 and March 10, 1932, NJSPM.

Lindbergh's whereabouts on Monday night: Whether Lindbergh actually did spend Monday night, February 29, 1932, at the Morrow mansion was not confirmed by anyone else staying there. Mrs. Morrow was on a trip and didn't return until the next morning. Anne's sister Elisabeth was there that night and told her mother on March 1 that Colonel and Mrs. Lindbergh "had not yet returned, as the baby had a slight cold." (From: statement of Mrs. Dwight W. Morrow, March 16, 1932, to Lt John J. Sweeney and Det. Hugh Strong, Newark Police, "Preliminary statements made to police 1932 March–April," YUCAL.) Betty Gow was also at the Morrow estate on Monday night and never mentioned seeing Lindbergh there.

"I didn't know where Colonel Lindbergh was": Anne Lindbergh . . . statement to Lieutenant John Sweeney, March 11, 1932, NJSPM.

All of the quotes from CAL are from Statement of Charles Lindbergh to New Jersey State Police, March 11, 1932, NJSPM.

All of the AML quotes on this page are from Statement of Anne Lindbergh March 13, 1932, NJSP, to Lieutenant Sweeney and Hugh Strong, Newark Police.

Lanphier would buy Madden's brewery: "People," *TIME,* June 26, 1933, 40; see also J. Anne Funderburg, *Bootleggers and Beer Barons of the Prohibition Era* (Jefferson, NC: McFarland & Co., 2014) 93, citing "Lanphier Heads Brewing Company," *NYT,* June 16, 1933.

"some assistance from inside": Gardner, *The Case That Never Dies,* 32, note 63, quoting JEH.

The March 16, 1932, note signed by CAL is in "Notes of authorization and identification for contacts, 1932," YUCAL.

"quite deaf" is from J. Edgar Hoover, Strictly Confidential "Memorandum for the Files" dated March 19, 1942, of interview with Lindbergh's close friend and business colleague at Transcontinental Air Major Thomas Lanphier at the Bureau's New York office. From Record Group 65 Classification 7-1, Box 2, Section 6, Serial No. 398, 3.

"The malfunctioning shutters": source Melsky, *Vol I,* location 387 and note 81 citing an unpublished manuscript of Mickey Rosner circa 1932, 30. See also "Shutters Down From Baby's Window," AP, March 18, 1932, *Valley Morning Star* (Harlingen, Texas) March 19, 1932, 1.

7. Hunches Backfire and Leads Go Nowhere

"to break the Lindbergh case within 48 hours": Melsky, *Vol I,* Kindle loc. 627, n. 163, citing J. M. Keith, Special Agent in Charge, FBI Memorandum for the Director, April 6, 1932, National Archives at College Park, Maryland.

"used to hide the baby for a scare": Melsky, *Vol I,* Kindle loc. 660, n. 167, citing Gow's unsigned/undated statement (c. March 1932) to Murray Garsson, NJSPM.

That heart-stopping prank: see Alan Hynd, "Everyone Wanted to Get Into the Act" reprinted in Alan Hynd, *Violence in the Night* (New York: Fawcett Books, 1995) 9–60. Betty Gow mentioned the prior incident in a handwritten description of her work history. NJPM, 1001, p. 2. See also, Gardner, *The Case That Never Dies,* 420, n. 34, Lanphier statement to J. Edgar Hoover, FBI files.

"Colonel Lindbergh promised I wouldn't be touched": Betty Gow undated statement March 1932, NJSPM. Melsky, *Vol I,* Kindle loc 666, n. 171 and 172, citing "Reveal Secrets of Lindbergh Baby Kidnapping in Investigation Made by 60 Federal Agents," *Chicago Tribune,* April 11, 1932, 2.

"began poking around in the ashes . . . ": Berg, *Lindbergh,* 263, citing J.M. Keith, Report to JEH, April 6, 1932, NJSPM.

"under no circumstances be arrested"; "extreme eccentricity": Reveal Secrets of Lindbergh Baby Kidnapping in Investigation . . . ," *Chicago Tribune,* April 11, 1932, 2.

Kelly reportedly told an investigator . . . : Report of Det. Sgt Zapolsky, Investigation for Governor Harold Hoffman re: Ex-Trooper Lewis, Feb 2, 1936, NJSPM.

Condon may have been steered toward Lindbergh by Owney Madden: "Chronology" FBI Summary Report (NY File: 62-3057), 21, www.archive.org.

The March 12, 1932, authorization is now part of the Yale collection: "Notes of authorization and identification for contacts, 1932," YUCAL.

AML told her mother that CAL was considering dropping the demand of proof their son was alive. ECM diary entry, March 24, 1932, "Diaries 1927–1936"; SCMFP, https://findingaids.smith.edu/repositories/2/archival_objects/143140.

"well and safe"; "Anne Morrow Lindbergh's skirts": Vitray, *Hullabaloo* 11, 71.

"this true account of a national tragedy": Vitray, *Hullabaloo,* dedication page.

Quotes are from John Brant and Edith Renaud, *True Story of the Lindbergh Baby Kidnapping,* 93, 115–116, and 272. The emphasis on *"And yet the most important clew of all time!"* is in the original.

"unless he died of exposure": Brant and Renaud, *True Story of the Lindbergh Baby Kidnapping,* 140.

Breckinridge asked ECM on April 30, 1932, if she had been asked to provide $150,000 in ransom money because he had reason to believe such a demand would be made on her (almost a month after Cemetery John took $50,000 on a false promise to produce the kidnapped child). ECM diary entry, April 30, 1932. "Diaries 1927–1936"; SCMFP, https://findingaids.smith.edu/repositories/2/archival_objects/143140. No such demand ever materialized, but Breckinridge's query occurred around the same time that Gaston Means was bilking heiress Evelyn Walsh McLean in Washington, D.C. out of more than $100,000 for the boy's safe return.

All quotes of Bureau agent J. M Keith re Henry Breckinridge as the "directing force" are from J. M, Keith, "Memorandum for the Director Re: Kidnapping of Charles A. Lindbergh, JR." [declassified March 18, 2003]. Record Group 65, Classification 7-1 Box 2, Section 9, NJSPM.

8. Wild Goose Chases

finding thumb guard: Whateley testimony, BRHT reel 1, part 10, p13 (1971); Gow testimony, BRHT Reel 1 Part 001, 49, (276-77); Walsh statement, Joint Conference, May 18, 1932 ,7 (Record Group 65m Records of the FBI, Box 5 , Section 18, Serial No. 1179); for FBI timeline, see, Fensch, Ed. *Top Secret,* 48.

March 30, 1932, authorization note signed by CAL for Condon: "Notes of authorization and identification for contacts 1932," YUCAL.

Lindbergh told a reporter he had already spent $200,000: "Lindbergh Borrowed Half of $50,000 Ransom; 'Broke' He Told Aid, Flier Informed Intermediary that Kidnaping Negotiations Cost $200,000 — Wealth Dissipated by Plunge in Market," *BDE,* May 16, 1932, 1.

$1.2 million estimated cost of investigation: Hoffman, "More Things I Forgot to Tell," LMAG July 7, 1938, PDF copy, NJSPM.

"no police interference. . .": Fisher, *The Lindbergh Case,* 77.

The bureau remained in the dark: Thomas J. Sisk, "Memorandum for the Director, Unknown Subjects: Kidnaping and Murder of Charles A. Lindbergh, Jr. June 8, 1934, 9 [declassified March 19, 2003], NJSPM.

Description of the ransom box: Henry Breckinridge, Grand Jury testimony, May 17, 1932, Bronx, New York, 24, NJSPM.

The fifteenth note was among the exhibits at the Hauptmann trial: Exhibit S-70, *Evidence from Hauptmann Trial* pdf, 71, NJSPM.

The description of the flight out to sea to look for the "Boad Nelly" is from Elmer L. Irey as told to William J. Slocum, *The Tax Dodgers: The Inside Story of the U.S. Treasury's War with America Political and Underworld Hoodlums* (New York: Greenberg Publishers, 1948), 79.

Prior pranks against the Breckinridges the first week after the kidnapping are mentioned in "Reveal Secrets of Lindbergh Baby Kidnapping in Investigation Made by 60 Federal Agents," *Chicago Tribune*, April 11, 1932, 2.

"not to be discouraged"; "a dead body than a live one": AML, *HGHL*, 238 [letter to ELLL, April 10, 1932].

CAL article in *Science* magazine: *Science*, New Series, Vol. 75, No. 1946 (Apr. 15, 1932) 415–416.

"immediate practical use"; "the kidnapping . . . rudely interrupted Col. Lindbergh's collaboration with the Nobel prizeman, Carrel.": "Medical Research Aided by Genius of Col. Lindbergh," May 7, 1932, *Science News-Letter*, Vol. 21, No. 578 (May 7, 1932), 294. According to author David Friedman, Lindbergh kept working on the article in the opening days of March. Lindbergh said he was at the Rockefeller Institute during the day on Tuesday March 1, 1932, but there is no other reference to him being there working on the article or otherwise on March 2 or beyond when the nationwide search had begun for his missing son.

Lindbergh was "tired of hearing about the kidnapping . . . : Melsky, *Vol. I*, Kindle loc 2788, n. 922, citing trial notes of Curtis, Law offices of C. Lloyd Fisher, NJSPM.

The weekend was described by CAL in his diary. The apartment where the Lindberghs stayed was at 2 East 72d St. CAL diary 1931–1932, entry dated May 8, 1932, "Diaries, 1912–1939 May 9," YUCAL.

Quote re the meeting in Woodlawn Cemetery, see Gardner, *The Case That Never Dies*, 66.

9. A Nation in Mourning

"almost open cooperation . . .": Nat Bodian, "Old Newark Memories: Newark in the Prohibition Era," http://newarkmemories.com/memories/597.php.

Quotes from William Allen are from "William Allen, Statement to the police," May 12, 1932, NJSPM.

"dogs or other animals . . .": E. J. Connelley Memorandum re "Unknown Subjects: Kidnapping and Murder Baby Charles A. Lindbergh Jr.," May 24, 1932, Memorandum 7-1 Box 5 Section 18, 1179., 5 [declassified March 18, 2003], NJSPM.

"75 yards": Melsky, *Vol I*, loc 2470, n. 814, citing NJSP Bulletin May 12, 1932 7:30 PM ; "75 feet" source: Melsky, *Vol. I*, loc 2332, n. 779, citing Jersey City PD Inspector Walsh and NJSP Lt. Arthur Keaten Report, "Investigation concerning the Kidnapping and murder of Charles A. Lindbergh Jr. In Hopewell NJ," dated May 12, 1932, NJSPM.

The April 5-mile radius search is described in HNS "personal file," unmarked folder, April 7, 1932, NJSPM.

The farmer is quoted at Gardner, *The Case That Never Dies*, 91.

Moran's work for Breckinridge as process server: Melsky, *The Dark Corners of the Lindbergh Kidnapping Vol. III* (Bloomington, Illinois: iUniverse, 2018), Kindle loc 1560, n. 320, citing Charles Maran's police statement Aug. 23, 1933, NJSPM.

"The baby is with Daddy": AML, *HGHL*, quoting her mother ECM, 246 [diary entry May 12, 1932].

Anne's letter to her mother-in-law: AML, *HGHL*, May 12, 1932 letter to ELLL.

"to know definitely . . ." AML, *HGHL* [diary entry May 12, 1932].

"Child Killed By Two Blows on Head," *The Daily Sentinel*, May 12, 1932, Grand Junction, Colorado, 1.

"Baby Lindy Found Beaten to Death," *NYDN*, May 13, 1932, 3, quoting a night bulletin from Colonel Schwarzkopf.

"Baby Lindy Found Beaten to Death," *NYDN*, 3, May 13, 1932.

"Not a damn thing . . . ": Falzini, *Their Fifteen Minutes*, 119.

10. At the Morgue

"Look-see" description of May 12, 1932, preliminary autopsy is from Swayze's taped interview, Sept. 19, 1977, NJSPM.

"odor made it impossible . . .": Dr. Charles Mitchell. Testimony (cross), BRHT, reel 1, part 007, 67 (1491), NJSPM.

Newspaper description of violent death: AP, "Two Blows on Head Brought Instant Death," *Honolulu Star Bulletin*, May 13, 1932, 1, quoting Dr. Mitchell using the same words attributed to a bulletin from Colonel Schwarzkopf, "It appeared as if some person held the baby tightly in his arms and deliberately hammered the head with the purpose of causing instant death."

"come apart of its own": Dr. Charles Mitchell. Testimony (cross), BRHT, reel 1, part 007, 73 (1502), NJSPM.

"a foreign substance . . .": Melsky, *Vol I*, loc 2695 n. 880, citing Mercer County Detective James Kirkham Grand Jury Testimony in Matter of Paul Wendel April 14, 1936, NJSPM.

one reporter took a photo: Melsky, *Vol I*, loc 2539, n. 830, citing Report No. 3 of Bergen County Detective George H. Foster. January 24, 1936, NJSPM.

Description of request for Betty Gow: Melsky, *Vol I*, Kindle loc. 2588, notes 845 and 846, citing Police Report of NJSP Lt. D. J. Dunn. May 16, 1932., NJSPM.

Dr. Mitchell stayed in the house: Melsky, *Vol I*, Kindle loc. 2616, n. 854, citing deposition of John Henry Conlon, July 10, 1981, NJSPM.

Gow's ID of the body: Dr. Charles Mitchell, testimony (cross), BRHT, reel 1, part 007, 72 (1501), NJSPM.

"towards the incisors...": Dr. Charles Mitchell, "Report on Unknown Baby" (preliminary autopsy), May 12, 1932, NJSPM.

"peculiar condition": "Says Shot Killed Lindbergh Baby; Single Bullet Caused Fractures of Skull, Physician Insists," *Delaware County Daily Times* (PA), May 14, 1932, 1.

"banged against a tree...": Fensch, *Top Secret*, 152, citing FBI summary of news accounts of Dr. Mitchell's statements to the press on May 12, 1932.

"Philip Van Ingen Statement taken Nov. 21, 1934, by Assistant Attorney General Robert Peacock," 2, NJSPM. In the widely distributed wanted poster, the description of his height should have been 2'9". [See Appendix II, Kennedy, *The Airman and the Carpenter*, 415. The mistake was corrected by an announcement from Col. Schwarzkopf within days, but never corrected on the poster.]

Infants' incisors generally appear by the age of one source: "Teething – Baby Teeth Order, http://kids.emedtv.com/teething/baby-teeth-order.html.

"little locks of hair"; "very light, flaxen hair": Microscopic examination would be done more than two years later. The lab then reported that the hair of the corpse matched that of locks saved from Charlie's February 1932 haircut, as well as wisps of hair in the debris found in the hollow under the corpse's head, and blond hairs removed from the burlap bag. From Philip Van Ingen Statement taken Nov. 21, 1934 by Assistant Attorney General Robert Peacock, 2. NJSPM; Fisher, *The Lindbergh Case*, 110.

Breckinridge agreed with him. Melsky *Vol I*, loc 2691, n. 884, citing Special Agent J. F. Carney. Memorandum for Special Agent in Charge T. F. Cullen. Re: Gaston B. Means; Norman T. Whitaker Larceny in the District of Columbia of $100,000.00 from Mrs. Evalyn Walsh McLean. April 28, 1933, 1, 4. Natl Archives at College Park, MD. Melsky, *Vol I*, n. 884.

"The condition of the body is such...": Dr. Van Ingen, handwritten note dated May 13, 1932, on stationery of Walter H. Swayze, Trenton, New Jersey, NJSPM.

"If someone were to... offer me $10 million: Melsky, *Vol I*, Kindle loc 2702, n. 885, citing Evalyn Walsh McLean Manuscript, Library of Congress. From Scaduto, *The Scapegoat*, 64, citing Hynd as his source.

References to what AML was told and her husband finding her in tears are from AML, *HGHL*, 248 [letter to ELLL May 12, 1932] and AML, *HGHL*, 249 [letter to ELLL May 14, 1932] and AML, *HGHL*, 248 [diary entry May 13, 1932].

"I don't think he knew anything about it": AML, *HGHL*, 249 [letter to ELLL May 14, 1932].

"His terrible patience and sweetness and silence — terrifying": AML, *HGHL*, 248 [diary entry May 13, 1932].

11. Ashes and Smoke

Crumpled newspaper page: "How Long Does It Take for Newspaper to Decompose?" https://www.refence.com/world-view/long-newspaper-decompose-6521e7c31173f18.

Frank Swayze announced a closed coffin: Melsky, *Vol I,* loc. 2774, n. 919 citing *The Lethbridge Herald,* May 13, 1932, "Parents to Remember Their son as Handsome, Smiling Little Chap; Coffin Sealed."

"subnormal": Ellis Parker, letter to Harold Hoffman, December 23, 1935, NJSPM.

Parker's consultation with pathologists re decomposition rate: Scaduto, *Scapegoat,* 65.

Lindbergh asked for a sharp instrument: Melsky, *Vol. I,* Kindle loc. 2826, n. 934, citing Mercer County Detective James Kirkham Grand Jury Testimony In the Matter of Paul Wendel, April 14, 1936, 53, NJSPM.

"I am perfectly satisfied that it is my child": "SCENES AND FIGURES IN CRIME OF THE CENTURY—THE LINDBERGH BABY MURDER—AS A NATION HUNTS KILLERS," *NYDN,* May 14, 1932, 18. Photo Caption: "Special detail of police clears path for the car carrying grief-stricken Col. Lindbergh to the under-taking establishment in Trenton, N.J., where yesterday—pale, haggard, but keeping himself well in hand—he viewed the body of the Eaglet." "I am perfectly satisfied that it is my child," he said. See also "LINDY WATCHES SON'S CREMATION,"*NYDN,* May 14, 1932, 6.

The baby's remains were delivered to a crematorium with no toxicology tests having been run. See Ahlgren and Monier, *The Crime of the Century: The Lindbergh Kidnapping Hoax,* 109.

Practice of paying for "unclaimed bodies" fit Parker's theory of a substitute corpse. See: Gareth Jones, "Unclaimed bodies are anatomy's shameful inheritance," *New Scientist,* April 15, 2014. If Parker believed that the corpse he saw in the morgue was a look-alike stolen from a nearby grave, he wasn't the only one to say so. In June of 1933, Arthur Hitner, who insisted he had insider knowledge of the crime, reported that the body identified as Charlie was actually stolen from a West Chester County cemetery and that the Lindbergh baby was still alive: *FBI Lindbergh Summary Report* (NY-62-3057), 387, www.archive.org.

The original May 14, 1932, autopsy report has disappeared, but a copy had already been made by the Bureau during an interview of Dr. Mitchell. The text has been preserved by the FBI: FBI Lindbergh Summary Report (NY-62-3057) 110 (Autopsy) www.archive.org.

"Sgt. Doyle" telephone call was recorded in the May 14, 1932 Call Log. Sheet #3. NJSPM. (May 14 was the same day Dr. Mitchell delivered his updated autopsy report to authorities.) Two days earlier, May 12, 1932 (the day the child's body was found), a "Sgt Doyle" was also listed as an officer at the gate to the Lindbergh estate, according to a May 1932 report by NJSP Trooper Herbert Lauterwald ("Police (Troop C) reports, 1932 March-June" YUCAL). Yet there was no Sergeant Doyle among the police personnel officially reported at the time, according to a list maintained in the NJSPM archives.

Lindbergh scattered the ashes: Berg, *Lindbergh,* 281.

"I hoped so I would bring that baby back": AML *HGHL,* 252 [May 17, 1932].

"We speak of the new baby . . .": AML, *HGHL,* 251 [May 15, 1932].

"The skull was not compressed . . .": Transcript attached to report of Special Agent E. J. Connelley, NJSPM [declassified March 13, 2003].

Schwarzkopf statement re Lindberghs' communication with the Breckinridges: Melsky, *Vol I*, loc 269, n. 44, citing NJSP Press Questions and Answers, Series No. 17. March 10, 1932, NJSPM.

No mention of telephone call: CAL testimony, BRHT, reel 1, part 000,74-75 (132–134) NJSPM. See also CAL statement to police, March 11, 1932, NJSPM.

"minute descriptions of the haunts . . . ": C. Lloyd Fisher, "The Case New Jersey Would Like to Forget," Part 7, *LMAG*, August 22, 1936, 4 [pdf], NJSPM.

Curtis's claim he signed a confession under duress: Falzini, *Their Fifteen Minutes*, 77. Also *FBI Summary Report* (NY File 62-3057), 386, www.archive.org.

Source of quotes and description of bureau agents' meeting with Col. Schwarzkopf on May 19, 1932: Thomas H. Sisk, "Memorandum for the Director," June 8, 1934, 8, NJSPM Record Group 65, FBI Records Category 7-1 [declassified March 19, 2003].

"Lindbergh Household and Employees": Fensch, *Top Secret*, 100–112.

AML quotes and quotes of CAL are from her diary entries: AML, *HGHL*, 251–256 [May 16–19, and May 22, 1932].

"a person, not a baby, gay, full of power, sure of himself . . . ": AML, *HGHL* [May 20, 1932].

They agreed her current pregnancy was like "starting all over again": AML, *HGHL*, 256 [May 22, 1932].

The Lindberghs had received from Dr. Carrel a letter of condolence for their tragic loss: Friedman, *The Immortalists*, 57, quoting AC letter to CAL mid-May 1932.

"had never been so close as they were at his birth — except now, at his death": AML, *HGHL*, 250.

"All too true": FBI Files Record Group 65, Classification 7-1, Box 2a, Serial No. A.

12. Bizarre Developments

Elisabeth was not told of her dire prognosis: AML, *HGHL*, 250.

The Feds could not verify state follow-up on the source of the ladder wood: Fensch, *Top Secret*, "Summary Report In Re Unknown Subjects Kidnaping and Murder of Charles A. Lindbergh, Jr. (N.Y. File 62-3057) Physical Evidence," 144.

"It is a crime how the State Police handled this piece of evidence": C. A. Appel, "Memorandum to the Director," May 24, 1932, Box 5, Classification 7-1, FBI Records, 1 [declassified March 18, 2003], NJSPM.

Quotes from Wilkins' May 1932 article are all from Horace V. Wilkins, "Lindbergh Kidnaping-Slaying Series of Bad Blunders from Start," *Brooklyn Daily Eagle*, May 29, 1932, 9, FBI Records, Classification 7-1 Record Group 65, NJSPM.

"extremely difficult if not impossible . . .": Squire Johnson to H. Norman Schwartzkopf [sic], March 10, 1932, NJSPM, Hoffman papers, Box 13. Discussion of the dropped investigation of Charles Schippel is from the same source. Johnson had also asked Colonel Schwarzkopf to follow up on a three-foot-long maple dowel he and a fellow investigator spotted in the corner of Lindbergh's study on March 10, 1932. It was of an uncommon size, but of the kind typically used for rolling oil cloth or rope for binding wheat or corn on a farm. What struck the two men was that the unusual diameter and hardness of that dowel were the "identical size and quality used in the dowels for assembly of the ladder."

Bureau could not do a comprehensive and intelligent investigation: T. J. Sisk, "Memorandum for the Director," June 8, 1934, 11 [declassified March 19, 2003], NJSPM.

Quotes from report on Violet Sharp suicide: Gardner, *The Case That Never Dies,* 107.

Mrs. Morrow publicly criticized Inspector Walsh: "Waitress Innocent Mrs. Morrow Says," *The Washington Post,* June 11, 1932. See also "Mrs. Morrow Believes Maid Innocent of Kidnaping Baby," *Brooklyn Times Union,* June 11, 1932, 1.

Nothing came of either accusation: Fensch, *Top Secret,* 115.

The description of C. Lloyd Fisher is from Falzini, *Their Fifteen Minutes,* 157–158.

Fisher's quotes about the prosecution and trial of Curtis are taken from his articles in *Liberty* magazine. See: C. Lloyd Fisher, "The Case New Jersey Would Like to Forget," *LMAG,* Part 1, August 1936, p 3/11 of PDF transcript, NJSPM.

Curtis's characterization of his conversations with two officers is taken from John Hughes Curtis, undated Trial Preparation Notes, NJSPM.

"Anyone who was on Lindy's side was a hero": Fisher, "The Case New Jersey Would Like to Forget," *LMAG,* Aug 22, 1936, part 6, NJSPM.

"The more I go into science . . .": AML, *HGHL,* 302 [diary entry August 18, 1932].

"all right" until her husband said: "He has a wart on his left toe": Berg, *Lindbergh,* 281.

Skean could not contain his excitement: AML, *HGHL,* 307 [August 30, 1932].

"but I clutch at them madly . . .": AML, *LROD,* 15 [February 24, 1933].

"he did not suffer, he did not know, a blow on the head": AML, *LROD,* 13 [Jan 30, 1933].

"There is the difference between men and women . . .": AML, *LROD,* 13 [February 5, 1933].

"The punctuation of anniversaries is terrible . . .": AML, *LROD,* 17 [diary entry February 27, 1933].

"entirely free for the first time in six years": AML, *LROD,* 22 [letter to ECM, March 17, 1933].

ACT THREE

1. Stymied

Anne told her sister Connie "made him happy...": AML, *LROD*, 151, 137.

"was in sheer terror" ... "never fly again": AML, *LROD*, 139–140.

One lowly corporal liaison to the Bureau of Investigation from NJSP: Letter to the Director, March 19, 1934, THS: MOB, March 19, 1934.

HNS letter of May 1, 1934 to J. Edgar Hoover and reply letter of May 3, 1934, from J. Edgar Hoover to HNS, FBI files, Record Group 65, 7-1, Box 14, section 66m series 3698, NJSPM.

CAL's restrictions on further interviews by the Bureau: AML, *LROD*, 26.

The Bureau Chief told his agents: quote is from JEH, "Memorandum for Mr. Tamm," July 18, 1934 [declassified March 19, 2003], NJSP 7-1 -4187, NJSPM.

2. An Elusive Suspect

Description of customer spending $10 certificate for produce at Levatino's stand: "Report of Investigation Concerning a Recovered $10.00 U.S. Gold Certificate, which is part of the Lindbergh Ransom Money," submitted by Cpl. William F. Horn, New Jersey State Police, Sept. 6, 1934, 1–2., NJSPM.

Taxi driver Perrone agreed with Condon that Cemetery John's accent was fake. See Gardner, *The Case That Never Dies*, 96.

Noel Behn theory re Nosovitsky. See Behn, *Lindbergh: The Crime*, 374-95.

Sources of striking similarities between Nosovitsky and Hitner:
a. Both were reportedly born in 1889.
AH: 1917-18 Draft Card (www.fold3.com); JN: Navy credential, Behn, 246
[AH may have falsely described his appearance. A draft card for JN listing an 1890 birth date in Russia is likely a forgery.]
b. Both were 5ft 10 with grey-ish eyes.
AH: FBI Summary: (NY File 62-3057) 389; JN: Behn, 246 & 387
c. Both used multiple aliases.
AH: FBI Summary (NY File 62-3057) 385; JN: Behn, 387.
d. Both were acquaintances of Gaston Means.
AH: FBI Summary (NY File 62-3057) 386; JN: Behn, 387
e. Both fraudulently claimed to be doctors.
AH: 1917–18 Draft card (www.fold3.com); JN: Behn, 379
f. Both were reportedly cosmetic scientists.
AH: FBI Summary (NY File 62-3057) 389; JN: Behn, 338
g. Both were identified as spies.
AH: "'Spy' Charge is Made at New Orleans Inquiry," *The Monroe News-Star*, September 14, 1934; JN: Behn, 377
h. Both had multiple convictions.
AH: FBI Summary (NY File 62-3057) 388–89; JN: Behn, 390–392.

Nosovitsky's self-reported history includes an unbelievable tale of his role in assassination attempts on the czar beginning when Nosovitsky was 15; daring escapes which left armed police officers dead; a stint in a Russian prison camp followed shortly after by a college education at the University of Kiev and the unnatural deaths of all of his immediate family members. (Behn, *Lindbergh: The Crime*, 378.) Nosovitsky's official documentation only dates back to a February 1916 application for American citizenship in which he fraudulently claimed to be a druggist and reported his nearest American relative was an "Uncle Sam." Behn noted, "fiction may well have bested fact regarding the origins of Jacob Nosovitsky." (Behn, *Lindbergh: The Crime*, 378.)

In contrast, newspaper reports and census records dating back to 1900 show that Arthur Linderman Hitner grew up as the son of an American reverend and his criminal history goes back to at least December 1907. Hitner's elaborate schemes included a fake suicide attempt with blank bullets and theatrical blood in order to win his wife back in 1911 – a con revealed when a doctor tried to "save" his life. ("Clever Scheme to Win Back his Wife — Arthur L. Hitner of Chapman Failed in his Efforts," *Lewisburg Journal*, 12 May 1911, 2.)

"Federal Prisoner Claims Knowledge of Lindbergh Kidnapping," *Ithaca Journal News*, June 8, 1933,13.

mug shot of Nosovitsky: Michael Melsky, https://lindberghkidnap.proboards.com.

3. The Most Hated Man in America

Quotes from arresting officers: Kennedy, *The Airman and the Carpenter*, 168.

"Great news . . . They've got him at last": Moseley, *Lindbergh*, 185, based on an interview of a friend who overheard the conversation between CAL and AML.

"Kill him, crucify him!": Kennedy, *The Airman and the Carpenter*, 194.

"I didn't know that anyone doubted it": Kennedy, *The Airman and the Carpenter*, 209, quoting Homer Cummings.

"much heavier [with] different eyes, hair, etc.": Hoffman, "What was wrong with the Lindbergh Case," *LMAG,* part nine, 1938, citing L. C. Turrou report, 60.

"LINDY CASE SOLVED: $13,000 RECOVERED," *The Paterson Evening News*, September 20, 1934, extra edition; *The Central New Jersey Home News*, Dec. 10, 1934, 1.

"three ring circus . . . side show": Gardner, *The Case That Never Dies*, 192, n. 48, citing September 26, 1934, Memorandum from JEH to Agent Tamm and September 27, 1934, memorandum from Tamm to JEH.

Letter ending Bureau's role: JEH letter to New Jersey Attorney General David Wilentz, November 19, 1, 1934,1–2 [declassified February 14, 2003], NJSPM.

Two examples of newspapers stating Levatino did not identify Hauptmann as his customer: "Hauptmann, German-American, Sullenly Reiterates Denial," *Indiana Gazette* (Indiana, PA), Sept. 21, 1934, 2. (Per this article, neither of the other two witnesses identified Hauptmann either. "Psychiatrist Gives Theory Why Lindy's Baby Was Kidnaped," *St. Louis Globe Gazette,* Jan. 28, 1935, 22) The newspapers that claimed Levatino did identify Hauptmann erroneously claimed three witnesses all testified that Hauptmann passed them $20 gold certificates. "TRIO PICKS HAUPTMANN AS PASSER $20 CERTIFICATES," *Corsicana Semi-Weekly Light,* Sept. 28, 1934, 22. (The customer Levatino described paid with a $10 bill, not $20.) Vendor Charles Aiello was approached the same day as Levatino. Officials noted that Aiello's account "tallied closely" with Levatino's. Ruby Altmann's encounter on September 8 was similar. (FBI Summary Report, Part 2, File 7-1-5142, Vol. 96, 10-15.) None of the three vendors ever testified.

Lindbergh testimony before the Bronx grand jury: Fisher, *Lindbergh Case,* 248; Gardner, *The Case That Never Dies,* 189 n. 38: Kennedy, *The Airman and the Carpenter,* 209.

"To see the man who kidnapped his son": Ross, *The Last Hero,* 215, quoting District Attorney Foley.

Condon still could not identify Hauptmann: "Cash No Link to Kidnapping Says Condon," *NYDN,* Sept. 22, 1934.

"Lindbergh Sleuths Make Up Theories to Suit All Tastes": *NYDN,* Sept. 28, 1934, 6.

Bureau led to believe only unusable smudges: January 18, 1934 letter to the Director from F. K. Fay, Special Agent in Charge, Department of Justice, U.S. Bureau of Investigation, New York, New York , FBI Record Group 65m 7-1, Box 11, Section 49, Serial No. 2825, NJSPM.

Erastus Hudson discussion with NJSP re Hauptmann's prints not being on the ladder, see Gardner, *The Case That Never Dies,* 344 and n. 45.

Quotes from the diary of Harold Nicolson: Nigel Nicolson, ed. Harold Nicolson, *Diaries and Letters 1930–1939,* (Collins, London/Atheneum: New York, 1966), 183 (October 1, 1934 entry) [emphasis in original].

"He plunged again into long conferences . . ." Kennedy, *The Airman and the Carpenter,* 249, quoting AML.

For details re Hauptmann's car, see Falzini, *Their Fifteen Minutes,* 17-19.

"suspicious pattern…" Noel Behn, *Lindbergh: The Crime,* 244.

For evidence police doctored records and secured false testimony re Hauptmann's work records in March and April of 1932 at the Majestic Apartments. See Scaduto, *Scapegoat,* 275-287 and Kennedy, *The Airman and the Carpenter,* 222-227.

4. Framing an Ironclad Case

The prosecution's felony-murder theory is set forth at reel 3, part 025, Brief for the State of New Jersey, Point V, 35-42, NJSPM.

"follow[ed] every detail of evidence and testimony . . ." Kennedy, *The Airman and the Carpenter,* 249, quoting AML.

Perrone's inability to identify Cemetery John: Kennedy, *The Airman and the Carpenter,* 124, citing police interview with Perrone c. May 1932. [Perrone: "I didn't pay any attention to anything." Police officer: Would you know him if you saw him? 'No, sir,"]. See also Gardner, *The Case That Never Dies,* 96–97, citing Perrone's May 1932 Grand Jury testimony that his mystery passenger had "kind of light brown eyes" (Hauptmann had blue eyes).

Perrone was "practically coerced" into identifying Hauptmann: Kennedy, *The Airman and the Carpenter*, 177; Gardner, *The Case That Never Dies*, 159–160.

Wilentz threatened Condon himself with prosecution: Kennedy, *The Airman and the Carpenter*, 233–235. Jim Fisher's account itself demonstrates undue pressure by Wilentz on Condon to change his testimony (*The Lindbergh Case,* 267). Condon's cousin later reported an additional threat was made. Investigators for the prosecution dug up an old, unsubstantiated claim Condon had molested one of his students. If he did not cooperate, the charge, even though hotly disputed, could be used to take away his pension. More recently, potential corroboration for this claim was made by a woman who said she was a family member. "At family discussion I did hear my Dad and Grandma Doyle say that Dr. Condon did say privately he really was unsure BRH was the kidnapper and when he did not want to identify him Dr. Condon was threatened with 1. implication and involvement in the kidnapping 2. loss of pension due to charges of "impropriaty [sp] with minors." This was so untrue. He was never, never improper." Patricia Doyle (self-identified as great-granddaughter of Dinny Doyle, who was John F. Condon's first cousin) subject: "The Condon Conundrum" posted Sept 14, 2006, at 4:55 p.m. on http://lindberghkidnap.proboards.com/

"You can surmise what you please": "Jafsie Damns Hauptmann as Ransom Taker," *NYDN*, October 24, 1934. See Fisher, *The Lindbergh Case*, 266–267.

"Condon Names Hauptmann as Ransom Taker," *Journal and Courier*, Lafayette, Indiana, Oct. 25, 1934, 1.

Since the landmark decision in *Brady v. Maryland*, 373 U.S. 83 (1963) the Supreme Court has required prosecutors to turn over to the defense potentially exculpatory evidence that the investigation turned up. The rationale for that constitutional decision was that the prosecutor's role is to seek justice in a fair trial, not to convict a defendant simply because he was arrested as a likely suspect. After the *Brady* decision, prosecutors could not legally play hide the ball to ensure a conviction of someone who might well be innocent.

5. Slew Footing Dr. Mitchell

Description of Gaston Means fraud trial: FBI Lindbergh Summary Report (NY File 62-3057), 386 (www.archive.org).

Testimony of Dr. Charles Mitchell, *United States v. Gaston Bullock Means and Norman Whitaker, Supreme Court of District of Columbia*, 265, May 9, 1933, NJSPM.

State Summation, BRHT, reel 3, part 23, 85(4584), NJSPM. The reenactment of the crime in May 1932 first suggested the possibility that the child hit his head against the house as the kidnapper descended with the child in the burlap bag.

Reconstructing the kidnap by ladder theory: Moseley, *Lindbergh*, 166, quoting Col. Schwarzkopf.

Schwarzkopf's willingness to lie for CAL: *New York Journal* interview February 15, 1935, quoted in Kennedy, *The Airman and the Carpenter*, 171, and Falzini, *Their Fifteen Minutes*, 83.

That small, roundish hole was first alluded to by Dr. Mitchell when talking to the press on the night of May 12 and then described by Dr. Mitchell in what Dr. Mitchell considered his official autopsy report, dated May 14, 1932; two days after the initial report on the "unknown baby" and one day after Lindbergh had identified the body as his son. This hole led directly to Dr. Mitchell developing the bullet theory he repeatedly shared with reporters through October 1934. [See FBI Lindbergh Summary Report, (NY File 62-3057) 110, www.archive.org).] At the Bronx grand jury proceedings in September 1934, Mitchell swore that he had never previously been told that a police officer had poked the skull after finding the corpse. Lindbergh himself had attended the Gaston Means trial in 1933 and knew that Dr. Mitchell had then testified that the bullet theory best explained the small hole behind the corpse's ear.

Dr. Mitchell rejected Schoeffel's grand jury testimony as absurd. He still considered the bullet theory plausible: Fisher, *The Lindbergh Kidnapping Case*, citing Dr. Baden [endnote 451, chap. 26, 454, chap. 33, n. 3).

"Col. Lindbergh Confronts Hauptmann," *NYDN*, Sept. 28, 1934, 4; see also Walter Swayze taped interview by NJSP Det. Sgt. Cornel Plebani, Sept. 19, 1977, NJSPM.

The skull was too thick and hard: "Search Continues for Bullet Clue," *The Philadelphia Inquirer*, September 30, 1934, 6e.

Police were sent to the site to look for a bullet, and the quote from Schwarzkopf: "Bullet Theory; Schwarzkopf Says Mitchell May Need to Supplement at *Trial*," "Lindbergh Identifies Hauptmann's Voice," *The Baltimore Evening Sun*, October 9, 1934, 6.

Hicks article: Robert Hicks, Specialist in Forensic Ballistics, "Ballistics vs. The Lindbergh Case," *The Police Reporter*, November 1934, 8, NJSPM. The report includes two contradictions of the FBI's own records. The agency had in its files a copy of the May 14, 1932, autopsy that described the bulletlike hole as ½ inch in diameter, not ¼ inch. In this published article, adding to public prejudice two months before the murder trial, Hicks also credited Lindbergh's identification of Hauptmann's voice at the confidential New Jersey grand jury proceedings when an internal FBI memorandum described that voice identification as not worthy of belief because of the physical distance and passage of time. Yet Hicks buttressed Dr. Mitchell in dismissing Lindbergh's theory of accidental death at Highfields — the premise for trying the death penalty case in Hunterdon County.

Hicks thought the small German pistol police had recovered from Hauptmann's home could have been the murder weapon. Yet Hicks mistakenly asserted that the skull had a ¼ inch hole behind the right ear when both the preliminary autopsy on May 12 and the final autopsy on May 14 specified it was a half-inch rounded hole. The May 14 report mentioned the bullet-like hole was about ½ inch; the May 12 did not mention a bullet, but that was when Dr. Mitchell asked Swayze to look for one in the brain because of the size of the hole and the nature and extent of the skull fractures.

Hauptmann's conviction was less assured in Mercer county: "Jersey Grand Due Jury to Act Today in Hauptmann Case," *NYT*, October 8, 1934, 2, 7.

confidential joint meeting with Colonel Schwarzkopf and members of the New York office of the Bureau: Transcript attached to report of Special Agent E. J. Connelley, NJSP 13 [declassified March 13, 2003], NJSPM.

Mitchell ID of corpse in Parker trial: "Parker to face Mercer Jurors for Fifth Time," *The Record*, April 15, 1936.

"I'd of been crazy to tangle with Lindbergh": Melsky, *The Dark Corners*, Vol 1, Kindle loc. 2490, n. 819.

6. Death House Reilly

"LINDY CASE SOLVED: $13,000 RECOVERED," *The Patterson Evening News*, Sept. 20, 1934; *The Central New Jersey Home News*, Dec. 10, 1934, 1.

Fawcett did not take kindly to being fired and unethically threatened to keep all the paperwork he had gathered for the defense until he was paid. (As of two weeks into the trial, he still had not turned them over to Reilly.)

Hearst had no doubt of Hauptmann's guilt or the reputation of "Death House" Reilly: Scaduto, *Scapegoat*, 121, 220 n. 60.

For more details on Hearst's treatment of Fatty Arbuckle and Leo Franck, see Lise Pearlman, *With Justice for Some: Politically Charged Crimes in the Early 20th Century That Helped Shape Today's America* (Regent Press 2017) Introduction and chapter 5.

Reilly "knew Hauptmann was guilty . . ." Hauptmann lay down and sobbed: Kennedy, *The Airman and the Carpenter*, 240 n. 2, citing Agent Thomas Sisk in a January 22, 1936, report from FBI Special Agent Tamm to J. Edgar Hoover, NJSPM. This casts suspicion on the purpose of the private meeting Reilly arranged with Atty. Gen. Wilentz in late November, 1934. Harry Whitney letter to David Wilentz, Nov. 20, 1934, https://lindberghkidnap.proboards.com.

A copy of the letterhead was maintained by the FBI together with a clipped newspaper article, "Ladder, Red Ink on Paper Used by Reilly in Fan Mail Replies," NJSPM.

"Hauptmann Obtains Fan-Mail Stationery," *Reading Times* (Reading, PA), January 10, 1935, 4. Reilly also got red ladder stationary for Hauptmann to use. From "Hauptmann Obtains Fan-Mail Stationery," *Reading Times* (Reading, PA), Jan 10, 1935, 4. ("Stationary printed in red ink and carrying a facsimile of the Lindbergh kidnap ladder has been obtained for Bruno Richard Hauptmann by Edward J. Reilly, chief defense counsel. He's going to use it in answering his 'fan mail,'" Reilly said.)

"Mr. Reilly had taken $2400 of the $2900 for his retainer . . .": C. Lloyd Fisher, *LMAG*, 1936, part 7, page 8, retyped copy, NJSPM.

Frederick Pope joined the team for the publicity: Falzini and Davidson, *New Jersey's Lindbergh Kidnapping and Trial*, 98.

Judge George Large switched sides: Melsky, *The Dark Corners of the Lindbergh Case, Vol. III* (Bloomington, Indiana: iUniverse, 2019) Kindle loc. 5671, n. 1151–1154.

Arthur Koehler work on ladder sources: Arthur Koehler (as told to Boyden Sparkes), "Who Made That Ladder?" *The Saturday Evening Post*, April 20, 1935, 10. See also Arthur Koehler, "Techniques Used in Tracing the Lindbergh Kidnaping Ladder," (U.S. Dept. of Agriculture Forestry Dept., Madison, Wisconsin, 1937).

The Harold Nicolson quotes of CAL and ECM are from Nigel Nicolson, ed., Harold Nicolson, *Diaries and Letters 1930–1939* (187, 190 (letters to his wife Vita, Nov. 7, and Nov. 23, 1934 [emphasis in original].

"not to disappoint C at the trial": AML, *LROD*, diary entry December 30, 1934.

7. Show Time

"the criminal": C. Lloyd Fisher, *LMAG*, part 7, page 9 transcription, NJSPM.

"Definitely Link Kidnap Ladder to Hauptmann's Home," *The Central New Jersey Home News*, Dec. 10, 1934, 1.

"one day closer to the electric chair": Scaduto, *Scapegoat*, 120.

"droves of sporting writers . . .": Kennedy, *The Airman and the Carpenter*, 256, quoting an editorial in the White Plains, New York, *Daily Reporter*.

"THEY HAVE RIGHT MAN, SAID COL LINDBERGH,*" BDE*, January 3, 1935, 3.

American Bar Association Canon 20 then addressed: "Newspaper Discussion of Pending Litigation. Newspaper publications by a lawyer as to pending or anticipated litigation may interfere with a fair trial in the Courts and otherwise prejudice the due administration of justice. Generally, they are to be condemned."

"Hauptmann would have needed a change of venue to Baghdad . . .": W. Dennis Duggan, The State of New Jersey v. Bruno Richard Hauptmann; Fairness of Trial, *Albany Bar Association Newsletter*, January 2004, http://www.lindberghkidnappinghoax.com/duggan.pdf.

"The only suspense was whether Hauptmann would get the chair or life": Scaduto, *Scapegoat*, 119, quoting Hynd, "Everybody wanted to get in on the Act," *True Magazine*, March,1949.

Dozens of locals interviewed two weeks into the trial believed Hauptmann was innocent, but that the jury would convict him anyway to avenge the death of the son of their hero. See Sevellon Brown, "Flemingtom Sees Hauptmann Innocent Journalism Student Sees in Survey," *Columbia Daily Spectator,* Vol. LVIII, No 68, January 17, 1935, 1.

Contrast of the way CAL looked at prosecution table and Hauptmann at the defense table: "Hauptmann's Chances Small, Say Observers," *BDE,* January 3, 1935, 11.

Fisher's objection overruled, to CAL seated at the prosecution table: C. Lloyd Fisher, "Various Things Done by the Prosecutor to Hinder and Hold Up the Defense," NJSPM.

8. Picking the Jury

"Very good type . . ." *LMAG,* part 11, "What Was Wrong" by Gov Hoffman, Hoffmann files, document 64, NJSPM. The gossip in the courthouse: Milton, *Loss of Eden*, 302. Colonel Schwarzkopf claimed it was his suggestion that Lindbergh wear the weapon because Schwarzkopf feared someone might try to assassinate Lindbergh. Schwarzkopf did not explain why he thought anyone would be tempted to commit such a crime, with heavy security present, in front of newsreel cameras, and with hundreds of reporters and other witnesses.

Wilentz's denial of giving CAL major role in prosecution: "Hauptmann's Chances Small, Say Observers," *BDE,* January 3, 1935, 11.

"any more than anybody else": Ahlgren and Monier, *The Crime of the Century*, 140. Among those dismissed was a painter overheard telling several other people he would "fix that fellow if he got a chance." See "Four Men and Six Women Selected as Jurors in Hauptmann Trial," *The Morning Post* (Camden, NJ), Jan. 3, 1935, 6. Another person was dismissed because her aunt was the landlady for Anna Hauptmann and her young son during the trial. The one who caused the most stir was a fellow who professed total ignorance of the case. When he admitted he might have heard something, Justice Trenchard dismissed him for cause.

9. Aiming for the Chair

David Wilentz, opening statement, BRHT, reel 1, part 000, 8(2-3), NJSPM.

AML testimony, BRHT, reel 1, part 000, 45-46(74-76), NJSPM.

Lindbergh largely agreed with Anne's testimony: Lindbergh specifically identified the June 1931 photo of his son that had been introduced into evidence the day before through Anne's testimony as what his son looked like when he disappeared on March 1, 1932. Lindbergh also affirmed that his son was then quite active and "entirely normal." BRHT, reel 1, part 000, page 66(115), NJSPM.

He heard a crashing sound: In his signed statement on March 11, 1932, Lindbergh said the couple went to the living room around 9 p.m. and went upstairs around 9:15 p.m. At trial, he modified that to five to ten minutes so it was more compatible with Anne's testimony that they spent at most five minutes in the living room before heading upstairs.

Now Lindbergh insisted Hauptmann was the lone perpetrator: Reilly did get Lindbergh to admit that at the time of Curtis's June 1932 trial he believed Curtis met at least three members of the kidnap gang. Prosecutor Hauck admitted at the time that the gang did exist and that Curtis told the truth about that.

Finding the ladder: Lindbergh testified on direct examination that he recalled that "it was Chief (Harry) Wolfe who, with his flashlight, found, located the ladder." (BRHT, reel 1, part 000, 51(87), NJSPM.) State Trooper Joe Wolf understood from the interviews he did on the night of March 1, 1932, it was Lindbergh who found the ladder.

Timing of when Lindbergh ran outside with his gun: At trial, Lindbergh testified that he instructed Whateley to call the sheriff and waited to hear that officers were on their way before heading outside with his gun. But that did not match the chronology established in the statements given to the state police that were never provided to the defense.

No details were elicited: On direct examination Lindbergh indicated he spent most of his time in New York on aviation business and decided to stay over in Englewood Monday night because he was working late and had more to do on Tuesday morning. On cross-examination he acknowledged spending some time on Monday at the Rockefeller Institute and the dentist in the afternoon. He was not asked what time he left the city. Nor was he asked where he called his wife from at 7:00 p.m. to say he would be late for dinner. He had to have already left the city in order to arrive home at 8:20 p.m.

Lindbergh's testimony re: what he heard while seated in his car outside St. Raymond's Cemetery: Later, when working on the appeal, Fisher went back to the graveyard where Condon said he met Cemetery John. To test Lindbergh's voice identification, Fisher placed one assistant where Lindbergh said he sat in the car. Fisher put another volunteer where Condon testified that "Cemetery John" had stood. The only way the substitute "Cemetery John" could be heard by someone where Lindbergh sat was if "Cemetery John" shouted at the top of his lungs, which itself distorts a person's voice. Fisher concluded that voice identification from that distance was simply not possible. Experts advised him that "the texture and tonal qualities of a voice" grow less distinguishable "every five feet." Fisher realized that Lindbergh's claim he could identify a voice nearly three years later would not have been true even if Lindbergh had sat in a car ten feet away from "Cemetery John." [C. Lloyd Fisher, "Voice Identification" Hoffmann File, NJSPM.]

editorial challenging the credibility of Lindbergh's hearing claim: Scaduto, *Scapegoat*, 127, citing *The New York Law Journal*.

JEH scoffing at Lindbergh's hearing claim: see Hoffman file, NJSPM, C. Lloyd Fisher, "Voice Identification." Lindbergh had previously told the New York grand jury the phrase he heard was "Hey Doc" and that he doubted he could identify who said it. Lindbergh insisted his memory was refreshed by hearing Hauptmann repeat the phrase in Foley's office. Yet before the New Jersey Grand Jury and at trial he used a different phrase and spoke with utmost confidence he would be taken at his word.

No one at Hauptmann's trial other than Lindbergh himself had any idea Lindbergh had been accused of brazenly committing perjury ten years earlier in a court battle over the principal asset in his father's estate. *In the Matter of the Appeal of the Wells-Dickey Trust Company Evangeline L. L. Lindbergh, widow, Charles A. Lindbergh, Jr, Eva Lindbergh Christie, and Louise Cooley Roberts (daughter of Lillian) First District Court, Seventh Judicial District*, MHSCAL. Lindbergh and his mother both lied on the stand to claim a homestead exemption on the basis that Evangeline and her husband had lived together as husband and wife on the farm property for three years before he died. They had separated for good more than 15 years earlier. That bitterly contested litigation caused a rift between Lindbergh and his half-sister Eva that lasted decades. Much later, Lindbergh admitted he had no intention of making the farm his permanent home when he and his mother left it for Wisconsin in 1920. Letter from Charles Lindbergh to Russell Fridley, Director, MHS, St. Paul, Minnesota, April 7, 1967, MHSCAL.

Attribution of crime to a gang and plaster cast made of Cemetery John footprint at cemetery: see Henry Breckinridge, Grand Jury Testimony, May 17, 1932, Bronx, New York, 25, 27, NJSPM.

Like Lindbergh, Condon never mentioned having seen another man acting as lookout: see, e.g., CAL, Statement to Inspector Walsh, May 20, 1932, NJSPM.

"Hauptmann wears a size nine shoe": Melsky, *Vol. II*, 277, n. 827, citing JEH Memorandum to Mr. Tamm, Sept. 25, 1934, National Archives, College Park, MD.

FBI possession of conflicting interviews of Condon, Hoffman: "What Was Wrong with the Lindbergh Case," Part 10, *LMAG*, April 2, 1938, 58, NJSPM.

Betty Gow did not see the ransom envelope until the police arrived: Betty Gow testimony, BRHT, reel 1, part 001, 48 & 67 (274-275 & 317), NJSPM.

10. More Damning Testimony

In Nov. 1933, Barr believed patron was American: "$5 bill B-35435796", NY File 62-3057, p. 240.

Wilentz opening statement re time and cause of death: "Dr. Chas. Mitchell will identify his statement, given to Col. Schwarzkopf as report of the autopsy, and will testify that the child died of a fractured skull, that death was immediate, that the child was dead when buried, and that the child was apparently dead since the first night." Untitled list of proposed witnesses' testimony and exhibits, NJSPM.

The "look-see" autopsy was the May 12, 1932, "Report concerning the finding of the body of Charles A. Lindbergh, Jr. in Mount Rose, N. J." NJSPM.

Overheard coaching of Dr. Mitchell: Melsky, *Vol. II*, 22, n. 77, quoting George G. Hawkes (1951) "Trial by Fury: The Hauptmann Trial," Princeton University Senior Thesis, 112, citing an interview with assistant defense counsel Fred Pope on March 3, 1951, New Jersey State Police Museum archives. See also Kennedy, *The Airman and the Carpenter*, 281.

Mitchell testimony in Gaston Means trial quoted in Melsky, *Vol II*, 22, n. 74, citing Charles Mitchell Testimony, *United States v. Gaston Bullock Means and Norman Whitaker, Supreme Court of District of Columbia*, 265, May 9, 1933.

Seery testified that he overheard Hauptmann say to Levatino at the jail, "Don't you remember me giving you this bill?" *BRHT*, Reel 1, part 007, 93(1540) NJSPM. The defense objected to no avail. Hauptmann denied ever saying that and Levatino never testified.

Ransom money was still showing up: Kennedy, *The Airman and the Carpenter*, 277.

Reporter Tom Cassidy's boast: Kennedy, *The Airman and the Carpenter*, 204–205.

Statement of Millard Whited made to Det. Robert Coar, Jersey City and Detective S. J. Leon, New Jersey State Police, April 26, 1932, NJSPM.

Charles Rossiter testimony: BRHT, Reel 1, part 10, (43-54), 2036-2047. In his September 22, 1934 statement Rossiter instead described a man about 5'6" with a slouched hat who resembled a different man's photo he had just seen in the newspaper (possibly Isidor Fisch). Report of Sgt. A. G. Varrelman re Rossier interview, September 22, 1934, NJSPM.

Hochmuth testimony: reel 1, BRHT, reel 2, part 002, (36) 450; statement given to Asst. Atty. Gen. Peacock Jan. 6, 1935, NJSPM. Hauptmann's car was blue – NJSP Det. Sgt. John Wallace Report on BRH arrest Sept 20, 1934. http://www.lindberghkidnappinghoax.com/wallacereport.pdf. Re Hochmuth's eyesight and Foley's concession, see, e.g., Kennedy, *The Airman and the Carpenter*, 225, 244. See also Hauptmann and Tolzmann (ed.), "*I am Innocent*," 110, 139. Hauptmann stated that on the morning of March 1, he went to the Majestic Apartments only to learn they did not need him that day. He went to the employment agency and spent the rest of that day in New York.

Observations re Anna Hauptmann's appearance: AML, *LROD*, 247.

Colonel Schwarzkopf knew the police offered Hauptmann spelling "help": Gardner, *The Case That Never Dies*, 161, note 46, October 26, 1934, HNS to J. Clark Sellers, accordion file General Handwriting, NJSPM.

The defense had only been given half a day to examine the prosecutor's expert reports: C. Lloyd Fisher, "What went wrong," NJSPM. Today, expert reports must be timely shared before trial to permit depositions; the authorities would also have to disclose that no prints they found belonged to belonged to Hauptmann. Kennedy, *The Airman and the Carpenter*, 213–214.

"You are conceding Hauptmann to the electric chair": Behn, *Lindbergh: The Crime*, 275 note 9, citing Whipple, *The Trial of Bruno Richard Hauptmann*, 228.

Summary of Koehler testimony: E. A. Tamm, MD, Jan. 23, 1935, NJSPM. To compare the grains he scraped the wood ends first to bring out similarities. He knew surface grains varied. Koehler, "Techniques Used in Tracing the Lindbergh Kidnapping Ladder," 4–6.

Potential suspects from those lines of inquiry had been abandoned without explanation: Gardner, *The Case That Never Dies*, 136.

missing floorboard: Melsky, *Vol. III*, Kindle loc. 5326, n. 1060, citing master carpenter Kevin Klein, message board post, April 26, 2007, lindberghkidnap.proboards.com.

He insisted he was being framed by police. In fact, in March of 1932 the ladder looked unused and made from new crates, not floorboards. See: "Builder Studies Ladders as Clue," *The Morning News*, Wilmington, DE, March 5, 1932, 5. No one wondered about the reason for 6'8 ½" rails. The first responders considered two sections of the ladder too short to reach the nursery window easily and all three came too high. So, the "kidnap" ladder was not made to size for the job. Nor did it make sense that it was designed to fit in Hauptmann's sedan. Standard American 6' rails would also have fit. Author Ludovic Kennedy called the attic plank theory "preposterous" and a total "fantasy." (*The Airman and the Carpenter*, 210, 220.) Crime reporter Anthony Scaduto had reacted similarly. (*Scapegoat*, 381-382). Kelvin Keraga reached the opposite conclusion in "Testimony in Wood: Analysis of the rail 16 evidence in the Lindbergh Kidnapping Summary Report 1.2," 2005, PDF, 14, 26, www.lindberghkidnappinghoax.com/keraga.pdf. (The ladder rails were almost exactly two meters long; crates of that length were common overseas. Metric "1 x 6" boards are 1.5mm thicker than US standard – 20.5 mm compared to 19mm. https://www.builderdepot.co.uk/25mm-x-150mm-planed-softwood-par-timber-6in-x-1in http://www.alsc.org/greenbook%20collection/ps20.pdf) The best way to tell whether rail 16 instead originated as part of the same floorboard as BRHT S-226 would be a wood DNA test on S-226 and rail 16 since both remain preserved in the NJSPM.

Hochmuth's "eyewitness" ID: A reporter later informed Gov. Hoffman about the pressure the police had put on the elderly man. See Russell Stoddard, Letter to Gov. Hoffmann, Melsky; lindberghkidnap.proboards.com. Hauptmann owned a blue sedan. Falzini, *Their Fifteen Minutes*, 17.

Chapter 11. The Defense

Hauptmann's prints not on the ladder: Erastus Mead Hudson, MD, "One Year After — A Scientific Verdict on the Lindbergh-Hauptmann Riddle," *LMAG*, April 3, 1937, 32–37, NJSPM.

Wilentz claim CAL touched ladder: BRHT, reel 2, part 20,6-7(3853-4), NJSPM.

Erastus Mead Hudson (Direct): BRHT, reel 2, part 019, 76(3798), NJSPM.

Sebastian Benjamin Lupica testimony: BRHT, reel 2, part 17, 42–52(3336-56), NJSPM.

Lupica recalled Hauptmann trial as a "sham": Ahlgren and Monier, *Crime of the Century*, 272–275.

Anna Hauptmann testimony: BRHT, reel 2, part 15, 32–33 (2917-2918), NJSPM.

Wilentz found little to impugn van Henke's testimony: Wilentz brought up that van Henke once operated a speakeasy and used a different last name and that Kiss illegally marketed his own rum. Investigators for the prosecution checked on Kiss's son and found that he was admitted to Bellevue Hospital late on the night of February 22, 1932. Wilentz tried to score a point that it was eight days before March 1, not seven. Lloyd

Fisher pointed out that the doctor visit lasted past midnight into the morning of Tuesday, February 23 — a week before March 1. In any event, Wilentz's effort to paint Kiss as mistaken about the date should have made little sense. Anna Hauptmann did not work at the bakery on Monday nights. Tuesday evening March 1, 1932, was when a man on the street wanted to claim the dog her husband was walking which was what Kiss had heard.

"blow dealt defense": "Baby Kidnapping Laid to Fisch and Violet Sharpe; Blow Dealt Defense," *Los Angeles Times*, February 2, 1935, 3.

Intimidation of Kloppenburg by Wilentz: Kennedy, *The Airman and the Carpenter*, 313–314, quoting Hans Kloppenburg.

Hans Kloppenburg testimony: BRHT, reel 2, part 017, 58 (3363), NJSPM.

Hauptmann's last two witnesses. Contractor Charles de Bisschop volunteered to pay his own way from out of state to testify after he saw Koehler's testimony in the newspaper. When de Bisschop viewed rail 16 he was certain it never had sat on joists. Veteran carpenter Evald Mielk noted the difference in color of rail 16 from the attic floorboard admitted as State Exhibit 226. Koehler still insisted they both came from the same tree. (See Kennedy, *The Airman and the Carpenter,* 319–320.) Actually, if rail 16 was a 2-meter-long crate made overseas its thickness and length made more sense. Planks processed in metric-based countries are about $1/16$ of an inch (1.5 mm) thicker than their American counterparts. (The finished height of a standard American "1 x 4" board = ¾ in. = 19.05 mm. The finished height of a metric " 1 x 4" = 20.5 mm. Although American standards have varied slightly since the 1920s it is likely the difference in standard thicknesses has not changed. Metric standard: (https://www.builderdepot.co.uk/25mm-x-150mm-planed-softwood-par-timber-6in-x-1in) American standard: PS 20-20 "American Softwood Lumber Standard" https://www.nist.gov/system/files/documents/2019/12/11/PS%20 20-20%20final%20WERB%20approved.pdf

Erastus Mead Hudson testimony, BRHT, Reel 2 part 19, 93-94(3832-34), NJSPM. Wilentz suggested to Hudson that the photos were taken of the original ladder rail which was now labeled "Rail 16" and wanted Hudson to confirm this was the same rail he tested in March 1932. Hudson testified he could not confirm from the photograph that this was the rail he tested and refused to take the word of the police that these photos dated back to that time. On Hudson's arrival at the Lindbergh farmhouse on March 13, 1932, he had been shocked to find the kidnap ladder simply gathering dust because the police thought it yielded no fingerprints. (Hudson, "A Scientific Verdict" *LMAG* pdf, 3, NJSPM). Hudson had then gone over every inch of the three-piece ladder. In testifying at the 1935 trial, Hudson remained certain that when he examined the ladder closely in mid-March of 1932 there was only one nail hole in that section of the rail. Yet one of the enlargements he was shown at trial of "Rail 16" had four nail holes in it.

George G. Wilton testimony, BRHT, reel 2, part 21, 35-40 (4110-4120), NJSPM. Kubler did not get assigned to the case until March 10, 1932 (reel 2, 19, 3673-80). He and Kelly took scores of other photos of the ladder that spring, which were not introduced at trial.

Harold Betts testimony: Betts admitted that he did not know when the four nail holes were created BRHT, reel, 2, part 021 (41-44), 4122-4129 at (44) 4128.

"the heat was off": Bates R. Raney, UPS, COL. LINDBERGH MADE THREE MYSTERIOUS TRIPS SINCE LAST MONDAY TO FIND HIS CHILD," Republican and Herald, Pottsville, Pennsylvania, March 10, 1932, 1,4.

Lupica's description of 1929 Dodge sedan: see Fensch, Top Secret, 153-163 and BRHT reel 2, part 017, (42-52) 3336-3357 and reports of NJSP Lt . John Sweeney of March 2, 1932; Det. Ellis Parker, April 4, 1932; Det. E.A. Haussling on Oct. 25, 1932; and Det. Louis Bornmann on Sept. 9, 1933, NJSPM. Col. Schwarzkopf kept a copy of Lupica's description of an unknown suspect in a 1929 Dodge sedan in his own file, obviously considering the sighting of a folded ladder in that car a key clue; yet he never had his men chase it down.

Wooden trunk removed by police after Hauptmann's arrest: Robert Conway, "'Innocent!' Hauptmann Tells Wife", *NYDN*, Jan. 1, 1935, 3,4 citing D.A. Hauck as his source that the trunk was added in 1933 – which was demonstrably false. Several witnesses had seen him with that trunk during 1931-1932. "Hauptmann Visited Georgia Islands in '32," *NYDN*, September 26, 1934, 8. Hauptmann built it for a 1931 summer trip as he describes in detail in his autobiography, *'I am Innocent'* (95, 139); see also Falzini, *Their Fifteen Minutes*, 17-19. Lupica told the press after Hauptmann's arrest that the car he saw had no trunk. "Crime One Man Job, US Holds" *NYDN*, September 22, 1934 , 8.

12. Condemned Without Mercy

Hauck statement re Millard Whited: reel 3, Part 023, (13) 4341.

Wilentz claims all evidence pointed to Hauptmann: reel 3, Part 023,(22-23) 4359-60.

Wilentz asserts there were 4 nail holes in rail 16 in early March, 1932: reel 3, Part 023 (30), 4374.

chisel might have been used "to crush the skull": Summation, BRHT, reel 3, part 023, 46 (4407), NJSPM. See Hoffman, "New Jersey Justice," February 5, 1938; Hoffman, "What was Wrong with the Lindbergh Case," *LMAG*, April 30, 1938, part 14, NJSPM. The chisel found in the yard had the initials "LK" and maybe "J" recently carved into it per the ER Squibb "Report of examination of Steel Chisel received in his office by H.A. Holaday from Detective Bornmann on October 17, 1932.", NJSPM , Melsky, *The Dark Corners*, Vol 3. loc. 3250, n. 678.

Justice Trenchard's charge to the jury: "The Court's Charge, Hauptmann Trial" BRHT, reel 3, part 023, 92-98 (4498-4511); part 024, 1-3 (4512-4516), NJSPM.

Lindbergh noticing Justice Trenchard's bias: see Nigel Nicolson, *Harold Nicolson: Diaries & Letters 1930-1939*, 196, quoting CAL [letter to wife, Feb. 14, 1935] (emphasis in original) Falzini, *Their Fifteen Minutes*, 137.

Trenchard criticism: Falzini and Davidson, *New Jersey's Lindbergh Kidnapping and Trial*, 114.

Judge W. Douglas Duggan, "Fairness on Trial," 11, http://lindberghkidnappinghoax.com/duggan.pdf; Kennedy, *The Airman and the Carpenter*, 338; "Justice Trenchard's Charge to Jury Stressing Burglary Element of the Case," *NYT*, February 14, 1935, 10.

The description of the Morrow/Lindbergh household listening to the radio and commenting on the verdict is from Nicolson, *Harold Nicolson's Diaries*,196–197.

Anne Morrow came to her mother's bedroom in tears on Monday morning, Feb. 11, 1935 after being severely scolded as a "failure" by her husband for not molding her conduct according to his dictates. ECM Diary, Feb. 11, 1935. SCMFP.

NOTE A TO PAGE 282 509

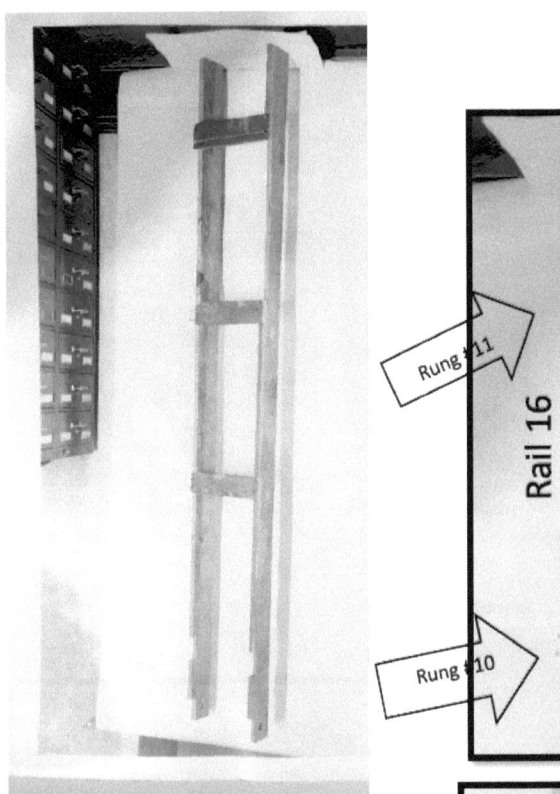

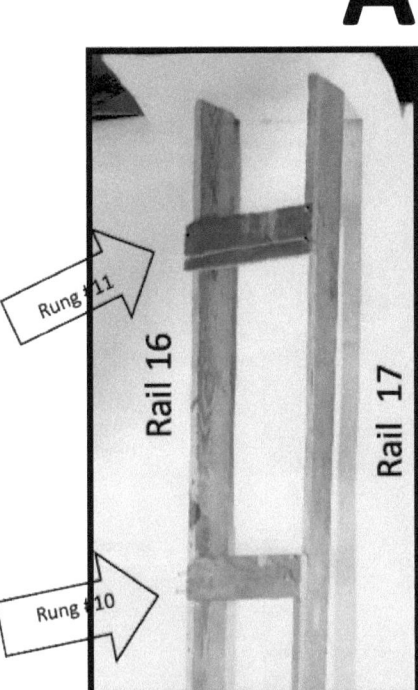

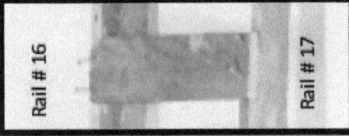
Closeup of rung # 10 with protruding nails attaching it to Rail #16

undated closeup of split in rung # 11

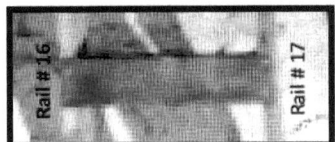
March 2, 1932 closeup of rung # 11

*Caption to photo of Justice Trenchard: Three sets of images of "kidnap ladder" labeled A, B and C. A is an undated police photo of the ladder showing rung #11 with two nails on each end attaching #16. The photo was taken before the police brought in wood expert Arthur Koehler in 1933. (Kelvin Keraga, Testimony in Wood: Analysis of the Rail 16 Evidence in the Lindbergh Kidnapping Summary Report," 2005, p. 12 and note 39, NJSPM). Images are from the Hoage Collection, UCLA. The New Jersey police had also taken pictures on March 2, 1932 which they later shared with Koehler. A closeup of rung #11 taken by the police on March 2 – the day after the kidnapping – does not indicate a visible split like the one in the undated photo. See Keraga, "Testimony in Wood," 1. (*New York Daily News *photos from March 2, 1932 show a similar difference indicating that the police caused the split in the rung sometime later.)*

Hauptmann Trial Exhibit 240

Sketch of the ladder made by state wood expert Arthur Koehler which he testified about at trial. When he first saw the ladder in 1933, the bottom half of rung #11 was already missing. The notch where the bottom of rung #11 had rested on rail #16 is exposed and only one nail is shown on either end of rung #11. (Keraga, "Testimony in Wood, 12 and note 39.) There is no thumb tack in the center of rung #11 — just as in the Hoage photo. There are no longer two nails sticking out where rung #10 attaches to rail #16. Image courtesy of the NJSTPM.

C

Third section

This photo of all three sections of the ladder marked with a tag was taken before the trial where it was introduced as an exhibit. The closeup below of rung #11 on the third section of the ladder shows it broken similarly to the sketch by Koehler. Rung #11 now has only one nail attaching it to rail #16, and the notch is exposed where the lower part of rung #11 previously appeared split. The bottom half of rung #11 is missing.

In the enlargement to the right, it is possible to see that rung #10 no longer has nails sticking out where it attaches to rail #16. Officer Wilton testified that he had first seen this section of the ladder when it looked like it did in the Hoage photo — with the protruding nails where it attached to rail #16. It was not the only change noted by witnesses for both sides in the appearance of the ladder at trial. The state also admitted that all fingerprints revealed by use of silver nitrate on the ladder had been washed off.

Closeup of rungs #10 and 11

13. Raising Doubts

Source of description of pool incident observed by Harold Nicolson: Milton, *Loss of Eden*, 424–425.

"nothing can be accomplished without taking any chance at all": Kennedy, *The Airman and the Carpenter*, 22, quoting Lindbergh.

"Without C., I would lose life . . .": AML, *LROD*, 313 [diary entry, September 17, 1935].

Every justice on the New Jersey high court was a colleague of Justice Thomas Trenchard, who tried the case: Trenchard had gone back to the high court but recused himself from participating in the review of Hauptmann's appeal. His brethren were not about to make this the first conviction ever reversed in Trenchard's long career. The current Chief Justice posed a special risk to the fair consideration of Fisher's arguments on appeal. At Boss Hague's request in 1932, Governor Hoffman's predecessor, Harry Moore, had appointed Hague's personal attorney Thomas Brogan an associate justice of the New Jersey Court of Errors and Appeals. A year later, Governor Moore promoted Brogan to Chief Justice. In getting the judicial appointments he wanted, Hague prized personal loyalty above all else. In one famous argument over a judicial candidate in the 1940s, then Governor Charles Edison wanted "a man of integrity." Hague yelled back: "The hell with his integrity, Charlie. What I want to know is, can you depend on the S.O.B. in a pinch?" See Thomas Fleming, "The Political Machine II: A Case History 'I am the Law,'" American Heritage, June 1969, Vol. 20, Issue 4, www.americanheritage.com. Hague had to be pleased that none of the scores of alleged errors detailed in Hauptmann's appeal gained any traction with the New Jersey high court headed by his own former lawyer.

Source of Anne's description of discussion of a new overseas extended trip with CAL for Pan Am: Series 2002-M-079, Box 15, folder 6, Diaries, "1970, undated," 226–228, 233, YUAML. (When Anne ultimately published her diary, these entries were omitted. Her family donated her diaries to Yale after her death.)

Ellis Parker had told Harold Hoffman the police "have got the wrong man": Hoffman, "What Was Wrong with the Lindbergh Case," February 5, 1938, "Jersey Justice," Week Two, *LMAG*, NJSPM.

The case "will soon be in our laps": Hoffmann "What Went Wrong with the Lindbergh Case," *LMAG*, Feb. 19, 1938, 47. See Behn, *Lindbergh: The Crime*, 317, n. 1.

Squire Johnson's request that Gov. Hoffman keep digging into the case: Gardner, *The Case That Never Dies*, 117.

The Bureau had been told state police had followed up on all potential suspects: Fensch, *Top Secret*, 98-99.

"unhappy, restless — must get away from Englewood": AML, *LROD*, Saturday (November 2, 1935), 595, quoting CAL.

Governor Hoffman announces he is reopening the case: Behn, *Lindbergh: The Crime*, 326, n. 9.

"Thousands of rumors" quoted from Harold Hoffman, signed official statement, December 7, 1935, NJSPM.

Going "abroad to England or Sweden . . . on 24-hours-notice": AML, *LROD*, 331, quoting CAL.

Request for confidential FBI files "preposterous": Memorandum to JEH from E. A. Tamm, December 10, 1935, FBI files, NJSPM [declassified February 14, 2003].

New ultraviolet technique; UV test suggests BRH framed, final test inconclusive: Robert Conway, "TESTS HINT LADDER 'FRAME UP' NAILED HAUPTMANN" *NYDN,* March 1, 1936, 3; Robert Conway, "'FRAME UP' BOTH SIDES CRY IN BRUNO LADDER CLASH", *NYDN,* March 27, 1936, 2; "Bruno's Wood Tested at Physics by Hoffman," *Columbia Daily Spectator,* Vol. LIX, No. 107, March 27, 1936, 1.

New evidence received by Gov. Hoffman: Anthony Scaduto, *Scapegoat,* 456–460; Kennedy, *The Airman and the Carpenter,* 153–154. Kennedy was skeptical of the Fisch evidence. Yet historian Lloyd Gardner notes that the steamship agent, George Steinweig, signed a statement on October 25, 1934, detailing the transaction, and Det. Ellis Parker investigated the claim and corroborated it with bank officials. See Gardner, *The Case that Never Dies,* 369 and n. 31. The failure by the police to list such a large transaction by Fisch could have been upon the request of Lindbergh and Breckinridge to cover up Fisch's role in disseminating the ransom money for which Fisch was also implicated by Cuban lawyer Arturo Gonzales. ["Cuban Offers Kidnap Clue," *The Tampa Times* (Tampa, Florida), Jan. 28, 1936, 7.]

Pastori swore he was told by a company official to keep his mouth shut: affidavit of Humberto Pastori, dated Feb. 27, 1936. From Leon Hoage collection of material about the Lindbergh kidnapping case (Collection 1066) UCLA Library Special Collections, Charles E. Young Research Library, UCLA.

14. "Old Smokey"

Postponement of execution three days due to grand jury proceedings: "2 NEW CLEWS BROADEN LINDY CASE; Wendel Kidnapper Confesses, Bills May Clear Bruno," *Indianapolis Star,* April 20, 1936, 1.

Hauptmann quote is from Bruno Richard Hauptmann, "Why Did You Kill Me?" *LMAG,* May 2, 1936. He ended the article: "I could not conceive in the face of such overwhelming proof [of innocence] that I could be held as the kidnaper of the Lindbergh baby. I was to learn to my bitter sorrow just how mistaken I really was."

"And so I sit, ten feet removed from the electric chair, and unless something can be done to aid me, unless something can be done to make someone tell the truth, or unless someone does tell it, I shall at eight o'clock Friday evening, in response to the call from my keepers, raise myself for the last time and shall walk that 'last mile," Hauptmann's dying statements are quoted both in Kennedy, *The Airman and the Carpenter,* 400, and Hoffman, Part 7, "The Crime, the Case, the Challenge," *LMAG,* "How Hauptmann died," March 12, 1938.

"BRUNO DIES IN CHAIR," *NYDN* (Extra Edition), April 4, 1936, 1.

"the bent of my mother's family . . ." Mosley, *Lindbergh: A Biography,* 205, quoting Nigel Nicolson, *Harold Nicolson's Diary,* 270–271.

The coded message from Breckinridge and its decoded contents are in YUCAL, May 29, 1936, letter from HSB to CAL. HSB conveyed a message from Colonel Schwarzkopf that he intended to "box and deliver to me [HSB] all your personal files" if not reappointed to head the NJSP by Hoffman in June 1936. HSB added, "If Hoffman reappoints him, he will take his time delivering the material." On May 29, 1936, Schwarzkopf wrote to HSB: that he would confer with Attorney General Wilentz and County Prosecutor Hauck on June 1, "at which time we will make arrangements in accordance with your request."

Quote from AML biographer Dorothy Herrmann is from Herrmann, *AML, The Gift of Life*, 177.

Photo kept by investigator Leon Hoage of the boy on a tricycle: source UCLA Hoage Collection. On the back of the photo an unidentified author (likely Hoage) wrote in pencil "Last File of US." "Lindbergh File" is written in black ink below. Hoage's wife, Lyra, sent the photo to the UCLA Law Library on Jan. 22, 1968 with a note that she had just come across it. UCLA accepted Lyra's offer to add it to the collection of her late husband's Lindbergh kidnapping investigation files that she had given UCLA five years earlier. In her 2011 blog post, Yasmin Damshenas, the UCLA archivist for the Leon Hoage collection, wrote that the boy on the tricycle was Charles Lindbergh, Jr. "shortly before the abduction," https://www.library.ucla.edu/blog/special/2011/11/04/evidence-in-the-crime-of-the-century. Michael Melsky, long-time Lindbergh researcher, author and administrator of the lindberghkidnap.proboard.com site, contends that the photograph is not Charlie, but "a picture sent by someone to the Governor thinking it might be the Lindbergh child." Michael Melsky, message board post, Dec. 24, 2014, lindberghkidnap.proboards.com, http://lindberghkidnap.proboards.com/thread/992/leon-hoage-files-ucla (Yet Hoage would likely have confirmed the ID with Dr. Van Ingen, Mrs. Morrow or her staff).

New York trial lawyer quoted at Hoffman, "What Was Wrong with the Lindbergh Case," *LMAG*, part 12, April 16, 1938, NJSPM.

Hoffman considered Whateley's sudden death suspicious: A minister called to visit Whateley told his son that Whateley conveyed a secret about the case that the minister felt duty-bound to keep confidential. See Melsky, *Vol II*, 9, n. 32, citing an unsigned list, undated, Hoffman Collection, NJSPM; *NYDN*, May 24, 1933, 12.

Hoffman's quotes are from Hoffman, "What Was Wrong with the Lindbergh Case," *LMAG*, part 12, April 16, 1938 and part 14, April 30, 1938, NJSPM PDF copy [emphasis in original].

Crowds gathered to see the hearse are described in Falzini and Davidson, *Images of America: New Jersey's Lindbergh Kidnapping and Crime*, 123-124.

"Old Smokey": see National Coalition to Abolish the Death Penalty, Innocence: Death Penalty Information Center https://deathpenaltyinfo.org/policy-issues/innocence

ACT FOUR

1. Kindred Spirits

The height of white supremacy since colonial days: Eric Foner, *Reconstruction: America's Unfinished Revolution* (New York: Harper & Row, 1988), 608.

Spanish-American War Hero Teddy Roosevelt: The unheralded all-black 24th Infantry played a pivotal role in winning the Battle of San Juan Hill for which Roosevelt was honored.

"THE AMERICAN FLAG etc." McKinley-Roosevelt Presidential Campaign Poster 1900: https://commons.wikimedia.org_Administration%27s_Promises_Have_Be/wiki.

"Defective germ plasm" quote is from Edwin Black, *War Against the Weak: Eugenics and America's Campaign to Create a Master Race* (Washington, D.C., Devon Press, 2003), 17.

Madison Grant quotes are from Madison Grant, *The Passing of the Great Race* (New York: Charles Scribner's Sons, 1916), 50.

The leading high school textbook was George W. Hunter, *A Civic Biology Presented in Problems* (New York: American Book Co., 1914), [Google Books, http://books.google.com/books?id=-yl.] Hunter instructed students on his view of the hierarchy of humans:
"The Races of Man. –
At the present time there exist upon the earth five races or varieties
of man, each very different from the other in instincts, social
customs, and, to an extent, in structure. These are the Ethiopian
or negro type, originating in Africa; the Malay or brown race, from
the islands of the Pacific; The American Indian; the Mongolian or
yellow race, including the natives of China, Japan, and the Eskimos;
and finally, the highest type of all, the Caucasians, represented by
the civilized white inhabitants of Europe and America." *A Civic Biology* at 261.

Nevins, *A Tale of Two "Villages,"* 44.

Dr. Laughlin had already convinced the U.S. Census Bureau to make him a special agent to create a master list of all persons held in custodial or charitable institutions — all of whom were already classified by the Census Bureau as "dependent, delinquent or defective": Black, *War Against the Weak*, 159. Included among the targets of Dr. Laughlin's model law for involuntary sterilization were those he labeled "criminalistic" (including the "delinquent and wayward"). His list included: *(b) The socially inadequate classes, regardless of etiology or prognosis, are the following: (1) Feeble-minded; (2) Insane (including the psychopathic); (3) Criminalistic (including the delinquent and wayward); (4) Epileptic; (5) Inebriate (including drug-habitués); (6) Diseased (including the tuberculous, the syphilitic, the leprous, and others with chronic, infectious and legally segregable diseases); (7) Blind (including those with seriously impaired vision); (8) Deaf (including those with seriously impaired hearing); (9) Deformed (including the crippled); and (10) Dependent (including orphans, ne'er-do-wells, the homeless, tramps and paupers).*

Harry Laughlin's "Model Eugenical Sterilization Law," reproduced by Asst. Prof. Alex Wellerstein of the Stevenson Institute of Technology, at http://alexwellerstein.com/laughlin/.

Buck v. Bell: Looking at the skewed record in the case then before the high court, Justice Holmes concluded that forced sterilization of 19-year-old Cary Buck was justified because "Three generations of imbeciles are enough." *Buck v. Bell* upheld 8-to-1 involuntary tubal ligation of teenager Carrie Buck as a procedure for the public benefit based only on a state-employed doctor labeling both Carrie (who had given birth to a baby after being raped) and her mother "feebleminded and promiscuous." (274 U.S. 200 at 207.) This characterization of the family later proved unfounded. In fact, the state of Virginia had given carte blanche to doctors it hired to decide who got that label and who did not, so "imbecile" might refer to a prostitute, as it did in the case of Cary Buck's mother. Dr. Laughlin, who drafted the model law, believed that millions of people deserving sterilization superficially appeared normal. Doctors were rarely questioned when they made that diagnosis of someone from a lower social class. The label of "imbecile" — however loosely defined — was clearly misapplied to Cary Buck and her baby.

"socially inadequate": Black, *War Against the Weak,* 159.

An economic and moral burden — Nevins, "Dr. Alexis Carrel, Medical Marvel & Moral Monster," self-published pamphlet, 10–11.

"serious menace . . . white races": AC, testimony to the American Breeders Association, 1911, cited in Nevins, "Dr. Alexis Carrel, "Medical Marvel & Moral Monster," self-published pamphlet, (undated) 10–11.

Ebeling had focused on human tissue: David Hamilton, *The First Transplant Surgeon: The Flawed Genius of Nobel Prize Winner Alexis Carrel* (Kindle ed. 2017), 320–321.

"If I could do the same tests on humans": Friedman, *The Immortalists,* 10, quoting AC.

"No real warmth": Walter S. Ross, *The Last Hero: Charles A. Lindbergh* (New York: Harper & Row, 1976), 368.

"Not all for the good": Ross, *The Last Hero,* 242.

"those who should be dead . . . kill off the worst . . . ": Nevins, *Meanderings in Medical History: Book Four,* 97, quoting AC.

2. The High Priest of Biology

"The high priest of biology" is a title used to describe AC in a long article in the *NYT Magazine* just after *The Culture of Organs* was published: "Carrel, at 65, is Deep in New Studies of Man: and Man, All of Him, is his One Interest," June 26, 1938, 3.

Unnecessary suffering: "Dog Torture Story Called Ridiculous," *NYT*, December 28, 1909, 16.

AC defended himself: Affidavit of AC, Rockefeller Institute Archives, FA 913, Box 2, folder 1, January 25, 1910.

He saved the infant daughter: "Five-Day Baby Saved By Blood Transfusion," *The Washington Times*, March 20, 1908, 6.

the lesser harm: Sydney A. Halpern, *Lesser Harms: The Morality of Risk In Medicine* (Chicago, Illinois: University of Chicago Press, 2004), 3–6.

Breakthroughs in addressing recurrent epidemics: Hamilton, *The First Transplant Surgeon*, 88.

Four out of five Nobel prizes: The context was very different then from now, though research scientists continue to push the boundaries in sometimes losing battles with animal rights activists. In 2018 activists forced the Department of Agriculture to terminate a program that involved killing thousands of cats by forcing them to eat contaminated meat. Opponents called the practice "kitten cannibalism." See "USDA Terminates Deadly Cat Experiments, Plans To Adopt Out Remaining Animals; https://www.npr.org/2019/04/02/709273861/usda-terminates-deadly-cat-experiments-plans-to-adopt-out-remaining-animals.

Loyal Davis, *Fellowship of Surgeons: A History of the American College of Surgeons* (American College of Surgeons: Chicago: 1993), 50–51. *The Philadelphia Press* headlined its Friday morning story on November 10 [1911]: 'Man's Kidney Transferred to Living Dog.'. . . Dr. Alexis Carrel gave an illustrated lecture on the technique and results of blood vessel anastomosis and explained the transplantation of a human kidney in a dog which lived for two years afterward." But see "Dr. Hammond Gives Patient New Kidney," *NYT*, Nov. 14, 1911, 2, which reported the opposite, that AC transplanted a dog's kidney to a man. *The Philadelphia Press* reported more details and appears more reliable.

AC inquiry about condemned men: "Would Experiment on Condemned Men; Dr. Carrel Believes the State Should Give Scientists The Right To Do So," *NYT*, July 25, 1909, C 2.

"The father of modern gynecology": Dr. Sims' tools included a shoemaker's awl used to maneuver fetal skulls. In the summer of 2017, a controversial Central Park statue dedicated to Dr. Sims wound up relocated in early 2018 to a cemetery in Brooklyn. See Olivia B. Waxman, "New York City Has Just Removed A Statue of Surgeon J. Marion Sims From Central Park, Here's Why," *TIME*, April 17, 2018; http://time.com/5243443/nyc-statue-marion-sims/.

Source of description of early 20th century human medical experiments: Susan Lederer, *Subjected to Science: Human Experimentation in America before the Second World War* (Baltimore & London: Johns Hopkins University Press, 1995).

Puerto Rican scandal: Two investigations found no ethical violations but an award in Rhoads's honor was later renamed because of his blatant racism. Douglas Starr, "Revisiting a 1930s Scandal: AACR to Rename a Prize," *Science* (April 25, 2003) Vol. 300, Issue 5619, pp. 573-74.

Tuskegee syphilis experiments: "Rockefeller, Johns Hopkins Behind Horrific Human Syphilis Experiments] Allege Guatemalan Victims in Lawsuit," April 1, 2015; https://www.prnewswire.com/news-releases/rockefeller-johns-hopkins-behind-horrific-human-syphilis-experiments-allege-guatemalan-victims-in-lawsuit-300059537.html.

The cultivation of tissues by AC and Burrows: Hannah Landecker, *Culturing Life: How Cells Became Technologies* (Harvard University Press: Cambridge, Massachusetts, 2007), 51–53.

Guthrie also considered for the 1912 Nobel prize: H. E. Stephenson, Jr., R. S. Kimpton, G. M. Masters, *America's First Nobel Prize in Medicine or Physiology: The Story of Guthrie and Carrel* (Midwestern Vascular Surgery Society; Boston, MA: 2000).

1912 *NYT* story re AC: "Carrel's Miracles in Surgery Win Nobel Prize," *NYT*, Oct. 13, 1912. AC suggested that future surgeons could "easily take such tissue in large quantities from the fresh cadavers of fetuses and cadavers. Whether he only used skin from infants who were already dead was not stated. "The results obtained by Tuffier, Magitot, and myself demonstrate that human tissues preserved in cold storage could be used in human surgery. Future investigators will show in what measure tissues of infants should be employed as grafts. The tissues actually used in human surgery, as cartilage, periosteum, skin and aponeuroses could easily be taken in large quantities from the fresh cadavers of foetuses and infants preserved in vaseline in cold storage." [AC quoted at American Medical Association annual conference at Atlantic City in June 1911.]

AC's films awed attendees and reporters: Landecker, *Culturing Life*, 85–86.

Replicating themselves generally 50 times: David Hamilton, *The First Transplant Surgeon: The Flawed Genius of Nobel Prize Winner Alexis Carrel* (Kindle ed. 2017), 320–321.

AC believed the best information came from humans themselves: Pietro Croce, *Vivisection or Science? An Investigation into Testing Drugs and Safeguarding Health* (Zed Books, 1999), 12. See diary entries in AC, *Jour après Jour*, 1893–1944 (Paris: Librairie Plon, Les Petits-Fils de Plon et Nourit, 1956), April 6 and 7, 1932.

newspaper clipping re chicken heart experiment: Georgetown University, AC Papers, Box 75, Section 19-3, Folder 193, dated "January 18, 1932." [Unsourced article called: "Chicken's Heart to 'Live Forever.'"]

Rockefeller Institute 2018 hybrid experiment: NBC News, "Why Scientists Created Human Chicken Hybrid Embryo," June 6, 2018; https://www.nbcnews.com/mach/science/why-scientists-created-human-chicken-hybrid-embryo-ncna880406 .

Era of medical paternalism: (Nevins, *A Tale of Two "Villages"*, 11): To understand that medical era one only need look at the work of one of AC"s valued colleagues, Dr. Henry Cotton, the director of New Jersey's oldest mental institution in Trenton. Back in 1915, Rockefeller Institute for Medical Research Director Simon Flexner reached out both to Princeton President Hibbard and to Dr. Cotton to help change the laws in New Jersey so research scientists like AC could avoid state oversight of vivisection experiments at its planned animal pathology laboratory near Princeton. For most of his 26-year career, Cotton was considered a national leader, much sought after by wealthy families for his experimental, surgical approach to curing mental illness. Dr. Cotton conducted thousands of invasive procedures on patients, including extraction of all teeth and partial colon removal, on the unsubstantiated theory he was eliminating "toxins" invading his patients' brains.

In his aggressive approach to surgery, Dr. Cotton frequently overrode both the objections of patients and their families, while hiding from the public a shocking mortality rate in the 1920s and early 1930s from major surgery of thirty to forty per cent. Through 1932, Cotton continued to fend off accusations of malpractice with the strong backing of

Commissioner Ellis of the State Board of Overseers. Cotton claimed that his patients were already at high risk when they came to him and that post-operative deaths from sepsis were not attributable to the major surgery he had just conducted. Cotton had obtained his job back in 1906 after the prior director of the Trenton mental institution was fired for "patient abuse and scandals" (See Nevins, *A Tale of Two Villages*, 8). One shudders to think what that doctor did to get ousted.

Skillman executives provided the exhibits: Back in 1911, Skillman's board members had played a leading role in drafting a pioneering state law to authorize involuntary sterilizations in New Jersey. The legislature then passed, by overwhelming vote, "An Act to Authorize and Provide for the Sterilization of Feebleminded (Including Idiots, Imbeciles and Morons), Epileptics, Rapists, Certain Criminals and Other Defectives." Governor Woodrow Wilson eagerly signed the bill into law. The procedure was immediately challenged by a test case involving a woman epileptic at Skillman whom the Board subjected to an involuntary salpingectomy (removal of a Fallopian tube) to prevent her from giving birth despite the fact her last epileptic seizure had been five years earlier. The New Jersey Supreme Court then became the first to declare a sterilization law unconstitutional. AC was on the sterilization committee. See Bleecker Van Wagenen, "Surgical Sterilization as a Eugenics Measure," *Journal of Psycho-Asthenics*, vol. xviii, June 1914, no. 4. See "Eugenics Records Office, Bulletin 10B, Feb. 1914, Harry H. Laughlin, *Report of the Committee to Study and Report on the Best Practical Means of Cutting Off the Defective Germ-Plasm in the American Population: II*. See *The Legal, Legislative and Administrative Aspects of Sterilization*, Eugenics Records Office, Cold Spring Harbor, Long Island, NY, 5, for a list of the committee members.

Skillman and Vineland remained laboratories for the next three decades: See Halpern, *Lesser Harms*, 76, 139, n. 31 and discussion and notes in Act Four, ch. 7, p. 344 and notes p. 523.

Voronoff argued for specialized hospitals: In an age long before Viagra, Dr. Voronoff became immensely popular among men with erectile dysfunction. In his 1920 book, *Life: A Study of the Means of Restoring Vital Energy and Prolonging Life*, Voronoff bemoaned the fact that he had to rely mostly on monkey testicles for experimentation because "prejudice and legislation are still opposed to [human donors]." He hoped for a time when sentimentality was replaced with "the lofty consciousness of a superior duty: the service of humanity even after death." See Serge Voronoff. *Life: A Study of the Means of Restoring Vital Energy and Prolonging Life* (New York: E.P. Dutton & Co., 1920), 86.

AC, *Jour après Jour*, 39 (May 4, 1925) (English translation by Leslie Pearlman).

The quoted journal entries are from AC, *Jour après Jour*, 53–54, 102 (July 29, 1929 and December 1931) (English translation by Leslie Pearlman).

3. A New Mission

Lindbergh put in long weeks: (Berg, *Lindbergh*, 224).

Almost anything that he wanted . . . his world fame": Joseph T. Durgin, S.J., *Hope for Our Time: Alexis Carrel on Man and Society* (New York: Harper & Row, 1965), 129.

Water bucket anecdote: Ross, quoting former Rockefeller Institute colleague of Lindbergh, Dr. Richard Bing, *The Last Hero*, 232.

CAL visit to Carnegie Institute: "Lindbergh Inspects Eugenics Exhibit at Cold Springs Harbor," *BDE*, January 22, 1931, 15.

The description of AC's lab and operations comes from *CO*, 80.

"Quick confident motions...": Friedman, *The Immortalists*, 33.

index and middle finger technique source: "Carrel's Man" *TIME* magazine September 16, 1935, 47.

"Nothing good about death": CAL, AV, 5.

"see across the border": Friedman, *The Immortalists*, citing CAL, AV, 134–135.

"one great eye": CAL, *SSL*, 390.

4. A Breakthrough at the Lab

Anonymous article: "APPARATUS TO CIRCULATE LIQUID UNDER CONSTANT PRESSURE IN A CLOSED SYSTEM," *Science*, Vol. 73, Issue 1899, 22 May 1931, 566.

"Virtual" motion picture source: "Albert Ebeling, "Biologist, 82; Expert on Body Cells Dies, Worked With Carrel," *NYT*, June 28, 1965, L28.

Wyckoff collaboration with CAL: CAL's 1932 diary mentions meeting with Wyckoff several times and taking him flying. CAL Diary 1931–1932, YUCAL. See George Corner's *A History of the Rockefeller Institute: 1901–1953*, 184, mentions Wyckoff's collaboration with AC's team. Theodore Malinin's biography of AC also references both AC's and CAL's ongoing working relationship with Wyckoff in the 1930s. See Theodore Malinin, *Surgery and Life: The Extraordinary Career of Alexis Carrel*, (New York: HBJ, 1979), 189.

"Bioengineering was in its infancy": Joyce Milton, *Loss of Eden: A Biography of Charles and Anne Morrow Lindbergh* (New York: Harper Collins Publishers, 1993), 202.

"never seen him as happy" ... he was "*very* secretive and shy": AML, *HGHL*, 243 [Letter to ELLL, April 29, 1932]. [Emphasis on "very" was Anne Morrow's.]

Mme. Carrel's NY visit and flight with CAL & Ebelings: CAL diary entry, Feb 22, 1932, YUCAL. Author David Hamilton's 2017 biography of AC mentions that AC had plans to have dinner with CAL on February 27, 1932. See David Hamilton, *The First Transplant Surgeon*, 382. But the Lindberghs dined on Saturday, February 27, and Sunday, February 28, at their farmhouse outside Hopewell only with the Breckinridges, so Leap Day, February 29, seems more likely. CAL did go to the lab that day and often dined with AC when in Manhattan. CAL sometimes worked all night at the Rockefeller lab, but he told his wife he spent Monday night at her mother's mansion in Englewood while Mrs. Morrow was away. This was not corroborated by Anne's sister Elisabeth who was at the mansion Monday night and told her mother that she believed CAL was then staying with Anne at the farmhouse. (Source: Mrs. Dwight Morrow statement to Lt Sweeney & Det. Strong, Newark PD March 16, 1932, YUCAL.)

Mme Carrel likely lent a hand: Perry, Vernon. P. "Charles A. Lindbergh 1902-1974" *In Vitro*, Sept-Oct, 1975, Vol. 11, No. 5, 247-250, 248.

5. The Landmark Artery Experiment

Carrel's department billed the institute: See "Microcinema" charge sheet, February 29, 1932, AC Papers, GUBSC. This sheet required a second page to include the high number of charges, while the other available 1932 charge sheets only needed one page.

two lab assistants would be assigned to photograph: AC & CAL, *CO*, viii.

Key members of Carrel's team included . . . : From April 1932 Report on Work, Division of Experimental Surgery, 87, AC Papers, GUBSC.

Parker's human fibroblast experiments including prior experiments with serum of a 14-month-old infant in 1931 (See April 1932 Report, 87, 101; also Parker, R. C., "Human serum, age and multiplication of homologous fibroblasts," *Science* (Aug. 14, 1931), vol. 74, 181–182.

For Dr. Parker's detailed description of carotid artery experiments, human serum preparation, and materials used in AC's lab: see Parker, *Methods of Tissue Culture* (New York: Paul B. Hoeber, 1938), 53–66.

Rockefeller Institute's lab workers wore rubber overshoes to avoid contamination: see J. R. Beach, "BACTERIOLOGICAL STUDY OF INFECTIOUS LARYNGOTRACHEITIS OF CHICKENS," (from the Department of Animal Pathology of The Rockefeller Institute for Medicine [received for publication July 28, 1931], 802.

CAL's unusually large feet: "[Lindbergh's] Feet: Large. When he arrived at the Embassy in France no shoes big enough were handy." Lindbergh's profile from *TIME* magazine's inaugural "Man of the Year" issue. "Heroes: Lindbergh" *TIME* magazine, January 2, 1928, no. 1, 10.

CAL 11D shoe size: Lindbergh donated his size 11D pair of civilian flying boots to the Smithsonian National Air and Space Museum where they were put on display at the Steven F. Udvar-Hazy Center in Chantilly, VA; https://airandspace.si.edu/collection-objects/boots-flying-civilian-charles-lindbergh-0.

Carrel's team prepared mica discs with plasma and phenol red . . . : see Parker, *MOTC*, chapter IX: "Hanging Drop Cultures" 85–97. For mica properties, see http://www.adhunikudyog.com/what_is_mica.php.

Parker's description of fibroblast experiments: Parker, *MOTC* (1938), 85–97.

AC's month-long carotid artery experiment: April 1932 Report on Work, 92–93, AC papers, Box 17, Sec. 19-1, folder 35, GUBSC.

Official history of the Rockefeller Institute: George W. Corner, *A History of the Rockefeller Institute (1901–1953): Origins and Growth* (New York: Rockefeller Institute Press, 1964), 233.

AC gave the lion's share of credit to CAL: April 1932 Report, 91–94, AC Papers, GUBSC.

CAL's diary entries for March and April: CAL kept a regular diary in 1932, but after February 24 there are no entries available until April 16, 1932 (This six-week period covers several significant events: Charlie's disappearance, Jafsie's involvement as go-between, and AC & CAL's month-long historic experiment — about which CAL had made regular updates in his diary up through February 24 preparing for it. Diaries, 1931–1932 (Diaries, 1912–1939 May 9), YUCAL.

Jour après Jour book jacket quote: Carrel's widow and book editors described the object of the two men's joint experiments as "tissus vivants transportés hors de leur milieu." AC, *Jour après Jour*, back cover [translation by Leslie Pearlman].

6. Hitler Embraces Carrel's "Ideal" Solution

A. A. Brill, "Is 'Mercy Killing' Justified?" with a reply to Dr. Alexis Carrel, November 25, 1935, *Vital Speeches of the Day*, December 16, 1935, Vol. 2, Issue 6, *The Important Addresses of the Leading Moulders of Public Opinion, Volume II, October 7, 1935 – October 1, 1936* (New York: The City News Publishing Co., Inc) 165–167.

The Germans made compulsory: Maurizio Meloni, *Political Biology: Science and Social Values in Human Heredity from Eugenics to Epigenetics* (New York: Palgrave MacMillan, 2016), 149, citing Stefan Kuhl, *The Nazi Connection: Eugenics, American Racism and German National Socialism* (Oxford: Oxford University Press, 1994).

Joseph De Jarnette quote: Egbert Klautke,"'The Germans are Beating us at our own Game': American Eugenics and the German Sterilization Law of 1933," http://discovery.ucl.ac.uk/1471934/3/Eugenics%20USA%20Germany%2010-2015%20HARVARD%20REVISED%20FINAL.PDF.

"eugenics" defined as putting to death undesirable people: Hamilton, *The First Transplant Surgeon*, 357–359, citing AC, *Man, The Unknown*, 318, n. 9.

"small, euthanistic institutions": AC, *Man, The Unknown*, 9, 16, 268, cited in Hamilton, *The First Transplant Surgeon*, 343, n. 16.

The ideal solution: *Der Mensch, das unbekannte Wesen*. DVA, Stuttgart (1937) as translated by Andrés Horacio Reggiani: *God's eugenicist: Alexis Carrel and the sociobiology of decline* (Oxford: Berghahn Books, 2007), 71, n. 49.

Foreshadowing Hitler's final solution: Hamilton, *The First Transplant Surgeon*, 369.

"the bent of my mother's family . . . ": Nicolson, *Harold Nicolson's Diary*, 270–271, quoting CAL.

"I am glad to have it known . . .": AML, *LROD*, June 1, 1935, 278.

AML quotes regarding her husband's scientific achievement: AML, *LROD*, June 1, 1935, 278.

"scary cult of personality": *Jesse Owens*. TV documentary. WGBH Educational Foundation, 2012. Presented on YALE TV 1, 9 July 2014.

Anne's description of Hitler. Eric Pace, "Anne Morrow Lindbergh, 94, Dies; Champion of Flight and Women's Concerns," *NYT*, February 8, 2001, A29, quoting a letter to her mother.

The Munich Accord was expected to produce lasting peace, with the agreement of France, Great Britain and Italy not to oppose Germany's annexation of Czechoslovakia on Hitler's promise he would not invade any other European country. The Czech people called it "The Munich Betrayal."

Carrel's problems with the new Director of Rockefeller Institute are described by Malinin, *Surgery and Life*, 176. Princeton University acquired the Rockefeller Institute's animal and plant pathology laboratories in the early 1950s; these buildings were repurposed as part of the James Forrestal Campus. See "Forrestal Campus" from Alexander Leitch, *A Princeton Companion*, copyright Princeton University Press (1978); https://etcweb.princeton.edu/CampusWWW/Companion/forrestal_campus.html

Letter from AC's head nurse Irene McFaul to Colonel and Mrs. Lindbergh, July 17 (1936?), Rockefeller Institute for Medical Research, 1931–1936, YUCAL.

AC speech re "the weak, the diseased, etc": cited in Nevins, *Meanderings in Medical History, Book Four*, 99.

"one of their own": Berg, *Lindbergh*, 323, n. 10, citing Rockefeller archive files.

7. The Culture of Organs

"nectar of immortality": Ilia Stambler, "India and the Tradition of Longevity," India Future Society, June 3, 2013; http://indiafuturesociety.org/longevity-and-the-indian-tradition/Articles re Lindberghs' trip to India and birth of Land: "Lindbergh Believed Surveying Air Route," *The Boston Globe*, April 6, 1937, 7; "Third son is Born to Lindberghs," *The Oakland Tribune*, May 24, 1937, 1.

"practically every important organ had been studied": Hamilton, *The First Transplant Surgeon*, 422, citing AC's speech at a meeting of the American Philosophical Society on April 21, 1938, in Philadelphia.

"out of all proportion": Ross, *The Last Hero*, 233.

The *NYT* reaction to AC's experiments: *"At 65, Deep in New Studies," NYT, NYT Magazine*, June 26, 1938, 3, 17.

Quote re improvements to perfusion designed by CAL: AC and CAL, *CO*, 14.

The official history noted that AC was not able to use his technique on humans: George W. Corner, *A History of the Rockefeller Institute: 1901–1953: Origins and Growth* (New York: Rockefeller Institute Press, 1964) 229.

"It happens today . . . ": AC and CAL, *CO*, 219.

"Although the cultivation of organs . . . ": AC and CAL, *CO*, 14.

"A forbidden field . . . ": AC and CAL, *CO*, 219.

Letter re "feeble-minded prospects" is quoted in Milton, *Loss of Eden*, 505, n. 5, citing letter from E. P. Earle to AC, Box 75, Sec. 311, AC Papers, GUBSC; see also Friedman, *The Immortalists*, 81. [The letter itself is now missing from GUBSC.]

"experiments on live humans . . . ": Friedman, *The Immortalists*, 81.

Another visiting doctor conducted pneumonia experiments at Skillman. In November, 1924, NY Health officials Dr. Abraham Zingher and David C. Bowen conducted scarlet fever experiments on 800 Skillman patients in the presence of then Commissioner of Institutions and Agencies Burdette Lewis and Superintendent David Weeks. "Scarlet Fever Test Given at Epileptic Village as Experiment," *Plainfield-Courier News*, November 5, 1924, 5. In the winter of 1936–1937, sponsored in part by the Rockefeller Foundation, Dr. Joseph Stokes, Jr., performed influenza experiments on human subjects at Skillman Village, Vineland Training School, and other New Jersey institutions. See Halpern, *Lesser Harms*, 76, 139, Chapter Three, n. 31.

Skillman death statistics: The high point was in 1929 when Skillman had 73 out of 158 investigated deaths for Somerset County — 46.2% of the county's total investigated deaths. "Report for Year is Presented by County Physician," *Plainfield Courier News*, Dec. 28, 1929, 7. In 1930, Skillman had 65 out of 159 investigated deaths for Somerset County (40.8% of the county's total investigated deaths. "County Physician Investigates 159 For County, Year," *Plainfield Courier News*, Jan. 12, 1931, 10. In 1931, Skillman had 56 out of 156 investigated deaths for Somerset County (35.9% of yje county's total investigated deaths.)" County Physician Reports for 1931," *Plainfield Courier News*, Jan. 2, 1932, 2. The county death report was not located for the year ending December 1932, which may have been due to the fact County Physician George Mack died in January. See "Dr. G. L. Mack Succumbs to Heart Attack," *Courier-News*, Jan. 17, 1933, 1. In 1933, Skillman had 60 out of 171 investigated deaths for Somerset County (35.08% of the county's total investigated deaths. "Autos Caused 23 Deaths in County," *Central New Jersey Home News*, Jan. 20, 1934, 5. The 1933 analysis was performed by a successor county physician.

8. The Highfields Center for the Science of Man

Something less grim: correspondence from Dr. Abraham Flexner to CAL, June 15, 1933, and reply from CAL to Dr. Flexner, June 19, 1933, with original papers of incorporation; Box 12, Abraham Flexner Papers, LOC.

"Lindbergh Welfare Plan Is Approved," *The Spring Lake Gazette, Spring Lake, N.J.*, June 29, 1933, 8; "Lindbergh Gift For Children Wins Family For Children Wins Thanks and Sympathy," *Asbury Park Evening Press*, July 15, 1933, 8, quoting the *Newark Evening Star*.

Simon Flexner is quoted in the *Wilkes-Barre Times Leader, Evening News* (Wilkes-Barre, PA), June 24, 1933, 12.

"tested and validated": Nevins, *A Tale of Two "Villages,"* 26.

Princeton University's support helped legalize Carrel's vivisection experiments. "Hibben Advocates Vivisection Law," *The Morning Post* (Camden, NJ) Feb 16, 1915; 11.

Skillman took no action for the next couple of years: Milton, *Loss of Eden*, 377.

CAL correspondence with Ellis: letter from Commissioner William J. Ellis to CAL at the Institute for Medical Research of the Rockefeller Foundation, January 18, 1938, and CAL reply letter, Series I, Box 10, Folder 287, YUCAL.

"hospital that could supply human tumors and human organs": copy of AC letter to Dr. Sherman, 2, Selected Correspondence: Incoming, YUCAL.

Signage at the World's Fair: Friedman, *The Immortalists*, 167.

AC's former team members at RIMR: Lederer, Zwick, Letter to CAL, September 20, 1939, YUCAL.

AC's complaints about RIMR management: AC letter to CAL, February 22, 1939, Select Correspondence (Incoming), 2, YUCAL.

Highfields brochure description is from Milton, *Loss of Eden*, 377–378.

"until the crisis has turned": Friedman, *The Immortalists*, 170, quoting CAL, *WJ*, 247.

9. From Hero to Villain

Breckinridge quit working for Lindbergh: Milton, *Loss of Eden*, 387.

"The bible of every American Nazi . . ." Max Wallace, *The American Axis: Henry Ford, Charles Lindbergh, and the Rise of the Third Reich* (New York: St. Martin's Press, 2003), 249 and n. 36, citing FBI Lindbergh FOIA file.

"yellow peril . . . ": Hamilton, *The First Transplant Surgeon*, 450.

"the Jewish problem . . . a surgeon with a knife": Mosley, *Lindbergh: A Biography*, 262, quoting CAL's radio talk in Detroit, Michigan.

Flexner quote: Nevins, "Abraham Flexner: A Flawed American Icon," 40 n. 16, citing Thomas Neville Bonner, *Iconoclast, Abraham Flexner and a Life in Learning*, (Baltimore, Maryland: The Johns Hopkins University Press, 2002), 294.

"messianic fervor . . . pro-Nazi traitor": Berg, *Lindbergh*, 7–8.

America First shut down: Krishnadev Calamur, "A Short History of 'America First'" *The Atlantic*, January 21, 2017, https://www.theatlantic.com/politics/archive/2017/01/trump-america-first/514037/.

10. Carrel's Fall From Grace

Right to procreate: *Skinner v. State of Oklahoma, ex. Rel. Williamson*, 316 U.S. 535 (1942), striking down as unconstitutional a compulsory sterilization law for selective repeat felons.

"potential for grim consequences": Max Wallace, *American Axis*, 296, 501.

Ouster of AC: *UP*, "French Health Chief Dismisses Carrel," *NYT*, August 29, 1944, 1; see Hertog, *Anne Morrow Lindbergh*, 538, n. 20.

"Group of Hitlers" quote "Dr. Alexis Carrel Ousted by French": *The Morning Post* (Camden, New Jersey), August 29, 1944, 1, 4.

"important new evidence against Carrel": *UP*, "Carrel Denies He Aided Germans," *NYT*, September 1, 1944, 4.

AC studied the effects of poison gases: Wallace, *American Axis*, 465, 499.

Former co-workers believed AC might have aided the Nazis: *UP*, "Carrel Denies He Aided Germans," *NYT*, August 31, 1944, 4.

AC's secretary reached out to Flexner who sent a telegram to Secretary of War Stimson acknowledged by his aide, John J. McCloy telegram to Simon Flexner, September 2, 1944. Simon Flexner papers, American Philosophical Society Library, Philadelphia, Pennsylvania. Stimson then sent orders to Eisenhower: Henriette Delaye-Dider Delorme, *Alexis Carrel – Humaniste chrétien 1873–1944 – Prix Nobel 1912*, (Imprimerie A.D.L.P, Chateau de Chanteloup, Arpajon, Apostolat des Éditions, 1963), 187.

CAL authorization to travel to Paris from military: U.S. Naval & Strategic Air Force authorizations for CAL, dated May 17, June 1, and June 10, 1945, YUCAL .

Donovan headed the OSS: *The Rockefeller Foundation,* Vol 1., No. 3, August 15, 1916; *Bulletin of the Rockefeller Foundation, Vol 1–6*. FDR had secretly put Donovan in charge of this new spy agency during World War II with double agents in France and other countries. (Donovan had started doing clandestine intelligence work for the U.S. government in 1914, when he was a member of the Rockefeller Foundation's War Relief Commission led by Herbert Hoover.) Douglas Waller, *Wild Bill Donovan: The Spymaster Who Created the OSS and Modern American Espionage* (New York: Free Press, 2011), 323–331.

Donovan proposed war crime trials: See Wallace, *American Axis*, 99, notes 35–36, citing the Nuremberg trial records. See also Hamilton, *The First Transplant Doctor*, 529.

Josef Mengele: The experiments of Dr. Josef Mengele were especially known for their cruelty. Nicknamed the "Angel of Death" for the prisoners he sent to the gas chamber, Mengele was also infamous for conducting genetics experiments by segregating nearly 1500 sets of twin children and subjecting one of each set to torture or disfigurement that often ended in death and then immediately killing the other twin to compare their autopsies. See Lucette Lagnado, *Children of the Flames; Dr. Josef Mengele and the Untold Story of the Twins of Auschwitz* (New York: Penguin Books, 1992); Gerald Posner and John Ware, *Mengele: The Complete Story* (New York: Cooper Square Press, 2000).

Forbidden human experiments: Joshua A Perper, Stephen J. Cina, (14 June 2010). *When Doctors Kill: Who, Why, and How.* Springer Science & Business Media. *ISBN 9781441913692.*

Selective adoption of the Nuremberg principles: Informed consent was the one standard all the countries agreed upon. "Nuremberg: Its Lessons for Today," The Schulberg/Waletzky Restoration, 2017, http://nurembergfilm.org/trial_nuremberg_principles.shtml. That standard is now set forth in the United Nations International Covenant on Civil and Political Rights and has also become a requirement imposed by the United States Department of Health and Human Services. U.S.H.H.S.§46.406: Research involving greater than minimal risk and no prospect of direct benefit to individual subjects, but likely to yield generalizable knowledge about the subject's disorder or condition.

HHS will conduct or fund research in which the IRB finds that more than minimal risk to children is presented by an intervention or procedure that does not hold out the prospect of direct benefit for the individual subject, or by a monitoring procedure which is not likely to contribute to the well-being of the subject, only if the IRB finds that:
(a) The risk represents a minor increase over minimal risk;
(b) The intervention or procedure presents experiences to subjects that are reasonably commensurate with those inherent in their actual or expected medical, dental, psychological, social, or educational situations;
(c) The intervention or procedure is likely to yield generalizable knowledge about the subjects' disorder or condition which is of vital importance for the understanding or amelioration of the subjects' disorder or condition; and
(d) Adequate provisions are made for soliciting assent of the children and permission of their parents or guardians, as set forth in §46.408.

Lindbergh worked closely with Mme. Carrel in reviewing Dr. Carrel's papers: Hamilton notes that "Carrel's friends discussed his life and works regularly, and they kept in touch with [his former assistant] Miss Crutcher." Hamilton, *The First Transplant Surgeon*, 527.

"Medical marvel"; "moral monster": Nevins, *Meanderings in Medical History, Book Four,* 94.

11. Lindbergh Secretly Achieves his Goal

Lindbergh moved to Darien, CT, which had restrictive covenants: In *The American Axis* at 368, author Max Wallace notes that at the time the Lindberghs moved there, Darien "was so notoriously anti-Jewish" that it served as the locale for the controversial 1947 Best Picture "Gentleman's Agreement," starring Hollywood leading man Gregory Peck.

Dr. Jekyll and Mr. Hyde: Mosley, *Lindbergh: A Biography*, 346.

"high and dry in an outmoded shell": AML, GFS, 78.

"she will never realize how much of this book she has written": CAL, *SSL*, acknowledgement.

"badly mated": Berg, *Lindbergh*, 509.

"the person who once tried to save the world . . . ": Friedman, *The Immortalists*, 263.

"Who is to say the record of future evolutionary ages will prove the black to be less progressive than the white?" quoted at Friedman, *The Immortalists*, 263.

splitting his time between his American and German families: See Rudolf Schroeck, *Das Doppelleben des Charles A. Lindbergh (The Double Life of Charles A. Lindbergh)*, (München: Wilhelm Heyne Verlag, 2005).

" . . . for he beat them blind": Moseley, *Lindbergh: A Biography*, 4.

ACT FIVE

1. Reassembling the Puzzle Pieces

The bird bones had been gnawed . . . none of the human bones had tooth/claw marks: see William M. Bass, "Skeletal Material Associated with the Lindbergh Kidnap Case," *American Journal of Human Biology* 3:613-616 (1991); see also *Affidavit of Dr. William Bass*, dated Nov. 25, 2019, Appendix A (attached). Dr. Bass was assisted by Dr. William Rodriguez III.

Quoting e-mail correspondence from California forensic artist Melissa Cooper to the author in July 2019.

Exposure to noise: Mark C. Lee, "Hearing Loss: Could It Happen to You?" *Plane & Pilot*, October 5, 2010 [updated February 6, 2016], https://www.planeandpilotmag.com/article/hearing-loss-could-it-happen-to-you/#.XDjSyfZFw2w. Lee asserts that it is still the case today that thirty per cent of aviators suffer permanent hearing loss, even wearing headsets.

AC diary entries Mar/Apr 1932: See AC, *Jour Après Jour*, 113–115. The summer before he had written in his diary: "When we consider biological phenomena solely by their physical-chemical side . . . we get an incomplete view of them. It is thus necessary to study the living structure, not only its physiological, physical and chemical reactions, but also its 'psyche,' that is to say, its power of adaptation, its capacity to modify its surroundings and finally to do things that are of no use to it, but are intended for the interest of all." July 29, 1929 entry, *ibid.*, 53–54 [translated from the French by Leslie Pearlman].

Evidence of ransom hoax: Rosner details how Breckinridge informed him at noon on Monday, March 7, that Phelan had just called to describe receipt in the mail of a third ransom note. (Lindbergh actually took Phelan's call on Sunday). Rosner said he then crafted a coded response for the Tuesday morning edition of the *New York American*. Gardner, *The Case that Never Dies*, 52. Yet the envelope containing the note was postmarked at 1 p.m. on March 7 and did not arrive at Breckinridge's office until March 8, 1932 – a day after the response ad was placed with the newspaper. (See Evidence from the Hauptmann Trial, pp.25-27. Trial Exs. S-21-23; Rosner, Morris, Untitled, unpublished mss., circa 1932, pp. 49-51, NJSPM.

"directly" and not by "anatomical and physiological study in . . . repose: AC, *Jour après Jour,* 116 (April 7, 1932) [translated from the French by Leslie Pearlman].

Dr. Parker had already published an article describing an operation on a neonate. Raymond Parker, "Human Serum, Age, and Multiplication of Homologous Fibroblasts" Science, Vol. 74, No. 1911 (Aug. 14, 1931), 181–182.

The Lindberghs spent the weekend in New York: CAL Diary (May 7–May 8, 1932), YUCAL.

"White cloth". Three suspicious men seen in the woods off the Hopewell-Princeton Road in early May 1932. Melsky, Vol III, loc 977, n. 197–199, Statement of Herman Veidt Jr. to Det. Degaetano and Trooper Wolf, NJSP, Oct 4, 1934. NJSPM.

2. The Squibb Lab Report

The Squibb lab report is attached as Appendix B. For Director Anderson's quote see: App. B, 442.

"Rubber" for left foot: See App. B, 452. 11 ¾ inch would correspond to shoe size 11-12 ½. See Famous Footwear chart: https://www.famousfootwear.com/App_Themes/Default/images/2009/fit_assistant/mens_brannock.pdf; Rubber overshoes then worn in high-end laboratories: J. R. Beach, "Bacteriological Study of Infectious Laryngotracheitis of chickens," J Exp Med (1931), 54(6), 801–808, 803.

Glove with "small white sand": See App. B, 452.

Slag could have been "boiler slag". The slag particles were found with cinder and coal dust. See App. B, 442. "Boiler slag" only produced by a specialized boiler. "Boiler slag" https://energyeducation.ca/encyclopedia/Boiler_slag

The burlap bag was traceable: It was later tracked to a shipment of Kraft powdered milk on August 16, 1930, that was later repurposed by Eastern States Milling Corporation for animal feed and shipped directly to farms on the East Coast, including New Jersey (source: Melsky, Vol III, loc 1090-1119, notes 221–226. A few cracked oats inside the bag (see App. B, 448) indicated this bag had likely been used to feed horses, which RIMR then raised for serum at its Princeton lab (see Corner, *A History of the Rockefeller Institute*, 284).

Bone in burlap bag also identified as infant foot bone: See App. B, 448.

"strip of lavender paper 2 ¾" x 3/8": See App. B, 443. 10mm x 70mm is a standard size: see FAH-Litmus Paper Blue 10mm x 70mm; https://www.amtech.co.nz/fah114 .html; Squibb sold litmus paper, including "neutral" (see E.R. Squibb & Sons, Squibb's Materia Medica (New York: Medical Dept, E.R. Squibb [1919], 148); Neutral litmus paper is light purple; https://www.leybold-shop.com/litmus-paper-violet-neutral-100-stri-ma91127.html).

white disc " 15/64 in by 17/64 in": See App. B, 444.

TIME review: "Medicine: Improved Centrifuge" *TIME,* Monday, Apr. 25, 1932; 28, www.time.com/vault Phenol Red used in Lindbergh's centrifuge experiments in AC's lab: CAL, "A Method for Washing Corpuscles in Suspension," *Science,* (April 15, 1932) 415-16 at 416.

Six mm coverslip discs are still available today: See BIPEE Round Coverslips, 6mm Microscope Cover Glass, https://www.amazon.com/BIPEE-CoverSlips-Microscope-0-13mm Thickness/dp/B00XXO9X4Ep.

"which looks very much like dried blood": See App. B, 444.

Similar blood-like substance found on both T-shirts: See App. B, 446

"three small red stains ... appearance of dye": See App. B, 451. Phenol Red common use. "Dyes Known in Early Ages, Help Civilizations Today," *Democrat & Chronicle* (Rochester, NY) May 5, 1929. Anderson's lab used Phenol in past blood experiments: Leonard, George F. "Thermal Coagulation Point of Blood and Serum." *Journal of Infectious Diseases* 21, no. 3 (1917): 249-53. Accessed July 16, 2020. www.jstor.org/stable/30084257.

Squibb made vaccines from survivors' blood serum for the State of New Jersey as a free service to combat polio: "Paralysis Epidemic Cost 134 Lives in New Jersey; Far Below Plague of 1916," *Courier News, Plainfield/Bridgewater,* New Jersey, Dec 8, 1931, 17.

tar-like substance ...: App. B, 449. Squibb itself sold tar oil: "Oil Tar Rectified," Squibb, Materia Medica (New York: Medical Dept, E.R. Squibb [1919]), 176. https://hdl.handle.net/2027/coo1.ark:/13960/t0qr5d57c. Rockefeller institute tar oil experiments with mice source: Hamilton, *The First Transplant Surgeon,* 330.

gloves with white and brown wrist hair 7/16 in: App. B, 449; hair same color/length found on shirt: App. B, 446; holes in fingertips: App. B, 449.

piece of board and 52 in. "originally white ... partly discolored black" cloth with five-inch x two-inch hole: App. B, 455.

six pieces of unidentified "waste material": App. B, 454.

an older man highly practiced in using a needle and thread: Carrel was by then likely well-known for that manual dexterity, a skill highlighted three years later in "Carrel's Man" *TIME* magazine, September 16, 1935, 47. See also Theodore Malinin, "Remembering Alexis Carrel and Charles Lindbergh," Int'l Heart Valve Summit, Vol. 23, No.1, 1996, 28, thij00028-0039.pdf

"black particles assumed to be of rubber ...": App. B, 447. Black rubber gloves like medical technicians then wore ...: AC and CAL, *CO,* 117, Plate XVI, fig. 22.

"Hauptmann wears a size nine shoe": Melsky, Vol. II, 277, n. 827, citing JEH Memorandum to Mr. Tamm, Sept. 25, 1934, National Archives, College Park, MD.

The Squibb lab and RIMR relationship: RIMR was a long-time, major customer of Squibb's. Abe Flexner, the brother of RIMR's first director Simon Flexner, was a featured guest speaker at the dedication in October 1938 of the Squibb Institute for Medical Research — created after RIMR decided to stop funding Carrel's staff and to force Carrel to retire. Abe Flexner was then fundraising chair for the proposed Highfields Center for the Science of Man, where Carrel and Lindbergh planned to conduct new tissue and culture experiments in partnership with Skillman Village. Just after Carrel left RIMR, Anderson opened Squibb's new virology department and hired Parker as its director. (See "New Laboratory Widens Study of Virus Ills; Dr. R.C. Parker, Biologist, Will Direct It," *NYT,* Aug. 30, 1939, L19). He soon brought aboard other ex-RIMR researchers. See *The Sunday Times* (*The Central New Jersey Home News*), New Brunswick, NJ, Oct. 9, 1938, 8.)

Dr. Anderson also conducted lethal animal experiments . . . shared belief in medical advancement . . . even if loss of life: ("Science Will Isolate Poliomyelitis Germ," *The Sunday Times (Central New Jersey Home News)*, New Brunswick, NJ, Sept. 20, 1931, 16.

3. Breckinridge, Fisch, and Cemetery John

Summary of B.D. letter: FBI Summary Report Re: Unknown Subjects (NY File 62-3057), 306-307, www.archive.org. (The "B.D." letter itself is missing from the reportedly complete records the FBI released to the public at the National Archives in College Park, MD.)

Breckinridge Statement to the police, September 28, 1934, NJSPM. His description of Isidor Fisch matches those on Fisch's naturalization papers. Two other Hopewell area witnesses also likely saw Fisch about the time of the kidnapping. Elwood Wilkins described a man of Fisch's height he stopped to help change a tire on a gray sedan with NY plates on March 1 or 2 on Greenwood Avenue in Hopewell near Broad Street. Wilkins also noticed a woman in the car. Elwood Wilkins, recorded statement, October 9, 1934. On September 22, 1934, the description Charles Rossiter gave of the stranger he saw could also have fit Isidor Fisch. Rossiter remembered the man differently at trial and helped convict Hauptmann. (Compare report of Sgt. A.G. Varrelman re Rossiter interview, Sept. 22, 1934 to Rossiter's testimony, BRHT, reel 1, part 10, (43-54), 2036-2047.)

"every possible thing . . .": Henry Breckinridge, Grand Jury Testimony May 17, 1932, Bronx, New York, 10, 30.

4. Reconstructing What Happened

"L'aviateur Charles Lindbergh . . .": Quote is from the back cover of *Jour Après Jour* [translation by Leslie Pearlman].

"feeble-minded prospects": Milton, *Loss of Eden*, 505, n. 5, citing letter from E. P. Earle to Alexis Carrel, Box 75, file 311, Carrel Papers, Georgetown University; see also Friedman, *The Immortalists*, 81. That letter has since gone missing from the Georgetown files.

"Sightings that night . . .": Lloyd Gardner, "New Looks at The Case That Never Dies—Most Asked Question," February 1, 2013, http://caseneverdies.blogspot.com/2013/02/most-asked-question.html.

Testimony of Bessie Mowat (Betty) Gow, BRHT, reel One, part 001, p. 273, NJSPM.

Koehler was unable to source the dowels found on the Lindbergh estate: "Report of Field Work on the Lindbergh Case by Arthur Koehler U.S. Forest Products Laboratory, Madison, Wisconsin." p. 4 (March 11, 1933). However, the dowel found in Lindbergh's study exactly matched standard Air Force pilot training supplies : "36 in. Dowel—birch or maple, ¾". Stock no. 7200-092960 Class 22". *Detailed Mock-up Information: Aileron and tab control system.* ST-1 (United States. Army Air Forces), 3. (books.google.com)

"He was just too big to bring down": Melsky, *Vol. 1*, location 3005, notes 889–990, citing *Under the Winter Sycamore* author Jim Bahm's account of what Detective Walsh told Bahm's uncle.

The unique "singnature" may have originated with a Leavenworth prisoner in a radio puzzle the inmate patented in 1931. One of Owney Madden's associates was at Leavenworth at the same time, so he could have made use of it. FBI Summary Report (N.Y. File 62-3057), 298–301, www.archive.org.

The team's comings and goings would not have attracted attention. Dr. Lillian E. Baker was an integral member of AC's staff since 1926. In addition to being in charge of the serum for perfusion experiments, she was known for her collaboration with Henry Simms at the Princeton Lab on his experiments: "The Preargnine in Edestin and its Resistance to Hydrolysis" (Department of Animal Pathology of the Rockefeller Institute for Medical Research, Princeton, N.J.), *Journal of General Physiology*, Nov. 20, 1928, 231–239, 236. https://doi.org/10.1085/jgp.12.2.231. A 1935 newspaper clipping in Carrel's file with a handwritten note from "H.O." at the institute's Princeton DAP lab, also indicated a close relationship between AC and staff member Herbert Osborn. A note to Carrel from H.O. presumably referred to Herbert Osborn, the only staff member with those initials in the plant pathology division of the Rockefeller Institute in New Jersey. See AC Papers, Box 75, Sec 19-3, Folder 231, GUBSC.

Sperm did not last long: CAL, *AV*, 392-394.

The team conducted human vivisections in 1931–32. AC's April 1932 report describes the subjects of the experiments performed by AC's surgical team over the past year as being alive when the operations commenced and discusses findings of strong similarities between chicken and human fibroblasts. See April 1932 Report on work, 87, AC Papers, Box 17 Sec 19-1, F 35, GUBSC.

Twentieth anniversary of the chicken-heart experiment: unsourced article called "Chicken's Heart to 'Live Forever,'" AC Papers, Box 75, Sec 19-3, Folder "January 18, 1932," GUBSC.

"state of repose": AC, *Jour après Jour*, 116 (April 7, 1932).

"Man has always feared the unknown . . .": AML, *HGHL*, 286, (letter to mother ECM, July 5, 1932, quoting CAL).

"It is really excellent, what he has done here": AML, *LROD*, 15, quoting AC.

Hauptmann began spending ransom money: Assuming Hitner was the mystery produce buyer he was likely directed to spend more ransom bills ostentatiously in the Bronx in early September 1934 to prompt a major sting operation to catch whoever else had just begun spending part of Fisch's share of the loot. (For sting that led to Hauptmann's arrest, see FBI Summary Report, part 2 File # 7-1-5412 of Vol. 96.)

Filming mostly a mystery: several film reels were stored in Lloyds Film Storage Vaults, Vault 2, 101 Harris Avenue, Long Island City, N.Y. See AC Papers, Box 9, Sec 7-5, Folder 39, GUBSC.

Raymond Parker, *Methods of Tissue Culture* (New York: Paul Hoeber, Inc. 1938), 129 [caption: *Figure 35. Cultures 5745 H1, 5744 H1, 5792 H2, and 6100 H1.*] Human leucocytes derived from the blood of four individuals and cultivated for seven days in 50 percent serum and Tyrode's solution. In each instance, the leucocytes were cultivated in their own serum. (A. Carrel unpublished experiments.) This reference to AC's unpublished human experiments does not appear in the third edition of Parker's *Methods of Tissue Culture* (New York: Harper and Row, 1961).

By the spring of 1932, it seems likely his lab team had reached numbered experiments in the 700s: AC and CAL, *CO*, Plate X description of carotid artery experiment #770.

5. Maggots and Chemicals Tell a Tale

The cause of the skull fracture and small hole behind the right ear: "Who Killed the Lindbergh Baby?" A PBS Nova Program. 2013. https://www.youtube.com/watch?v=vSYvcm0t-vOE&t=768s

Cushing's 1909 shunt experiment: see Courtney Pendleton, B.S., Hasan A. Zaidi, B.S., George Jallo, M.D., Aaron A. Cohen-Gadol, M.D., M.Sc., and Alfredo Quiñones-Hinojosa, M.D.,"Harvey Cushing's use of a transplanted human vein to treat hydrocephalus in an infant in the early 1900s", *J. Neurosurgical Pediatrics* (2010) 5:423-427.

Dr. Speth concluded that the maggots found in a few small masses of soil, in which two small human bones were also found, most likely were attracted by the odor of the decomposition fluid. As such, they were more than likely deposited by so-called dung flies (the flies directly deposit maggots, bypassing the egg stage), either at the woodsy scene or later while the soil was being dried on strainers at the Squibb lab. (See Appendix C p. 6.) William Allen said in his statement on May 12: "The body . . .was too far gone to know if it was a boy or a girl [and] was either decomposed or had been eaten by animals." When his co-worker Orville Wilson came out of the truck to see, Allen said, 'Look here, here lies a child or a baby.' I looked on the ground . . . and said, "That is what it is, it surely is a child. . . . We stayed there about five minutes or more and in looking over the body we noticed that it lay in a sort of a a shallow hole . . .. It seemed to me as if somebody had put the body there and attempted to cover it up with leaves and dirt . . ." NJSPM.

Andrew Zapolsky quote, reel 7, Testimony of Andrew Zapolsky, 1453-58 NJSPM.

Report of Andrew Zapolsky and James Fitzgerald, May 12, 1932, NJSPM.

"[Acme Photographer Pat] Candido stated that he did not see [any] maggots but that there was terrific odor emanating from the body," Report of George Foster to Gov. Harold Hoffman, January 1936, NJSPM.

May 12, 1932 Autopsy of "Unknown Baby": Testimony of Dr. Charles Mitchell, BRHT, reel 1, part 007,62-75, NJSPM.

Dr. Speth's sleuthing paid off: Online research led Dr. Speth to discover that in 1924 a doctor working under Dr. Roy D. McClure discovered that tannic acid could be used successfully doctor working under Dr. Roy D. McClure discovered that tannic acid could be used successfully in the treatment of burns — an innovation for which Dr. McClure would receive an award in 1937 from the Societe Internationale de Chirurgie in Paris (https://www.henryford.com/about/culture/history/people/mcclure). McClure had worked as an intern with Dr. Carrel back in 1907, assisting in animal transplant experiments. Dr. Speth discovered that tannic acid was used extensively at Carrel's lab in both tissue culture work and histological staining and helped to fix tissue stains, especially iron and silver stains, to better see cell structures under a microscope. Ebeling, "A pure strain of thyroid cells and its characteristics," *Journal of Experimental Medicine* (1925) 41 (3):337–346, 339 (www.rupress.org). It was also used by doctors battling polio during the 1930s. Although Dr. Albert Sabin, who created the oral polio vaccine, did not come to work at the Rockefeller Institute until 1935, Dr. Raymond Parker, who also did significant work on a cure for polio, had been working in Carrel's lab since the 1920s.

Tannic acid turns cells blue: Ebeling, "A pure strain of thyroid cells and its characteristics," *Journal of Experimental Medicine* (1925) 41 (3):337–346, 339 (www.rupress.org).

6. What Lindbergh Valued Most in Life

"genetic inheritance"; "critical importance": Berg, Lindbergh, quoting CAL, 529.

One "remarkable" exception: Brian Horrigan, "'My Own Mind and Pen': Charles Lindbergh, Autobiography and Memory," Minnesota Historical Society, Spring 2002, 3.

Quotes from Jovanovich: William Jovanovich, Foreword to *AV*, xiii–xiv. Lindbergh had very specific concerns about both the contract and the wording of a letter to the Trustees of Yale regarding the terms under which his private papers would be placed in its archives. He not only insisted that Jovanovich personally edit the manuscript but also that if Jovanovich were to die, the project would be turned over to one of Jovanovich's own sons to finish.

Widow AML thanked for photos: Judith Ann Schiff, Foreword, *AV*, xviii.

"unforgiving of the most trivial mistake": Mosley, *Lindbergh: A Biography*, xxii.

"the most painful memories . . . ": Berg, *Lindbergh*, 33.

"at least two generations . . . afflicted with mental illness": Berg, *Lindbergh*, 529.

"In Carrel, spiritual and material values were met . . . " CAL, *AV*, 17.

7. Accidental Admissions?

Consciousness of guilt: see, e.g., *Al-Adahi v. Obama*, 613 F. 3d. 1102, 1107 (D.C. Cir. 2010.)

"a tragedy took place . . ."; "all material values": CAL, *AV*, 17–18

Jury instructions on credibility of witnesses: See, e.g., *The Mueller Report*, Volume II, Kindle ed. loc. 7548.

Description of his first born: CAL, *AV*, 139–140 and 142.

Repeatedly derided Charlie as "it": Brant and Renaud, *True Story of the Lindbergh Kidnapping*, 12.

He was also quite agile: At Hauptmann's trial, Lindbergh testified that when his son disappeared he was "entirely normal." Lindbergh also identified his son's birthday photo (put in evidence the day before) as what his son looked like on March 1, 1932. See BRHT, reel 1, part 0, page 66.

CAL criticizing inaccuracy in Ross biography: CAL August 1, 1968 letter re Ross errata, MHSCAL, 38.

"I went upstairs . . .": CAL, *AV*, 139.

What happened when he went outside with his gun: Lindbergh testified in 1935 that he ran outside with his gun as soon as Olly Whateley completed his first call to the police. (BRHT, reel 0, p. 86). But in Lindbergh's signed statement to the New Jersey State Police, he said he waited upstairs while Whateley made that call. See Lindbergh Statement, March 11, 1932, NJSPM.

That could have been when a rail cracked: Lindbergh also wrote to Ross in 1968 that "the broken ladder, as I recall, was found immediately under the nursery window. All such details can be checked with police and court records." (CAL MHS, letter re Ross errata, 39.) Apparently, Lindbergh chose not to fact-check himself because those records not only reflected where in the yard the ladder parts were found in the yard, but when he called state police headquarters to report that find. Lindbergh testified at Hauptmann's murder trial that he recalled that it was Hopewell Police Chief Harry Wolfe who found the ladder in the yard with his flashlight. (Hauptmann trial transcript, reel 1 part 0, p. 87.) Lindbergh called the state police at 10:53 p.m. to report that they had just found the ladder. State Trooper Joe Wolf arrived shortly thereafter. His report indicated that Lindbergh found the ladder in the yard *before* Whateley called the police. (Cpl. Joseph A. Wolf, "Major Initial Report," March 1, 1932, p.3, NJSPM.)

"I realized there was no use going into the woods . . .": CAL, *AV,* 139.

Safari where abandoned baby elephant spotted: CAL, *AV,* 279–281.

8. Conclusion

Infanticides by parents, Jon Benet Ramsey case: Michael Newton, *The Encyclopedia of Unsolved Crimes* (New York: Checkmark Books, 2004), 257.

Dillinger admiration: Frank Rich, "Bernie Madoff is No John Dillinger," *NYT,* Opinion page, July 4, 2009, 8, citing *Detective* magazine poll 1933–34.

Epilogue

Fatal flaws in Jim Fisher's analysis of the Lindbergh kidnapping case: First, Fisher states as a given that the New Jersey State Police conducted a thorough investigation. That is an astonishing assertion given key evidence the police deliberately abandoned the search for, such as the 1929 Dodge with local plates driven by Suspect No. 1 on the night of the kidnapping, and the mystery fingerprints found on the inside joint of the ladder. Second, Fisher assumes no evidence related to the kidnap/murder was fabricated, nor any evidence that supported Hauptmann's innocence suppressed. This was demonstrably untrue, as belated access through the Freedom of Information Act to confidential records of the state police and the FBI helped uncover. Third, Fisher defended the trial as being "as fair as could be expected under the circumstances," which is damning with faint praise. The extremely biased media coverage leading up to and during the trial incited the crowd surrounding the courthouse to the fervor of a lynch mob.

Fourth, Fisher states there is "no hard evidence to support the notion that Hauptmann was aided in the crime by accomplices." (Fisher, *The Lindbergh Kidnapping,* 5.) Fisher admits, "No one saw Hauptmann snatch the baby from his crib and no one, save the killer, witnessed the child's death." In fact, no reliable witness ever placed Hauptmann in the neighborhood of the Lindbergh estate. (At least two other witnesses did place Isidor Fisch in that vicinity during the week of the kidnapping, but neither of them were called to testify.) Lastly, Fisher asserts that the corpse was that of Lindbergh's son without addressing the disappearance of the May 14, 1932, final autopsy report. It raised serious questions about the timing and manner of death inconsistent with Dr. Mitchell's trial testimony against Hauptmann. Fisher also fails to consider that Lindbergh prevented complete analysis of the corpse in the pending homicide case by immediately cremating the remains without legally-required toxicology tests.

J. Edgar Hoover tracking secrets of famous Americans: After the FBI Chief died in 1972, rampant speculation about his own hypocrisy severely compromised his legacy. Hoover's aide and longtime inseparable companion Clyde Tolson inherited the bulk of Hoover's estate and secret files on public figures from Presidents to movie stars, dissidents, and civil rights leaders like Martin Luther King, Jr.. Reportedly, the day Tolson died in mid-April of 1975, FBI agents raced to his house to retrieve the explosive cache. Lise Pearlman, *The Sky's the Limit: People v. Newton, the REAL Trial of the 20th Century?* (Berkeley, California; Regent Press, 2012) 288–289.

"some assistance from inside"; "The two men never completely trusted each other": Gardner, *The Case That Never Dies*, 32 and notes 63–64, citing Hoover, "Memorandum for File," March 19, 1932; *Chicago Daily Tribune*, April 11, 1932.

Discovery of new evidence by Mark Falzini: Gardner, *The Case That Never Dies*, 413–414.) Falzini made another important discovery about the acceptance by modern historians as gospel that Hauptmann had previously committed a burglary with a ladder as a teenager in Germany. Falzini discovered that the allegation first appeared in a book by George Waller, *Kidnap: The Story of the Lindbergh Case* (New York: Dial Press, 1961). Waller's unsubstantiated assertion was then accepted by a number of later authors, including historian Lloyd Gardner, *The Case That Never Dies*, 165, and law professor Douglas Linder, creator of the website "Famous Trials." Linder lists the supposed "fact" that Hauptmann had been convicted in Germany of a burglary involving "a second-story job using a ladder" as key evidence of his guilt of the 1932 kidnapping of the Lindbergh baby — i.e., that was Hauptmann's modus operandi [https://famous-trials.com/hauptmann/1397-keyevidence]. Falzini checked the 1935 trial record and found no allegation that Hauptmann had committed a prior burglary with a ladder. Attorney General Wilentz would clearly have used such information if it existed. The state obtained Hauptmann's criminal record in November 1934 from German police and had it translated. The methods of entry were detailed in that report. Two involved breaking a window with a crowbar. Once, Hauptmann climbed in an open window. Nowhere is it indicated in the German police records that Hauptmann ever gained entry via the second floor or that he used a ladder. (See Translation of records of Bruno Richard Hauptmann obtained from the County Court at Bautzen, record numbers 1 A 96/19 and A1 309/25 by Emil M. Keney, Essex County Court Interpreter, November 2, 1934, NJSPM.)

"Episode 3: The Vanished": AHC, "Chasing Conspiracies," 2016, https://www.ahctv.com/tv-shows/chasing-conspiracies/.

The parallels are striking: for critique of "Dark Phoenix," see Mick LaSalle, "Troubled mind of a superhero: When mental illness makes dark impulses irresistible," *San Francisco Chronicle Datebook*, June 7, 2019, E-1, 7.

Ludovic Kennedy quote is from Kennedy, *The Airman and the Carpenter*, 6.

Quotes of AML are from Hertog, *Anne Morrow Lindbergh*, 5, 8, 165, 474.

SOURCES

BOOKS

Ahlgren, Gregory, and Monier, Stephen, *Crime of the Century: The Lindbergh Kidnapping Hoax* (Boston: Banden Books, 1993)

Alfieri, Megan, "Studying the Lindbergh Case: A Reference Guide to the Evidence Used in the Bruno Richard Hauptman Trial" (West Trenton, New Jersey: State Police Museum & Learning Center, 2007)

Bak, Richard, *Lindbergh: Triumph and Tragedy: An Illustrated Biography* (Dallas, Texas: Taylor Publishing Company, 2000)

Baldwin, Neil, *Henry Ford and the Jews: The Mass Production of Hate* (New York: Public Affairs, 2003)

Behn, Noel, *Lindbergh: The Crime* (New York: Penguin Books, 1995)

Berg, A. Scott, *Lindbergh* (New York: Berkley Books, 1999)

Brant, John, and Renaud, Edith, *True Story of the Lindbergh Kidnapping* (New York: Kroy Wren Publishers, Inc., 1932)

Burrough, Bryan, *Public Enemies: America's Greatest Crime Wave and the Birth of the FBI, 1933–34* (New York: Penguin Books, 2004)

Cahill, Richard T., Jr., *Hauptmann's Ladder: A Step-by-Step Analysis of the Lindbergh Kidnapping* (Kent, Ohio: Kent State University Press, 2014)

Carrel, Dr. Alexis, *Jour après Jour: 1893–1944* (Paris: Librairie Plon, 1956)

_____ *Man, the Unknown* (New York: Harper Brothers, 1935)

Carrel, Alexis, and Lindbergh, Charles A., *The Culture of Organs* (New York: Paul B. Hoeber Inc., Medical Book Department of Harper & Brothers, 1938)

Condon, Dr. John F., *Jafsie Tells All! Revealing the Inside Story of the Lindbergh-Hauptmann Case* (New York: Jonathan Lee Publishing Corp., 1936)

Corner, George W., *A History of the Rockefeller Institute: 1901–1953 Origins and Growth* (New York: The Rockefeller Institute Press, 1965)

Davis, Keith S., *The Hero: Charles A. Lindbergh and the American Dream* (Garden City, New York: Doubleday & Company. Inc., 1959)

Falzini, Mark W., *Their Fifteen Minutes: Biographical Sketches of the Lindbergh Case.* (New York: iUniverse, Inc., 2008)

Falzini, Mark W., and Davidson, James, *Images of America: New Jersey's Lindbergh Kidnapping and Crime* (Charleston, SC: Arcadia Publishing, 2012)

Fass, Paula S., *Kidnapped: Child Abduction in America* (New York: Oxford University Press, 1997)

Fensch, Thomas (ed.), *Top Secret: FBI Files on the Lindbergh Baby Kidnapping* (The Woodlands, Texas: New Century Books, 2001)

Fisher, Jim, *The Ghosts of Hopewell: Setting the Record Straight in the Lindbergh Case* (Carbondale, Illnois: Southern Illinois University Press, 1999)

_____ *The Lindbergh Case* (New Brunswick, New Jersey: Rutgers University Press, 1987)

Friedman, David M., *The Immortalists: Charles Lindbergh, Dr. Alexis Carrel, and Their Daring Quest to Live Forever* (New York: HarperCollins, 2007)

Funderburg, J. Anne, *Bootleggers and Beer Barons of the Prohibition Era* (Jefferson, NC: McFarland & Company, Inc., 2014)

Gardner, Lloyd C., *The Case That Never Dies: The Lindbergh Kidnapping* (New Brunswick, New Jersey: Rutgers University Press, 2004)

_____ *The Crime of the Century: The Enduring Mystery of the Lindbergh Kidnapping* (Now and Then Reader, LLC: Kindle, 2015)

Geary, Rick, *The Lindbergh Child: America's Hero and the Crime of the Century* (New York: Nantier, Beall, Minoustchine, 2008)

Halpern, Sydney A., *Lesser Harms: The Morality of Risk in Medical Research* (Chicago & London: The University of Chicago Press, 2004)

Hamilton, David, *The First Transplant Surgeon: The Flawed Genius of Nobel Prize Winner Alexis Carrel* ([Hackensack, New Jersey; London, England; Singapore: World Scientific Publishing Co. Pte Ltd. 2017)

Hatle, Elizabeth Dorsey, *The Ku Klux Klan in Minnesota* (Charleston, South Carolina: The History Press, 2013)

Hauptmann, Bruno Richard, Tolzmann, Don Heinrich (ed.), *"I am Innocent": A Statement in the Death Cell* (Kindle ed. 2016).

Herrmann, Dorothy, *Anne Morrow Lindbergh: A Gift for Life* (New York: Ticknor & Fields, 1992)

Hertog, Susan, *Anne Morrow Lindbergh: Her Life* (New York: Nan A. Talese Doubleday, 1999)

Hixson, Walter L., *Charles A. Lindbergh: Lone Eagle* (New York: Pearson Education, Inc., 2007)

Kennedy, Ludovic, *The Airman and the Carpenter: The Lindbergh Kidnapping and the Framing of Richard Hauptmann* (New York: Viking Penguin Inc., 1985)

Larson, Bruce L., *Lindbergh of Minnesota: A Political Biography* (New York: Harcourt Brace Jovanovich, Inc., 1971, 1973)

Lindbergh, Anne Morrow, *A Gift From the Sea* (New York: Pantheon Books, 1955, 1975)

_____ *Bring Me a Unicorn: Diaries and Letters of Anne Morrow Lindbergh, 1922-1928* (New York: Harcourt Brace Jovanovich, Inc., 1992)

_____ *Hour of Gold, Hour of Lead* (New York: Harcourt Brace, & World, 1973)

_____ *Locked Rooms and Open Doors* (New York: Harcourt, Brace Jovanovich, 1974)

Lindbergh, Charles A., *Autobiography of Values* (San Diego, California: A Harvest Book, Harcourt, Inc., 1992)

_____ *Boyhood on the Upper Mississippi: A Reminiscent Letter* (St. Paul, Minnesota: Minnesota Historical Society, 1972)

_____ *The Spirit of St. Louis* (New York: Scribner, 1953)

_____ *"WE": The Daring Flyer's Remarkable Life Story and His Account of the Transatlantic Flight that Shook the World* (Guilford, Connecticut: The Lyons Press, 1927)

Lindbergh, Reeve, *No More Words: The Story of My Mother, Anne Morrow Lindbergh* (New York: Simon & Schuster Paperbacks, 2001)

Melsky, Michael, *The Dark Corners of the Lindbergh Kidnapping, Volume I* (West Conshohocken, PA: Infinity Publishing, 2016)

_____ *The Dark Corners of the Lindbergh Kidnapping, Volume II* (Bloomington, IN: iUniverse, 2018)

_____ *The Dark Corners of the Lindbergh Kidnapping, Volume III* (Bloomington, IN: iUniverse, 2019)

Milton, Joyce, *Loss of Eden: A Biography of Charles and Anne Morrow Lindbergh* (New York: Harper Collins Publishers, 1993)

Mills, Robert Lockwood, *The Lindbergh Syndrome, Heroes and Celebrities in a New Gilded Age* (Tucson, Arizona: Fenestra Books, 2005)

Mosley, Leonard, *Lindbergh: A Biography* (Garden City, New York: Doubleday & Company, 1976)

Nevins, Michael, *A Tale of Two "Villages": Vineland and Skillman, NJ* (Bloomington, Indiana: iUniverse Inc., 2009)

_____ *Meanderings in Medical History: Book Four* (Bloomington, IN: iUniverse, 2016)

Norris, William, *A Talent to Deceive: Who Really Killed the Lindbergh Baby?* (Davenport, Florida: Synergybooks, 2007)

Parker, Raymond C. Ph. D., *Methods of Tissue Culture* (New York: Paul B. Hoeber Inc., Medical Book Department of Harper & Brothers, 1938)

_____ *Methods of Tissue Culture, 2nd ed. rev.* (New York: Paul B. Hoeber Inc., Medical Book Department of Harper & Brothers, 1950)

_____ *Methods of Tissue Culture, 3rd ed.* (New York: Hoeber Medical Division, Harper & Row Publishers, 1961; third printing, 1964)

Raatma, Lucia, *Charles Lindbergh: Pilot* (Chicago: Ferguson Publishing Company, 2000)

Saddleback Educational Publishing, Graphic Biography, *Charles Lindbergh* (Irvine, California: Saddleback Educational Publishing, 2008)

U.S. Department of Justice, *The Lindbergh Kidnapping Case As Told by the FBI* (Bayside, New York: A.J. Cornell Publications, 2016)

Vitray, Laura, *The Great Lindbergh Hullabaloo: An Unorthodox Account* (New York: William Faro, Inc., 1932)

Wallace, Max, *The American Axis: Henry Ford, Charles Lindbergh, and the Rise of the Third Reich* (New York: St. Martin's Press, 2003)

Whitman, James Q., *Hitler's American Model: The United States and the Making of Nazi Race Law* (Princeton and Oxford: Princeton University Press, 2017)

Zorn, Robert, *Cemetery John: The Undiscovered Mastermind of the Lindbergh Kidnapping* (New York: The Overlook Press, Peter Mayer Publishers, Inc., 2012)

ARCHIVES

American Philosophical Society Library (Philadelphia, PA)
- Simon Flexner Papers

Georgetown University Library Booth Family Special Collections (Washington D.C.)
- Alexis Carrel Papers

Library of Congress (Washington, D.C.)
- Susan Hertog Collection related to Anne Morrow Lindbergh
- Breckinridge Family Papers
- Abraham Flexner Papers
- Robert Helyer Thayer Papers

Minnesota Historical Society (St. Paul, MN)
- Charles Fremont Dight Papers
- Charles A. Lindbergh and Family Papers

National Archives (College Park, MD)
- Records of the Federal Bureau of Investigation Record Group 65: Investigative Case Files 7-1 The Lindbergh Kidnapping Case (1932–1982)

National Archives (Kansas City, MO)

New Jersey State Archives (Trenton, NJ)

New Jersey State Police Museum Center and Archives (West Trenton, NJ)

Princeton University Library (Princeton, NJ)
- Alexis Carrel
- William Jovanovich Papers–Charles & Anne Lindbergh Files – (1910–1995)
- Charles A./Anne M. Lindbergh Papers

Rockefeller Archive Center (Sleepy Hollow, NY)
- Rockefeller University Collections (formerly Rockefeller Institute for Medical Research)

Smith College Library – Sophia Smith Collection of Women's History (Northampton, MA)
- Anne Morrow Lindbergh Papers
- Morrow Family Papers

Stanford University Libraries Dept. of Special Collections (Stanford, CA)
- Noel Behn Papers

The Van Harlingen Historical Society

UCLA Library Special Collections (Los Angeles, CA)
- Leon Hoage Collection

Yale University Archives (New Haven, CT)
- Anne Morrow Lindbergh Papers
- Charles Augustus Lindbergh Papers

ONLINE SOURCES (copies of original documents)

www.ancestry.com

www.archive.org

www.familysearch.org

https://lindberghkidnap.proboards.com/

www.lindberghkidnappinghoax.com

www.newspapers.com

www.nytimes.com (New York Times website and Archives)

www.rupress.org (Rockefeller University Press Archives) ONLINE

INDEX

A

Adam, Archie 111
Allen, William xviii, 167, 174, 405
America First 354–56, 411
American Bar Association 167, 174, 405
American Breeders Association ("ABA") 302, 348
American Eugenics Society 34, 64, 302–03, 335, 366
American Genetics Association 34, 302, 390
American Medical Association 302, 362
Anderson, John 111, 379

B

Baker, Lillian xv, 319, 325, 329
Banks, Septimus xii, 200
barnstorming 24, 33, 45
Bass, William M. 371, 380, 407, 432–38
"B.D." 387
Beaumont's Code 311
Beaumont, William 311
Behn, Noel 112, 213, 221
Bennett, Floyd 43
Benny, Jack 247
Berg, A. Scott 35, 316, 356, 413
Bird Aviation Company 68, 145
Bitz, Irving xiv, 122, 145, 149
Borelli, Edilberto 289
Bornmann, Lewis J. xiii, 99, 242, 263–64, 288
Bowlus, Hawley 57
Brandt, Karl 361
Breckinridge, Aida De Acosta xii, 11, 44, 50, 64–65, 83–86, 99, 137, 142, 372
Breckinridge, Henry advisor to Lindbergh xii, xiv, Act I, ch. 4–11; Acts II & III *passim*; Act V, ch.1, 3, 4 *passim*, 426; background, 62; and eugenics movement, 64, 391; and Isidor Fisch, 387–89; Highfields Board, 347; split from Lindbergh 354

Brewster, Kingman 355, 411
Brigham, Carl 303
Brill, A. A. 335
Brinkert, Ernest 200
British Information Services 354
Brooklyn Daily Eagle 197, 227
Brooks Field 14
Broun, Heywood 247
Bruno, Harry 33
Buck v. Bell 35, 303
burlap bag evidence 168–72, 185, 232, 234, 260, 378–84, 390, 400, 423
Burrows, Montrose 310–11
Bush, Oscar xiii, 100–01, 120, 123–24, 130, 378, 395
Byrd, Richard 26, 43
Byrne, Brendan 371

C

Cain, N.J. State Trooper 119, 130
Capone, Al 121, 155, 169
Cardozo, Benjamin 307
Carlen, Lovisa Jansdotter (See also Lindbergh, Louisa) xi, 15, 411
Carmody, Thomas 185
Carnegie Institute Eugenics Records Office 303
Carrel, Alexis xv, 158, 192, 204, 208–10, 285, 287, 292; Acts IV & V, *passim*; 430–31
Carrel, Madame Anne 208–09, 312, 326, 329, 332
Cassidy, Tom 262
Catano, Philip 130
Cemetery John vi, Act II, ch. 8, *passim*; Act III, ch. 2–4, 6, 9, 11, *passim*, 387, 397, 402, 415, 424–25, 427
Central Intelligence Agency (CIA) 360
Chamberlin, Neville 338
Charles, Crown Prince of Sweden 15
"Chasing Conspiracies" 429
Children's Aid Society of N.Y. 347
Chilton, Connie 44, 58, 81

Chippewa 16, 23
Churchill, Winston 308
Coar, Robert 169, 170, 179, 196
Condon, John F. ("Jafsie") xiv, Act II, ch.6–8 *passim*; 182, 203–04; Act III, ch.2–13, *passim*, 382, 385–87, 392, 397, 402, 427
Conlon, John 179
Conover family 123
Coolidge, Calvin 27, 29, 37, 72, 122
Cooper, Melissa 372
Cravatt, Robert 252
Crutcher, Kathleen 359
Culture of Organs, The vi, 322, 334, 340–46, 349, 362, 397, 402
Cumming, Hugh 8
Cummings, Homer 217
Cummings, Marie 70, 148, 191
Curtis, John Hughes xiv, xv, Act II, ch.8, 9, 11,12, *passim*; 209, 214, 231, 233, 240, 249, 256, 332, 377–78, 392, 418, 424

D

"Dark Phoenix" 430
Darrow, Clarence 247
Davis, Kenneth 14–15
De Jarnette, Joseph 335
Depression, The 1, 2, 10, 63, 68, 155, 292, 307, 344, 380, 391, 422, 425–26
Dillinger, John 425
Dobson–Peacock, H. 159, 190, 202, 214, 231
"Doctors' Trial, The" 361
Donovan, William ("Wild Bill") and Henry Breckinridge xiv, 122–23, 392; and Lindbergh 122–23, 145, 149, 355; and Owney Madden 122–23; and Nosovitsky, 213; Nuremburg trial role 360–61; OSS 360–61
Doyle, Sergeant 188

E

Earhart, Amelia 54, 56
Earle, E. P. 343–44
Ebeling, Albert xv, 306, 318, 325, 351
Einstein, Albert 301
Eisenhower, Dwight 360, 365

Ellis, William J. 347
Eugenics 34–35, 64, Act IV, ch. 1, *passim*; 348, 354, 358, 361

F

Falzini, Mark 126, 276, 429
Faulkner, J. J. 212–13, 289
Fawcett, James 218, 221, 238
FBI xiv, 3, 128, 196, 217, 241, 289, 291, 373, 423, 425, 427–28
Federal Bureau of Investigation ("FBI") (See also Bureau of Investigation)
Ferber, Edna 247
Fisch family 272
Fisch, Isidor xiv, Act III, ch. 3,4, 6, and 10–13, *passim*; 387, 389, 392, 398, 408, 424
Fisher, C. Lloyd xv, counsel for John Curtis, 168, 202–03; counsel for Hauptmann Act III, ch. 6–14, 428
Fisher, Jim 168, 428
"Fitter Families for Future Firesides" 34–35
Fitzgerald, James xiii, 168–171, 196, 405–08
Flexner, Abraham "Abe" 347, 350–51, 356
Flexner, Simon xv, 301, 342, 347–49, 359
Fogarty, John 32, 100, 132, 181
Foley, Samuel 218–19, 229
Ford, Henry 40, 339, 355–57
Foundation for Aeronautical Research 30
Franck, Leo 238
Freedom of Information Act ix, 427–28
French Foundation for the Study of Human Problems 353
Friedman, David 343–44, 365

G

Gardner, Lloyd xvii, 122, 395, 429–30
Garsson, Murray xiv, 148–49, 170, 373
Gasser, Herbert 338–39
Gift from the Sea 365
Gold certificates 155–56, 159, 212, 218, 220–21, 224, 228
Gonzales, Arturo 288–89
Gow, Bessie Mowat ("Betty") xi, Act I, ch. 1, 8–10, *passim*; Act II, ch.6–11, *passim*, 1, 2,6, , 200; 256, 258–59, 373–74, 376, 394–96, 416–20, 429

Guggenheim, Harry 30–33, 36–37, 45, 356
Gurney, Harlan ("Bud") 33
Guthrie, Charles 310
Guthrie, Woodie 356

H

Hague, Frank ("Boss") xiv, 112–13, 118–19, 126
Hahn, Elmer 152
Hall of Science 350
Hamilton, David 343
Hammond, Alfred 110–11, 226, 288
Harcourt, Brace & Jovanovich 411
Harding Administration 122
Harper & Row 366
Hart, B. H. Lidell 3
Hauck, Anthony ("Tony") xv, 203, 225, 230, 233, 251, 277, 386
Hauptmann, Anna Schoeffler ix, xv, 238, 240, 246, 254, 270–71, 273, 292, 295, 371
Hauptmann, Bruno Richard ix, xiv, xv, 2, Act III, ch. 3–14, Act V, Epilogue, *passim*; Appeal 284–87; arrest 216–17; Gov. Hoffman reinvestigation of guilt 284–94, criminal record 220; execution 291–98; and Isidor Fisch 216, 271–72, 278; "Why Did You Kill Me?" 291; and wife Anna ix, 217, 240, 292, 371
Hauptmann, Manfred ("Bubi") xv, 254
Hauptmann trial jury 233, 236, 250–51
Hawks, Everett 59
Hearst, William Randolph 31, 100, 129, 130, 150, 238–39, 257, 271, 281
Herrmann, Dorothy 293
Hertog, Susan 10, 431, 474–76
Hicks, FBI Agent 233, 291
Highfields (see next entry)
Highfields Center for the Science of Man (See also Science of Man Institute) 234, 347–53, 395
History Channel, The 372
Hitler, Adolph vi, Act IV, ch. 6, 9, 10 *passim*, 410
Hitner, Arthur xiv, 190, 214, 392, 397, 408, 424
Hoage, Leon xiii, 90, 293
Hochmuth, Amandus 262, 265, 279
Hockenbury, Philip 252

Hoffman, Harold ix, xiii, 264–65, 284, 286–94, 426
Holmes, Oliver Wendell 303
Holmes, Sherlock 112, 131, 409
Home Box Office (HBO) 410, 430
Hoover, Herbert 36, 44, 54, 64, 149–50, 185
Hoover, J. Edgar Bureau Director xiv, 128; FOIA discoveries 427–29; Hauptmann's appeal 287; Hauptmann's arrest 217; Hauptmann's trial 257, 261, 263; and Gov. Hoffman 289; kidnapping investigation 152, 196–201, 209–13, 241; and Lanphier interview 145–46, 372–73; Lindbergh Law 201
Hopf, Otto 316
Horrigan, Brian 410
Hour of Gold, Hour of Lead 417
Hudson, Erastus Mead xv, New Jersey State Police fingerprint expert 219–20, 241–42, 392, 398, 419; trial expert witness for Hauptmann, 263, 268, 270, 272, 277; and Gov. Hoffman 284
Hurley, Lee 74
Hydrocephalus 60, 77, 404, 430

I

Immortalists: Charles Lindbergh, Dr. Alexis Carrel, and Their Daring Quest to Live Forever, The 343
Irey, Elmer xiv, 149, 155, 156, 157
Iron Cross 339

J

Jefferson Memorial Museum 42
Johnsen, Henry "Red" 145, 149
Johns Hopkins University 311
Johnson, Squire 199, 284, 286, 372, 396
Jovanovich, William 411–12, 414

K

Katzen-Ellenbogen, Edwin 362
Keaten, Arthur xiii, 98, 169, 170, 203, 232, 234, 291, 405

Keith, J. M. 152
Kelly, Frank xiii, 98, 99, 149, 272
Kennedy, Ludovic ix, 431
Kidnapping Act I, ch. 1, *passim*; Acts II–V, *passim*
Kidnapping site floor plan xviii–xix
Kidnap poster 117, 129, 139, 372
Kilgallen, Dorothy 281
Kipling, Rudyard 302
Kirkham, James 179, 181–82
Kiss, Louis 271
Kloppenburg, Hans 218, 221, 271, 276
Koehler, Arthur xv, 242, 263–64, 266, 287–88, 399
Kubler, Louis 171, 272
Kulikowski, William 130

L

Ladder evidence 3, Act II *passim*, ch. 1–7, 11–12; Act III, ch. 3–14 *passim*; Act V, ch. 1, 4, 7 *passim*; 423, 426, 428
Lambert, Albert 56, 62
Lambert Field 24–25
Lamb, John xiii, 132, 136, 168–69, 179, 291, 386
Land, Charles xi, 370, 408
Land, Evangeline xi
Lanigan, Joseph 230
Lanphier, Thomas 145, 146, 372–73
Large, George K. 230
Larson, Bruce 411
Laughlin, Harry 303, 317
Leap Day 1932, 329
Le Bourget Field 26, 30
Lederle Laboratories (and members of AC team) 350–51
Leibowitz, Sam 247
Lend-Lease Act (WWII) 355
Leon, Sam, 179
Leopold and Loeb 388
Leukocytes (human experiment by AC) 402–03
Levatino, Salvatore 212–14, 216, 218, 241
L'Homme, cet Inconnu (see also *Man, The Unknown*), 307, 354
Liberty Magazine 291
Lindbergh, Anne Morrow, *passim*, affair 365; author and diarist 48, 210, 242, 284, 355, 364; and Breckinridges 64, 66 138, 160; CAL Jr.'s birth 58–60, 304, 390; and CAL Jr. as toddler 73–89, 372, 391; CAL Jr.'s death 173–74, 182–83, 188–89, 191–93, 204–05, 416; and Dr. and Mme. Carrel, 204, 209, 326, 336–37, 340–41, 400–01; China trip 70–72, 415; engagement 46–49; flight training 68–69, 145; family tree xi, xii; Garson investigation 148–49; and Hitler, visiting Nazi Berlin 337, 339; Hauptmann prosecution 220, 243– 281; Hauptmann's execution 304; hearing ability 146; on Highfields board 347–49; and household staff 63, 70; kidnapping Act I, ch. 1, Act II, ch. 1–6, *passim*, 327, Act V, ch. 1, 4 *passim*, 417; husband's last illness 411–12; interviews by Hertog 431; interview by Kennedy 431; marriage 50–55, 206, 391, 413; meeting Lindbergh 37– 46, 113; and daughter Anne 355; daughter Reeve 3, 360, 367, 421; and son Jon 204–05, 283–84, 287, 340–41, 366; and son Land 340, 357, 366–368; and son Scott 357, 368; overseas travel plans fall 1935 284–88; political views 337, 354–55; relationship with parents 49, 355; post WWII 364–66; relationship with mother–in–law 18, 78; royal couple 50; and sister Connie 355; and sister Elisabeth 58, 209, 216, 301, 415; and Violet Sharp 200–01
Lindbergh, August (See Mansson, Ola) 15–16, 20, 421
Lindbergh, Charles August ("C.A.") (See also Mansson, Karl August) 15–23, 421
Lindbergh, Charles Augustus *passim*; America First 354–56; army training 14–15, 23–24; author 33, 158, 320, 364, 367, 410–22; carpentry experience 20–22, 58; and Henry Breckinridge Act I, ch. 4–11, Acts II & III; Act V, ch.1, 3, 4 *passim*, 426; and Alexis Carrel,158, 192, 204, 209–10, 285, 287, 292; Acts IV and V, *passim*; 430–31; and Anne Carrel 326, 329, 340–41, 362; and Cemetery John 156, 218–19, 256–57; centrifuge

improvements 158, 326; commercial pilot 24–26; Commissioners Earle and Ellis contacts 343, 347–49; and Condon 145–58; and Curtis 58–61, 166, 189–90, 377; deathbed 411–14; engagement 46–49; and eugenics 34–36; family tree xii; farming 21–22; Hauptmann prosecution Act III, ch. 3–14; Hauptmann trial testimony 256–57; kidnap investigation, Act I, ch. 1, Act II, *passim*; morgue ID of CAL Jr. 186; and grandfather Charles Land, 20, 22, 370, 406, 408; CAL Jr. attitude toward 73–74, 77–78. 81–8, 410, 413, 416, 423; Dwight Morrow, Sr. 49, 55, 58; and Elisabeth Morrow, 39–41, 43–44, 205, 209, 243, 301, 317; perfusion experiments 316–34, 340–46; perjury evidence 226–27, 257, 415–16; political ambition 54, 292; post WW II life 362; WWII 353–60; and German children 365; Unknown Person No. 1 (Suspect No. 1), 3, 426, 431; and *Up!* 430; upbringing 16–23; wedding 52–53

Lindbergh, Charles Augustus, Jr. ("Little Charlie") analysis of death scene evidence (by Dr. Speth) 404–409, 458–72; (by Squibb) 379–85; analysis of foot and hand bones (Dr. Bass) 371, 432–38; autopsy and reports 177–88; birth 59; corpse xx, ,167–88, 371, 381, 399–400; death certificate 195; diet 328; existence unmentioned to siblings, 366–67; family tree xi; haircut 82–83, 91; father's attitude toward 73–74, 77–78. 81–8, 410, 413, 416, 423; health 59–61, 82; Highfields Center founded in honor of 347–48; homicide trial, Act III ch.7–12 *passim*; kidnap investigation Act II, Act III, ch. 3–6, *passim*; kidnapping, Act I, ch.1, Act V, ch. 1,4, 7 *passim*; Little School 76, 81; life 63–65, 70, 76–89; photos of (corpse) xx, 184, 472; (at one) 91, 128 , 253; (as a toddler) 90, 293; possible photo of CAL Jr.'s carotid artery 346; prenatal air travel 56–58; 399–400; testimony of medical examiner 231–35, 261

Lindbergh dogs (see also Skean and Wahgoosh) xii, 68, 80, 133, 170, 192
Lindbergh, Evangeline Lodge Land xi, 13, 17–23, 40, 52, 61, 78, 138, 173, 287, 316
Lindbergh, Jon xi, 204–05, 283–84, 287, 340–41, 367–68
Lindbergh Kidnapping Case As Told by the FBI, The 427
Lindbergh, Land xi, 357, 366–68, 340–41
"Lindbergh Law, The" 201
Lindbergh, Louisa (See Carlen, Lovisa Jansdotter) xi, 15–17, 411
Lindbergh, Reeve xi, 39, 366–67, 422
Lindbergh, Scott xi, 35, 316, 356–57, 366, 368, 413
Lindbergh: The Crime 213
Listen! The Wind 210
Little School, The (see also ERMM) 76, 81, 83, 90
Lodge, Edwin A. xi, 17, 316–17
Lovejoy, Owen 347–48
Love, Philip ("Red") 30
Lupica, Sebastian "Ben" 108–10, 129, 144, 199, 221, 270, 275, 374–75, 393, 421

M

MacDonald, Carlisle 33
Madden, Owen ("Owney") xiv, 121–22, 137, 145, 149, 169, 392
Mafia 169
Mansson, Karl August (see also Lindbergh, "C. A.") xi
Mansson, Ola (See also Lindbergh, August) xi, 15–16, 365
Man, The Unknown 285, 307, 335, 359
Maran, Charles 172
Maxwell, Elsa 247
McKinley, William 302
McLean, Evalyn Walsh 231
Means, Gaston xiv, 190, 214, 231, 234, 261, 392
Mengele, Joseph 361
Methods of Tissue Culture 321, 323–24, 329–331, 333, 403
Milton, Joyce 326
Minnesota Eugenics Society 34
Minnesota Historical Society 410
Mitchell, Billy (Colonel) 27

Mitchell, Charles (Medical Examiner) vi, 177–88, 231–35, 241, 260–61, 388, 400–09, 423, 425, 428
Mitchell, William (US Attorney General) 201
Moffatt, Sergeant Warren 169–72
Moore, Harry (New Jersey Governor) xiii, 72, 97, 111–113, 118, 126, 135, 229
Morgan, Aubrey 205, 209, 354, 355
Morgan Bank 155
Morgan, Constance ("Connie") Morrow (see also Morrow, Constance); xii, 354
Morgan, Elisabeth Reeve (Morrow) xii, 205, 209, 216, 243
Morgan, J. P. 36–37
Morgan, J. P. & Associates 122, 155, 213
Morrow, Alice 40
Morrow, Constance "Connie" (see also Morgan, Constance) 37, 40, 43, 45, 47–49, 53, 68, 116, 197, 209
Morrow, Dwight, Sr. xii, 8, Act I, ch. 4–8 *passim*, 74, 159, 201, 205, 213, 220, 243, 279–80, 283, 292, 348
Morrow, Dwight, Jr. xii, 37, 47, 58, 116, 201
Morrow, Elisabeth Reeve (See also Morgan, Elisabeth) xii, 8, 37–47, 52, 58, 73–74, 76, 90, 117, 197, 301, 317, 391, 413
Morrow, Elizabeth Cutter ("Tee") xii, 8, Act I, ch. 4–10 *passim*, Act II ch. 2–12 *passim*, 243, 279–80, 284, 287, 336, 355, 372, 416
Mosley, Leonard 15, 364

N

Nazis Act IV ch. 6–11 *passim*, 410
Nevins, Michael 363
New Jersey Board of Pardons 284, 286, 290
New Jersey State Police x, xiii, xviii–xviii , 327 Act I, ch. 1 *passim*; Acts II & III *passim*, 327, Act V *passim*, 428, 431
New York Police Department (NYPD) 156, 212, 214, 216, 242, 387, 389, 415, 424
Nicolson, Harold 220, 243, 279–81, 283–84, 336, 367
North to the Orient 71, 243, 283

Nosovitsky, Jacob xiv, 213–215, 231, 289, 408
Nuremberg trials (see also "The Doctors' Trials") 360–362

O

Office of Strategic Services (see also OSS) 122, 360
"Old Smokey" vi, 291, 298
Olympics 31 (1920), (1928); 337, 356 (1936)
Orteig Prize 24–25, 43
O'Ryan, John 217
OSS (see Office of Strategic Services)

P

Pan American Airways 44, 55, 365
Parker, Ellis xiii, 111–13, 146, 185–87, 235, 284, 286, 288, 293, 390, 396
Parker, Raymond xv, 321, 323–24, 329–333, 402–03
Passing of the Great Race, The 303
Pastori, Humberto 289
Perfusion experiments Act IV ch. 3 – Act V ch. 4 *passim*, 414
Perrone, Joseph 226, 256
Persaud, Raj 430
Pershing, John (General) 37
Phelan, James "Jim" 122, 136
Philosopher's Club 306, 377
PIXAR 430
Plot Against America, The 410, 430
Pope, Fred 240, 261, 274
Post, Wiley 283
Princeton (town) 62, 102, 110, 131–32, 135, 378, 394, 397, 400, 421
Princeton Academy 108, 110
Princeton Institute for Advance Study 347
Princeton University 9, 31, 62, 67, 69, 83, 85, 87, 99–100, 108, 303, 316, 349
Princeton Rockefeller Institute satellite lab (see RIMR Princeton)
Prohibition 71, 112, 170, 238
Public Broadcasting System (PBS) 404
Pulitzer Prize 320, 335, 364, 411

R

Ramsey, JonBenet 425
Ransom box 155–56 489
Ransom demands/correspondence 154–156, 159, 213, 220, 241, 263, 269, 402, 424, 429
Ransom money xiv, 10, Act II ch. 1 – Act III ch. 13 *passim*, 376, Act V ch. 3 – ch 4 *passim*, 420, 424–429
Reilly, Edward ("Death House") vi, xv, 237–42, 247–48, 256–58, 260–63, 271–273, 278, 284
RIMR (see Rockefeller Institute for Medical Research)
RIMR Princeton lab 316, 319, 382, 391–393, 397–400
Roberts, Lillian Lindbergh (CAL's half-sister) xi
Rockefeller Institute for Medical Research ("RIMR") see also Rockefeller University and RIMR Princeton Lab) xv, 158, 192, 197, 243, 285, Act IV ch. 1 – Act V ch. 4 *passim*, 426
Rockefeller, John 36
Rockne, Knute 67
Rogers, Ginger 247
Rogers, Will 81–82, 116, 283
Roosevelt, Eleanor 281
Roosevelt, Franklin Delano 220, 292, 350, 353, 355, 357, 410, 425
Roosevelt, Theodore "Teddy" 35, 302
Root, Alva xii, 83–6, 133, 142
Root, Oren xii, 83, 85, 87, 99
Rosecrans, Egbert 240, 273
Rosemary's Baby 318
Rosen, Dr. John 364, 366
Rosner, Morris "Mickey" xiv, 122, 128, 137, 145–146, 155, 182
Ross, Walter 307, 413, 417
Rossiter, Charles 262
Roth, Philip 410, 430
Runyan, Damon 247
Ruth, Babe 14
Ryan Aircraft 26, 57

S

Salk polio vaccine 329
Sanger, Margaret 35
Santos–Dumont, Alberto 44

Scaduto, Anthony ix
Schippell, Charles 199
Schoeffel, Charles 98, 121, 127, 232
Schwartz, Lauren 404, 430
Schwarzkopf, H. Norman ("Blackburn") xiii, 12, 97–8, Acts II & III, V ch. 1–4 *passim*, 415
Science 158
Science News–Letter 158
Scotland Yard 118, 127, 373, 423, 428
Scottsboro Boys 217
Sharp, Violet xii, 87, 200, 258, 262, 294
Shaw, George Bernard 36
Shek, Chiang–Kai 71
Simpson, O. J. 2
Sims, J. Marion 311
Sioux 16
Sisk, Thomas 226
Skean xii, 68, 80, 83, 87, 131, 133, 147, 192, 205, 305, 394
Skillman Village for Epileptics 62–64, 102–03, 110–11, 119, 130, 135, 137, 151, 188, 199, 226, 286, 288, 314, 344, 347–351, 362, 377, 389, 392–93, 395, 397, 421, 424
Smith College 37, 42, 116
Smith, Delos 135–36
Snake Pit, The 344
Sourland Mountain Farm, Inc. 347
Spaeth, Eva Lindbergh xi
Speth, Peter vii, 404–409, 458–472
Spirit of St. Louis, The (book) 320, 364, 411
"Spirit of St. Louis" (plane) 7, 26, 29, 37, 44, 57, 158
Spitale, Salvatore xiv, 122, 145, 149
Squibb Report vii, 379–83, 407, 424, 439–457
Steep Ascent, The 357
Stimson, Henry 360
St. Johns, Adela Rogers 257, 271
Stockton, Richard, III 230
Stout, Harry 203
St. Raymond's Cemetery 154–156, 165, 236, 258, 271, 276, 288, 389
Swayze, Frank 179–81, 185–86, 232
Swayze, Walter 171–74, 177–82, 184–88, 195, 232, 234, 260–61, 400, 404

T

Thayer, Robert "Bob" 122–23
Titus, Livingston 167
Top Secret: FBI Files on the Lindbergh Baby Kidnapping 427
Training School for Feeble-minded Boys and Girls (see Vineland Village) 348
Transcontinental Air Transport (see also Trans World Airlines) 44, 55, 145
Trenchard, Thomas xv, 248–49, 272, 278–79, 282
True Story of the Lindbergh Kidnapping 150–51
Truman, Harry 360
Tuskegee Experiment 311, 362

U

Uelmen, Gerald 2
"Unknown Person No. 1" 3, 108, 110, 375, 421
"UP!" 430

V

Van Henke, August 271
Van Ingen, Philip 60, 64, 75, 82, 181–82, 186–87, 284, 428
Veidt, Herman 378, 400
Vichy government (see also WWII) 353–54, 358
Vineland Village (See also Training School for Feeble-minded Boys and Girls)) 314, 343, 348
Vitray, Laura 59, 100, 129, 136, 150, 160
Voronoff, Serge 314

W

Wahgoosh (the Lindberghs' N.J. pet) xii, 68, 83, 85, 102, 131, 133, 395
Wahgoosh (CAL pet as teen) 23
Walsh, Harry xiii, 118, 169–71, 196, 201, 203, 231, 234, 260, 291, 396, 405–06, 409
Wartime Journals of Charles A. Lindbergh, The 367
Wave of the Future, The 355

Wendel, Paul 235, 291
Whateley, Aloysius ("Olly") xii, Act I ch. 1, 7–11 *passim*, Act 2, ch. 1–8,12 *passim*; 258, 294, 395–96
Whateley, Phoebe Mary ("Elsie") xii, Act I, ch. 1, 7–11 *passim*, 258–59, 420
Whited, Millard 262, 277
Whitehead, Peter 121
White House Conferences on Child Health and Protection 64, 304, 348
Wilentz, David xv, 218, 225–34, 242, 247–48, 251–56, 260–62, 268–72, 277–89, 293, 380, 402
Wilkins, Horace V. 131, 197–98
Williamson, Charles xiii, 95, 97, 168–69, 406
Wilson, Orville 167–68, 170–71
Wilson, Woodrow 21, 31
Wilton, George 272, 277
Wolf, Joe xiii, 97–99, 101, 105, 117, 141–42, 420
Wolfe, Harry xiii, 95–96, 111, 118, 124, 168–169, 396, 406, 415
Woodlawn Cemetery 156, 162, 398
World's Fair (1939) 350–352
World War I xiv, 37, 122, 202, 221, 308, 312, 356, 360, 390
World War II 3, 122, 351, 360–62, 365, 367
Wright Brothers 22
Wright, Orville 36
Wyckoff, Ralph xv, 326, 329, 351

Y

Yale University 91, 354–55, 370, 411–12

Z

Zapolsky, Andrew xiii, 168–71, 260, 405, 407–08
Zwillman, Abner "Longy" 169–70

ACKNOWLEDGMENTS

This is another long-term book project I began more than a decade ago. I have a great many people to thank for generously sharing their time and expertise along the way. Proceeding in rough chronological order of experts whose knowledge I have tapped, I am extraordinarily appreciative of Professor Emeritus Lloyd Gardner of Rutgers University and New Jersey State Police Museum archivist Mark Falzini, both of whom I first met when I was gathering material about the Lindbergh kidnapping case for my 2012 book, *The Sky's the Limit: People v. Newton, The Real Trial of the 20^h Century?* The methodically researched books they have written were of tremendous value in getting me started and the feedback and insights they have provided as I researched and wrote about the Lindbergh kidnapping were invaluable. This was only made possible because of New Jersey Gov. Brendan Byrne's executive order in 1981 making public all of the State Police's Lindbergh kidnapping files to be held in a museum that Mark Falzini now administers. Mark Falzini is truly an archivist's archivist, unstintingly giving of his time to assist any and all researchers of the collection he oversees. Lloyd Gardner is one of the most dedicated historians I have ever met, always devoted to ferreting out the truth wherever it leads.

I gained extraordinary insights from the university archives and many other books on the Lindberghs and the kidnapping included in the sources I consulted. Key sources included: *Liberty* magazine articles by Gov. Harold Hoffman, C. Lloyd Fisher and Bruno Richard Hauptmann; the extensive notes of investigator Leon Hoage archived at UCLA; the contemporaneous books on the kidnapping investigation by Laura Vitray and John Brant and Edith Renaud; Anne Morrow Lindbergh's and Elizabeth Cutter Morrow's diaries and the diaries of Harold Nicolson; Anthony Scaduto's book, *Scapegoa*t; Ludovic Kennedy's book, *The Airman and the Carpenter;* and Noel Behn's book, *Lindbergh: The Crime*. I owe an enormous debt of gratitude as well for the decades of research by biographers A. Scott Berg, Leonard Mosley, Kenneth Davis, Dorothy Hermann, Joyce Milton and Susan Hertog, all of whose books provided shrewd observations and telling anecdotes about Charles and Anne Lindbergh. David Friedman's book *The Immortalists: Charles Lindbergh, Dr. Alexis Carrel, and Their Daring Quest* *to Live Forever* provided a major boost to my understanding of the case. But I wanted to give special thanks to three modern authors for having the privilege of consulting their work in researching this book: Greg Ahlgren and Stephen Monier, *Crime of the Century: The Lindbergh Kidnapping Hoax* and Michael Melsky, author of the three volumes, *The Dark Corners of the Lindbergh Kidnapping*.

Ahlgren and Monier gave a fresh look at the evidence about the kidnapping based on their combined expertise in criminal law and conducted an invaluable interview of Sebastian Lupica. Their focus on Lindbergh's suspicious behavior was my first real window into a different approach to solving the kidnap/murder. Michael Melsky's books added great depth to my understanding of the case. His work reflects years of diving into musty shelves of stored documents and digesting their contents to benefit both followers of his popular "Lindbergh Kidnapping Discussion Board" [lindberghkidnap.proboards.com] and authors like myself who could never have replicated the exceptional effort Melsky put into shedding light on those dark corners. Thanks as well to his Discussion Board co-administrator Amy. I also want to thank Ronelle Delmont, the creator of Lindberghkidnappinghoax.com, which posts numerous original documents about the case that were of great use in researching my book. Special thanks to Don Heinrich Tolzmann for chasing down, completing and republishing in English Hauptmann's autobiography: *I am Innocent, A Statement in the Death Cell.*

I am grateful as well to forensic artist Melissa Cooper for her invaluable expertise in comparing photos of Charles Lindbergh, Jr. at age one and newspaper pictures of the missing 20-month-old the following March. Special thanks to hardware store owner Richard Hubbard for sharing nearly 50 years of expertise with lumber and carpentry, which convinced him the poorly made "kidnap" ladder was likely constructed from crate slats, not floorboard from Hauptmann's landlord's attic and not fashioned by the same skilled carpenter (Hauptmann) who built his own garage. Thanks so much to my nephew Aram Schiffman, a superb woodworker in his spare time from his career as a medical systems engineer, who also shed light on the unlikelihood that one rail of the "kidnap" ladder originated as part of a floorboard from an attic.

I wish to thank as well my early "sounding boards" for this project, retired federal judge, D. Lowell Jensen, and my friend Barry Scheck, co-director of the Innocence Project. I am indebted to medical ethics expert Dr. Michael Nevins, who loaned me key materials from his collection. Other doctors who provided me with much-needed insight into the victim's health issues, cause of death and post-mortem issues include pediatrician Dr. Jane Pardee, forensic pathologist Dr. Judy Melinek, retired anesthesiologist Dr. Mark Rosen, neurosurgeon Dr. Phiroz Tarapore, and (via e-mail) Scottish Dr. David Hamilton (author of *The First Transplant Surgeon: The Flawed Genius of Nobel Prize winner Alexis Carrel*). I also wish to thank Joel Parrott, President and CEO of CA Conservation Society: Oakland Zoo, for viewing the police photos taken of the corpse found in the woods on May 12, 1932 and sharing his opinion the scene did not reflect what he would expect from a wild animal attack. Special thanks to Dr. William M. Bass, III, the legendary founder of the Body Farm, who graciously reviewed key documents and provided an affidavit for the book after welcoming my daughter, grandson and myself into his home for a memorable visit. I am especially indebted to forensic pathologist Dr. Peter Speth, who, since early 2019, has devoted innumerable hours of advice and skill as a devil's advocate to test my theory. Dr. Speth not only provided a detailed medical opinion worthy of Sherlock Holmes, he offered editing suggestions on the book as a whole. I appreciate as well that he reached out to consult other medical and anthropological experts, including Dr. Bass and others listed in Dr. Speth's declaration. My thanks to these other experts for giving of their own time to help Dr. Speth solve enduring puzzles about the condition of Charles Lindbergh, Jr.'s corpse. What I cherish most is Dr. Speth's and his wife Helge's friendship with both my daughter Jamie and me that blossomed over the past year and a half.

Profuse thanks to my editor Amy Ettinger for her amazing editing talent (she teaches creative writing at Stanford University and is the author of *Sweet Spot: An Ice Cream Binge Across America*) and thanks as well to her husband author Dan White (*The Cactus Eaters* and *Under the Stars: How America Fell in Love with Camping*). Dan both deftly edited my prior books and offered his own comments to complement Amy's editing suggestions for this book. Thanks to my lawyer Peter Franck for both his sage advice and enthusiastic support. Thanks also to Larry

Weissman and Sascha Alper of Brooklyn Literary and freelance editor Wendell Jamieson for their feedback that confirmed my determination to get this book out this year. I wish to thank graphic artist Emily Burch once again for her talent in creating the book cover, and to express appreciation once more to Mark Weiman of Regent Press and Suzanne Waligore for all their hard work and belief in this project, to Christopher Bernard and Natalie Wollenweber for their copyediting skills, to Paul Veres for his cartography work, to Marilyn Springel for her work on the bibliography, and to Jamie Harkar for her editing suggestions and recommendation that I add a cast of characters. I am thankful to all who have offered corrections to the book where I have inadvertently made misstatements in my attempt to separate fact from fiction in this extraordinarily murky saga and, particularly, to Wayne McDaniel for his eagle-eye in spotting errors that crept in despite my best efforts. A big thank you as well to publicist Rob Nissen and my film agent Scott Tiffany for their ongoing promotional efforts.

Heartfelt appreciation always to my daughters, Amalia "Mali" Benvenutti Glasgow for research help, cheerleading and marketing suggestions and Anna Benvenutti Hoffmann for her contributions as a valuable sounding board in analyzing legal issues and for her help in reaching out to forensic experts; to my sister Leslie for helping with archival research, her translations from the French, editing suggestions and staunch cheerleading; and to my husband Peter Benvenutti for all of his support and encouragement in myriad ways throughout the long birthing process of this book.

Most of all, I need to thank my research assistants – volunteer Katy Lee, college students Diego Esparza, Raegan Loheide, Isabel Sherman, Natasha Raynovich and my chief research assistant, my daughter Jamie Benvenutti. Without Jamie supervising other researchers, conducting her own painstaking and inspired research, reviewing the manuscript for factual accuracy, and contributing her incisive analysis of key data, this book would not have included much of the most powerful evidence I was privileged to incorporate. That said, any mistakes in interpreting the results of research are solely my responsibility and the opinions expressed herein are my own. If I have left anyone out whom I should have thanked, my apologies.

The following pages describe other critically acclaimed books by the author and the prize-winnng documentary she is co-producing.

The Sky's The Limit: People v. Newton, The REAL Trial of the 20th Century?
(Regent Press 2012)

2013 Winner – International Book Award for books on law
2013 Silver Award Benjamin Franklin IBPA award Multiculturalism
2013 Finalist International Book Award for U.S. History

"Lise Pearlman's account of the tinderbox setting enveloping the trial of Huey Newton perfectly captures how much can be stake for an entire community – even a nation – in a single trial." — **BARRY SCHECK**
Co-Director, The Innocence Project

American Justice on Trial: *People v. Newton*
(Regent Press 2016)

Best Book Awards Law 2017

"A Life-changing True Story" — **W.A.V.E. Media**

"A clear . . . exposition of the quest for justice and equality . . . [in] a trial that illuminates the racial divide of a nation."
— **MELVIN NEWTON**
Prof. Emeritus Ethnic Studies, Merritt College
(Huey Newton's older brother)

"The definitive book on the 1968 Huey Newton death penalty trial"
— **LOWELL JENSEN**
Newton Prosecutor

"Critical reading . . . for anyone wishing to become involved with activism in our current, turbulent political climate."
—**ASSENA FAIRUZ**
AUTHOR OF *As It Ought to Be*

In 2015, Pearlman appeared in Director Stanley Nelson's PBS documentary, *The Black Panthers: Vanguard of the Revolution* as a nationally recognized expert on the 1968 trial that transformed the American "jury of one's peers" from the traditional 12 white men to the diverse panels of men and women that Americans often take for granted today. In addition to writing books, she is the co-producer of a nonprofit documentary project, *American Justice on Trial: People v. Newton*, which won a civil rights award and is expected to be completed and released in 2021. www.americanjusticeontrial.com

www.lisepearlman.com
https://www.facebook.com/LPAuthorAndSpeaker/

With Justice for Some: Politically Charged Criminal Trials in the Early 20th Century that Helped Shape Today's America
(Regent Press 2017)

5 STAR REVIEWS
Finalist for 2018 Best Book Award for books on social change -

"An expertly curated tour through some of our nation's greatest legal scandals – a pleasure to read." — SETH ROSENFELD,
AUTHOR OF *Subversives: The FBI's War on Student Radicals, and Reagan's Rise to Power.*

"Armed with a razor-sharp legal mind and imbued with a sense of fairness for all, retired Judge Lise Pearlman examines a dozen landmark trials in U.S. history . . . [and] paints a searing portrait of a society divided by class, caste, race and creed." — JONAH RASKIN,
AUTHOR OF *A Terrible Beauty: The Wilderness of American Literature*

"Judge Pearlman breathes life into historical topics that remain highly relevant today." — RICHARD TRUMKA,
AFL-CIO President

Call Me Phaedra: The Life and Times of Movement Lawyer Fay Stender
(Regent Press 2018)

International Book Awards Winner Best Biography

"Diligently researched and carefully written . . Pearlman's biography accords Fay the recognition she deserves as a seminal criminal defense lawyer at a pivotal moment in the history of the California prison system." — JONAH RASKIN,
Counterpunch

"Moving, well-written at times poetic."
— ROBERT RICHTER,
Award-winning Documentary Filmmaker and lifelong friend of Fay Stender

"A necessary remembrance of an amazing woman."
— PENNY COOPER,
Member of the California Trial Lawyers Hall of Fame

With Justice for Some: Politically Charged
Criminal Trials in the Early 20th Century
That Helped Shape Today's America